A COMMITMENT TO PRIVATE INTERNATIONAL LAW

UN ENGAGEMENT AU SERVICE DU DROIT INTERNATIONAL PRIVÉ

A COMMITMENT TO PRIVATE INTERNATIONAL LAW

Essays in honour of Hans van Loon

UN ENGAGEMENT AU SERVICE DU DROIT INTERNATIONAL PRIVÉ

Mélanges en l'honneur de Hans van Loon

The Permanent Bureau of the Hague Conference
on Private International Law

Le Bureau Permanent de la Conférence de La Haye
de droit international privé

intersentia

Cambridge – Antwerp – Portland

Intersentia Publishing Ltd.

Trinity House | Cambridge Business Park | Cowley Road
Cambridge | CB4 0WZ | United Kingdom
Tel.: +44 1223 393 753 | email: mail@intersentia.co.uk

Distribution for the UK:
NBN International
Airport Business Centre, 10 Thornbury Road
Plymouth, PL6 7PP
United Kingdom
Tel: +44 1752 202 301
Email: orders@nbninternational.com

Distribution for the USA and Canada:
International Specialized Book Services
920 NE 58th Ave Suite 300
Portland, OR 97213
USA
Tel.: +1 800 944 6190 (toll free)
Email: info@isbs.com

Distribution for Austria:
Neuer Wissenschaftlicher Verlag
Argentinierstraße 42/6
1040 Wien
Austria
Tel.: +43 1 535 61 03 24
Email: office@nwv.at

Distribution for other countries:
Intersentia Publishing nv
Groenstraat 31
2640 Mortsel
Belgium
Tel.: +32 3 680 15 50
Email: mail@intersentia.be

A Commitment to Private International Law – Essays in honour of Hans van Loon.
Un engagement au service du droit international privé – Mélanges en l'honneur de Hans van Loon.
The Permanent Bureau of the Hague Conference on Private International Law
Le Bureau Permanent de la Conférence de La Haye de droit international privé

ISBN 978-1-78068-150-4
D/2013/7849/49
NUR 822

British Library Cataloguing in Publication Data. A catalogue record for this book is available from the British Library.

PREFACE

Hans van Loon has been at the forefront of private international law for well over a quarter of a century. Since joining the Hague Conference on Private International Law in 1978, he has presided over remarkable growth of the Organisation and significant changes to how it operates. He has been involved in the development of nine Hague Conventions, two of which are fast approaching 100 Contracting States, as well as the revision of the Statute of the Hague Conference. In his time as Secretary General, he has seen the Organisation's membership grow from 44 to 72 Members (with more than 60 non-Member States now party to at least one Hague Convention), which has turned the Hague Conference into a veritable world organisation. The continued relevance of the Hague Conference in the 21st century owes much to the commitment of Hans van Loon to private international law and his awareness of its role in a broader social context.

This *Liber Amicorum* is a collection of contributions from friends and colleagues who have shared the negotiating table with Hans van Loon at various diplomatic sessions, collaborated with him on seminars and academic pursuits around the globe, and worked alongside him at the Permanent Bureau. Its pages are testament to a long and respected career, as well as to the meaningful relationships that Hans van Loon has developed along the way with academics, judges, practitioners and government officials from various legal backgrounds.

The members of the Permanent Bureau, both past and present, all of whom have been privileged to work closely with Hans van Loon and experience his energy and passion, wish to thank him for all that he has done for the Hague Conference in these changing times. We wish him all the best for his retirement and future endeavours.

Members of the Permanent Bureau

PRÉFACE

Hans van Loon a passé bien plus d'un quart de siècle aux avant-postes du droit international privé. Depuis qu'il a rejoint la Conférence de La Haye de droit international privé en 1978, l'Organisation a connu une croissance remarquable, et son fonctionnement a été marqué par d'importants changements. Hans van Loon a pris part à l'élaboration et au développement de neuf Conventions de La Haye, dont deux frôlent de près les 100 États contractants, ainsi qu'à la révision du Statut de la Conférence de La Haye. Entre sa nomination au poste de Secrétaire général et aujourd'hui, le nombre de Membres de l'Organisation est passé de 44 à 72 (et plus de 60 États non membres sont désormais Parties à l'une au moins des Conventions de La Haye), faisant de la Conférence de La Haye une organisation véritablement mondiale. Le fait que la Conférence de La Haye reste d'actualité au 21e siècle tient en grande partie à l'engagement de Hans van Loon au service du droit international privé et à sa volonté d'inscrire le rôle de la Conférence dans un contexte social plus vaste.

Ces *Mélanges* sont un recueil de contributions d'amis et de collègues qui ont côtoyé Hans van Loon à la table des négociations lors de différentes sessions diplomatiques, ont collaboré avec lui lors de séminaires ou aux fins de travaux universitaires à travers le monde et ont travaillé à ses côtés au sein du Bureau Permanent. Cet ouvrage retrace l'histoire d'une carrière longue et reconnue, et atteste des liens significatifs que Hans van Loon a tissés tout au long de son parcours avec des universitaires, des juges, des praticiens et des employés gouvernementaux de différentes cultures juridiques.

Les anciens membres et membres actuels du Bureau Permanent, qui ont tous eu la chance de travailler en étroite collaboration avec Hans van Loon et ont été les témoins privilégiés de sa formidable énergie et de sa passion pour son métier, souhaitent le remercier chaleureusement de tout ce qu'il a fait pour la Conférence de La Haye en cette période de changements. Nous lui adressons nos meilleurs vœux pour sa retraite et ses projets futurs.

Les Membres du Bureau Permanent

FOREWORD

Hans van Loon, when he joined the Permanent Bureau in 1978, brought the breath of law practice, as well as youth, into the building at Number 2c Javastraat, The Hague, in which Special Commissions met – only a long block from the Peace Palace, where the Plenary Sessions of the Hague Conference on Private International Law took place. He came from four years of practice with the distinguished Hague law firm of Blackstone, Rueb and van Boeschoten, but he had behind him already internships at Strasbourg with the Directorate of Legal Affairs of the Council of Europe and the Secretariat of the European Commission of Human Rights, as well as law studies at the Universities of Utrecht and Leiden and at the Graduate Institute of International Studies in Geneva.

Hans became the junior member of the Permanent Bureau of four statutory members, replacing Matthijs H. van Hoogstraten, who had practiced law in Deventer during the World War II occupation of the Netherlands, revived the Hague Conferences in 1951 from his post as a lawyer at the Netherlands Foreign Ministry, and in 1955 had become the first appointed Secretary General of this new intergovernmental organization [IGO].

The mission of the Hague Conference is "to work for the progressive unification of the rules of private international law". The vehicles of this work are multilateral treaties.

Hans brought with him from among his commitments as a lawyer a case in which he acted for the applicant before the European Commission and Court of Human Rights, *Winterwerp v. the Netherlands*, 6301/73 (1979) ECHR 4; (1981) ECHR 7. Thus, for some time after his arrival at the Permanent Bureau, the breath of practical law practice under an international treaty [the European Convention for the Protection of Human Rights and Fundamental Freedoms] followed him through the front door of the offices at Javastraat 2c – and at times even settled on the couch in the entry foyer.

The retirement of van Hoogstraten and the elevation of Georges Droz to the post of Secretary General brought on a reordering of tasks for the upcoming

14th Plenary Session in October of 1980, and Hans – assigned to replace Droz for the third leg of piecemeal revision of the Hague Convention of March 1, 1954 on Civil Procedure – quickly showed his skills as a lawyer and diplomat. He steered to a successful conclusion the work of negotiation and drafting of the Hague Convention on International Access to Justice, which was adopted on October 25, 1980 [concurrently with the Convention on the Civil Aspects of International Child Abduction, which was under the responsibility of this author] and then was immediately signed by several countries.

The Access to Justice Convention would include chapters dealing with (1) legal aid, (2) security for costs and enforcement of orders for costs, (3) copies of entries and decisions, and (4) physical detention and safe-conduct and – because it was a revision of parts of the 1954 Convention – might have an impact on countries which were Parties to the 1954 Convention but were not Member States of the Hague Conference. Thus, the Second Commission of the 14th Session was made up not only of delegations from 25 Member States of the Hague Conference, but also of delegations, attending by invitation, from four countries which were not Member States: Hungary, Morocco, the Holy See and the Union of Soviet Socialist Republics.[1] This 1980 Convention as of now has entered into force for 26 States Parties, the most recent being Brazil on February 1, 2012.

While none of the foregoing invited countries has ratified the 1980 Convention on International Access to Justice, Hungary, Morocco and the Russian Federation are now Members of the Hague Conference. This experience not merely initiated Hans to the idea that participation by non-Members could end up by bringing new Member States into the Hague Conference. It gave him experience in shepherding a multilateral treaty to adoption by a group which included *ad hoc* Members, Parties to a treaty under revision, who were exercising the rights of Member States of the IGO for this process only.

Ten years later – after having worked successfully from beginning to result on the elaboration of Hague Conventions on trusts[2] and on succession to the estates of deceased persons – Hans dreamed up and made a process a reality that led

1 Their instruments of accession to the 1954 Convention on Civil Procedure had been deposited with the Netherlands Foreign Ministry on the following dates: Hungary – May 21, 1965; the Holy See – August 25, 1966; the Union of Soviet Socialist Republics – October 28, 1966; Morocco – December 22, 1971.

2 On a personal note, this author was in close collaboration with Hans van Loon for the preparation of the initial report on the Trusts project, which was a joint report in order to reflect one author's training and experience in a common-law legal system [Texas] which has trusts in its law and the other author's training and experience in a jurisdiction [the Netherlands] which does not have trusts, but has legal devices employed for fiduciary purposes which do not have

to invitations to a broad range of interested countries to participate *ad hoc* in drawing up a brand new treaty, with full rights to speak, write proposals and vote as though they were Member States. Hans worked out the details of creating a fund to assist a number of countries with the costs of participation at The Hague, which for many was a new and unfamiliar venue. In so doing he demonstrated a talent for obtaining voluntary contributions for the financing of useful projects which had previously been unknown to the more tradition-bound members of the Permanent Bureau, including the author of this foreword. The result was the Convention of May 29, 1993 on Protection of Children and Co-operation in Respect of Intercountry Adoption, which now has 89 States Parties and – like the Child Abduction Convention – keeps on growing.

This kind of vision of the Hague Conference's mission led naturally to the elevation of Hans van Loon to the post of Secretary General in 1996, when Georges Droz retired. Hans has continued to carry forward this vision with tenacity and skill as a lawyer and diplomat – serving the interests of children and families by promoting the spread and the effective implementation of family-law treaties, while promoting the benefits to commercial organizations or individuals that come from reducing the obstacles to international trade and migration.

The kind of flexibility that allowed countries to act in the capacity of *ad hoc* Members is one of the advantages that can arise from being a small organization, but it also requires personal flexibility and adherence to a vision on the part of the individuals carrying out the organization's work. Hans van Loon has had both of these traits, from the time when he first galloped up three flights of steep stairs at the Permanent Bureau's offices in 1978 – bursting with vigor and enthusiasm – to now when he approaches retirement while still travelling all over the world, having most recently opened the Conference's Asia Pacific Regional Office in the Hong Kong Special Administrative Region of the People's Republic of China. This follows his earlier establishment of a regional presence of the Hague Conference in Buenos Aires, Argentina, to serve Latin American States. During his tenure as Secretary General, the Conference has grown from 41 to 71 Member States, while revising its Statute to update its governance structure and to allow the European Union to become its first Member Organisation, which happened in 2007. Its current headquarters building at Scheveningseweg 6 – within eyeshot of the Peace Palace – is bursting at the seams with useful activity in all areas of private international law.

---

the all-encompassing scope of the English trust. Hans was a remarkably patient collaborator, while this author dithered over nuances of this historic structure.

Lecturing all across the world, including the Hague Academy of International Law and the Organization of American States' *Curso de Derecho Internacional* at Rio de Janeiro, Hans van Loon is Doctor *honoris causa* at the University of Osnabrück, Germany, *Officier de l'Ordre National du Mérite* in France, Officer in the Order of Orange Nassau in the Netherlands, and has received an award for his work from the US Congressional Coalition on Adoption.

Hans van Loon has done all of this while he and his supportive wife, Carola, were raising a family of three children, who have diverse interests. Being himself the son of a medical doctor, and having found his own life's work in the law, he has offered his children much freedom to pursue their natural bents.

While one wants to express the hope that retirement from the responsibilities of serving as Secretary General will give him more time to spend with his family, it is not possible to avoid harboring the hope that his multiple talents will continue to find useful avenues of expression – given his continuing mental and physical vigor. This book is testimony by his friends of their admiration of his accomplishments and at the same time an outline of some of the ideals which have inspired Hans during his career at the Permanent Bureau. Work always remains to be done – particularly in the vineyard of international legal and administrative cooperation – and Hans van Loon has set out many beacons to steer our successors in their efforts to improve the lot of the human community.

Adair Dyer — January 2013

Former Deputy Secretary General,
now Attorney at Law in private
practice, Austin, Texas, USA

CONTENTS

BIOGRAPHY HANS VAN LOON

Hans van Loon has been the Hague Conference's Secretary General since 30 June 1996 and steered the Organisation during a time of global expansion and transformation.

He studied law and sociology at the University of Utrecht, and international law and international relations at the University of Leiden and at the Graduate Institute of International Studies, Geneva (1966–1973). Following a traineeship with the Council of Europe (European Commission of Human Rights), he was admitted to the Bar in The Hague and practiced law with the Supreme Court of the Netherlands, acting also before the European Court of Human Rights (case of *Winterwerp v. The Netherlands*, 1979, 1981). He was an Honorary Secretary of the Executive Board of the Netherlands Branch of the International Law Association (1977–1986).

He joined the Permanent Bureau of the Hague Conference on 15 September 1978, combining his international functions until 1996 with those of Executive Secretary of the Netherlands Standing Government Committee on Private International Law, where he initiated, and was responsible for, the scientific organisation of the Committee's work on the codification of private international law in the Netherlands (which would ultimately lead to Book 10 Civil Code). He also was a Substitute Judge in the Hague District Court (1984–1996).

He contributed to the development of the following international Conventions within the Hague Conference:

Convention of 25 October 1980 on International Access to Justice
Convention of 1 July 1985 on the Law Applicable to Trusts and on their Recognition
Convention of 22 December 1986 on the Law Applicable to Contracts for the International Sale of Goods;
Convention of 1 August 1989 on the Law Applicable to Succession to the Estates of Deceased Persons;
Convention of 29 May 1993 on Protection of Children and Co-operation in Respect of Intercountry Adoption (which he initiated)

Convention of 19 October 1996 on Jurisdiction, Applicable Law, Recognition, Enforcement and Co-operation in respect of Parental Responsibility and Measures for the Protection of Children;
Convention of 13 January 2000 on the International Protection of Adults;
Convention of 5 July 2006 on the Law Applicable to Certain Rights in Respect of Securities held with an Intermediary;
Revision of the Statute of the Hague Conference (effective 1 January 2007);
Convention of 23 November 2007 on the International Recovery of Child Support and Other Forms of Family Maintenance;
Protocol of 23 November 2007 on the Law Applicable to Maintenance Obligations

He taught at the Hague Academy of International Law (Summer 1993, Seminar for Advanced Studies 2012), at its external programs in San José (Costa Rica, 1995) and Abu Dhabi (UAE, 2010), the XXXIIth Session of the OAS Course on International Law (Rio de Janeiro, 2005), and at the University of Florida (Fall 1988). He lectured on the Hague Conference and its work at universities and academic institutions worldwide, and (co-) organised numerous international symposia concerning subject matters of (private) international law with other intergovernmental organisations, governments, and academic institutions, including on subjects such as the outlook for private international law after the fall of the Berlin Wall, damage to the environment, human rights, Islamic law, transfrontier family relations across the Mediterranean and beyond, registered partnerships, Internet and E-commerce.

He has widely published on numerous topics of private international law. He is a doctor *honoris causa* of the University of Osnabrück (Germany, 2001).

He was an expert consultant to the Governments of Costa Rica, Romania, Albania, Guatemala and Cambodia, as well as to the Senate of Paraguay, and to other international organisations (UNICEF, UNHCR), concerning international legal co-operation, in particular concerning Hague Conventions.

He was elected an Associate Member of the *Institut de Droit International* (2009). He has been a Member of the European Group of Private International Law since its inception (1991), and is an honorary Member of the *Asociación Americana de Derecho Internacional Privado* (ASADIP, 2007).

PUBLICATIONS BY / PAR HANS VAN LOON

ACADÉMIE DE DROIT INTERNATIONAL, RECUEIL DES COURS

- "International Co-operation and Protection of Children with regard to Intercountry Adoption", in *Recueil des Cours, Volume 244* (1993-VII), pp. 195–456 (1995).

STUDIES IN PREPARATION OF INTERNATIONAL CONVENTIONS / ETUDES PRÉPARATOIRES POUR DES CONVENTIONS INTERNATIONALES

- « Rapport sur l'adoption d'enfants originaires de l'étranger/Report on Intercountry Adoption of Children », in Hague Conference on Private International Law / Conférence de La Haye de droit international privé, *Proceedings of the Seventeenth Session/Actes et documents de la Dix-septième session (1993), Tome II* (1994), pp. 11–119, (also translated into Spanish/également traduit en espagnol).
- "Report on trusts and analogous institutions/Rapport sur les trusts et institutions analogues", (co-author/co-auteur), in Hague Conference on Private International Law/Conférence de La Haye de droit international privé, *Proceedings of the Fifteenth Session/Actes et documents de la Quinzième session (1984), Tome II* (1985), pp. 10–108, (also translated into Japanese; également traduit en japonais).
- "Succession in private international law-Prospective Study/Droit international privé des successions-Étude prospective", in Hague Conference on Private International Law/Conférence de La Haye de droit international privé, *Proceedings of the Sixteenth Session/Actes et Documents de la Seizième (1988), Tome II*, (1990), pp. 140–161 (Supplementary Notes / Notes complémentaires, *ibidem*, pp. 106–139, pp. 196–201; 202–205; 206–217; 222–231).

STUDIES WRITTEN FOR THE INTERNATIONAL LAW ASSOCIATION / ÉTUDES ÉCRITES POUR LA INTERNATIONAL LAW ASSOCIATION

- "International Adoption of Children", in International Law Association, *Report of Sixty-Fourth Conference* (Queensland, 1990), pp. 362–386;
  Idem, *Report of the Sixty-Third Conference* (Warsaw, 1988), pp. 570–665.

ARTICLES

- "The Hague Conference on Private International Law: Asser's Vision and an Evolving Mission", in *NIPR* (Nederlands Internationaal Privaatrecht), Vol. 30/3, pp. 358–361 and also published in *Hague Yearbook of International Law / Annuaire de La Haye de droit international*, Vol. 24, 2011, p. 3.
- "Internationale Kinderontvoering – Mensenrechten en IPR", in Th. M. de Boer *et al.*, eds. *Strikwerda's Conclusies* (Deventer, Kluwer, 2011), pp. 297–309
- "The Citizen in the Face of Legal Diversity – New Challenges for International Law in an Age of Globalization", in *Forum, proceedings of the first Saint-Petersburg International Legal Forum*, (St Petersburg, International Legal Forum Foundation, 2011) pp. 24–28 (in English and Russian).
- « Conférence de La Haye de droit international privé », in *Répertoire international Dalloz*, 2011
- "Internationale geschillenbeslechting", in Niemeijer *et al*, *Internationalisering, veiligheid en recht* (The Hague, Ministerie van Justitie, 2010), pp. 34–36.
- "A European Law Institute? – A perspective from The Hague", in Cafaggi F., Francini F., Micklitz H.-W., Poiares Maduro M., eds. *A European Law Institute? – Towards Innovation in European Legal Integration* (Florence, European University Institute, 2010), pp. 67–79.
- "The accommodation of religious laws in cross-border situations: the contribution of the Hague Conference on Private International Law", in *Cuadernos de Derecho Internacional* (March 2010), Vol 2, No 1, pp. 261–267.
- "The Need for Global Co-operation in the Field of Private International Law: India and the Work of The Hague Conference" in *International law: Issues and Challenges.* (Gurgaon: Hope India Publications, 2009), vol. 2 pp. 105-117.
- "Legal diversity in a flat, crowded world: the role of the Hague Conference", in *Revue hellénique de droit international* (2009), Vol 62, No 2, pp. 495–509, also published in *International Journal of Legal Information*, (2011), Vol 39, No 2, pp. 172–185).
- « Vers un nouveau modèle de gouvernance multilatérale de la migration internationale – réflexions à partir de certaines techniques de coopération développées au sein de la

Conférence de La Haye », in *Vers de nouveaux équilibres entre ordres juridiques. Liber Amicorum Hélène Gaudemet-Tallon*, (Paris : Dalloz, 2008), pp. 420–434.

- "The European Community and the Hague Conference on Private International Law", (with Andrea Schulz), in Martenczuk, B., and van Thiel, S., eds., *Justice, Liberty, Security: New Challenges for EU External Relations* (Brussels: Brussels University Press, 2008), pp. 257–299.
- "Bridging cultural differences between Western and religious legal systems - the contribution of the Hague Conference on Private International Law", in Vriesendorp, D., Nelissen F.A., Wladimiroff M., eds., *The Hague Legal Capital? Liber in Honorem W.J. Deetman* (The Hague: Hague Academic Press, 2008), pp. 15–22.
- "Remarks on the needs and methods for governance in the field of private international law - at the global and the regional levels", in Cafaggi, F., Muir-Watt, H., eds., *Making European Private Law - Governance Design*, (Cheltenham: Edward Elger Publishing, 2008), pp. 197–208.
- "40 years of Private International Law", in Ribbelink, O., ed., *Forty Years of international Law - on the occasion of 40 years of the T.M.C. Asser Instituut*, (The Hague: T.M.C.Asser Instituut, 2007), pp. 15–21.
- "La Conferenza dell'Aia di Diritto Internazionale Privato e il Notariato Latino. Una missione comune nell'era della globalizzazione e dell'integrazione regionale", in Unione Internazionale del Notariato, *Il ruolo del Notariato nello spazio giuridico internazionale* (Roma: IPSOA, 2007), pp. 5–17.
- « Quelques aspects de la mondialisation dans le domaine des conflits de juridictions », in *Travaux du Comité français de droit international privé*, années 2004–2006, pp. 227 et s.
- « L'actualité de la Convention de La Haye relative à la loi applicable au trust et à sa reconnaissance », in *Mélanges en l'honneur de Mariel Revillard - Liber Amicorum* (Paris : Éditions Defrénois, 2007), pp. 323–341.
- "Unification of private international law in a multi-forum context",in E.M.Kieninger, ed., *Denationalisierung des Privatrechts? Symposium anlässlich des 70. Geburtstages von Karl Kreuzer* (Tübingen: Mohr Siebeck, 2005), pp. 33–52.
- "The Hague Conference on Private International Law: An Introduction", in van Krieken, P.J., and McKay, D., eds., *The Hague: Legal Capital of the World* (The Hague: T.M.C. Asser Press, 2005), pp. 518–526.
- "Global and Regional Cooperation in the Field of Private International Law: A Challenge for the Hague Conference", *Japanese Yearbook of Private International Law* 7 (2005), pp. 2–19.
- "The Hague Conference on Private International Law and its Relevance to the UN Convention on the Rights of the Child" in E. Verhellen, ed., *Understanding Children's Rights*, (Ghent: Ghent University, 2004), pp. 243–352.
- "The implementation and Enforcement of the Hague Convention of 25 October 1980 on the Civil Aspects of International Child Abduction in comparative perspective:

It's Japan's move!", *Gender Law and Policy Annual Review 2*, (2004) (The Tohoku University 21st Century COE Program), English, pp. 189–209; Japanese, pp. 123 - 137.
- "The Hague Conference on Private International Law in an Age of Increasing Globalisation and Regional Integration", *Pravna Misal 4*, 2003, pp. 45–61 (in Bulgarian).
- "International Governance and Institutions: What Significance for International Law? Balancing Global and Regional Perspectives", Keynote address, in *Proceedings of the 11th Annual Meeting of the Australian New Zealand Society of International Law*, 2003, p. 8–14.
- "The Hague Convention of 1st July 1985 on the Law Applicable to Trusts and on their Recognition", in Prum, A. et Witz, C., éd., *Trust et fiducie, la Convention de La Haye et la nouvelle législation luxembourgeoise*, (Paris: Édition Montchrestien, 2005), pp. 19–33.
- "The Hague Conference on Private International Law: Current problems and perspectives", in *La Codificación del Derecho Internacional - Cursos de Derecho Internacional y Relaciones Internacionales de Vitoria-Gasteiz*, 2002, pp. 21–41.
- "Anders denken over kinderrechten: de betekenis van de Haagse Verdragen over internationaal privaatrecht", in *Tijdschrift voor Jeugdrecht en Kinderrechten*, 3, extra editie, (2002), pp. 18–21.
- "The Hague Conference on Private International Law in a time of Globalisation: New Challenges and New Conventions in the fields of Civil Procedure and Applicable Law", in Baur, J.F., Manzel, H.-P., eds., *Systemwechsel im europäischen Kollisionsrecht*, Fachtagung der Bayer-Stiftung für deutsches und internationales Arbeits-und Wirtschaftsrecht am 17. und 18. Mai 2001, (München: Verlag C.H. Beck, 2002), pp. 193–203.
- "Law, International Commerce and the Formulating Agencies - the Future of Harmonisation and Formulating Agencies - A Perspective from the Hague Conference", in I. Fletcher, L. Mistelis, M. Cremona, eds., *Foundations and Perspectives of International Trade Law*, (London: Sweet and Maxwell, 2001), pp. 67–72.
- "Les conflits de garde au sein des couples bi-nationaux", in *Enfants d'Europe, Enfants du monde*, Actes des Deuxièmes Journées Européennes du Droit de Nancy (Nancy, 2000), pp. 31–38.
- "Globalisation and The Hague Conference on Private International Law", *International Law Forum du droit international* 2 (2000), pp. 230–234.
- "Recent Developments in International Treaty Law on the Protection of Children", *International Family Law* (1999), pp. 91–95.
- "One Hundred Years of Activity of the Hague Conference on Private International Law in the Field of Family Law", *Japanese Yearbook of Private International Law*, 1999, p. 95–116.

- "Synthesis of the Discussions at the European Conference on Monitoring Children's Rights", in E. Verhellen, ed., *Monitoring Children's Rights*, (The Hague etc.: Martinus Nijhoff, 1996), pp. 211–221.
- "A bird's eye view of the Hague Convention of 29 May 1993", in E. Verhellen, ed., *Understanding Children's Rights* (Ghent: University of Ghent, 1996), pp. 389–395.
- "Unification and Co-operation in the Field of International Family Law: A Perspective from The Hague" in Borrás, A, Bucher, A., Struycken, T, Verwilghen, M., eds, *E Pluribus Unum. Liber Amicorum Georges A.L. Droz*, (The Hague etc.: Martinus Nijhoff, 1996) pp. 173–190.
- « Les Conventions de la Conférence de La Haye (I) », in Rubellin-Devichi, J. et Frank, R., *L'Enfant et Les Conventions internationales*, (Lyon : Presses Universitaires de Lyon, 1996), pp. 49–69.
- "What New Conventions There May Be: A Perspective From The Hague" in Lowe, N., Douglas, G., eds., *Families Across Frontiers*, International Society of Family Law 8th World Conference, Cardiff 1994 (The Hague: Kluwer, 1996), pp. 855–868.
- "Het Haags Verdrag van 29 mei 1993 inzake internationale adoptie", in E.Verhellen, ed., *Rechten van kinderen in de wereld* (Gent: Universiteit Gent, 1996), pp. 149–167.
- "Os Aspectos Legais da Adoção Internacional e a Proteção da Criança – Relatório da Associação de Direito Internacional", in *Uma vida dedicada ao Directo. Homenagem a Carlos Henrique de Carvalho*, (São Paulo: Editora Revista dos Tribunais, 1995), pp. 241–254.
- "Hague Convention of 29 May 1993 on Protection of Children and Co-operation in Respect of Intercountry Adoption", *The International Journal of Children's Rights* 3, 1995, pp. 463–468.
- "Inleiding", in Frohn, E.N., Hennis, E., eds., *Staatscommissie IPR, Geselecteerde Adviezen – naar een afgewogen IPR*, (Den Haag: T.M.C. Asserinstituut, 1995), pp. IX–XVI. Also drafted various consultation papers included in this Collection for the Government of the Netherlands on private international law, e.g. on / A également rédigé de nombreux avis, inclus dans ce Recueil, destinés au Gouvernment néerlandais, notamment sur :
  - The application of imprisonment for debt of foreigners/La contrainte par corps contre les étrangers (1980), pp. 311–315;
  - The law applicable to maritime and inland navigation issues/ La Loi applicable aux questions de droit maritime et de navigation intérieure (1981), pp. 284–301;
  - Declaratory judgments concerning the validity of foreign legal relationships/ Jugements déclaratifs concernant la validité de relations juridiques établies à l'étranger (1982), pp. 15–19;
  - The law applicable to family names and first names/La loi applicable aux noms et aux prénoms (1985), pp. 19–27;

  - The Hague and Luxembourg Conventions on child abduction and their implementation/ Les Conventions de La Haye et de Luxembourg sur l'enlèvement international d'enfants et leur mise en œuvre (1985), pp. 176–188;
  - The Rome Convention of 19 June 1980 on the law applicable to contractual obligations/ La Convention de Rome du 19 juin 1980 sur la loi applicable aux obligations contractuelles (1985), pp. 231–238;
  - International divorce proceedings/Les procédures en matière de divorce international (1986), pp. 108–112;
  - The law applicable to the celebration and the recognition of the validity of marriages/La loi applicable à la célébration et la reconnaissance de la validité des mariages (1987), pp. 124–134;
  - International access to Justice / L'accès international à la justice (1987), pp. 315–325;
  - The law applicable to international sales contracts / La loi applicable aux contrats de vente internationale (1990), pp. 238–241;
  - Legislative jurisdiction on the Dutch part of the continental shelf outside the territorial sea / La compétence législative sur la partie néerlandaise du plateau continental en dehors de la mer territoriale (1990), pp. 245–252;
  - Private international law aspects of insolvency / La faillite en droit international privé (1981;1990) pp. 303–309;
  - The law applicable to international trusts and their recognition / La loi applicable au trust et sa reconnaissance (1991), pp. 255–261.
- « Genèse et Historique de la Convention du 29 mai 1993 », in Association Louis Chatin pour la défense des droits de l'Enfant, *Actes du Colloque « L'adoption internationale »*, (Paris : Cour de Cassation, 1994) pp. 9–17.
- "Honderd jaar Haagse Conferentie voor internationaal privaatrecht", *Nederlands Internationaal Privaatrecht*, édition spéciale / special issue (1994), pp. 5–10
- "The Hague Conference – its origins, organization and achievements", *Svensk Juristtidning* 4 (1993), pp. 293–307
- "Het 'dubbele aangezicht' van Haagse verdragen: volkenrechtelijke en nationaal-rechtelijke aspecten", *Rechtsgeleerd Magazijn Themis*, 4/5,1993), 196–210
- "Introduction", in C. von Bar, ed., *Perspektiven der Internationalen Privatrechts nach dem Ende der Spaltung Europas*, (Cologne: Carl Heymans Verlag, 1993), pp. 7–9
- "De wisselwerking tussen internationaal privaatrecht en rechten van de mens", in *Grensoverschrijdend privaatrecht. Opstellen aangeboden aan Mr. J. van Rijn van Alkemade*, (Deventer: Kluwer, 1993), pp. 135–148.
- "Introductory Note on the Hague Convention of 29 May 1993 on Protection of Children and Cooperation in Respect of Intercountry Adoption", in *Uniform Law Review*, 1993, Vol. I/II, pp. 76–81
- "Intercountry Adoption of Children: A Challenge for International Co-operation to Protect Children's Rights", *Hague Yearbook of International Law* (1992), pp. 137–163

- "Family Relations in a Mobile Society – Private International Law Issues", in *Contemporary International Law Issues: Sharing Pan-European and American Perspectives*, ASIL/NVIR Proceedings, (Dordrecht: Kluwer, 1992), pp. 218–225.
- « L'application pratique de la Convention de Bruxelles aux Pays-Bas », *Gazette du Palais* (Paris, Nos 2,3, janvier 1991), pp. 17–20.
- "Some Comments on the Declaration of Human Responsibilities for Peace and Sustainable Development", in Brenes-Castro, A., ed., *Seeking the True Meaning of Peace*, Conference Proceedings and Post-Conference Contributions, (San José: University of Peace Press, 1991) pp. 422–432.
- "Naar een wereldwijd verdrag over adoptie van kinderen uit het buitenland", in *Interlandelijke adoptie (Preadvies Thijmgenootschap)*, (Zwolle: W.E.J. Tjeenk Willink, 1990), pp. 57–68
- "Ter inleiding: iets over de Haagse Conferentie voor Internationaal Privaatrecht en de Haagse Verdragen", in Joppe I.S., de Lange, K.D., Westbroek.W., *Twee Haagse Verdragen*, (Deventer: Kluwer, 1990), pp. 1–10.
- "The Increasing Significance of International Co-operation for the Unification of Private International Law", in *Forty Years On: the Evolution of Postwar Private International Law in Europe*, (Deventer: Kluwer, 1990), pp. 101–122.
- "The Hague Convention on the Law Applicable to Succession to the Estates of Deceased Persons", *Hague Yearbook of International Law* 2, (1989), pp. 48–66.
- "Die Haager Konferenz und Ihre Bestrebungen zur Reform des Internationalen Erbrechts", *Mitteilungen der Rheinischen Notarkammer*, (Heft Nr 1/2, Januar/Februar 1989), pp. 9–12.
- « Quelques réflexions sur l'unification progressive du droit international privé dans le cadre de la Conférence de La Haye », in Erauw J., Bouckaert B., Bocken H., Gaus H., Storme M., ed., *Liber memorialis François Laurent 1810–1887*, (Bruxelles : E. Story-Scientia, 1989), pp. 1133–1149.
- "Der Entwurf einer Konvention über die Rechte des Kindes im Kontext anderer internationaler Übereinkommen", AGJ Mitteilungen *Forum-Jugendhilfe*, (Bonn: No 3–4, 1988), pp. 28–32.
- "Towards a Convention on the Law Applicable to Succession to the Estates of Deceased Persons", Hague *Yearbook of International Law* 1, (1988), pp. 270–279.
- "The Hague Conventions on Private International Law", in F.G. Jacobs & S. Roberts, eds., *The Effect of Treaties in Domestic Law*, (London: Sweet and Maxwell, 1987), pp. 221–251.
- "Overzicht der Nederlandse rechtspraak – Internationaal Privaatrecht – Overeenkomsten (1980–1986)" (with/avec M.V. Polak), *Weekblad voor Notarisambt en Registratie* 1987, Nrs. 5820 and 5821
- "Het gevaarscriterium", in RIAGG, *Verslag Symposium "Het gevaarscriterium"*. 1987, pp. 27–32.

- « La nouvelle loi néerlandaise sur la nationalité », *Revue critique de droit international privé* (1986), pp. 182–192.
- "Feasibility study on the law applicable to contractual obligations/Étude prospective sur la loi applicable aux obligations contractuelles", in Hague Conference on Private International Law/Conférence de la Haye de droit international privé, *Proceedings of the Fifteenth Session/Actes et documents de la Quinzième session (1984), Tome I* (1986), pp. 98–113 (cf *Proceedings of the Seventeenth Session/Actes et Documents de la Dix-septième Session (1993), Tome I*, pp. 154–157)
- "De erkenning van trusts", Landelijk Notarieel Studentenblad *A la Minuut*, 56, (1986), pp. 4–9.
- "De Vijftiende Zitting van de Haagse Conferentie voor Internationaal Privaatrecht", *Nederlands Juristenblad* (1985), pp. 573–579.
- "Anglo-Amerikaanse trusts en het Nederlandse recht, Aanrakingspunten met het Nederlandse recht", in *Mededelingen NVIR* (1983), 87, pp. 43–111.
- "Nationaliteit en personeel statuut", *Nederlands Juristenblad* (1983), pp. 449–450.
- "Internationale alimentatie", *Advocatenblad* (1982), pp. 124–130; pp. 141–144.

ANNUAL REVIEWS / REVUES ANNUELLES

- "The Hague Conference on Private International Law – Work in Progress", Annual contributions, in Bonomi A., *et al.*, eds., *Yearbook of Private International Law*, 1999-2010: Vol XII (2010), pp. 419–433; Vol VII (2005), pp. 240–247; Vol VI (2004), pp. 237-245; Vol V (2003), pp. 169–175; Vol IV (2002), pp. 219–226; Vol III (2001), pp. 237–244; Vol II (2000), pp. 169–178; Vol I (1999), pp. 205–214.
- "Hague Conference on Private International Law – Work in…", Annual overviews of the work of the Hague Conference, in *Hague Yearbook of International Law/Annuaire de La Haye de droit international*, 1988 – 2005: 2005 (pp. 197–205); 2004 (pp. 359-367); 2003 (pp. 299–314); 2002 (pp. 273–279); 2001 (pp. 281–289); 2000 (pp. 307–315); 1999 (pp. 337–340); 1998 (pp. 271–274); 1997 (pp. 269–271); 1996 (pp. 241–242); 1995 (pp. 209–228); 1994 (pp. 325–341); 1993 (p. 293); 1992 (pp. 279–283); 1991 (pp. 339-341); 1990 (pp. 286–288); 1989 (pp. 354–355); 1988 (pp. 470–471).

FOREWORDS / PRÉFACES

- "Préface", in UIHJ (Union Internationale des Huissiers de Justice et Officiers Judiciaires), *Si l'Union m'était contée...1952–2012*, p. 7, novembre 2012
- Welcoming letter, in *Collection of Conventions of the Hague Conference on Private International Law*, Beijing 2012, (in Chinese).

- "Preface", in *International Family Law* Special Issue in Honour of William Duncan, [2012] IFL 1–134.
- "Preface"/"Prefácio", in G. Tagle de Ferreyra, F.J.Forcada Miranda, M.Seone de Chiodi, *La Restitución Internacional de Niños* (Córdoba, Argentina: Nuevo Enfoque Jurídico, 2011), pp. 13–21.
- "Palabras previas – Los desafíos actuales de la Conferencia de La Haya con especial atención a América Latina – algunas relexiones y suggerencias", in Fernández Arroyo D.P., N.González Martín, eds., *Tendencias y Relaciones Derecho Internationcional Privado Americano Actual* (Jornadas de la ASADIP 2008) (Mexico: Editorial Porrúa, 2010), pp. XIII–XVII.
- "Prefácio", in Grandino Rodas J., de Campos Monaco G.F., eds., *Conferência da Haia de Direito Internacional Privado: A Participação do Brasil* (Brasilia: Fundação Alexandre de Gusmão, Ministério das Relaçoes Exteriores, 2007) pp. XV–XXI (English pp. XXIII–XXVIII).
- "Foreword", in Svantesson D.J.B., *Private International Law and the Internet*, (Alphen aan den Rijn: Kluwer Law International, 2007), pp. XIII–XV.
- "Foreword", in Lowe N., Everall M., Nicholls M., *International Movement of Children,* Law Practice and Procedure (Bristol: Jordan Publishing, 2004), pp. v–vi.
- "Foreword", in Selman P., ed., *Intercountry Adoption, Developments, trends and perspectives* (London: British Agencies for Adoption and Fostering, 2000), pp. 1–2.
- "Preface", in Detrick S., and Vlaardingerbroek P., eds., *Globalization of Child Law, the Role of the Hague Conventions* (The Hague etc.: Kluwer Law International, 1999), pp. VII–IX.

SELECTION OF PUBLICATIONS UNDER THE NAME OF THE PERMANENT BUREAU OF THE HAGUE CONFERENCE / QUELQUES PUBLICATIONS AU NOM DU BUREAU PERMANENT DE LA CONFÉRENCE DE LA HAYE

- « Some reflections on the Present State of Negotiations on the Judgments Project in the Context of the Future Work Programme of the Conference/Quelques réflexions sur l'état actuel des négociations du projet sur les jugements dans le contexte du programme de travail future de la Conférence », in Hague Conference on Private International Law/Conférence de La Haye de droit international privé, *Proceedings of the Nineteenth Session/ Actes et Documents de la Dix-neuvième session (2001/2002), Tome I* (2008), pp. 428–435.
- « Some reflections of the Permanent Bureau on a general convention on enforcement of judgments/Quelques réflexions du Bureau Permanent sur une convention générale sur l'exécution des jugements », in Conférence de La Haye de droit international privé/Hague Conference on Private International Law, *Actes et Documents de la Dix-*

septième session/Proceedings of the Seventeenth Session (1993), Tome I, (1995), pp. 231–239.

- « Note sur la compétence judiciaire et la reconnaissance et l'exécution des décisions en matière de successions/Note on judicial jurisdiction and recognition and enforcement of decisions in matters of succession upon death », *ibidem*, pp. 220–227.
- Practical Handbook on the operation of the Hague Convention of 18 March 1970 on the Taking of Evidence Abroad in Civil or Commercial Matters / Manuel pratique sur le fonctionnement de la Convention de La Haye du 18 mars 1970 sur l'obtention des preuves à l'étranger en matière civile ou commerciale (Antwerp/Anvers : Maklu, 1984)
- Practical Handbook on the operation of the Hague Convention of 15 November 1965 on the Service Abroad of Judicial and Extrajudicial Documents in Civil or Commercial Matters/Manuel pratique sur le fonctionnement de la Convention de La Haye du 15 novembre 1965 relative à la signification et la notification à l'étranger des actes judiciaires et extrajudiciaires en matière civile ou commerciale (Antwerp/Anvers : Maklu, 1983).

EDITED BOOKS / TRAVAUX DIRIGÉS

- With / avec Doek J.E. and / et Vlaardingerbroek P., *Children on the Move*. How to implement their right to family life (The Hague: Martinus Nijhoff), 1996.
- With / avec van Eeuwijk, P.C.Th.M., *Identiteitsproblemen bij Adoptiekinderen*, (Amsterdam/Lisse: Swets & Zeitlinger), 1989.

TOWARDS GLOBAL HARMONIZATION OF CONFLICT-OF-LAWS RULES IN THE AREA OF SECURED FINANCING: THE CONFLICT-OF-LAWS RECOMMENDATIONS OF THE UNCITRAL LEGISLATIVE GUIDE ON SECURED TRANSACTIONS

Spyridon V. BAZINAS*
Senior Legal Officer, International Trade Law Division, Office of Legal Affairs (which serves as the Secretariat of UNCITRAL)

INTRODUCTION

In many countries around the world, the substantive law on security interests in movable assets, tangible and intangible, is out of date, and presents gaps and inconsistencies.[1] The main reason is that markets typically move faster than the law. This does not necessarily mean that the law does not evolve at all or that markets function outside legal boundaries. Often market participants and practitioners rise to the challenge and, with the assistance of courts, fill the gaps and settle the inconsistencies in the law. The law applicable to security interests in movable assets presents still more complex problems, in particular where it intersects with substantive law on assets such as bank accounts, securities, letters of credit and intellectual property, or with insolvency law.

* The views expressed in this article are the personal views of the author and do not necessarily represent the views of the United Nations or UNCITRAL.

1 For a critical discussion of, for example, English secured transactions law, see Roy Goode, *Commercial Law* (edited and fully revised by Ewan McKendrick), 4th edition, Penguin Books, London, 2010, 718. For the English Law Commission's reform proposals, see http://lawcommission.justice.gov.uk/areas/company-security-interests.htm.

The UNCITRAL Legislative Guide on Secured Transactions (the "Secured Transactions Guide" or the "Guide"), which was adopted by the United Nations Commission on International Trade Law ("UNCITRAL" or the "Commission"),[2] at its 40th session in 2007, represents an effort to modernize and harmonize both substantive and conflict-of-laws rules with respect to security interests in movable assets, tangible and intangible (with few exceptions).[3] The Supplement on Security Interests in Intellectual Property (the "Intellectual Property Supplement" or the "Supplement"), adopted by UNCITRAL at its 43rd session in 2010, is intended to achieve in addition coordination between secured financing and intellectual property law.[4] Both texts deal also with insolvency-related issues in a way that is consistent with the UNCITRAL Legislative Guide on Insolvency Law (the "Insolvency Guide").[5]

With respect to receivables, the Secured Transactions Guide incorporates the provisions of the United Nations Convention on the Assignment of Receivables in International Trade (the "Receivables Convention").[6] The relationship between the UNCITRAL texts on security interests and those prepared by the Hague Conference on Private International Law ("the Hague Conference) and the

2 For a brief description of UNCITRAL and its work, see www.uncitral.org/en-index.htm.

3 United Nations publication, Sales No. E.09.V.12 (www.uncitral.org/uncitral/en/uncitral_texts/security/Guide_securedtrans.html). (www.uncitral.org/uncitral/en/uncitral_texts/payments/Guide_securedtrans.html).

4 United Nations publication, Sales No. E.11.V.6 (www.uncitral.org/uncitral/en/uncitral_texts/payments/ip-supplement.html).

5 United Nations publication, Sales No. E.05.V.10 (www.uncitral.org/uncitral/en/uncitral_texts/insolvency/2004Guide.html).

6 United Nations publication, Sales No. E.04.V.14, www.uncitral.org/uncitral/en/uncitral_texts/payments/2001Convention_receivables.html. For a brief discussion of the Convention, see Spiros V. Bazinas, Richard Kohn and Louis Del Duca, Facilitating a cost-free path to economic recovery – Implementing a global uniform receivables financing law, *Uniform Commercial Code Law Journal*, Vol. 44, No. 3 (July 2012), 277–316. It is true that the Receivables Convention has not been widely implemented as such (www.uncitral.org/uncitral/en/uncitral_texts/security/2001Convention_receivables_status.html). The reasons range from the inability of several States to ratify the Convention before they modernize their domestic law to ensure that both domestic and foreign assignees will have the same rights, to the prolongation of the discussion in the EU with regard to the law applicable to the proprietary effects of assignments and to the delay associated with the legislative process in many States. However, some are too quick to draw from that fact the conclusion that "there is no sign that the UN Convention will come into force in the near future" (see Trevor C. Hartley, "Choice of law regarding the voluntary assignment of contractual obligations under the Rome I Regulation", *ICLQ*, vol. 60, January 2011, 52). The US signed the Convention in 2003 and in 2010 announced that it will soon ratify it. There are clear signs that the imminent US ratification will be soon followed by a number of ratifications, as a result of which the Convention will enter into force. In addition, a number of States (e.g. Belgium, Canada, New Zealand and USA) already have the assignor's law in their domestic law. Moreover, in 2007 UNCITRAL confirmed the assignor's law and now that a number of States are implementing the Guide (*infra* footnote 11), they are introducing into their domestic laws the rules of the Convention, which have been incorporated in the Guide. Thus, the influence of the Convention, including the assignor's law, is bound to increase.

International Institute on the Unification of Private Law ("UNIDROIT") is dealt with in a joint publication by the three organizations.[7] The Secured Transactions Guide and the Intellectual Property Supplement will be soon complemented by the UNCITRAL Technical Legislative Guide on the Implementation of a Security Interests Registry, which is expected to be completed by UNCITRAL at its 46th session in 2013.[8] Upon completion of the draft Registry Guide, the Commission plans to prepare a model law based on the general recommendations of the Secured Transactions Guide and consistent with all the texts prepared by UNCITRAL on secured transactions.[9]

The Secured Transactions Guide includes commentary and recommendations dealing in a comprehensive way with a wide range of issues that should be addressed by a legislator in a law dealing with security interests in movable assets, tangible and intangible. The commentary discusses various workable approaches and their comparable advantages and disadvantages and explains the recommendation made on each issue. As a result, the Guide combines the certainty of the recommendations with the flexibility of the commentary, and can thus be used by States with different legal systems and at different levels of economic development.[10]

Each chapter of the commentary and the recommendations of the Guide contains a general part that applies to all types of movable asset and a specific part that applies to certain types of asset (such as receivables, bank accounts negotiable instruments, negotiable documents and letters of credit). The Supplement is also an intellectual-property specific text that qualifies the general commentary and the recommendations of the Guide as they apply to security interests in intellectual property. Thus, each State can use the parts of the Guide that it needs most without necessarily having to adopt both the general and all the asset-specific recommendations of the Guide in their entirety.

The Guide deals with security interests in all types of movable asset, tangible (such as equipment and inventory) and intangible, such as receivables and

7 United Nations publication, Sales No. V.12-51563-May 2012, www.uncitral.org/uncitral/en/uncitral_texts/payments/2011UNCITRAL_HCCH_Unidroit_texts.html.

8 See A/67/17, para. 100 (www.uncitral.org/uncitral/commission/sessions/45th.html). For the draft Registry Guide see documents A/CN.9/WG.VI/WP.54 and Addenda 1-6 (www.uncitral.org/uncitral/en/commission/working_groups/6Security_Interests.html).

9 See A/67/17, para. 101. For the first draft of the model law, see documents A/CN.9/WG.VI/WP.55 and Addenda 1-4 (same website as in footnote 8).

10 It should be noted that the Guide has already influenced the new Personal Property Security Acts of a number of countries, including Australia, Columbia, Ghana, Malawi and Mexico. It has also influenced Book IX of the Draft Common Frame of Reference of the Principles, Definitions and Model Rules of European Private Law, the OHADA Uniform Securities Act and the Secured Transactions Toolkit of the World Bank Group.

rights to payment of funds credited in a bank account (with few exceptions).[11] Security interests include all types of interest securing the payment or other performance of an obligation, including retention-of-title rights and financial-lease rights. Security interests may secure all types of obligation, present or future, determined or determinable, including fluctuating obligations and obligations described in a generic way. They may encumber specific assets or all of the assets of a grantor, present and future, including a changing pool of assets. Security interests may be created or acquired by any legal or natural person, including a consumer. However, the law recommended in the Guide cannot affect rights under consumer-protection law (recommendation 2).[12]

The conflict-of-laws chapter of the Guide (chapter X) is particularly important. In the best case scenario, the harmonization of substantive secured transactions law will take time. Until that time, there is a need to ensure that a security interest validly created under the law of a State will be upheld by a court in another State (this is particularly important for quasi-security devices, such as retention-of-title sales, that are often found to be ineffective when the relevant goods cross national borders). But even after the harmonization of substantive law, conflict-of-laws rules will still be necessary, at least, to determine the State whose requirements will apply (e.g. in which jurisdiction a notice about a particular security interest should be made effective against third parties by registration). In any case, where harmonization of substantive secured transactions law is not possible, harmonization of conflict-of-laws rules is generally thought to be the second-best solution.

More specifically, the conflict-of-laws chapter of the Guide includes general recommendations with respect to the law applicable to the mutual rights and obligations of the parties to the security agreement (in the terminology of the Guide, the grantor and the secured creditor), as well as to the creation, third-party effectiveness, priority and enforcement of a security interest in a tangible and in an intangible asset. It also includes specific recommendations with respect to the law applicable to security interests in proceeds and in specific types of

11 The Guide does not apply to: (a) securities, payment rights arising under financial contracts governed by netting agreements other than receivables owed on the termination of all outstanding transactions or payment rights arising under foreign exchange transactions (recommendation 4, subparas. (c)-(e)); (b) aircraft, railway rolling stock, space objects and ships or other similar categories of mobile equipment if matters covered in the law are covered in national law or international agreements adopted by the State enacting the law (recommendation 4, subpara. (a); (c) to intellectual property, if the provisions of the law are inconsistent with law relating to intellectual property (recommendation 4, subpara. (b)); or (d) immovable property, it does apply, however, to attachments to immovable property (see recommendation 5).

12 For a discussion of the salient features of the Guide, see Spiros V. Bazinas, "The UNCITRAL Legislative Guide on Secured Transactions – Key Objectives and Fundamental Policies", *Uniform Commercial Code Law Journal*, Vol. 42, No. 2 (February 2010), 123–155.

movable asset, such as a right to payment of funds credited to a bank account and a right to receive the proceeds under a letter of credit (the Supplement added a conflict-of-laws recommendation on security interests in intellectual property). Finally, the conflict-of-laws chapter of the Guide deals with general conflict-of-laws issues, such as *renvoi* and public policy and internationally mandatory rules. The purpose of this contribution is to discuss some key aspects of the (general, not the asset-specific) conflict-of-laws recommendations of the Guide.

I. CHARACTERIZATION AND SCOPE OF CONFLICT-OF-LAWS RECOMMENDATIONS

Under the Guide, the term "security interest" (the term "security right" is used in the Guide for the purpose of using consistent terminology in all language versions) means "a property right in a movable asset that is created by agreement and secures payment or other performance of an obligation, regardless of whether the parties have denominated it as a security right" (Introduction to the Guide, section B). While the Guide explains the term "security right" for the benefit of the reader, neither the substantive nor the conflict-of-laws recommendations define that term. So, the scope of the conflict-of-laws recommendations depends on the characterization of a right as a security right.

In view of its character as "soft law", the Guide is based on the assumption that the characterization of a right or interest as a security interest will normally reflect the substantive secured transactions law in a State (chapter X of the Guide, para. 10). Thus, in principle, a court or other authority will use its own law whenever it is required to characterize an issue for the purpose of selecting the appropriate conflict-of-laws rule.

Under the Guide, the applicable conflict-of-laws rule depends on whether an issue is characterized as an issue of creation (i.e. effectiveness between the parties), an issue of effectiveness against third parties (i.e. parties other than the grantor and the secured creditor), an issue of priority among competing claimants or an issue of enforcement. The term "priority" in the Guide means essentially the right of a competing claimant to be paid first (Introduction, section B). The scope of the term "priority" under the Guide also depends on the meaning of the term "competing claimant", which in the Guide refers to other secured creditors, transferees of encumbered assets, judgment creditors and the administrator in the insolvency of the grantor (Introduction, section B).

If a State adopts both the substantive and conflict-of-laws recommendations of the Guide, the exact scope of the conflict-of-laws rules will depend on the scope of the substantive law rules. Similarly, if a State implements the recommendations of the Guide in their entirety, questions, for example, relating to the form and the contents of the security agreement will be qualified as an issue of creation and a question relating to registration will be qualified as an issue of third-party effectiveness.

If, however, a State implements only the conflict-of-laws recommendations of the Guide, the scope of its conflict-of-laws rules may be different from the scope of its substantive law rules, depending, for example, on whether that State follows a functional approach (subjecting all transactions that perform security functions to the secured transactions rules). If this is not the case, the question arises as to whether the conflict-of-laws rules will apply to transactions, such as retention-of-title sales and financial leases. Irrespective of whether a State follows a unitary approach (with a unitary concept of "security interest") or not, the Guide recommends that the conflict-of-laws rules applicable to security interests should apply to those transactions as well (recommendation 201). Otherwise, the conflict-of-laws rules could not cover all priority conflicts, including those between a secured creditor and a retention-of-title seller or financial lessor. The result would be lack of certainty as to the law applicable to those other priority disputes or lack of predictability as a different law might apply depending on the nature of the transaction giving rise to the priority dispute. For the same reason, the Guide recommends that even outright sales of receivables should be covered, at least to a limited extent. The reason is that outright sales are often used in receivables financing transactions (such as factoring and securitization) and may create an interest that would be in competition with a security interest. To avoid interfering with the intent of the parties to these important financing practices though, the Guide does not re-characterize them as secured transactions (chapter I, paras. 30 and 31, and recommendations 3 and 208).

The scope of the conflict-of-laws rules may also be different in other respects from the scope of its substantive law rules, depending on whether that State draws a distinction between the creation of a security interest (effectiveness as between the parties) and its effectiveness against third parties (the Guide draws a clear distinction between creation and third-party effectiveness; chapters II, paras. 2–7, and III, paras. 6–8). If a State does not draw such a distinction, the scope of the conflict-of-laws rules may be difficult to determine since creation and third-party effectiveness may be characterized as one issue. No real problem would arise though if both creation and third-party effectiveness were referred to one and the same law. This is generally the case in the Guide with both tangible and intangible assets (recommendations 203, 208 and 218), but not with proceeds (recommendation 215).

In all cases, the conflict-of-laws recommendations of the Guide apply only to the property aspects of security interests, that is, the creation, third-party effectiveness, priority and enforcement of a security interest (including in the case of insolvency), and are thus mandatory.[13] The personal obligations of the parties to the security agreement will normally be governed by the law chosen by the parties and, in the absence of a choice of law by the parties, by the law governing the security agreement. That law will be determined by the conflict-of-laws rules dealing with the law governing contractual obligations such as, for example, the Rome I Regulation. This is the approach recommended in the Guide (chapter X, para. 61 and recommendation 216).

II. LAW APPLICABLE TO SECURITY INTERESTS IN TANGIBLE ASSETS

With respect to the law applicable to the creation, third-party effectiveness and priority of a security interest in a tangible asset, the Guide recommends the generally accepted law of the State in which the asset is located – *lex rei sitae* or *lex situs* (recommendation 203). With respect to the law applicable to the enforcement of a security interest in a tangible asset, the Guide also recommends the generally accepted law of the State in which enforcement takes place – *lex fori*, which would normally be the State in which the asset is located (recommendation 218, subpara. (a)).

The main reasons why the *lex rei sitae* is generally accepted are that: (a) it provides certainty and predictability with respect to the law applicable; (b) the connecting factor corresponds to the reasonable expectations of the parties that may be affected by a secured transaction; and (c) it is simple to apply.[14] The other advantage of this approach is that, in view of its broad scope, it can be applied in all States irrespective of whether they distinguish between creation and third-party effectiveness. The main disadvantage of this approach is that, in the case of a transaction that involves multiple encumbered assets located in different States, it will result in the application of the law of more than one State to one and the same transaction. This means cost (and, in the case of future assets, uncertainty), which the secured creditor will most likely factor into the terms of the security agreement and thus will be borne by the grantor (the borrower).

The Guide offers, however, a nuanced approach to the law applicable to security interests in mobile assets, assets subject to specialized registration, assets rights which are embodied in a negotiable document, assets in transit or to be exported and negotiable instruments.

[13] Michel Deschamps, "Conflict-of-Laws Rules for Security Rights: What should be the best rules", in Horst Eidenmüller and Eva-Maria Kieninger (eds.), *The Future of Secured Credit in Europe*, De Gruyter Recht, 2008, 285.

[14] Deschamps, *ibid*, 286–288.

In the case of assets that by their very nature may cross national borders, the law applicable is the law of the State in which the grantor is located (recommendation 204). In the case of such assets, the *lex rei sitae* would result in the application of the law of more than one State. If all those States were known at the time of the conclusion of the security agreement, the result would still be more costly. If they were not known or if the encumbered asset was unexpectedly sold to a buyer in a third State, the uncertainty and the risk would be such that the financing transaction could not take place at all or could take place at a very high cost to cover the risk that a security interest that was effectively created and made effective against third parties under one law could be found to be ineffective under the law of another State.

With respect to assets that are subject to a specialized registration system (for example, a ship, aircraft or motor vehicle), the applicable law is the law of the State under whose authority the registry is maintained or the title certificate issued (recommendation 205). The advantage of this approach is that it results in the application of the law of a single State that is most closely connected with the asset and thus corresponds to the expectations of the parties.

Where a security interest in a tangible asset is made effective against third parties by delivery of possession of a negotiable document covering those assets and such a security interest is in competition with a security interest made effective against third parties by another method, the law applicable to priority is the law of the State in which the document (not the assets) is located (recommendation 206). This approach is mainly intended to give full effect to the negotiability of the document by meeting the expectations of the parties that derive their rights from the document.

With respect to export goods, the question is whether the law of the State of origin or the law of the State of destination would apply. To ensure that the security interest will be effective in any case, the Guide recommends that the security interest will be effective if it is created and made effective against third parties under either law (recommendation 207). However, to avoid creating uncertainty as to the law applicable to priority, priority is referred to the law of the State in which the asset is located at the relevant time (recommendation 203).

In this connection, it should be noted that the Guide usefully clarifies the time relevant for determining location. As to the question whether a security interest has been created, the relevant time is the time of the putative creation of the security interest; for third-party effectiveness and priority though, the relevant time is the time when the issue arose (recommendation 220, subpara. (a)). This approach also addresses the question of the law applicable where the location of an asset changes after a security interest in the asset was created. There is only one case in which the law applicable prior to a change of location continues to apply. If all competing interests were created and made effective against third parties before the change of location, then creation, third-party effectiveness and priority would be subject to the law applicable before the change of location (recommendation 220, subpara. (b)). This approach has the advantage that it meets the expectations of all parties involved.

As to security interests in negotiable instruments, the Guide recommends an interesting approach. The basic rule is the *lex situs*, that is, the law of the State in which the negotiable instrument is located. This is in line with the expectations of all parties and preserves the negotiability of the instrument. However, where a security interest in a negotiable instrument may be made effective against third parties by registration under the law of the State in which the grantor is located, that law will govern the question whether the security interest has been made effective against third parties (recommendation 211). Thus, whether registration in the State of the grantor's location is effective is to be determined according to that State's law. Still, to avoid frustrating the expectations of third parties in the jurisdiction where the instrument is located, the Guide recommends that the creation and priority of such a security interest remains subject to the *lex situs* of the instrument (recommendation 203).

III. LAW APPLICABLE TO SECURITY INTERESTS IN INTANGIBLE ASSETS

In the case of intangible assets (with the exception of bank accounts, letters of credit and intellectual property which are subject to special conflict-of-laws rules),[15] the law applicable to the creation, third-party effectiveness and priority of a security interest is the law of the State in which the grantor is located (recommendation 208). The law applicable to the enforcement of such a security interest is the law governing priority with the result that the law of the grantor's location also applies to enforcement (recommendation 218, subpara. (b)).

In this connection, it should be noted that priority among competing security interests in the Guide is understood as priority among security interests in the same assets *granted by the same grantor* (recommendation 76), not by different grantors. Thus, in the case where A creates a security interest in its receivables in favour of X, sells the receivables to B and B creates a second security interest in the same receivables in favour of Y, the dispute between X and Y is not a priority conflict between two secured creditors. In other words, there cannot be two grantors owning the same asset and potentially two applicable laws. Under the Guide, the law of the grantor's location governs the question whether transferee B takes the receivables subject to the security interest of secured creditor X. The

[15] Recommendations 210–212, and 248.

extent of the rights granted by transferee B to its secured creditor Y is left to other law that would generally result in those rights not being higher than the rights of B (*nemo dat*).

The grantor's law approach recommended in the Guide with respect to intangible assets has the advantage that it refers all property law issues to a single law, even in the case of a security interest in a pool of assets that are located in different States (which is the typical scenario, for example, in a receivables financing transaction).[16] Appropriate location rules deal with the change of the grantor's location after the creation of a security interest. In this case, generally the location at the time of creation determines the law applicable to creation and the location at the time a third-party effectiveness or priority issue arises determines the law applicable to third-party effectiveness or priority (recommendation 220, subparagraph (a)).

Another advantage of the grantor's law is that, for example, in the case of a receivable where the debtor of the receivable is located in a State other than the State of the grantor's location, the grantor's law is still the relevant law for third-party effectiveness and priority issues. This result does not prejudice the rights of the debtor of an encumbered receivable as the rights and obligations of the debtor are separate from questions of third-party effectiveness and priority, and as such, by definition, do not concern the debtor of the receivable.[17] And the Guide makes this distinction clear, subjecting the rights and obligations of the debtor to the law governing the receivable and third-party effectiveness and priority to the law of the grantor's location (recommendations 208 and 217).[18]

An additional advantage of the grantor's law is that it is easy to determine, even in the case of a security interest in assets that do not exist at the time of the creation of the security interest (that is, in future assets). In this connection, it is worth noting that, under the Guide, the grantor's location is the grantor's place of business and, where the grantor has places of business in more than one State, the State in which the grantor has its central administration (real seat, recommendation 219, as well as article 5, subpara (h) of the Receivables

---

16 See Hartley, *supra* footnote 6, 53. As to the problems with the assignor's law identified by Hartley (change of principal place of business by the assignor, assignments by joint assignors and successive assignments), the Guide has resolved the first with recommendation 220, suggested a practical solution to the second by referring to transactions where, for example, a syndicate of banks is represented by a lead bank/agent (Guide, chapters II, para. 37, IV, para. 30) and resolved the third by treating it as a question whether a transferee (and all those who acquire rights from a transferee) obtain the encumbered assets subject to an already existing and effective security interest.

17 See Roy Goode, "Security Assignment of Receivables in Cross-Border Transactions", Lecture to DLA Piper (www.dlapiper.com/dla-piper-london-hosts-lecture-by-professor-sir-roy-goode-10-26-2011/).

18 Walsh, "Receivables Financing and the Conflict of Laws", *Dickinson Law Review*, Vol. 106:1, 194.

Convention). While this may not be the case in all situations, the real seat of the grantor is normally easy to determine and not so easy to change.[19]

Referring to the place of the central administration (a concept similar to the centre of main interests) of the grantor results in the law of the State in which the main insolvency proceedings with respect to the grantor are most likely to be opened. Thus, the law applicable to security interests and the law applicable to insolvency proceedings will be the law of one and the same jurisdiction (and the possibility of a secondary insolvency proceeding or the exception of rights *in rem* in Article 5 of the European Insolvency Regulation does not seriously weaken this argument).[20] This addresses to a large extent the risk that, in the case where a security interest is most relied upon (that is, in the case of the grantor's insolvency), the applicable law will be set aside as contrary to the public policy or the internationally mandatory rules of the forum where insolvency proceedings will be opened. Any other approach to this issue is exposed to that risk and, as a result, cannot ensure certainty of the law applicable where this certainty is mostly needed. The law governing the contract of assignment is clearly unacceptable as it would result in the assignor and the assignee choosing the law that would govern the rights of third parties, in a way that would not be transparent to third parties.[21] The law governing the receivable, that is, the law governing the contract from which the receivable arises is equally unacceptable, at least for most receivables. In the typical receivables financing transaction where a pool receivables is involved, the law governing the receivables could result in the application of several laws to the same transaction; and, to the extent future receivables are involved, what that law might be would not be clear even to the parties of the transaction at the time of the transaction.[22] Similarly, referring to the law of the *situs* for receivables (the place of payment or of the debtor's domicile) also fails to ensure certainty and transparency of the applicable law in the case where it is mostly needed, namely in the case of the insolvency of the grantor/assignor (the borrower). Contractual arrangements to place the receivables in a particular jurisdiction (to ensure the application of a certain law) may well not be worth even the paper they are written on.

It should be noted that the grantor's law approach does not apply to securities and payment rights arising under financial contracts or foreign

---

19 For a discussion and generally positive evaluation of the grantor's law approach, see Ulrich Drobnig, "Die Kollisionsnormen des Legislative Guide for Secured Transactions von UNCITRAL (2007)", in *Die richtige Ordnung, Festschrift für Jan Kropholler zum 70. Geburtstag*, herausgegeben von Dietmar Baetge, Jan von Hein und Michael von Hinden, Mohr Siebeck, Tübingen, 2008, 542.

20 Peter Mankowski, „Zessionstatut v. Recht des Zedentensitzes-Ergänzende Überlegungen zur Anknüpfung der Drittwirking von Zessionen", *IPRax* 2012, Heft 4, 301.

21 Catherine Walsh, *supra* footnote 19, 171.

22 Walsh, *ibid*, 173.

exchange transactions, as these types of transaction are excluded from the Guide (recommendation 4, subparas. (c)-(e)) and the Receivables Convention altogether (Article 4, para. 2). This approach does not apply either to bank accounts, letters of credit or intellectual property as the Guide includes special rules with respect to these types of asset (recommendations 210, 212 and 248) and the Receivables Convention excludes them (Article 4, para. 2) or does not apply (to intellectual property).

It should also be noted that, with respect to the law applicable to a security interest in the case of insolvency, the Guide recommends that the commencement of insolvency should not displace the conflict-of-laws rules that determine the law applicable to the property law aspects of a security interest. However, this rule is subject to the application of the insolvency law of the State in which insolvency proceedings are commenced (*lex fori concursus*) to issues such as avoidance, treatment of secured creditors, ranking of claims or distribution of proceeds (recommendation 223). This recommendation is designed to strike a balance between the law applicable to security interests in general and the law applicable to insolvency proceedings.

The European Commission published recently a study prepared by the British Institute of International and Comparative Law.[23] The study states that overall 44% of the stakeholders favour the law of the assignor's habitual residence, 30% favour the law of the underlying claim and 11% prefer the law chosen by the assignor and the assignee, and that a vast majority of stakeholders favour a uniform EU solution (which will apply to transactions involving even non-EU parties if the forum is an EU member State).[24] Yet, the study recommends first a solution based on the law of the contract chosen by the assignor and the assignee, except in the case of an assignment of future receivables,[25] next a solution based on the law applicable to the assigned claim, again except in the case of an assignment of future receivables,[26] and only as a third solution the law of the assignor's habitual residence, except in the case of receivables from financial contracts!

In any case, all three proposals contain so many conditions and exceptions that certainty and transparency of the law applicable are not achieved to any acceptable degree and certainly not as much as the past EU Commission's proposal for an Article 13(3) of the Rome I Regulation. [27] Only that past EU Commission proposal would ensure a coordinated approach not just with the

23 Http://ec.europa.eu/justice/civil/files/report_assignment_en.pdf.

24 *Ibid*, 4.1.4.

25 *Ibid*, 5.2.1.

26 *Ibid*, 5.2.2.

27 *Ibid*, 5.2.3. For a critical analysis of the BICL study, see Eva-Maria Kieninger, "Das auf die Forderungsabtretung anzuwendende Recht im Licht der BIICL-Studie", *IPRax* 2012, Heft 4, 289.

Receivables Convention but also with the many national laws that have had for a long time or have recently adopted a modern secured transactions law based on the Guide. This coordinated approach is in the interest of all stakeholders in receivables financing to avoid the application of different laws depending on the forum in which the issue arose.[28] In this context, it should be noted that, at its 45th session in 2012, UNCITRAL reiterated its appeal to the EU Commission for a coordinated approach to avoid the application of different laws.[29]

IV. LAW APPLICABLE TO SECURITY INTERESTS IN PROCEEDS

An instance where not all issues are referred to a single law relates to security interests in proceeds of encumbered assets (and proceeds of proceeds). To meet the reasonable commercial expectations of the parties with rights in the original encumbered assets, the Guide recommends one law for the creation (continuation) of a security interest in proceeds, that is, the law applicable to the security interest in the original encumbered asset from which the proceeds arose; and, to protect the interests of third parties that may have extended credit against the security of the proceeds as original encumbered assets, the Guide recommends a different law for the third-party effectiveness and priority of a security interest in proceeds, that is, the law applicable to the third-party effectiveness and priority of a security right in the same kind of asset as the proceeds (recommendation 215)

As a result, for example, if the original encumbered asset is inventory, the inventory is sold and the proceeds generated from the sale are in the form of receivables, the creation of a security interest in the receivables is referred to the law of the State in which the inventory is located at the time of the putative creation of the security right (recommendations 215 and 220, subpara. (a)). However, in this same example, the third-party effectiveness and priority of the security interest in the receivables is referred to the law of the State in which the grantor is located at the time the issue arises (recommendations 215 and 220, subpara. (a)).

This rule cannot be applied in a forum State that has not implemented the substantive law recommendations of the Guide and does not distinguish between creation (effectiveness between the parties) and third-party effectiveness, but treats a security interest upon its creation as effective against all parties (*erga omnes*). In such a forum State, creation would include third-party effectiveness

[28] For the value of a uniform conflict-of-laws rule, see Michel Deschamps, "La Convention des Nations Unies sur la cession de créances dans une perspective canadienne", *Banque & Droit*, no. 90 – juillet-août 2003, 40.

[29] See A/67/17, para. 168 (www.uncitral.org/uncitral/commission/sessions/45th.html).

and both issues would be referred to the law applicable to the security interest in the original encumbered assets.

V. LAW APPLICABLE TO THE MUTUAL RIGHTS AND OBLIGATIONS OF THE PARTIES

With respect to matters that relate to the mutual rights and obligations of the parties to (the contractual aspects of) a security agreement, the application of the principle of party autonomy is generally accepted and is in line with the expectations of the parties. Thus, these issues are under the Guide subject to a law other than the law governing property matters. This is the law chosen by the parties and, in the absence of a choice of law, to the law governing the security agreement (recommendation 216).

The conflict-of-laws chapter of the Guide does not attempt to provide a conflict-of-laws recommendation as to the law governing the security agreement since this is not, strictly speaking, a secured transactions issue and is typically dealt with in codifications dealing with the law applicable to contractual obligations. However, the commentary refers to various conflict-of-law rules applicable to contractual obligations, such as the Rome Convention on the Law Applicable to Contractual Obligations, which, in article 4, para. 1, includes the close-connection test (chapter X, paras. 12 and 61).[30]

CONCLUSIONS

The Guide addresses in a comprehensive way the law applicable to security interests in movable assets, tangible and intangible (with few exceptions). The commentary discusses the relevant policy issues and the ways in which they could be addressed with their advantages and disadvantages; and the legislative recommendations relate to a conflict-of-laws rule that could be included in national law.

The Guide recognizes that conflict-of-laws rules are necessary to ensure that a security interest effectively created and made effective against third parties under the law of a State would be recognized under the law of another State, which may foresee different creation and third-party effectiveness requirements. The Guide also admits that conflict-of-laws rules would be necessary even if substantive

[30] The Guide also deals with the IX. Law applicable to the rights and obligations of third-party obligors (recommendation 217), order public and mandatory rules (recommendation 222) and renvoi (recommendation 225).

law were harmonized, at least, to determine the State whose requirements would apply to issues such as, for example, registration.

Some of the relevant conflict-of-laws recommendations of the Guide simply codify generally recognized notions (e.g. the *lex rei sitae* with respect to security interests in tangible assets).

Other conflict-of-laws recommendations of the Guide follow practical approaches adopted in many jurisdictions (e.g. the law of the grantor's location for security interests in intangible assets with limited exceptions), or include alternatives (e.g. the law of the State in which the bank account is maintained or the law governing the account agreement for security interests in rights to payment of funds credited to a bank account). Yet other recommendations break new ground (e.g. the combination of the *lex protectionis* and the grantor's law for security interests in intellectual property rights).

With respect to intangible assets, such as receivables, the Guide follows the approach of the Receivables Convention and recommends the law of the grantor's location (place of business, place of central administration or habitual residence). Receivables arising from securities, financial contracts and foreign exchange transactions are excluded from the scope of the Guide altogether and bank accounts, letters of credit and intellectual property are the subject of special, asset-based conflict-of-laws recommendations.

The grantor's law approach has a number of advantages, including that it results in the application of a single law to property aspects of a secured transaction (even where a pool of assets are encumbered), which is easy to determine (even in the case of future assets) and, most importantly, is the law of the State in which the main insolvency proceeding is typically opened with the respect to the grantor, and thus does not run the risk of being set aside as manifestly contrary to the public policy or the mandatory rules of the insolvency forum.

POST *NEULINGER* CASE LAW OF THE EUROPEAN COURT OF HUMAN RIGHTS ON THE HAGUE CHILD ABDUCTION CONVENTION

Paul BEAUMONT
Professor, University of Aberdeen

Lara WALKER
research assistant and PhD candidate, University of Aberdeen

This book is a tribute to Hans van Loon, whom Paul Beaumont has known since they first met at The Hague Conference in 1996. Paul has a great regard for Hans as a private international lawyer. Hans has done excellent work notably on Intercountry Adoption, Trusts and the Judgments Project. On many occasions Paul has seen how clearly and quickly Hans sees the technical problems with proposals made during meetings in the Hague Conference. Hans truly is a world class technician in the development of private international law conventions. He cares passionately about his subject and sees very clearly its relevance to the real world.

Hans was an enthusiast for Paul Beaumont's Hague Academy lectures in 2008 (which he attended) and therefore it is with great pleasure that this chapter builds on Paul's work in those lectures on the jurisprudence of the European Court of Human Rights on the Hague Child Abduction Convention. In the published version of the lectures Paul concluded that:

> 'the Court has modernised the Hague Convention by saying that all decisions must be taken in a way that is consistent with the "best interests" of the child but it has done so in a way that accepts that the drafters of the Hague Convention created limited exceptions to return in Articles 13 and 20 that exhaustively determine when it is in the child's best interests not to be returned. The Court has avoided the various extremes of, on one hand, virtually writing out the Article 13 exceptions and being more zealous to restore the *status quo ante* than the drafters and, on the

> other hand, of allowing the Article 13 exceptions to be greatly broadened in their scope by introducing a new freestanding exception that the child should not be returned when it is not in his or her best interests. The Court was clearly tempted at one point to do the latter but has wisely resisted the temptation and in doing so continued to make the Hague Convention effective and fit for purpose.'[1]

Since then the position of the European Court of Human Rights (ECtHR) appears to have changed in relation to the Hague Abduction Convention. Some of the case law indicates that there should be a full assessment of the best interests of the child in return proceedings. This is beyond the scope of the summary return mechanism intended by the Convention, and instead begins to turn into a full review of the merits of the custody arrangement.

This position first began to change in the Grand Chamber decision in *Neulinger*,[2] and since then there appears to be some inconsistencies in the case law. Although the decision in *Neulinger* was satisfactory, the reasoning of the Grand Chamber was not as clear and precise as it had been in the earlier case law.[3] It was hoped that in the following decisions the Court would give a narrow construction to *Neulinger* but this has not been the case.

Raban v *Romania*[4] was the next case to be heard by the ECtHR concerning the child abduction Convention. In the case there was a rather dubious interpretation of Articles 3 and 13(b) of the Convention in the domestic proceedings in Romania and a non-return order was made. When the case was brought to the ECtHR the Court did not take a strict interpretation of the Articles in the Hague Convention, as it had in previous cases,[5] but simply agreed with the interpretation of the Romanian court.[6] Following this there have been a number of other cases before the ECtHR and we can see an inconsistency of interpretation.

---

1 P Beaumont, 'The Jurisprudence of the European Court of Human Rights and the European Court of Justice on the Hague Convention of International Child Abduction' (2008) 335 *Recueil des cours* 12, 102.

2 *Neulinger and Shuruk* v *Switzerland* (App No 41615/07) ECHR 6 July 2010, and see L Walker, 'The Impact of the Hague Abduction Convention on the Rights of the Family in the case-law of the European Court of Human Rights and the UN Human Rights Committee: The Danger of *Neulinger*' (2010) 6 *Journal of Private International Law* 649, 665–671.

3 For an analysis of the earlier case law see: A Schulz, 'The 1980 Hague Child Abduction Convention and the European Convention on Human Rights' (2002) 12 *Transnational Law and Contemporary Problems*, 355, P Beaumont, n 1 and L Walker, n 2.

4 *Raban* v *Romania* (App No 25437/08) ECHR 26 October 2010.

5 For example, see the Court's interpretation of Article 3 of the Hague Convention in *Monory* v *Romania and Hungary* (App No 71099/01) ECHR 5 April 2005.

6 For an analysis of the decision in *Raban* see, L Walker and P Beaumont, 'Shifting the Balance Achieved by the Abduction Convention: The Contrasting Approaches of the European Court of Human Rights and the European Court of Justice' (2011) 7 *Journal of Private International Law* 231, 232–239.

PROCEEDINGS INITIATED BY THE ABDUCTING PARENT

X v *Latvia* was heard by the third chamber in December 2011.[7] The Court held by five votes to two that there had been a violation of Article 8 of the Convention by the Latvian authorities. The case was referred to the Grand Chamber. The hearing took place on 10 October 2012, and we are currently awaiting the decision of the Grand Chamber.[8] The facts of the case are relatively complicated. The child was born in Australia in 2005, and although the father's name was not given on her birth certificate the applicant and the child lived with the father, T, in his flat. On 17 July 2008 the applicant removed the child from Australia and took her to Latvia. On 6 November 2008 the Australian Family Court decided that T and the applicant had joint parental responsibility for the child since she was born. The Latvian Central Authority received a request for the return of the child to Australia under the Hague Convention on 22 September 2008.

The Riga City Zemgale District Court ordered the return of the child to Australia on 19 November 2008. The mother appealed this decision on the basis that she had been the sole guardian of the child when she left Australia and that the return of the child would expose her to psychological harm. The Riga Regional Court upheld the decision of the lower court on 26 January 2009. In reaching its decision the court recognised that the aim of ordering a return under the instrument was not to separate the parties but rather to have a proper custody hearing in the State of the child's habitual residence.[9] It is considered that the Latvian courts reached the correct result in this case. The applicant had no reason not to return to Australia with the child because she was an Australian national and had the right to reside, work and move freely in Australia. Therefore Article 13(1)(b) should not be applicable. Also as the father was exercising custody rights at the time of the removal, as the Latvian authorities considered that the Australian parental responsibility order confirmed that the father had parental responsibility rather than establishing his parental rights.[10]

However, after the return was ordered, the actual enforcement of the order was not handled very well.[11] A bailiff lodged an application for enforcement of the order and the applicant asked for suspension of the order. A hearing was

---

7 *X* v *Latvia* (App No 27853/09) ECHR 13 December 2011.

8 A webcast of the hearing is available at www.echr.coe.int/ECHR/EN/Header/Press/Multimedia/Webcasts+of+public+hearings/webcastEN_media?id=20121010-1&lang=en&flow=high, accessed 15 October 2012.

9 *X* v *Latvia*, n 7, para. 21.

10 See the arguments of the Latvian Government in *X* v *Latvia*, n 7, para. 50.

11 On a positive note however, the Latvian Ministry of Justice has set up a working group to propose necessary amendments to the laws on execution of orders. (*X* v *Latvia*, n 7, para. 29).

scheduled for April 2009. However, on 14 March 2009 the father re-abducted the child and took her back to Australia.

The majority of the ECtHR considered that the approach of the Latvian courts, when reaching their decisions to return the child to Australia, lacked in-depth examination of the entire family situation and of a whole series of factors, therefore rendering the interference disproportional within the meaning of Article 8(2) of the Convention.[12] The majority considered that there were a variety of reasons for this. In particular it was believed that the Regional Court 'did not review the psychological report, disregarding its clear conclusions with respect to particular ties between the mother and the child, and the risk of psychological harm in the event of separation'.[13] However, in the view of the minority the Latvian court did pay attention to the risk of separation but did not give any weight to it because there was no clear reason why the mother should not return to Australia with the child.[14] As the full text of the relevant part of the judgment of the Latvian court is not reproduced in the ECtHR report it is unclear how this matter was dealt with.[15] What is clear, however, is that the mother would have had no problems returning to Australia and she did in fact return there. Therefore, it is hoped that the Grand Chamber focuses on this fact and holds that there was no violation of Article 8. The mother was free to return to Australia and entitled to seek employment there and obtain social benefits[16] so there was no risk of psychological harm to the child from being separated from her mother unless the mother acted unreasonably by refusing to go back to Australia with her child.

The approach taken in the dissenting opinion in *X* is preferable to the majority decision. The task of assessing the best interests of the child belongs primarily to the national authorities,[17] because they often have the benefit of having direct contact with all the parties. 'It is not the job of this Court to take the place of the competent authorities in determining whether a decision concerning a child's residence would expose him to psychological harm.'[18] The Court should simply be assessing whether adequate procedures have been followed and there were no arbitrary or unreasonable conclusions. 'As is clear from the case file, the national courts took into account all the relevant principles and, on the basis of

12 *X* v *Latvia*, n 7, para. 78.
13 *Ibid*, para. 71.
14 *Ibid*, dissenting opinion of Judges Myjer and López Guerra.
15 *Ibid*, para. 21 does quote the relevant part of the judgment of the Riga Regional Court but has some words omitted. The part that is reproduced suggests that the reason the psychologist's report was not given any weight by the Riga Regional Court was because it was making a return order under the Hague Convention and not deciding on the merits of custody.
16 *Ibid*, dissenting opinion and Government argument noted in para. 53.
17 See, *Neulinger and Shuruk* v *Switzerland* (App No 41615/07) ECHR 6 July 2010, para. 138.
18 *X* v *Latvia* (App No 27853/09) ECHR 13 December 2011, dissenting opinion of Judges Myjer and López Garcia.

the evidence examined, concluded that there was no reasonably-founded concern that the child's return to Australia would subject her to a risk of any kind.'[19] Despite this the majority was not happy with the Latvian court's examination of the case. The dissenting judges consider that

> 'the majority has substituted its assessment concerning the best interests of the child for the assessment of the national courts in their reasoned and non-arbitrary judgments, but without having had ... the benefit of direct contact with the parties concerned or with the evidence examined in the proceedings. In our opinion, the majority has assumed a function going beyond the competence of this Court. In this case, the Latvian courts duly assessed the behaviour – including the (lack of) cooperation with both the Australian and Latvian authorities by the applicant herself – and the personal circumstances of the parties, the relevant provisions of national law and Australian law and the foreseeable consequences that returning to Australia would have on the child as well as the position of the applicant if she likewise decided to return to Australia, with regard to her freedom of movement, employment and social benefits.'[20]

The approach taken in the dissenting opinion is sensible and in line with state practice under the Hague Convention. There cannot be perceived to be a grave risk of harm simply because the abducting parent would rather not return to the country of origin. Unless there is a clear reason that the abducting parent cannot return to the state of origin,[21] issues of harm to the child on separation from the abducting parent are irrelevant. It is hoped that the decision of the Grand Chamber will rectify this.

The Court took a similar approach to *X* in the case of *B*.[22] The child was born in America and had dual Belgian and American citizenship. Her father was American and her mother had been living in America since she was three but was a Belgian national. The child had lived exclusively with her mother until she was four years old. The parents agreed to share custody of the child, and a court in Florida upheld the agreement in May 2008. The mother and the child left the United States in October 2008 and went to live in Belgium. In March 2010 the Ghent court of first instance held that the child should not be returned because the exception in Article 13(1)(b) had been met. This decision was overturned

---

19 *Ibid.*

20 *Ibid.*

21 'An inability for the abducting parent to contest the merits of the custody of the child in that forum, perhaps because of criminal prosecution or a denial of entry due to visa restrictions, would seem to justify a decision not to return the child in terms of Article 13(1)(b).' (P Beaumont, n 1, 62).

22 *B* v *Belgium* (App No 4320/11) ECHR 10 July 2012. Regrettably this judgment is only available in French. The authors are grateful to their colleague, Dr Anatole Boute, for his assistance as a native speaker with translation.

by the Ghent court of appeal in December 2010. A further appeal was lodged before the Court of Cassation, but this was dismissed on 10 November 2011.[23] The American courts had awarded the father custody of the child, whilst proceedings in the Belgian courts were ongoing.

As far as it is clear from the facts, just as in the *X* case, the mother was arguing that the child should not be returned because this would put the child in an intolerable situation. Several psychological reports were put forward; however it would appear that they only identified a risk of harm in the situation that the child would be separated from the mother. The mother should have no problem returning to the United States with the child, because she had lived there since she was three years old so she must have sufficient ties and connections with the country.[24]

In its assessment the Court took several factors into account. The Court highlighted that all parties had been heard before the national courts, and the court had several psychological reports as evidence as well as a video of a meeting between the father and the child.[25] The ECtHR suggested that the Belgian courts rejected the reports, in substance, simply on the basis that they had been established by the mother and that the video between the child and the father showed no difficulties between them. The Court believed that the Belgian authorities could have had their own reports drawn up if they wished (however, this would have created more delays). It was also mentioned that the Belgian courts should have considered reports from the U.S. authorities.[26] In addition, to not considering the reports properly (even though they received evidence from all the parties) the Court also believed that the Belgian courts did not properly consider whether the mother could accompany the child back to the U.S., because it had been alleged that she could face criminal sanctions on return.[27]

Thirdly, since the child had already been in Belgium for two years, at the time of the decision of the court of appeal, the Court believed that the court of appeal should have taken into account the child's current situation and whether the passage of time meant that she was settled into her new environment. They

23 It is unfortunate that there were three stages of appeal before the national courts. It would be more suitable if national authorities only allowed one appeal in abduction proceedings in order to stop the abductor benefiting from the passage of time by initiating numerous appeals.

24 However, there is a reference to criminal sanctions in the case, but it was alleged that these risks were unfounded. We will not comment on this aspect of the case as the facts are not clear. However, we do not think a mother should be made to return if the risk of criminal proceedings is real. If the Belgian authorities had any doubts about the safety of the mother on return then it would have been beneficial if they had sought an undertaking from the US authorities that the mother would not face criminal sanctions if she were to return and cooperate with the authorities. (see note 21).

25 *B* v *Belgium*, n 22, para. 68.

26 *Ibid*, para. 72.

27 *Ibid*, para. 73.

reprimanded the court of appeal for following the text in Article 12 and refusing to consider this, since the child had been in Belgium for less than a year when the proceedings started.[28] The ECtHR should not be encouraging national courts to be considering factors such as the passage of time, where the Abduction Convention does not require it. This will mean that the abducting parent can beat the system and make an illegal situation legal, simply by making numerous appeals in order to allow the child time to settle into their new environment. This trend has to be stopped if the Abduction Convention is to remain effective, and the situation needs to be resolved expeditiously as the Convention requires.[29] The Court further highlighted that it took eleven months for the Court of Cassation to give a decision. This is far too long, especially when the case had already been dealt with at two other levels. National authorities either need to put a limit on appeals in Abduction Convention cases or make sure they are given preference over other cases so that they are dealt with expeditiously, in order to prevent the situation where the child becomes settled in their new environment. The same could be said for the ECtHR in reference to Abduction cases, where the delay is generally longer than at the national level.[30]

Despite complaining about the delay the Court then reprimands the court of appeal for not examining the case in a more thorough way because it had sufficient time to do this.[31] Clearly, children should not be returned when this is not in their best interests because one of the Article 13 exceptions applies. However, the ECtHR cannot demand an in-depth examination of all the facts, which requires obtaining many reports, more like actual custody proceedings, while at the same time requiring the national courts to deal with the case expeditiously. There has to be a middle ground whereby when national courts hear sufficient evidence to establish whether any of the Article 13 exceptions apply there should be no examination of the entire situation. It is believed that the ECtHR is not finding this balance at the moment. The majority of the Court concluded in *B*, that the court of appeal did not examine clearly whether there was a risk within Article 13(b) and therefore the return of the child could not be considered as being necessary in a democratic society.[32]

---

28 *Ibid*, para. 74. See Article 12 of the Abduction Convention, which allows other factors to be taken into consideration, such as whether the child is settled into the new environment, but only if the application is made after a year has passed. The Court also wrongly took this factor into account in *Raban* v *Romania*, n 4. See, L Walker and P Beaumont, n 6, 235.

29 See Articles 2,11 and 12 of the Abduction Convention.

30 See P Beaumont, n 1, at pp. 79–80. In relation to the latest case law *Neulinger* – 2 years 10 months, *Raban* – 2 years 5 months, *B* – 1 year 6 months, *MR and LR* – 2 months, *Shaw* – 2 years 6 months, *Karrer* – 1 year 11 months and *X* has currently taken 3 years and 7 months but we are still waiting for the final decision.

31 *B* v *Belgium* n 22, para. 75.

32 *Ibid*, para. 76.

The dissenting Judges Berro-Lefèvre and Karakas, heavily criticise the reasoning and opinion of the majority. Firstly they note that the Ghent court of appeal took into account all the evidence and heard all the parties and looked at declarations from other acquaintances, the child's school and the priest. The court also observed that the US authorities took care to ensure the gradual entry of the father into the child's life and had observed agreements between the parties that were made during the mediation process. The court believed that neither the father nor his family would be negative or threatening towards the child and that the father could take care of his daughter. The dissent then highlights that the majority, after deciding that the court of appeal had not exhaustively examined the case,[33] then criticises this examination for several reasons. The dissent believes that in taking this approach the majority substituted their conclusions on the best interests of the child for those of the court of appeal and acted as a judge of fourth instance.[34]

The dissent believes that the case is totally different from *Neulinger* because the father had been granted custody by the U.S. authorities, and the father was taking an active interest in the child including visiting the child in Belgium. Due to the fact that the Belgian courts undertook a thorough examination and the case can be distinguished from *Neulinger*, the dissent believes that the interpretation of the Abduction Convention by the majority is beginning to put the future of the Convention at risk. The dissent considers that the finding of a violation now becomes the norm because the Court substitutes its opinion for that of the national authorities simply because of the effect of time passing.[35] The dissent highlights that the Convention is meant to prevent the wrongful removal of children and the philosophy is that the *status quo ante* should be resumed as quickly as possible in order to avoid the legal consolidation of a factual situation that is originally wrongful.[36] This has to be true and therefore it is imperative that the ECtHR stops creating a wrongful incentive for parents to appeal, in the knowledge that the European Court is likely to find a violation of Article 8 simply because of the passage of time caused by those appeals and is likely to instruct the national authorities to suspend any return order when the abducting parent brings an application to the ECtHR.

Further, the dissent believes that the ECtHR's current approach of requiring an in-depth examination of the entire family situation is wrong. To impose on the internal authorities an in-depth examination of the entire family situation in every case of this type makes no sense; there would be no difference between

---

33 The dissent believed this examination was meticulous and detailed, and should not be regarded as insufficient or arbitrary.

34 *B* v *Belgium*, n 22, 28.

35 *Ibid*, 29.

36 *Ibid*.

Convention procedures where rapidity is required and the in-depth procedures of a ruling on the custody, access and residence of the child.[37] The dissent considers that this approach empties the Convention of its substance and purpose and takes note of the Explanatory Report in deciding that Article 13 should be interpreted strictly and in doing so emphasises that a grave risk of harm under Article 13 should not be constituted only by the separation from the parent that wrongfully removed or retained the child.[38] The dissent in *B* made some very good arguments and highlighted that the approach of the Court, when assessing applications by the abducting parent, is no longer consistent with the underlying philosophy of the Hague Convention. It would be beneficial if the Grand Chamber paid attention to these arguments when reaching its conclusion in the *X* case.

It would also be useful for the Grand Chamber to find that there is no violation of Article 8 in the *X* case in order for the decision to be consistent with *MR and LR* v *Estonia*.[39] The case concerned a wrongful retention of the child in Estonia. As in *X* there was an expert psychologist report which indicated that if the child was returned to Italy without the mother then this would cause 'serious mental suffering'.[40] The county court considered that on the basis of the evidence they could not conclude that there was actual abuse by the father to the child or the mother. They also importantly and clearly stated that; 'pursuant to the Hague Convention the child was not returned to the other parent but to the other country; therefore, the court did not find the first applicant's arguments about the separation of mother and child relevant.'[41] The Court of Appeal upheld the decision of the county court considering that with the spirit of the Hague Convention the best way of protecting the best interests of the child was a swift return to her habitual environment. This also assisted to fulfil the purpose of 'ensuring that parents would not take their children unlawfully to another country.'[42] The appeal court also agreed that concerns about the separation of the child and the mother were unfounded.

Unlike in *X* and *B*, the ECtHR were happy with the national courts' assessment and held, by a majority, that the application in *MR and LR* was manifestly unfounded.[43] In reaching this conclusion the Court considered that the applicant herself had sufficient ties with Italy and therefore believed that 'by dismissing the first applicant's arguments concerning her impossibility to return

37 *Ibid.*
38 *Ibid.*
39 (App No 13420/12) ECHR 15 May 2012.
40 *Ibid*, see para. 12.
41 *Ibid*, para. 15.
42 *Ibid*, see para. 19.
43 *Ibid*, see para. 50. The ECtHR dealt with the matter in a very short time for them, only two months! (see note 30) If the ECtHR dealt with all these cases so efficiently, this would be a better outcome in keeping with the philosophy of the Hague Convention.

to Italy the domestic courts did not overstep their margin of appreciation.'[44] It was further noted that there appeared to be nothing arbitrary about the domestic courts' assessment, and there was nothing to suggest that the authorities did not strike a fair balance between the competing interests. Importantly the Court clarified that 'the proceedings in question did not involve any determination of the parents' custody rights, which are subject to the proceedings in Italy'.[45]

The outcome in *MR and LR* is better than that in *X*. Although the language used by the Estonian courts may be clearer than that used by the Latvian courts in *X*, the approach taken by the Latvian courts was in no way arbitrary and the correct decision was reached.[46] Both mothers could easily return to the country of origin and, in *X*, the applicant was even an Australian national. Therefore, the approach taken by the dissenting judges in *X*, *B* and the majority in *MR* which clarifies that the decision of the national courts, who may have the benefit of direct contact with the parties, should be considered correct unless it is arbitrary, has to be preferred. It is hoped that the Grand Chamber follows this approach and dismisses the application in *X*, in order to maintain the spirit of the Hague Convention which is to prevent the unlawful removal of the child from its country of habitual residence. Any other finding would result in the abducting parent benefiting from their wrongdoing, and thus being able to usurp the Abduction Convention simply due to the passage of time.[47]

APPLICATIONS MADE BY THE LEFT BEHIND PARENT

In *Karrer* v *Romania*,[48] instead of the abductor making an application to the ECtHR, it was the left behind parent. The parents were married in Austria in 2004 and their child was born there in 2006. They separated in 2008 and divorce proceedings were initiated in Austria. In February 2008 the Salzburg District Civil Court granted the mother, KT, an interim injunction against the father seeking his removal from the family home on grounds of violent behaviour. On 25 July 2008 the father was found not guilty of inflicting bodily harm against KT.

44 *Ibid*, para. 48.
45 *Ibid*, para. 49.
46 The ECtHR also has the benefit of the knowledge that the Latvian courts generally do not function by mechanically ordering a return in all cases, because in the earlier case of *Ŝneersone and Kampanella* v *Italy* (App No 14737/09) 12 July 2011, the Latvian court had in fact refused to return the child on the basis of Article 13(1)(b). This case will not be discussed in the present work as the case concerned Brussels II*a* and was not a pure Hague Child Abduction case.
47 See the dissenting opinion in *B* n 22 discussed above at pp. 24–25, where the risk posed to the future of the Convention is explained.
48 (App No 16965/10) ECHR 21 February 2012.

In September 2008 KT took the child with her to Romania. On 25 November 2008 the Salzburg District Civil Court granted the father temporary sole custody of the child until the divorce was finalised. At the time the case was heard by the ECtHR divorce proceedings were pending before the Romanian Courts.[49]

The father submitted a request for the return of the child to Austria on 30 September 2008. In a judgment of January 2009, that was not communicated until May 2009, the Bucharest County Court ordered the return of the child to Austria. However, the Bucharest Court of Appeal overturned the decision of the lower court in July 2009, holding that the return of the child to Austria would expose her to physical and psychological harm within the meaning of Article 13(1)(b). The court based this on the fact that it had been alleged that the father had been violent towards KT and that the Salzburg court had granted her an interim injunction. However, the court failed to acknowledge that the father had already been acquitted of the criminal charges in relation to the alleged violence and had even been awarded temporary sole custody of the child by the Salzburg courts. The court also seems to have failed to consider whether or not the mother could safely return to Austria and what her position would be there.[50] It also appears that the Romanian Central Authority did not have any direct contact with the father.

The father lodged a complaint before the ECtHR on the basis that the case had not been dealt with expeditiously, he had not been heard and the Romanian Central Authority had not represented his interests properly. The ECtHR considered that, in its assessment of the child's best interests, the Romanian court did not make any reference to the child's current family situation it simply relied on an expired interim injunction. In addition the witness testimonies relied on only came from KT and her parents. 'No attempt appears to have been made to contact the first applicant [father] in order to hear his position on this matter [and] there was no analysis of the implications of a possible return'[51] of the child to Austria. It is also acknowledged that the case file contained controversial pieces of evidence and therefore 'giving the first applicant the opportunity to present his case either directly or through written submissions was of paramount importance for ensuring the fairness of the decision-making process.'[52]

The Court confirmed its case law that if Hague Abduction cases are not handled urgently then the 'passage of time can have irremediable consequences for the relations between the children and the parent who does not live with

49 *Ibid*, paras 7–13.
50 *Ibid*, see paras 46 and 47.
51 *Ibid*, para. 47.
52 *Ibid*, para. 53.

them'.[53] The Court was not content that the Hague return proceedings before the Romanian courts lasted eleven months.

The Court unanimously concluded that there had been a violation of Article 8 of the Convention by the Romanian authorities because; 'the decision-making process at the domestic level was flawed as on the one hand no in-depth analysis was conducted with a view to assessing the child's best interests and on the other hand the first applicant was not given the opportunity to present his case in an expeditious manner as required under Article 8 of the Convention interpreted in the light of the Hague Convention'.[54]

There was no clear reason why Article 13(1)(b) should have applied and therefore the child should not have been returned to Austria. It is good that the Court has referred back to its earlier case law highlighting that applications under the Hague Convention should be dealt with expeditiously.[55] However, it is slightly contradictory to insist on an in-depth analysis on the one hand and a quick outcome on the other. The former suggests that the court of refuge must make a full analysis of the best interests of the child as though it was a custody hearing which should not be the case.[56]

Terrible delays in enforcement of a Hague return order by the national authorities are evident in *Shaw* v *Hungary*.[57] In January 2008 the child was wrongfully retained by the mother in Hungary. Hague proceedings began on 12 March 2008. The proceedings were heard by three courts and a final decision to return the child was given on 18 November 2008.[58] But the return order was never enforced.

When assessing the case the ECtHR referred back to its earlier case law on the Hague Convention which requires that 'the national authorities have taken all necessary steps to facilitate the execution as can reasonabl[y] be demanded in

---

53 *Ibid*, para. 54. See also P Beaumont, n 1, 47–50.

54 *Karrer* v *Romania* (App No 16965/10) ECHR 21 February 2012, para 55.

55 In relation to this it is important to point out that the cases that are going to the ECtHR are usually taking years to conclude (see n 30 above), which in the end is often leading to a skewed result because once the child has been in the state of refuge for two or more years it is harder to justify the application of the Hague Convention as it is designed to prevent this from happening. Therefore, by the time the ECtHR makes a decision, it is often no longer possible to remove the child from the environment they are now settled in. The ECtHR should not grant an interim order preventing the return of the child unless it guarantees to decide the case within 2 months.

56 As the Court rightly considered in *MR and LR* v *Estonia*, n 39, para. 49.

57 (App No 6457/09) ECHR 26 July 2011. The Court sets out the sad tale of the failure to enforce the return order at paras. 13–32 of its judgment.

58 Although numerous appeals in Hague proceedings should be avoided, the proceedings only took 9 months to go through the national courts, which compared to some of the other cases, as well as any references to the ECtHR is not actually that long. However, the ECtHR chose to reproach the Hungarian authorities for the delays in the hearing (see paras 70–71).

the special circumstances of each case'.[59] This is good because the longer the child stays away from their habitual residence the harder it is to justify a return there as their links to that country begin to diminish and they develop closer ties to the state of refuge.[60] The Court found that the Hungarian authorities failed to 'take adequate and effective measures for the enforcement of the return order' because they had 11 months to make it happen before the mother disappeared with the child, they imposed only one small fine on the mother and they did not enforce the order when they arrested her .[61] Therefore, there was a violation of Article 8.

It is useful that the Court is still finding a violation of the rights of the left behind parent where there has been a delay or a failure to return the child. These cases are not detrimental to the Hague Convention, and should in fact help for it to be implemented correctly, because the delay in proceedings before the ECtHR has no effect on the location of the child. In these situations the national authorities should be trying to return the child and the proceedings by the left behind parent should not affect this. The problem is the other way around when the delays in the ECtHR are holding up the enforcement of the return order and therefore allowing a wrongful situation to become legitimate.

CONCLUSION

There are two major problems with the current approach of the ECtHR. Firstly proceedings are taking too long, which has an even greater impact when the ECtHR is reaching its decisions on the basis of the passage of time. Secondly, the Court is insisting on an in-depth examination of the entire family situation, to such an extent that the proceedings become akin to custody proceedings, therefore creating another reason why the cases cannot be dealt with expeditiously.

In order for the Hague Convention to continue to be a workable and successful instrument in Europe, the ECtHR must conform to the purpose and the text of the Convention. The Convention requires that national courts use the 'most expeditious procedures available.'[62] Article 11 also exemplifies that return proceedings should be dealt with expeditiously. This is supposed to constitute two elements: 'firstly, the use of the most speedy procedures known to their legal system; secondly, that applications are, so far as possible, to be granted priority

[59] *Ibid*, para. 65. For a full analysis of the earlier case law of the ECtHR on enforcement and delays in the context of the Hague Convention see P Beaumont, n 1, 27–50, and L Walker, n 2, 650–659.

[60] See above (especially the dissenting opinion in *B*) and how the abducting parent can now use this to their advantage.

[61] *Shaw* v *Hungary*, n 57, paras 73 and 74.

[62] Hague Abduction Convention, Article 2.

treatment.'[63] The European Court of Human Rights should be required to deal with child abduction cases in the same way as national courts. The Court of Justice of the European Union even has an urgent procedure that it uses for certain cases, including child abduction cases, to ensure that they are dealt with as quickly as possible.[64] Therefore, it is argued that the ECtHR has to create a system for hearing Child Abduction cases urgently in about 2 months as it did in the *MR and LR* v *Estonia* case.

The ECtHR has to take care not to place too much emphasis on the passage of time, and it also has to realise that separation from the primary carer is not on its own sufficient to justify the non return of the child.[65] In addition the Court also has to remember that the child is returning to the State of habitual residence and not to the left behind parent,[66] so that a proper custody hearing can be held in the correct place.

Instead of distinguishing return proceedings from custody proceedings the Court is insisting on an in-depth analysis of the entire family situation in order to ascertain the child's best interests in Convention proceedings, thus almost equating them to custody proceedings.[67] Requiring national courts to order extra reports, which the national courts do not think are necessary in order to determine if the child should be returned will only add to the length of time that procedures are taking, therefore making it more difficult to return the child. In Hague Convention return proceedings the national courts should be deemed to be upholding the best interests of the child when they make a good faith attempt to interpret and apply the provisions of that Convention in accordance with its aims and objectives. The ECtHR should stop acting like a final court of appeal by substituting its opinions for those of the national courts and delaying procedures in cases where it is imperative that cases are dealt with more quickly. The result is often that the child is caused more harm and the *status quo ante* can no longer be resumed.

---

63 Perez Vera Explanatory Report, para. 104.

64 This is an urgent preliminary ruling procedure that applies to the area of freedom security and justice and it came into effect on 1 March 2008. See http://curia.europa.eu/jcms/upload/docs/application/pdf/2009-03/cp080012en.pdf, accessed 25 October 2012. The Court deals with these cases in an average of 2.5 months, see the CJEU Annual Report 2011, see http://curia.europa.eu/jcms/jcms/Jo2_7000/.

65 The Court needs to deal with the exceptions properly. The intention is that 'they are interpreted in a restrictive fashion if the Convention is not to become a dead letter. In fact, the Convention as a whole rests upon the unanimous rejection of this phenomenon of illegal child removals and upon the conviction that the best way to combat them at an international level is to refuse to grant them legal recognition.' (Perez Vera Report, para. 34).

66 See the assertions of the national court in *MR and LR* v *Estonia* (App No 13420/12) ECHR 15 May 2012, para. 15.

67 See the dissent in *B*, n 22 above, at pp. 24–25.

OF LUDDITES AND LUMINARIES: THE USE OF MODERN TECHNOLOGIES UNDER THE HAGUE LEGAL CO-OPERATION CONVENTIONS*

Christophe Bernasconi
Deputy Secretary General of the Hague Conference on Private International Law

Mayela Celis
Senior Legal Officer at the Permanent Bureau

Alexander Kunzelmann
Legal Officer at the Permanent Bureau

INTRODUCTION

Hans van Loon's tenure at the Hague Conference on Private International Law ("Hague Conference") coincided with marked changes in the way in which civil and commercial relationships – and intergovernmental organisations – function as a result of advances in information and communication technology. Since becoming Secretary General in 1996, the number of households with computers has doubled in the United States ("US"), and increased ten-fold in China. Statistics on internet connectivity are even more telling; according to the International Telecommunications Union, the number of internet users has risen from below 30% of the population to over 70% in developed economies over the past decade, and from below 3% to almost 30% in developing economies. The internet is today much faster and more reliable, and supports new ways of social networking as well as a multi-trillion dollar digital economy.

* The Legal Co-operation team would like to thank Ms Tsjatsja Westerveld, Peter Nygh intern at the Permanent Bureau, for her assistance with the drafting of this article.

What if we wind back the clock to when Hans began at the Hague Conference in October 1978? The "Apple 2" personal computer had just been released,[1] telex was at the height of fashion, and fax machines were only starting to take off. Formal correspondence with Member States was all done by post, and documents were dictated and carefully transcribed by typewriter. The Permanent Bureau became a computerised environment in the late 1980s, but even then, there was no internal network or internet access. These did not arrive until the late 1990s, along with e-mail and the launch of the Hague Conference website. Although Hans has not been an aficionado of modern technology in his personal life (he would not be seen in an airport lounge browsing on the latest version of a fancy tablet computer, or tweeting latest developments), he has always fostered and supported initiatives to ensure that the Hague Conference and its work keep pace with technological change.

This contribution outlines just some of these initiatives. It will focus on the Hague Legal Co-operation Conventions, and look at the use of modern technologies under the *Hague Convention of 5 October 1961 Abolishing the Requirement of Legalisation for Foreign Public Documents* ("Apostille Convention"), the *Hague Convention of 15 November 1965 on the Service Abroad of Judicial and Extrajudicial Documents in Civil or Commercial Matters* ("Service Convention") and the *Hague Convention of 18 March 1970 on the Taking of Evidence Abroad in Civil or Commercial Matters* ("Evidence Convention"). In light of the upcoming Special Commission on the practical operation of the Service and Evidence Conventions, this contribution will mainly focus on the use of modern technologies under these Conventions.[2]

1. THE LEGAL CO-OPERATION CONVENTIONS AND THE USE OF MODERN TECHNOLOGY

A. INTRODUCTION TO THE LEGAL CO-OPERATION CONVENTIONS

In Hague Conference parlance, the "Legal Co-operation Conventions" refer to the three Conventions designed to replace the *Hague Convention of 1 March 1954 on Civil Procedure* – the Service Convention, Evidence Convention, and Access

---

1 See in contrast one of the worst tech predictions of all time: "There is no reason anyone would want a computer in their home" (Ken Olson, President of Digital Equipment Corp., 1977).

2 For more information on the e-APP see the Bibliography tab on the "Apostille Section" of the Hague Conference website at <www.hcch.net>.

to Justice Convention – as well as the Apostille Convention.[3] Before examining the role played by modern technology in these Conventions, it is useful to recall their operation.

The Apostille Convention currently has 104 Contracting States, making it the most widely ratified and acceded to of all the Conventions adopted by the Hague Conference.[4] The objective of the Convention is to facilitate the cross-border circulation of public documents by: (a) abolishing the often cumbersome, time-consuming and costly process of legalisation; and (b) replacing it with a single formality, the issuance of an Apostille by the Competent Authority designated by the Contracting State where the public document has been issued. The number of Contracting States is expected to continue to rise as States in Latin America, Southeast Asia and East Africa take note of the Convention's benefits, particularly in terms of regional economic integration, cross-border trade, and foreign investment.

The Service Convention provides a global framework for co-operation in the cross-border service of judicial and extrajudicial documents, by providing the channels of transmission to be used whenever a document is to be transmitted from one Contracting State to another Contracting State for service in the latter. The Convention does not provide substantive rules on the actual service of process, which remains a matter for the internal law of each State. The Convention has 67 Contracting States and has been described as the "most important multilateral convention" in the field of transnational service of process.[5]

The Evidence Convention establishes methods of co-operation for the taking of evidence abroad in civil and commercial matters and currently has 57 Contracting States. The Convention provides a means of overcoming differences in civil and common law systems with respect to the taking of evidence, and provides two separate mechanisms for evidence in one Contracting State to be taken, for use in proceedings in another Contracting State: (a) by letter of request (Chapter 1); and (b) by diplomatic official, consular agent or commissioner (Chapter 2).

---

3 These four Conventions are not the only Hague Conventions that establish mechanisms of legal co-operation, with several key Conventions concluded in the area of international child protection including the 1980 Child Abduction Convention, the 1993 Intercountry Adoption Convention, the 1996 Child Protection Convention, and the 2007 Child Support Convention. The success of these Conventions is due, in large part, to the legal co-operation mechanisms they establish, and in whose development Hans has played a pivotal role.

4 Conclusion & Recommendation No 1 of the 2012 Special Commission meeting. It is remarkable to note that of all the States that have joined the Apostille Convention until now, almost 40 percent have done so in the last decade.

5 *Dicey, Morris and Collins on the Conflict of Laws*, 13th ed. p. 197.

B. THE USE OF MODERN TECHNOLOGY IN GENERAL

Hans has played a defining role in monitoring the work carried out by the Hague Conference in respect of the Hague Legal Co-operation Conventions. It was Hans who prepared the first editions of the handbooks on the Service and Evidence Conventions, and who oversaw the organisation of almost every meeting of the various Special Commissions convened to review the practical operation of these Conventions. With Hans' support, we realised the challenges and potential for the use of modern technologies in the everyday operation of the Legal Co-operation Conventions.

Soon after Hans became Secretary General, the Permanent Bureau of the Hague Conference organised a series of conferences on the relationship between private international law and information and communication technologies. In June 1997, the Permanent Bureau, in association with the Molengraaff Institute of Private Law at the University of Utrecht, hosted an international colloquium entitled "Internet: Which Court Decides, Which Law Applies?" in honour of Michel Pelichet, former Deputy Secretary General of the Hague Conference.[6] Following the colloquium, the Permanent Bureau, in conjunction with the University of Geneva (Switzerland), held a round table discussion in September 1999, which brought together over 100 experts representing different sectors of electronic commerce ("e-commerce") to discuss issues of jurisdiction and applicable law arising out of e-commerce and internet transactions.[7] The final event in the series took place in The Hague in October 2004, and involved the collaboration of the Hague Conference, the Government of the Netherlands, and the International Chamber of Commerce ("ICC"), and focussed on the legal aspects of e-commerce transactions. These conferences enabled the Hague Conference to proceed with developing new instruments and servicing existing instruments with greater awareness of the realities of modern life.

In a 2000 paper outlining the challenges posed by globalisation for the Hague Conference, Hans observed that existing Hague Conventions, in particular the Apostille, Service and Evidence Conventions, were witnessing the effects of the exponential growth of electronic data interchange, the internet, and e-commerce.[8] These observations were followed in 2003 by a meeting of the Special Commission,

---

6 The proceedings from the colloquium are published in a 1998 book by the same name, edited by K. Boele-Woelki.

7 For more on this event, see Electronic Data Interchange, Internet and Electronic Commerce, *Preliminary Document No 7 of April 2000 for the attention of the Special Commission of May 2000 on general affairs and policy of the Conference*, available on the Hague Conference website < www.hcch.net >.

8 Van Loon, Hans, Globalisation and The Hague Conference on Private International Law, *International Law Forum du droit international*, Vol. 2, 2000, p. 232.

which was convened to review the practical operation of the Apostille, Service and Evidence Conventions. At this meeting, a whole session was set aside to discuss the "impact of new technologies".

In its Conclusions & Recommendations, the Special Commission emphasised that the reviewed Conventions "operate in an environment that is subject to important technical developments".[9] Recognising that these developments could not have been foreseen at the time the Conventions were adopted, the Special Commission noted that "the spirit and letter of the Conventions do not constitute an obstacle to the usage of such technologies"; quite the contrary, the Special Commission noted that "their application and operation can be *further improved* by relying on such technologies".[10]

On the back of these observations, and to ensure that the Hague Legal Co-operation Conventions remain relevant and effective in modern times, the Permanent Bureau has promoted the implementation of the electronic Apostille Program ("e-APP") under the Apostille Convention, and continues to explore the possibility of using modern technologies under the Service and Evidence Conventions, namely the electronic transmission of documents and taking of evidence by video link respectively.

C. ELECTRONIC APOSTILLE PROGRAM ("e-APP")

To ensure that the Apostille Convention continues to facilitate the international circulation of public documents for individuals and companies engaged in cross-border transactions, the authentication system it establishes must keep pace with the changing environment in which it operates. In this regard, new technologies are changing how traders and investors operate, and are enabling governments to provide citizens with public services online and issue them with public documents in electronic form.

The electronic Apostille Program (e-APP) is designed to bring the operation of the Apostille Convention into the 21st century through the application of modern technologies.[11] The aim of the e-APP is to promote and assist in the implementation of low-cost, operational and secure software, for the issuance of *e-Apostilles* and the operation of *e-Registers* accessible online by recipients seeking to verify the origin of e-Apostilles and paper Apostilles. Each component is standalone, and States are free to implement either or both of them. At the same

9 Conclusion & Recommendation No 4 of the 2003 Special Commission meeting.
10 Ibid (emphasis added).
11 For more information on the Apostille Convention, and the e-APP in general (incl. Conclusions & Recommendations of the Special Commission, Fora and Regional Meetings), see the "Apostille Section" of the Hague Conference website at <www.hcch.net>.

time, a number of e-APP States have opted to implement a comprehensive system that incorporates both components, thereby allowing Apostilles to be issued and registered at the click of a button.

In 2006, the Permanent Bureau, with the support of the NNA, launched the (then) electronic Apostille Pilot Program during the 2006 Special Commission (now the Council) on General Affairs and Policy of the Hague Conference. The launch followed the *International Forum on e-Notarization and e-Apostilles* in May 2005, which was jointly organised by the International Union of Latin Notaries and hosted by the NNA. Since then, the e-APP, with Hans's unremitting support, has gone from strength to strength, with the e-APP forum now a regular feature on the Hague Conference calendar, and the number of e-APP States continuing to grow. As a sign of this success, the word *pilot* was removed from its title in January 2012, and the program is now referred to as the *electronic Apostille Program*.

Since its launch in 2006, the e-APP has been implemented by over 150 Competent Authorities from 16 Contracting States, with Uruguay being the latest State to join at the end of 2012. In addition, approximately 20 other States have indicated that they are currently studying at least one of the e-APP components, including States that are in the process of joining the Convention. At present, approximately 35,000 e-Apostilles have been issued by participating Competent Authorities (using a comprehensive implementation of the e-Apostille component) and 22 e-Registers are in operation across the globe.

D. ELECTRONIC TRANSMISSION AND SERVICE UNDER THE SERVICE CONVENTION

An increasing number of jurisdictions representing different legal traditions are accepting that judicial documents may be served by electronic means, notably by e-mail. Although service by electronic means is a matter for internal law, where it is generally viewed as a form of substituted service to be ordered when personal service is not possible, the phenomenon of "e-service" may bring into play the operation of the Service Convention where foreign parties are involved.

The use of electronic methods of transmission under the Service Convention was first considered by Commission V of the 1999 Geneva Round Table. More recently, the use of electronic means of transmission was considered at the 2003 meeting of the Special Commission,[12] and again at the 2009 meeting, and both meetings took into account and further developed the findings of

[12] Conclusions & Recommendations No 59–64 of the 2003 meeting of the Special Commission.

Commission V.[13] The Special Commission concluded that "the transmission of documents internationally for the purposes of the Convention can and should be undertaken by IT-Business methods including e-mail". With regard to the main channel, the Special Commission acknowledged that electronic means of transmission could be used for communications between a requesting party and a forwarding authority, communications between a forwarding authority and a Central Authority of a requested State, and retransmission of the certificate of execution by the designated authority. In particular, e-mail and fax may be used for informal communications between the forwarding authority and the Central Authority once a request for service has been transmitted. With regard to service using modern technologies, the Special Commission noted that "a small number of States Parties had revised their domestic law to make reference to service using modern technologies such as email and fax". However, it further noted that at that time there had been only a few cases allowing this form of service, and typically only as a last resort.

It is important to distinguish between, on the one hand, *transmitting* documents under the Service Convention and *serving* them on the addressee. The main channel of transmission does not govern the actual service of documents *per se*; what needs to be served remains a matter of the requesting State and how the documents are to be served remains a matter for the law of the State addressed. Therefore, although documents may be transmitted to Central Authorities by electronic means, it is still up to that Central Authority to determine how to proceed with the service in accordance with its own laws under Article 5(1)(a), which may include service by electronic means. In addition, it is open to the applicant to request the Central Authority to serve the documents electronically as a "particular method of service" pursuant to Article 5(1)(b).

Direct service by electronic means may nevertheless be realised under the postal channel. Under the "functional equivalence" approach, the 'postal channels' may include modern technologies such as e-mail. Article 10(a) provides that the Convention does not interfere with the freedom to send judicial documents, by postal channels, directly to persons abroad, provided that the State of destination does not object. Here, a number of commentators have voiced their support for the view that the postal channel covers service by e-mail. However, if transmissions and service are to be carried out only by electronic means, it is crucial that Contracting States are able to ensure that security requirements are guaranteed, and that the defendant is protected in light of the requirements of due process concerns and Article 15 of the Convention.

To address the security requirements and due process concerns when using electronic mail under Article 10(a), one approach could be the use of e-post services

[13] Conclusions &Recommendations No 37–39 of the 2009 meeting of the Special Commission.

delivered by the International Postal Union. A recent study by the International Postal Union entitled, "Measuring postal e-services development", reveals the developments in the range of e-post services delivered to customers around the world using information and communication technology, including the sending of electronic messages.[14] Admittedly, the emergence of internationally accepted e-post services does not overcome objections raised by a Contracting States to any use of postal channels to serve documents, which can only be addressed through continued dialogue between States, especially at the Special Commission level. However, it opens up interesting new possibilities for further study, and ensures that the issue will remain on the agenda of future meetings of the Special Commission for some time to come.

i. Is e-mail considered an "address" for the purposes of the Service Convention?

The scope of the Convention in Article 1 states that the Service Convention does not apply when the address of the person to be served is not known. A question arises as to whether under the "functional equivalence" approach, the term "address" ought to include the "electronic address" (e-mail) of the recipient. We believe that an e-mail address is incapable of allowing an authority to determine whether there is occasion to transmit a document abroad and thus whether or not the Convention applies (and whether a State is a Contracting State to the Service Convention). In addition, recent court decisions show that States are very cautious when ordering substituted service by e-mail (when the defendant's physical address is not known) and have only done so when certain criteria are met.

Another approach to this issue of geographical connection, proposes that as e-mail servers make the contents of e-mails available to the recipient wherever he or she is physically located, e-mail should be treated as a transmission of a document into the country where the defendant will open the e-mail and read the documents.[15] However, other commentators contend that Article 1 refers only to a defendant's physical address, and where this is not known, the Convention will not apply.[16] Whether an electronic address is capable of signifying a geographical connection, as required by Article 1, remains an issue that will need to be

[14] International Postal Union. *Measuring postal e-services development – A global perspective* (January 2012) available at <www.upu.int/en/activities/electronic-services/publications.html> (last accessed on 23 January 2013).

[15] Folkman, Ted, The year in Review I: Service by Email Under the Hague Service Convention, *Letters Blogatory* <http://lettersblogatory.com/2011/12/16/service-by-email> (last accessed on 12 October 2012).

[16] See, Schultz, Andriana, Superpoked and Served: Service of Process Via Social Networking Site (2009) *University of Richmond Law Review*, Vol. 43, 1497, p. 1522.

considered by Contracting States if electronic methods of transmission are to be used under the Service Convention.

ii. *Case law developments on service by electronic means on foreign defendants*

Recent cases involving foreign defendants before common law courts in the United Kingdom ("UK"), Australia, the U.S. and Canada have shown that these courts will only order electronic service by e-mail, as a means of alternative service or substituted service, where traditional methods of service have been unsuccessful, or where the defendant has been evasive.[17]

In the Civil Procedure Rules in the UK and Australia, and in practice in the U.S. and Canada, judges consider specific factors when exercising their discretion to make an order for alternative service, including: whether reasonable steps have been taken to attempt to serve the respondent by permitted means, whether the use of e-mail is a preferred method of communication by the defendant, whether service by e-mail would be just and would be likely to bring the document to the attention of the defendant (addressing any concerns of due process), and the level of the defendant's attempts at evasion.[18] Aside from service by e-mail, a number of national courts in these jurisdictions have exercised their discretion to make an order for alternative service, and ordered service by Facebook and other social networking sites, such as Twitter, after consideration of the specific factors of the case.[19]

New developments in e-service of documents are not exclusive to common law jurisdictions. Increasingly, civil law countries are amending their laws to provide for e-service of documents and are setting up technology to enable

17 See, *Crystal Decisions (UK) Limited v Vedatech Corporation* [2004] EWHC (ch) 1872 (England); *LeBlanc v Whitma* 2005 ABQB 568 (Canada); *Rio Properties Inc. v Rio International Interlink* 284 F.3d (9th Cir. 2002) (United States); *Williams-Sonoma Inc v Friendfinder Inc.*, No. 06-6572, 2007 WL 1140639 (N.D.Cal. April 17, 2007) (United States).

18 See, *Bryne v Howards* [2010] FMCAfam 2009 (Australia); *Broadfoot v Diaz* 245 B.R. 713 (United States).; Also see generally, D. P. Stewart & A. Conley, E-mail service on foreign defendants: time for an international approach?, (2006–2007) 38 *Georgetown Journal of International* 755.

19 See, *MKM Capital Property Ltd v Corbo and Poyser* (ACT Supreme Court) (No. 608 of 2008) (Australia); *Blaney v Persons Unknown* (2008) (England); *Knott v Sutherland* (5 February 2009), Edmonton 0803 02267 (Alta. Q.B.M.) (Canada); *Axe Market Gardens Limited v Axe* CIV-2008-485-2676, High Court Wellington, 16 March 2009 (New Zealand); *AKO Capital LLP & Another v TFS Derivatives & Others* (unreported), UK High Court, 17 February 2012 (England). While the previous cases were decided in common law jurisdictions, the view that service by Facebook is an acceptable way of serving documents is gradually gaining ground. In this regard, Quebec, a mixed jurisdiction of civil law and common law, has also allowed service by Facebook in *Boivin & Associés c. Scott*, 2011 QCCQ 10324, par. 5 (Canada) and *Droit de la famille* — 111764, 2011 QCCS 3120 (Canada).

service by electronic means.[20] France is one of the States at the forefront of these developments and provides an example of one method of civil procedure reform to allow for the secure, electronic service of documents. Recent amendments to the *French Civil Procedure Code* and other domestic laws allow for the service of documents via electronic means, provided that certain conditions are met. Generally, electronic service can take place in domestic cases, provided the recipient has previously given his or her consent to documents being transmitted via electronic means. Also, electronic service of documents should offer *at least* equal safeguards as those provided by personal service of documents in paper form, which includes: reliability of the identification of the parties participating in the electronic transmission, integrity of the documents, the security and the confidentiality of the information exchanged, keeping a record of the transmission, and the possibility to establish with certitude the dates of sending and receipt of the documents.[21]

Electronic service was implemented in practice, following the adoption of the decree of 28 August 2012 which set out the technological requirements for e-service by the *huissiers de justice* (the French term for a bailiff or judicial officer). On 10 January 2013, the *Chambre nationale des huissiers de justice* launched the website "e-palais" (<https://www.e-palais.fr/>), which is a secure electronic platform for the service of documents (*actes du palais*) to lawyers, public prosecutors and court clerks.[22] Documents are electronically signed and stamped by the relevant *huissier de justice* using this platform. The platform then alerts the recipient, who can easily access the documents after entering a login name and password.[23]

Accordingly, this platform provides adequate safeguards as it ensures the identity of the parties participating in the transmission by use of a login name and password, as well as the integrity of the documents, and confidentiality of the information exchanged through the secure portal. Further, as a defendant must agree and register to be served via the e-portal, this approach addresses concerns of due process and whether the method of communication will provide

---

20 Brazil amended its civil procedure code in 2006 to allow defendants to register with the courts to be served electronically, by posting the documents on a web portal (Lei No. 11.419 de Dezembro de 2006, available at <www.trt02.gov.br/geral/tribunal2/Legis/Leis/11419_06.html>). See also France (Décret n° 2012-366 du 15 mars 2012 relatif à la signification des actes d'huissier de justice par voie électronique et aux notifications internationales), Spain (Spanish Code of Civil Procedure Law 1/2000 provides for service by electronic means), Italy (Presidential Decree 2001/123 provides for **electronic transmission** as a means of effecting service) and Romania (*Code of Civil Procedure allows service by fax and electronic means).*

21 Article 748-6 of the French Civil Procedure Code available at <www.legifrance.gouv.fr/> (last accessed on 23 January 2013).

22 See Article 672 of the French Civil Procedure Code.

23 A similar platform has been implemented by the *Chambre des huissiers de justice du Québec*, see < https://notabene.huissiersquebec.qc.ca/ >.

the defendant with notice. However, some commentators have suggested that as a defendant must first agree to be served electronically, this approach does not address situations in which only an e-mail-address exists for an evasive defendant. Regardless of any limitations, French reforms demonstrate that domestic courts are attempting to adjust service and civil procedure rules to accommodate modern technologies.

A similar approach using an electronic portal could be envisaged for the transmission of documents to be served abroad under the Hague Service Convention. *Huissiers* could transmit documents to be served abroad under Article 10(b) or (c) via: 1) a national platform to which a *huissier* in the foreign jurisdiction has also access; 2) two platforms maintained in two different jurisdictions but which are interoperable and allow for exchange of documents among the two jurisdictions; 3) an international platform operated by an international organisation (*e.g*,, the International Union of Judicial Officers) that can be accessed by *huissiers* in multiple jurisdictions. In addition, *huissiers* can execute incoming requests for service electronically under the main channel of transmission (Art. 5(1)(a) and (b)). Given that the consent of the recipient, or his lawyer, is required in advance, it would generally not be possible to apply this electronic transmission for service of process (unless parties have given their consent in contract or otherwise). However, this approach could nevertheless be applied for the remaining notifications necessary during the proceedings, including appeals.

E. TAKING EVIDENCE BY VIDEO-LINK UNDER THE EVIDENCE CONVENTION

The use of video-link technology to facilitate the taking of evidence abroad under the Evidence Convention has been an issue of considerable interest among Contracting States and practitioners in the 21st century. The advantage of this technology is that it allows a party, their representative, or a witness to appear or testify remotely in judicial proceedings. Given the borderlessness of transmission networks, such as the internet or telephone networks, video-links may be used where the remote location is within the same territory as the court or abroad. By overcoming distance, video-links offer potential savings in the time, cost, inconvenience, and environmental impact of physically attending court, and can therefore improve the efficiency of judicial proceedings.

A number of States, both Contracting and non-Contracting States to the Evidence Convention, have made provision under their internal law for hearings to take place by video-link. These include Australia, Canada, Czech Republic, Finland, France, Germany, Ireland, Japan, New Zealand, Norway, Poland, the

Russian Federation, Singapore, Spain, the UK, and the U.S.[24] In other States, the ability to conduct hearings by video-link has been read into existing legislation.[25] In addition, a number of States that allow for video-links have issued practice notes or directives on the modalities of their use, such as technical requirements for transmission of the audio-visual signal, facility set-up (for the courtroom and remote location), persons required to attend at either location, roles and responsibilities of parties involved, and guidance on how to optimise the use of equipment.

As with e-service, the use of video-links to take evidence is generally considered in exceptional and limited circumstances. In principle, internal civil procedure rules prefer evidence to be given in open court, where witness testimony can be more closely analysed. Accordingly, where the taking of evidence by video-link is provided for under national law, it tends only to be permitted in limited circumstances and subject to the discretion of the court and/or agreement of the parties.

In some States, the law expressly extends the use of video-links to the taking of evidence abroad.[26] The cross-border use of video-links to take evidence is also provided for in regional instruments, such as the 2001 *EU Evidence Regulation*[27] and the 2010 *Ibero-American Convention on the Use of Videoconferencing*. The latter, which is still to enter into force, is expressly motivated by considerations of the "importance of expanding the use of new technologies as a tool to assist the administration of justice in an expedient, efficient and effective manner". It is also relevant to note that the use of video-links to take evidence abroad is being promoted in other international fora. For instance, the UN Office on Drugs and Crime has been studying the issue as a means to improve international co-operation

---

24 See, *e.g.*, *Federal Court of Australia Act 1976* (Cth), s. 47A (Australia). Federal Courts Rules, SOR/98–106, r. 88(2) (Canada); Instruction of the Ministry of Justice No 505/2001, § 11a (Czech Republic); Code of Judicial Procedure, Ch. 17, s. 34a (Finland); *Code de l'organisation judiciaire*, Article L111–12 (France); *Code of Civil Procedure*, § 128a (Germany); *Civil Law (Miscellaneous Provisions) Act 2008*, s. 26 (Ireland); *Code of Civil Procedure*, Act No. 109 of 26 June 1996, Article 204 (Japan); *High Court Rules*, r. 10.24 (New Zealand); Dispute Act (Act of 17 June 2005 no. 90 relating to mediation and procedure in civil disputes), s. 13-1 (Norway); Code of Civil Procedure, Article 235, §2 (Poland); Federal Law No. 228-FZ of 27 July 2010 (Russian Federation); Evidence Act, s. 62A (Singapore); *Ley Orgánica 6/1985 del Poder Judicial*, Article 229(3) (Spain); *Civil Procedure Rules*, r. 32.3 (England and Wales); *Federal Rules of Civil Procedure*, r. 43(a) (United States).

25 See, *e.g.*, India, where although the India Evidence Act, 1872 does not make provision for the taking of evidence by video-link, the Supreme Court of India has found that in certain circumstances, its use is permissible within the framework of those rules: *State of Maharashtra v Praful B. Desai*, (2003) 4 SCC 601 (India). In Israel, cl. 13(a) of the Evidence Ordinance 1971 has been interpreted to encompass the authority to order examination by video-link: *Smith Kline Beecham plc v Uniform* 56(6) PDI 865 (Israel).

26 See, *e.g.*, *Federal Court of Australia Act 1976* (Cth), s. 47A(5) ("This section applies whether the person giving testimony is in or outside Australia…").

27 Council Regulation (EC) No 1206/2001 of 28 May 2001.

under the Convention against Transnational Organised Crime and is currently developing a guide to assist prosecutors, magistrates and judges in obtaining testimony by video-link. The International Law Association has also contributed to the discussion, stating in the 2008 *Paris-Rio Guidelines of Best Practice for Transnational Group Actions* that "modern means of videoconferencing must be considered" for hearing witnesses "each time that no aspect of the case requires that the testimony be given by another means".

In light of these developments, what role can the Evidence Convention play? The use of video-links under the Evidence Convention was first raised at the 2003 meeting of the Special Commission. Summing up discussions, the Chair observed that: (a) the use of video-links does not appear to be contrary to the Convention; (b) the use of video-links may not be contemplated under the law of all Contracting States; and (c) States that allow for the use of video-links find the technology useful and encourage its use under the Convention. At its meeting in 2009, the Special Commission, upon consideration of a document drawn by the Permanent Bureau entitled *The taking of evidence by video-link under the Hague Evidence Convention*, concluded that "the use of video-links and similar technologies to assist the taking of evidence abroad is consistent with the current framework of the Convention".[28]

With regard to Chapter I of the Convention taking evidence by way of Letters of Request, the Special Commission noted that: (a) the Convention permits judicial personnel of the requesting authority, parties and their representatives to be present by video-link at the execution of the Letter of Request; (b) the Convention does not preclude judicial personnel of the requesting authority from being present at the execution of the Letter of Request; and (c) the Convention permits a video-link to be used to assist in the execution of a Letter of Request (where the law of the requested State permits such use). In this sense, video-links may be used in much the same way as they are used under Article 10 of the *EU Evidence Regulation*. This method is referred to as the "indirect" taking of evidence as it is not the court before which proceedings are pending that takes the evidence, but the authorities of the State that execute the Letter of Request.

The Special Commission also noted that video-links may be used to assist in the taking of evidence under Chapter II. Although it is less likely to imagine situations where a diplomatic officer or consular agent would be called upon to use video-links to take evidence, assuming that the officer/agent and evidence are located in the same territory, there might be potential for the cross-border use of video-links in situations where evidence is taken by a commissioner. This of course may not be the case in larger States with remote regions. In this regard,

28 See, *Preliminary Document No 6 of December 2008*, which is available in the "Evidence Section" of the Hague Conference website at <www.hcch.net>.

Article 17 of the Convention provides that a commissioner (generally a court-appointed judge, court officer, consular agent or lawyer) may "take evidence in the territory of a Contracting State" in aid of proceedings commenced in the courts of another Contracting State. Permission by the Contracting State where the evidence is to be taken is required. Applying the "functional equivalence" approach endorsed by the Special Commission, it could be argued that Article 17 of the Evidence Convention allows a judge or court officer physically located in the courtroom of one Contracting State to use a video-link to take evidence in the territory of the other Contracting State. This approach (as well as the drafting) parallels the EU Evidence Regulation, which expressly provides for a member of judicial personnel or some other designated person physically located in one Member State to use a video-link to "take evidence directly in another Member State". If such an approach were to be accepted, it would certainly allow the Evidence Convention to keep pace with new methods of taking evidence abroad.

The idea of appointing a presiding judge as commissioner to take evidence by video-link was recently considered in proceedings before the Federal Court of Australia. In the case of *Joyce v Sunland Waterfront (BVI) Ltd*,[29] the Court was asked to appoint the presiding judge to examine a witness in the United Arab Emirates. The witness was unable to attend the court in person because he was the subject of ongoing criminal investigations in the UAE and had surrendered his passport as a condition of bail. At first instance, the Court acknowledged the "ingenuity" of the request, yet refused to grant the request on the grounds that the prior consent of the UAE had not been obtained. On appeal, the Full Court ordered the video-link to go ahead nonetheless. Although the case did not involve the Evidence Convention (the UAE is not a Contracting State), it suggests that courts in Contracting States may be willing to use the commissioner function in Article 17 of the Evidence Convention to directly take evidence abroad by video-link.

Any such course of action would need to fulfill the conditions set out in Article 17, namely that (a) the State where evidence is to be taken has given its permission, and (b) the commissioner complies with any conditions specified in the permission. Moreover, Article 17 of the Convention must apply as between the Contracting States involved; the Evidence Convention allows Contracting States to exclude all or part of Chapter II in their relations with other Contracting States, and approximately 25% of Contracting States have excluded the operation of Article 17 (whether specifically or by general exclusion of Chapter II).

In working towards the next meeting of the Special Commission, the Permanent Bureau will continue to monitor developments at a national and international level.

29 *Joyce v Sunland Waterfront (BVI) Ltd* [2011] FCAFC 95 (19 August 2011) (Australia).

CONCLUSION

It is quite remarkable how much the Hague Legal Co-operation Conventions have kept pace with developments in modern information and communication technology. Each of these instruments was concluded in a paper environment at a time when the use and impact of modern technologies could not have been foreseen. So far, the Conventions – drafted in neutral terms that can embrace modern developments – have not needed to be revised to embrace the use of such technologies. The continuing success of the Hague Legal Co-operation Conventions owes a lot to Hans's commitment to post-Convention services and his openness to new horizons.

(CROSS-BORDER) SURROGATE MOTHERHOOD: WE NEED TO TAKE ACTION NOW!

Katharina BOELE-WOELKI
Professor of Private International Law and Comparative Law at Utrecht University, the Netherlands
Extraordinary Professor at the University of the Western Cape, South Africa

I. A PRESSING PROBLEM

This contribution is aimed at providing some information about an area where in Europe and beyond different answers and solutions are provided as regards the ethical, medical, physical, psychological and legal questions which usually arise. Many scholars from various disciplines have tackled the phenomena;[1] evidently this small tribute to Hans van Loon in admiration of his enduring advocacy for more international cooperation in the interest of children only addresses some legal issues by exemplifying the problem with a few Dutch cases. They are thorny and complicated. It will not come as a surprise that not only in the Netherlands are there specialized lawyers who only deal with the topic of this contribution, and that is (cross-border) surrogate motherhood.

1. COMBINATIONS OF OFFSPRING

Two developments have transformed surrogacy into a battlefield on which parents fight for their rights as legal parents: The rise of the Internet on the one hand – sperm and eggs as well as surrogates and donors can be easily found

---

[1] See, e.g., Olga B.A. VAN DEN AKKER, "Psychosocial aspects of surrogate motherhood", *Human Reproduction Update*, 2007, 53–62.

and 'ordered' from different parts of the world[2] – and, on the other hand, the development and popularity of assisted reproductive technology (ART), in particular the emergence of in-vitro fertilization (IVF).[3] Research has shown that in particular infertile women voice a spiralling of preferences. They prefer a full biological link to a partial link, which in turn they prefer to no genetic link at all as in adoption.[4] As a result, with the options of full or part biological offspring available to infertile persons, adoption tends to be seen as an option of last resort, or a second-best choice.[5]

Theoretically there are nine possible combinations of offspring resulting from surrogate arrangements, where the gestation in all instances is with the surrogate mother. These combinations include two types of surrogacy: genetic surrogacy, which refers to the surrogate using her eggs, and gestational surrogacy, which refers to the combinations where the eggs of the intended mother or a third woman (a donor) are used.[6]

2. CONFRONTING PARENTAGE LAW: A NATIONAL, REGIONAL AND GLOBAL PROBLEM

Commercial surrogacy is forbidden in the vast majority of countries; in some states, however, only mediation by means of a professional practice or company and the publication of supply and demand requests concerning surrogacy arrangements are penalized,[7] whereas in others also persons directly involved in

---

2 The documentary *Google Baby*, a film by Zippi Brand Frank in 2009, about the journey across three continents tells the story of the baby production industry in the age of globalization. Western couples order eggs and sperm via the Internet and the surrogacy is outsourced to India, where women carry and give birth to children in order, for example, to be able to pay for the repair of their roof or for the education of their own children.

3 In 2010, the British scientist Robert G. EDWARDS received the Nobel Prize for the development of in-vitro fertilization, which makes it possible to treat infertility which afflicts more than 10% of all couples worldwide. In 1978 the first baby conceived with IVF was born after a full-term pregnancy. IVF had moved from a vision to reality. It is an established therapy when sperm and egg cannot meet inside the body.

4 See Olga B.A. VAN DEN AKKER, "Psychosocial aspects of surrogate motherhood", *Human Reproduction Update* 2007, 55.

5 See Karen SMITH ROTABI and Nicole FOOTEN BROMFIELD, "The Decline in Intercountry Adoptions and New Practices of Global Surrogacy: Global Exploitation and Human Rights Concerns", *Affilia: Journal of Women and Social Work* 27(2), 2012, 129–141.

6 See Olga B.A. VAN DEN AKKER, "Psychosocial aspects of surrogate motherhood", *Human Reproduction Update* 2007, 53–54.

7 See the comparative report for the Dutch Ministry of Justice completed in 2011 by Katharina BOELE-WOELKI et al., *Draagmoederschap en illegale opneming van kinderen*, serie *Familie & Recht* no. 4, Boom Juridische Uitgevers – The Hague 2012.

surrogacy commit a crime.[8] As regards altruistic surrogacy also a great deal of legal uncertainty exists. Legislators, judges and civil registrars are struggling to find solutions since in the vast majority of jurisdictions surrogacy has not been regulated by statute. Generally, from a legal point of view, the mother who has given birth to the child is the legal mother. This is the surrogate mother who has conceived, carried, delivered but agreed to relinquish the baby.[9] How can commissioning parents become legal parents? Can persons involved in surrogacy enter into an agreement on parentage? Is such a contract enforceable?

In cross-border cases, we are confronted with, for instance, a couple living in the Netherlands who request the Civil Registrar to register a birth certificate drawn up in the Ukraine which indicates the couple as the parents. The Civil Registrar has no proof that the woman has given birth to the child, he only knows that in the Ukraine, which is the most surrogate-friendly country in the East, commissioning parents, upon their request, are registered as legal parents if at least the husband has a genetic link with the child.[10] Is this status obtained abroad to be recognized? Or – to take a different situation – how do we deal with a French birth certificate which only indicates one of the male couple as the father but no mother? The child was born in France where the Dutch surrogate mother gave birth to the child anonymously.[11] In this case the child cannot trace

---

8 See Mary Keyes, "Cross-border Surrogacy Arrangements", *Australian Journal of Family Law* 2012, 28–50.

9 A totally different question has arisen within the context of employment. The European Court of Justice will soon deal with the position of intended mothers who have a baby through a surrogacy arrangement. Recently, preliminary questions were posed about their requests to receive maternity leave. Case C-167/12, OJ 30.6.2012, C 194/9 and Case C-363/12, OJ 13.10.2012, C 311/5. In these cases reference is made to the Treaty on the Functioning of the European Union, to the Charter on Fundamental Rights of the European Union, to Directive 2006/54/EC of the European Parliament and of the Council of 5 July 2006 on the implementation of the principle of equal opportunities and the equal treatment of men and women in matters of employment and occupation, to Council Directive 2000/78/EC OF 27 November 2000 establishing a general framework for equal treatment in employment and occupation, to Council Directive 92/85/EEC of 19 October 1992 on the introduction of measures to encourage improvements in the safety and health at work of pregnant workers and workers who have recently given birth or are breastfeeding and to Directive 2006/54/EC of the European Parliament and of the Council of 5 July 2006 on the implementation of the principle of equal opportunities and equal treatment of men and women in matters of employment and occupation.

10 Article 123 on Establishing Maternal and Paternal Affiliation in Case of Medically Assisted Procreation and Ovum Implantation of the Ukraine Family Code provides:

1. If the wife is fertilized by artificial procreation techniques upon written consent of her husband, the latter is registered as the father of the child born by his wife.
2. If an ovum conceived by the spouses is implanted to another woman, the spouses shall be the parents of the child.
3. Whenever an ovum conceived by the husband with another woman is implanted to his wife, the child is considered to be affiliated to the spouses.

11 This case was decided by the District Court of The Hague on 14 September 2009, *LJN* BK1197. The Court held that the French birth certificate was contrary to Dutch public policy. As a

his or her origins which in turn violates the child's rights guaranteed by the UN Convention on the Rights of the Child.[12] While none of the international human rights conventions[13] explicitly address surrogacy, they each address rights crucial in this context, such as the right to health, the right to support, the right to know one's origins and the right to a family.[14]

Due to the increase in surrogacy cases with cross-border implications both European and international organisations are considering whether and how to take action. The European Parliament, for instance, has commissioned a comparative study on the regime of surrogacy in the EU Member States.[15] It will however be difficult to ascertain the exact numbers of surrogacies that have taken place and the number of those cases that have crossed national borders.[16] How many children have been born out of a surrogacy arrangement can only be estimated. Various organisations are engaged in front-line work such as Population or Inhabitant Registration Offices, Civil Registrars, Immigration and Naturalisation Services, the Central Authorities for Adoption, the Embassies abroad and Child Protection Boards. In the majority of countries a clear reporting system does not exist. Finally, at the global level the Hague Conference on Private International Law is carrying out studies on the legal issues surrounding the cross-border aspects of surrogate maternity.[17]

---

consequence the child has no legal parents.

12 See on the protection of children's right to know one's origins at the international and regional level, Richard Blauwhoff, *Foundational Facts, Relative Truths*, Intersentia – Antwerp 2009, 43–100.

13 Such as the Covenant on Economic, Social and Cultural Rights, the Convention on the Elimination of all Forms of Discrimination Against Women, the European Convention on Human Rights and the Convention on the Rights of the Child.

14 See Barbara Stark, "Transnational Surrogacy and International Human Rights Law", *International Law Students Association Journal of International & Comparative Law* 2012, 1–16 (3, 8–10).

15 Service Contract – 127527–2012 of 21 April 2012: The aim of the study is to tackle only the legal aspects of surrogacy. It shall analyze how Member States approach surrogacy, in order to establish which problems stem from the fact that there are legal gaps in relation to surrogacy in some Member States, to analyze how the judiciary in practice resolves these problems, and to assess whether the EU should adopt uniform rules in this field.

16 See Ian Curry-Sumner and Machteld Vonk, "The Netherlands, National and International Surrogacy: An Odyssey", *The International Survey of Family Law* 2011, 259–280.

17 See Hague Conference Permanent Bureau, "Private International Law Issues Surrounding the Status of Children, Including Issues Arising from International Surrogacy Agreements", Preliminary Document No. 11 of March 2011 for the attention of the Council of April 2011 on General Affairs and Policy of the Conference and Hague Conference Update: Permanent Bureau of the Hague Conference on Private International Law, International Family Law 2011, 338–339.

II. WANTED: SURROGATE MOTHER

A Dutch TV documentary recently addressed the dilemmas of surrogacy with the expressive title "Wanted: Surrogate Mother". In five episodes four couples were shown who desperately want a child with the help of a surrogate mother. Two male and two heterosexual couples told their stories in a surprisingly frank and disarming manner. How far do they go in realizing their desire to have a child? What are the reasons for involving another woman to give birth to a child with which at least one of them is genetically linked? What are the reasons for surrogate mothers to give the gift of life? Is it the compensation that they obtain or do they do it for purely altruistic reasons?[18] If the financial compensation is the main reason should we not be concerned about the possible exploitation of these women?[19]

The legal implications of the stories of the four couples in the Dutch documentary include the following.

1. A SAME-SEX COUPLE FIND A SURROGATE IN THE NETHERLANDS

The first couple, Sven and Jeroen from Amsterdam, find a surrogate mother in the Netherlands. Cindy is happily married and has two children. The eggs of a good friend of the male couple are fertilized with Sven's sperm and are placed in Cindy's uterus. This takes place in Cyprus since in the Netherlands IFV treatment is only possible if the sperm and the egg are derived from the commissioning couple. Moreover, the couple must be heterosexual and must live in the Netherlands. Cindy gives birth to twins in the Netherlands. She and her husband are legal parents by operation of law. How do Sven and Jeroen become the legal parents of the children? To begin with, the transfer of full parental rights will not occur against the will of any of the parties involved. Cindy has no legal duty to hand over the twins, nor

---

18 The most prolific surrogate mother lives in England. She has given birth to twelve children within thirteen years, on each occasion receiving an estimated £25,000 to 30,000 per child; see www.worldrecordacademy.com/human/most_prolific_surrogate_mother-world_record_set_by_Carole_Horlock_90113.htm (accessed on 10 January 2013). Another extreme example concerns a compulsory surrogacy which happened in the United States where a woman was mistakenly inseminated with another couple's embryos during an IVF procedure. In so doing this woman unwittingly became a surrogate mother for this other couple's child while giving away her last opportunity, due to her age, for a healthy pregnancy that could have resulted in another child; see abcnews.go.com/Health/carolyn-sean-savage-embryo-mix-now-expect-twins/story?id=13318708 (accessed on10 January 2013).

19 See Emily Stehr, "International Surrogacy Contract Regulation: National Governments' and International Bodies' Misguided Quests to Prevent Exploitation", *Hastings International and Comparative Law Review* 2012, 253–287.

are Sven and Jeroen under a legal duty to accept both children. Their agreement to do otherwise is not enforceable. The male couple can only gain full parental status through joint adoption. However, before the twins can be adopted by the intentional parents, Cindy and her husband will first have to be divested of their parental responsibilities. The divestment of parental responsibilities under Dutch law is a child protection measure that is used in cases where parents are unable or unfit to look after the child. Cindy and her husband cannot apply to the court to be divested; this can only be requested by the Child Care and Protection Board and the Public Prosecution Service. Then the court must positively ascertain that the legal parents are unable or unfit to raise the child(ren) in question. To date, the Dutch Supreme Court has not yet had the opportunity to decide on divestment in the context of surrogacy. However, decisions by various Courts of Appeal allow for the discharge of surrogate parents on the ground that they did not intend to have the child for themselves. If the divestment procedure is successful, Sven and Jeroen may be attributed with joint guardianship which is similar to parental responsibility. If they then have taken care of the twins together for one year they may file for an adoption order with the court. Specific post-surrogacy adoption rules do not exist and the normal adoption procedure is to be followed. If Sven and Jeroen did not involve the Child Protection Board before the birth of the twins, transferring parental rights from Cindy and her husband to the male couple is a lengthy procedure of which the outcome is uncertain.[20] If in Cyprus or any other country the IVF treatment of Cindy would not have been possible, the Dutch authorities would not be confronted with a situation that is not regulated by Dutch parentage law. This results in friction and legal uncertainty for all parties involved, in particular for the children.

2. THE MOTHER OF THE INTENDED MOTHER

The second couple cohabit. Jacinta cannot become pregnant, because she was born without a uterus. However, her ovaries produce eggs and it is possible to fertilize them with the sperm of her partner Charles. But where does one find a surrogate mother who one can trust and who will give away the child? In the Netherlands the legal mother has to waive her rights and duties as a legal mother in a legal procedure in order to make the adoption of the child possible. The most trustworthy person is Jacinta's mother Willeke, who is 55 years old.[21] She wants

20 See on the steps to be followed Ian Curry-Sumner and Machteld Vonk, "The Netherlands, National and International Surrogacy: An Odyssey", *The International Survey of Family Law* 2011, 265–266.

21 This situation is not unusual. See www.dailyherald.com/article/20120907/news/709079711/photos/AR (accessed on 10 January 2013) about a woman, aged 53, who gave birth to her

to carry the child of her daughter and undergoes extensive hormone treatment. For an in-vitro fertilization in the Netherlands she is too old, but in a clinic in the Czech Republic different rules apply. The mother, daughter and her partner go there for two treatments, but without success. Later, it transpires that the medical diagnosis of the Czech doctors was incorrect. The mother could never have become pregnant due to a medical intervention which she had undergone many years previously. Jacinta continues to search for a surrogate mother who she can trust.

If the treatment would have been successful – it happens that women in their sixties or even seventies can give birth to a child – the child would most likely have been born in the Netherlands. Charles could recognize the child and become the legal father since he is not married to Jacinta.[22] The child would have been related to her genetic mother Jacinta as a sister or a brother. He or she would have been a first degree descendent in terms of inheritance rights like Jacinta until Willeke would have been divested of her rights as a legal mother in court and until Jacinta and Charles would have adopted the child. If the relationship between Jacinta and Charles would in the meantime have come to an end, Jacinta, who has the same biological ties with the child as Charles, would be left empty-handed. Charles could refuse to give consent to the adoption by Jacinta. These kinds of cases have resulted in legal proceedings in Norway and Sweden.[23] The position of the commissioning mother whether married to the man or not, who can recognize the child of the birth-giving mother, is weak. She is totally dependent upon continuing the relationship with the father.

3. THE COUPLE WITH THREE CHILDREN WHO WANT A FOURTH CHILD

Musetta and Hotze have three children. They passionately wish to enlarge their family with another child of their own. However, Musetta lost her uterus during the birth of her third child. Her friend Jolanda offers to carry the child. In the Netherlands the transfer of the embryo, which is genetically linked to the couple, cannot take place. The intended parents and the surrogate mother travel to Latvia where such treatment is possible. However, the embryo is rejected and Jolanda does not want to undergo further treatment. Musetta is hurt and has

own grandchild since her daughter was diagnosed with cervical cancer and underwent a hysterectomy.

22 If he would be married to Jacinta he would not be able to recognize the child under Dutch law unless he has a close relationship with that child, Article 1:204 (1)(c) Dutch Civil Code.

23 See Maarit Jänterä-Jareborg, Surrogacy in Scandinavia – in particular Sweden, *Swedish national report for the International Law Association working group* (not yet published).

no understanding of Jolanda's decision at all. They end up by being no longer on speaking terms. Musetta does not give up. She has heard of the world's first successful transplantation of a uterus, which took place in Turkey. She consults the Turkish physicians in Istanbul and asks whether she could qualify for such an operation. She does not. Many other infertile women are lining up who do not yet have any children. Apart from the uterus transplantation the surrogate agreement raises the question whether a couple has a legal and probably enforceable right to have a child with whom they have full or part biological links. This question is not new. It has always been posed in the context of adoption, where generally there is no genetic link between the adoptive parents and the child except in cases of step-parent adoption. Today, adoption is considered to be a child protection measure; in earlier days adoption was made possible to prevent the extinction of a family. The right to adopt is not unlimited. Specific requirements are prescribed by legal rules. Under many jurisdictions a couple with three children would qualify to adopt a child, but their wish to have a fourth child does not necessarily include the right to have their own child with medical assistance or, more explicitly, the right to involve a surrogate mother. Such a right cannot be enforced through a court order. This we consider to be one step too far and it would not even be acceptable to "solve" the problem of infertile women. Besides, theoretically, legal rules should not make a difference between a couple with no children and a couple which already have three children.[24] Practically, however, IVF treatment and uterus transplantation are only for those women who "deserve" the treatment. Hospitals make their own rules on selection and obviously in fields such as organ donation the medical staff take their own decisions.

4. THE SAME-SEX COUPLE THAT ARE TOO OLD TO ADOPT

Finally, Hein and Erik. They have been trying to adopt a child for many years, but without success. In the meantime they have exceeded the age of 46 which, in principle, is the maximum age for adopting under Dutch law. Their last chance is to look for a surrogate mother in India. They visit a clinic where the IFV treatment can take place and where surrogate mothers are living during their pregnancy. They are advised that if they would decide on surrogacy two women would be fertilized with the sperm of one of them, that they must take into account that due to the hormone treatment of these women twins would be conceived and that they probably would end up with four children instead of one. This alarms

[24] Noticeably, the many responses to the TV blog regarding this couple with three children of their own are mostly one of outrage.

them. Moreover, they feel totally uncomfortable during their visit to the clinic seeing the many surrogates waiting for the delivery in overcrowded rooms. In the end, they remain undecided; they postpone the decision although their wish to have a child remains overwhelmingly strong. If they would finally decide to try surrogacy they would encounter difficult legal problems. Only one of them will be genetically linked with the child or the children. Under the law of India the surrogate mother will most likely be registered as the legal mother and either Hein or Erik will be registered as the legal father. How can they travel to and enter the Netherlands with the child? The registration of one of them as the legal father in India does not automatically lead to the child acquiring Dutch citizenship.[25] The Dutch embassy generally refuses to provide a Dutch passport since the legal fatherhood as registered in India will not be recognized due to the Dutch rules on private international law. Lengthy procedures are to be expected in which the Dutch couple also have to take into account their own situation as foreigners in India who need a visa.[26]

Suppose that Eric and Hein would not go to India but to California, where surrogacy clinics extensively advertise on the Internet how easy it is to have a child with the help of a surrogate mother and that this would not cause legal problems since they would both be indicated as the legal parents of the child on the birth certificate. However, upon their return to the Netherlands they would be surprised because their status as legal parents would not be recognized in the Netherlands either. Not only in the Netherlands would recognition be denied, but also in many other European countries. In 2011, the French *Cour de cassation*, for example, delivered three judgments[27] which ruled that foreign surrogacy agreements violate French public policy. In each of the three cases, the child or children were born in a state of the United States where the practice was lawful, like in Minnesota and California.[28] Two issues were to be decided: (1) did the American judgments violate French public policy, and (2) if so, should they nevertheless be recognized as a consequence of the rights of the French couples and of the children afforded by international conventions? All three judgments gave the same reasons: The American birth certificate could not be mentioned in the French civil status registry because the foundation of the birth certificate was a foreign judgment

25 Currently, the Surrogacy (Regulation and Control) Bill of 2012 is pending in India, according to which foreigners can only 'hire' a surrogate mother if they provide an undertaking that their country ensures legality of such a child. In addition, it will be required that the child will get the citizenship of the foreign country.

26 See District Court of The Hague 10 January 2011, *LJN* BP 0426, in which a temporary passport was granted so that the legal father was able to return to the Netherlands with the child.

27 Decisions of 6 April 2011, Nos. 369, 370, 371.

28 See Barbara Stark, "Transnational Surrogacy and International Human Rights Law", *International Law Students Association Journal of International & Comparative Law*, 2012, 1–16.

which violated French public policy. Surrogacy agreements violate a fundamental principle of French law which determines that civil status is inalienable. Pursuant to this principle, one may not derogate from the law of parenthood by contract. This outcome neither violates Article 8 of the European Convention on Human Rights, as the children have a father in any case (i.e. the biological father), a mother under the law of the relevant US state, and may live together with the French couple in France; nor does the outcome violate Article 3-1 of the UN Convention on the Rights of Children. One might challenge the fact that the children may live in France but they are not to be granted French citizenship in the absence of registration in the French civil status registry. Proceedings before the European Court of Human Rights have been commenced. In this context it is worth mentioning that male couples who have adopted a child in the United States and who seek recognition of the adoption order in France will fail. In June 2012 the French *Cour de cassation* ruled that foreign decisions allowing adoption by a same-sex couple are contrary to French public policy.[29] French registries may not provide that a child has parents of the same sex. The filiation relationship between the child and his/her biological parents may not be severed.

III. IN THE MIDST OF FINDING THE RIGHT WAY FORWARD

The four Dutch cases which where shown on TV in 2012 illustrate among many other considerations and dilemmas the legal obstacles which people encounter when they embark on a surrogacy adventure. The personal and private insights that the persons divulged made it possible to sympathise with all the persons involved. However, sympathy is insufficient to solve their problems. Legal solutions are needed. But which solutions are the best, most desirable, most effective and enforceable solutions? The number of complicated surrogacy cases is endless. Each jurisdiction can enumerate leading cases.[30] They not only involve far-away jurisdictions like India and California, but to an increasing extent East-European

[29] Decisions of 7 June 2012, Nos. 755, 756: "Attendu qu'est contraire à un principe essentiel du droit français de la filiation, la reconnaissance en France d'une décision étrangère dont la transcription sur les registres de l'état civil français, valant acte de naissance, emporte inscription d'un enfant comme né de deux parents du même sexe."

[30] See e.g. Jinske Verhellen, "Intercountry surrogacy: a comment on recent Belgian cases", *Nederlands Internationaal Privaatrecht* 2011, 657–662; Santiago Álvarez González, "Efectos en España de la gestación por sustitución llevada a cabo en el extranjero", *Anuario Español de Derecho Internacional Privado* 2010, 339–377 and Teun Struycken, "Surrogacy, a New Way to become a Mother? An Issue of Private International Law that may Affect Good Relations among States", in: *Hague Academy of International Law, The 90th Birthday of Boutros Boutros Ghali*, Martinus Nijhoff Publishers 2012, pp. 235–254.

countries and various Member States of the European Union. In this context it has been rightly stated by a Member of the European Parliament that since this method of reproduction is authorized or laid down by law in a number of Member States, whilst in other Member States it is prohibited by law, the resulting unequal legal treatment within the EU encourages trafficking, including, in particular, to third countries. Therefore a coordinated stance within the EU is needed on this sensitive issue.[31] But there are many more concerns.

At this stage, nobody has been able to provide a clear-cut solution to the demanding problem of transnational surrogacy. Currently, family law in Europe and beyond is in the midst of finding the right way forward. We are debating the phenomenon. Courts have indicated various directions in cases where statutory rules are lacking.[32] They have provided some guidelines. Most importantly, in finding the best solutions several comparative studies have been undertaken and will be finalized in the near future.[33] Before regulating surrogacy we need to know everything about all the possible situations that may occur. Most notably, national legislators should not only look to other jurisdictions for inspiration but should try to find solutions which work in relation to other jurisdictions. Besides, it would be short-sighted to legislate only at the national or regional level (within the EU) since we are confronted with a global problem. Moreover, taking into account the surrogate mother's interest should not overshadow the interests of future children who are designed to be born into a surrogacy construction.[34] They are the most vulnerable of all the persons concerned. In the best interest of the child specific questions evidently arise: Who is legally responsible? What if the intended parents split up? What if they change their minds or die? What if the baby is premature or has health problems? What if the baby has health problems resulting from the surrogate's drug use or alcohol intake during pregnancy? How will the child deal with her unusual origins?[35] At any rate, States should only offer surrogacy services if it has been established that there is no risk for the child

[31] Member of the European Parliament Question no. 42 by Ivo Belet (H-000096/11).

[32] See Bettina Heiderhoff, „Der gewöhnliche Aufenthalt von Säuglingen", *Zeitschrift für Internationales Privat- und Verfahrensrecht* 2012, 523–526.

[33] See Katarina Trimmings and Paul Beaumont, "International Surrogacy Arrangements: An Urgent Need for Legal Regulation at the International Level", *Journal of Private International Law 2011, 627–647.*

[34] See Laura Bosch, "Kinderrechten in een Petrischaaltje, De waardigheid van wenskinderen bij commercieel hoogtechnologisch draagmoederschap", *Tijdschrift voor Familie- en Jeugdrecht* 2012, 153–159.

[35] See Barbara Stark, "Transnational Surrogacy and International Human Rights Law", *International Law Students Association Journal of International & Comparative Law*, 2012, 1–16 (6).

of falling into a legal vacuum having regard to the laws of the commissioning parents' home country.[36]

Hence, joined forces are indispensable on all sides and legal scholars and practitioners in (international) family law are called upon to contribute to this challenging undertaking. The Hague Conference on Private International Law has rightly put this pressing problem on its agenda.[37] In the interest of children born through surrogacy international cooperation is needed now!

[36] See Maarit Jänterä-Jareborg, Surrogacy in Scandinavia – in particular Sweden, Swedish national report for the International Law Association working group (not yet published). See also Barbara Stark, "Transnational Surrogacy and International Human Rights Law", *ILSA Journal of International & Comparative Law,* 2012, 1–16 (16): "Problems can be rectified by requiring intending parents to prove before entering into a surrogacy arrangement that the resulting child will be granted citizenship in the state where her intending parents live and that they, in fact will be legally recognized as her parents in that state."

[37] See Rolf Wagner, „Abstammungsfragen bei Leihmutterschaft in internationalen Sachverhalten, Bemühungen der Haager Konferenz für Internationales Privatrecht", *Zeitschrift für das Standesamtswesen* 2012, 294–300.

SOME REFLECTIONS ON MULTICULTURALISM, APPLICATION OF ISLAMIC LAW, LEGAL PLURALISM AND THE NEW EU SUCCESSION REGULATION

Michael BOGDAN
Professor of Comparative and Private International Law, University of Lund, Sweden

1. INTRODUCTION

Most European countries have today a sizeable minority consisting of first or second generation immigrants, frequently including many Moslems. To take Sweden as an example, pursuant to unofficial estimates (official figures do not exist, as questions regarding religious beliefs are not posed in Swedish official population surveys), out of about ten million inhabitants of Sweden there are today between 250,000 and 400,000 Moslems, even though the religious feelings of most of them are probably not much stronger than the rather lukewarm allegiance of the majority population to the Protestant (Lutheran) faith, constituting until recently the State Church of Sweden. Most immigrants proclaiming themselves to be Moslems probably perceive Islam more as a cultural phenomenon or as a way of life rather than a religion in the strict sense of the word.

In the former colonial superpowers, such as France of Great Britain, because of obvious historical reasons the number of Moslems, both in terms of the number of individuals and in terms of proportion of the total population, is substantially higher. In many European countries there are voices pointing out that the society is becoming, or has in fact already become, multicultural and that the dominant majority culture should no longer have the monopoly of influence and be imposed on minorities with a radically different cultural heritage.

Many of the Moslems in Europe originate from countries whose family and succession law is wholly or to a substantial extent based on the tenets of the Islamic religion. In its theological form, Islam is of course independent of any recognition by the State, but in many countries its rules (or some of them), as interpreted by the local legislator, have been elevated (or degraded, depending on the opinion of the commentator) to positive law, recognized and upheld by the power of the State. The rules of family and succession law are normally very closely connected with the culture, religion and ethical values as they have developed in the society concerned. The current family and succession law of most European countries reflect usually a combination of traditional Christian values (such as the principle of monogamy) and modern concepts of human rights and freedoms (such as equal rights of men and women, equal rights of all children regardless of whether born in or out of wedlock, and religious freedom). Islamic rules of family and succession law, both in their "pure" theological form and as they are implemented in many Islamic countries, differ in several respects from these ideals. To mention just a few examples regarding succession, pursuant to Islamic law daughters inherit only half of the portions inherited by sons, children born out of wedlock do not inherit at all, and non-Moslems cannot inherit from Moslems.

The rising number of Moslem inhabitants forces more and more frequently the courts of the European countries to resolve their family and succession disputes. This gives rise to the question of whether and to what extent the European courts should apply Islamic (Moslem) law or at least take it into account in some way.[1] The use of Islamic law can in principle take two forms. It can be applied as foreign law pursuant to the conflict rules of private international law of the forum country (see section 2 below). Another possibility is to introduce, into the substantive law of the forum country, special parallel rules inspired by Islamic law and intended for those cases where the person(s) concerned are Moslems (see section 3 below). In addition, Islamic law has sometimes to be taken into account by European courts as a fact even when they apply their own law which has no Islamic background at all, for example when a dispute arises concerning the interpretation of an agreement on an Islamic bride-price (*mahr*), entered into by a Moslem couple who are Swedish citizens with habitual residence in Sweden; the

1 The use of Islamic law by the courts and other authorities of European countries must be distinguished from the various forms of private jurisdiction exercised within the Islamic religious communities in Europe. For example, it is generally known that many Moslem married couples living in Sweden, after having obtained a divorce decree from a Swedish court of law, go through Islamic divorce proceedings, normally in the form of a repudiation (*talak*) of the wife by the husband certified by a local Moslem priest (*imam*). From the viewpoint of Swedish law, the repudiation is a private matter with no legal consequences, but it may be of great practical importance if the couple wish to be regarded as divorced also in their country of origin. It occurs also that a Moslem couple living in Sweden go through a Moslem marriage ceremony not recognized by Swedish law; in the eyes of their relatives and other members of their community they are married while in the eyes of Swedish law they are mere "cohabitees" (the cohabitation itself has, nevertheless, some important legal consequences pursuant to Swedish law).

agreement would most probably be governed by Swedish law but Islamic law may be adduced as a proof of the intentions of the parties.

2. APPLICATION OF ISLAMIC LAW PURSUANT TO CONFLICT RULES OF PRIVATE INTERNATIONAL LAW

Many of the cases where Islamic law is referred to in European courts deal with situations having an international (cross-border) dimension due to the connections between the persons involved and their country of origin, in particular when the case concerns immigrants who have retained the citizenship of that country. The conflict rules of private international law of many – albeit not all – continental European countries have traditionally been based on the application to family and succession matters of the law of the country of citizenship (*lex patriae*). This used to be, and to some extent still is, the case of Sweden as well, even though the law of the country of habitual residence has been successively gaining importance and can today be said to prevail. This development is certainly connected with the transformation of Sweden during the twentieth century from a country of emigration, trying to preserve its legal ties to Swedish citizens who have moved abroad, to a country of immigration, wishing to assimilate the numerous foreigners residing habitually within its borders.

On 27 July 2012, a new EU Regulation No 650/2012 of 4 July 2012 "on Jurisdiction, Applicable Law, Recognition and Enforcement of Decisions and Acceptance and Enforcement of Authentic Instruments in Matters of Succession and on the Creation of a European Certificate of Succession" was published in the Official Journal of the European Union.[2] When it starts to apply,[3] this Regulation will unify the conflict rules of the EU Member States (with the exception of Denmark and possibly also the United Kingdom and Ireland) in the field of succession law. The conflict rules of the Regulation apply irrespective of whether they lead to the application of the law of a Member State or not (see Article 20), which means that there is no room left for national, autonomous conflict rules of the Member States for "non-European" situations. The main, general conflict rule of the Regulation is found in its Article 21: the law applicable to the succession as a whole will be the law of the country in which the deceased had his habitual residence at the time of death, unless, "by way of exception", it is clear from all the circumstances of the case that, at the time of death, the deceased was manifestly

[2] OJ 2012 L 201 p. 107.

[3] Pursuant to its Article 83(1), the Regulation shall apply to the succession of persons who die on or after 17 August 2015.

more closely connected with another country, in which case the law of that country will apply (this exception may have in mind, for example, those cases where the deceased died very short time after the change of habitual residence). The law designated by this conflict rule will govern most matters of succession law, including the determination of the beneficiaries and their respective shares, the capacity to inherit, disinheritance and disqualification by conduct, the disposable part of the estate and other restrictions on the disposal of property upon death, the obligation to restore or account for gifts received during the deceased's lifetime, etc.

The principal conflict rule of the Regulation is thus based mainly on the application of the law of the country of habitual residence, regardless of the nationality (citizenship) of the person(s) concerned. The reasons for the designation of habitual residence as the main connecting factor are stated, in an excessively summary fashion, in Recital 23 of the Regulation, referring to the increasing mobility of citizens and the need to ensure the proper administration of justice and that a genuine connection exists between the succession and the Member State of the forum (Article 4 grants the courts of the Member State in which the deceased had his habitual residence at the time of death primary jurisdiction to rule on the succession).

The main conflict rule in Article 21 is modified by Article 22, which gives persons possessing the citizenship of a country other than that of their habitual residence the right to choose as the law governing their succession the law of the country of their citizenship. It is not possible to choose another law, such as the law of the country where the assets are located or where the choice was made, and it appears that the choice must comprise the succession as a whole, i.e. mot merely a part of it. The choice must be made expressly in a will or an agreement as to succession or be demonstrated by the terms of such a disposition. On the other hand, a person possessing citizenship of more than one country may choose the law of any of them, regardless of whether or not one of the citizenships is that of the country of the forum.

The right to choose the *lex patriae* as the law governing the succession constitutes a concession to the nationality principle favoured by some Member States, especially those with substantial emigration leading to a large number of their citizens residing habitually abroad. The combination of the main conflict rule based on habitual residence and the right to choose the law of the country of nationality[4] has the advantage of disarming, to a large extent, criticism accusing

[4] A similar combination is used also in Regulation No 1259/2010 of 20 December 2010 Implementing Enhanced Cooperation in the Area of the Law Applicable to Divorce and Legal Separation, OJ 2010 L 343 p. 10, where the main conflict rule leading to the application of the law of the country where the spouses are habitually resident at the time the court is seized

the conflict rule of violating the Treaty on the Functioning of the European Union (TFEU). The mandatory use of habitual residence as the only connecting factor could, it might be argued, constitute an obstacle hindering indirectly the exercise of the right of EU citizens to move and reside freely within the EU (Article 21 TFEU), as it could discourage them from moving their habitual residence to a Member State whose succession law they dislike, while the mandatory use of citizenship as the sole connecting factor could be perceived as a discrimination on grounds of nationality, forbidden by Article 18 TFEU.

These positive features of the new conflict rules do not, however, mean that the rules are satisfactory in all respects, in particular with regard to the compromise making habitual residence the main connecting factor and using citizenship as an optional connecting factor for those persons who possess the nationality of a country other than that where they habitually reside.

In the course of some 40 years I have been involved in researching and teaching Swedish private international law, I have consistently advocated a more general transition to the application of the law of the country of habitual residence (*hemvist*). My main arguments were partly based on my personal experiences as an immigrant and my preference for the ideology of assimilation, but had even more to do with the obvious practical advantages of applying the law of the country where the person concerned lives and works and where his or her legal problems concerning family and succession will have to be resolved by local courts. I have, furthermore, assumed that almost all immigrants adapt their values and way of life relatively quickly to those prevailing in their new country of habitual residence and that the application of the law of that country will relatively soon correspond to their expectations.

I must confess, however, that I have recently been compelled to change my views on this point. The above-mentioned arguments may have been correct and relevant twenty or more years ago, but their weight has weakened considerably since then, especially regarding the succession issues concerning non-European (most often Moslem) immigrants.

The immigration of today, in particular from non-European countries, differs in some respects substantially from the traditional one. A few decades ago, moving to another country, and especially to another continent, meant a dramatic breach with the cultural environment of the migrant. Contacts with the country of origin weakened relatively fast, whereas the contacts with the culture, including legal culture, of the new country were very intense, thanks to exposures to it in the workplace or school. Today a relatively high portion of non-European immigrants remain isolated from the rest of the Swedish society even after many

(Article 8) can be contracted out by the parties by agreeing on, *inter alia*, the law of the country of nationality of either spouse at the time the agreement is concluded (Article 5).

years of habitual residence in the country, for example many Moslem women who have never worked outside of home, speak no Swedish, and sometimes do not even leave the apartment except in the company of a male family member. The rising number of immigrants from the Middle East has converted certain suburbs of larger cities, for instance Malmö, into cultural enclaves dominated by Islamic culture, whose inhabitants are exposed to an intense social control and pressure not to deviate from their traditional values and way of life. Some Moslems enrol their childred in private Moslem schools in order to protect them from sexual education and from physical training together with children of the opposite gender; it is true that most Moslem children from the immigrant suburbs go to communal schools, but often end up in classes where all or almost all other pupils are Moslem.

Of particularly great importance for preserving dominant cultural ties with the country of origin rather than acquiring such ties with the country of the new habitual residence are the modern communications, such as satellite television, Internet, inexpensive phone calls, etc. Intercontinental flights, which a few decades ago were beyond the reach of large segments of the population, have become so affordable that yearly family visits in the country of origin are common.

The change of the country of habitual physical presence does not, consequently, necessarily lead to a change in the cultural environment any more. This is one of the reasons why the ideology of legal assimilation is today more and more replaced with the ideology of multiculturalism, stressing the legitimacy of the desire of many immigrants to preserve, to the largest possible extent, their own culture, including their own family and succession law. As it was put by a Swedish sociologist during a television interview, it cannot be required of a recently immigrated Moslem that he or she should start thinking as a Lutheran Protestant. It can therefore be argued that he or she should not be unvoluntarily subjected to family and succession rules that he or she finds strange and does not understand.

The problem is not limited to non-European migrants coming to Europe, as the same questions can be asked in connection with European citizens moving permanently to non-European countries, for example a Swedish doctor working and living, together with his Swedish family, in Saudi Arabia. Even though he may have lived in that country for many years and has undeniably habitual residence and closest connections there, the legal and cultural differences between Sweden and Saudi Arabia are of such a magnitude that is can be doubted whether he has adapted to the values of Saudi Arabia to such an extent that subjecting him to the family and succession law of the country of his habitual residence is appropriate.

All this weakens substantially the arguments in favour of the application, in the field of family and succession law, of the rules of the country of habitual residence, and strengthens arguments in favour of applying the law of the country of citizenship, normally identical to the country of the immigrant's origin.[5] Among Nordic legal writers, the Norwegian professor Helge J. Thue was one of the first to take notice of this development.[6] In spite of the fact that Norwegian private international law was firmly based on the application of the *lex domicilii*, he argued strongly for the application of the law of the country of citizenship. He stressed, however, that his proposal was not related to the nationalism that characterized the arguments in favour of the same conflict rule put forward more than 160 years ago by the great Italian partisan of the nationality principle, professor Mancini. The opposite is true, as Thue saw in the application of the law of the country of citizenship a feature making private international law "a law of tolerance" in relation to foreign concepts of law and justice. A multicultural approach, preferring the application of the law of the country of citizenship to the application of the law of the country of habitual residence, is advocated, specifically in the context of the role of Islamic succession law in Sweden, by Mosa Sayed.[7]

A reasonable solution might possibly be achieved by means of a compromise between the two alternatives. The compromise found in Articles 21 and 22 of the new EU Succession Regulation (see above) may certainly be useful, but it hardly constitutes the optimal and ultimate solution to the problem, because it presupposes a relatively advanced legal knowledge and therefore probably will not be used on a larger scale. The Swedish doctor in the fictitious example above has presumably access to legal expertise sufficient to enable him to find out about his options and to make an informed choice of the applicable law, but the same can hardly be said of an average Moslem immigrant in a Swedish suburb.

In the experience and practice of European courts, the main cultural borderline in the field of succession law goes between on the one hand the laws of European countries, especially the Member States of the European Union, and on the other hand the laws of the Islamic countries. The compromise stipulated in the EU Succession Regulation may be quite appropriate for conflicts between laws of the various Member States of the European Union,[8] but it should have been reversed in cases concerning succession of persons who are habitual residents

[5] If and when the immigrant becomes a naturalized citizen of the new country and gives up his original nationality, there are good reasons for a change in the applicable law as well. The case of double nationality is too complicated to be dealt with in detail in this short paper, but it is submitted that the nationality of the forum country should not automatically be given priority when it comes to designating the applicable law.

[6] See Helge J. Thue, *Internasjonal privatrett. Personrett, familierett og arverett. Alminnelige prinsipper og de enkelte reguleringer*, Oslo 2002, pp. 106–116.

[7] See Mosa Sayed, *Islam och arvsrätt i det mångkulturella Sverige. En internationellt privaträttslig och jämförande studie*, Diss. Uppsala 2009.

[8] The same can to some extent be said about conflicts involving non-European "Western" nations, such as the U.S. or Australia.

and/or citizens of non-member countries, where citizenship should serve as the main connecting factor, combined with the right of the person involved to opt for the law of the country of habitual residence. It is true that this would amount to having different conflict rules for intra-EU and extra-EU situations, but a similar dualism has been in use for decades in the Nordic countries without causing any difficulties worth mentioning.[9]

3. ISLAMIC LAW AS A COMPONENT OF THE LEX FORI

Of course, the acquisition of the citizenship of the country of the immigrant's new habitual residence is not a guarantee of a full-scale or substantial cultural integration, at least not in Sweden, where naturalization does not presuppose any knowledge of the Swedish society, any command of the Swedish language or any oath or declaration of allegiance to the Swedish Constitution or the values on which that Constitution is based. It is true that naturalization requires normally several years of residence in the country, which vouches probably for at least some adaptation, but for many naturalized Swedes Swedish family and succession law remains incomprehensible and strange. On the other hand, the application of foreign law to Swedish citizens habitually residing in Sweden is hardly an acceptable alternative.[10]

It is therefore reasonable to ask whether a multicultural society such as Sweden should not introduce special parallel rules of domestic, substantive family and succession law, in order to accommodate the Moslem segment of its population. This is not a question about the application of the law of a particular foreign Islamic country, but rather about the enactment of parallel *Swedish* rules, generally inspired by Islamic law and intended primarily for Swedes of the Moslem faith.

The existence of such legal pluralism, characterized by parallel substantive rules for different categories of persons within the framework of a single national

[9] The Nordic Convention of 19 November 1934 between Denmark, Finland, Iceland, Norway and Sweden comprising Private International Law Provisions on Succession, Wills and Estate Administration (as amended) stipulates as a main rule that succession of Nordic citizens habitually residing in the Nordic area is governed by the law of the Nordic country of habitual residence of the deceased. The designation of the law governing the succession of non-Nordic citizens and/or residents is left to be regulated by the private international law of the Contracting State of the forum; in Sweden this means, pursuant to Act 1937:81 on Certain International Relationships concerning Estates of Deceased Persons, in principle the application of the law of the country of which the deceased was a citizen at the time of death. The 1937 Act will in due course be replaced by the EU Succession Regulation (see above).

[10] Cases of double or multiple citizenships are not dealt with here.

legal system, is not rare in non-European countries, such as Israel or Morocco. In fact, the new EU Succession Regulation takes their existence into account in its Article 37, stipulating that any reference to the law of a State having two or more sets of rules applicable to different categories of persons in respect of succession shall be construed as referring to the set of rules determined by the rules of that State or, in the absence of such rules, the set of rules with which the deceased had the closest connection. In Europe however, such inter-personal conflicts of law are very unusual, but it deserves to be mentioned that the chairman of the association of Swedish Moslems sent as early as in 2006 a letter to the leaders of Swedish political parties, where among other things he proposed the enactment of a separate Swedish family law for Moslems. More international attention was attracted by Rowan Williams, the Archbishop of Canterbury, who was reported as having declared in one of his speeches in February 2008 that English law would have to make room for the application of Islamic principles to Englishmen of Islamic faith.

The creation of such parallel sets of substantive law rules might seem like an attractive proposition, in particular from the point of view of the adherents of multiculturalism, but it could, it is submitted, cause serious difficulties. The parallel rules would have to take into consideration the views of the various schools of Islam, which it itself would not be an easy task. If applied consistently, such system would furthermore require the determination of the religious and cultural allegiance of each person, even against his or her will or after his or her death. Such determination would necessarily often have to be based on indirect and unreliable evidence and result in a more-or-less arbitrary guesswork. It could even be abused, especially if the religious or cultural identity were allowed to vary depending on which rule the person(s) involved preferred in the particular case. Of course, one could make the parallel rules applicable only to those persons who have expressly opted for a Moslem "status", but this would not work for those persons who lack the knowledge and/or the energy required for making an informed choice.

4. FINAL REMARK

The application or taking account of Islamic family and succession law in Europe gives rise to a number of interesting questions, but I shall in the following focus on merely one of them. As mentioned at the outset, some of the Islamic principles are difficult to reconcile with the values prevailing in modern European societies, such as the equality, in the eyes of the law, of men and women. It is clear that the application of foreign law, whether Islamic or not, must be refused if it would be manifestly incompatible with the public policy (*ordre public*) of the forum, for example as defined in the constitutional provisions of the forum country. As practically all European countries are parties to the European Convention for the Protection of Human Rights and Fundamental Freedoms from 1950, it can be assumed that the application of Islamic law would also be refused whenever it would violate that Convention. Member States of the European Union have also to consider the Charter of Fundamental Rights of the EU, to the extent it is applicable.

It must, however, be stressed that far from all of the Islamic family and succession rules are unacceptable from the European point of view. Islamic rules, just like any other foreign law, must be studied and evaluated in their context, because something that at a superficial look might seems shocking can at a closer look appear to be fairly reasonable. For example, the Islamic bride-price (*mahr*) may remind one of a purchase of a bride, but it serves usually as the wife's economic security, compensating for the husband's right to dissolve the marriage at any time by a unilateral act. A time-limited marriage, permitted by Iranian law, may seem incompatible with the European concept of marriage, but if concluded for a long fixed period, such as 99 years, it protects the wife from a unilateral repudiation at any time by the husband. As the wife does not have the right to repudiate the husband and it is very difficult for her to get a divorce against the husband's will, a marriage limited to a few years gives her a chance to discontinue or re-negotiate the matrimonial bond. The smaller inheritance share of daughters as compared to that of sons constitutes an overt discrimination against women on grounds of their gender, but in some Islamic legal systems it is compensated by the fact that only sons are legally obligated to take care of the parents in their old age, etc. It is thus necessary to examine the effects of the applicable Islamic rule under the circumstances of the individual case under scrutiny rather than to make general pronouncements about the acceptability of this or that provision.

The degree of tolerance to be shown by today's European multicultural societies towards Islamic values and legal culture is a highly sensitive and controversial political issue. It is an important task of comparative law to provide the decision-makers with relevant and correct information, not least by demonstrating that the common prejudices about Islamic family and succession law are not always well-founded.

CONFÉRENCE DE LA HAYE ET UNION EUROPÉENNE – SYNERGIES DANS LE DOMAINE DU DROIT DES SUCCESSIONS

Andrea BONOMI
Professeur à l'Université de Lausanne

1. QUELQUES REMARQUES SUR LES RELATIONS ENTRE LA CONFÉRENCE DE LA HAYE ET L'UNION EUROPÉENNE

Au cours des deux décennies pendant lesquelles Hans van Loon a guidé, avec beaucoup de compétence et de sagesse, le Bureau Permanent de la Conférence de La Haye, il a été confronté à l'essor, de plus en plus conquérant, du droit international privé de source européenne. Depuis 2000, un imposant corpus de règlements européens a vu le jour, se substituant progressivement aux systèmes nationaux des Etats membres de l'Union européenne. Par cette intense production législative, l'Union s'est investie de compétences croissantes, et souvent exclusives, pour la négociation et la conclusion de conventions internationales dans le domaine des conflits de lois et de juridictions. Par ce biais, elle a assumé un rôle souvent déterminant pour l'issue des travaux au sein de la Conférence de La Haye, ce qui a conduit à lui conférer un statut de membre *sui generis* de cette organisation.

Universalisme et régionalisme ne faisant pas toujours bon ménage, il existe un sentiment diffus selon lequel la montée en puissance du droit international privé européen n'est pas très propice à l'unification de ce domaine à l'échelle mondiale. Comme on le rappelle volontiers, les Etats européens ont traditionnellement été parmi les principaux artisans et bénéficiaires des conventions de La Haye ; leurs besoins en termes d'uniformisation étant désormais largement assouvis au plan régional, leur engagement au sein de la Conférence paraît désormais plus chancelant. Par ailleurs, l'élaboration de solutions consensuelles au sein de l'Union européenne étant souvent le fruit de longues et âpres négociations entre les Etats membres, ceux-ci manifestent parfois une certaine réticence à s'impliquer dans l'élaboration de textes à vocation universelle, si et dans la mesure où cet exercice peut remettre en cause l'acquis européen.

Cependant, cette vision pessimiste n'est sans doute pas partagée par le récipiendaire de ces Mélanges, et cela à juste titre. En effet, dans un monde globalisé les besoins de coordination entre les droits nationaux dépassent largement les frontières européennes, comme en témoignent les développements législatifs et jurisprudentiels dans plusieurs pays de l'Asie, de l'Afrique et de l'Amérique latine. Plusieurs initiatives récentes du Bureau Permanent[1] montrent bien qu'une certaine conception « eurocentrique » de la Conférence est aujourd'hui largement dépassée. Par ailleurs, l'activisme des institutions de l'Union européenne, notamment de la Commission, loin d'être nuisible aux travaux de la Conférence, peut s'avérer très profitable lors de la négociation d'instruments à vocation universelle. Il convient de noter, enfin, que l'unification du droit international privé au sein de l'Union peut également faciliter les travaux au sein de la Conférence ; en effet, les solutions élaborées pour jeter un pont entre les droits parfois très divergents des Etats membres peuvent être une bonne source d'inspiration pour des textes de portée plus large.

Dans cette perspective, j'essayerai de montrer que le Règlement européen sur les successions, récemment adopté[2], loin d'écrire le mot de la fin aux efforts d'harmonisation engagés dans ce domaine, pourrait relancer des objectifs plus ambitieux, dont la Conférence de La Haye pourrait encore une fois se faire le porte-drapeau.

2. LE RÈGLEMENT EUROPÉEN SUR LES SUCCESSIONS ET LES PERSPECTIVES D'HARMONISATION À L'ÉCHELLE GLOBALE

Le Règlement européen sur les successions sonne définitivement le glas des espoirs liés à l'entrée en vigueur de la Convention de La Haye sur la loi applicable aux successions à cause de mort du 1er août 1989. A vrai dire, les perspectives de ce texte étaient déjà mauvaises, voire inexistantes. Avec l'adoption du Règlement européen, la Convention deviendra inapplicable même aux Pays-Bas, seul Etat qui l'avait ratifiée et qui en appliquait les règles en vertu d'une loi de 1996.

1 Nous pensons notamment à la création de bureaux régionaux en Amérique latine (à Buenos Aires, depuis 2005) et en Asie (à Hong Kong, en 2012). Cf. le Rapport sur l'Amérique latine – Etat du Bureau de la Conférence de La Haye en Amérique latine, *Doc. info.* n° 3 d'avril 2012.

2 Règlement 650/2012/UE du Parlement européen et du Conseil du 4 juillet 2012 relatif à la compétence, la loi applicable, la reconnaissance et l'exécution des décisions, et l'acceptation et l'exécution des actes authentiques en matière de successions et à la création d'un certificat successoral européen, JO L 201, du 27 juillet 2012, p. 107–134.

Toutefois, il serait faux de dresser un constat d'échec des initiatives de la Conférence dans le domaine du droit des successions. En effet, la Convention de 1989 et les autres textes élaborés à La Haye ont sans doute pavé la voie au législateur européen, celui-ci s'en étant largement inspiré (2.1). Par ailleurs, l'œuvre d'unification du droit international privé des successions est loin d'être achevée : la Conférence de La Haye serait bien inspirée de prendre le relais de l'Union européenne, afin de jeter un pont entre l'Europe et les autres systèmes du monde (2.2).

2.1. LE RÈGLEMENT EUROPÉEN ET LES INSTRUMENTS ADOPTÉS PAR LA CONFÉRENCE DE LA HAYE EN MATIÈRE DE SUCCESSIONS

Le Règlement européen puise largement dans les instruments élaborés à La Haye en matière de successions.

Des emprunts importants ont été faits, tout d'abord, à la Convention de 1989. A l'instar de ce texte, le Règlement a opté pour la méthode unitaire en adoptant, comme critère de rattachement principal, la dernière résidence habituelle du défunt (art. 21 par. 1 RS, art. 3 par. 1 et 2 de la Convention)[3]. Comme dans la Convention, ce critère peut être écarté par le biais d'une clause d'exception (art. 21 par. 2 du Règlement, art. 3 par. 2 de la Convention). Le renvoi de la loi applicable à la loi d'un Etat tiers est accepté aux mêmes conditions qu'à l'article 4 de la Convention (art. 34 par. 1 point b RS). Le choix de la loi applicable par le *de cujus* est également permis et son régime reflète à plusieurs égards celui de la Convention (art. 22 RS, art. 5 de la Convention). Des règles très semblables sont prévues pour la recevabilité et la validité des pactes successoraux (art. 25 RS, art. 8 à 12 de la Convention). Le champ d'application ratione materiae et les matières exclues sont définies de manière semblable dans les deux textes (art. 1er RS, art. 1er de la Convention). Enfin, plusieurs règles ponctuelles du Règlement ont été reprises, à quelques modifications près, de la Convention : tel est le cas des dispositions relatives aux régimes successoraux particuliers, aux comourants et aux biens en déshérence (art. 30, 32 et 33 RS, art. 15, 13 et 16 de la Convention).

Quant à la Convention de La Haye du 5 octobre 1961 sur les conflits de lois en matière de forme des dispositions testamentaires, les solutions qu'elle consacre sont reprises telles quelles dans le texte même du Règlement, qui les étend ainsi aux Etats membres non parties à la Convention (art. 27 RS).

Certes, le Règlement va plus loin que la Convention et s'en éloigne à plusieurs égards.

[3] Art. 21 par. 1 du Règlement, art. 3 de la Convention.

En premier lieu, il ne régit pas uniquement la loi applicable mais également la compétence juridictionnelle, la reconnaissance et l'exécution des décisions et des transactions judiciaires, ainsi que l'acceptation et l'exécution des actes authentiques, des domaines non couverts par les conventions de La Haye (chapitres II, IV et V RS). En outre, le certificat successoral européen qu'il institue (chapitre VI RS) est réglé de manière beaucoup plus détaillée, et produit des effets plus importants, que le certificat prévu par la Convention de La Haye du 2 octobre 1973 sur l'administration internationale des successions. En dépit de quelques faiblesses, la réglementation de ces aspects constitue sans doute un pas en avant par rapport aux textes élaborés à La Haye.

En ce qui concerne plus spécifiquement la loi applicable, en revanche, les solutions européennes ne sont pas toujours meilleures que celles issues des travaux à La Haye. Certes, au plan du rattachement objectif, la solution du Règlement, qui fait de la résidence habituelle le seul critère de rattachement objectif, sous réserve de la clause d'exception, paraît préférable ; en effet, la solution de la Convention de 1989, en vertu de laquelle la loi nationale était applicable à la succession lorsque la résidence habituelle du défunt n'avait pas été établie au moins cinq ans avant le décès (art. 3 par. 2 et 3), était, de l'avis général, trop compliquée. En revanche, la solution conventionnelle est préférable en ce qui concerne le choix de la loi ; le Règlement, qui admet la désignation de la loi nationale du *de cujus* mais exclut celle de la loi de sa résidence habituelle, est trop restrictive. En outre, s'il est sans doute positif que les règles de forme de la Convention de 1961 soient étendues aux pactes successoraux (art. 27 RS), à l'inverse l'extension aux autres dispositions à cause de mort des règles relatives à la recevabilité et à la validité au fond des pactes successoraux (art. 24 RS) paraît moins heureuse. La définition beaucoup plus large du domaine de la loi successorale, englobant également les questions d'administration et de liquidation de la succession (cf. l'art. 23 RS, beaucoup plus large que l'art. 7 de la Convention), est en principe positive mais elle soulève également quelques problèmes complexes. Enfin, on peut douter que l'admission généralisée du renvoi à la loi de l'Etat du for ou à la loi d'un autre Etat membre (art. 34 par. 1 point a RS) constitue toujours la bonne solution, notamment lorsqu'il aboutit à une scission successorale.

Quoi qu'il en soit, sur tous ces points, les instruments de La Haye ont sans doute été de grande utilité pour le législateur européen qui a pu tirer profit des expériences antérieures.

2.2. LE RÈGLEMENT EUROPÉEN COMME TREMPLIN POUR UN NOUVEL INSTRUMENT UNIVERSEL SUR LES SUCCESSIONS

Si le Règlement européen bénéficie largement des travaux menés au sein de la Conférence, il pourrait à son tour constituer un tremplin pour relancer les travaux d'harmonisation du droit international privé des successions à l'échelle universelle.

Cette suggestion peut paraître utopique, si l'on tient compte à la fois de l'adoption récente du texte européen et du succès mitigé des principales conventions de La Haye élaborées dans ce domaine. Cependant, un tel projet répond à un réel besoin, qui subsiste à l'adoption du Règlement (a) ; en outre, il pourrait bénéficier des accomplissements du texte européen ainsi que de certaines expériences faites pendant la négociation de celui-ci (b).

a) Le besoin de coordination des droits en matière de successions existe à l'échelle globale. Depuis longtemps, la circulation des personnes et des investissements n'est plus limitée à quelques régions du monde. La globalisation a accentué ce phénomène et la crise économique des dernières années l'a probablement encore renforcé. Les migrations motivées par des raisons économiques ne sont plus uniquement orientées sur l'axe sud-nord (des pays « pauvres » vers les pays industrialisés) mais prennent une dimension plus complexe ; ainsi, de plus en plus de jeunes européens, souvent bénéficiant d'une bonne formation, vont tenter leur chance dans des pays émergents. De même, la croissance encore soutenue de certains pays du sud attire des capitaux et d'autres investissements à la recherche de bonnes rémunérations. Ces phénomènes économiques sont destinés à multiplier, à l'avenir, les cas de successions transfrontières à l'échelle mondiale. Si plusieurs Etats non européens étaient déjà prêts, entre les années 50 et 80, à s'engager sur la voie de l'élaboration de conventions internationales dans le domaine successoral, leur intérêt ne pourra que s'accroître à l'avenir.

Le Règlement européen n'est applicable que dans les Etats membres de l'Union européenne et ne répond évidemment pas aux besoins des Etats tiers. Qui plus est, il ne permet même pas de régler entièrement le problème des successions transfrontalières au sein de l'Europe. En effet, le Royaume-Uni et l'Irlande, qui ont participé très activement aux négociations, ont finalement renoncé à exercer leur droit d'*opt in* ; à l'instar du Danemark, ils ne sont donc pas liés par ce texte. L'occasion de jeter un pont entre les systèmes successoraux des pays de *common law* et des pays de tradition civiliste a donc été perdue. Qui mieux que la Conférence de La Haye pourrait reprendre ce défi, comme elle avait su le faire avec la Convention de 1985 sur le trust ? Au sein de la Conférence, le Royaume-Uni et l'Irlande ne seraient pas isolés et pourraient plus facilement négocier, avec le soutien d'autres Etats anglo-saxons, des solutions pragmatiques permettant de tenir compte des particularités du droit successoral de *common law*.

Notons enfin que le Règlement, loin de résoudre les problèmes de coordination entre les Etats liés et les Etats tiers, aura parfois pour effet d'accentuer ces problèmes.

Tel sera l'effet de certaines solutions qui ont été retenues en matière de conflits de juridictions. Ainsi, lorsque le défunt a sa résidence dans un Etat tiers, l'article 10 de ce texte accorde aux juridictions de l'Etat membre du lieu de situation des biens successoraux des compétences très étendues, qui englobent parfois la totalité de la succession[4] ; ces règles sont susceptibles de multiplier les conflits avec les juridictions d'Etats tiers. Ces conflits ne peuvent pas être évités en application des règles sur la litispendance ou la connexité, car ces mécanismes ne sont disponibles, en vertu des articles 17 et 18 du Règlement, que dans les relations entre Etats membres. Enfin, la limitation facultative de la procédure prévue, dans un but de coordination, à l'article 12 du Règlement est soumise à la condition que la décision de la juridiction saisie dans un Etat membre ne puisse pas être reconnue ou exécutée dans l'Etat tiers du lieu de situation des biens, ce qui suppose un pronostic de reconnaissance très délicat, à la lumière des règles de reconnaissance en vigueur dans l'Etat tiers concerné.

Au plan des conflits de lois, si l'admission du renvoi (art. 34 RS) favorise sans doute la coordination, le choix de loi de l'article 22 du Règlement peut créer des conflits avec les Etats tiers qui ne reconnaissent pas (ou pas encore) l'autonomie de la volonté en matière successorale.

Une convention internationale à vocation universelle pourrait prévenir ces conflits, en excluant dans les relations entre les Etats parties les compétences trop étendues, en établissant des mécanismes pour prévenir les procédures parallèles et des règles harmonisées sur la reconnaissance des décisions, en introduisant le choix de la loi applicable. Rappelons que les thèmes de la compétence judiciaire, de la reconnaissance et de l'exécution des décisions en matière de successions figurent depuis longtemps parmi les possibles sujets de travaux futurs de la Conférence[5].

---

4 Tel est le cas lorsque le défunt avait la nationalité de cet Etat ou y avait eu sa résidence habituelle antérieure dans les cinq ans qui ont précédé la saisine du tribunal (art. 10 par. 1 points a et b). En l'absence de ces conditions, la compétence des juridictions de l'Etat du lieu de situation est limitée aux biens situés dans cet Etat (art. 10 par. 2).

5 Ce sujet figure régulièrement parmi les possibles sujets non prioritaires de travaux futurs depuis le début des années 1990 : cf. les Conclusions de la Commission spéciale de mai 2000 sur les affaires générales et la politique de la Conférence, Doc. prél. n° 10 de juin 2000, p. 13, ainsi que les Conclusions et Recommandations adoptées par le Conseil sur les affaires générales et la politique de la Conférence (17–20 avril 2012), point 23. Cf. aussi la Deuxième mise à jour de la Note sur la compétence judiciaire et la reconnaissance et l'exécution des décisions en matière de successions, note établie par le Bureau Permanent Doc. prél. n° 4 de mars 2000.

b) L'élaboration d'un instrument à vocation universelle pourrait être favorisée par les solutions retenues dans le Règlement européen. Comme nous l'avons relevé, ce texte reprend un certain nombre de principes qui étaient déjà à la base de la Convention de La Haye de 1989 et qui pourraient, probablement, recueillir un consensus assez large.

Ainsi, l'approche unitaire peut compter, à l'intérieur même des pays dualistes, sur un très fort soutien. Du reste, cette solution avait été admise sans trop de contestation dans la Convention de 1989, et l'échec de celle-ci est probablement imputable à d'autres raisons. De même, lors des négociations du Règlement européen, le Royaume-Uni et l'Irlande étaient assez enclins à renoncer au dualisme, leur opposition s'étant focalisée sur d'autres aspects plus ponctuels, notamment l'application de la loi successorale à l'administration de la succession ainsi qu'au rapport et à la réduction des libéralités (« clawback »).

De même, les avantages du choix de la loi applicable à la succession sont aujourd'hui largement admis dans un nombre grandissant de pays. L'admission assez prudente de ce choix par le Règlement pourrait faire des adeptes bien au-delà des frontières européennes. Un tel développement serait sans doute bienvenu, car il permettrait d'asseoir la planification successorale sur des bases plus solides.

Enfin, l'élaboration d'une convention serait probablement facilitée par l'abandon, dans l'instrument européen, de la nationalité comme critère de rattachement objectif. Avec les Etats arabes et le Japon, plusieurs Etats de l'Europe continentale étaient jusqu'à présent le principal bastion de la nationalité ; la solution compliquée de l'article 3 de la Convention de La Haye de 1989 s'explique principalement par la réticence de plusieurs pays européens à renoncer à ce critère. En dépit des perplexités que la résidence habituelle suscite en matière successorale, ce critère est susceptible de recueillir à l'échelle mondiale un bien plus large consensus que la nationalité. Du reste, même les pays encore favorables à l'application de la loi nationale pourraient s'accommoder de la faculté offerte au *de cujus* d'élire cette loi.

En revanche, il paraît plus difficile qu'un consensus puisse se former entre les Etats de *civil law* et de *common law* quant au domaine d'application de la loi régissant la succession. L'approche très large de l'article 23 du Règlement a été l'un des points qui ont amené le Royaume-Uni à ne pas participer à l'adoption du texte. Cela ne constitue cependant pas un obstacle pour une convention universelle, puisque l'instrument de 1989 prévoyait déjà, à son article 7, une solution suffisamment souple pour consentir la coexistence d'approches différentes.

Au-delà des principes, les solutions retenues ou discutées lors de l'élaboration du Règlement européen en relation avec des questions plus ponctuelles pourraient également alimenter une future convention de La Haye.

Tel est le cas de l'article 29 du Règlement, relatif à la nomination et aux pouvoirs d'un administrateur de la succession conformément à la loi du for : cette disposition, introduite principalement pour tenir compte des particularités de la procédure de *probate*, n'a pas suffit pour convaincre le Royaume-Uni et l'Irlande à participer au Règlement, mais elle peut constituer une bonne base de discussion pour une solution globale.

La recherche d'un compromis avec les pays de *common law* avait également conduit, pendant les négociations, à envisager des solutions intéressantes quant à la loi applicable au rapport et à la réduction des libéralités consenties par le *de cujus* de son vivant. Pour tenir compte de l'hostilité anglo-saxonne à la remise en cause, par effet de ces règles, du transfert de propriété résultant d'un acte à l'origine valable (« clawback ») il avait été proposé, entre autres, de soumettre cette question à la loi qui aurait été applicable à la succession au moment de la libéralité (« loi successorale hypothétique »)[6] ; cette solution n'a finalement pas été retenue dans le texte final du Règlement, mais elle pourrait constituer l'une des briques d'un compromis plus large.

*

* *

En conclusion, les efforts d'unification du droit international privé engagés par la Conférence de La Haye et par l'Union européenne, loin d'être mutuellement nuisibles, peuvent et doivent converger vers l'objectif unitaire d'assurer une meilleure coordination des systèmes juridiques nationaux, à l'échelle régionale et universelle. L'exemple des successions à cause de mort montre que, si les instruments adoptés à La Haye ont nourri de manière importante les travaux des institutions européennes, l'inverse est également souhaitable. Hans van Loon a toujours œuvré pour promouvoir les synergies entres ces deux organisations ; cet esprit de collaboration a sans doute marqué son mandat de Secrétaire général.

---

6 J. Harris, "The Proposed EU Regulation on Succession and Wills : Prospects and Challenges", *Trust Law International*, 2008, p. 199 ; A. Dutta, "Succession and Wills in the Conflict of Laws on the Eve of Europeanisation", *RabelsZ*, 2009, p. 583.

THE PROTECTION OF THE RIGHTS OF CHILDREN AND THE RECOGNITION OF *KAFALA*

Alegría Borrás
Professor of Private International Law,
University of Barcelona (Spain)

I. INTRODUCTION

According to Article 20, paragraph 1 of the United Nations Convention on the Rights of the Child, "[a] child temporarily or permanently deprived of his or her family environment, or in whose own best interests cannot be allowed to remain in that environment, shall be entitled to special protection and assistance provided by the State". In paragraph 3 it is added that "[s]uch care could include, inter alia, foster placement, *kafalah* of Islamic Law, adoption or if necessary placement in suitable institutions for the care of children. When considering solutions, due regard shall be paid to the desirability of continuity in a child's upbringing and to the child's ethnic, religious, cultural and linguistic background". From this article, it is possible to extract three elements: (1) the best interest of the child is to remain in his family environment and, when this is not possible, a system of protection has to be established; (2) there are different systems of protection and *kafala* is not the same as adoption or other measures of protection; (3) in any case, continuity in the child's ethnic, religious, cultural and linguistic background is desirable.

In this context, I recall one of the first works by Hans Van Loon that I had the opportunity to read at the very beginning of the negotiations on the 1993 Hague Intercountry Adoption Convention. It was his preliminary report on intercountry adoption[1] in which attention is paid to the constant core interests of Hans: the protection of human rights and, in particular, the protection of the

1 J.H.A. Van Loon, "Report on the intercountry adoption", Preliminary document no. 1 of April 1990, *Actes et documents de la XVIIe Session,* Tome II, Adoption – Cooperation.

rights of children. As is well known, *kafala* is a particular institution of Islamic law for the protection of children, which has been implemented in different ways in different Islamic countries. In recent times, some Islamic countries have established clearer rules concerning *kafala*, or new interpretations of this institution, usually hardening the conditions for 'foreigners' (those living outside the country in which the *kafala* is to be ordered) wishing to undertake a *kafala*. In the great majority of Muslim countries, adoption is forbidden: it is *haram*. Other Muslim countries accept adoption only for certain groups of persons, depending upon their religion. However, some Muslim countries have introduced adoption into their laws.[2] Finally, in many cases a *kafala* constituted in a Muslim country is "converted" into adoption in a European country.

The current situation provides us with a good opportunity to underline certain points which have arisen over the years, from the 1993 Hague Intercountry Adoption Convention to the 1996 Hague Child Protection Convention and, above all, concerning the protection of human rights and the best interests of the child.

II. THE STARTING POINT: THE EXCLUSION OF *KAFALA* FROM THE 1993 HAGUE INTERCOUNTRY ADOPTION CONVENTION

The starting point in the aforementioned Report of Hans Van Loon was the United Nations Declaration of 1986 and the United Nations Convention of 1989.[3] In both texts, the best interests of the child is recognised as the paramount principle which should govern the placement of children outside their families, nationally and internationally. In addition, Article 20 of the UN Convention stresses the importance of paying due regard to the child's background. It was in the context of defining the limits of the 1993 Hague Convention, under construction at that point in time, that Hans devoted some attention[4] to the "Islamic exception", qualifying it as a "cross-cultural problem". According to his explanation, the most broadly prevailing interpretation in Islamic societies is that the Koran introduced a prohibition of the artificial creation of family ties (*nasab*) by *tabanni*, a widespread practice in pre-Islamic times which led to a complete integration of a child into a new family, including the imposition of the same marriage prohibitions as for biological relatives. In fact, it was because of these marriage prohibitions that the Prophet at first declined the offer of Zaid, his adopted son,

---

2 It seems that only Tunisia, Turkey and Indonesia allow adoption.

3 Van Loon Report, *cit.*, pp. 91-92. Afterwards, also in J.H.A. Van Loon, "International co-operation and protection of children with regard to intercountry adoption", *Recueil des Cours*, tome 244 (1993), pp. 209 ss.

4 Van Loon Report, *cit.*, pp. 25-26.

to marry Zaid's wife. After Zaid had repudiated his wife, Zaynab, the Prophet married her. In this situation, the *tabanni* practice could not be maintained since this marriage was only possible if the adoption of Zaid had not created a link of filiation. Consequently, the Koran explicitly provides that adopted sons shall not be held as natural ones and shall not be named after their adopters. As Van Loon says, Islamic jurists have concluded from this that, in addition, adoption cannot produce any other effects, such as marriage prohibitions, inheritance rights and that indeed it cannot confer the status of being a legitimate child, which means that adoption, as we know it, "cannot exist in Islamic law".

Paragraph 3 of the Preamble to the 1993 Hague Convention expressly recognises "that intercountry adoption may offer the advantage of a permanent family to a child for whom a suitable family cannot be found in his or her State of origin". This means that the Convention, as a starting point, only applies to give "a permanent family to a child", which is not the case with *kafala*. A proposal of Egypt to add a new paragraph to the Preamble with a reference to, "the other alternatives and forms of child care, *e.g.* foster placement and kafala as enshrined in Islamic law, and the need to promote international co-operation therein"[5] was not accepted. The expert representing Egypt,[6] in his remarks on the draft Convention, stressed the need for co-operation in relation to other forms of child care and stated that they expected "that the draft recognises the other alternatives of taking care of the child, as the one recognised by the Islamic Law, which we certainly consider to be in the best interest of the child". And he added that, "the Draft accepted, as I interpret it, the principle of 'subsidiarity', and we did expect to see such recognition of the other alternatives having their place in the body of the Convention". He was therefore of the opinion that all these possibilities had to be included in the 1993 Convention. But, really, the place for *kafala* is not in the 1993 Hague Intercountry Adoption Convention but in the 1996 Hague Child Protection Convention.

The 1993 Hague Intercountry Adoption Convention was adopted on 29 May 1993 and this is why it is so significant that on 6 September 1993 Morocco became a Member of the Hague Conference on Private international law.[7] It was clear that they were expecting the Hague Conference to deal with *kafala* in the future. With Morocco a Member of the Hague Conference, Charfi's statement that the

5 Working document 124. In the discussion, another proposal was also discussed, not relevant from our perspective.

6 Annex to the Report of the Special Commission of 1992, *Actes et documents of the XVII Session*, p. 243.

7 González Beilfuss, C., "La aceptación del Estatuto de la Conferencia de La Haya por Marruecos y sus consecuencias", *Revista Española de Derecho internacional*, 1994, pp. 451 ss.

"Muslim world remains alien to the Hague Conference" would no longer apply.[8] The inclusion of Morocco in the Membership of the Hague Conference was an important fact taking into account the number of Conventions prepared by the Conference relating to family matters and, in particular, to matters related to the protection of children. In this regard, two facts have to be underlined: the 1996 Hague Child Protection Convention and the so-called "Malta Process".[9] This is not the place to talk about the "Malta Process" but, in relation to *kafala*, it is important to examine the main points of the 1996 Hague Convention.

III. THE STATUS OF *KAFALA* IN THE HAGUE CONFERENCE: THE 1996 HAGUE CHILD PROTECTION CONVENTION

During negotiations on the 1996 Convention, the Moroccan delegation was particularly active. The members of the delegation were conscious of the fact that *kafala* had its place in the Convention and, in order to inform other delegations who were unfamiliar with the institution, they introduced Working Document No 10[10] explaining the procedure of *Kafala* as set out in the Moroccan law of 10 September 1993 on abandoned children. It was really an informative document not to be lightly dismissed. From this document, it was clear that a *kafala* is not the same as an adoption, which would be forbidden by Islamic law, and that a *kafala* produces no effect on the parent-child relationship. As a result, the child does not become a member of the family of the *kafil*. *Kafala* is accorded by a decision of the guardianship judge or administrative commission to a public or social institution or to a Muslim family which will then take care of the child and receive delegation of guardianship over the child.

For the first time, *kafala* is mentioned in a Hague Convention. In fact, Article 3 establishes that, among the measures referred to in Article 1, the following is included: "*e)* the placement of the child in a foster family or in institutional care, or the provision of care by *kafala* or an analogous institution". This provision

[8] Charfi, M., "L'influence de la religion dans le droit international privé des pays musulmans", *Recueil des Cours,* tome 203, 1987, pp. 336-337; Jahel, S. "La lente acculturation du droit maghrébin de la famille dans l'espace juridique français", *Revue internationale de Droit comparé,* 1994, p. 43.

[9] On these questions, Borrás, A., "Europa: entre la integración y la multiculturalidad", *Derecho islámico e interculturalidad* (Z. Combalía - M.P. Diago - A. González-Varas, coordinadores), Madrid, 2011, pp. 23 ss.

[10] Proposition of the delegation of Morocco, on the *"Procédure de la* Kafala, *telle qu'elle est établie par la loi du 10 septembre 1993, relative aux enfants abandonnés"*, and also the Lagarde Report on the Convention, *Actes et documents de la XVIII Session,* tome II – protection des enfants, pp. 230-231 and 547.

was undoubtedly influenced by the solutions established in Chapter IV of the 1993 Convention on adoption, in line with the proposal of the Netherlands,[11] which takes into account the possibility that this placement could take place in another Contracting State. It is to this end that a procedure is established in Article 33 and a sanction for non-compliance with the procedure is established in Article 23: that is, non-recognition of the placement. The discussion on these rules was difficult.[12] It was Ms van Iterson, from the Netherlands, who introduced the proposal, explaining that the objective of the rule was to avoid the refusal of recognition of a placement of a child, in a case where the placement was to take place in a Contracting State different from the State where decision concerning the placement was taken. The proposal provoked a negative reaction from Mr. Helin (Finland), who considered the formulation of the rule too rigid and also from Prof. Picone, who considered that it was sufficient to have the possibility for co-operation in the Convention, but the introduction of a compulsory system was not warranted. M. Idrissi-Bichr (Morocco) considered that the proposal of the Netherlands was positive, as it provided guarantees for the displaced child, and he questioned Ms van Iterson as to how the proposed system would work. Ms van Iterson answered that the system would work following the example of Chapter IV of the 1993 Hague Intercountry Adoption Convention with the objective of ensuring that the placement could take place. In this situation, the Chairman took a vote.[13] The result regarding what is now Article 23, 2, f) was 12 votes in favour, 8 against and 8 abstentions. The result concerning what is now Article 33 was 12 votes in favour, 9 against and 7 abstentions.[14] Although the text was adopted, it is clear that there was no consensus. At this point, Prof. Duncan, then delegate of Ireland, enquired whether the drafting Committee could consider certain "details" of Working document No 89, in the sense that a direct obligation should not be imposed on the Central Authority. Prof. Picone regretted that this point had not been raised prior to the vote, but he was not in favour of according the Drafting Committee the power to change the merits of the proposal. At this point, the chairman, Mr Pirrung (Germany), ruled the discussion closed on this

11 Working document No. 59 of the Delegation of the Netherlands, redrafted in Working document No. 89, of the delegation of the Netherlands, supported by the delegations of Spain, Ireland, Switzerland, Belgium, Luxembourg and Sweden, *Actes et documents de la XVIII Session,* Tome II – Protection of children, p. 258.

12 See Minutes No. 16, *Actes et documents de la XVIII Session,* Tome II – Protection of children, p. 406.

13 At that moment, the Hague Conference worked under the rule of majority and not of consensus, as is now the case after the modification of the Statute of the Hague Conference on Private International Law.

14 There is a mistake in the Minutes, as it says that the number of abstentions was also 9. The Chair corrected the result in his intervention in the second reading, on Minutes No 25, *Actes et documents de la XVIII Session,* Tome II – Protection of children, p. 472.

point, although he recognised that "the discussion was proceeding very quickly" and "that situations such as this would inevitably arise". The only possibility available was an amendment during the second reading.

And this was indeed the case, with the delegations of France, Italy, Portugal, the Slovak Republic and the United Kingdom proposing to delete both rules.[15]

The intervention of Mr Sturlese (France) underlined that the result of the previous vote had been ambiguous and that the rule would involve the introduction of a very heavy procedure. For him, this procedure was good for adoption, but not for the placement of a child in a situation that could be very provisional. According to the rules then in force, an absolute majority was needed to reopen the discussion and it was not reached, as only 13 votes[16] were expressed in favour of reopening the discussion. The result was very close, but it had to be accepted according to the rules then in force, although it would have not been the case nowadays with the system of consensus. In any event, we shall see afterwards if the system is good or not in the case of *kafala*.

Morocco was the first country to sign the 1996 Convention, on the same day as the adoption of the text, 19 October 1996, and as a sign of its satisfaction at having *kafala* included in the Convention. The Convention entered into force on 1st January 2002 in the Czech Republic, Monaco and Slovakia and in Morocco on 1st December 2002. Although all the Member States of the European Community (at that time) signed the Convention jointly on 1st April 2003, two facts delayed their ratification of the Convention. First, the competence of the European Union concerning the protection of children; and secondly, the fact that the 1996 Convention does not have a "REIO clause" to allow the European Union itself to ratify the Convention. This is the reason why a decision of the Council of the European Union was adopted authorising certain Member States to ratify, or accede to the 1996 Convention, in the interest of the European Union.[17] According to Article 3 of this Decision, the intention was for Member States to

15 Working document No. 144, *Actes et documents de la XVIII Session,* Tome II – Protection of children, p.293.

16 It is now quite difficult to remember how many delegations there were at that moment in the room. But supposing that there were the same number that voted on the proposal, the absolute majority would have been 15 votes, as the total number of votes expressed was 28.

17 Council Decision of 5 June 2008 authorising certain Member States to ratify, or accede to, in the interest of the European Community, the 1996 Hague Convention on Jurisdiction, Applicable Law, Recognition, Enforcement and Cooperation in respect of Parental Responsibility and Measures for the Protection of Children and authorising certain Member States to make a declaration on the application of the relevant internal rules of Community law, *OJ* L 151, of 11 June 2008. This is not the place to go into all of the different situations of all the Member States at that point in time, which required a complicated decision. On this issue, Borrás, A., "Europa: entre la integración y la multiculturalidad", *Derecho islámico e interculturalidad* (Z. Combalía – M.P. Diago – A. González-Varas, coordinadores), Madrid (Ed. Iustel), 2011, pp. 23-43.

deposit simultaneously the instruments of ratification or accession "if possible before 5 June 2010". As it was not possible for all the Member States to finish their internal procedures on ratification or accession by this date, each of them deposited their instrument of ratification or accession when they were ready. At the time of writing, the last ratification of a Member State of the European Union was the ratification of Sweden, the Convention entering into force for this country on 1st January 2013. From the Member States of the EU, only the ratifications of Belgium and Italy are yet to take place. As to the success of the 1996 Convention, 39 States are Parties at the time of writing, with the Russian Federation and Lesotho being the last States to accede. The Convention will enter into force for these States on 1st June 2013.

IV. THE DIFFICULT RELATIONSHIP BETWEEN *KAFALA* AND ADOPTION

It is a rather frequent situation nowadays for children coming from Islamic countries to be given in *kafala* to a couple residing, during the process of constitution of the *kafala*, in the Islamic country, with the couple, in the majority of cases, having converted to Islam recently. Shortly afterwards, the *kafils* and the *makful* come back to the country where the *kafils* live habitually, where they expect either the *kafala* to be "converted" into an adoption or, as this is not possible in the great majority of cases, for an adoption to take place *ex novo*, as they are different institutions and without equivalent effects.[18] As a consequence, this situation differs from the case in which the *kafils* are Muslim and belong to the family of the child and are authorised to live in a foreign country.

In these situations, the attitude of the Spanish authorities has been much more permissive than others. It is true that, for example, the French authorities have Article 370-3 of the *Code civil*, as modified by the Law of 16 February 2001, in the sense that the adoption of Maghrebian children whose national law prohibits adoption is only possible if the child was born and habitually resides in France, a rule which has given rise to well-known decisions of the *Cour de Cassation*.[19] Similarly, Spanish law is not as well-prepared as the Belgian *Code civil*, where

18 In the vast bibliography on the institution and the problems in Europe, P. Diago, "La *kafala* islámica en España", *Cuadernos de Derecho transnacional*, 2010, marzo, pp. 138 ss. For a more general overview, see A. Borrás, "Les ordres plurilégislatifs dans le droit international privé actuel », *Recueil des Cours*, volume 249 (1994-V), pp. 145 ss.; A. Borrás, « La sociedad europea multicultural : la integración del mundo árabe", in *El Islam Jurídico y Europea* (A. Borrás-S. Mernissi, eds.), Barcelona, 1998, pp. 163 ss.

19 Comments on the law, by P. Lagarde « La loi du 6 février 2001 relative à l'adoption internationale : une opportune clarification », *Revue critique de Droit international privé*, 2001, pp. 275 ss. Among the judgments of the *Cour de cassation*, there were two decisions of 10 October 2006,

Article 361-5[20] contains detailed regulation for the adoption, in Belgium, of children coming from these countries.

Without mentioning the rich debate surrounding Spanish Law on the matter of international adoption, as it is not the object of this contribution,[21] it is worth pointing out that Article 34 of [INSERT] deals with institutions such as *kafala* constituted by foreign authorities, which do not produce a link of filiation, and puts them at the same level as foster care in Spain, in accordance with the *Resolución – Circular* of the *Dirección General de los Registros y del Notariado* of 15 July 2006, which defines *kafala* as "an institution for the protection of children equivalent to foster care in Spain". This correctly allows for the rejection of a visa application on the part of the family regrouping with children given in *kafala*, as there is no custody *(patria potestad)* (Judgment of the *Tribunal Supremo* of 9 December 2011) or, for the same reason, it allows for the denial of the right to opt for Spanish nationality (Decision of the *Dirección General de los Registros y del Notariado* of 29 March 2011). Equally correct is the decision of the *Tribunal Supremo* of 10 February 2009,[22] awarding an orphan's pension to two abandoned Moroccan children given in *kafala* by a Moroccan authority to a Moroccan couple when one of them died.

On the contrary, there are a large number of cases which, broadly speaking, repeat the scheme of the decision of the *Audiencia Provincial de Barcelona* 153/2011, of 27 June 2011.[23] In this case, a child born in Morocco was declared abandoned and was given in *kafala* to a Spanish couple, resident in Spain, who fulfilled, in principle, the requirements of Moroccan Law. The Moroccan Court authorised the child to travel to Spain to reside with the *kafils*. Adoption was not authorised in the first instance by the judge in Morocco. However, it was authorised by the *Audiencia Provincial* without the proposal of a Public Entity and after less than one year of residence in Spain, on the basis that it was in the best interests of the child and there was a positive report on the integration of the child in the new family environment. These are procedures which could be qualified as "conversions" of *kafala* to adoption. There is little control of such procedures in the country of origin, where requirements for adoption do not exist

revoking the adoption of two children coming from Morocco and Algeria, given in *kafala*. The doctrinal debate on the rule is not mentioned here.

20 Drafted according to the law of 6 December 2005.

21 For a general overview, R. Arenas – C. González Beilfuss, "La Ley 54/2007, de 28 de diciembre, de adopción internacional: entre la realidad y el deseo", *Revista Electrónica de Estudios Internacionales,* nº 17, 2009. S. Adroher, "La nueva regulación de la adopción internacional en España. Comentarios generales a la Ley 54/2007, de 28 de diciembre, de los 'Santos Inocentes'", *Revista crítica de Derecho inmobiliario,* 2009, 11, pp. 13-56.

22 Comments by A. Rodríguez Benot en *Anuario Español de Derecho internacional privado, 2009,* pp. 929 ss.

23 Comments by Ch. Oró en *Revista Española de Derecho internacional,* 2012, 1, pp. 217 ss.

because the country does not know or recognise adoption, or in the receiving State, where the authorities should be at least as rigorous as in other cases of international adoption. This situation occurs very frequently in Spain with a lot of children coming from Morocco, a country which, besides a couple, also allows a single woman to be a *kafil*.[24] Furthermore, the result of this is that we can speak of a "limping adoption" as the adoption is valid in the country of constitution but invalid in the child's country of origin.

As I said at the beginning, in recent times a noticeable hardening of the laws in Muslim countries has taken place, or, at least, a modifying of the existing rules,[25] or of the application of such rules. The latter occurred when the Moroccan Ministry of Justice gave instructions to the Public Prosecutor to strictly supervise the requirements for *kafala*: that is, for the child to be educated in the Muslim religion and for the *kafil* to have his/her/their habitual residence in Morocco. This last requirement has given rise to problems for some Spanish families, who were part-way through undertaking a *kafala* in Morocco.

In this situation, lots of questions can be raised. For example, when the certificate of eligibility and suitability is prepared in Spain, is it for *kafala* or for adoption? Is there really a transfer of the habitual residence of the *kafils* to Morocco? Is there really a conversion to Islam? Do the authorities in Morocco or in other Muslim countries ignore these matters? What happens regarding the pledge to educate the child in the Islamic religion? Under what conditions is the child authorised to come to Spain under the regime of *kafala?* What happens concerning the follow-up of the *kafala*?

This is the reason why I consider that the moment has arrived to dissociate the institutions of *kafala* and adoption, respecting in this way the content of both institutions, respecting the internal laws in force and, in the case of States Party to the 1996 Hague Convention, respecting the procedure established in this Convention.

In fact, Article 23 of the 1996 Hague Convention, after stating that "the measures taken by the authorities of a Contracting State shall be recognised

---

[24] Favoured also by associations as in Catalonia "Amics dels infants de Marroc" (friends of children of Morocco). See www.amicsinfantsmarroc.org, where they offer only advice in order to facilitate the constitution of a *kafala* in Morocco and, among the documents which have to be prepared, we have the certificate of suitability for *kafala*, the certificate of residence in Morocco during the procedure and the certificate of conversion to Islam. On these problems, see A. Quiñones – A. Rodríguez Benot – H. Zekri – J. Ouhida, *Kafala y adopción en las relaciones hispano-marroquíes,* Madrid, 2009, in particular, pp. 171 ss.

[25] It is possible, for example, to think about the consequences for international adoption of the new *Code des personnes et de la famille* of Mali (Loi n° 2011-087, of 30 December 2011), as Mali is a Contracting State to the 1993 Hague Convention. In fact, it is important to underline that being a Party to the Convention does not oblige a country to undertake international adoptions. See *The implementation and operation of the 1993 Hague intercountry adoption Convention. Guide to good practice. Guide No 1,* The Hague, 2008, pp. 21-25.

by operation of law in all other Contracting States", in paragraph 2, lists the situations in which recognition "may however be refused". As it is stated in the Explanatory Report drafted by Prof. Lagarde,[26] "it is to be noted that this paragraph 2 authorises the refusal of recognition, but does not impose it". Among the grounds for non-recognition, the following is included, "*f)* if the procedure provided in Article 33 has not been complied with". Article 33, as we shall have occasion to see, establishes a "mandatory procedure of consultation where the authority of a contracting State contemplates a measure of placement of the child, for example by *kafala,* which has to be carried out in another Contracting State. Article 23, paragraph 2, sub-paragraph f), avoids placing the State, in which the measure of placement is to be carried out, before a *fait accompli,* and authorises it to refuse recognition if the procedure for consultation has not been followed".[27]

Article 33 establishes a procedure for consultation in cases where a child has to be placed in a country different to the country where the measure is adopted. As the Lagarde Report underlines, it is "the only procedure for obligatory consultation provided by the Convention".[28] According to this article, when the authority which has jurisdiction under Articles 5 to 10 contemplates the provision of care by *kafala* in another Contracting State, this authority has to consult with the Central Authority or other competent authority of the receiving country, transmitting a report on the child together with the reasons for the proposed provision of care. The decision on *kafala* in the requesting State may only be taken after the authorities in the requested State have given their consent, "taking into account the child's best interests", in the terms of paragraph 2 of Article 33. As we have seen, the sanction for non-compliance with this consultation procedure is the possibility of non-recognition of the *kafala* or other placement in the requested State.

V. FINAL REMARKS

The objective of considering the matters set out above was to emphasise some of the elements which are integrated in the protection of the best interests of the child. As I mentioned at the beginning, paragraph 3 of Article 20 of the United Nations Convention on the Rights of the Child, upon considering solutions for an abandoned child, states that "due regard shall be paid to the desirability of continuity in a child's upbringing and to the child's ethnic, religious, cultural and linguistic background". If a child has been given in *kafala,* according to

[26] Lagarde Report, *cit.* paragraph 121, p. 585.
[27] Lagarde Report, *cit.*, paragraph 127, p. 587.
[28] Lagarde Report, *cit.*, paragraph 143, p. 593.

his religious and cultural background, it is necessary to respect the procedure described in the 1996 Hague Convention. What is not respectful of the child's religious and cultural background is to permit an adoption which is not allowed by the law of the child's country of origin. As I have already pointed out, the introduction of Article 33 of the 1996 Hague Convention was not easy but, in my view, it is positive from the perspective of achieving continuity in a child's upbringing, particularly concerning such a serious issue as religion.

This does not mean that the adoption of a Muslim child has to be prohibited in all cases, but the cases in which it is allowed must be clearly identified and clearly regulated, paying close attention to the very strict and special conditions specific to each case.

JURISDICTIONAL DEVELOPMENTS AND THE NEW HAGUE JUDGMENTS PROJECT

Ronald A. Brand
Professor of Law and Director, Center for International Legal Education, University of Pittsburgh School of Law

I. INTRODUCTION

Jurisdiction and the recognition and enforcement of judgments have seldom been far from the agenda at the Hague Conference on Private International Law over the past two decades. The jurisdiction and judgments project that began in 1992 concluded in 2005 with the Hague Convention on Choice of Court Agreements.[1] The fact that the result was less ambitious than the original scope of the negotiations led to further consideration of the question of judgments recognition by the Council on General Affairs and Policy of the Hague Conference in 2012.

The original jurisdiction and judgments project has at times been described as a failed effort.[2] In fact, that project probably ended just where it should have begun, with a focus on jurisdiction by consent in the Convention on Choice of Court Agreements. That Convention enshrined the single most acceptable basis of jurisdiction – consent by the parties – in a treaty that should become the litigation

1 Convention on Choice of Court Agreements, available at www.hcch.net/index_en.php?act=conventions.text&cid=98. The jurisdiction and judgments project began with a May 5, 1992 letter from Edwin Williamson, Legal Adviser to the U.S. Secretary of State, to the Secretary-General proposing the negotiation of a multilateral convention on the recognition and enforcement of judgments. See *Some Reflections of the Permanent Bureau on a General Convention on Enforcement of Judgments*, Prel. Doc. No. 17, May 1992. See also Ronald A. Brand, "Enforcement of Judgments in the United States and Europe", 13 *J. L. & Com.* 193, at 195 and 208 (1994).

2 See, e.g., James P. George, "Enforcing Judgments Across State and National Boundaries: Inbound Foreign Judgments and Outbound Texas Judgments", 50 *S. Tex. L.Rev* 399, 424 (2009) ("In the wake of the Hague Judgments Convention failure, in 2005 the Hague Conference produced the Hague Convention on Choice of Court Agreements").

partner to the successful United Nations Convention on the Recognition and Enforcement of Foreign Arbitral Awards (the New York Convention).[3]

The Hague Conference has once again taken up discussion of the "Judgments Project," with exploratory work considered by an Experts' Group, and the 2012 establishment of a Working Group "whose initial task shall be to prepare proposals for consideration by a Special Commission in relation to provisions for inclusion in a future instrument relating to recognition and enforcement of judgments, including jurisdictional filters."[4] The Experts' Group has also been asked to give further consideration in relation to matters of jurisdiction.[5]

Even if new jurisdictional instruments are not pursued, a principal question in any new judgments project is the relationship between jurisdiction and the recognition and enforcement of foreign judgments. The difficulty encountered in negotiating common rules of jurisdiction contributed significantly to the limitation of the results of the earlier negotiations to a Convention on Choice of Court Agreements. While the new project should be limited to the recognition and enforcement of judgments, any resulting instrument will nevertheless have to deal indirectly with matters of jurisdiction. Thus, because existing differences in approach to jurisdiction will necessarily affect any possible outcome of a new Hague judgments project, it is important both to remember the differences that affected the earlier negotiations and to consider subsequent developments that have highlighted those differences.

The principle differences in jurisdictional approaches have been defined largely by the legal systems in the United States and the European Union. In this paper, I begin by reviewing those differences and the manner in which they created difficulty in the earlier negotiation of a convention on jurisdiction and judgments. I will then consider subsequent developments in jurisdictional law in both the United States and the European Union. I will conclude with comments about the implications of those developments for any future negotiations on judgments recognition.

II. THE LAST TIME AROUND: JURISDICTIONAL DISJUNCTION AND RECOGNITION

The jurisdiction and judgments negotiations which were generated in 1992 and culminated with the Convention on Choice of Court Agreements in 2005

3 United Nations Convention on the Recognition and Enforcement of Foreign Arbitral Awards, done at New York, June 10, 1958, 330 U.N.T.S. 38 ("New York Convention").

4 Hague Conference on Private International Law, Conclusions and Recommendations Adopted by the Council on General Affairs and Policy, ¶¶ 17 (17-20 April 2012).

5 *Id.* ¶ 18.

originally sought agreement on rules of direct jurisdiction as well as rules on the recognition and enforcement of judgments.[6] This led to consideration of the differences between existing bases of jurisdiction in varying legal systems. Those from outside the United States were concerned with expansive U.S. concepts of general jurisdiction–based on "minimum contacts" beyond simple domicile. They sought to cut back this jurisdictional reach during the negotiations. Similarly, states outside Europe sought protection from the exorbitant bases of national jurisdiction that were made inapplicable within Europe by the Brussels Convention[7] and then the Brussels I Regulation.[8]

These two very different sets of jurisdictional rules reflect different legal systems, different core values, and resulting different approaches to the concept of judicial jurisdiction itself, as well as different approaches to the persons sought to be protected in a legal system through jurisdictional rules. The most obvious difference is between the civil law system of continental Europe, reflected in the Brussels regime for jurisdiction and judgments, and the common law system of the United States. While the European system implements rules through legislation designed to reflect social values, the U.S. common law system focuses on equitable results in judicial decisions applied to specific parties and circumstances. The former focuses on predictability and efficiency, and the latter on equity in individual cases. While the results of the application from either system when applied to the same set of facts may be similar to the results from the other system, the paths to those results clearly differ.

In the United States, a second distinction sets jurisdictional analysis apart even from its common law brethren. The case law of the United States Supreme Court has made clear that jurisdiction is a constitutional matter, requiring analysis of the Due Process rights of the defendant under the Fifth and Fourteenth Amendments of the United States Constitution.[9] Thus, even after a jurisdictional

---

6 *See, e.g.*, Interim Text – Summary of the Outcome of the Discussion in Commission II of the First Part of the Diplomatic Conference (6-22 June 2001), prepared by the Permanent Bureau and the Co-reporters, *available at* www.hcch.net/index_en.php?act=publications.details&pid=3499&dtid=35.

7 European Convention on Jurisdiction and Enforcement of Judgments in Civil and Commercial Matters, done at Brussels, 27 September 1968, 33 OJ (C189/1) 1 (28 July 1990) (consolidated and updated version of the 1968 Convention and the Protocol of 1971, following the 1989 accession of Spain and Portugal), ["Brussels Convention"]. The Convention was also subject to the Convention on the accession of the Republic of Austria, the Republic of Finland and the Kingdom of Sweden, done at Brussels, 29 November 1996, 40 OJ (C15/1) (15 January 1997). It was generally replaced by the Brussels I Regulation in 2001.

8 Council Regulation (EC) No 44/2001 of 22 December 2000 on Jurisdiction and the Recognition and Enforcement of Judgments in Civil and Commercial Matters, OJ L 12/1, 22 December 2000 ("Brussels I Regulation").

9 For an explanation of U.S. concepts of Due Process in the context of the Hague negotiations on jurisdiction and judgments, see Ronald A. Brand, "Due Process, Jurisdiction and a Hague Judgments Convention", 60 *U. Pitt. L.Rev.* 661(1999).

statute has been applied,[10] a court must determine whether the application of that jurisdictional rule offends the Due Process rights of the defendant over whom jurisdiction is being asserted.

The Due Process analysis required by the United States Supreme Court provides a defendant-oriented approach to jurisdiction, while the Brussels Regime in Europe has provided a plaintiff-oriented system of analysis in many cases. In the United States, it is the Due Process rights of the defendant that ultimately are the focus of the jurisdictional analysis. Thus, it is jurisdiction as a power-based concept ("jurisdiction over the defendant") that is at issue, not jurisdiction as a matter of judicial competence to hear a case. In Europe, on the other hand, recent developments have made clear that the Brussels regime, while starting with a focus on the defendant in its general jurisdiction rule of Article 2, has taken on a plaintiff-centered orientation. This is seen in the plaintiff-friendly protective rules for consumers, employees, and insured parties.[11]

Any effort to co-ordinate judgments recognition rules necessarily requires consideration of the jurisdictional bases of authority of the court from which the judgment originates. When those bases of authority are colored by (1) basic differences between civil law and common law approaches to judicial analysis, (2) differences in the extent to which jurisdiction is a constitutional matter, and (3) differences in focus on the interests of plaintiffs and defendants, the problems of co-ordination are easily multiplied.

III. RECENT DEVELOPMENTS AND THEIR IMPACT ON NEW JUDGMENTS NEGOTIATIONS

The 2001 Hague Conference turn from a comprehensive convention on jurisdiction and judgments to a Convention on Choice of Court Agreements was a wise one given the very deep divide between existing systems of jurisdiction and the unlikely possibility of either harmonization or unification of those rules on a global basis. The question in 2013 is whether conditions are such that it is possible

---

10 Analysis of *in personam* jurisdiction in U.S. courts generally involves a two-step process, beginning with the application of the state long-arm statute, to determine if there is statutory jurisdiction. The second step is the constitutional analysis by which it is determined whether the exercise of jurisdiction allowed by state statute in the particular case is within the limits of the Due Process Clause. Jurisdiction in the federal courts is governed by Rule 4(k) of the Federal Rules of Civil Procedure. Rule 4(k)(1)(A) authorizes a federal district court to borrow the jurisdictional powers of state courts in the state where it is located.

11 See Ronald A. Brand, "Access-to-Justice Analysis on a Due Process Platform, review of Christopher A. Whytock and Cassandra Burke Robertson, Forum Non Conveniens and The Enforcement of Foreign Judgments" 112 *Col. L.Rev. Sidebar* 76 (2012), available at www.columbialawreview.org/assets/sidebar/volume/112/76_Brand.pdf.

to return to an effort to reconcile both jurisdiction and judgments recognition on a global basis or even to craft an instrument on judgments that takes into account existing divergent rules of jurisdiction.

Events after the 2005 completion of the Convention on Choice of Court Agreements demonstrate even greater divergence between the U.S. and European systems of judicial jurisdiction. In the United States, developments have come primarily through the common law evolution of the law of jurisdiction in the Supreme Court. In Europe, development has continued in a civil law mode through the December 2012 completion of the Recast of the Brussels I Regulation.

A. DEVELOPMENTS IN THE UNITED STATES

In June 2011, the United States Supreme Court decided two cases that many had hoped would provide clear guidance to courts, litigators, and transactions lawyers on matters of jurisdiction over foreign defendants in U.S. courts. In *Goodyear v. Brown*,[12] the Court addressed questions of general jurisdiction. The case was brought in North Carolina by the parents of a young man who died in a bus accident outside Paris, France. Alleging that tire defects had caused the accident, the plaintiffs sued Goodyear USA (an Ohio corporation), as well as Goodyear subsidiaries in Luxembourg, Turkey, and France. The subsidiaries all contested jurisdiction. Because no events leading to the cause of action arose in, or out of contacts with, North Carolina, the plaintiffs were relying on theories of general jurisdiction. The North Carolina courts found general jurisdiction to exist on a stream of commerce analysis, but the Supreme Court, in a unanimous opinion by Justice Ginsburg, reversed, holding that a "connection so limited between the forum and the foreign corporation ... is an inadequate basis for the exercise of general jurisdiction," as it "does not establish the 'continuous and systematic' affiliation necessary to empower North Carolina courts to entertain claims unrelated to the foreign corporation's contacts with the state."[13]

The *Goodyear* opinion both clarifies the limits of general jurisdiction and draws lines between those limits and the type of contacts often relied upon to support specific jurisdiction:

> Flow of a manufacturer's products into the forum may bolster an affiliation germane to *specific* jurisdiction, ..., but ties serving to bolster the exercise of specific jurisdiction do not warrant a determination that, based on those ties, the forum has general jurisdiction over a defendant. A corporation's "continuous

12 __ U.S. __, 131 S.Ct. 2846 (June 27, 2011).

13 *Id.* at 131 S.Ct. 2851.

> activity of some sorts within a state," *International Shoe* instructed, "is not enough to support the demand that the corporation be amenable to suits unrelated to that activity." [14]

Prior to the *Goodyear* decision, the primary distinction between U.S. and European concepts of general jurisdiction rested on the difference between simple domicile and the carrying on of continuous and systematic business activity in the forum state. The former– enshrined in Article 2 of the Brussels I Regulation as *the* basis of general jurisdiction in Europe–is a simple and predictable connecting factor. The latter is more amorphous, but arguably more equitable in an age of instant communication through an electronic "presence" in a state, ease of travel on a global basis, and the legal fiction of the corporate "person." Much of the jurisprudence of the United States Supreme Court during the latter half of the twentieth century recognized that a corporation has no single place of being, but is present where its officers and employees engage in continuous and systematic activity – and thus is subject to general judicial jurisdiction in any such state.[15] Both the European and the U.S. rules recognize that a corporation may be sued under concepts of general jurisdiction where the corporation *is*; they differ on how one determines where the corporation *is* for this purpose. For Europe it is a predictable, but limited, determination of domicile. For the United States, it is a more amorphous and expansive determination of where the corporation is actually engaging in business activity.

The *Goodyear* opinion arguably brings the United States closer to Europe on questions of general jurisdiction. By stating that "[a] court may assert general jurisdiction over foreign (sister-state or foreign-country) corporations to hear any and all claims against them when their affiliations with the State are so "continuous and systematic" as to render them essentially at home in the forum State,"[16] the Court brought the U.S. concept of corporate "home" closer to the European concept of domicile. The Court did not move all the way to a simple domicile test, but came close by comparing the corporate home to the natural person's domicile. "For an individual, the paradigm forum for the exercise of general jurisdiction is the individual's domicile; for a corporation, it is an equivalent place, one in which the corporation is fairly regarded as at home."[17] Whether there is any room between these concepts of domicile and home remains to be seen. Footnote 6 of the *Goodyear* opinion is likely to receive focus in the further development of whether any distinction continues to exist:

---

14 *Id.* at 131 S.Ct. 2849.
15 *See* Brand, *supra* note 9, at 683-84.
16 *Goodyear*, at 131 S.Ct. 2851.
17 *Id.* at 131 S.Ct. 2846.

> In the brief they filed in the North Carolina Court of Appeals, respondents stated that petitioners were part of an "integrated world-wide efforts (sic) to design, manufacture, market and sell *their tires* in the United States, including in North Carolina." ... Read in context, that assertion was offered in support of a narrower proposition: The distribution of petitioners' tires in North Carolina, respondents maintained, demonstrated petitioners' own "calculated and deliberate efforts to take advantage of the North Carolina market." ... As already explained, ... , even regularly occurring sales of a product in a State do not justify the exercise of jurisdiction over a claim unrelated to those sales.[18]

On the same day that it decided the *Goodyear* case, the Supreme Court also issued its decision in *J. McIntyre Machinery, Ltd. v. Nicastro.*[19] *Nicastro* was a specific jurisdiction case in which a New Jersey resident sued a United Kingdom manufacturer of scrap metal machines in New Jersey state court for injuries sustained when one of the machines, purchased by the plaintiff's employer, allegedly malfunctioned and caused serious injury.

Under the special jurisdiction rules found in Article 5 of the Brussels I Regulation, the *Nicastro* case would have created no significant problems. Article 5(3) clearly states that a person domiciled in a Member State may be sued "in matters relating to tort, delict or quasi-delict, in the courts for the place where the harmful event occurred or may occur."[20] The European Court of Justice has made clear that this rule means that "the defendant may be sued, at the option of the plaintiff, either in the courts for the place where the damage occurred or in the courts for the place of the event which gives rise to and is at the origin of that damage."[21] Thus, under the type of jurisdictional rules available in Europe, jurisdiction in New Jersey would have been a rather simple matter.[22]

---

18 *Id.* at 131 S.Ct. 2857 n 6.

19 __ U.S. __, 131 S.Ct. 2780 (27 June 2011).

20 Brussels I Regulation, *supra* note 8, Article 5(3).

21 *Bier v. Mines de Potasse d'Alsace* [1976] E.C.R. 1741.

22 While the Brussels I Regulation continues to apply primarily to cases involving defendants domiciled in EU Member States, national law of Member States includes similar rules, sometimes by simply incorporating the rules of the Brussels regime. *See, e.g.*, Law Reforming the Italian System of Private International Law, Law 31 May 1995, n. 218, *English translation at* 35 I.L.M. 760 (1996). Article 3 of the 1995 Law provides:
Article 3
(Scope of jurisdiction)
1. Italian courts shall have jurisdiction if the defendant is domiciled or resides in Italy or has a representative in this country who is enabled to appear in court pursuant to Article 77 of the Code of Civil Procedure, as well as in the other cases provided for by law.
2. Italian courts shall further have jurisdiction according to the criteria set out in Sections 2, 3 and 4 of Title II of the Convention on Jurisdiction and the Enforcement of Judgements in Civil and Commercial Matters with Protocol, signed in Brussels on 27 September 1968, enforced by Law No. 804 of 21 June 1971, with amendments in force for Italy, including

In the United States, the matter is not so simple. Nor is the law left clear after *Nicastro*. While six Justices agreed that New Jersey did not have jurisdiction over the UK manufacturer, they did so in divided opinions that provide no clear majority rule. In a three-Justice dissent written by Justice Ginsburg, the contours of the diverging opinions were clearly delineated:

> A foreign industrialist seeks to develop a market in the United States for machines it manufactures. It hopes to derive substantial revenue from sales it makes to United States purchasers. Where in the United States buyers reside does not matter to this manufacturer. Its goal is simply to sell as much as it can, wherever it can. It excludes no region or State from the market it wishes to reach. But, all things considered, it prefers to avoid products liability litigation in the United States. To that end, it engages a U.S. distributor to ship its machines stateside. Has it succeeded in escaping personal jurisdiction in a State where one of its products is sold and causes injury or even death to a local user? Under this Court's pathmarking precedent in *International Shoe Co. v. Washington*, and subsequent decisions, one would expect the answer to be unequivocally, "No." But instead, six Justices of this Court, in divergent opinions, tell us that the manufacturer has avoided the jurisdiction of our State courts, except perhaps in States where its products are sold in sizeable quantities.

This situation is the result of the application of the Fourteenth Amendment Due Process Clause to jurisdictional reach of each of the individual states of the United States. While many states have long-arm statutes that look much like Article 5(3) of the Brussels I Regulation,[23] they may not extend a state's jurisdictional reach beyond what is allowed by the Due Process Clause. Thus, the ultimate determination is the Constitutional one, and the Supreme Court has now limited that reach significantly for purposes of specific jurisdiction, but without clear guidance regarding the test of its limits.

While the divergent opinions in *Nicastro* make it difficult to define a clear rule for future cases, it does make clear that the jurisdictional reach of U.S. courts is far more limited than in countries that have rules such as those found in the Brussels I Regulation.[24] It thus allows corporations to structure their transactions and relationships in order to avoid tort jurisdiction in the United States under

---

when the defendant is not domiciled in the territory of a contracting State, with respect to any of the matters falling within the scope of application of the Convention. With regard to other matters, jurisdiction shall be also determined according to the criteria laid down for territorial jurisdiction.

23 For example, 42 *Pa. Cons. Stat.* § 5322(a)(4) provides that "Causing harm or tortious injury in this Commonwealth by an act or omission outside this Commonwealth" constitutes "transacting business" within Pennsylvania sufficient to subject a person to specific personal jurisdiction.

24 *Supra* note 22.

circumstances that would clearly result in jurisdiction existing in a European court. The protection provided to a defendant by the Due Process Clauses has clearly been expanded beyond past boundaries, with the ultimate limits yet to be determined.

B. DEVELOPMENTS IN THE EUROPEAN UNION

In the European Union, developments have moved in the opposite direction, making it more likely that foreign defendants will be subject to jurisdiction in the courts of EU Member States. The Commission's original 2010 draft Recast of the Brussels I Regulation would have removed the discriminatory operation of the Regulation that allows jurisdiction over defendants domiciled outside Europe under exorbitant national jurisdiction rules that are prohibited when the defendant is domiciled in an EU Member State.[25] The Recast Regulation 1215/2012,[26] as finally approved, jettisoned the extension of the Regulation to external defendants. Thus, bases of jurisdiction such as Article 14 of the French Civil Code (providing for general jurisdiction over foreign defendants when the plaintiff is a French citizen) and Article 23 of the German Code of Civil Procedure (providing for general jurisdiction over a foreign defendant based on the presence of property owned by the defendant within the German jurisdiction–regardless of the value of the property) remain available against foreign defendants, with no equivalent of the U.S. Due Process limitation to protect them.

Not only did the final Recast of the Brussels I Regulation fail to rectify the pre-existing discriminatory application of national jurisdictional rules against foreign defendants, it also extended one of the internal jurisdictional benefits provided to certain classes of plaintiffs so that it will be available as well against defendants from outside the European Union. Article 16 of the Brussels I Regulation provides that "[a] consumer may bring proceedings against the other

25 Article 3 of the Brussels I Regulation protects defendants domiciled in an EU Member State from the operation of national jurisdictional rules found to be objectionable. Article 4 provides that those rules continue to apply against defendants domiciled outside the European Union. The Commission originally proposed the deletion of Article 4 and a new Article 3(2) that would make defendants domiciled outside the EU subject to the same jurisdictional rules as those domiciled within the EU, subject to some additional rules in Section 8 of Chapter II of the Regulation. Proposal for a Regulation of the European Parliament and of the Council on jurisdiction and the recognition and enforcement of judgments in civil and commercial matters (Recast), COM(2010) 748 final of 14 December 2010.

26 Regulation (EU) No 1215/2012 of the European Parliament and of the Council of 12 December 2012 on jurisdiction and the recognition and enforcement of judgments in civil and commercial matters (recast), OJ L 351/1, 20 December 2012 ("Recast Regulation"). Under Article 81, the Recast Regulation "shall apply from 10 January 2015, with the exception of Articles 75 and 76, which shall apply from 10 January 2014."

party to a contract either in the courts of the Member State in which that party is domiciled or in the courts for the place where the consumer is domiciled."[27] Under the existing regime, this provision applies only to defendants domiciled in the Member States of the European Union.[28] The Recast Regulation, however, extends the consumer jurisdiction rule to defendants from outside the European Union in Article 18(1), stating that "[a] consumer may bring proceedings against the other party to a contract either in the courts of the Member State in which that party is domiciled or, *regardless of the domicile of the other party*, in the courts for the place where the consumer is domiciled."[29] This may well open European courts to consumer litigation on a scale not seen prior to the effective date of the Recast Regulation. On the other hand, given the dearth of reported consumer cases under the existing rules within the European Union – probably because most consumer claims are really too small to take to court – it may be that this is another of those rules that creates theoretical problems with little practical impact. Nonetheless, it is consistent with a pro-plaintiff orientation that sharply contrasts with the general pro-defendant orientation resulting from Due Process analysis in the United States.

IV. WHAT IS EASY MAY NOT ALWAYS MATTER SO MUCH

If the Convention on Choice of Court Agreements is widely ratified and implemented, then any complementary legal instrument prepared at the Hague Conference and dealing with judgments must begin with rules on recognition and enforcement when the parties have not consented to jurisdiction. The problem is that those jurisdictional bases most uniformly applied across the globe may well be those for which recognition and enforcement in a foreign court is least important.

Some bases of jurisdiction are common to most legal systems. For example, it is commonly understood that a defendant may be sued in the courts of his state of domicile for matters that arise anywhere.[30] This is the basic concept of general jurisdiction. It is also commonly understood that the courts of a state have exclusive jurisdiction over the determination of rights that exist only within

---

27 Brussels I Regulation, *supra* note 8, Article 16(1).

28 See *Id.* Article 3(1) ("Persons domiciled in a Member State may be sued in the courts of another Member State only by virtue of the rules set out in Sections 2 to 7 of this Chapter").

29 *Id.*, Article 18(1) (emphasis added).

30 See, e.g., the discussion of the *Goodyear* case in the U.S. Supreme Court, *supra* notes 12-18 and accompanying text, and the discussion of Article 2 of the Brussels I Regulation, text following note 14, *supra*.

the territory of that state or which are necessarily created by and thus governed by that state alone.[31] Thus, title to immovable property located in State X normally is a matter exclusively reserved for determination by the courts of State X, and the existence or validity of a patent issued by State X is a matter exclusively reserved for determination by the courts of State X.

It should not be difficult to agree that judgments rendered by a court in the state of the defendant's domicile, or judgments determining title to immovable property located in the state of the originating court, should be entitled to respect in the form of recognition and enforcement in the courts of other states. At the same time, however, it is precisely the connection between the forum state and the defendant (for purposes of general jurisdiction), or the property which is the subject of the dispute (for purposes of *in rem* jurisdiction), that make it more likely that the assets on which the ultimate enforcement will depend are located in the state in which the judgment was granted. Thus, it is other bases of jurisdiction which are less uniform across the globe that are most likely to be important for judgments recognition purposes.

Assuming the Convention on Choice of Court Agreements becomes widely ratified, and that negotiators at The Hague can draft an instrument that leads to easier recognition of judgments based on domicile as a general jurisdiction nexus and common bases of exclusive jurisdiction, that still would not resolve the real issue that probably matters most in the judgments recognition realm: recognition of judgments in tort cases based on specific jurisdiction ("special jurisdiction" in the European lexicon). This is the type of judgment for which jurisdiction is likely to exist in one country but for which the defendant and the defendant's assets are most likely to be found in another country.

As the discussion above indicates, it is specific/special jurisdiction in tort cases that has moved farther apart, not closer together in the United States and Europe. While the direction of the Brussels I Regulation and Recast Regulation has focused on the rights of the plaintiff, making it easier in some cases to find jurisdiction over a foreign defendant, the United States Supreme Court has focused on the interests of the defendant, making it more difficult to obtain jurisdiction in similar situations. Until this process results in these two major players in the jurisdiction and judgments equation moving closer together, rather than farther apart, any real progress on judgments will not be easy, and any hope of progress on common rules of jurisdiction seems ephemeral at best.

[31] See, e.g., Brussels I Regulation, *supra* note 8, Article 22; Recast Regulation, *supra* note 26, Article 24.

LA MIGRATION DE L'ÉTAT CIVIL

Andreas Bucher
Professeur honoraire de l'Université de Genève
Membre de l'Institut de droit international

L'apport du droit international privé à la maîtrise de la migration internationale des personnes a toujours été une préoccupation majeure du Secrétaire général de la Conférence de La Haye.[1] L'ambition avec laquelle Hans van Loon a animé ce projet est à la mesure de sa générosité. Sa vision a porté loin. Comment le droit international privé pouvait-il être absent de la « gouvernance » de la migration des populations et des personnes, le phénomène social international le plus important de notre époque ? Et comment pouvait-on ne pas proposer aux Etats de s'inspirer des procédures de coopération entre Etats et Autorités centrales, qui sont au cœur de la plupart des conventions des récentes années ? Faute de vision, les Membres de la Conférence n'ont pas voulu s'engager dans un champ d'activité dont les dimensions leur paraissaient imprévisibles. Il n'en demeure pas moins que le monde attend du progrès et des solutions. Celles-ci peuvent être divisées en deux thèmes : la coopération entre les autorités et la protection des personnes en migration. Ce second aspect mérite aujourd'hui une attention prioritaire, car la Conférence dispose déjà de l'expérience dans la gestion des relations entre autorités à travers les frontières.

La protection de la personne migrante peut être divisée à son tour en un volet personnel et un volet économique. Le premier est commenté ici, car il nous semble toucher les populations à plus grande échelle. Sans pour autant ignorer le second. En effet, si la Conférence s'est occupée de la migration des enfants à des fins d'adoption ou de placement à l'étranger, n'existe-t-il pas des raisons pour qu'elle s'intéresse également au transfert temporaire ou circulaire de travailleurs, ainsi qu'à la régulation de l'intervention des intermédiaires dans un processus au

1 Cf., en dernier lieu, le document préliminaire n° 7 à l'attention du Conseil sur les affaires générales et la politique (février 2010) ; Hans van Loon, « Vers un nouveau modèle de gouvernance multilatérale de la migration internationale », in *Liber amicorum Hélène Gaudemet-Tallon*, Paris 2008, p. 419–434.

sein duquel l'individu se trouve souvent démuni ? Le regard ne devra donc pas s'arrêter au statut personnel et familial, mais s'élargir au statut économique des personnes vulnérables dans un contexte migratoire.

I. MISE EN PERSPECTIVE

Ledit volet personnel de la migration ne vise pas au premier abord la protection des personnes vulnérables dans un contexte familial, telle qu'on la trouve au centre des Conventions sur la protection des enfants et des adultes. Il s'agira de protéger toute personne dans son aspiration légitime au respect de ses droits fondamentaux lorsqu'elle est l'objet d'une migration transfrontalière. Ces droits doivent préserver l'identité et l'état civil des personnes ; ils doivent garantir également un seuil minimum de conditions de vie.

Arrêtons-nous un instant pour bien assimiler le changement de perspective. On parle de « migration » et non plus de la paire « immigration » et « émigration ». Ces termes ont été associés, dans le droit international privé depuis plus d'un siècle, aux principes de la nationalité et du domicile. Comme l'a été le sort de ces termes, ces deux principes ont été recalés dans la hiérarchie des valeurs des relations privées internationales. De nos jours, l'intérêt porte prioritairement sur la reconnaissance, à travers les frontières, de l'état des personnes créé dans un Etat. Alors que l'harmonie des décisions était un sujet de première importance pour des méthodes de droit international privé centrées sur la détermination de la loi applicable, ce thème a passé à l'arrière-plan du fait de son manque de pertinence au regard des facilités créées et se développant pour favoriser le respect des décisions étrangères sans que soit vérifié, après coup, quelle loi était initialement applicable.

Dans un contexte de migration des personnes, ce changement dans la perception du rôle du droit international privé se manifeste. Le respect des personnes passe devant l'intérêt des Etats au respect de leurs propres lois. L'harmonie des décisions est importante, certes, mais elle n'a pas pour but de parvenir à l'application d'une loi unique. Elle commande dorénavant le respect, par les Etats, de l'identité d'une personne telle que déterminée dans un Etat. L'harmonie se transforme en droit individuel, alors qu'elle était auparavant un objectif de politique législative poursuivi par chaque Etat indépendamment. Cette politique étant d'emblée placée en position d'échec, le thème des « rapports juridiques boiteux » était apprécié des auteurs de l'époque comme une fatalité, alors qu'aujourd'hui, on ne voit plus pourquoi un tel état des choses devrait faire partie, en quelque sorte « par nature », du droit international privé.

Il est tout aussi certain, cependant, que cette nouvelle perspective ne peut offrir d'elle-même les solutions à venir ; elle ne fait que mieux en percevoir la nature. La migration des personnes à travers les frontières est, et restera toujours, une migration à travers des ordres juridiques différents. S'il convient de protéger la personne face à cette diversité, on n'y parviendra pas en postulant le rapprochement des législations, ni même en exigeant une harmonisation des lois nationales au niveau d'un seuil minimal, encore qu'il n'est pas inutile de rappeler qu'un tel objectif paraisse déjà plus réaliste. En revanche, on doit pouvoir soutenir une vision qui consiste à amener les Etats à respecter des droits relevant d'un seuil minimal tels qu'ils ont été acquis par la personne dans un autre Etat avant d'avoir été exposée au processus de migration.

II. UN SEUIL MINIMAL DE RESPECT DES PERSONNES

Le plancher minimal devant intéresser tout ordre juridique par rapport aux personnes est la protection de leur identité et la garantie de leur survie, économique et sociale. Ces principes n'ont pas à être créés ; même formulés un peu différemment, ce sont des fondements largement reconnus. Il leur manque cependant une élaboration plus précise de leur contenu et de leurs effets juridiques. Ce défaut est davantage apparent dans le contexte migratoire qu'il ne l'est dans un contexte purement interne, moins accessible aux regards extérieurs. Or, sans substance, ces principes restent vides et ne peuvent remplir leur but. La Conférence pourrait donc y trouver un terrain d'activité dans les matières étant de son ressort. Celles-ci portent surtout sur le domaine personnel et familial, tandis que la mise en place de garanties de survie, respectivement de lutte contre l'exploitation, en particulier des personnes les plus vulnérables tels les femmes et les enfants, est une préoccupation majeure d'autres organisations ; cela semble inspirer à la Conférence plutôt une position de retrait ou de réserve.

D'aucuns diront que le haut niveau de travail et d'expérience de la Conférence de La Haye en matière de droit international privé n'est ainsi pas suffisamment sollicité. Même si l'argument était vrai, il n'a guère de sens, le programme de la Conférence étant loin d'être surchargé par des projets de ce niveau. En réalité, le fait qu'un projet s'attache à rendre concrète une protection relevant des droits fondamentaux ne veut nullement dire que l'excellence du savoir-faire de la Conférence ne soit pas mise à contribution. La perfection à laquelle on pense en évoquant le tableau de toutes les Conventions de La Haye est de type européen. Les conventions sur la loi applicable, par exemple, n'ont pas rayonné dans le monde si l'on observe le faible nombre des Etats parties, la plupart européens. Les conventions qui remplissent largement le palmarès de la Conférence sont des conventions de procédure et de coopération, dans des matières dans lesquelles le droit international privé remplit essentiellement une fonction opérationnelle, impliquant un engagement important d'autorités administratives. Leur rôle tend à croître d'autant plus que les conventions sur la loi applicable manquent progressivement de soutien du fait de l'appropriation de leur matière par l'Union européenne. La Conférence doit à nouveau rayonner au plan mondial. Or, pour ce faire, ce sont les droits fondamentaux et leur mise en œuvre qui doivent attirer l'intérêt de la Conférence, avant de songer à gravir des échelons vers des règles juridiques plus perfectionnées. On comparera dès lors la Conférence d'aujourd'hui à celle de ses débuts à la fin du XIXe siècle. Les conventions de l'époque portaient sur des questions plutôt ponctuelles de procédure, sur le mariage et la tutelle ; des sujets bien circonscrits, actuels sans être particulièrement attractifs, et appelant des solutions simples, qui ne nécessitaient aucun travail de « suivi ». Aujourd'hui, il ne s'agit pas de refaire le passé, mais de s'en inspirer afin de réagir avec sagesse et modération aux défis auxquels la Conférence est confrontée.

Une migration s'effectuant dans des conditions humaines acceptables requiert le respect des personnes. Celle-ci se compose de signes d'identité et d'un noyau familial. Leur reconnaissance est un gage de protection à un niveau très élémentaire, certes, mais qui est loin de constituer une évidence à l'échelle universelle. A cet effet, l'enregistrement de l'état civil est fondamental. Sans état civil constaté officiellement, la personne risque de ne pas être reconnue, voire ne pas exister d'un point de vue juridique. L'impossibilité de retrouver l'acte de mariage a donné lieu à des drames du temps de Napoléon Ier déjà.[2] De nos jours, l'expérience se tourne vers des illustrations révélant l'exploitation et le dénuement des personnes. La Conférence a déjà été confrontée à de telles situations dans le contexte particulier des enfants dont l'évacuation d'une zone de conflit armé ou de catastrophe doit être envisagée.[3] Dans un tel cas de trouble, si les forces d'évacuation peuvent arriver rapidement sur le terrain, il faut savoir que les trafiquants d'enfants ne sont pas loin non plus, se servant faussement d'une banderole de service humanitaire. Il est donc de toute première importance de veiller à ne pas séparer les enfants de leurs parents sans avoir pris toutes les précautions permettant de préserver les détails de leur identité, des pièces d'état civil du pays étant pour cela primordiaux. Car sans identité, l'enfant risque de se faire mener rapidement sur le chemin de l'adoption ou d'autres formes de trafic, dont il ne sortira qu'après des recherches laborieuses, si tant est qu'il y parvienne. La migration à travers les frontières devient alors forcée, faute pour l'enfant et sa famille d'avoir pu disposer de moyens d'identification.

---

[2] On conseillera la lecture de la narration passionnante de Michel Verwilghen, *D'amours fous en querelles d'héritage : Trois surprenantes affaires judiciaires au temps de Napoléon* Ier, Bruxelles 2011.

[3] Cf. la Recommandation de 1994 concernant l'application de la Convention sur l'adoption aux enfants réfugiés, Annexe A au Rapport de la Commission spéciale de 1994 ; Conclusions et Recommandations de la Commission spéciale de 2012, n° 38–40.

Or, cet exemple n'est pas unique. On connaît de nos jours l'extrême difficulté de connaître l'âge et l'origine de certains demandeurs d'asile. Sur un autre plan, l'absence d'enregistrement des enfants à leur naissance peut être une cause facilitant des mariages forcés, du fait que l'acte de naissance n'est établi qu'après la « cérémonie », la mariée étant faussement rendue majeure afin d'échapper à la vigilance des autorités du pays ou lors de la migration vers des pays étrangers dits civilisés[4]. On songera également, en sus de l'exemple cité du risque d'être livré en adoption, aux cas très nombreux de familles déchirées par des événements de guerre ou de catastrophe, qui éprouvent tant de peine à retrouver leurs proches car ils ne peuvent pas accéder à un registre permettant de connaître et de tracer leur identité. Les familles réunies ne représentent qu'une partie du monde. Une autre est composée de familles dispersées à travers les frontières et les continents, qui ne parviennent pas à se retrouver faute de pouvoir emprunter le bon chemin. Or, pour ce faire, l'enregistrement de l'état civil constitue une aide précieuse. Il peut exister d'autres obstacles difficiles à franchir, certes, mais ce n'est pas une raison pour ne pas tenter d'éliminer celui résultant de l'impossibilité d'effectuer un « family tracing » au moyen de pièces d'état civil reconnues internationalement.

La Conférence pourrait fonder ses travaux sur un principe déjà bien ancré en droit international : obliger les Etats à procéder à l'enregistrement de mariages et de filiations. D'après la Convention sur les droits de l'enfant du 20 novembre 1989, « l'enfant est enregistré aussitôt sa naissance » (art. 7). De son côté, la Convention de New York du 10 décembre 1962 sur le consentement au mariage, l'âge minimum du mariage et l'enregistrement des mariages prévoit que « tous les mariages devront être inscrits par l'autorité compétente sur un registre officiel » (art. 3).[5]

Cependant, faute d'être complétés par des modalités pratiques appropriées, ces principes n'ont guère été transcrits par les Etats aussi largement qu'il le faudrait. Il conviendrait donc de convier les Membres et les Etats non membres afin de les inviter à consacrer plus concrètement dans un instrument de droit international l'obligation des Etats de mettre à disposition un service d'enregistrement de l'état civil. Un tel service doit pouvoir délivrer des documents constatant ceux des éléments de l'état civil dont on estimera la mention nécessaire en prévision de leur utilisation à travers les frontières. Parmi ces éléments, on devra trouver la date et le lieu de naissance, le nom de la personne ainsi que, eu égard aux Conventions mentionnées, le lien de filiation maternelle et paternelle et le mariage. Cet état civil sera celui établi dans l'Etat qui délivre la pièce. Il sera très important d'envisager un document plurilingue et électronique, mais ne comportant pas

[4] Cf. Filiz Sütçü, *Zwangsheirat und Zwangsehe*, Frankfurt a.M. 2009, p.161.

[5] Cette obligation est rappelée dans la Résolution 1468 (2005) du Conseil de l'Europe sur les mariages forcés et les mariages d'enfants (n° 14.2.2).

plus d'informations que celles jugées indispensables. Par ailleurs, face à leurs obligations de droit international, les Etats doivent traiter leurs éventuelles réticences liées à la protection des données sous la forme de modalités assortissant l'enregistrement, sans mettre en cause le principe lui-même.

III. L'ÉTAT CIVIL INTERNATIONALISÉ

1. LES BESOINS DE BASE

Sous l'angle international, il se posera la question des effets d'un tel document à l'étranger. Dans un premier temps, il conviendra de ne pas donner à la question une portée trop ambitieuse. Car le seul fait de constater que dans un Etat, celui de la confection de la pièce, un certain nombre de faits d'état civil soient déterminés au regard de l'ordre juridique de cet Etat, constitue déjà un soutien utile lorsque, même à l'étranger, la personne voudra faire état de son identité. Même si, dans un autre Etat, cette identité, ou certains de ses éléments, ne sont pas reconnus, tels un mariage ou un lien d'adoption, il n'en demeure pas moins que la pièce est apte à démontrer que dans l'Etat d'origine, cette identité existe bel et bien.

Dans un cadre de négociation entre Etats, il faudra faire un pas de plus et obtenir, à l'instar de la pratique de nombreux pays, que la force probante des pièces d'état civil confectionnées selon un modèle consacré soit reconnue, sous réserve de contestations judicaires visant les droits individuels constatés dans l'acte. Cependant, même si l'on n'y parvient pas, dans un premier stade peut-être, la simple adoption d'un document uniforme d'état civil dont toute personne peut requérir la délivrance de la part des autorités de son pays sera déjà un grand succès. Car l'usage d'une pièce au format uniforme nourrit la confiance dans le fonctionnement des autorités des pays impliqués au point qu'un jour ils accepteront plus facilement d'en reconnaître également la force probante devant leurs juridictions et sur leur territoire.

L'enregistrement internationalement généralisé de l'état civil permettrait d'ailleurs de servir de fondement à un système assurant à toute personne une possibilité de rétablir le contact avec la famille. Certes, cela sera autrement plus compliqué que le seul enregistrement des naissances et des mariages, mais à tout projet ambitieux, il faut un début.

On pourrait alors intégrer un complément économique : la protection de base des personnes s'articule au moyen du respect de son état civil, mais elle rend également nécessaire la garantie de conditions de vie décentes. La migration économique ne doit pas laisser l'individu isolé et sans ressources dans un pays étranger n'offrant aucun accueil, le seul encadrement étant « fourni » par des employeurs et des intermédiaires sans scrupules. Le traçage des familles connaît aussi son volet économique : une condition de vie élémentaire du travailleur à l'étranger consiste à lui permettre l'accès à des moyens de transfert simple et économique des fonds à sa famille restée dans son pays d'origine. Or, en l'état, notre monde pousse à la globalisation des économies, et on s'en félicite, mais lorsqu'il s'agit d'offrir aux travailleurs le renvoi de leurs gains, on en reste aux multiples déclarations d'intention de tous les organismes qui croient avoir un mot à dire à ce sujet, sans aucun suivi dans l'exécution. On constate ainsi qu'au plan économique les besoins sont aussi basiques qu'au niveau de l'état civil.

Certes, à ce stade, le droit international privé n'est guère visible. Peu importe. L'ambition du résultat vaut mieux que l'ambition du texte parfait. Celui-ci, perfectionné et compliqué, manquera sa cible car il ne pourra pas attirer des ratifications en nombre respectable. De toute manière, l'effectivité des actes à travers les frontières, aussi faible soit-elle, apporte un progrès du point de vue du droit international privé, pour lequel le respect des personnes constitue un objectif primordial.

On ajoutera que dans sa phase initiale de pénétration sur le territoire d'un pays étranger, la migration ne fait pas véritablement appel au droit international privé ; elle ne le fait qu'à un niveau subordonné, qui n'attire guère l'attention. En effet, les travailleurs, réfugiés ou voyageurs sont accueillis juridiquement par le nom et les liens de famille qu'ils portent avec eux, au moyen de leurs pièces d'identité.[6] Leur état civil est celui de l'Etat national ayant délivré ces documents. Cela ne viendrait à l'esprit de personne, notamment dans la pratique administrative de l'immigration, de vérifier ces données personnelles au regard de la loi désignée par les règles ordinaires de conflits de lois de l'Etat d'accueil. Ces règles ne deviennent d'actualité qu'à partir du moment où la personne entend nouer des relations juridiques sur le territoire de cet Etat. Jusqu'à ce moment, la force probante des documents officiels de l'Etat de provenance offre à la personne une présence juridique suffisante.

2. LA RECONNAISSANCE

Il est vrai, cependant, qu'au-delà du respect de la force probante des actes de l'état civil, la suite naturelle consisterait à assurer également la reconnaissance des rapports de droit civil et familial consacrés dans de tels actes. Cet objectif sera plus difficile à atteindre. Il faudra s'y engager dans un deuxième temps, avec la patience et la persévérance qui conviennent. Si l'on fait abstraction du cadre européen, où l'on pense que tout est déjà parfait, il est loin d'être évident que l'on parvienne à satisfaire une telle ambition dans les autres régions du monde. Il

[6] En Suisse, on a appelé cela le principe du « sac à dos ».

faudrait d'abord viser l'essentiel : la reconnaissance des rapports de famille nés à l'étranger que l'Etat requis connaît également dans son droit, ainsi que ceux dont il peut accepter l'accueil dans son système juridique. Cette position est en retrait par rapport à l'idéal d'un système ayant banni toute révision au fond. Mais elle est réaliste, malgré ce que des Européens au regard étriqué sur ce monde vont dire. On comparera la Convention adoption de 1993, qui implique l'acceptation au préalable de l'adoption ordonnée dans l'Etat d'origine (art. 17), et la Convention mariage de 1978, qui commande la reconnaissance des mariages sans égard à la loi appliquée (art. 9). On connaît le succès de la première et l'échec de la seconde. Cela montre la voie.

Au plan mondial, il est illusoire de vouloir placer tous les systèmes de droit sur pied d'égalité et de prôner l'acception généralisée de tout rapport de droit familial en provenance de n'importe quel système. La barrière de l'ordre public ne suffit pas : soit elle est trop élevée (avec le soutien du mot « manifestement »), soit elle peut être franchie trop facilement, auquel cas elle rend l'ensemble méconnaissable. Il faudra ainsi entourer les notions de relations familiales, profitant du système de reconnaissance, par des définitions permettant d'écarter les situations que certains Etats ne peuvent accepter, quitte à ce qu'ils puissent le faire plus tard. Ce sont des concessions à faire si l'on veut sauver l'essentiel. Mieux vaut un modeste succès qu'un échec. Et ce succès ne serait peut-être pas aussi modeste que l'on pourrait le croire : la Convention d'adoption est proche de l'introduction d'un système de codécision des Etats concernés dans le cas particulier, créant un rapprochement qui a rendu la clause de l'ordre public inutile dans la quasi-totalité des cas.

Une telle approche ne doit pas détourner l'attention portée à des institutions connues dans certains pays alors qu'elles rencontrent des réactions de rejet dans d'autres. Ainsi, la Conférence se heurte à l'objection d'une minorité d'Etats qui l'empêchent de s'intéresser à la protection des couples vivant en partenariat ou en union libre, en se servant de l'exigence, mal comprise, du consensus au détriment des Etats qui font valoir un intérêt légitime à faire progresser l'unification du droit en faveur de couples méritant le respect.

Lorsqu'il y a lieu de réagir face à des divergences trop sensibles entre législations en contact dans le cas particulier, le droit international privé réagit habituellement par un refus de la reconnaissance de rapports juridiques nés d'un système « étrange », auquel l'Etat requis est « hostile ». Et lorsqu'un tel Etat est placé en négociation et rencontre le même problème, il tentera d'inclure dans l'instrument des clauses de refus de reconnaissance, spécifiques de préférence, générales faute de mieux, telle que la réserve de l'ordre public.

Pourtant, cette approche va à contre-courant d'une tendance qui soutient le respect de situations de droit individuel valablement nées dans un autre pays, leur titulaire ayant un droit fondamental ou, tout au moins, un intérêt légitime à vivre sous un statut juridique unique qui caractérise son identité en tant que sujet de droit. Il paraît inopportun de s'engager dans l'élaboration d'un instrument de reconnaissance en visant d'emblée à y inclure des situations de rejet générant des rapports juridiques boiteux à travers les frontières.

3. L'AUTOLIMITATION

Or, cette réaction de rejet se produit en aval du processus. Elle tend à empêcher le rapport de droit concerné de répandre ses effets à l'étranger. Une autre réaction pourrait être placée en amont, tendant à empêcher la situation « hostile » de naître dans l'Etat d'origine. Cela ne fait pas habituellement partie du droit international privé ; pourtant, cela existe. Il faut distinguer deux niveaux. Au plan de la gestion des relations individuelles, il peut être convenu qu'un Etat n'accepte de créer une relation de famille qu'à la condition qu'elle soit ensuite reçue dans un autre Etat, particulièrement lié aux personnes concernées. Cela revient à une codécision pour laquelle la Convention adoption de 1993 présente un modèle, auquel on ajoutera l'exemple du placement transfrontière et de la kafala selon l'article 33 de la Convention sur la protection des enfants de 1996.

Au plan général, la solution consiste à ce qu'un Etat « exportateur » de rapports de famille, qui rencontre l'hostilité d'Etats étrangers, accepte de ne pas les autoriser sur son territoire s'ils concernent des personnes ayant des liens étroits avec de tels Etats, du fait de leur domicile ou de leur nationalité, par exemple. L'Etat d'origine, sans renier une institution ancrée dans son droit, acceptera ainsi d'y associer une autolimitation de son champ d'application par rapport à certains cas d'extranéité qu'il conviendra de définir. De nos jours, on pourrait regretter, par exemple, que l'on aie décidé en 1993 d'exclure l'adoption d'enfants par des couples de même sexe du champ de la Convention. On aurait également pu prévoir, en rassurant autant les pays qui y sont hostiles, que l'Etat d'origine n'autorise une telle adoption qu'à la condition qu'elle soit acceptée par tous les pays concernés par le cas particulier. Une convention traitant du partenariat serait peut-être mieux perçue si elle prévoyait qu'un Etat accepte de ne pas procéder à l'enregistrement d'une telle union si celle-ci heurte les sensibilités d'Etats étrangers avec lesquels le couple est étroitement lié.

Il serait sans doute plus aisé d'aborder le sujet délicat des maternités de substitution par la négociation si celle-ci incluait une telle démarche de retenue de la part des Etats acceptant un tel procédé. Ces Etats ne vont pas adhérer à un traité les obligeant à cesser d'autoriser de telles pratiques, malgré les recommandations savantes qui leur seront prodiguées pour les y encourager, comme les Etats censés être les « receveurs » ne vont pas surmonter aisément leur hostilité et joindre un instrument les obligeant à devenir plus accueillants. En revanche, les Etats « producteurs » pourraient se montrer sensibles au fait que le « conflit de lois » ainsi provoqué dans certains pays étrangers hostiles est extrêmement sérieux, notamment sous l'angle de l'intérêt de l'enfant. Au lieu d'un système fondé sur des décisions prises au cas par cas, comme pour l'adoption, on aurait ainsi une réglementation plus générale consacrant des hypothèses déterminées dans lesquelles l'Etat d'origine du processus y renoncera afin d'éviter à l'enfant l'hostilité, juridique et sociale, qu'il rencontrera dans d'autres Etats ayant déclaré qu'ils refuseront de l'accueillir.[7]

La migration venant de certains pays profondément ancrés dans des cultures religieuses confrontent les pays laïcs, ou autrement détachés de traditions anciennes, au phénomène des mariages forcés et des mariages d'enfants. Certes, du point de vue de ce second groupe de pays, on peut soit refuser la reconnaissance de tels mariages, soit les soumettre à une procédure d'annulation engagée d'office sitôt le couple entré sur le territoire de l'Etat requis.[8] Il n'en demeure pas moins qu'une telle intervention ne permet pas d'effacer le mariage comme il le faudrait, car il continuera d'exister dans le pays étranger de sa célébration et il laissera des traces même dans l'Etat qui y est « hostile », ne serait-ce que par le fait, par exemple, que l'annulation du mariage produit ses effets uniquement *ex nunc* ou que l'existence d'un mariage antérieur puisse encore être reconnue dans les registres de l'état civil. Le conflit de lois et de civilisations ne peut être résolu par le seul Etat d'accueil et d'immigration. L'Etat d'origine, pour sa part, estimera que c'est trop lui demander d'effacer des traditions ancrées profondément dans la population. En revanche, un tel Etat pourrait être prêt à renoncer à l'exercice de pratiques dont il sait qu'elles vont heurter de front les sensibilités de pays étrangers vers lesquels le couple projette de se rendre pour s'y établir. Il ne s'agit pas, pour l'instant, de dessiner des solutions. On reconnaîtra cependant qu'une telle approche peut mettre les Etats plus à l'aise pour entamer un dialogue, suivi d'une négociation.

4. LE MORCELLEMENT

La migration ne sera pas pour autant débarrassée de ses conflits de lois. Car des rapports de famille créés dans un Etat malgré l'hostilité d'autres Etats vont rester un sujet d'actualité aussi longtemps que les personnes et les familles traversent les

[7] A la lecture du Rapport préliminaire sur les problèmes découlant des conventions de maternité de substitution à caractère international à l'attention du Conseil (document préliminaire n° 10, mars 2012), la Convention adoption de 1993 apparaît comme modèle prédominant (cf. n° 46, 50, 58–63). Il est prématuré de diriger le débat vers ce seul type d'instrument.

[8] Cf. la Résolution 1468 (2005) du Conseil de l'Europe sur les mariages forcés et les mariages d'enfants (n° 14.2.4 à 6).

frontières. Pour atténuer les conflits qui en résultent et les inconvénients frappant les familles, il conviendrait de se détacher des concepts de type institutionnel et de s'attacher à les morceler afin de trouver des solutions pour chacun de leurs effets, pris isolément. En effet, suivant une tradition juridique remontant au XIXe siècle, on attribue une valeur intrinsèque à des concepts tels que le « mariage » et la « filiation », l'idée étant que ces relations portent en elles-mêmes la force de générer un ensemble d'effets juridiques particuliers directement rattachés au concept de base. Or, si cela peut s'expliquer dans le contexte d'une structure de droit fermée et se suffisant à elle-même, il ne doit pas en être ainsi nécessairement. On pourrait également, au lieu de reconnaître ou de refuser de reconnaître un rapport de famille en tant que tel, régler uniquement le sort de certains de ses effets, sans prendre position sur l'accueil ou le refus de l'institution qui leur sert de support. La Conférence en a l'expérience en matière d'obligations alimentaires, lorsqu'elle a tiré, en 1956 déjà puis à nouveau en 1973 (art. 2), une ligne de séparation entre le droit aux aliments, d'une part, et le rapport de filiation, d'autre part, l'obligation alimentaire étant régie par la Convention de manière autonome, tandis que la filiation suit un régime de droit national. On citera également l'exemple de l'adoption, dont la Convention de 1993 admet, certes, qu'elle entraîne la reconnaissance d'un nouveau lien de filiation, mais en n'adressant qu'un seul de ses effets, la responsabilité parentale des parents adoptifs (art. 26 al. 1 lit. a et b). On peut donc morceler le statut familial et n'en assurer la reconnaissance à l'étranger que pour les parties moins offensives, laissant les autres livrées au clivage entre législations si tant est que le noyau est sauvegardé.

Il apparaît en effet que des institutions familiales qui rencontrent une hostilité certaine dans certains pays parviennent néanmoins à y pénétrer avec certains de leurs effets. Le thème est classique s'agissant de la polygamie, dont certains effets, tels le droit aux aliments ou les droits successoraux peuvent passer le filet de l'ordre public, tandis que le concept de la pluralité de femmes mariées est rejeté, fermement même. Une approche similaire pourrait inspirer une réflexion sur le sort des unions se situant hors du mariage traditionnel. Il n'y a pas lieu, en effet, de viser directement la reconnaissance de telles unions en tant qu'institution juridique. Un progrès serait déjà acquis si l'on acceptait le respect de leurs effets sur une échelle internationale, en évitant des controverses qui deviennent politiques et délicates dès que l'on entend promouvoir l'institution en tant que partie de l'état civil.[9] Le débat sur les maternités de substitution pourrait également profiter d'un tel apport de réalisme. En effet, on ne parviendra pas à unir les Etats sur un

9 La réflexion pourrait être animée par l'arrêt de la Cour de cassation française du 8 juillet 2010 (*Rev. crit.* 2010 p. 747), acceptant l'exequatur d'une décision américaine qui partage l'autorité parentale entre la mère biologique et l'adoptante de l'enfant, sans dire que la création d'une double parenté de même sexe soit ainsi validée. On tiendra compte, également, de la kafala qui ne crée pas de lien de filiation, tout en permettant à la famille d'accueil de prendre toute

modèle d'effets internationaux en termes de filiation, qu'il s'agisse de celle de la mère porteuse ou de celle des parents receveurs.[10] En revanche, si l'accent est mis sur l'intérêt d'un enfant qui ne doit pas subir de sanction du fait de son mode de naissance, on pourrait peut-être parvenir à ce que les parents d'accueil puissent exercer la responsabilité parentale et l'obligation alimentaire à l'égard de l'enfant et que celui-ci puisse porter leur nom, sans que le rapport de filiation fasse l'objet d'une reconnaissance de plein droit, avec effet d'état civil reporté sur le registre.

Ce qui compte en définitive, c'est de soutenir la migration des personnes grâce à des solutions marquées par leur humanité plutôt que par leur rigueur conceptuelle. La Conférence y parviendra et Hans van Loon lui aura ainsi légué ce qui caractérise au mieux sa riche personnalité.

---

décision dans l'intérêt de l'enfant (cf. Cour européenne des droits de l'homme, arrêt du 4 octobre 2012, *Harroudj c. France*, n° 43631/09, § 51).

10 C'est pourtant l'axe de raisonnement du document préliminaire n° 10 de mars 2012, cité (cf. n° 33–37, 39, 48, 53–55). Il conviendrait également de ne pas associer de trop près le sort de l'enfant à la sanction d'une convention de maternité de substitution dans un Etat d'accueil qui interdit celle-ci et la frappe de nullité. Si les parents ont passé outre cette prohibition, ce n'est pas à l'enfant d'en subir les conséquences.

LA CONVENTION SUR LES ASPECTS CIVILS DE L'ENLÈVEMENT INTERNATIONAL D'ENFANTS ET LES DROITS DE L'ENFANT

Jacques Chamberland
juge, Cour d'appel du Québec[1]

Moi, mes souliers ont beaucoup voyagé,
Ils m'ont porté de l'école à la guerre.
J'ai traversé sur mes souliers ferrés
Le monde et sa misère.

Moi, mes souliers (1950)
Félix Leclerc, 1914-1988

INTRODUCTION

Le thème de ce *liber amicorum* offert à mon collègue et ami Hans van Loon à l'occasion de sa retraite du poste de Secrétaire général de la Conférence de La Haye de droit international privé nous invite à réfléchir sur le droit international privé et ses interactions avec les droits de l'homme.

J'ai choisi de cibler mon propos sur la *Convention sur les aspects civils de l'enlèvement international d'enfants* (25 octobre 1980) (la Convention de 1980) en abordant deux sujets bien précis, le droit de l'enfant à ce que les décisions le concernant soient prises dans son meilleur intérêt et le droit de l'enfant d'être entendu dans toute procédure l'intéressant.

[1] L'auteur tient à remercier Me Sarah Messerli, auxiliaire juridique à la Cour d'appel du Québec, pour son aide dans la préparation de ce texte.

Les vers que je cite en exergue de ce texte sont ceux d'un troubadour canadien, originaire du Québec, Félix Leclerc. Je les ai choisis pour vous donner le goût de connaître l'œuvre de ce grand poète québécois bien sûr, mais également parce qu'ils auraient pu être les paroles d'un enfant déplacé ou retenu illicitement à l'étranger.

La Convention de 1980 vise à protéger l'enfant contre les effets nuisibles d'un déplacement illicite à l'étranger, ou de son non-retour, et, à cette fin, établit des procédures en vue de garantir son retour immédiat dans l'État de sa résidence habituelle. La procédure mise en place est simple : sauf quelques exceptions bien définies, l'autorité judiciaire ou administrative de l'État où se trouve l'enfant ordonne son retour immédiat, l'objectif étant que toutes les questions relatives à sa garde soient débattues dans l'État de sa résidence habituelle.

Dans le préambule de la Convention de 1980, les États signataires se déclarent « profondément convaincus que l'intérêt de l'enfant est d'une importance primordiale pour toute question relative à sa garde ».

À l'époque, il existait déjà plusieurs instruments juridiques internationaux visant à promouvoir les droits de l'enfant et de la famille et la nécessité de les protéger.

La Déclaration des droits de l'enfant du 26 septembre 1924 (la Déclaration de Genève) affirme, dans son préambule, que « l'humanité doit donner à l'enfant ce qu'elle a de meilleur ».

La Déclaration universelle des droits de l'homme du 10 décembre 1948 déclare, à son alinéa 16(3), que la famille constitue « l'élément naturel et fondamental de la société et a droit à la protection de la société et de l'État ».

La Déclaration des droits de l'enfant du 20 novembre 1959 énonce le principe voulant que, dans l'adoption de lois destinées à protéger l'enfant, l'intérêt supérieur de celui-ci doive être « la considération déterminante ».

Le Pacte international relatif aux droits civils et politiques du 16 décembre 1966 reprend l'idée que la famille (à l'article 23.1) et l'enfant (à l'article 24.1) ont droit à la protection de la société et de l'État.

Le Pacte international relatif aux droits économiques, sociaux et culturels du 16 décembre 1966 reprend le même thème (à l'article 10.1 et 10.3).

Le 2 septembre 1990, la *Convention relative aux droits de l'enfant du 20 novembre 1989* (la CRDE) entre en vigueur. Il s'agit d'un instrument juridique international majeur, ratifié par la quasi-totalité des États membres de l'Organisation des Nations Unies.

La Convention énonce plusieurs principes d'importance : le fait que, dans toutes les décisions le concernant, le meilleur intérêt de l'enfant doive être « une considération primordiale » (article 3.1); le droit de l'enfant séparé de ses parents ou de l'un d'eux d'entretenir régulièrement des relations personnelles et des contacts directs avec ses deux parents (article 9.3); et enfin, le droit de l'enfant d'exprimer librement son opinion sur toute question l'intéressant et donc, d'avoir la possibilité d'être entendu dans toute procédure judiciaire ou administrative l'intéressant (articles 12.1 et 12.2).

La Convention confirme également l'engagement de la communauté internationale à prendre des mesures pour lutter contre les déplacements et les non-retours illicites d'enfants à l'étranger, y compris la conclusion d'accords bilatéraux ou multilatéraux ou l'adhésion aux accords existants (articles 11.1 et 11.2).

Il existe donc déjà une certaine forme de dialogue entre les grands instruments juridiques internationaux et la Convention de 1980. Celle-ci traduit, dans le contexte bien précis du déplacement illicite d'un enfant à l'étranger, ou de son non-retour, la conviction des États que l'intérêt de l'enfant est d'une « importance primordiale » pour toute question relative à sa garde. La CRDE confirme à son tour explicitement l'importance de la Convention de 1980 dans la lutte contre les déplacements et les non-retours illicites d'enfants à l'étranger en invitant les États à adhérer aux accords multilatéraux existants ; elle reprend également le vocabulaire de cette convention – « une importance primordiale » – rédigée sous les auspices de la Conférence de La Haye de droit international privé, pour bien situer l'intérêt de l'enfant – « une considération primordiale » – dans les décisions le concernant.

L'INTÉRÊT DE L'ENFANT

Le *Code civil du Québec* énonce le principe voulant que toutes les décisions concernant l'enfant soient prises « dans son intérêt et dans le respect de ses droits » (article 33). Cette règle fait écho, en droit national québécois, au principe énoncé dans la CRDE.

S'appuyant sur cette règle, certains voudraient que le retour de l'enfant dans l'État de sa résidence habituelle et le rétablissement de la situation existant avant son déplacement à l'étranger soient toujours subordonnés au principe voulant que toute décision le concernant soit prise dans son meilleur intérêt.

Avec respect pour l'opinion contraire, je crois que ce serait là faire fausse route et que cela minerait, à plus ou moins long terme, les fondements mêmes de la Convention de 1980. Je m'explique.

La Convention propose une procédure sommaire visant, sauf exceptions, à assurer le retour immédiat de l'enfant dans l'État de sa résidence habituelle. L'État saisi de la demande de retour et l'État requérant sont-ils liés par la Convention ? L'enfant a-t-il moins de 16 ans ? L'enfant avait-il sa résidence habituelle dans l'État requérant avant son déplacement ? Le déplacement de l'enfant à l'étranger, ou son non-retour, est-il illicite au sens de la Convention ? Advenant une réponse positive à chacune de ces questions, le juge *doit* ordonner le retour immédiat de l'enfant sauf si l'une ou l'autre des quelques exceptions conventionnelles – six en tout – s'applique.

La procédure est simple et ne commande pas, en principe, l'examen des questions relatives au meilleur intérêt de l'enfant, cet examen étant réservé au débat sur le fond du droit de garde.

En d'autres mots, l'intérêt supérieur de l'enfant dont l'on demande le retour n'est généralement pas au cœur de l'étude que la Convention de 1980 exige du juge.

S'agissant en quelque sorte d'un moyen préliminaire relatif à l'identification de la juridiction où le débat sur la garde de l'enfant se tiendra – l'équivalent d'une exception déclinatoire[2] en droit civil québécois – il serait clairement contre-productif de subordonner la décision du juge à la prise en considération du meilleur intérêt de l'enfant, sauf bien sûr lorsque le parent ravisseur invoque une exception liée à la situation personnelle de l'enfant (par exemple, une allégation voulant qu'il existe un risque grave que le retour de l'enfant l'expose à un danger physique ou psychique ou le place dans une situation intolérable).

Et même là, l'enquête du tribunal doit être limitée à ce qui est strictement nécessaire pour trancher l'argument. L'allégation d'une exception au principe du retour de l'enfant ne doit jamais servir de prétexte à une étude exhaustive de ce qui constituerait le meilleur intérêt de l'enfant dans le contexte d'une décision concernant sa garde. Ce serait une erreur grave, voire une erreur fatale, que d'encourager les juges à procéder à une telle étude (qui exige la prise en considération, outre les besoins moraux, intellectuels, affectifs et physiques de l'enfant, de son âge, de sa santé, de son caractère, de son milieu familial et des autres aspects de sa situation) au stade somme toute préliminaire de la demande de retour.

La position que je défends ici n'est pas nouvelle.

Elle reflète précisément, je crois, l'intention des rédacteurs et des États signataires de la Convention de 1980.

Dans son Rapport explicatif, la professeure Elisa Pérez-Vera décrit les risques qu'il y aurait à invoquer la norme juridique du « meilleur intérêt de l'enfant » dans l'étude des demandes de retour (paragr. 21 et 22). Elle conclut que l'intérêt de l'enfant ne doit pas servir de « critère correcteur de l'objectif conventionnel qui vise à assurer le retour immédiat des enfants déplacés ou retenus illicitement » (paragr. 23).

---

[2] Exception d'incompétence, moyen par lequel le défendeur prétend que la juridiction devant laquelle il a été assigné est incompétente et lui demande de se dessaisir (Gérard Cornu, Association Henri Capitant, *Vocabulaire juridique*, P.U.F. 1987, 6e édition mise à jour « Quadrige » : 2004, juin, p. 267).

Je souscris tout à fait à cette façon de voir les choses.

La Convention de 1980 participe à la lutte contre le fléau des enlèvements internationaux d'enfants. Cette lutte est inspirée par le désir de protéger les enfants en se faisant « l'interprète de leur véritable intérêt » (paragr. 24) et, en cas de déplacement ou de non-retour illicites, en prévoyant un mécanisme conventionnel simple assurant la réintégration immédiate de ces enfants dans leur milieu de vie habituel, sauf quelques exceptions bien ciblées.

Dans ce contexte, je considère que la décision de la Cour européenne des droits de l'homme (Grande Chambre) dans *Neulinger and Shuruk v. Switzerland*, (App. No 41615/07) [2010] ECHR 1053, [2011] 1 FLR 122, constitue un faux pas dans la mesure où elle laisse entendre que les autorités judiciaires saisies d'une demande de retour doivent procéder à un examen en profondeur de la situation familiale et du bien-être de l'enfant afin de décider du sort de la demande de retour.

Je partage plutôt le point de vue plus mesuré et, à mon avis, plus fidèle au texte et à l'esprit de la Convention de 1980 exprimé par la Cour suprême du Royaume-Uni dans *Re E (Children)*, [2011] UKSC 27, [2011] 2 FLR 758. Il serait inapproprié de procéder à un examen en profondeur de la situation familiale dans le contexte d'une demande de retour.

Malheureusement, ce qui me semble aller de soi dans le contexte conventionnel actuel est loin de faire l'unanimité. Depuis la décision *Neulinger*, plusieurs autres décisions de la CEDH vont dans le même sens, par exemple, *X v. Latvia (Application No 27853/09, CEDH – 13 décembre 2011*, affaire entendue le 1er octobre 2012 par la Grande Chambre de la CEDH, en délibéré), *Karrer v. Romania (Application No 16965/10, CEDH – 21 février 2012), MR and LR v. Estonia (Application No 13420/12, CEDH – 15 mai 2012), Ilker Ensar Uyanik c. Turquie (Requête no 60328/09, CEDH – 3 mai 2012), B c. Belgique (Requête No 4320/11, CEDH – 10 juillet 2012*, à noter la remarquable dissidence des juges Berro-Lefèvre et Karakas).

Heureusement, certaines décisions font contrepoids à cette tendance à mon avis néfaste pour la Convention de 1980 et, à plus ou moins long terme, pour la lutte contre la multiplication des enlèvements internationaux d'enfants par leurs parents.

Dans *Re S (A Child)*, [2012] UKSC 10-14 mars 2012, la Cour suprême du Royaume-Uni réitérait la position claire qu'elle avait exprimée l'année précédente dans *Re E (Children)*. Ni la Convention de 1980, ni l'article 8 de la Convention européenne des droits de l'homme ne justifient d'étudier en détail la situation familiale complète et l'intérêt de chacune des personnes qui la composent, tel que suggéré dans *Neulinger*. En fait, ce serait carrément inapproprié de le faire (voir également, dans le même sens, une décision de la Cour d'appel du Québec, *Droit de la famille – 1222*, 2012 QCCA 21 – 12 janvier 2012).

En terminant, je souligne que dans l'arrêt *Canadian Foundation for Children, Youth and the Law c. Canada (Procureur général)*, [2004] 1 R.C.S. 76, 2004 CSC 4, affaire portant sur la validité constitutionnelle d'un article du *Code criminel* canadien prévoyant que le père ou la mère (de même que l'instituteur) est fondé à employer une force raisonnable pour corriger un enfant, la Cour suprême du Canada rejette l'argument selon lequel « l'intérêt supérieur de l'enfant » figure parmi les « principes de justice fondamentale ». Il s'agit d'un principe juridique important, mais pas d'une condition essentielle à l'exercice de la justice ; il peut même être subordonné à d'autres intérêts en cause dans l'administration de la justice. La juge en chef du Canada, s'exprimant pour la majorité, conclut que « "l'intérêt supérieur de l'enfant" est un principe juridique très puissant dans de nombreux contextes. Cependant, il ne constitue pas un principe de justice fondamentale » (paragr. 12).

L'intérêt de l'enfant peut être subordonné à d'autres intérêts, selon les contextes. C'est, je crois, le cas en matière d'enlèvement international d'enfants et d'application de la Convention de 1980.

LE DROIT DE L'ENFANT D'ÊTRE ENTENDU

Le *Code civil du Québec* exige du juge, « chaque fois qu'il est saisi d'une demande mettant en jeu l'intérêt d'un enfant », qu'il lui donne la possibilité d'être entendu si son âge et son discernement le permettent (article 34). Cette règle fait écho, en droit québécois, au principe qu'énoncent les articles 12.1 et 12.2 de la CRDE : l'enfant qui est capable de discernement a le droit d'exprimer librement son opinion sur toute question l'intéressant, cette opinion devant être dûment prise en considération eu égard à son âge et à son degré de maturité ; il faut donc lui donner la possibilité d'être entendu dans toute procédure judiciaire ou administrative l'intéressant.

La question qui se pose est celle de savoir si le droit d'être ainsi entendu est à ce point absolu que le juge doive toujours et en toutes circonstances donner à l'enfant la possibilité de l'exercer dans le contexte d'une demande de retour présentée en vertu de la Convention de 1980.

Dans son rapport explicatif (paragr. 30), la professeure Pérez-Vera aborde brièvement la question dans le cadre de l'exception qui reconnaît à l'enfant le droit de s'opposer à son retour (l'article 13, deuxième alinéa) :

> De surcroît, la Convention admet aussi que l'avis de l'enfant sur le point essentiel de son retour ou de son non-retour puisse être décisif, si d'après les autorités compétentes il a atteint un âge et une maturité suffisante. Par ce biais, la Convention donne aux enfants la possibilité de se faire l'interprète de leur

> propre intérêt. Évidemment, cette disposition peut devenir dangereuse si son application se traduit par des interrogatoires directs de jeunes qui peuvent, certes, avoir une conscience claire de la situation, mais qui peuvent aussi subir des dommages psychiques sérieux s'ils pensent qu'on les a obligés à choisir entre leurs deux parents. Pourtant, une disposition de ce genre était indispensable étant donné que le domaine d'application de la Convention *ratione personae* s'étend aux enfants jusqu'à leur seizième anniversaire ; il faut avouer que serait difficilement acceptable le retour d'un enfant, par exemple de quinze ans, contre sa volonté. D'ailleurs, sur ce point précis, les efforts faits pour se mettre d'accord sur un âge minimum à partir duquel l'opinion de l'enfant pourrait être prise en considération ont échoué, tous les chiffres ayant un caractère artificiel, voire arbitraire ; il est apparu préférable de laisser l'application de cette clause à la sagesse des autorités compétentes.

La Convention de 1980 donne alors à l'enfant la possibilité de se faire l'interprète de son propre intérêt. Mais la mise en garde est sérieuse ; il faut faire preuve de prudence pour éviter de placer l'enfant dans une situation où il peut avoir l'impression que le « système » le force ainsi à choisir entre ses deux parents.

Il faut également être vigilant pour détecter les situations où l'enfant n'est en définitive que le porte-parole d'un parent, ce dernier s'étant au fil du temps, des gestes et des paroles, acquis la loyauté de l'enfant (voir, sur ce point, les inquiétudes exprimées par Sarah Cecilie Finkelstein Waters dans *Reflections on Primary Caretakers and the Child's Voice in Hague Convention Cases*, IBA Family Law Newsletter, September 2012, pp. 40-42, et par le juge Nicholas Wall dans un article intitulé « *The Voice of the Child in Hague Proceedings : an English Perspective* », La Lettre des juges, Tome VI, Automne 2003, p. 20-23).

L'emphase mise sur le droit des enfants d'être entendus dans le cadre des procédures qui les intéressent ne doit pas nous amener – parents, avocats et juges – à transférer sur les épaules de l'enfant le sort de la demande de retour, ou à donner à cet enfant l'impression qu'il en est ainsi.

L'exception prévue au deuxième alinéa de l'article 13 de la Convention de 1980 n'est pas la seule où le droit de l'enfant d'être entendu ne pose pas de difficulté de principe. L'exception du risque grave que présenterait son retour au lieu de sa résidence habituelle (article 13, premier alinéa, point b)) et celle relative à son intégration dans son nouveau milieu (article 12, deuxième alinéa) complètent la liste.

À ces exceptions, on peut possiblement ajouter une autre situation où le juge pourrait tenir compte des souhaits de l'enfant. Il s'agit de celle où le juge est satisfait de l'existence d'une exception, mais où il doit tout de même exercer sa discrétion pour décider d'ordonner ou non le retour de l'enfant. Il pourrait alors, selon les circonstances, être bien avisé d'obtenir le point de vue de l'enfant, avec toutes les précautions requises par la situation.

Dans un article intitulé « *La voix de l'enfant dans les procédures fondées sur la Convention de La Haye : perspective française* », publié dans La Lettre des juges, Tome VI, Automne 2003, p. 18-20, la juge Celeyron-Bouillot exprime l'avis qu' « au stade de la procédure de retour, procéder à l'audition de l'enfant revient à l'inviter à cautionner, directement ou indirectement, un procédé qui est *a priori* jugé inapproprié par les instances internationales » (p. 19). Après avoir noté que l'audition de l'enfant dans un tel contexte de conflit familial est de nature à le perturber encore plus, elle conclut :

> Si nous arrivons à nous convaincre qu'ordonner le retour d'un enfant dans son pays d'origine, ce n'est pas le replacer dans la situation antérieure, mais redonner une chance que le conflit familial trouve le règlement qu'il aurait dû trouver naturellement, le juge du retour n'a aucune raison de procéder à l'audition de l'enfant. Ce n'est que s'il décide de ne pas ordonner le retour et qu'il devient alors compétent pour statuer sur l'organisation de la vie de l'enfant qu'il peut, et je pense doit dans ces circonstances particulièrement douloureuses pour les enfants, procéder à leur audition.

À l'exception de ces cas où l'on cherche à savoir si l'enfant s'oppose à son retour, s'il y a un danger associé à ce retour ou si l'enfant s'est intégré dans son nouveau milieu, je ne crois pas qu'il soit ni requis ni sage de procéder à l'audition de l'enfant qui a l'âge et le discernement voulus pour être entendu.

Bref, sauf les exceptions conçues en fonction de l'intérêt même de l'enfant visé par la demande de retour, les opinions et vœux de l'enfant ne sont pas pertinents à l'établissement des faits spécifiques propres à la demande de retour (le déplacement illicite, la résidence habituelle, etc.).

Il ne faut pas perdre de vue non plus qu'en matière d'enlèvement international d'enfants, l'accent est placé sur une résolution rapide des affaires et sur le retour rapide de l'enfant. Il est important – et on ne le rappellera jamais assez – que les procédures ne se prolongent pas inutilement et ne se transforment pas en bataille rangée entre les parents, au détriment de l'enfant. La nécessité d'une résolution rapide de cette étape préliminaire que constitue le choix de la juridiction qui sera saisie du fond de la garde milite également contre la mise en œuvre dans tous les cas, et sans égard aux circonstances, du droit de l'enfant à être entendu.

En somme, et en quelque sorte paradoxalement, la demande de retour formée en vertu de la Convention de 1980 ne soulève pas toujours une question intéressant l'enfant.

CONCLUSION

La Convention de 1980 vise à protéger l'enfant contre les effets nuisibles d'un déplacement illicite à l'étranger ou de son non-retour dans l'État de sa résidence habituelle.

Il s'agit du moyen choisi par la communauté internationale pour lutter contre le fléau de l'enlèvement international d'enfants par un parent contre le gré de l'autre parent.

La Convention de 1980 n'est cependant qu'un des éléments du bouclier mis en place par la communauté des nations pour assurer la protection internationale de l'enfant, dont la CRDE qui reconnaît explicitement l'existence d'accords bilatéraux et multilatéraux visant à lutter contre les déplacements illicites d'enfants à l'étranger. Cette reconnaissance explicite m'amène à dire que les grands principes que la CRDE énonce doivent nécessairement être interprétés et mis en œuvre de manière à préserver l'intégrité et l'efficacité des accords existants en matière de lutte contre les déplacements illicites d'enfants par l'un des parents vers l'étranger.

La volonté que toutes les décisions concernant un enfant soient prises dans son meilleur intérêt ne doit donc pas avoir pour effet de miner les fondements mêmes de la Convention de 1980. Son succès dépend de son efficacité ; sa raison d'être dépend de son succès. Ce serait une grave erreur de subordonner les demandes de retour au principe voulant que toute décision concernant l'enfant soit prise dans son meilleur intérêt et d'en faire un principe absolu.

Ce serait également une erreur de reconnaître à l'enfant le droit d'être entendu dans toutes les demandes de retour, peu importe le contexte. La nature préliminaire de la demande de retour ne le commande pas. Le risque de transférer ainsi sur les épaules de l'enfant le sort de la demande est toujours présent. Toutes les demandes de retour ne soulèvent pas une question intéressant l'enfant. La mise en œuvre du droit de l'enfant d'être entendu doit être limitée essentiellement aux exceptions conçues en fonction de l'intérêt même de l'enfant visé par la demande de retour.

DIVORCE – A FUNDAMENTAL RIGHT?

Harry DUINTJER TEBBENS
Dr. jur., former Head of Division, Legal Service, European Parliament, Brussels

1. INTRODUCTION

To compare the fact of life that Hans van Loon departs from the Hague Conference on Private International Law with a "divorce" would certainly be inappropriate, even when a divorce by mutual consent is meant. Perhaps one could speak of a legal separation in that Hans will be released from his duty to cohabitate with the Conference and its Permanent Bureau, but that metaphor too is hardly suitable: he will surely remain in close proximity, if not in a geographical at least in a spiritual sense, to this fascinating and meritorious organisation aimed towards smoothing the contacts of a legal nature between individuals, enterprises or authorities worldwide.

No, my choice of topic for the present collection of essays in his honour is induced by another fact of life: the number of divorces of couples in an international context is increasing in Europe.[1] The entry into force in June 2012 – for half of the Member States – of a European Union Regulation (Rome III) on the law applicable to divorce (and legal separation) provides an opportunity to enquire to what extent a right to divorce exists today, going beyond the *favor divortii* prevailing in many legal systems. By way of overture I will also say a few words about the law in one dissenting Member State, The Netherlands. Due to space constraints, the emphasis will be on the law governing divorce, but for some digression into questions of jurisdiction or recognition of foreign divorces.

A major limitation imposed by the scope of the Rome III Regulation is that attendant issues concerning maintenance claims, custody of minor children or liquidation of matrimonial property – however important or even decisive in practice – will have to be left aside.

---

1 Green paper on applicable law and jurisdiction in divorce matters of 14 March 2005, COM(2005) 82, para. 1.

2. DIVORCE IN DUTCH PRIVATE INTERNATIONAL LAW

A. BACK TO THE LEX FORI

Since a leading case decided by the Dutch Supreme Court back in the early years of the last century[2] Dutch private international law for divorce has moved almost in a full circle. At the time a divorce could, as a matter of public policy, only be pronounced under Dutch law even between two foreigners. During the following decades the judge-made law developed into a bilateral conflicts rule using the common nationality as the main connecting factor – a factor qualified by a test of effectiveness. Failing an effective common nationality, various ancillary rules came into play, in practice often leading to domestic Dutch law. In the latter part of the last century the rule was further refined and in 1981 the legislature introduced a limited form of party autonomy.[3] Today, under the new Dutch Private International Law Code of 2011,[4] the choice of connecting factors for divorce is such that the Dutch substantive law of divorce will almost always be applied. When one climbs the "ladder" of connecting factors in Article 10:56 a clear prominence of Dutch law transpires: only if the spouses have chosen the law of a common foreign nationality and they both still have a real social link (*maatschappelijke band*) with the relevant country, will a Dutch court apply the corresponding foreign law. Since the jurisdiction rules at the same time require a certain connection of at least one spouse with the Netherlands, the conditions for applying foreign law will rarely be fulfilled. These new rules codify in fact the judicial practice that had developed under the previous Act of 1981.

B. A RIGHT TO DIVORCE

Under domestic Dutch law either spouse has the right to obtain a divorce even if the other spouse contests the irretrievable breakdown of the marriage. In Dutch/foreign marriages the Dutch courts may be tempted to "assist" the Dutch spouse in exercising this right even if the personal law of the other spouse would oppose the divorce. An intriguing case in point, although turning upon jurisdiction rather than choice of law, was decided in 2005 by The Hague Court of Appeal.[5]

---

2. *Hoge Raad*, 13 December 1907, W. 8636.
3. Act of 25 March 1981, *Stb.* 166; noted, A. Wendels, 29 *NILR* 1982, 401 f.
4. Book 10 of the Civil Code, enacted by Act of 19 May 2011, *Stb.* 272, in force as of 1 January 2012. English translation by ten Wolde *et al.*, 13 *YBPIL* 2011, 657 f.
5. Judgment of 21 December 2005, *NIPR* 2006, 101.

The parties, a Maltese man and a Dutch woman, had married in Malta and were still habitually resident there when they wanted to divorce. They filed a common petition containing a choice for Dutch law to a court in The Netherlands. However, the first instance court decided that it lacked jurisdiction under the relevant EU Regulation,[6] as well as under Dutch law. On appeal, the petition was granted. The appellate court noted that the wife, "as a Dutch citizen", was entitled to obtain a divorce, but that the Regulation attributed jurisdiction solely to the Maltese courts – thereby in fact thwarting her right to have "access to justice" (and to get a divorce), that is, a right guaranteed by Article 6 of the European Human Rights Convention. It then argued that the fundamental rights form part of Community law and decided to dis-apply the EU Regulation in order to be able to enforce the wife's right to divorce. Turning to the Dutch rules of international jurisdiction the court construed broadly the rule of *forum necessitatis* that allowed it to take jurisdiction if proceedings abroad "prove to be impossible."[7] It also noted that a Dutch divorce decree could be recognised in Malta because of the Dutch nationality of one of the spouses. The court then affirmed its jurisdiction and, on the basis of the expressed choice by the parties for Dutch law, granted the divorce.

The court develops an interpretation *praeter legem* of the European Convention's right of "access to justice" so as to include a right to divorce and to oust the EU common jurisdiction rules.[8] This reasoning is open to criticism, yet the result might be defended – if one assumes the existence of a (fundamental) right to divorce.

3. DIVORCE IN THE EUROPEAN UNION

A. LARGE JURISDICTION AND RECOGNITION OF DIVORCES

Unlike many other private international law topics that gained momentum only after the Amsterdam Treaty had brought about a substantial extension of Community competence in 1997, divorce had already come in the picture in the previous era of co-operation at the intergovernmental level. A significant contribution to the preparation of an instrument in this area came from the

6 Regulation 1347/2000 of 29 May 2000, OJ L 160/19 (Brussels II).

7 Article 9 C. Civ. Proc., sub b) : according to the legislative materials, this includes the case where proceedings in another country are "very burdensome" for the parties. In the instant case, the wife could have brought about jurisdiction of the Dutch court under the EU Regulation by residing for six months in the country, but as the Court noted, she "declined to use such artifice."

8 See for a critical comment, E. Jayme & Ch. Kohler, *IPRax* 2006, 548.

Groupe européen de droit international privé (GEDIP). It is worthy of note that divorce and other family matters were among the very first topics that the GEDIP took up following its creation in 1991. It produced a draft text for a convention in 1993, known as the "Heidelberg draft"[9] that was fed into the preparations of an EC Working Party. As a result the Council adopted the Convention concerning judicial jurisdiction and recognition and the enforcement of decisions in matrimonial matters (the "Brussels II Convention").[10] This Convention did not come to life, as the shadows of the Amsterdam Treaty loomed over it already when it was adopted in 1998. But it was reincarnated in a EC regulation in 2000 without changes as to its substance; that regulation in turn was replaced by the current one adopted in 2003 and in force since 2005 (Brussels II *bis*).[11]

The Brussels II *bis* Regulation provides divorce litigants with a large access to court. Its Article 3 offers no less than six heads of jurisdiction, on the basis mainly of connections between the forum and the spouses through their (former) habitual residence. Article 3(2) has an extraterritorial pretention, in that it allows a *forum patriae communis* for EU citizens wherever in the world they reside. Thus, European expats residing in a country with an inconvenient legal system should always be able to obtain a "European" divorce. Moreover, under Article 7 the Member States retain their own jurisdictional rules to provide a forum if the Regulation's generous rules do not designate one.

The recognition regime too is very liberal. Few grounds for refusal are open to the State where a sister State divorce is invoked; refusal cannot be founded on the fact that the foreign court applied another law than the one designated by the choice-of-law rules of the requested State, nor on the fact that the domestic law of that State would not have allowed the divorce in the same circumstances. Yet, the public policy exception is still available as a safety valve although it will probably not often be successfully invoked. When, during some years, Dutch law made it possible to convert a marriage into a registered partnership and then terminate the latter by a simplified non-judicial procedure, other Member States signalled that such a way of dissolving a marriage would be contrary to their public policy.[12]

The Brussels II *bis* Regulation essentially promotes the right of access to a court hearing a petition for divorce in the European Union, yet does not guarantee that a divorce will actually be granted. This depends of course on the law that the court deems applicable.

---

9 See for the text M. Fallon et al. (eds), *Building European Private International Law (Twenty Years' Work by GEDIP)*, 2011, 52, with commentary by P. Lagarde, *ibid.* 61.

10 Convention of 28 May 1998, OJ C 221,18 and Explanatory Report by A. Borràs at 27 f.

11 Regulations 1347/2000 (*supra*, note 6) and 2201/2003 of 27 November 2003, OJ L 338/1.

12 Procedure known as *'flitsscheiding'* ('flash divorce'), banned, *e.g.*, in Italy by ministerial circular, see *Riv.d.i.p.p.* 2008, 1189.

B. A STEP TOWARDS COMMON CHOICE-OF-LAW RULES

Shortly after the Brussels II *bis* Regulation came into force the Commission suggested in a Green Paper[13] that the time had come to complete it by common rules on the law to be applied to divorce and separation. The large choice of courts open to the diligent claimant favoured indeed forum shopping and it was thought that common choice-of-law rules would reduce this phenomenon. The Commission made a formal proposal in 2006 that would introduce the faculty for the parties to a divorce to choose, with certain limitations, the competent court and the applicable law.[14] However, the discussions in the Council Working Group showed fundamental differences between the Member States as to the approach taken by the Commission for the rules to apply in the absence of choice by the parties. While a majority supported the idea to designate laws on the basis of the content-neutral close connection criterion (combinations of habitual residence and nationality of the spouses), a group of Member States, including Sweden as its most determined voice, preferred to always apply their own substantive law or, at least, to keep their national choice of law rules.[15] The Netherlands too adhered to this latter view, which was explicitly endorsed by the Dutch Standing Committee on Private International Law.[16] These Member States feared that under the proposed regulation foreign law would have to be applied more often – especially foreign law that was less liberal in granting divorce than their own.

When it became clear that the required unanimity[17] for this topic could not be reached, half a dozen Member States asked the EC Commission to initiate a procedure for enhanced co-operation[18] in order to continue the project solely with the willing States. The Commission took its time to reflect upon the desirability to use this exceptional procedure for the first time in the area of family law. A drawback of this move was that it would bypass the normal procedure in the sensitive domain of family law which as a matter of principle called for unanimity, and that it would inevitably lead to a Europe "*à géométrie variable.*" Ultimately, the Commission decided to go ahead, and by the end of 2010 a Regulation, also known as "Rome III", was adopted for fourteen Member States.[19] It applies in those

13 See note 1.
14 Document COM(2006) 399 of 17 July 2006.
15 See for an account of the discussions, N.A. Baarsma, "European choice of law on divorce (Rome III): Where did it go wrong?", *NIPR* 2009, 9 f.
16 Opinion of October 2010, stressing the strong *favor divortii* basis of the Dutch conflict rules.
17 For family law matters under Article 67(5) EC, now Article 81(3)(2) TFEU.
18 Article 20 TEU and Article 326 f. TFEU.
19 Regulation 1259/2010 of 20 December 2010, OJ 2010, L 343/10.

States only as of 21 June 2012. It is not our purpose to examine the Regulation in depth, but just to highlight some of its salient features.[20]

C. THE ROME III REGULATION

Rome III is not only a peculiar instrument because it binds (so far) only half of the EU Member States. It also introduces limited party autonomy for divorce, thereby substantially modifying the choice of law system of several participating Member States. Moreover, it provides for some puzzling mechanisms to avert the consequences of its scheme in certain specific fact patterns.

The core chapter of the Regulation opens with the faculty for the spouses to agree on one out of four options for the law to govern their divorce, Article 5. They may choose the law of (i) the State where both spouses habitually reside, (ii) the State of their last habitual residence where one of them still resides, or (iii) the State of which either spouse is a national. For all three options the relevant connection must exist at the time of the agreement and not, as one might expect, the time the court is seized. The legislature wants to already permit the choice during the marriage or even as part of an ante-nuptial agreement; it remains to be seen whether this will often happen in practice. I suspect that a marriage contract will very seldom include a choice of law for a possible future divorce. And when a marriage goes wrong and there are substantial financial interests at stake, it seems more likely than not that the spouses will be divided as to which law to choose for divorce, so that no choice will be made at all. In any event, this generosity shows that the drafters laid considerable weight on legal foreseeability for the spouses. The fourth option is for the law of the forum State – a practical option that combines well with the various forum selection possibilities offered to the claimant by the Brussels II *bis* Regulation.

We find the same connecting factors back in Article 8 when it comes to the law applicable in the absence of choice by the spouses – but here they are placed in a hierarchical order and must be fulfilled at the time the court is seized. They form a "ladder" to be checked out by the court, the first connection being the parties' habitual residence in the same State; failing this, their last common habitual residence with some additional conditions; failing this, their common nationality (*i.e.*, more restricted than in case of choice by the parties); and lastly, again, the law of the forum. Whereas under Article 5 the spouses will no doubt use the options open to them, if at all, by taking into account the content of each eligible law, Article 8 for one operates in a content-neutral fashion.

[20] For comments on Rome III see e.g., P. Orejudo Prieto de los Mozos, *La Ley*, 31 July 2012, and the authors cited *infra*, note 22.

D. RESULT-CORRECTIVE RULES

However, the Regulation has some corrective devices in store that are anything but neutral. As we will see, they are conceived as different forms of one and the same desire to promote a kind of standardised European divorce, to the exclusion of "deviating" ways to dissolve a marriage.

Under Article 10, the law of the forum applies instead of the law chosen by the spouses or the otherwise applicable law, in two instances. The first is when the designated law "makes no provision for divorce." This situation has become largely irrelevant upon the introduction of divorce in Maltese law in 2011,[21] since very few legal systems do not permit divorce at all. Yet, in spite of its small practical impact, this rule is significant in that it amounts in the eyes of several commentators to creating a sort of "fundamental right to divorce"[22]: in the European Union no one should be denied the right to divorce.

The second ground to apply forum law is when the originally designated law "does not grant one of the spouses equal access to divorce (...) on grounds of their sex." The background of this rule is mainly a fear for laws inspired by or applying Islamic law principles, including rules on repudiation that only the husband can initiate; but the rule could also affect Jewish law.[23] It is remarkable that even the informed choice of two spouses for their common national law, say the law of Somalia, has to be discarded if the forum in the European Union finds that access is unequal in that law. The text of Article 10 seems to indicate that an abstract inequality in the law is sufficient, yet there would seem to be no discrimination when in the given case, the wife voluntarily consents to the procedure initiated by the husband. In any event, whether the test to be applied is abstract or concrete, in either case it is likely to be a difficult task for a court to research a foreign law or practice on this issue. I note in this context that there is no uniform "Islamic law", and that for example Moroccan law knows other ways to dissolve a marriage than repudiation.[24] However, the burden upon the court could be somewhat alleviated in so far as the discriminated spouse would have to identify the lack of equality.

---

21 Civil Code (Amendment) Act , Act XIV of 2011, *Government Gazette of Malta*, 29 July 2011, no. 18784, Suppl.

22 In this sense P. Hammje, "Le nouveau règlement (UE) n° 1259/2010 du Conseil du 20 décembre 2010 mettant en œuvre une coopération renforcée dans le domaine de la loi applicable au divorce et à la séparation de corps", *Rev.crit.d.i.p.* 2011, 291, 333; Ch. Kohler, "Le choix de la loi applicable au divorce- Interrogations sur le règlement "Rome III" de l'Union européenne", in H. Kronke & K. Thorn (eds), *Grenzen überwinden – Prinzipien bewahren, Festschrift für Bernd von Hoffmann*, 2011, 208, at 212; U. P. Gruber, "Scheidung auf Europäisch – die Rom III-Verordnung", *IPRax* 2012, 391.

23 Only the husband can deliver a *get*-letter initiating divorce.

24 K. Kreuzer, "Sharî'a -Staaten und Menschenrechten", 61 *Rev. Hell. Dr. Int.* 2008, 363, at 370; F.J.A. van der Velden, "Het nieuwe Marokkaanse Wetboek van Familierecht", *NIPR* 2005, 4, 7.

If the foreign law passes the abstract test, but in the case in hand a gender-based inequality is in fact (in whatever way) established, it remains probably open to the court to resort to the traditional public policy clause which is still available under Article 12 of the Regulation – so at least I read the second sentence of Recital 24 whose wording is not crystal clear. A disturbing feature of Article 10 is that it does not give the court any discretion nor require any connection with the forum State beyond the jurisdictional one under the Brussels II *bis* Regulation. For example, if the jurisdiction of the court is based on the last habitual residence where only one spouse still resides, resorting to the forum's own law under this rigid rule of anti-discrimination may seem excessive. To this extent a narrower 'fundamental' right appears to take shape in Article 10: the right to what has been called an "egalitarian divorce."[25]

Next, the Regulation provides in Article 13 a corrective rule which dispenses a Member State from the duty to pronounce a divorce under the choice-of-law rules, if its internal law, (i) does not know the concept of divorce, or (ii) does not recognise the type of marriage in issue as "marriage", so that an essential condition for divorce is lacking. The first limb was meant to accommodate the law of Malta, but as noted above,[26] divorce has since been introduced in this country and the contemplated situation can no longer arise. The second limb refers to the emancipated type of marriage that allows persons of the same sex to marry and that today exists in a minority of Member States only. The faculty for other Member States to refuse to divorce such couples seems paradoxical, in that the Regulation tends to impose a common concept of "European" divorce, while at the same time accepting fundamentally different concepts of "marriage" to co-exist.[27] This provision is also difficult to reconcile with Article 1(2), b) of the regulation, which leaves it fully – without reserving Article 13 – to the national rules of private international law whether to recognise the validity of the marriage which is to be dissolved by divorce. If under the former Article a Member State with a liberal recognition policy would recognise a foreign same-sex marriage although it does not in its domestic law allow such marriages, Article 13 nevertheless permits its courts to refuse to pronounce a divorce as if the case were a purely internal one.[28]

The effect of Article 13 is particularly unfortunate when the couple can only find a court having jurisdiction in a Member State where same-sex couples cannot marry. Gruber[29] gives the example of a Spanish man and an Italian man

25 P. Hammje, *loc. cit.* (note 22), at 335.
26 Note 21.
27 P. Hammje, *loc.cit.* (note 22), at 332.
28 The EC Commission considered this rule as 'a derogation that negates the very purpose of the enhanced cooperation' agreed upon in the Council, see Council document 17046/10 of 26 November 2010.
29 Gruber, *loc. cit.* (note 22), at 390.

marrying in Spain and moving later to Italy. The Spanish courts no longer have jurisdiction, the Italian courts do, but they may invoke Article 13 in order not to have to divorce the couple. He suggests remedying this "intolerable" situation by allowing the Spanish courts to rely on their national jurisdictional rules via Article 7 Brussels II *bis* as a last resort, since the Italian courts' competence cannot lead to the desired divorce. An alternative solution might be to have this *déni de justice* cured in Italy: the Italian court could decide not to use the faculty given in Article 13, and pronounce the dissolution of the Spanish same-sex marriage (provided, of course, that Italian private international law so allows) on the basis of Article 6 ECHR, since the applicants would otherwise be denied access to justice. This would be in line with the approach of the Dutch court referred to above (2. B), but it does appear to overstretch the potential of Article 6. *De lege ferenda* the gap in judicial protection should be filled by adding a *forum necessitatis* to the Brussels II *bis* Regulation. Actually, in the final stage of the adoption of Rome III both the Council and the European Parliament did invite the Commission to make a proposal to this effect.

4. DIVORCE AND THE EUROPEAN CONVENTION FOR HUMAN RIGHTS

It is common ground that neither the European Convention nor its Protocols permit to construe a right to divorce. Article 12 of the Convention does state the right to marry[30] which arguably embraces the right to remarry after divorce. However, the same Article refers to national law for the conditions for a (new) marriage, which may include the not unreasonable condition that a previous divorce must have been recognised. Moreover, as the European Court recently held in *Gas & Dubois v. France*, the Convention does not oblige national law to allow same-sex couples to marry,[31] which makes a general right to divorce nugatory for them.

One might argue that Article 8 of the Convention is concerned not just with the situation where individuals assert their right to family life – seen as a factual matter more than in the formal dress of a "marriage", but that it also includes or implies the right to withdraw from a married status and pursue his or her private life as they see fit and without unjustified interference by the State. As far as I know, however, the European Court of Human Rights has not recognised

30 Article 9 of the Charter of Human Rights of the EU also embodies 'the' right to marry etc, but unlike the ECHR does not refer to 'men and women' as the subjects of this right, thereby leaving room for same-sex marriages.

31 ECtHR, judgment of 15 March 2012, no. 25951/07, § 66.

such a "right."[32] This is understandable since changing a person's marital status will normally involve some form of State control and in exercising this control the State enjoys a certain margin of appreciation.

Similarly, the State may edict reasonable conditions for recognising a divorce obtained abroad, such as requiring that the divorce was granted by a court after proceedings in which both spouses participated or could have participated. Thus, the Court held in *Green and Farhat v. Malta*[33] that Malta was not bound to recognise an annulment of marriage by mere conversion of the Maltese wife to Islam in Libya, because the conditions for recognition were not fulfilled even though the wife had remarried in Libya and lived there for twenty years with a Libyan man. The right to family life with a (second) spouse did not outweigh the interests of the State to ensure that marriages of its citizens were terminated with consideration for the (first) spouse.

The Convention does not in itself require a divorcee status acquired abroad to be recognised, but rather imposes a balancing of public and private interests.[34]

5. CONCLUDING REMARKS

A. A QUALIFIED RIGHT TO DIVORCE

By the combined effect of its neutral and its corrective rules the Rome III Regulation does in practice create a right to divorce according to the conditions of whatever substantive law (whether or not of a EU Member State) governs – as long as the parties are a traditional couple and the divorce is "egalitarian."

The right is not generally open to same-sex couples, in so far as neither European human rights law nor European Union law oblige States to confer on them the right to marry in the first place.[35] The European Court of Justice has yet to decide whether the notion of "marriage" in the Brussels II *bis* Regulation includes a marriage between two persons of the same gender.[36]

The public policy exception is fully operational, not only in regard to non-EU States, but also between Member States to guarantee respect for, and thereby

32 In its judgment of 18 December 1987, no. 11329/85, *F.* v. *Switzerland*, § 38, the Court held that the Convention did not require national legislation to allow divorce.

33 Decision of 6 July 2010, no. 38797/07; noted, P. Kinsch, 13 *YBPIL* 2011, 37, 42, L. d'Avout, *Rev. crit.d.i.p.* 2011, 672.

34 Cf. P. Kinsch, "Droits de l'homme, droits fondamentaux et DIP", *Rec. Cours*, vol. 318 (2005), 96 f.; id., *Rev.crit.d.i.p.* 2011, 817, 820.

35 See note 31.

36 The Commission proposal concerning matrimonial property regimes appears to use a gender-neutral concept of marriage, COM(2011)126 of 16 March 2011.

perpetuate, essential differences in the evolution of the law on this issue.[37] The limited acceptance of same-sex marriages reflects a serious divide within the Union and beyond; it impacts directly on the scope of a right to divorce. So, the right to divorce can scarcely be labelled "fundamental" in the absence of an equally generalised right to marry.

Under the universalist banner of Rome III, divorce law of non-Member States qualifies in principle for application, but it is nonetheless disqualified if that application implies gender discrimination, in which case the "tainted" divorce is replaced by an egalitarian one of European make.

B. THE FRAGMENTATION OF INTERNATIONAL DIVORCE LAW

The inconvenient truth emerging from this rapid survey is that legal practitioners dealing with international divorce litigation in Europe are confronted with a startling multiple fragmentation:

- The rules governing jurisdiction and choice of law are different for divorce requests and for closely related issues such as parental responsibility, maintenance or matrimonial property.
- Basically different concepts of the institution of marriage in substantive law hamper a liberal let alone universal regime of the granting of divorce and its recognition in other States.
- Different sets of rules apply in Member States participating and in each of those staying out of the Rome III Regulation.

The actions taken in this field by the EU legislature bear some resemblance to an Echternach procession: two steps toward mutual recognition and common conflict rules are followed by a backward step to save national sensibilities. This may be inevitable in an area where society and the law evolve at a different pace among twenty-eight Members of a Union.[38] Yet, it does prompt questions such as: was legislation at EU level opportune and appropriate? Has the presumed risk of forum shopping diminished to any significant extent? It is far from certain that these questions merit an affirmative answer.

37 Article 67(1) TFEU; see Ch. Kohler, "Le droit de l'Union européenne face à la diversité culturelle: tensions et solutions", 62 *Rev.Hell. Dr.Int.* 2009, 473, 489, Th. M. de Boer, in A. Malatesta *et al.* (eds), *The external dimension of EC private international law in family and succession matters*, 2008, 295, 323–327, and J. Meeusen, *ibid.*, 331 f.

38 In the U.S. too, States opening marriage to same-sex couples neighbour States enacting "Defense of Marriage" Acts.

REFLECTIONS ON THE MALTA PROCESS

William DUNCAN
Former Deputy Secretary General of the Hague Conference on Private International Law

PRELIMINARY REMARKS

My first opportunity to work with Hans van Loon was during the negotiations on the *1993 Hague Convention on Protection of Children and Co-operation in Respect of Intercountry Adoption* (the 1993 Hague Convention), for which he was the responsible member of the Permanent Bureau of the Hague Conference. He had persuaded the Hague Conference to take on what was then regarded as a controversial subject for the Conference. His outstanding report laid the firm foundation for the successful outcome to the negotiations. His diplomatic skills, his inclusive approach, the willingness to listen, his determination to find practical solutions, all helped to secure a Convention which now enjoys the confidence of both States of origin and receiving States, and has attracted ratifications and accessions at an unprecedented rate. I was later to learn how much, with these same qualities, Hans van Loon had contributed to Hague Conventions in all of the very diverse areas in which the Hague Conference works. His expertise in private international law is as broad as it is deep. In the area of international child protection, which is the subject-matter of this short essay, he has combined a deep concern for the interests of families and children with his considerable expertise in the Hague Conventions generally, and has always shown a willingness and ability to think beyond the traditional boundaries of private international law to find solutions that are workable and will make a difference to the lives of children and their families. During his time as Secretary General, responsible for the very broad programme of work now undertaken by the Hague Conference, it has been his vision and commitment which has steered the Hague Conference towards its now global mission. He is a precious talent and an exceptional man.

THE MALTA PROCESS

One task of private international law, to which Hans van Loon has always been committed, is that of finding practical means of legal co-operation between States having diverse legal cultures yet sharing common problems. The Malta Process, initiated by the Hague Conference in 2004, has just such a purpose. Its focus is on cross-frontier family law issues involving certain Hague Convention States (Parties to the 1980 Hague *Convention on the Civil Aspects of International Child Abduction*) and non-Hague Convention States from the Islamic world whose laws are based on or influenced by Sharia law *(hereafter referred to as Sharia-influenced States)*. The more specific objective was to work towards the more effective resolution of cross-frontier parental disputes concerning children, in particular cases involving the removal or retention of children across borders and more generally cases where contact between a parent and child had been disrupted. Improvements in cross-border cooperation were to be explored at all levels, from the establishment of workable frameworks for legal and administrative cooperation to improved communication between judges and other officials concerned in resolving international family disputes

The increase in international and intercultural marriage is a world-wide phenomenon, and efforts to improve legal cooperation in resolving the consequences of breakdown have been going on for some time. Some earlier research by the Hague Conference had found that a number of efforts to establish bilateral forms of co-operation between Hague Convention and Sharia-influenced States were not working well. A number of States within the Hague Conference wanted to explore the possibilities for improved legal co-operation, and so the Malta Process began, in the form of a dialogue which has involved a slowly increasing number of Hague Convention and Sharia-influenced States.

UNDERSTANDING DIFFERENCES

The bridging of cultural divides requires first an understanding of differences and, in the case of legal cultures, some appreciation of the reasons why similar problems are addressed in different ways.

To speak of diversity when examining the legal systems represented in the Malta Process is something of a simplification. Family and child protection laws are at very different stages of development in the various legal systems. Substantive rules relating to matters of child custody and contact differ, sometimes markedly. Shariah law itself is the subject of many different schools of interpretation. In addition, there is a wide range of other background factors which need to be borne in mind, some of them having ethical or political foundations and some of them arising from more mundane, but equally important, practical and resource considerations.

The accepted level of State intervention in family life tends to be less in States whose legal systems are influenced by Shariah law. There are two broad reasons for this, the one having ethical or religious foundations, the other having to do with limited capacity to intervene in States with less-developed child protection regimes. The reluctance to subject family relationships to interference by the State reveals itself in a strong preference for the voluntary settlement of family disputes through mediation and similar techniques. Undeveloped enforcement machinery is another common phenomenon.

The process of secularization of family law and family dispute resolution, which is almost complete in many western legal systems, either has not occurred or is occurring at a different pace in Sharia-influenced systems. This reveals itself also in the sphere of private international law and the choice of connecting factors for jurisdictional and applicable law purposes in family law. The connecting factors developed in the context of the Hague Conventions (such as "habitual residence") tend to be based on the actual links between an individual and a legal system. These are not so readily absorbed in legal systems which place more emphasis on allegiance (nationality) or faith (religion).

The phenomenon of parallel systems of family law occurs in a number of countries concerned. These usually exist to facilitate the members of different religions and they may be accompanied by a "civil" alternative. The Hague Conference is familiar with this phenomenon and has made allowance for it in its modern Conventions, but it does add to the complexity.

While there is wide adherence in all the countries concerned in the Malta Process to universal principles (such as those set out in the *UN Convention of 20 November 1989 on the Rights of the Child (UNCRC)*) there are often significant differences in their interpretation and application. Thus, while the principle of non-discrimination set out in Article 2 of the UNCRC, is accepted there may be differences of view about what constitutes equal treatment, for example in relation to the status of a child born outside marriage.

The processes of law reform differ from country to country and in the case of some Sharia-influenced States it is not easy to identify or access the sources of authority which have the power or the capacity to deliver effective reforms in family or child law.

COMMON CONCERN TO FIND SOLUTIONS

Despite these differences in legal context, the countries involved in the Malta Process have been quick to recognise a common interest in resolving cross-frontier family conflicts, especially where children are affected. The important role played by judges in the dialogue has helped to identify this common interest through their shared experience of family conflict in their respective courts. Each country has experience of similar problems, even though demographic factors may alter the lenses through which these problems are viewed.

There is no country involved in the Malta Process which would not prefer to have at hand better methods of resolving international family disputes and more effective international co-operation towards that end. Apart from the damage to family relationships these disputes can sometimes lead to diplomatic embarrassment, or even take on a political colour. The failure to resolve them can have more general consequences for relations between States.

Understandings were reached about how the dialogue should proceed, which became hallmarks of the Malta Process:

- Mutual respect, and acceptance of the need for better understanding between the different legal systems.
- A balance of existing Hague Convention and Sharia-influenced States.
- A willingness to accept, and even to celebrate, certain differences between the legal systems concerned.
- An understanding that solutions should be found by consensus.
- A willingness to explore compromise.
- Acceptance of the urgent need to find means of cooperation which will provide children and their families with firm, speedy, predictable, accessible and just procedures for the settlement of cross-border family disputes.

SHARED PRINCIPLES

There was, therefore, a common concern to move forward, but were there any shared principles that could provide a basis for dialogue and eventual resolution of the problems? This question has been at the centre of the Malta Process and the three Malta Declarations (available on the website of the Hague Conference) reveal a substantial core of common ground.

With regard to fundamental principles there is clear acceptance of the principle embodied in Articles 9 and 10 of the UNCRC that the child has a right to maintain personal relations and direct contact with both parents on a regular basis. Recognition of the value of the parent / child relationship and of the damage which can result when that relationship is disrupted provides a solid basis for co-operation, a fact already evidenced by the success of the 1980 *Hague Convention on the Civil Aspects of International Child Abduction.*

As far as concerns legal co-operation, the Malta Process has led to the re-affirmation of the essential legal foundations for cross-border judicial co-operation, namely:

- the need for agreement on the bases for the exercise of jurisdiction in international cases;
- a readiness to respect (recognise and, if appropriate, enforce) decisions made on those bases by foreign courts.

It cannot be claimed that the Malta Process has resolved in any definitive way what should be the common bases for the exercise of jurisdiction. Nevertheless, it is notable that there is an increasing willingness among the Sharia-influenced States to explore in this respect the potential value of the modern Hague Children's Conventions, and in particular the *1996 Hague Convention on Jurisdiction, Applicable Law, Recognition, Enforcement and Co-operation in Respect of Parental Responsibility and Measures for the Protection of Children* (the 1996 Hague Convention). This Convention, with its explicit rules on jurisdiction based on the idea that the primary responsibility for making decisions concerning children rests with the authorities of the country where the child actually lives ("habitual residence"), may eventually be seen as offering the best prospects for a fair, a neutral and a workable foundation for legal co-operation between Sharia-influenced and other legal systems.

CONSTRUCTING NETWORKS

Agreed rules on international competence cannot alone produce successful international co-operation. Networking is needed among those whose responsibility it is to breathe life into those instruments. At the administrative level, focal points are needed in each country ready to co-operate with one another in the exchange of general and case-specific information. They are also needed as a "window" through which applicants from abroad may obtain information about available services and procedures, and as a "door" through which they may be helped to gain access to such services and procedures. Within the current Hague Children's Conventions, such bodies exist in the form of "Central Authorities", and they have over many years proved their value in international legal co-operation. They have been equally successful in other areas of legal co-operation. Within the Malta Process, specific proposals have been developed for the establishment of central contact points designed to facilitate the use of mediation as a means of resolving international disputes concerning children. (See below, where it is suggested that the potential benefits of establishing central contact points go beyond mediation.)

Another vital network to be fostered is that comprising judges from the different countries and cultures. If cross-border legal co-operation is to succeed, and in particular if international instruments are to be applied effectively to that end, those who have the responsibility to apply and interpret these instruments need to understand and trust one another. Decision making at the international level often requires judges to place confidence in their counterparts in other jurisdictions. The decision, for example, to cede jurisdiction to a foreign court or to order the return of a child to a foreign country is made easier if the decision maker is familiar with and has some confidence in the procedures which will be applied when the case, or indeed the child, moves from one jurisdiction to another. The Malta Process has placed great emphasis on the need to foster judicial networking at the international level. The rapidly developing International Hague Network of Judges (IHNJ) offers one vehicle for this movement. Although the IHNJ was originally conceived as supporting the operation of the existing Hague Children's Conventions, it was soon recognised that the IHNJ has an important role also in forging links with and between judges from non-Hague Convention countries. At the same time much work continues to be done in forging networks and good cross-border working relationships between judges at regional and bilateral levels. This is particularly the case in Latin America and Europe. Every opportunity should be taken to involve judges from the Shariah-influenced States in networking with their colleagues abroad. Nothing can contribute more to the development of mutual understanding between the different legal systems.

WHERE NEXT FOR THE MALTA PROCESS?

For some, the measure of success of the Malta Process will be the number of accessions by Sharia-influenced States to existing multilateral instruments such as the 1980 and 1996 Hague Conventions. The recent accession by Morocco to the 1980 Hague Convention (already a Party to the 1996 Hague Convention) has been a highlight. But it may take some time before a substantial number of Sharia-influenced countries take the plunge and enter the full formal framework provided by the Hague Conventions.

In this writer's opinion, it does not follow that the Malta Process has failed or that it is time to bring it to a conclusion. No doubt the long term objective, and the one which will best serve the interests of children and their families is to have operating clear and binding legal structures which should offer family members an accessible predictable and effective means of resolving disputes at the international level. In short, what is needed is a rule of law? The Malta Process is helping the move in that direction and will continue to do so, albeit principally by means of bilateral and regional meetings.

In the meantime much can be done to continue the process of confidence building, and to explore other possibilities for improved co-operation, including by means of alternative forms of dispute resolution. One particular initiative currently being conducted within the Malta Process involves the facilitation of mediation to optimise the possibilities for international family disputes to be resolved by agreement between the parties. The Malta Process has in particular emphasised the value and importance for each country of establishing a central contact point to provide information concerning existing mediation facilities and how to access them. This is an important initiative, not only because it will provide an avenue of hope for family members, but also because it will help in the process of forging links and building the trust that is needed if more formal legal structures are to be developed. It is recognised that mediation is not a panacea, and mediation which is not conducted "in the shadow of the law" has its limitations, not least because a legal framework is needed to help ensure that agreements reached are respected.

The idea of a network of central contact points to facilitate access to mediation could be expanded. Why should these central contact points not have more general functions in relation to matters of cross-border child protection? For countries that are still reluctant or find it difficult to undertake the legal obligations which come with accession to the 1980 and 1996 Hague Conventions there may, nevertheless, be value in joining a developing global network of child protection units or authorities based in each country and having responsibility for cross-border child protection matters more generally. The functions of such units would be to co-operate with one another in matters of cross border child protection and to provide information to applicants from abroad about existing child protection facilities and procedures, and how to access them. Initially, therefore, the obligations could be light and need not involve a heavy deployment of resources. In effect, the principal obligation would be to establish a unit, probably within an existing Ministry, with responsibility for cross-border child protection matters. Contact details would need to be publicised and kept up to date.

This idea emerges, almost organically, from structures and arrangements which are already in place in many countries. States Parties to the 1996 Hague Convention already have established Central Authorities with a wider and more explicit range of responsibilities for co-operation with other States in child protection matters. Under the 1980 Hague Convention, as well as the 1993 Hague Convention on inter-country adoption, Central Authorities are established which, along with procedural responsibilities have the duty to co-operate with one another in specialised areas of child protection. Outside the framework of the

Hague Conventions there are many other countries which, at Departmental or Ministerial level, are organised in a way which could adapt easily to the idea of a central unit or contact point for international child protection matters.

There is no suggestion here of re-inventing any wheels. The idea is rather to offer to non-Hague Convention countries the opportunity to experience and benefit from a certain level of international networking at the administrative level.

A more or less informal network of this kind, operating in both Hague and non-Hague Convention countries could have many advantages. Within the framework of the Malta Process the creation of such contact points, already envisaged in relation to mediation, could provide the possibility of better co-operation in resolving individual cases, whether or not mediation is a possible or preferred option. The contact points could also provide a focus for consideration of more intensive co-operation at regional or global levels. Outside the Malta Process, there are many countries and regions (Southern Africa is one that springs to mind) which could benefit from the implementation of an informal network of this kind. In the end, co-operation will be more effective if it has a firm legal basis such as that provided by the 1996 Hague Convention. Nevertheless, the establishment of a less formal network would not only be valuable in itself, but might also serve in some countries as a preparatory step in the direction of more formal cooperation.

CONCLUSIONS

Bridge-building can be a slow process. Constructing systems of international legal co-operation can also be slow, especially when it involves countries that do not know each other well and do not have a record of effective co-operation. Building the right legal framework for co-operation is essential and the Hague Children's Conventions are designed for that purpose. But it is not alone enough. If the Malta Process has taught us anything, it is that the development of mutual trust and understanding matters not only for the effective implementation of legal instruments, but also as a prelude to their adoption. The construction of networks, at the judicial and administrative levels should be viewed as both a concomitant of and a precursor to more formal legal arrangements. These networks have a value in their own right, and set the stage for the closer forms of co-operation.

Without effective international co-operation the prospects for the resolution of cross-border disputes concerning children is bleak. Differences within the family are reflected in lack of trust and mutuality between legal systems. When they do not co-operate with one another, legal systems often become part of the pathology of family breakdown. This is why the Malta Process is so important.

LE DROIT INTERNATIONAL PRIVÉ DE LA FAMILLE ET LES DROITS FONDAMENTAUX DE L'ENFANT : LE CHOC QUI FAIT CHIC ?

Bernard DUTOIT
Professeur honoraire de la Faculté de droit et des sciences criminelles de l'Université de Lausanne
Ancien directeur du Centre de droit comparé et européen

EN PRÉAMBULE : COEXISTENCE DU DROIT INTERNATIONAL PRIVÉ ET DES DROITS DE L'HOMME ?

Le contenu de plus en plus substantiel des droits de l'homme en général et des droits fondamentaux concernant l'enfant en particulier (cf. la Convention européenne des droits de l'homme, ci-après CEDH et la Convention sur les droits de l'enfant, ci-après CDE) soulève la question (elle aussi fondamentale !) de l'articulation du droit international privé et des droits de l'homme.

Faut-il opter pour une perspective pessimiste selon laquelle l'universalisme et la globalisation croissante des droits de l'homme toucheraient le droit international privé au cœur dans sa fonction de respect de l'altérité et des différences qu'il s'agit d'articuler les unes par rapport aux autres dans un esprit d'ouverture et de respect mutuel[1] ? Ou bien au contraire, dans une vision plus positive, ne sied-il pas plutôt d'admettre que la concrétisation des droits de l'homme dans une situation internationale relève d'abord et au premier chef du

[1] En ce sens, cf. par exemple H. FULCHIRON, « Droits fondamentaux et règles de droit international privé : conflits de droits, conflit de logiques ? », in : *Le droit au respect de la vie familiale au sens de la Convention européenne des droits de l'homme* (F. Sudra, directeur publication), Bruxelles 2002, p. 353 ss. Comme tenants d'une conception négative des droits de l'homme, cf. aussi M. VILLEY, *Le droit et les droits de l'homme*, 1983, p. 13 et J. CARBONNIER, *Droit et passion du droit sous la Ve République*, 1996, p. 56.

droit international privé et non des impératifs de la CEDH dont les exigences, lorsqu'une affaire internationale est en cause, doivent passer par le tamis du droit international privé ? En effet, sa fonction essentielle, qui est de faire jouer les couleurs contrastées des différents droits en un vitrail cohérent, ne s'efface pas, au contraire, du fait qu'une réglementation internationale des droits de l'homme a vu le jour. Certes, la CEDH par exemple va donner la même couleur à un certain nombre de droits nationaux en la matière et la fonction du droit international privé résidera moins dans l'articulation de couleurs législatives différentes que dans le filtrage des droits de l'homme à travers les particularités d'une situation internationale, de telle sorte que le vitrail reste cohérent et ne fasse pas l'objet de distorsions regrettables.

Par ailleurs, il faut souligner que la CEDH laisse souvent aux Etats « une marge nationale d'appréciation », de telle sorte qu'une contextualisation qui doit se faire à travers le droit international privé s'impose *in casu* dans l'application des droits de l'homme[2]. En effet, ceux-ci constituent un processus à la fois dynamique, évolutif et interactif qu'il convient d'insérer correctement dans les situations internationales. Paradoxalement, l'universalisme des droits de l'homme doit du reste se conjuguer aujourd'hui avec la diversité culturelle élevée au rang de patrimoine commun de l'humanité (cf. la Déclaration de l'UNESCO de 2001 et la Convention de 2005).

Et l'on reconnaîtra qu'« une fois acquise son autonomie et débarrassé d'une quête d'identité, le droit international privé se plie, comme d'autres branches du droit, à la nécessité d'une ouverture au regard des droits fondamentaux »[3]. Qu'une fonction de filtrage (ou de contextualisation) puisse se substituer à une fonction d'articulation n'enlève rien à l'existence ni à la nécessité du droit international privé. On précisera encore que les droits de l'homme exercent sur le droit international privé une double influence : directe d'une part, en ce sens que le droit international privé doit rendre effectives dans une situation internationale les garanties du droit matériel incluses dans les droits de l'homme, influence indirecte d'autre part, en ce sens que la finalité des règles de conflit de lois et de juridictions doit respecter les droits de l'homme, sans qu'il en résulte pour autant l'imposition d'un contenu matériel déterminé de ces règles.

Si donc une coexistence (pacifique) s'impose entre droit international privé et droits de l'homme, il ne paraît pas inutile de se demander quel est l'impact des

---

2 Cf. M. Delmas-Marty/A.Supiot, « L'internationalisation du droit : dégradation ou recomposition », *Revue Esprit*, novembre 2012, p. 35 ss, spécialement p. 38-45 sur le statut des droits de l'homme.

3 Rigaux/Fallon, *Droit international privé*, 3e éd., Bruxelles, 2005, n° 212 ; cf. aussi B. Fauvargue- Cosson, « Droit comparé et droit international privé : la confrontation de deux logiques à travers l'exemple des droits fondamentaux », *Revue internationale de droit comparé* 2000, p. 797 ss.

droits fondamentaux de l'enfant sur le droit international privé moderne de la famille, et cela sous l'angle de la compétence internationale des tribunaux (§ 1), des règles de conflit de lois (§ 2) et de la reconnaissance et de l'exécution des jugements étrangers (§ 3)[4].

1. DROITS FONDAMENTAUX DE L'ENFANT ET COMPÉTENCE INTERNATIONALE DIRECTE DES TRIBUNAUX

La question qui se pose est la suivante : qu'exigent les droits fondamentaux (de l'enfant) du point de vue de la compétence internationale directe des tribunaux ?[5]

D'un point de vue général, le droit à un procès équitable, qui englobe évidemment l'accès à la justice, postule l'admission d'un for de nécessité (par exemple art. 3 LDIP) pour éviter un déni de justice au détriment du demandeur. A l'inverse, on peut se demander si la théorie anglo-saxonne du *forum non conveniens,* qui permet à un tribunal normalement compétent selon la *lex fori* de se dessaisir, au motif qu'il existerait un autre tribunal considéré comme mieux placé en l'espèce pour s'occuper de l'affaire, n'entame pas indûment le droit du demandeur à l'accès à la justice. Mais l'équilibre des droits du demandeur et des droits du défendeur, qu'implique un procès équitable, a pour conséquence que de son côté le défendeur doit être protégé contre des compétences dites exorbitantes, qui n'ont pas un lien suffisant avec la cause (cf. par exemple *le forum arresti,* art. 4 LDIP ou paragraphe 23 ZPO, supprimé dans le Règlement Bruxelles I)[6].

Qu'en est-il des règles pouvant être discriminatoires en raison de la nationalité ? Elles ne sauraient en principe être admises (cf. par exemple les fameux art. 14 et 15 CCF). A cet égard, la Cour EDH a jugé que « seules des considérations très fortes peuvent amener la Cour à estimer compatible avec la Convention une différence de traitement exclusivement fondée sur la nationalité »[7]. Ainsi, la compétence d'un tribunal fondée, à titre principal, sur la nationalité de l'une des

---

[4] Sur la problématique abordée dans le présent article, on signalera notamment F. MARCHADIER, *Les objectifs généraux du droit international privé à l'épreuve de la CEDH*, thèse, Limoges, 2005 ; S. BRUINIER, *Der Einfluss der Grundfreiheiten auf das IPR*, Berne, 2003; P. KINSCH, « Droits de l'homme, droits fondamentaux et droit international privé », *Recueil des cours de l'Académie de droit international*, t. 318 (2005) p. 9-332.

[5] II est important de signaler ici l'existence de Theseus : base de données sur la jurisprudence de la Cour EDH à l'égard des enfants, 1968-2012.

[6] On signalera au passage que certaines compétences spéciales de l'art. 5 du Règlement Bruxelles I, notamment l'art. 5, n° 4, de même que l'art. 4, pourraient soulever des problèmes à cet égard. Mais cette question ne concerne pas la présente contribution.

[7] CEDH, arrêt du 16 septembre 1996, *Gaygusuz*, requête n° 17371/90, Rec. 1996-IV, p. 1142, par. 42.

parties devrait violer le droit à un procès équitable et un correct accès à la justice. En effet, deux plaideurs se trouvant dans la même situation pourraient, l'un se voir reconnaître la compétence du tribunal s'il a la nationalité de l'Etat du for, et l'autre, se la voir refuser s'il n'a pas cette nationalité. Dans le domaine du droit de la famille (et non pas directement des droits de l'enfant), l'article 3, 6e chef de compétence, du Règlement Bruxelles II bis (JOUE L 338/5 du 23 décembre 2003) qui, en matière de divorce, de séparation de corps et d'annulation du mariage, prévoit la compétence des tribunaux de l'Etat membre sur le territoire duquel se trouve « la résidence habituelle du demandeur s'il y a résidé depuis au moins six mois immédiatement avant l'introduction de la demande et s'il est soit ressortissant de l'Etat membre en question, soit, dans le cas du Royaume-Uni et l'Irlande, s'il y a son domicile », paraît bien octroyer au demandeur (même si on peut en comprendre les raisons) un privilège exorbitant. En revanche le « for d'origine », tel que le connaît le droit international privé suisse (cf. art. 67 LDIP pour la constatation ou la contestation de la filiation, art. 76 LDIP pour l'adoption, art. 80 LDIP pour les effets de la filiation), même s'il se réfère au « lieu d'origine » de la personne intéressée, constitue en réalité un for de nécessité parfaitement acceptable du point de vue de la CEDH.

En ce qui concerne la compétence internationale directe des tribunaux dans les matières touchant aux droits de l'enfant, il ne semble pas que l'impact des droits fondamentaux soulève de réels problèmes, étant admis que la compétence internationale des tribunaux de l'Etat de la résidence habituelle de l'enfant est très largement reconnue.

2. DROITS FONDAMENTAUX DE L'ENFANT ET RÈGLES DE CONFLIT DE LOIS

II convient de se demander aussi quel est l'impact des droits fondamentaux de l'enfant sur l'application du droit désigné par les règles de conflit de lois du for.

On ne s'arrêtera pas sur une évidence (même si elle a pu être contestée[8]), à savoir que le système des règles de conflit de lois n'est pas mis en cause par l'émergence des droits de l'homme. En effet, toutes les règles de conflit raisonnablement envisageables sont compatibles avec le principe d'égalité, quelle que soit leur structure (bilatérale, unilatérale, matérielle, *interest analysis*). Même le rattachement du statut personnel à la nationalité de l'intéressé n'est pas discriminatoire en lui-même car la règle de conflit de lois est la même pour tous. Le principe d'égalité se révèle tolérant par rapport au contenu de la règle de conflit

8 Cf. Ch. Engel, « Ausstrahlungen der Europäischen Menschenrechtskonvention auf das Kollisionsrecht », RabelsZ. 1989, p. 21-24.

de lois. Du reste, le rattachement à la loi nationale de l'intéressé a trouvé, en droit international privé postmoderne, du moins chez certains auteurs[9], une actualité nouvelle, en ce sens que ce rattachement permet de valoriser l'identité culturelle de la personne.

Quant au fonctionnement de la règle de conflit de lois, l'effet dit atténué de l'ordre public, au stade de l'application du droit étranger par le juge du for (cf. art. 17 LDIP en Suisse) relève de critères objectifs et non discriminatoires. Ainsi, lorsqu'un juge suisse est placé devant une situation qui a été régulièrement créée à l'étranger selon le droit applicable et qui fait l'objet d'une question préalable (effets successoraux, soumis au juge suisse à titre principal, d'un mariage polygamique), ledit juge donne un effet atténué à l'ordre public suisse qui n'admet pas le mariage polygamique, mais en reconnaît *in casu* les effets successoraux, et cela selon un critère objectif et non discriminatoire.

En ce qui concerne la théorie dite de la « Binnenbeziehung » (ordre public de proximité), selon laquelle l'ordre public, au stade de la loi applicable par le juge du for, n'intervient que si les liens territoriaux entre la cause et le for sont suffisamment étroits, il faut admettre que le lien entre nationalité et/ou résidence habituelle d'une part et bénéficiaire de l'ordre public d'autre part, peut apparaître comme problématique. Ainsi la Cour de cassation française a jugé que les lois prohibant l'établissement d'un lien de filiation n'étaient pas contraires à l'ordre public français, à moins qu'elles ne privent un enfant français ou résidant habituellement en France du droit d'établir sa filiation (cf. RCDIP 1993, p. 620). Mais si la question se pose, à titre préalable, à propos d'un enfant étranger non résident en France et soumis à une telle loi, l'ordre public ne sera pas invoqué, de façon discriminatoire.

Sur cette toile de fond, il importe de se demander quelles règles matérielles l'intérêt de l'enfant – qui constitue un droit fondamental[10] – impose au législateur national, de telle sorte qu'une loi étrangère rendue compétente par les règles de droit international privé du for et ne respectant pas les exigences de ce droit fondamental devra être évincée par recours à l'ordre public (cf. art. 17 LDIP en Suisse). En d'autres termes, quel contenu concret donner à ce droit fondamental qu'est l'intérêt de l'enfant ?

Un intérêt majeur de l'enfant a trait à la protection et au respect de la vie familiale (art. 8 CEDH), entendue au sens très large de « lien familial de fait » englobant aussi les relations hors mariage[11], y compris même les rapports entre

---

9 Cf. E. Jayme, « Identité culturelle et intégration : le droit international privé postmoderne », *Recueil des cours de l'Académie de droit international*, t. 251 (1995), p. 9-268.

10 Cf. art. 11, al. 1 Constitution fédérale suisse, art. 3 CDE.

11 CEDH, *Johnston*, arrêt du 18 décembre 1986, requête n° 9697/82, Série A, n° 112, par. 55-58.

personnes liées par des liens familiaux *de facto* sans avoir cohabité[12]. Dès lors qu'une telle vie familiale est constatée, l'intégration de l'enfant dans sa famille doit être rendue possible[13]. Ainsi, l'enfant naturel doit pouvoir établir son lien de filiation avec chacun de ses parents[14]. De son côté, le père biologique doit disposer d'un moyen procédural effectif pour faire valoir sa paternité[15]. A l'inverse, le père légal doit pouvoir agir en désaveu pour l'enfant qui n'est pas le sien[16]. La Cour EDH a eu l'occasion de préciser aussi que les relations entre un enfant et ses grands- parents étaient couvertes par l'article 8[17], ainsi que les relations entre un enfant né hors mariage et son père naturel[18]. De même le Tribunal fédéral suisse a protégé les relations entre un enfant et son père de fait sans lien biologique ni adoption, en considérant que celui qui a été frauduleusement inscrit dans les registres comme père, mais qui a exercé sa fonction parentale durant onze ans, ne commet pas un abus de droit lorsqu'il dépose une plainte pour enlèvement de mineur contre celle qui est inscrite comme mère, alors même qu'il avait participé avec elle à l'obtention frauduleuse de l'inscription[19].

A l'intégration de l'enfant dans sa famille ainsi largement entendue correspond son droit d'être élevé par ses parents et d'être ensemble avec eux. Des mesures internes qui les en empêchent constituent une ingérence dans les droits protégés à l'article 8, y compris le non-retour de l'enfant dans son foyer d'origine après avoir vécu un certain temps avec ses grands-parents[20].

L'attribution de l'autorité parentale a suscité une abondante jurisprudence. La garde de l'enfant ne peut dépendre de considérations religieuses[21], par exemple de l'appartenance d'un parent aux Témoins de Jéhovah, ni de l'orientation sexuelle d'un parent[22].

---

12 CEDH, *Barrehab*, arrêt du 21 juin 1988, requête n° 18535/91, série A, n° 138, par. 21 ; *Guhl*, arrêt du 19 février 1996, Rec. 1996-I, p. 159, par. 32.

13 CEDH, *Gnadoré*, arrêt du 19 septembre 2000, requête n° 40031/98, Rec. 2000-IX, p. 407, par. 51.

14 Cf. aussi art. 7, al. 1 CDE ; ATF, 20 février 2002, arrêt 5P. 466/2011, cons 5c.

15 CEDH, *Rozanski*, arrêt du 18 mai 2006, requête n° 55339/00, par. 67-80.

16 CEDH, *Shofman*, arrêt du 24 novembre 2005, requête n° 74826/01, par. 40-46 ; *Mizzi*, arrêt du 12 janvier 2006, requête n° 26111/02, Rec. 2006-I, p. 125, par. 111-115.

17 CEDH, *Scozzari*, arrêt du 13 juillet 2000, requêtes n°s 39231/98 et 41963/98, Rec. 2000-VIII, p. 401, par. 221.

18 CEDH, *Nylund*, arrêt du 29 juin 1999 , requête n° 27110/95, Rec. 1999-VI, p. 394.

19 ATF 128 IV 154.

20 CEDH, *Bronda*, arrêt du 9 juin 1998, requête n° 40/1997/1824/1030, Rec. 1998-IV, p. 1476, par. 51.

21 CEDH, *Hoffmann*, arrêt du 23 juin 1993, requête n° 12875/87, Série A, n° 255-C, par. 30-36 ; *Palan- Martinez*, arrêt du 16 décembre 2003, requête n° 64427/01, Rec. 2003-XII, p. 303, par. 32-49.

22 CEDH, *Salguario da Silva Monta*, arrêt du 21 décembre 1999, requête n° 33290/96, Rec. 1999-IX, p. 331, par. 31-36.

S'agissant de l'attribution de l'autorité parentale, la Cour EDH a dû préciser si une législation nationale, allemande (§ 1626a, al. 2 et 1672 BGB) ou autrichienne (art. 166 et 176 ABGB) par exemple, qui n'accorde l'autorité parentale à un père non marié que si la mère y consent violait l'article 8 CEDH sur le droit au respect de la vie familiale. Dans l'arrêt Zaunegger[23], puis dans l'arrêt Sporer[24], la Cour EDH a jugé qu'une législation nationale qui accorde de plein droit l'autorité parentale uniquement à la mère de l'enfant ne violait pas l'article 8 CEDH, interprété à la lumière de la Convention de La Haye de 1980 sur l'enlèvement international d'enfants, pour autant qu'elle autorise le père non investi de l'autorité parentale à demander au juge national compétent la modification de l'attribution de cette autorité. Ainsi donc, une législation qui ne prévoirait aucune possibilité pour le père naturel d'obtenir l'autorité parentale sans l'accord de la mère constituerait une discrimination injustifiée selon l'article 14 CEDH en combinaison avec l'article 8 CEDH. Ainsi en va-t-il des législations allemande et autrichienne précitées. Il est clair désormais que l'autorité parentale relève du contenu de l'article 8 CEDH[25].

De son côté, la CJUE eut à se pencher sur la même question, le mode d'attribution de l'autorité parentale se posant à titre de question préalable dans une affaire d'enlèvement d'enfant[26] : comment le Règlement Bruxelles II bis, du 27 novembre 2003 (JOUE L 338 du 23 décembre 2003), doit-il être interprété à la lumière de l'article 7 de la Charte des droits fondamentaux de l'Union européenne, qui correspond à l'article 8 CEDH ? En l'espèce, la législation irlandaise n'accorde pas au père naturel automatiquement un droit de garde sur son enfant ; il faut pour cela que ce droit lui soit conféré par un accord entre les parents ou par une décision de justice[27]. La CJUE a repris la jurisprudence de la Cour EDH en l'affaire Zaunegger en jugeant qu'« il s'ensuit que, aux fins de l'application du Règlement n° 2201/2003, pour déterminer le caractère illicite du déplacement de l'enfant, lequel est emmené dans un autre Etat membre, par sa mère, le père naturel de cet enfant doit avoir le droit de s'adresser à la juridiction nationale compétente,

---

[23] CEDH, *Zaunegger*, arrêt du 3 décembre 2009, requête n° 22028/04, FamPra.CH 2010, p. 213, n° 14.

[24] CEDH, *Sporer*, arrêt du 3 février 2011, requête n° 35637/03.

[25] Cf. en sens contraire pour la Suisse, ATF 123 III 445, cons. 2b/bb, qui considère que l'autorité parentale commune après divorce n'est pas commandée par l'art. 8 CEDH.

[26] Le caractère illicite du déplacement d'un enfant dépend uniquement de l'existence d'un droit de garde conféré par le droit national applicable, en violation duquel le déplacement a eu lieu (cons. 44). Mais une telle interprétation est-elle compatible avec l'art. 7 de la Charte des droits fondamentaux de l'Union européenne si le droit national applicable en l'espèce ne donne pas au père naturel automatiquement le droit de garde sur son enfant ?

[27] Cf. Status of Children Act 1987, Sec. 11 et Children Act 1997, Sec. 4. Pour un aperçu de droit comparé des législations européennes concernant l'autorité parentale, cf. K. Boele-Woelki/F. Ferraud/Cr. Gonzalez Beilfuss/M. Jantera-Jareborg/N. Louve/D. Martiny/W. Printens, *Principles of European Family Law regarding Parental Responsabilities, European Family Law Series* n° 16 (2007), Oxford.

avant le déplacement, afin de demander qu'un droit de garde de son enfant lui soit conféré, ce qui constitue l'essence même du droit d'un père naturel à une vie privée et familiale dans un tel contexte » (cons. 55). Et la CJUE de préciser que « en revanche, le fait que le père naturel ne soit pas, à la différence de la mère, automatiquement détenteur d'un droit de garde de son enfant au sens de l'article 2 du Règlement n° 2201/2003 n'affecte pas le contenu essentiel de son droit à la vie privée et familiale, pour autant que le droit énoncé au point 55 du présent arrêt est sauvegardé » (cons. 57)[28]. Ainsi, la réglementation irlandaise précitée ne viole pas l'ordre public européen incorporé dans la Charte des droits fondamentaux de l'Union européenne.

De son côté, le Tribunal fédéral suisse, s'agissant de l'attribution de l'autorité parentale au père selon le droit iranien applicable en l'espèce (art. 8, al. 3 et 4 de la Convention d'établissement irano-suisse du 25 avril 1934), a jugé qu'une telle attribution n'était compatible avec l'ordre public suisse (cf. art. 11, al. 1 Constitution fédérale et l'art. 9, al. 1 CDE) que si cette solution constituait la meilleure voie pour l'enfant[29].

Il convient de noter que la réglementation suisse actuelle de l'attribution de l'autorité parentale ne correspond pas aux exigences des arrêts Zaunegger et Sporer précités de la Cour EDH. En effet, lorsque la mère n'est pas mariée avec le père, l'autorité parentale appartient à la mère (art. 298, al. 1 CCS). Selon l'article 298 a, al. 1 CCS, l'autorité parentale conjointe n'est possible que sur requête conjointe des père et mère et pour autant que cela soit compatible avec le bien de l'enfant et qu'ils soumettent à la ratification de l'autorité tutélaire une convention qui détermine leur participation à la prise en charge de l'enfant et la répartition des frais d'entretien de celui-ci. Ainsi aucune autorité parentale commune n'est possible sans l'accord de la mère et aucune voie judiciaire n'est ouverte au mari[30]. Telle est précisément la situation condamnée par la Cour EDH dans les arrêts Zaunegger et Sporer.

Conscient du problème, le législateur suisse procède actuellement à la révision du droit relatif à l'autorité parentale. Dans son Message du 16 novembre 2011 concernant une modification du Code civil suisse (autorité parentale)[31], le Conseil fédéral a adapté le droit suisse aux exigences de la Cour EDH. Certes, il ne s'est pas prononcé pour une autorité parentale conjointe automatique

[28] CJUE, arrêt du 5 octobre 2010, aff. C-400/10, PPJ, *McB. c. L.E.* et observations K. Siehr in *IPRax* 2012, p. 316 ss.

[29] ATF 123 III 250 et *Revue suisse de droit international et européen* 2003, p. 389-394, observations Bucher.

[30] Cf. Ph. Meier, « L'autorité parentale conjointe : l'arrêt de la Cour EDH Zaunegger c. Allemagne – quels effets sur le droit suisse ? » *Revue de la protection des mineurs et des adultes*, 2010, p. 246 ss ; M. Widrig, « Elterliche Sorge – ein Grundrecht ? », in : *Jusletter* du 23 juillet 2012.

[31] Feuille fédérale 2011, p. 8315 ; la Commission des affaires juridiques du Conseil national s'est saisie de ce projet le 29 juin 2012.

s'agissant de parents non mariés. Celle-ci n'est accordée que sur la base d'une déclaration commune pour autant que le père ait reconnu l'enfant (art. 298 a, al. 1 nouveau CCS). Jusqu'au dépôt de la déclaration, l'enfant reste soumis à l'autorité parentale exclusive de la mère. Toutefois, « lorsqu'un parent refuse le dépôt de la déclaration commune, l'autre parent peut s'adresser à l'autorité de protection de l'enfant du lieu de domicile de l'enfant » (art. 298 b., al. 1 nouveau CCS). L'autorité parentale conjointe est prioritaire dans la mesure où ladite autorité « institue l'autorité parentale conjointe, à moins que la sauvegarde des intérêts de l'enfant ne commande que la mère reste seule détentrice de l'autorité parentale ou que cette dernière soit attribuée exclusivement au père » (art. 298 b, al. 2 nouveau CCS). Selon l'article 133 nouveau CCS, la même réglementation s'applique à l'attribution de l'autorité parentale après divorce.

On remarquera que le projet du Conseil fédéral s'adapte a minima aux exigences de la Cour EDH, mais maintient une inégalité de départ entre mari et femme, en n'admettant pas une attribution automatique de l'autorité parentale au père naturel dès la reconnaissance de l'enfant, ainsi que l'avait prévu l'article 298 de l'avant-projet[32].

Il est intéressant de noter que le Tribunal fédéral suisse a jugé que l'article 12 CDE concernant le droit de l'enfant d'être entendu était directement applicable[33] et l'emportait par conséquent sur les règles suisses relatives à l'audition des enfants. Ainsi une règle de conflit de lois ou de juridictions conduisant à l'application d'un droit ou à la compétence d'un tribunal ne respectant pas l'article 12 CDE se heurterait à l'ordre public du point de vue suisse[34].

On relèvera pour clore ce chapitre que la vie familiale englobe aussi des intérêts matériels[35]. Dans le domaine des successions par exemple, la distinction entre enfants légitimes et enfants adultérins dans l'accès à la succession doit être considérée comme discriminatoire[36].

3. DROITS FONDAMENTAUX DE L'ENFANT ET RECONNAISSANCE ET EXÉCUTION DES JUGEMENTS

II convient de noter d'abord que le refus, par l'Etat requis, de la reconnaissance et de l'exécution d'un jugement peut constituer une ingérence dans le droit à un procès équitable (art. 6 CEDH) et dans le droit au respect de la vie privée et

[32] Cf. dans le même sens l'art. 372 CCF.

[33] ATF 124 III 90 et 124 II 361.

[34] Cf. Bucher in *Semaine judiciaire* 2006 II p. 282-285.

[35] CEDH, *Merger et Cros*, arrêt du 22 décembre 2004, requête n° 68864/01, par. 46.

[36] Même arrêt, par. 33.

familiale (art. 8 CEDH). En effet, l'Etat requis ne peut opposer des obstacles qui dépassent les exigences de ces articles, par exemple soumettre la reconnaissance et l'exécution d'un jugement à l'existence d'un traité en la matière entre l'Etat d'origine et l'Etat requis (ainsi qu'il en va en Russie) ou exiger la réciprocité ou encore pratiquer la révision au fond. Sous l'angle de l'article 6 CEDH, il faut considérer que l'exécution du jugement fait partie intégrante du procès[37] et que l'Etat requis ne peut lui faire indûment échec en refusant d'exécuter la décision étrangère. Sous l'angle de l'article 8 CEDH, les liens de famille ne sauraient être limités dans la protection que leur confère cette disposition par le refus de l'Etat requis de leur donner effet, s'agissant d'Etats partageant les mêmes valeurs.

Toutefois, le refus de reconnaissance et d'exécution d'un jugement étranger présente une autre face, à savoir non plus une ingérence dans les droits protégés par les articles 6 et 8 CEDH, mais tout au contraire la protection même de ces droits, lorsque la décision étrangère ne les respecte pas. Le point d'insertion de l'effectivité de ces droits se trouve dans la réserve de l'ordre public que l'Etat requis oppose à la décision étrangère.

S'agissant de l'article 6 CEDH, l'Etat requis a le devoir de refuser de reconnaître et d'exécuter un jugement étranger non conforme aux garanties de cette disposition. Dans l'affaire Pellegrini précitée[38], la Cour EDH a estimé, à propos d'une déclaration de nullité de mariage prononcée par le Vatican (Tribunal de la Rote) que « les juridictions italiennes ont manqué à leur devoir de s'assurer, avant d'ordonner l'exequatur à l'arrêt de la Rote romaine, que, dans le cadre de la procédure canonique, la requérante avait bénéficié d'un procès équitable. Il y a donc violation de l'article 6 § 1 de la Convention » (§ 47). On notera que la Cour EDH a imposé aux autorités italiennes l'obligation de respecter l'article 6 CEDH, s'agissant d'une décision émanant d'un Etat non contractant à la CEDH, le Vatican en l'espèce. Ainsi donc désormais il faut considérer que le même standard relatif à l'équité procédurale s'applique, peu importe que l'on ait affaire à un jugement émanant d'un Etat contractant ou non. Au contraire, le Tribunal fédéral suisse a appliqué le standard minimal à la reconnaissance et à l'exécution d'une décision émanant d'Etats tiers à la CEDH ou même d'Etats membres, au sens de l'ordre public atténué de la reconnaissance, interprété de manière restrictive, l'ordre public procédural n'étant même pas examiné d'office (art. 27 al. 2 LDIP)[39].

---

[37] Cf. notamment CEDH, *Hornsby*, arrêt du 19 mars 1997, requête n° 18357/91, Rec. 1997-II, p. 495, par. 40 ; *Pellegrini*, arrêt du 20 juillet 2001, requête n° 30882/96, Rec. 2001-VIII, p. 353, n°s 40-48 ; *Romanczyk*, arrêt du 18 novembre 2010, requête n° 7618/05, par. 53-55 ; *Papue*, arrêt du 27 mai 2010, requête n° 44476/04, par. 35.

[38] Sur cet important arrêt, cf. J.-F. FLAUSS, « L'exequatur des jugements étrangers devant la Cour européenne des droits de l'homme », in : *Mélanges Dutoit*, Genève, 2002, p. 69 ss.

[39] Cf. ATF 116 II 625, cons. 4 (reconnaissance d'un jugement américain); ATF 111 la 12, cons. 2a (reconnaissance d'un jugement iranien) ; ATF 126 III 327, cons 2b (reconnaissance d'une décision libanaise) ; ATF 126 III 101, cons. 3b (reconnaissance d'un jugement italien). Tous

Un problème d'articulation de l'article 6 CEDH se pose ainsi non seulement avec l'ordre public national, mais encore, dans le cadre de l'Union européenne, avec les Règlements « Bruxelles I » et « Bruxelles II bis » dont les exigences, en matière d'ordre public, sont nettement moins sévères que celles qui sont consacrées dans la jurisprudence Pellegrini[40]. Faut-il considérer que les jugements rendus dans les Etats membres de l'Union européenne dans les matières relevant desdits Règlements sont soumis aux exigences du procès équitable, au sens de l'article 6, al. 1 de la CEDH, sous le contrôle de la Cour EDH ? Peut-on admettre qu'un jugement national en matière de reconnaissance et d'exécution des jugements ne respectant pas l'article 6 CEDH, et cela au bénéfice de la législation communautaire, puisse faire l'objet d'un contentieux devant la Cour de Strasbourg[41] ? Cette problématique dépasse le cadre du présent article. On relèvera toutefois que les Règlements précités sont postérieurs à la CEDH et devraient donc pouvoir l'emporter sur celle-ci, dans la mesure où l'on pourrait considérer que, au moins implicitement, les Etats membres ont adopté des règles particulières quant au recours à l'ordre public en matière de reconnaissance et d'exécution des jugements en vue de faciliter leur circulation et d'éviter des situations juridiques boiteuses. Mais il demeure une contradiction fondamentale entre la sévérité de l'article 6 CEDH tel qu'interprété par la Cour de Strasbourg et le caractère exceptionnel du recours à l'ordre public (interprété strictement) dans les Règlements « Bruxelles I » et « Bruxelles II bis ».

En ce qui concerne l'article 8 CEDH et notamment la réunion des parents à leurs enfants, cette disposition présente également deux faces. D'une part, l'Etat requis ne peut faire un contrôle allant au-delà de l'article 8 CEDH et s'opposer à une reconnaissance au motif que le tribunal d'origine ne satisfait pas aux exigences de compétence indirecte de l'Etat requis[42]. D'autre part, les règles de droit international privé de l'Etat requis doivent satisfaire aux exigences de l'article 8 CEDH.

S'agissant de l'importante question de l'enlèvement international d'enfants, couverte par l'article 8 CEDH, celui-ci doit être interprété notamment en tenant

---

ces arrêts sont antérieurs à la décision Pellegrini de la Cour EDH du 20 juillet 2001. Dans des arrêts postérieurs à cette date (arrêt 5A- 633/2007, du 14 avril 2008, cons. 2 et arrêt du 26 janvier 2005 (ATF 131 III 182, cons. 4) concernant respectivement la reconnaissance de jugements américain et kosovar, le Tribunal fédéral n'a fait aucune allusion à un impact possible de la jurisprudence Pellegrini sur sa conception de l'ordre public en matière de reconnaissance des jugements.

40 Cf. art. 34 Règlement « Bruxelles I » et art. 22 et 23 Règlement « Bruxelles II bis ».

41 Sur ces questions, cf. FLAUSS, art. cité en note 38, p. 82 ss.

42 CEDH, *Wagner*, arrêt du 28 juin 2007, requête n° 76240/01, par. 131-136, *RCDIP* 2007, p. 807 : les règles luxembourgeoises de conflit de lois en matière d'adoption ne tiennent notamment pas compte de la réalité sociale en l'espèce et d'un statut juridique valablement créé au Pérou ; le refus de reconnaître le jugement étranger d'adoption viole l'art. 8 CEDH.

compte de la Convention de La Haye du 25 octobre 1980 sur les aspects civils de l'enlèvement international d'enfants et de la Convention relative aux droits de l'enfant[43]. La Cour EDH a précisé qu'elle était compétente « pour contrôler la procédure suivie devant les tribunaux internes, en particulier pour rechercher si, dans l'application et l'interprétation de la Convention de La Haye, ceux-ci ont respecté les garanties de la Convention, notamment de son art. 8 »[44]. Concrètement, la Cour de Strasbourg recherche si les autorités nationales ont pris « toutes les mesures que l'on pouvait raisonnablement exiger d'elles pour faciliter l'exercice du droit de garde, de l'autorité parentale et de visite reconnus à un parent par la législation applicable ou résultant de décisions judiciaires »[45]. C'est notamment à propos de la procédure d'urgence en vue du retour de l'enfant (art. 11 Convention de La Haye) que la Cour EDH a eu à examiner si les autorités nationales avaient fait preuve de la rapidité et de la diligence nécessaires[46].

La Cour EDH a souligné aussi que le retour de l'enfant ne constituait pas un droit absolu, appliqué de façon automatique. Ainsi l'écoulement d'une période de plus de vingt mois avant la prise de décision sur le retour de l'enfant ne permet plus le rétablissement du *statu quo ante*[47].

A propos de l'article 20 de la Convention de La Haye, qui dispose que le retour de l'enfant « peut être refusé quand il ne serait pas permis par les principes fondamentaux de l'Etat requis sur la sauvegarde des droits de l'homme et des libertés fondamentales », il faut noter que cet article est rarement appliqué[48], car la Convention tente de favoriser le retour de l'enfant. Ainsi, le Tribunal fédéral suisse a jugé que, pour que l'article 20 s'applique, il fallait que la violation de ces principes fondamentaux soit grave et liée directement à la situation en cas de retour de l'enfant[49], l'atteinte à ces principes ne pouvant résulter par ailleurs de la seule restitution de l'enfant[50]. On pourrait imaginer l'application de l'article 20 par exemple si, lors de la procédure d'attribution du droit de garde, l'enfant devait être exposé à une discrimination grave et prévisible, ou encore si le parent ravisseur devait être empêché de participer à la procédure sur le droit de garde.

---

[43] CEDH, *Neulinger/Sheruk*, arrêt du 6 juillet 2010, requête n° 41615/07, par. 132 ; *Ignaccolo-Zenide*, arrêt du 25 janvier 2000, requête n° 31679/96, Rec. 2000-1, p. 205, par. 95 ; *Iglesias*, arrêt du 29 avril 2003, requête n° 56673/00, Rec. 2003-V, p. 247, par. 51 ; *Maire*, arrêt du 26 juin 2003, requête n° 48206/99, Rec. 2003-VII, p. 309, par. 72.

[44] CEDH arrêt *Neulinger/Sheruk* précité, par. 133 ; cf. aussi *Bianchi*, arrêt du 22 juin 2006, requête n° 7548/04, par. 82 ; *Carlson*, arrêt du 6 novembre 2008, requête n° 49492/06, par. 68.

[45] CEDH, arrêt *Carlson* précité, par. 69.

[46] Cf. CEDH, arrêt *Carlson* précité, par. 76 ; arrêt *Bianchi* précité, par. 94 ; arrêt *Monory*, du 5 avril 2005, requête n° 71099/01, par. 82.

[47] CEDH, *Macready*, arrêt du 22 avril 2010, requêtes n°s 4824/06 et 15512/08, par. 65.

[48] Peut-être le contenu de plus en plus substantiel de l'art. 8 CEDH serait-il de nature à infléchir cette tendance.

[49] ATF 133 III 694.

[50] ATF 123 II423, cons 2b.

Enfin, l'exécution du retour, une fois ordonnée, doit être assurée, même, le cas échéant, en recourant à des mesures coercitives[51].

On peut se demander pour terminer si, en matière familiale, la reconnaissance et l'exécution des jugements ne pourrait pas être fondée directement sur l'article 8 CEDH, et non pas sur des règles de droit international privé, afin d'éviter la survenance de rapports familiaux boiteux reconnus dans un Etat mais non dans un autre[52]. Si séduisante que puisse paraître cette solution, elle nous semble ne pas devoir être suivie, sauf peut-être dans le cadre d'un processus d'intégration[53]. Pourquoi procéder à l'opération chirurgicale de l'amputation du droit international privé, alors que le patient pourrait encore fort bien marcher sur ses deux jambes ? En effet, le droit international privé connaît suffisamment de techniques de validation exceptionnelle de situations boiteuses, qui devraient suffire par rapport aux exigences des droits de l'homme. Au nombre de ces techniques, on citera au premier chef l'admission de la primauté de l'ordre juridique étranger grâce à la reconnaissance de situations valablement acquises à l'étranger, sans contrôle de la loi appliquée à l'étranger par rapport aux règles de conflit du for[54]. D'autres voies encore, plus ponctuelles, existent en vue d'articuler entre eux les systèmes juridiques et d'éviter les situations boiteuses, par exemple la protection des droits acquis à l'étranger, la validation d'une situation à la suite d'un changement ultérieur de loi applicable (conflit mobile), le rattachement, dépendant ou non, de la question préalable. En fin de compte, même en matière familiale, il convient de garder au droit international privé et aux droits de l'homme leur place respective dans une correcte articulation de ces deux voies juridiques.

EN GUISE DE CONCLUSION

A la lumière de ce bref examen des rapports entre droit international privé et droits fondamentaux de l'enfant, la question posée en préambule prend, à notre sens, un relief particulier. En effet, si difficile soit-elle dans certains cas, la coexistence de ces deux branches du droit nous paraît essentielle. Au cours des pages qui précèdent s'est posée en filigrane la question suivante : comment les

---

51 Cf. CEDH, arrêt précité *Ignaccolo-Zenide*, par. 106.

52 Cf. sur cette problématique, A. Bucher, « La famille en droit international privé », *Recueil des cours de l'Académie de droit international* t. 283 (2000), p. 96-115.

53 Cf. les art. 21 ss du Règlement « Bruxelles II bis » pour l'Union européenne.

54 Cf. sur cette problématique, P. Lagarde, « Développements futurs du droit international privé dans une Europe en voie d'unification : quelques conjectures », *RabelsZ.* 2004, p. 225 ss ; P. Mayer, « Les méthodes de la reconnaissance en droit international privé », in : *Mélanges Lagarde*, 2005, p. 547 ss ; P. Picone, « Les méthodes de coordination entre ordres juridiques en droit international privé », *Recueil des cours de l'Académie de droit international* t. 276 (1999), p. 227-231.

arrêts de la Cour de Strasbourg, qui concrétisent les articles 6 et 8 CEDH et qui sont rendus dans des affaires opposant un particulier à un Etat donné (avec ou sans élément d'extranéité), vont-ils par la suite être source d'une règle à appliquer dans un contexte international, au triple niveau de la juridiction compétente, du droit applicable ou de la reconnaissance et de l'exécution des jugements ?

Face à un arrêt de la Cour EDH, un pont doit être jeté entre la CEDH (et la jurisprudence y relative) et l'espace international dans lequel elle a vocation à s'appliquer. Or ce pont ou cette médiation ne peut provenir que du droit international privé, qui permet aux droits de l'homme d'embarquer sur les eaux des relations internationales.

Il reste à souhaiter que ces eaux ne soient pas trop tumultueuses mais aussi que la barque des droits de l'homme ne soit pas inutilement chargée au point de rendre la navigation difficile. Trop de droits de l'homme pourrait tuer les droits de l'homme.

STRATEGIC VISION AND COMMON SENSE IN THE HAGUE CONVENTIONS SINCE 1950 (MID-TWENTIETH CENTURY)

Adair Dyer
Attorney at Law, Austin, Texas
Formerly Deputy Secretary General of the Hague Conference on Private international Law

I. INTRODUCTION – PROCEDURAL AND SUBSTANTIVE HUMAN RIGHTS

Tobias M.C. Asser, the Dutch lawyer, professor and statesman who founded the Hague Conference on Private International Law (hereinafter referred to as "the Hague Conference"), despite his preference for laying out general principles first,[1] had a pragmatic view of both the public and private spheres of activity and promoted mutually supportive progress in both spheres through the medium of multilateral international treaties. Private international law treaties came to fruition first, following the First and Second Sessions of the Hague Conference (1893 and 1894), with a draft on civil procedure – based on a Dutch draft – and texts on various aspects of family law. Following the First Hague Peace Conference (1899, the text stressing humanitarian objectives), and the entry into force of the 1896 Hague Convention on Civil Procedure, the Third and Fourth Conferences on Private International law (1900 and 1904) achieved the elaboration of five family law treaties and a more sophisticated treaty on civil procedure – focused on (a) service of process which provided actual (rather than fictional) notice to a defendant abroad, (b) taking of evidence abroad by Letter of Request, (c) protection of foreign defendants from discriminatory practices regarding the

[1] See A. Eyffinger, *T.M.C. Asser (1838–1913) Founder of The Hague Tradition*, T.M.C. Asser Press (The Hague, 2011), at 36–38.

provision of security for costs, counterbalanced with international enforcement of judgments for costs, (d) free legal aid, and (e) a ban on discriminatory physical detention of the foreign party (*contrainte par corps*).

The family law treaties, based primarily on the then prevailing European view that the nationalities of the family members should play a dominant role in determining disputes among them, had a less clear axis for purposes of protection of human rights. But one of them, the *Hague Convention of 12 June 1902 on the Guardianship of Minors*, opened a narrow breach in this system by giving alternative roles to the law of the child's "habitual residence" in its Articles 2, 3 and 9 – foreshadowing developments beginning in the 1950s that recognized children as being subjects of law, rather than mere objects of legal protection.

The selection of Asser for the Nobel Peace Prize in 1911[2] and the opening of the Peace Palace in The Hague in 1913, housing the Permanent Court of Arbitration, masked to some extent the disappointments in respect of international cooperation which signaled the breakdown of the hopes that had led Andrew Carnegie to finance the physical structure of this mansion dedicated to international law.

The beginning of World War I in 1914 marked a definitive end to such hopes as they had existed. The end of this war gave rise to new institutions – notably the League of Nations – and the Peace Treaties closing out the war revived among the formerly hostile powers only one of the Hague Conference's treaties in the field of family law, the aforementioned Convention on the Guardianship of Minors. This selection of children's law as a special priority foreshadowed the drafting by the League of Nations of its Declaration of the Rights of the Child (1924), and eventually the United Nations Declaration on the Rights of the Child (1959) and its Convention on the Rights of the Child (General Assembly, 1989).

The failure of the Hague Conference's Fifth Session (1925) and its Sixth Session (1928) to cure the problems raised by the use of nationality as the determinant criterion in the treaties on family law led to impasse which deepened during the periods of armed conflict in Europe during the 1930s and 1940s. Only with the advent of a practical program of 'progressive unification' of private international law, under the leadership of Amsterdam Professor J. Offerhaus and the Conference's first permanent Secretary General, Matthijs H. van Hoogstraten – a less flamboyant and ambitious personality than Asser, but a realistic promoter of limited goals – did the Hague Conference acquire a Statute (drafted and adopted at the Seventh Session, in 1951, entered into force July 15, 1955) and become an established intergovernmental organization (IGO).

Human rights was not by name a part of the Hague Conference's program, but the contents of the areas in which the Conference worked led, in time, back

2 *Id.*, at 85–86.

to expression of the types of ideals which Asser had favored. In particular, after drawing up two treaties dealing with financial support for children living in countries away from those of one or both of their parents, the Conference went on to paint a whole new panoply of "The Hague Children's Conventions" (title of a compact disc issued by the Permanent Bureau of the Hague Conference which contained the complete published legislative history of three children's law treaties) that burnishes its accomplishments with a range of instruments catering to children's needs when their families are divided across frontiers, or even oceans.

The development of this work in the field of child protection and nourishment has been carried on, since van Hoogstraten's retirement in 1978, by Secretary General Georges A.L. Droz (1978–1996) and – with even more emphasis on the human rights aspects of The Hague Children's Conventions – by Secretary General Hans van Loon. Not to be forgotten is the close cooperation offered by successive Presidents of the Netherlands Standing Government Committee on Private International Law following Professor Offerhaus: Professors L.I. de Winter, J.C. Schultsz, A.V.M. Struycken and P. Vlas.

II. THE REVIVAL OF THE HAGUE CONFERENCE IN THE 1950s

After the doldrums of the 1930s and 1940s for cooperation in respect of private international law, work resumed with the invitations issued by the Netherlands Government for the Hague Conference's Seventh Session in 1951. The task was to take up again the effort started by T.M.C. Asser and rebuild from the beginning.[3] Only the 1905 Convention on Civil Procedure and the 1902 Convention on the Guardianship of Minors remained as hopeful bases for rebuilding.

A. THE 1954 CIVIL PROCEDURE CONVENTION

The Hague Conference's new devotion to modest advances, step by step, was perfectly characterized by its revival at the Seventh Session (1951) where the 1905 Convention's substantive provisions were repeated word for word in the newly adopted text which became the 1954 Convention on Civil Procedure. (That Convention, like all texts adopted by the Hague Conference before 1964,

[3] The official texts of Hague Conventions adopted beginning in 1951, including the Conference's Statute, are reproduced in the *Recueil des Conventions/Collection of Conventions (1951–2009)*, edited by the Hague Conference's Permanent Bureau.

was drafted in the French language; some expressions from the title or the text of any such Convention have been translated into English for the purpose of simplification of references in this article.)

The reason for simply repeating the text of the 1905 Convention in a new instrument was drawn from public international law. Some nations viewed hostilities as terminating all relations between Parties to an international treaty unless they expressly revived such relations. Other countries viewed treaty relations as only being suspended during the period of hostilities.

This was the importance of the express revival of the Hague Guardianship Convention in the World War I Peace Treaties of Versailles (1919, 225 L.N.T.S. 317–318, Art. 282), Saint-Germain (1919, 226 L.N.T.S. 98–100, Art. 234) and Trianon (1920, 6 L.N.T.S. 188, Art. 217). Other Hague Conventions, which were not expressly revived,[4] were left with a patchwork of Parties – some of which had suspended relations only while hostilities continued, others having terminated relations and not expressly revived them.

The approach shepherded through by van Hoogstraten simply cut the Gordian Knot of public international law which had been created by war, recreating the treaty in its own image. This approach avoided the treaty-law nuances of final termination or temporary suspension of the 1905 Convention, simply offering a new treaty to be ratified.

B. THE HAGUE CONFERENCE'S STATUTE AND SECRETARIAT

The Statute when it entered into force on 15 July, 1955 created an IGO, the Hague Conference on Private International Law, and a small Permanent Bureau (PB) to prepare and service its meetings and its texts. The Permanent Bureau was initially limited to three members, all of whom had to have different nationalities, which number could be enlarged after consultation with the Member States. When the author of this article retired in 1997, there were still only four PB members – one having been added when English was introduced as a second official language.

The PB is characterized by the personal responsibility assumed by its appointed Members, who sign the reports and questionnaires issued by the Hague Conference in the process of preparing a new international Convention. Their stewardship of the treaties drawn up within the Conference extends to the work

[4] *Convention pour régler les Conflits de lois en matière de mariage; Convention pour régler les Conflits de lois et de juridictions en matière de Divorce et de Séparation de Corps; Convention concernant les Conflits de lois relatifs aux Effets du Mariage sur le droit et les devoirs des époux dans leurs rapports personnels et sur les biens des époux; Convention concernant l'Interdiction et les mesures de protection analogues.*

involved in organizing Special Commission meetings held to study the operation of particular treaties, and finding possible ways to improve the effectiveness and defend the integrity of such instruments.

C. THE CHILD MAINTENANCE (SUPPORT) CONVENTIONS

Another area in which needed work could be done by drawing on work started in the past was cooperation between countries in providing and collecting funds for support of children. This work had been commenced earlier in other organizations, and the Hague Conference's Eighth Session, in 1956, had before it three texts: (a) the Rome Draft, proposed by UNIDROIT (*AVANT-PROJET D'UNE CONVENTION POUR LA RECONNAISSANCE ET L'EXÉCUTION A L'ÉTRANGER DES DÉCISIONS EN MATIÈRE D'OBLIGATIONS ALIMENTAIRES*); (b) the Geneva Draft recommended by the United Nations (*CONVENTION TYPE SUR L'EXÉCUTION A L'ÉTRANGER DES OBLIGATIONS ALIMENTAIRES*); and (c) the 1956 New York Convention of the United Nations (*CONVENTION SUR LE RECOUVREMENT DES ALIMENTS A L'ÉTRANGER*).[5] Following World War II, dislocation of families had caused many more children to be separated from parents by frontiers, and there was a desperate need for legal facilities to simplify and ensure the provision of maintenance for them.

The two Hague Conventions that came out of the Eighth Session on this topic, *Convention du 24 octobre 1956 sur la loi applicable aux obligations alimentaires envers les enfants* and *Convention du 15 avril 1958 concernant la reconnaissance et l'exécution des décisions en matière d'obligations alimentaires envers les enfants*, worked in tandem with the 1956 UN New York Convention to the benefit of thousands of children. Each is replaced, between Parties to the corresponding later Convention, (a) by a treaty drawn up at the Hague Conference's Twelfth Session that expanded the scope of coverage to adult maintenance, or (b) by a treaty drawn up at the Hague Conference's Seventeenth Session.[6]

The least that can be said is that the Hague Conference has given repeated attention for more than a half century to the need for adequate and up-to-date tools for international recovery of child support. These form part of the Conference's core mission.

5 These three texts are reproduced in *Documents relatifs a la Huitième Session*, 3 au 24 octobre 1956 (Imprimerie nationale/La Haye/1957), at 169–184.

6 Hague Convention of 23 November 2007 on the International Recovery of Child Support and Other Forms of Family Maintenance; Hague Protocol of 23 November 2007 on the Law Applicable to Maintenance Obligations.

D. THE 1955 SALE OF GOODS CONVENTION

Undertaken at the Seventh Session in 1951, the *Hague Convention of 15 June 1955 on the Law Applicable to the International Sale of Goods* is the shortest text in the COLLECTION OF CONVENTIONS (1951–2009), its 12 articles, in French only, occupying only 3 pages of the Collection.

Building on work undertaken at the Fifth Session (1925) and the Sixth Session (1928), which had been synthesized into a compact text by a Special Commission meeting held on May 28, 1931, the Seventh Session adopted this text with some modifications.[7]

This result exemplifies the genius for simplification, producing modest advances, that characterized van Hoogstraten, who once told the author of this article that a person could achieve many good things if he is willing for someone else to take the credit.

The Hague Conference's Conventions in the fields of commercial law and tort law are beyond the scope of this article, since they do not directly impact human rights. This brief sketch of the 1955 Convention is included because it was an essential part of the Conference's rebuilding in the 1950s, and because it illustrates the values of simplicity and limited scope – which later characterized, in particular, the 1980 Child Abduction Convention (see footnote 12 and PART IV(A), below).

III. "PROGRESSIVE" UNIFICATION OF PRIVATE INTERNATIONAL LAW

The Statute of the Hague Conference, in Article 1, expresses its mission as follows: "The purpose of the Hague Conference is to work for the progressive unification of the rules of private international law." The failure to mention codification is intentional. The new organization, created in 1955 was to pursue a step-by-step process – not towards the over-arching structure of a code, but rather by filling in the chinks with modest improvements.

[7] See Lipstein, "One Hundred Years of Hague Conferences on Private International Law", 42 *I.C.L.Q.* 553, 616 (1993).

A. THE 1961 APOSTILLE CONVENTION

The most successful Hague Convention, the *Hague Convention of 5 October 1961 Abolishing the Requirement of Legalisation for Foreign Public Documents*[8] (104 States Parties as of 29 December, 2012) resulted from a suggestion offered by the Council of Europe. It was not a brilliant intellectual breakthrough, but rather a pedestrian effort to simplify the authentication of public documents issued in one country, for use before the courts or administrative authorities of another country. The documents authenticated by the model form for the *apostille* which is annexed to this Convention, which consists of only 15 articles, range, for example, from court judgments to patents and trademark registrations to birth or marriage certificates and oaths taken before a notary public. It was one of the first two Hague Conventions to have an official English text, the French text prevailing in case of divergence. (Beginning in 1964, the English text of each Convention has had equal authenticity as the French text.)

The wide geographical spread of this treaty is testimony to the significance of basic advances achieved in routine legal processes, which help to reduce the friction caused in international trade or migration or litigation by nation-state boundaries.

B. THE 1961 CHILD PROTECTION CONVENTION

Only one of the Hague Conference's Conventions drawn up before 1951 has been interpreted and applied in a case brought before an international court. The case of the Netherlands vs. Sweden (popularly known as the "Boll case"), resulted in the decision of the International Court of Justice reported at 1958 I.C.J. 55 (November 28).[9] The ICJ'S decision pulled the teeth of the 1902 *Hague Convention on the Guardianship of Minors* by exempting measures of child protection taken by public authorities, leaving only the French concept of *tutelle* as a greatly narrowed base for the treaty's scope. The Hague Conference's response was to draft a new Convention replacing (in its Article 18) the 1902 Convention with a new treaty which broadened the scope to "measures" for the protection of minors – both as to the minor's person and his or her property.[10]

It is not the intention of the author of this article to expound on all of the innovations of the 1961 Convention, which, in destroying the 1902 Convention's

8 *Collection of Conventions (1951–2009)* at 60.

9 See Dyer, "The Internationalization of Family Law", 30 *U.C. Davis Law Review* 625, 631 (1997).

10 *Convention du 5 octobre 1961 concernant la compétence des autorités et la loi applicable en matière de protection des mineurs.* This was the last treaty of the Hague Conference adopted only in French.

dominance given to the law of the child's nationality, replaced it with a precarious balance between the laws of the child's habitual residence and nationality. (The spread of dual nationalities among children in multinational families soon created even more stress on the application of the nationality principle.) The Commission drawing up this text at the Conference's Ninth Session, in 1960, had in the preliminary draft an article dealing with "fraudulent displacement" of a child, but in the end voted to delete the article in its entirety.[11] This problem reappeared in the 1970s and led to the elaboration of the 1980 *Hague Child Abduction* Convention ("the Child Abduction Convention)[12] (see also Section II.D, *supra*). The 1961 Convention has been replaced in full by the *Hague Convention of 19 October 1996 on Jurisdiction, Applicable Law, Recognition, Enforcement and Co-operation in Respect of Parental Responsibility and Measures for the Protection of Children.*

IV. VISIONARY DETOURS ALONG THE ROAD TO CO-OPERATION

By the mid-1970s, the face of international unification of law was changing, with the European Communities expanding both in number of countries and in willingness to undertake important legal unification projects, while the United Nations Commission on International Trade Law (UNCITRAL) was producing important texts on contracts for the international sale of goods and on international arbitration. The Council of Europe was working on a Convention on the recognition and enforcement of custody decisions, which, after addition of articles on restoration of custody, became its Convention No. 105, adopted in May of 1980.

Tending the vineyard of private international law required attention to completing the triptych of treaties updating and replacing in stages the *1954 Hague Convention on Civil Procedure*, the *Hague Convention of 15 November 1965 on the Service Abroad of Judicial and Extrajudicial Documents in Civil or Commercial Matters* having been adopted at the Tenth Session, in 1964, and the *Hague Convention of 18 March 1970 on the Taking of Evidence Abroad in Civil or Commercial Matters* at the Eleventh Session, in 1968, leaving the topics of legal aid, security for costs and physical detention of a defendant to be brought together in a third treaty.[13] Canada, which had joined the Hague Conference in 1968, came

11 *Actes et documents de la Neuvième session, 1960, Tome IV*, at 149.
12 *Collection of Conventions (1951–2009)* at 281.
13 Hague Convention of 25 October 1980 on International Access to Justice, *Collection of Conventions (1951–2009)* at 300.

to the meeting of the Special Commission on Future Work, in January of 1976, and proposed a treaty on 'legal kidnapping'.

A. THE 1980 CHILD ABDUCTION CONVENTION

The response to the Canadian proposal at the Hague Conference's Thirteenth Session, in October of 1976, was broadly positive – despite the work on custody decisions which was already underway at the Council of Europe. Georges Droz, who was then Deputy Secretary General, had written a note for the Thirteenth Session showing the interest in the topic. Given the Council of Europe's geographical limits at the time, it was clear that there were many cases of abduction by one parent to or from countries that were not members of that IGO. The Hague Conference only had 28 Member States at the time, but these included countries from North and South America, Asia and Africa in addition to a strong base in Western Europe and some countries of Eastern Europe (Yugoslavia, Turkey, Greece and Czechoslovakia).

When Georges Droz was selected (in October 1977) to succeed Matthijs van Hoogstraten as Secretary General upon his retirement in 1978, the author of this article was assigned to prepare a Report and Questionnaire addressed to the Governments of the Member States on the topic of legal kidnapping. A couple of days were spent in discussions at the Geneva headquarters of International Social Service, whose officers from several national branches had practical experience with the legal difficulties for families when one parent decided unilaterally to take the child or children and remove them abroad from their place of habitual residence. Meanwhile, this author had become aware of a proposal introduced at the Council of Europe's Committee on Children's Law by the Swiss Delegation favoring rapid action to obtain the return of the child or children without any decision being taken on their custody by the authorities of the state of refuge.

All of the above went into the preparation of the *Report and Questionnaire on international child abduction by one parent*,[14] along with extensive research on the comparative law and procedures of child custody, as well as on the legislative histories of the *Hague Convention of 5 October 1961 concerning the powers of authorities and the law applicable in respect of the protection of infants*, the USA's Uniform Child Custody Jurisdiction Act (1968) and the Canadian Extra-Provincial Custody Orders Enforcement Act (1974), before the Report and Questionnaire were issued to the Governments of the Hague Conference's Member States in August 1978.

[14] *Actes et documents de la Quatorzième session, 1980, Tome III* at 9–60.

The germ of the Swiss proposal at Strasbourg was taken as a basis, and Special Commission meetings were held in 1979 at which Professor Elisa Pérez-Vera of Spain was chosen to be the Hague Conference's first female *Rapporteur*, and the final text of the Child Abduction Convention was adopted and signed at the Peace Palace on October 25, 1980 – following which Professor Pérez-Vera drew up her remarkable Explanatory Report on the Convention which has been cited by courts all around the world. This is the first of the Hague Conference's Conventions to mention expressly "the protection of human rights and fundamental freedoms" – which mention appears in its Article 20. Its text has a laser-like focus on a single remedy – return of a child who has been wrongfully removed or retained, as rapidly as possible, leaving custody and access questions to be decided after return.

This treaty was brought into force on 1 December 1983 subsequent to the first three ratifications – those of Canada, France and Portugal – which were followed closely by Switzerland's ratification. The treaty has 89 States Parties as of 30 December 2012.

B. THE 1993 INTERCOUNTRY ADOPTION CONVENTION

Sometimes the vision of one person is determinative as to whether there will be a needed improvement in international law and procedures. This was not the case with the Hague Child Abduction Convention, which, when it was proposed by Canada, drew immediate strong support from a broad number of delegations.

To the contrary, when Hans van Loon first suggested looking into a new treaty on intercountry adoption of children, it was clear that many of the countries whose participation would be needed were not Member States of the Hague Conference and that many of those same countries would find it excessively expensive to send delegations to The Hague, when their norm might be to be represented at IGOs of worldwide scope only by delegations sent to the United Nations' installations in New York and Geneva.

Thus, the preliminary question was how to obtain meaningful representation on this topic from a broad majority of the countries having children coming into their territories to join adopting parents, or having children departing before or after adoption.

Hans van Loon surmounted those problems and brought together at the Peace Palace in The Hague in June of 1990 a broad mix of lawyers and judges and social workers, in roughly equivalent numbers of men and women (which was unusual), who were dedicated to finding ways to provide families for children who need them.

The result, after three more years of work, was the *Hague Convention of 29 May 1993 on Protection of Children and Co-operation in Respect of Intercountry Adoption*, which has 89 States Parties as of 30 December, 2012. This was the first of the Hague Conventions to key itself on the United Nations Convention on the Rights of the Child (CRC). Its Preamble refers expressly to that treaty, adopted by the U.N. General Assembly on November 20, 1989. Article 21 of the CRC expresses certain criteria for adoption systems. The Hague Convention, since its entry into force on May 1st 1995, has brought great advances to the legal protection of the children adopted and to all of the parents involved.

The Explanatory Report on the 1993 Convention was written by Professor Gonzalo Parra-Aranguren, who has also served as an elected Member of the International Court of Justice, the judicial branch of the United Nations.

V. THE STRATEGIC MISSION OF THE HAGUE CONFERENCE

As it has developed over the more than six decades that have passed since the Hague Conference took up its work again at its Seventh Session (1951), this organization has shown a particular facility for protecting human rights, without advertising that expression. Even the newest treaty on recovery of child support (see footnote 6, above), prepared after fifty years of work by the Conference in this vineyard, refers in its Preamble to Articles 3 and 27 of the CRC, finally mentioning the human rights aspect of the Conference's work on the collection of child support. This adds to the mention of Article 21 of the CRC in the Intercountry Adoption Convention and to the mention of human rights and fundamental freedoms in Article 20 of the Child Abduction Convention, the latter of which is indirectly referred to in Article 11 of the CRC.

The fact that, adding to this battery of treaties protecting children, there is the general child protection treaty, the 1996 Hague Convention,[15] which expressly refers in its Preamble to the CRC and has 39 States Parties as of 31 December, 2012, shows that it is time to admit that promotion and protection of the human rights of children form an integral part of the Conference's core mission.

This should not take away any of the importance of the Conference's battery of procedural treaties on service of process, taking of evidence and access to justice. Assuring better and fairer operation of the justice system for adults involved in international litigation is a worthy task for the Hague Conference, which goes

15 Hague Convention of 19 October 1996 on Jurisdiction, Applicable Law, Recognition, Enforcement and Co-operation in Respect of Parental Responsibility and Measures for the Protection of Children, *Collection of Conventions (1951–2009)* at 397.

back to the ideals which inspired T.M.C. Asser when he founded the Conference and brought forward its early treaties on civil procedure.

Finally, the Conference has a comprehensive mission to reduce unnecessary obstacles and expenses burdening international commerce and the free migration of people. The fact that its little *apostille* is used to reduce trouble and expense in the international use of public documents as among 104 countries is a remarkable demonstration of what the Conference's delegates achieved at the Ninth Session in 1960.

Conventions on the law applicable to product liability[16] and on sales of goods have provided a facility for regional groupings, even when they have not achieved worldwide acceptance. The treaty on trusts,[17] to which Hans van Loon made essential contributions, has been useful for a certain number of dispersed jurisdictions. All of these efforts have added to a building process of unified private international law which continues.

VI. THE EXTRAORDINARY VISION OF HANS VAN LOON: HIS FOCUS ON HUMAN RIGHTS WITHOUT NEGLECT OF ORDINARY LEGAL ISSUES

Hans van Loon has been a key member of the Hague Conference's Permanent Bureau since his arrival in 1978, coming from a distinguished private law firm in The Hague. His ascension to the post of Secretary General in 1996, after having completed the remarkable task of bringing the Intercountry Adoption Convention to fruition in 1993, has led to the flowering of the Hague Conference – bringing his vision of international cooperation to nearly every corner of the globe. With a practical view of ordinary legal issues, he has brought an idealistic and extraordinary vision of possible achievements for the welfare of human beings to bear on the obstacles that arise. It is a pleasure to contribute to this book of articles in his honor.

16 Hague Convention of 2 October 1973 on the Law Applicable to Products Liability, *Collection of Conventions (1951–2009)* at 202.

17 Hague Convention of 1 July 1985 on the Law Applicable to Trusts and on their Recognition, *Collection of Conventions (1951–2009)* at 330.

HERMENEUTIC DIALOGUE BETWEEN ROME I AND ROME II: GENERAL PRINCIPLES AND ARGUMENTATIVE RULES

Francisco J. GARCIMARTÍN ALFÉREZ
Professor of Private International Law at the University Autónoma of Madrid

I. INTRODUCTION

One of the main functions of Private International Law is to guarantee harmony of decisions (*internationaler Entscheidungseinklang*): the same law should apply to a case, irrespective of the competent court. *Ex ante,* this ensures cross-border continuity of subjective rights – contractual and proprietary – and, therefore, lowers transaction costs in the international market. *Ex post,* it discourages opportunistic behaviours, in particular a race between the parties to the courts.[1]

Such harmony of decisions calls for two elements: common rules, *i.e.* a set of uniform conflict of law rules, and a common framework of interpretation.

In the European Union (EU), and in the area of civil and commercial matters, the Rome I[2] and Rome II[3] Regulations lay down a set of common conflict of law rules. The first is for contractual obligations and the second for non-contractual obligations, including unjust enrichment, *negotiorum gestio* and pre-contractual liability. Moreover, both texts have a universal scope of application. They apply irrespective of whether the case is linked to the EU or not (Article 2 of Rome I and Article 3 of Rome II). Leaving aside certain exclusions, both instruments establish an *EU conflict of law code* for contractual and non-contractual obligations. This set

[1] See, recently, elaborating this idea with regard to the Rome Regulations and with further references, G.-P. Calliess, in Calliess (ed.), *Rome Regulations,* 2011, at 1–6.

[2] Regulation (EC) No 593/2008 of the European Parliament and of the Council of 17 June 2008 on the law applicable to contractual obligations (Rome I), OJ L 177/6, 4.7.2008.

[3] Regulation (EC) No 864/2007 of the European Parliament and of the Council of 11 July 2007 on the law applicable to non-contractual obligations (Rome II), OJ L 19/40, 31.7.2007.

of common rules ensures harmony of decisions, which is crucial for any market to function properly. As correctly stated in Recital 6 of both Rome I and Rome II Regulations, "the proper functioning of the internal market creates a need... for the conflict-of-law rules in the Member States to designate the same national law irrespective of the country of the court in which an action is brought".

However, together with such legal uniformity, it is essential to ensure *uniform interpretation and application* of instruments. There is no real uniformity if each Member State interprets and applies the common instruments in a different way, *i.e.* according to its own parameters. Uniform texts must be uniformly interpreted and applied. There are marginal exceptions (see Recital 8 of Rome I and Recital 10 of Rome II), but these must remain exceptions to the general rule.

Uniform interpretation requires, in turn, two elements: common rules of interpretation and an institutional guarantee. The latter, *i.e.* the *institutional guarantee*, is provided for by the European Court of Justice (ECJ) which has the last word on the interpretation of EU texts: any national judge can submit a preliminary question on instruments to that court.[4] Furthermore, the ECJ or national judges, when interpreting EU instruments, must apply common cannons of interpretation, *i.e.* the same standards of interpretation and construction and with the same hierarchy. In principle, this involves applying traditional rules or criteria of interpretation adapted to the nature of the text. Literal or textual, teleological, systematic and historical cannons must be adapted to the fact that we are dealing with European instruments.[5] Thus, for example, the literal criteria calls for taking into account the authentic versions of text in different languages. Together with those four criteria, the comparative law aspect may play a relevant function. The case law of the ECJ has progressively elaborated on the content of such cannons of interpretation and the interplay among them.[6] These can be characterized as the EU law interpretative framework.

It is worth noting that this interpretative framework is likely to have a more important function in EU law than in national law. The EU lawmaking process has certain peculiarities that may lead to legal texts with more ambiguities and gaps. The texts are negotiated at different levels, in different languages, and with different legal backgrounds in mind. Furthermore, EU institutions are more prone to look for compromises between many conflicting groups of interests and

4 See Article 267 of the Treaty on the Functioning of the European Union.

5 See, with regard to the Rome Regulations in particular, Calliess, *loc.cit.*, at 12–14; R. Plender/M. Wilderspin, *The European Private International Law of Obligations*, 3rd ed., 2009, at 33–44.

6 See, recently, ECJ case C-190/11, at www.curia.europe.eu, giving special weight to the genetic and teleological cannons of interpretation. Also, and with further references, D. Coester-Waltjen, "Die Rolle des EuGH im internationalen Privat-und Verfahrensrecht", in E.M. Kieninger/O. Remien (eds.), *Europäische Kollisionsrechtsvereinheitlichung*, 2012, p. 77 *et seq.*, at 83–87.

States with varying political clout.[7] In several cases, the interest in having a final text involves the introduction of calculated ambiguities and gaps. Many issues are left, therefore, for the courts to resolve.[8] Naturally, the same holds for EU Private International Law (EU PIL). In addition, the fragmentation of instruments is one of the main flaws of the current system of EU PIL. This part of EU law consists of different pieces of legislation adopted in very different contexts and times.[9] As a result, a qualified effort is called for to restore consistency to the legal system through legal scholarship and judicial interpretation.

The purpose of this work is to contribute to this "judicial dimension" of EU PIL and, in particular, to suggest some of the principles that should govern the hermeneutic relationships between the Rome I and Rome II Regulations. We may call these principles: (i) the *principle of complementarity*; (ii) the *principle of autonomy and continuity of concepts*; and (iii) the *principle of hermeneutic reciprocity*. From these three principles, we can deduce six "meta-argumentative rules". These function as rules on the *burden of argumentation* which may make application of the positive norms less costly and, therefore, prove useful for lawyers and judicial practice. These argumentative rules may complement the substantive principles underpinning EU PIL, such as party autonomy (see, e.g. Arts. 3.1 Rome I, 14 Rome II or 23 Brussels I), the protection of weaker parties, i.e. consumers and employees (see e.g. Arts. 6 and 8 Rome I, 14.2 Rome II or 8–17 Brussels I), the protection of general interests (see e.g. Arts. 9 Rome I and 16 Rome II) or the principle of certainty and predictability (see e.g. Recital 6 Rome I and Rome II, or 11 Brussels I).

Nevertheless, before moving to those principles and rules, it may be pertinent to place this contribution within the context of this Liber Amicorum to Hans van Loon. A common and coherent interpretative framework ensures the consistency of the legal system and, therefore, not only the proper functioning of the internal market but also, more importantly, the rule of law. The rule of law protects contractual and proprietary rights and provides the necessary predictability to do business and enter into social and economic relationships. This includes the protection of private rights *vis-à-vis* arbitrary or irrational interpretation of the

---

7 See, with many examples, P. Mankowski, *Interessenpolitik und europäisches Kollisionsrecht*, 2011, *passim*.

8 At least, my limited personal experience is that at the EU level, the number of decisions adopted by "compromise" (and, therefore, to satisfy as many Member States and lobbies as possible, even at the expense of internal coherence and consistency) and the issues left for the courts to resolve is much higher than at the internal or national level. This implies that the interpretation and construction process fulfils a more relevant function.

9 See, *i.a.*, J. Basedow, "EC Conflict of Laws – A Matter of Coordination", in L. De Lima Pinheiro, *Seminário internacional sobre a comunitarizacao do direito internacional privado*, 2005, p. 19 *et seq.*, at 30; U. Liukkunen, "Managing Legal Diversity in the EU: The Case of Subject-Specific Conflicts Rules", *E.Rev.P.L.*, 4–2012, p. 1045 *et seq.*, at 1068.

law by governmental agencies or judges. State authorities' interpretation of the law must be rational, predictable and consistent. Only then can human beings foresee the consequences of their decisions and are the courts publicly accountable for their decisions. This condition also encompasses the cross-border dimension of human activities. Accordingly, conflict of law rules are also governed by the test of rational, predictable and consistent interpretation. This paper attempts to contribute to the elaboration of an EU PIL interpretative framework which meets those conditions.

II. PRINCIPLE OF COMPLEMENTARITY

Rome I and Rome II are two complementary instruments. The starting point for the legislator is that both texts dovetail. In the area of civil and commercial matters, the intention is to encompass all personal obligations and, therefore, to establish a common set of EU conflict rules applicable to all cross-border personal obligations, i.e. rights *in personam* as oppose to rights *in rem*.[10] The two instruments mirror at the conflict of laws level, the canonical distinction in Roman law, *omnis enim obligatio vel ex contractu nasciturus vel ex delicto.* Obligations derive either from a contract or a tort. Rome I applies to contractual obligations, whereas Rome II applies to non-contractual obligations in the broadest sense of the term. It includes torts, *negotiorum gestio*, unjust enrichment and *culpa in contrahendo* (Article 2.1 Rome II).

It is true that there may be exceptions, i.e. personal obligations, that are explicitly excluded from the scope of those instruments (see Article 1.2 of both texts),[11] or implicitly as may be the case of the *actio pauliana* (ECJ as. C-261/90). But these are exceptions. The starting point is that principle of complementarity: what is not included in one instrument is *prima facie* included in the other. There are, in principle, no gaps between them. It is an "either / or" system. Accordingly, we can formulate the first argumentative rule in the following terms: *in principle, the law applicable to a personal (in personam) obligation shall be determined either under the Rome I or the Rome II Regulation, unless the interested party (or judge) proves otherwise.* As an "in principle" sentence, it does not mean that all personal obligations are included either under the Rome I Regulation or under the Rome II

[10] The contraposition between rights *in rem* and rights *in personam* is habitual in the case law of the ECJ (see, e.g., C-294/92, at www.curia.europe.eu). On the idea of complementarity, see also B. Haftel, "Entre Rome II at Bruxelles I: l'interprétation communautaire uniforme du règlement Rome I", *Clunet*, 2010, p. 761 *et seq.*, at 775; S. Leible, *Rom I und Rom II: Neue Perspektiven im Europäischen Kollisionsrecht*, 2009, at 43–47; E. Lein, "The new Rome I/Rome II/Brussels I Synergy", *YbPIL*, 2008, p. 177 *et seq.*, at 189; D. Coester-Waltjen, *loc.cit.*, at 93.

[11] Mainly, but not only, family and successions matters.

Regulation. It only means that the argumentative burden rests on those – the courts or the parties – who posit that an obligation *in personam* is included neither in the Rome I Regulation nor in the Rome II Regulation.

The "either/or" approach implies that there are no gaps but also no overlaps between the two instruments. Therefore, the same cause of action is governed either by the Rome I Regulation or by the Rome II Regulation, but not by both Regulations at the same time. A plaintiff cannot arbitrarily choose. There is no concurrent liability *at the conflict of law level.* A claim based on a personal obligation should be confined to one instrument exclusively.[12]

Furthermore, and in line with the case law of the ECJ with regard to Brussels I, there is a certain hierarchy between the two instruments. First, we have to see whether Rome I applies and, if not, whether Rome II applies. We may say therefore that Rome II applies by default. Or, in other words, the concept of tort or quasi-delict is residual.[13] What is not characterized as a contractual obligation should – again, in principle – be characterized as a tort.

According to the ECJ, matters relating to torts cover all actions which seek to establish the liability of a defendant and which are not related to a 'contract' within the meaning of Article 5 (1) (see e.g. cases 189/87, C-261/90, C-96/00 or C-167/00). And a contract implies a situation in which there is an obligation "freely assumed by one party towards another" (*ibid.*): an intentional and voluntary act by one party towards another. The Case law of the ECJ with regard to Articles 5.1 and 5.3 of the Brussels I Regulation[14] can be applied to the relationships between Rome I and Rome II.[15]

The *Réunion européenne* case is a good example to illustrate this way of reasoning. The case arose within the context of carriage of goods from Melbourne (Australia) to Rotterdam (The Netherlands) by sea by a person different from the one who issued the bill of lading. The ECJ based its decision on two ideas. First, Article 5.1 of the Brussels I Regulation ("matters relating to contract") was not applicable, since the defendant – i.e. the actual maritime carrier – had not freely assumed an obligation *vis-à-vis* the beneficiary of the bill of lading. And, secondly, Article 5.3 applied since this provision covers "all actions which seek to establish the liability of a defendant *and which are not related to a 'contract' within the meaning of Article 5(1)* [emphasis added]". In principle, and as a mere

---

12 Though authors maintain different views on this issue, see e.g. Plender/Wilderspin, *loc.cit,* at 70–74; A. Dickinson, *The Rome II Regulation,* 2008, at 185–191; E. Lein, *loc.cit.*, at 197.

13 Plender/Wilderspin, *loc.cit.*, at 56; see also Dickinson, *loc.cit.*, at 173; I. Bach, in P. Huber (ed.), *Rome II Regulation,* 2011, at 36; E. Lein, *loc.cit.*, at 189–190; MünchKommBGB/Junker, "Art. 1 Rom II-VO", *RdNr* 14–15.

14 Council Regulation No 44/2001, of 22 December 2000 on jurisdiction and the recognition and enforcement of judgment in civil and commercial matters.

15 This is also an "in principle" interpretative rule; see *infra*, footnote 20.

argumentative rule, we can apply the same approach to the interplay between Rome I and Rome II.

Thus, we can formulate the second interpretative rule in the following terms. *If an obligation derives from an agreement freely assumed by one party towards another, the law applicable should be determined by the Rome I Regulation. Otherwise, the law applicable should be determined by the Rome II Regulation, unless the interested party proves that the corresponding personal obligations cannot be characterized as a tort either.*

IV. PRINCIPLE OF AUTONOMY AND CONTINUITY OF CONCEPTS

The next interpretative principle is the principle of *autonomy* and *continuity* of concepts: the legal concepts used by the EU PIL instruments must be understood or interpreted autonomously and must have the same meaning in all of them. Autonomous interpretation is a corollary of the uniformity of the legal framework. Should the concepts be interpreted by reference to national law, the uniform application of the instrument would be jeopardized. This idea is well supported in the case law of the ECJ with regard to the Brussels I Regulation and does not need to be reiterated.[16] Thus, we can directly formulate the third argumentative rule: *the legal concepts used by the Rome I and the Rome II Regulations must be uniformly interpreted and, therefore, understood autonomously, not by reference to national law, unless the texts explicitly or implicitly require otherwise* (Arts. 8 Rome I and 10 Rome II). Accordingly, *the argumentative burden lies upon those who propose a non-autonomous interpretation.*

Furthermore, the starting point is the continuity of concepts, i.e. that the same legal concepts have the same meaning in the two Regulations, Rome I and Rome II, and in the Brussels I Regulation, and naturally in other EU instruments on PIL such as certain Directives or the Regulation on insolvency proceedings.[17] A concept appearing in different provisions of EU PIL instruments should generally be read in the same way each time it appears.[18] This is likely the main aspect of the requirement for consistency between the three instruments referred to in Recitals 7 of both Rome I and Rome II: "the scope of application

16 See recently, ECJ case C-190/11, at para. 28: "*It must be recalled that the concepts used in the Brussels I Regulation… must be interpreted independently, by reference principally to the system and objectives of the regulation, in order to ensure that it is uniformly applied in all the Member States*".

17 Regulation (EC) 1346/2000 of 29 May 2000 on insolvency proceedings.

18 See also in family matters, Recital 10 of Regulation (UE) No 1259/2010 of 20 December 2010, Rome III.

and the provisions" of those instruments "should be consistent" and applied to a particular case in Recital 17 Rome I ("the concept of 'provision of services' and 'sale of goods' should be interpreted in the same way as when applying Article 5 of Regulation No 44/2001"). The same idea is expressed in Recital 24 of the Rome I Regulation as regards the concept of "directed activities" as a condition for applying the consumer protection rules in Article 15 of the Brussels I Regulation and Article 6 of the Rome I Regulation.[19] Accordingly, we can formulate a fourth argumentative rule: *the same legal concept is presumed to have the same meaning in the three instruments.* Again, this is not an absolute principle. It does not mean that the same concept must always have the same meaning. The presumption may be rebutted. It only means that the argumentative burden lies upon those who propose that the same concept should be interpreted differently.[20]

This has two consequences. First, the legal definitions included in one text can be extended to the other. For example, the definition of *lois de pólice* or overriding mandatory rules included in the Rome I Regulation is applicable to the same concept in the Rome II Regulation. The legislator's intention with the definition contained in Article 9(1) of the Rome I Regulation was to prevent national judges from invoking Article 9 to frustrate application of the Regulation's general conflict of law rules. Article 9 only encompasses "ordo-political rules", i.e. *Eingriffsnormen.* Those *"the respect of which is regarded a crucial by a country".* The same holds for Article 16 of the Rome II Regulation.[21]

Secondly, the case law of the ECJ with regard to Brussels I should also be applied *in principle* to Rome I and Rome II. Therefore, the interpretation given by the ECJ with regard to concepts such as: (i) Civil and commercial matters (e.g. cases C-172/91, C-167/00, C-271/00, C-266/1, C-265/02, C-292/05);

---

19 This concept has been strongly criticized by legal scholars, but this is the cost of the piecemeal approach of the EU legislator. In the drafting of the Rome I Regulation, the EU legislator was conditioned by the solutions taken in the Brussels I Regulation and the Rome II Regulation. This has a positive aspect (since it ensures consistency among the different instruments) but also a negative aspect (since it replicates the flaws).

20 The differences may be more justified with regard to the Brussels I Regulation, since the nature of the rules are different. There are hermeneutic criteria which apply to Articles 5.1 and 5.3 of the Brussels I Regulation that do not apply to the Rome I and Rome II Regulations. The idea, for example, that Articles 5.1 and 5.3 of the Brussels I Regulation *"should be interpreted in such a way as to enable a normally well-informed defendant reasonably to predict before which courts... he may be sued"* (ECJ, *i.a.*, case C-26/91, at para 18) or that those provisions respond to *"a close link between the court and the action"* (Recital 12 Brussels I) cannot obviously be used in the context of the Rome I and Rome II Regulations. This aspect is very relevant when rebutting the principle of continuity of concepts. See, *i.e.*, MünchKommBGB/Martiny, "Vor Art. 1 Rom I-VO", RdNr 15c; Coaster-Waltjen, *loc.cit.*, at 99 or recently and with many examples, J. Lüttringhaus, "Übergreifende Begrifflichkeiten im europäischen Zivilverfahrens- und Kollisionsrecht", *Max Planck Private Law Research Paper*, No 12/16, *passim.*

21 See, *i.e.*, A. Dickinson, *loc.cit.*, at 634; J. von Hein, in Calliess (ed.), *loc.cit.*, at 565; S. Leible, *loc. cit.*, at 62; A. Fuchs, in Huber (ed.), *loc.cit.*, at 355; MünchKommBGB/Junker, "Art. 16 Rom II-VO", *RdNr* 13.

(ii) Contractual matters (cases 34/82, 9/87, C-26/91, C-51/97); (iii) Torts (cases C-189/87, C-261/90C-96/00, C- 167/00 (iv) Provisions of services and sale of goods (cases C-533/07, C-381/08, C-19/09); (v) Consumer contracts (cases C-96/00, C-464/01, C-27/02, C-180/06, C-585/08); (vi) Tenancy of immovable property (cases C-73/77, C-280/90, C-8/98); (vi) Employment contracts (case C-266/85), (vii) Place of damage (189/08: the words 'place where the harmful event occurred' designate the place where the initial damage occurred as a result of the normal use of the product for the purpose for which it was intended), and so on, must also apply to the same concepts used in the Rome I or the Rome II Regulations.

V. PRINCIPLE OF HERMENEUTIC RECIPROCITY

The other side of the coin is the mismatches between the two (or three, including Brussels I) instruments. Certain provisions are included in one instrument yet omitted or drafted differently in another. Taking into account the particularities of the legislative process within EU institutions, it is more difficult to formulate rules for the interpretative consequences that could be drawn from disparate provisions than it is for those drawn from parallel concepts and provisions. To see why, we can identify two kinds of differences between the texts. For lack of better wording, I will call them *conscious or voluntary differences* and *unconscious or involuntary differences.*[22] Naturally, to characterize a difference as conscious or unconscious it is not enough to look at a single sentence or text. We have to look at its sense and policy. Analysis of the lawmaking process, i.e. the legislative history (*travaux préparatoires)*, and the recitals may on many occasions prove extremely useful.

Conscious differences, as their name suggests, are made on purpose and the intention of the lawmaker is to depart from the solution adopted in the other rules or instruments. In certain cases, they can also be characterized as eloquent silences. The legislator acted intentionally and purposefully in the disparate inclusions or exclusions.

The examples we can give in this respect are very obvious. (i) In matters relating to torts, Article 4.1 Rome II does not used the term "the place where the harmful event occurred", as in Article 5.3 Brussels I, but the term "the country where the damage occurs". The intention is very clear: whereas the event causing the damage is relevant to determine jurisdiction (Brussels I), it is not to determine the applicable law (Rome II). Rome II, unlike Brussels I, does not follow the so-called principle of ubiquity. The reason lies in the different function of the two provisions. Article 5.3 Brussels I is based on a close link between the courts and

[22] See also E. Lein, *loc.cit.*, at 191.

the action in order to facilitate the sound administration of justice (Recital 12 Brussels I). Article 4.1 Rome II is based on a balance between the interest of the person who has sustained the damage and the person claimed to be liable (Recital 16 Rome II); and it also guarantees that each State can rule on the standards of behaviour within its boundaries and gives an incentive to persons to internalize the consequences that their conduct may cause abroad. (ii) With regard to overriding mandatory provisions, the difference between Rome I and Rome II is also clear. Whereas Article 9.3 Rome I envisages the application of overriding mandatory provisions of a third country, Article 16 Rome II only refers to the overriding mandatory rules of the forum. This difference is also eloquent. The EU legislator understands that in the area of tort, overriding mandatory provisions of a third country play a marginal function, that it is in part fulfilled by Article 13 (rules of safety and conduct). Thus, unlike Article 9.1 Rome I, *Article 9.3 Rome I cannot be extended or applied by analogy to Rome II.* (iii) Note that there are also conscious or voluntary differences within the text of a single instrument. Thus, for example, the escape clause contained in Article 4.3 Rome I is drafted differently than the escape clause contained in Article 8.4 of the same instrument. The latter text is more flexible than the text of the former. In particular, the adverbs "clearly" and "manifestly" are not included in Article 8.4. The legislator's intention was to give more leeway to judges when dealing with employment contracts, where the interests and the policies at stake may be different than in those contracts governed by the general rule of Article 4.

Accordingly, we can formulate a fifth argumentative rule: *Conscious or voluntary differences, i.e. which are the intention of the EU legislator, must be interpreted as eloquent silences and therefore a contrario.*

Conversely, there are also *unconscious or involuntary differences*, which do not reflect an intention by the EU legislator to have different solutions in Rome I and Rome II. This kind of divergence must be interpreted by extension or analogy, giving preference to the solutions adopted in the Rome I Regulation, since this was the last instrument and was negotiated "in the shadow" of the other instruments.

We can give three or four examples to illustrate this idea. (i) The principle established by Recital 8 of the Rome II Regulation ("This Regulation should apply irrespective of the nature of the court or tribunal seized") also applies to the Rome I Regulation. This clarification may be relevant with regard to State contracts not excluded from the scope of this instrument.[23] (ii) Rome II does not contain rules on assignment of claims or set-off. But this is not eloquent silence on the part of the legislator. It is a *lacuna* that should be filled by applying the corresponding rules of the Rome I Regulation. Therefore, (a) in the case of an

23 See, F. Garcimartín, "The Rome II Regulation: On the way towards a European Private International Law Code", *EuLF*, 3-2007, p. 77 *et seq.*, at 80.

assignment of a non-contractual claim, the law applicable to such claim governs its assignability, the relationship between the assignee and the debtor, the conditions under which the assignment can be invoked against the debtor and whether the debtor's obligations have been discharged (see Article 14.2 Rome I). (b) The right to set-off two non-contractual obligations shall be governed by the law applicable to the claim against which the set-off is asserted (see Article 17 Rome I). (iii) With regard to multiple liability, Article 16 Rome I contains a sentence that is not included in the parallel provision of Rome II, i.e. Article 20. This is not eloquent silence on the part of the legislator either. The rule of Rome I should be applied by analogy. In principle, the solution is the same in both instruments: if a creditor has a claim against several debtors who are liable for the same claim, and one of the debtors has already satisfied the claim in whole or in part, the law governing the debtor's obligation towards the creditor also governs the debtor's right to claim recourse from the other debtors. In other words, the debtor who pays determines the law applicable to the right of reimbursement by the other debtors. However, the Rome I Regulation introduces an additional sentence aimed at protecting the legitimate expectations of the co-debtors: "The other debtors may rely on the defences they had against the creditor to the extent allowed by the law governing their obligations towards the creditor". For example, the other debtors may invoke the limitation period under the law governing their obligation as a defence against the right to reimburse. The same principle should apply in relation to Article 20 of Rome II by analogy.[24] Article 16 *in fine* Rome I is a good example of those provisions of this instrument that were negotiated with the intention of closing a non-voluntary gap raised by the former instrument, *i.e.* in the Rome II Regulation.

Accordingly, we can formulate the sixth argumentative rule on the following terms: *Unconscious or explanatory differences must be interpreted by analogy, taking the Rome I Regulation as the point of reference.*

V. CONCLUSIONS

This paper is a contribution to the "judicial dimension" of EU PIL. We have elaborated some of the principles that should govern the hermeneutic relationships between the Rome I and Rome II Regulations. We have called these principles: (i) the *principle of complementarity*; (ii) the *principle of autonomy and continuity of concepts*; and (iii) the *principle of hermeneutic reciprocity.*

[24] See, *i.a.*, MünchKommBGB/Junker, "Art. 20 Rom II-VO", *RdNr* 15; D. Baetge, in Calliess (ed.) *loc. cit.*, at 599.

From these three principles, we have deduced six argumentative rules, as rules concerning the *burden of argumentation*, which may reduce the costs of application of the norms and, therefore, may prove useful for lawyers and for judicial practice. These argumentative rules are the following:

(i) In principle, the law applicable to a personal (in personam) obligation shall be determined either under the Rome I or the Rome II Regulation, unless the interested party (or judge) proves otherwise.
(ii) If an obligation derives from an agreement freely assumed by one party towards another, the law applicable should be determined by the Rome I Regulation. Otherwise, the law applicable should be determined by the Rome II Regulation, unless the interested party proves that the corresponding personal obligations cannot be characterized as a tort either.
(iii) The legal concepts used by Rome I and Rome II must be uniformly interpreted and, therefore, understood autonomously, not by reference to national law, unless the texts explicitly or implicitly require otherwise.
(iv) The same legal concept is presumed to have the same meaning in the three instruments, Brussels I, Rome I and Rome II. This presumption, however, can be rebutted.
(v) Conscious or voluntary differences between the two instruments, i.e. Rome I and Rome II, which reflect the intention of the EU legislator, must be interpreted as eloquent silences and therefore a contrario.
(vi) Unconscious or explanatory differences must be interpreted by analogy, taking the Rome I Regulation as the point of reference.

INDIVIDUALISME ET MONDIALISATION : ASPECTS DE DROIT INTERNATIONAL PRIVÉ DE LA FAMILLE

Hélène Gaudemet-Tallon
Professeur émérite de l'Université Panthéon-Assas (Paris II)
Membre de l'Institut de Droit international

« *L'humanité est une entreprise surhumaine* »
Giraudoux, *Intermezzo*, acte III, scène 1

Il n'est pas nécessaire d'être philosophe, sociologue ou psychologue pour prendre conscience des transformations radicales de notre monde en ce début de XXIème siècle. En particulier, on assiste à la fois à la proclamation de la valeur de chaque être humain, de sa dignité, de sa liberté, et, en même temps, à une évolution des modes de vie, tous touchés d'une façon ou d'une autre par la « mondialisation », le brassage des populations, les migrations et déplacements volontaires ou subis. Le juriste est directement concerné et particulièrement le spécialiste de droit international privé : ce double mouvement de promotion de l'individu et d'internationalisation toujours plus intense l'oblige à innover. Ce phénomène est flagrant en droit international privé de la famille et a été au cœur des préoccupations de Hans van Loon. En effet, Hans van Loon, comme le montre sa brillante carrière à la Conférence de La Haye de droit international privé, s'est toujours intéressé à l'être humain en tant que tel, et souvent au plus fragile, l'étranger, le migrant ou encore celui que le droit qualifie « d'incapable », et a œuvré pour que les individus et les rapports qu'ils entretiennent entre eux puissent s'épanouir de la meilleure façon possible au niveau international. Evoquant Hans van Loon, c'est tout naturellement que les mots d'individualisme (au sens d'humanisme, de prise en compte de chaque personne) et de mondialisation me sont venus à l'esprit.

Les lignes qui suivent sont avant tout un témoignage d'admiration et d'amitié à l'égard du dédicataire de ces mélanges mais voudraient aussi indiquer quelques unes des façons dont le droit international privé de la famille prend en compte les transformations du monde contemporain. Le droit international privé de la famille doit en effet relever un double défi, celui de la montée de l'individualisme (I), et celui de la mondialisation croissante (II).

I. LE DROIT INTERNATIONAL PRIVÉ DE LA FAMILLE AU DÉFI DE LA MONTÉE DE L'INDIVIDUALISME

Deux phénomènes doivent être mis en évidence : le déclin des rattachements traditionnels au profit de l'autonomie de la volonté (A) et l'affirmation des « droits de l'homme » (B).

A. DÉCLIN DES RATTACHEMENTS TRADITIONNELS AU PROFIT DE L'AUTONOMIE DE LA VOLONTÉ

Le statut personnel, statut individuel ou rapports familiaux, était traditionnellement soumis, dans les pays qui ne relevaient pas d'un système de *Common Law*, à la loi nationale. Et, lorsque les membres d'une même famille avaient des nationalités différentes, on recourait à la loi du domicile commun.

Mais chacun sait que le rattachement à la nationalité est de plus en plus contesté. Il apparaît souvent que retenir la loi de la nationalité d'une personne n'est pas la meilleure solution, en particulier, lorsqu'il s'agit de protéger cette personne qui peut se trouver dans un Etat dont elle n'a pas la nationalité. Le rattachement à la nationalité pose aussi problème dans les cas, de plus en plus fréquents, de plurinationalité chez une même personne, ou de différences de nationalité entre les membres d'une même famille. Enfin, on s'est demandé si le rattachement à la nationalité n'était pas une atteinte aux droits de l'homme, lesquels sont attribués sans que l'on puisse fonder une discrimination sur la nationalité (v. *infra B*), ou encore au droit de l'Union européenne en ce qu'il serait contraire à l'article 18 TFUE[1].

Depuis plusieurs dizaines d'années, le rattachement à la résidence habituelle a souvent remplacé le rattachement à la nationalité, en particulier lorsqu'il faut protéger une personne incapable, qu'il s'agisse d'un mineur ou d'un majeur. Mais ce rattachement fait, lui aussi, l'objet de critiques[2]. En premier lieu parce qu'il est impossible de définir la résidence habituelle, elle dépend d'éléments de fait qui

---

1 V. M-J. Puljak, *Le droit international privé à l'épreuve du principe communautaire de non discrimination en raison de la nationalité*, *PUM* 2003, préf. Y. Lequette.

2 V. J. Heymann, *Le droit international privé à l'épreuve du fédéralisme européen*, Economica 2010, préf. H. Muir Watt, spéc. n° 441 à 445 ; v. toutefois pour une défense mesurée des rattachements tantôt à la nationalité, tantôt à la résidence habituelle : B. Audit, « Les avatars de

varient au gré des espèces. Aucune loi, aucun règlement de l'Union européenne, aucune convention internationale, n'en a donné de définition et, comme l'écrit A. Bucher, « la notion semble insaisissable »[3]. Ce rattachement est aussi critiqué, en second lieu, parce que, les personnes se déplaçant de plus en plus facilement et de plus en plus souvent, leur résidence habituelle est susceptible de changer plusieurs fois au cours de leur vie, ce qui nuit à la permanence requise lorsqu'il s'agit de statut personnel. Enfin, on peut encore remarquer qu'une même personne peut avoir deux résidences habituelles (l'une professionnelle, l'autre familiale par exemple), et qu'au sein d'une même famille, il arrive que la résidence habituelle soit différente pour chacun des membres du couple ou que celle du couple ne coïncide pas avec celle des enfants.

Enfin nationalité et résidence habituelle sont liées aux éléments constitutifs de l'Etat : ses nationaux, et son territoire. Or l'Etat, même s'il reste la cellule de base de la société internationale, subit aussi un certain déclin dans la mesure où le cadre étatique est souvent trop étroit, qu'il s'agisse de politique étrangère, d'économie ou de droit[4].

Un moyen de remédier aux insuffisances soit de la nationalité, soit de la résidence habituelle surgit alors : laisser l'individu choisir la loi à laquelle il entend voir soumis son statut personnel, ainsi que ses intérêts patrimoniaux (obligations alimentaires, régimes matrimoniaux et successions)[5].

Le phénomène n'a rien d'étonnant : il n'est que la traduction en droit international privé d'un profond mouvement des droits internes en faveur de l'autonomie de la volonté. En droit interne, il suffit de rappeler les multiples formes que peut adopter le couple désireux de vivre en commun (mariage, PACS, union libre), les figures variées de séparation entre lesquelles il a le choix, la possibilité d'avoir hors mariage des enfants qui auront les mêmes droits que ceux nés durant le mariage, la possibilité d'avoir recours à des procréations médicalement assistées, d'adopter[6]. En droit patrimonial de la famille une place importante a toujours été reconnue à la volonté individuelle : contrat de mariage, possibilité de changer de régime matrimonial, possibilité d'organiser sa succession grâce à des donations-partages et à des testaments (avec encore en droit français la limite de la réserve). Cette promotion de la volonté individuelle en droit interne ne pouvait

la loi personnelle en droit international privé contemporain », *in Le Monde du Droit, Ecrits en l'honneur de Jacques Foyer*, Economica 2008, p. 49 et s.

3 *La famille en droit international privé*, Rec. cours Acad. La Haye tome 283 (2000) n° 17.

4 V. en particulier sur ce thème : J. Guillaumé, « L'affaiblissement de l'Etat-Nation et le Droit international privé », *LGDJ* 2011, 750 p. , préf. C. Grare-Didier.

5 J. Guillaumé voit même dans « l'autonomie de la *volonté, la méthode principale du droit à la mobilité internationale* », *op.cit.* p. 284 et s.

6 V. Y. Lequette, « Quelques remarques sur le pluralisme en droit de la famille », *in Liber amicorum G. Champenois, Defrénois* 2012, p. 523 et s.

pas être sans effet en droit international privé[7]. Ainsi, de plus en plus souvent, le droit international privé laisse aux personnes une option de législation. Déjà en 1987 l'Institut de Droit international avait proposé qu'une option soit possible entre loi nationale et loi du domicile[8] ; cette option a de nouveau été proposée par l'Institut en 2005 spécifiquement en matière familiale[9]. Certains auteurs ont développé cette idée d'une possible autonomie de la volonté en matière de statut personnel[10]. L'idée est maintenant retenue en droit positif par de nombreuses législations[11], et les règlements de Droit international privé de l'Union européenne admettent une option de législation s'agissant du divorce (art. 5 du règlement Rome III), des obligations alimentaires (v. art. 7 et 8 du Protocole de La Haye du 23 novembre 2007 auquel renvoie l'art. 15 du règlement 4/2009) ou encore des successions (art. 22 du règlement 650/2012) ; et il en sera de même pour les régimes matrimoniaux (art. 16 de la proposition du 16 mars 2011). La convention de La Haye de 1989 sur la loi applicable aux successions avait déjà admis cette *professio juris.*

Il ne s'agit pas d'une liberté totale de choix comme celle admise pour les contrats mais d'options de législation : le législateur national, européen ou international propose un choix entre diverses lois qui ont toutes un rattachement objectif avec la situation en cause (loi de la nationalité ou de la résidence habituelle d'une des personnes en cause, résidence actuelle ou dernière résidence habituelle, loi du for etc.). C'est qu'en effet, pour le statut personnel, il est apparu impossible de laisser les parties choisir n'importe quelle loi, car le rattachement à un ordre juridique étatique reste fort. Il peut s'agir d'un Etat auquel la personne est liée par sa nationalité, ou par sa résidence habituelle actuelle ou passée, mais un lien (de souveraineté ou de territorialité) est nécessaire. De plus, le droit international privé a toujours à sa disposition les outils traditionnels de l'ordre public pour lutter contre des agissements prohibés par le droit français (par exemple pour refuser de reconnaître des actes d'état civil étrangers établis à la suite d'une gestation pour

---

7 V.P. Courbe, « L'influence des réformes du droit de la famille sur le droit international privé », *in Liber amicorum H. Gaudemet-Tallon,* Dalloz 2008, p. 703.

8 *Annuaire de l'Institut*, session du Caire.

9 *Annuaire de l'Institut*, session de Cracovie, résolution « Différences culturelles et ordre public en droit international privé de la famille », adoptée après le rapport de P. Lagarde.

10 V. par exemple, C. Labrusse, « La compétence et l'application des lois nationales face au phénomène de l'immigration étrangère », *Trav. Com.fr.DIP* 1975-1977, p. 111 ; J.-Y. Carlier, *Autonomie de la volonté et statut personnel*, Bruylant 1992 ; P. Gannagé, « La pénétration de l'autonomie de la volonté dans le droit international privé de la famille », *Rev .crit.DIP* 1992, p. 425 et s. Est très réservé sur le rôle de la volonté en droit international privé de la famille, D. Bureau, « L'influence de la volonté individuelle sur les conflits de lois », *in L'avenir du Droit, Mélanges en l'honneur de F. Terré*, Dalloz 1999, p. 285 et s.

11 V. par exemple, l'art. 9.2 du Code civil espagnol, l'art. 55.2 de la loi belge du 16 juillet 2004.

autrui[12] ou d'une adoption par un couple homosexuel[13]) et des lois de police (qui s'imposeront s'agissant de mesures d'assistance éducative à l'égard de mineurs se trouvant en France).

Ainsi, finalement le droit international privé concilie de façon assez heureuse l'autonomie de la volonté des intéressés et le maintien d'une empreinte étatique justifiée.

Mais le droit international privé de la famille doit faire face à une autre difficulté : l'influence croissante des « droits de l'homme ».

B. L'AFFIRMATION DES DROITS DE L'HOMME

Les droits de l'homme (et nous incluons sous ce vocable les « droits fondamentaux »[14]) sont proclamés dans de nombreux instruments nationaux, européens[15] et internationaux, instruments bien connus qu'il est inutile de détailler. Le respect de ces droits conduit parfois à écarter l'application classique du droit international privé.

Une première manifestation de l'influence des droits de l'homme se révèle dans ce qu'on a appelé la « clause spéciale d'ordre public » qui a pour but de reconnaître un droit à une personne ayant des liens de proximité avec le for (nationalité ou résidence) alors que la loi désignée par la règle de conflit la priverait de ce droit. Ainsi la Cour de cassation française a jugé qu'une femme française et résidant en France avait droit au divorce même si la loi désignée par la règle de conflit ignorait le divorce[16], ou qu'un enfant français ou résidant habituellement en France avait le droit de voir sa filiation établie même si la loi désignée par la règle de conflit

12 Cass. civ. 1ère 6 avril 2011, pourvoi n° 10-19053, ép. Mennesson, *Rev.crit.DIP* 2011, 722, 1ère esp. note P. Hammje ; *Rev.trim.dr.civ.* 2011, 340, obs. J. Hauser ; *contra* CA Rennes 21 fév. 2012, *D.* 2012, AJ. 878, obs. A. Minkovic ; *Rev.trim.dr.civ.* 2012, 304, obs. J. Hauser ; *AJFam.* 2012, 226 obs. Siffrein-Blanc.

13 Cass. civ. 1ère 7 juin 2012, deux arrêts, n° pourvoi 11-30261 et 11-30262, qui invoquent les « principes essentiels du droit français » ; *D.* 2012, p. 1992, note D. Vigneau et les articles de L. d'Avout p. 1973 et F. Millet, p. 1975 ; *Rev.trim.dr.civ.* 2012, 522, obs. J. Hauser. Cette jurisprudence est appelée à changer si le législateur français, comme il en est fortement question (décembre 2012) admet le mariage entre personnes de même sexe.

14 V. P. Kinsch, *Droits de l'homme, droits fondamentaux et droit international privé, Rec. cours Acad. La Haye,* tome 318, 2005 ; F. Marchadier, *Les objectifs généraux du droit international privé à l'épreuve de la Convention européenne des droits de l'homme*, Bruylant 2007, préf. J.-P. Marguénaud.

15 Sous ce terme d' « européens », il faut inclure aussi bien la Convention de sauvegarde des droits de l'homme et des libertés fondamentales du Conseil de l'Europe (1950) que la Charte des droits fondamentaux de 2000 adoptée par l'Union européenne. Sur la cohérence entre ces deux textes, *Charte des droits fondamentaux et Convention européenne des droits de l'homme*, Bruylant 2012 (dir. L. Coutron et C. Picheral).

16 Cass. civ. 1ère , 1er avril 1981, *JDI* 1981, 812, note D. Alexandre. Et déjà avec la même inspiration, Cass. civ. 8 mars 1938, Fontaine, *Rev.crit.DIP* 1938, 653, note H. Batiffol ; *DP* 1939.I.17, note

l'en empêchait[17]. Cette clause spéciale d'ordre public figure aussi dans des lois de droit international privé. On citera, à titre d'exemple l'article 17 al. 1 EGBGB (permettant le divorce si l'époux demandeur est de nationalité allemande)[18].

L'emprise des droits de l'homme sur le droit international privé se manifeste encore lorsque le juge s'estime compétent et applique sa loi sans que les règles de conflits de juridictions ou de conflits de lois soient évoquées. C'est alors l'idée de « mise en œuvre sans condition des droits fondamentaux... »[19] qui s'impose. Une illustration parfaite en est donnée par l'arrêt *Moukarim* : la Cour de cassation décide que les juges français sont compétents et la loi française applicable pour connaître du sort d'une jeune nigériane qui était seulement de passage en France et avait réussi à échapper à ses employeurs britanniques qui la tenaient en esclavage[20]. Dans le même ordre d'idée, la Conférence de La Haye avait proposé dans son avant-projet de convention sur la compétence et les jugements étrangers la possibilité pour un Etat d'exercer sa compétence pour les actions civiles fondées sur une violation des droits de l'homme (art. 18-3)[21] dès lors que le demandeur se trouvait dans cet Etat. Et les Etats-Unis ont une règle analogue avec *l'Alien Tort Claims Act*[22].

Le droit de la nationalité, bien que relevant en principe du législateur national, peut être affecté par la Convention européenne des droits de l'homme puisque la

Nast ; *Grands arrêts de la jurisprudence française de Droit international privé,* par B. Ancel et Y. Lequette, Dalloz 5ème éd. 2006, n° 17.

17 Cass. civ. 1ère 10 fév. 1993, *Rev.crit.DIP* 1993, 620 note J. Foyer ; *JDI* 1994, 124, 1ère esp. note I. Barrière-Brousse.

18 V. aussi l'art. 46 du décret-loi hongrois n° 13/1979 sur le droit international privé, privilégiant la loi hongroise pour régir la filiation et les obligations alimentaires concernant un enfant hongrois ; ou encore, pour le divorce, l'art. 61 para. 3 de la LDIP suisse faisant prévaloir la loi suisse lorsque la loi nationale est prohibitive et que l'un des époux est suisse.

19 J. Guillaumé, *op.cit.* n° 885.

20 Cass. soc. 10 mai 2006, *Rev.crit.DIP* 2006, 856, note E. Pataut et P. Hammje ; *JCP* 2006.II.10121, note S. Bollée ; *Rev.des Contrats* 2006, 1260, note P. Deumier ; *JDI* 2007, 531, note J.-M. Jacquet ; *D.* 2007, Pan. 1751, obs. P. Courbe.

21 Sur ce sujet, v. C. Kessedjian, « Les actions civiles pour violation des droits de l'homme. Aspects de droit international privé », *Trav.Com.fr.DIP* 2002-2004, p. 151. Il faut rappeler ici l'arrêt de la Cour internationale de justice dans l'affaire *Allemagne c. Italie* du 3 février 2012, qui a estimé que l'immunité juridictionnelle de l'Etat allemand s'opposait à ce que la justice italienne connaisse de la demande de victimes du travail forcé pendant la seconde guerre mondiale, et de l'exequatur d'une décision grecque qui condamnait l'Allemagne à des réparations envers de telles victimes : l'immunité l'emporte sur un « droit fondamental ». V. l'article de H. Muir Watt, « Les droits fondamentaux devant les juges nationaux à l'épreuve des immunités juridictionnelles », *Rev.crit.DIP* 2012, 539 et les obs. de A. Geslin et G. Le Floch, *Chron.de jurisp.de la CIJ, JDI* 2012, p. 1585.

22 H. Muir Watt, « Privatisation du contentieux des droits de l'homme et vocation universelle du juge américain : réflexions à partir des actions en justice des victimes de l'holocauste devant les tribunaux des Etats-Unis », *Rev.internat.dr.comp.* 2003, 883 ; et du même auteur, « Les enjeux de l'affaire Kiobel : la responsabilité des multinationales au regard des droits de l'homme », *Communic. au Comité fr. de DIP du 27 janv. 2012,* à paraître *in Trav. du Comité.*

Cour de Strasbourg, si elle n'a pas proclamé un « droit à la nationalité », n'exclut pas qu'un « refus arbitraire de nationalité puisse, dans certaines conditions poser un problème sous l'angle de l'article 8 de la Convention en raison de l'impact d'un tel refus sur la vie privée de l'intéressé »[23]. Et, combinant l'article 8 à l'article 14 (prohibition des discriminations) la Cour a, dans un autre arrêt[24], condamné Malte qui faisait produire des effets différents en matière de nationalité selon que l'enfant était né dans ou hors mariage. Il serait donc fort possible que l'affirmation de la Cour de cassation française selon laquelle « les articles 8 et 14 de la Convention européenne des droits de l'homme ne peuvent faire échec au droit qu'a chaque Etat de déterminer les conditions d'accès à la nationalité »[25] soit censurée par la Cour de Strasbourg[26].

Enfin on peut voir encore une manifestation de l'influence des droits de l'homme dans le recours systématique, s'agissant des enfants, à la notion d'« intérêt supérieur de l'enfant ». La Convention de New York sur les droits de l'enfant du 26 janvier 1990 dispose en son article 3-1 que « Dans toutes les décisions concernant les enfants... l'intérêt supérieur de l'enfant doit être une considération primordiale ». Il en résultera que tant les règles de conflits de juridictions que les règles de conflits de lois devront être lues et appliquées au regard de cette exigence première : l'intérêt supérieur de l'enfant. Cette notion figure tant dans les conventions de La Haye (v. art. 8 et 22 de la convention de 1996 sur la protection des enfants ainsi que le préambule de la convention de 2007 sur le recouvrement des aliments) que dans la Charte des droits fondamentaux de 2000 (art. 24 al. 2) ou encore dans le règlement communautaire Bruxelles IIbis (art. 15). La Cour européenne des droits de l'homme a jugé qu'il fallait appliquer l'article 13 b) de la convention de La Haye de 1980 sur les enlèvements d'enfant sous l'angle de l'intérêt de l'enfant au sens de l'article 3 de la Convention européenne des droits de l'homme[27]. On peut reprocher à la notion d'être assez vague, et surtout cet intérêt supérieur de l'enfant risque d'être apprécié de façon

23 CEDH 12 janv. 1999, req. 31414/96, *Karassev c. Finlande.*

24 CEDH 11 octobre 2011, req. 53124/09, *Genovese c. Malte*, sur lequel v. F. Marchadier, *Rev.crit.DIP*, 2012, 61.

25 Cass. civ. 1ère 14 mars 2012, pourvoi n° 11-15290, *Rev.crit.DIP* 2012, p. 553, note F. Marchadier.

26 En ce sens, note F. Marchadier préc. spéc. p. 558 à 560.

27 V. spéc. CEDH 6 déc. 2007, Req. n° 39388/05, *Maumousseau and Washington c. France,* avec l'article de F. Marchadier à la *Rev.crit.DIP* 2007, p. 677 et s. Et sur ce que l'art. 13 b) de la convention de La Haye de 1980 sur l'enlèvement d'enfants intègre implicitement une référence à l'intérêt de l'enfant, v. A. Bucher, La famille en droit international privé, *Cours spécial Acad. La Haye tome 283 (2000),* spéc. N 47 ; La dimension sociale du droit international privé, *Cours général Acad. La Haye,* tome 341 (2009), n° 294 et du même auteur, « L'intérêt de l'enfant pénètre la convention sur l'enlèvement », *in Liber amicorum H. Gaudemet-Tallon,* Dalloz 2008, p. 683 et s.

différente selon l'autorité saisie et selon l'affaire en cause[28]; il n'en demeure pas moins qu'il est heureux que l'intérêt de l'enfant puisse éventuellement tenir en échec toute règle de conflit de juridictions ou de conflit de lois dont l'application se révèlerait malheureuse dans un cas donné.

On constate ainsi que les droits de l'homme, dans la mesure où ils ont vocation à s'appliquer à tout individu, obligent les règles de droit international privé à s'effacer si leur mise en œuvre ne garantit pas correctement la protection du droit en cause[29].

Mais le droit international privé doit relever non seulement le défi de l'individualisme mais aussi celui de la mondialisation.

II. LE DROIT INTERNATIONAL PRIVÉ DE LA FAMILLE AU DÉFI DE LA MONDIALISATION CROISSANTE

La réponse du Droit international privé de la famille à la mondialisation se concrétise à la fois par une plus grande internationalisation des sources (A) et par l'apparition d'une méthode nouvelle, la méthode de la reconnaissance des situations (B).

A. L'INTERNATIONALISATION DES SOURCES

Le droit international privé, et nul ne s'en étonnera, a toujours eu, à côté des sources nationales, des sources internationales importantes. La Conférence de La Haye a joué un rôle particulièrement important à ce sujet puisque sept conventions furent déjà adoptées entre 1893 et 1904, conventions qui ont toutes été remplacées par des conventions plus modernes. Mais ce qui nous paraît significatif est que sur la trentaine de conventions qui figurent dans la dernière édition du recueil publié

---

28 Pour la difficulté qu'il y a à apprécier dans chaque espèce l'intérêt supérieur de l'enfant, v. par ex. : CEDH 15 mars 2012, Req. n° 25951/07, *Gas et Dubois c. France*, *Rev.trim.dr.civ.* 2012, p. 275 obs. J.-P. Marguénaud et p. 306 obs. J. Hauser : selon la Cour, la France a le droit de refuser l'adoption d'un enfant par un couple de lesbiennes. L'intérêt de l'enfant est-il préservé ? (v. les obs. J.-P. Marguénaud) ; ou encore CEDH 4 oct. 2012, req. n° 43631/09, *D.* 2012, 2392 ; N. Fricero, *Procédures 2012, comm. 327* : s'agissant d'un enfant recueilli en vertu d'une *kafala*, le refus de l'adoption n'est pas contraire à l'art. 8 de la Convention européenne des droits de l'homme.

29 Pour une étude très complète dans une perspective critique, v. Y. Lequette, « Le droit international privé et les droits fondamentaux », *in Libertés et droits fondamentaux*, 18ème éd. Dalloz 2012 (dir. R.Cabrillac, M.-A. Frison-Roche et T. Revet) p. 115 et s. On se reportera aussi au bel article prémonitoire de Ph. Francescakis, « Droit naturel et Droit international privé », *in Mélanges offerts à J. Maury*, Dalloz & Sirey 1960, tome 1 p. 113 et s.

par le Bureau Permanent de la Conférence[30], dix-huit portent sur des questions de droit de la famille (patrimonial ou extrapatrimonial) auxquelles il faut ajouter le protocole du 23 novembre 2007 concernant aussi le droit de la famille (protocole sur la loi applicable aux obligations alimentaires) ; en particulier, de 1989 à 2007, ce sont cinq conventions et un protocole qui ont été adoptés en matière familiale, textes pour lesquels le rôle de Hans van Loon a été déterminant[31]. On notera que quatre de ces conventions concernent des personnes méritant une protection spéciale[32] : l'enfant, le majeur incapable, le créancier d'aliments, autant d'individus particulièrement vulnérables sur la scène internationale et pour lesquels le droit étatique ne peut suffire.

Ce développement des sources non-étatiques est également flagrant au niveau régional de l'Union européenne. Si l'on discute encore de la légitimité de l'intervention du législateur communautaire, ce paraît être un débat déjà dépassé. En effet les règlements européens concernant le droit international privé de la famille se sont multipliés : dès 2000, le règlement Bruxelles II traitait de la compétence et de la reconnaissance des jugements en matière de divorce et de responsabilité parentale à l'égard d'enfants communs dans la mesure où la question de responsabilité parentale était liée au divorce, texte rapidement remplacé en 2003 par le règlement Bruxelles IIbis qui s'étend à toutes les questions de responsabilité parentale concernant tous les enfants. Plus récemment le règlement 4/2009 de 2008 régit le droit international privé[33] des obligations alimentaires, le règlement Rome III du 20 décembre 2010 décide de la loi applicable au divorce et le règlement 650/2012 du 4 juillet 2012 établit un droit international privé européen des successions. Et sont encore à venir un règlement sur le droit international privé des régimes matrimoniaux[34] et un autre sur celui des effets patrimoniaux des partenariats enregistrés[35].

Dorénavant, devant statuer dans un litige à caractère international, le juge aura le plus souvent à appliquer, non pas le droit international privé du for, mais telle ou telle convention internationale, tel ou tel règlement communautaire. Et la meilleure façon de résoudre les litiges internationaux en matière familiale n'est-elle pas d'avoir un droit international privé de source internationale (ou au moins régionale) afin d'éviter que les réponses diffèrent selon le juge saisi ? Reste

---

30 *Recueil* édité par le Bureau Permanent de la Conférence (1951-2009) : le statut de la Conférence, 37 conventions et un protocole.

31 Rappelons que H. van Loon, entré comme Secrétaire à la Conférence de La Haye en 1978, en devint le Premier Secrétaire en 1988, et Secrétaire Général depuis 1996.

32 Convention de 1993 sur l'adoption, de 1996 sur la protection des enfants, de 2000 sur la protection des adultes et de 2007 sur le recouvrement international des aliments.

33 L'expression « droit international privé » signifie que le règlement traite à la fois de la compétence judiciaire, de la loi applicable et de la reconnaissance des jugements.

34 Proposition de la Commission du 16 mars 2011, COM (2011) 126 final.

35 Proposition de la Commission du 16 mars 2011, COM (2011) 127 final.

que la coexistence de sources à vocation universelle telles que les conventions de La Haye et de sources régionales telles que les règlements européens dont la portée est nécessairement plus limitée risque de soulever des difficultés. Il y a toutefois déjà des efforts de coordination louables. Par exemple, pour déterminer la loi applicable en matière d'obligations alimentaires le règlement 4/2009 renvoie purement et simplement au Protocole de La Haye du 23 novembre 2007 ; et s'agissant de la reconnaissance des décisions, le chapitre IV du règlement 4/2009 établit deux régimes selon que la décision a été rendue dans un Etat membre de l'UE lié ou non par le Protocole de La Haye[36].

Certains Etats ont bien compris l'utilité des sources internationales et les ont parfois intégrées dans leur droit étatique : c'est le cas de la Suisse dont la loi fédérale sur le Droit international privé de 1987 intègre les conventions ratifiées par la Suisse dès lors que ces conventions s'appliquent sans exiger ni réciprocité ni lien particulier du rapport juridique avec un Etat contractant[37]. Allant encore plus loin le législateur italien en 1995 a eu recours à la technique de la « référence amplifiante »[38] : ainsi a-t-il été décidé (art. 42) que la protection des mineurs serait *dans tous les cas* soumise à la Convention de La Haye de 1961 et que la loi applicable aux obligations alimentaires d'origine familiale (art. 45) serait *dans tous les cas* déterminée par la Convention de La Haye de 1973. Récemment, le 19 mai 2011[39], la loi néerlandaise sur le droit international privé indique, à plusieurs reprises, que ses articles sont destinés à mettre en œuvre telle ou telle convention internationale ou tel ou tel règlement communautaire[40] ; cette omniprésence des sources internationales dans la loi du 19 mai 2011 n'étonne pas si l'on observe que les Pays-Bas sont l'Etat qui a ratifié le plus de conventions de La Haye.

---

36 V. aussi la coordination entre le règlement Bruxelles IIbis et la Convention de La Haye de 1996 sur la protection des mineurs (art. 61 du règlement Bruxelles IIbis) ; ou encore entre le règlement Bruxelles IIbis et la Convention de La Haye de 1980 sur l'enlèvement international d'enfants (art. 11 du règlement Bruxelles IIbis).

37 V. A. Bucher, « La LDIP et les conventions internationales », *in Mélanges en l'honneur du Professeur Von Overbeck*, Fribourg 1990, p. 265 et s.

38 A. Giardina, « Les caractères généraux de la réforme », *Rev.crit.DIP* 1996, p. 1 et s.

39 V. la traduction française du texte in *Rev.crit.DIP* 2012, p. 674 pour les Dispositions générales, la suite de la loi devant paraître dans le n°4/2012 de cette même revue.

40 Mise en œuvre de la convention de Munich (CIEC) de 1980 sur la loi applicable au nom et au prénom (art. 18) ; mise en œuvre des Conventions de La Haye de 1978 sur la reconnaissance du mariage et sur la loi applicable aux régimes matrimoniaux (art. 37 et 43) ; mise en œuvre de la convention de La Haye de 1970 sur la reconnaissance des divorces (art. 54) ; on relèvera aussi l'art. 113, qui dispose que la protection des enfants est régie par la Convention de La Haye de 1961 (qui sera dorénavant la convention de 1996), par le règlement Bruxelles IIbis, et par la loi du 16 février 2006 « portant mise en œuvre des instruments internationaux en matière de protection internationale de l'enfance » ; l'art. 114 sur l'enlèvement d'enfants renvoie aux conventions de Luxembourg du 20 mai 1980, de La Haye du 25 octobre 1980 et au règlement Bruxelles II bis. Citons enfin l'art. 115 sur la loi applicable aux obligations alimentaires qui renvoie au Protocole de La Haye du 23 nov. 2007 ainsi qu'aux conventions de La Haye de 1956 et de 1973.

Le développement des sources internationales, même s'il engendre de nouvelles difficultés qui ne sont pas toutes résolues, semble constituer la réponse adéquate à la mondialisation croissante : personnes et familles vivant des situations internationales sont de plus en plus difficilement rattachées à un ordre étatique unique ; plutôt que d'avoir à gérer au mieux la coexistence, au pire la confrontation, entre sources étatiques différentes, il paraît préférable d'avoir recours à des sources internationales dont l'effet unificateur est bénéfique.

C'est aussi cette mondialisation croissante qui contribue au développement d'une méthode nouvelle, celle de la reconnaissance des situations.

B. UNE MÉTHODE NOUVELLE : LA RECONNAISSANCE DES SITUATIONS

A côté de la reconnaissance des décisions judiciaires, phénomène bien connu et étudié depuis longtemps, est apparue à l'aube du XXIème siècle une nouvelle méthode : celle de la reconnaissance des situations. De nombreux écrits y sont déjà consacrés en France et à l'étranger. Après avoir rappelé brièvement en quoi consiste cette méthode, et en me limitant toujours au droit de la famille, je voudrais montrer comment elle est une réponse à la mondialisation[41].

Il s'agit de donner effet à une situation qui s'est constituée à l'étranger sans avoir nécessairement fait l'objet d'un jugement. Parfois cette situation se sera « cristallisée »[42] par l'intervention d'une autorité publique étrangère (par exemple la célébration d'un mariage) ; on peut aussi imaginer des cas dans lesquels il n'y a pas eu intervention d'une quelconque autorité, mais la situation aura été vécue à l'étranger et on devra la reconnaître en France (par exemple la qualité d'enfant de telle ou telle personne établie par la simple possession d'état[43]). La caractéristique de cette méthode est de « se passer d'un critère déterminé de validité au regard

---

41 En me limitant à certains articles particulièrement importants en langue française, je citerai : P. Lagarde, « Développements futurs du droit international privé dans une Europe en voie de formation : quelques conjectures », *RabelsZ* 2004, 225 ; et du même auteur, « La reconnaissance mode d'emploi », *in Liber Amicorum H. Gaudemet-Tallon*, Dalloz 2008, p. 481 ; P. Mayer, « Les méthodes de la reconnaissance en droit international privé », *in Mélanges en l'honneur de P. Lagarde*, Dalloz 2005, p. 547 ; G-P. Romano, « La bilatéralité éclipsée par l'autorité. Développements récents en matière d'état des personnes », *Rev.crit.DIP* 2006, p. 457 ; S. Bollée, « Domaine de la méthode de la reconnaissance mutuelle », *Rev.crit. DIP* 2007 p. 307 ; Ch. Pamboukis, « La renaissance-métamorphose de la méthode de la reconnaissance », *Rev.crit.DIP* 2008, p. 513 ; A. Bucher, « De la reconnaissance mutuelle au droit à l'identité », rapport présenté au GEDIP en septembre 2009 et repris dans le *Cours général de La Haye* préc. note 27, p. 282 et s. ; G. Goldstein et H. Muir Watt, « La méthode de la reconnaissance à la lueur de la Convention de Munich du 5 septembre 2007 sur la reconnaissance des partenariats enregistrés », *JDI* 2010,1085.

42 Expression empruntée à P. Mayer, in *Les méthodes de la reconnaissance*, art. préc. note 41.

43 V. D. Bureau et H. Muir Watt, *Droit international privé*, PUF, 2ème éd. 2010, n° 581.

de l'ordre juridique du for »[44] ; et « sans exclure nécessairement tout contrôle de la qualité du rattachement, cette méthode se préoccupe bien plus de l'effectivité des situations acquises que de leur conformité à un paramètre préconçu »[45]. Cette méthode a été adoptée par certaines conventions internationales : la convention de La Haye du 14 mars 1978 (en vigueur mais pas en France) prévoit à son article 9 que « Le mariage qui a été valablement conclu selon le droit de l'Etat de la célébration , ou qui devient ultérieurement valable selon ce droit, est considéré comme tel dans tout Etat contractant sous réserve des dispositions de ce chapitre » ; les conventions de la Commission internationale de l'état civil de Vienne (12 septembre 2000), d'Antalya (16 septembre 2005) et de Munich (5 septembre 2007)[46] admettent, de façon analogue, la reconnaissance respectivement du changement de sexe, du nom et des partenariats enregistrés. La Commission de Bruxelles a publié le 14 décembre 2010 un Livre vert intitulé « Moins de démarches administratives pour les citoyens : promouvoir la libre circulation des documents publics et la reconnaissance des effets des actes de l'état civil »[47] qui montre son intérêt pour cette méthode. On trouve aussi des applications de cette méthode en jurisprudence : la Cour de justice des Communautés européennes l'utilise lorsqu'elle oblige les autorités allemandes à reconnaître le nom d'un enfant de nationalité allemande mais né au Danemark et inscrit au registre d'état civil sous le double nom de son père et de sa mère, conformément à la loi danoise, mais contrairement à la loi allemande[48]. La Cour européenne des droits de l'homme en fait également usage lorsque, dans l'arrêt *Wagner*, elle oblige le Luxembourg à reconnaître une adoption prononcée au Brésil alors que n'a pas été respectée la règle de conflit luxembourgeoise[49] ; et la même juridiction s'en inspire encore dans l'arrêt *Negrepontis-Giannisis*[50] en contraignant la Grèce à reconnaître une adoption prononcée aux Etats-Unis. Dans ce dernier cas la Cour de Strasbourg fonde sa décision non pas sur la seule existence du jugement américain mais sur des facteurs montrant la réalité de la situation vécue. Il ne s'agit donc pas seulement

[44] G. Goldstein et H. Muir Watt, art. préc. note 41, n° 2.

[45] G. Goldstein et H. Muir Watt, art.préc., *eod.loc.*

[46] La convention de Vienne est en vigueur en Espagne et aux Pays-Bas, les conventions d'Antalya et de Munich ne sont pas encore en vigueur. Voir déjà la convention de Luxembourg de 1967 sur la reconnaissance des décisions relatives au lien conjugal (en vigueur dans certains Etats mais pas en France), et la convention de Madrid de 1990 sur la reconnaissance et la mise à jour des livrets d'état civil (en vigueur en France).

[47] COM (2010) 747 final.

[48] CJCE 14 oct. 2008, *Grunkin-Paul,* aff. C-353/06, Europe 2008, comm. n° 431, obs. L. Idot ; *Rev.crit.*DIP 2009, 80 note P. Lagarde : *JDI* 2009, 203, note L. d'Avout ; *D.* 2009, 845, note Fr. Boulanger ; *JCP* 2009.II.10071, note A. Devers.

[49] CEDH 28 juin 2007, *Wagner c. Luxembourg,* D. 2007, 2700, note F. Marchadier ; *Rev.crit.DIP* 2007, 738, note P. Kinsch ; *JDI* 2008, 183, note L. d'Avout.

[50] CEDH 3 mai 2011, *Negrepontis-Giannisis c. Grèce, Rev.crit.DIP* 2011, 889 et l'art. de P. Kinsch p. 817.

de libéraliser les conditions de reconnaissance d'un jugement étranger, mais bien de reconnaître une situation vécue par les personnes en cause. En France, si la méthode n'est pas formellement reconnue, on citera toutefois un jugement du Tribunal de grande instance de Paris du 10 mai 1990 que l'on peut déjà analyser en « reconnaissance » d'un divorce entre un Français et une Thaïlandaise, par simple déclaration des époux devant l'officier d'état civil de Thaïlande à Londres[51]. De plus certaines décisions, en se fondant sur la notion d'ordre public atténué, arrivent au même résultat : reconnaissance d'une situation personnelle créée à l'étranger et étant concrètement vécue par les intéressés. Ainsi, par exemple, la Cour de cassation a admis l'exequatur en France d'un jugement américain qui partageait l'autorité parentale entre deux femmes qui vivaient en couple et avaient eu un enfant[52].

Si se développe cette méthode de la reconnaissance, et particulièrement pour tout ce qui concerne le statut personnel, c'est sans aucun doute parce que la plus grande mobilité des personnes, la « mondialisation » de leurs vies obligeait à trouver cependant le moyen d'assurer la permanence de leur statut personnel[53]. Pendant longtemps c'est la compétence de la loi nationale pour régir le statut personnel qui était destinée à assurer cette permanence. Mais on sait que le rattachement à la nationalité n'a plus les faveurs du droit positif contemporain. On lui préfère souvent le rattachement à la résidence habituelle complété par le jeu de l'autonomie de la volonté (v. *supra* I A), et ce dans un souci de réalisme : la loi de la résidence habituelle ou la loi choisie sont considérées comme devant avoir un lien plus fort avec l'intéressé que la loi nationale. Mais l'inconvénient du rattachement à la résidence habituelle (et à la loi choisie lorsque le choix peut être modifié) est précisément de ne pas assurer la permanence du statut personnel alors que cette permanence reste indispensable. La méthode de la reconnaissance s'avère donc utile pour répondre au défi de la mondialisation. On ne peut mieux faire ici que de citer Paul Lagarde : estimant que le rattachement à la loi nationale envisageait la permanence « de façon abstraite », il poursuit : « A une époque de grande mobilité des personnes, ne faut-il pas considérer la permanence d'une façon plus

---

51 *Rev.crit.DIP* 1991, 391, note H. Muir Watt.

52 Cass. civ.1ère, 8 juillet 2010, pourvoi n° 08-21.740, *Rev.crit. DIP* 2010, 747, note P. Hammje ; *JCP* 2010 II 1502, obs. A. Devers et p.2216, note Fulchiron ; *Rev.trim.dr.civ.* 2010, 547, obs. J. Hauser. Mais il peut aussi y avoir refus de reconnaissance : v. par ex. Cass. civ. 1ère, 1er décembre 2011, pourvoi n° 10-27864, *Rev.crit.DIP* 2012, 339, note crit. P. Lagarde : la Cour estime que l'ordre public s'oppose à ce qu'un mariage polygamique en Algérie, alors qu'un premier mariage en France avec une Française n'était pas dissous, produise effet en France ; ou encore Civ. 1ère 7 juin 2012 préc. note 13.

53 Dans la discussion actuelle en France quant à l'admission du « mariage pour tous » (v. le projet de loi du 7 novembre 2012) un argument en faveur de la possibilité de mariage entre personnes du même sexe est la difficulté à laquelle on se heurte en refusant de reconnaître le mariage d'un Français célébré à l'étranger avec une personne du même sexe.

concrète ? Si un événement affectant le statut d'une personne s'est effectivement produit dans un Etat donné, comme l'attribution d'un nom, la conclusion d'un mariage ou d'un partenariat, le besoin de permanence se porte sur cet événement et demande qu'il soit reconnu dans les autres Etats dans lesquels la personne concernée possède ou possèdera des liens »[54].

Cette méthode de la reconnaissance, dont les contours et le mécanisme devront encore être précisés, permettra donc au droit international privé de la famille de mieux s'adapter à la nouvelle donne internationale. Dans la mesure où personnes et familles se déplacent de plus en plus souvent et de plus en plus facilement et où pourtant le statut de la personne et de sa famille ne doivent pas changer avec chaque franchissement de frontière, la reconnaissance des situations devrait se révéler une réponse utile à la mondialisation.

Ainsi, comme toute branche du droit, le droit international privé de la famille s'adapte aux grandes tendances qui caractérisent le monde en ce début de siècle : l'individualisme qui se concrétise par la prise en compte de plus en plus fréquente de la volonté individuelle et l'affirmation des droits de l'homme ; mais aussi la mondialisation avec l'essor des sources internationales et le développement de la méthode de la reconnaissance. Hans van Loon de par sa personnalité et de par ses fonctions à la Conférence de La Haye a joué un rôle essentiel dans cette adaptation et les juristes du monde entier lui en sauront gré.

Décembre 2012

[54] Art. préc. *in Liber amicorum H. Gaudemet-Tallon*, spéc. n° 13 p. 491. V. dans le même sens A. Bucher, *Cours général* préc. note 27, n° 197 et s., 222 et s. ; M. Ho-Dac, *La loi du pays d'origine en droit de l'Union européenne*, Bruylant 2012, préf. S. Sana-Chaillé de Néré, spéc. n° 728 et s.

THE FRUITS OF THE JUDGMENTS PROJECT

David GODDARD QC
Barrister, New Zealand

The Hague Conference's Judgments Project had its origins in a 1992 proposal to undertake work towards a "mixed convention" on jurisdiction and enforcement of judgments in civil and commercial matters.[1] Almost 10 years later, in 2001, a Diplomatic Conference prepared an "Interim Text" which reflected the considerable progress made on many issues, but which also identified significant differences of view that remained on a number of key issues. Following that Diplomatic Conference a decision was made not to continue work on the broader project, but rather to focus on specific issues where agreement was likely to be achieved.

Although the Judgments Project did not result in the single comprehensive mixed convention that was originally contemplated, it has been a fruitful source of inspiration for further work in the field. The purpose of this paper is to describe some of the progeny of the Judgments Project: those that have already come into existence, and those that are yet to come.

THE JUDGMENTS PROJECT: AN OVERVIEW

The objective of the Judgments Project was to prepare a multilateral convention on jurisdiction and judgments applicable to all civil and commercial proceedings, inspired by the Brussels and Lugano Conventions. The basic structure envisaged was a "mixed convention" which addressed both jurisdiction and judgments, with:

1 See P Beaumont, "Hague Choice of Court Agreement 2005: Background, Negotiations, Analysis and Current Status" (2009) 5 *Journal of Private International Law* 125; R A Brand and P M Herrup, *The 2005 Hague Convention on Choice of Court Agreements* (Cambridge University Press, 2008) esp at 5–10.

- a white list of required grounds of jurisdiction;
- a black list of prohibited grounds of jurisdiction;
- provision for the exercise of grounds of jurisdiction provided for under national law that were not on the white list or the black list (sometimes referred to as a "grey list" – though no list of such grounds was to be included in the Convention);
- rules governing parallel proceedings;
- provision for enforcement and recognition of judgments given by a court of a contracting state with white list jurisdiction (coupled with a prohibition on enforcement/recognition of judgments founded on black list grounds).

The interim text arrived at by a Diplomatic Conference in 2001 contained hundreds of square bracketed provisions, reflecting unresolved differences of opinion on how best to address a range of issues. It seemed most unlikely that some of those differences could be bridged. But there was a core set of issues that seemed more likely to be tractable, and an informal Working Group was established to recommend which of these should be the subject of future work.

The Working Group proposed further work on choice of court clauses in commercial contracts, and prepared a draft text of a choice of court convention. That proposal resulted in the adoption of the Choice of Court Convention in 2005.

THE CHOICE OF COURT CONVENTION

The Convention on Choice of Court Agreements is the best known offshoot of the Judgments project.[2] The goals of the Choice of Court Convention have been described by the Permanent Bureau as:

- providing legal certainty and predictability with respect to choice of court agreements;
- becoming the litigation equivalent of the 1958 New York Convention on the Recognition and Enforcement of Foreign Arbitral Awards.

The Choice of Court Convention applies to civil and commercial matters, with certain exclusions including consumer and employment contracts. In broad outline, the Convention:

- introduces a presumption that an agreement designating the court of a contracting state as the forum for resolution of disputes between the parties

[2] Www.hcch.net/index_en.php?act=conventions.text&cid=98.

is exclusive, unless the agreement provides otherwise (reversing the current common law presumption);
- requires a court designated in an exclusive choice of court agreement (the chosen court) to hear the dispute;
- requires a non-chosen court to suspend or dismiss proceedings;
- provides for recognition and enforcement of final decisions of the chosen court;
- includes an optional regime for recognition and enforcement of judgments founded on a non-exclusive choice of court agreement.

The Convention is not yet in force at the time of writing (January 2013), but has been signed by the U.S. and the EU and acceded to by Mexico. Ratification by the EU is expected in the near future. Implementing legislation is being prepared in the U.S. A number of other states are actively working towards ratification. The Convention will come into force when two States have ratified, or acceded to, the Convention.

THE TRANS-TASMAN PROCEEDINGS REGIME

A regional initiative whose roots can also be traced to the Judgments Project is the Trans-Tasman Proceedings regime.[3] In 2003, recognising the importance of the objectives of the Judgments Project, and conscious that any multilateral instrument in this field would take time to develop and would fall short of what could be achieved in the trans-Tasman context, the Governments of Australia and New Zealand established a Working Group to look at the potential for adoption of a trans-Tasman regime for allocation of forum and enforcement of judgments, based on the Australian inter-state arrangements set out in the Service and Execution of Process Act 1992 (Cth) (SEPA). The Working Group reported in 2006, recommending a trans-Tasman regime broadly along these lines.[4] In the words of the Working Group Final Report:

> The Working Group's central recommendation is that a 'trans-Tasman regime', modelled on the *Service and Execution of Process Act 1992* (Cth), be introduced as

---

[3] Indeed its earliest seeds were sown at a Judgments Project meeting in Ottawa in 2001, in discussions between the writer and the late Dr Peter Nygh of Australia. See also David Goddard, "Trans-Tasman Legal Coordination – The Next Frontiers" (paper presented to Australian and New Zealand Society of International Law Conference 2003, Wellington NZ) available at http://law.anu.edu.au/anzsil/conferences/2003/2003proceedings.pdf.

[4] Www.ema.gov.au/www/agd/agd.nsf/Page/Publications_Trans-TasmanCourtProceedingsandRegulatoryEnforcement-December2006.

> between the two countries. The proposed regime would allow initiating process in civil proceedings issued out of a court in Australia or New Zealand to be served in the other country, with the same effect as if service had occurred in the country of issue. Currently, a range of judgments of Australian and New Zealand courts can be registered and enforced by a court in the other country. We propose that the range of enforceable judgments be broadened, and that judgments only be refused enforcement if they conflict with the public policy of the other country.
>
> The proposed trans-Tasman regime would be supported by wider use of teleconference and video link technology to enable remote appearances in trans-Tasman proceedings. The Working Group recommends that, for appearances in civil proceedings, a party in the other country (and their lawyer) be allowed to appear by telephone or video link with the leave of the court in most cases, and as of right in an application for a stay of proceedings, on the grounds that a court in the other country is more appropriate to decide the dispute.
>
> Some of the Working Group's recommendations would improve regulatory enforcement between Australia and New Zealand. Civil pecuniary penalties from one country would be enforceable in the other unless specifically excluded. Criminal fines imposed for certain regulatory offences in one country would be enforceable in the other in the same way as a civil judgment debt.

A treaty giving effect to these recommendations was signed in July 2008, and legislation to implement the arrangement has been enacted in both New Zealand and Australia. The new trans-Tasman arrangement is expected to come into force in 2013, when the necessary rules of court have been finalised.

Key features of the arrangement include:

- the plaintiff can serve civil proceedings issued in one country in the other country, without the need to establish any particular connection between the proceedings and the forum;
- the defendant can apply for a stay of proceedings on the grounds that a court in the other country is the more appropriate court for the proceeding. This *forum conveniens* approach applies in all proceedings except where there is an exclusive choice of court agreement to which the Hague Choice of Court Convention would apply: the legislation requires that such clauses be respected by the parties;
- a judgment from one country can be registered in the other. It will have the same force and effect, and can be enforced, as a judgment of the court where it is registered;
- a judgment can be refused enforcement in the other country only on public policy grounds. Other grounds, such as breach of natural justice, would have to be raised with the original court;

- a judgment can only be varied, set aside or appealed in the court of origin. The court of registration would be able to stay enforcement to allow this to happen;
- all final civil judgments, including non-money judgments, will come under this regime (with a small list of exceptions, and the potential to add to these by agreement over time);
- civil penalty judgments are enforceable under the regime, unless expressly excluded (there is provision for a "negative list" to be adopted, and added to over time);
- fines for breach of specified regulatory statutes are also enforceable under this regime, as if they were civil judgments in favour of the State in which they were rendered (there is a "positive list" which can be added to over time);
- there is increased provision for parties and counsel to appear by video or telephone link from the other country. There is a right to appear remotely for applications for a stay (without the need for counsel to be admitted in the forum hearing the application). For other remote appearances, the leave of the court is required;
- the existing arrangements for giving evidence remotely between the two countries, which have been in place for some years now and which work well, are expanded and streamlined in a number of respects;
- Australian and New Zealand courts have authority to grant interim relief in support of proceedings in the other country's courts.

The ability of the trans-Tasman working group to reach agreement on these arrangements for civil proceedings without too much difficulty was the product of a number of factors:

- both countries have long experience of a system which is relatively permissive in terms of service of proceedings, with the ability to serve any proceedings in the jurisdiction and broad criteria for service out of the jurisdiction, coupled with a judicial discretion to decline jurisdiction where another court is more appropriate (or, in the context of service abroad of Australian proceedings, clearly more appropriate). The new model has as its foundation this *forum conveniens*-centred approach;
- both countries have a high level of confidence in the ability and willingness of the courts of the other country to apply a structured discretion in relation to the grant of a stay;
- both countries have a high level of confidence in the ability of the courts of the other country to address, through appeals or other mechanisms, concerns about process issues raised in relation to a judgment given in that country;
- travel between the two countries is relatively simple and inexpensive;

- there are effective arrangements for giving evidence between the two countries;
- there is a reasonable level of comfort that remote appearances by parties and counsel can be made to work, at least for preliminary hearings;
- Australia has had some 15 years' experience with the SEPA model, and few concerns have been encountered in practice in relation to civil proceedings and judgments.

The provisions on enforcement of civil penalties and fines are the product of these factors coupled with extensive economic links and a commitment to developing a trans-Tasman "Single Economic Market", which make cooperation on these dimensions important, and have fostered a high level of regulatory coordination.

It would be difficult to extend the trans-Tasman approach to civil proceedings to other countries in the absence of the special factors identified above. In particular, it seems unlikely that this model could be extended to the many countries that do not already employ a *forum conveniens* approach to the regulation of exercise of jurisdiction. It is possible that there will be a gradual extension of the trans-Tasman regime over time, but it does not provide a template for a global arrangement. Rather, it illustrates the potential for regional arrangements that are inspired by, and build on, multilateral initiatives.

FUTURE PROGENY OF THE JUDGMENTS PROJECT

THE OBJECTIVES OF FURTHER WORK IN THIS FIELD

The objectives that underpinned the Hague Conference's work on the Judgments Project remain at least as compelling now as they were 20 years ago when that project began:

- to ensure that proceedings are determined in an appropriate forum, consistent with the fair and efficient determination of the dispute between the parties;
- to reduce uncertainty in relation to the forum in which a dispute will be heard and determined, and the cost associated with disputes about which forum a dispute should be heard in;
- to facilitate the enforcement of judgments rendered by an appropriate court, and thus enhance certainty and reduce costs associated with cross-border dispute resolution.

These objectives are consistent both with broader access to justice and quality of justice goals, and the more prosaic, but nonetheless very important, goal of reducing uncertainty and costs associated with cross-border dealings, including cross-border trade.

These same objectives underpin the Choice of Court Convention, the Trans-Tasman Proceedings regime, the (recently revised) European instruments on jurisdiction and judgments, and a number of other bilateral and regional initiatives. They also inspire the work that the Commonwealth Secretariat is currently undertaking to develop a new model law for Commonwealth countries on recognition and enforcement of judgments.[5]

However it remains the case that there is no widely ratified global instrument that is designed to pursue these objectives, despite the increasing global interconnectedness that we observe today as a result of increasing cross-border movement of people, increasing cross-border trade, and the global reach of the internet. The importance of these objectives, and the absence of any such global instrument, suggest that useful work remains to be done in this field. What might that work look like?

SOME OPTIONS FOR FUTURE WORK

One possibility is to seek to pick up where the Judgments Project left off, and to continue work on both jurisdiction and judgments. There are some additional heads of jurisdiction (apart from choice of court) that are sufficiently uncontroversial that it may be possible to reach agreement both on the exercise of jurisdiction on those grounds, and on the enforcement of resulting judgments.[6]

The informal working group established by the Hague Conference to suggest a path forward after the 2001 diplomatic conference considered proposals to include in the next round of discussions provisions relating to the defendant's forum, consent/waiver/submission, and counterclaims. These were topics on which considerable progress had been made. However the Working Group considered that in the interests of maximising the prospects of success of future

---

5 A draft model law is expected to be considered by Commonwealth Law Ministers at their 2014 meeting. See Commonwealth Secretariat "Commonwealth Practice in the Recognition of Foreign Judgments" (presented at the Meeting of Senior Officials of Commonwealth Law Ministries, London, 1–3 October 2007); Commonwealth Secretariat, "The Recognition And Enforcement Of Foreign Judgments" (presented at Meeting of Senior Officials of Commonwealth Law Ministries Marlborough House, London, 18–20 October 2010); "Communiqué" (Meeting of Senior Officials of Commonwealth Law Ministries Marlborough House, London, 20 October 2010). These papers are available at www.thecommonwealth.org/.

6 For a discussion of potential topics for further work prepared shortly after the 2001 Diplomatic Conference see David Goddard, "Rethinking the Judgments Convention – a Pacific Perspective" *Yearbook of Private International Law 2001*, Volume 3 (2001), pp. 27–62.

negotiations, and completing the work within a reasonably short period, the focus of the next round of work should be solely on exclusive choice of court agreements.

So one option for further work would address the remaining issues on that list, and seek to develop a convention which provides that the defendant's home forum will exercise jurisdiction (unless that would be inconsistent with a choice of court agreement), and that judgments given in that forum will be enforced elsewhere. Consent to the exercise of jurisdiction short of a contractual choice of court (eg by submission, or by bringing proceedings in the forum in question on the same matter) also seems a relatively uncontroversial basis for the exercise of jurisdiction, and for the enforcement of resulting judgments, which could be provided for in such a convention. But it may be difficult to extend an agreed "white list" of grounds of jurisdiction much beyond this. And even in this relatively limited sphere, the concerns which influenced the informal Working Group, which would need to be carefully considered before embarking on further work along these lines, include:

- the utility of a convention providing for the exercise of jurisdiction on these grounds. There are few (if any) countries in which these heads of jurisdiction are not available, subject to the ability of the courts to decline jurisdiction on *lis pendens* or *forum non conveniens* grounds;
- the need to regulate the priority of these different grounds of jurisdiction, and more generally to address the circumstances in which a court may, or must, decline to exercise jurisdiction on one of these grounds in favour of proceedings before another court;
- the utility of an enforcement regime confined to these topics alone. Most if not all common law countries enforce money judgments from the defendant's home jurisdiction or from a jurisdiction to which the defendant has submitted, and recognise and give effect to (via estoppel principles) non-money judgments from that jurisdiction – both as against the defendant, and as against the plaintiff (who has submitted to the jurisdiction of the court, by proceeding there). There is a patchwork of treaty arrangements between common law and civilian countries providing for enforcement and recognition of civil and commercial judgments, and where such arrangements exist, they almost invariably provide for enforcement or recognition of judgments in these categories. There would be benefits in having a single modern instrument to govern such enforcement, expanding the number of countries in which judgments given on these grounds are enforced, extending enforcement to non-money judgments, and simplifying and speeding up the process for enforcement of such judgments. But it would be more satisfactory if these benefits could be achieved in a wider set of circumstances, not restricted to this very narrow set of grounds of jurisdiction.

The treatment of non-exclusive choice of court agreements in the Choice of Court Convention suggests another possible path forward – the development of a judgments enforcement convention coupled with one or more "optional chapters" on jurisdiction. The optional "direct" jurisdiction chapter(s) would be coupled with a "core chapter" providing for enforcement and recognition of judgments grounded on a list of acceptable "indirect" heads of jurisdiction. This list of indirect heads of jurisdiction grounding enforcement is likely to be more extensive than any list of direct heads of jurisdiction that could command widespread acceptance.

It seems likely that the opt-in nature of the direct grounds of jurisdiction in the optional chapter(s) would take some of the pressure off the formulation of those grounds. But a number of challenges are likely to remain:

- the issue of declining jurisdiction – in what circumstances is a court with white list jurisdiction permitted or required to decline to exercise that jurisdiction?
- the priority of different grounds of jurisdiction. In practice it is not possible to draft each basis of jurisdiction on a stand-alone basis: they intersect, and some challenging issues arise about the hierarchy that will be applied. If different countries sign up to different chapters, this may become quite complex;
- the strong desire of some States to include a "black list" of prohibited grounds of jurisdiction in any future convention concerned with jurisdiction and judgments.

Another variant on the "optional chapter" approach would be to combine work on a binding instrument in areas where consensus can reasonably readily be achieved with work on a non-binding instrument, such as a model law, in other more challenging areas. The experience of the UNCITRAL Model Law on International Commercial Arbitration[7] suggests that in the field of cross-border dispute resolution a great deal can be achieved by work on a non-binding instrument, which:

- enables countries to share their expertise, and exchange information about their policy goals and their concerns in this field;
- can accommodate a greater degree of difference between participants, especially (but not only) on matters of detail;
- facilitates higher quality domestic laws;
- addresses the capacity issues that affect the ability of many countries to undertake effective domestic law reform in this technical and complex field;

7 Www.uncitral.org/pdf/english/texts/arbitration/ml-arb/06-54671_Ebook.pdf.

- enhances commonality across domestic regimes, reducing information costs and uncertainty.

Work on a model law could potentially include the full range of topics tackled in the original Judgments Project. But even in this context, it would probably be prudent to begin by focusing on areas where progress is likely to be made without too much difficulty, and expanding the scope of the project incrementally, adding new issues as and when each prior set of issues has been successfully addressed.

One issue that would merit careful consideration is the need for reciprocity in any such regime. For many countries, an improved framework for deciding when to exercise jurisdiction, and which judgments to enforce, is desirable even if others do not adopt a similar framework. The goal of assisting such countries would be an important one in any model law drafting exercise: the focus need no longer be on reciprocal enforcement alone (though the model law might include, as an option for countries that prefer to proceed on the basis of reciprocity, a model reciprocity provision).

NEXT STEPS

Work is now under way to explore the potential for a new Hague Convention on enforcement of judgments, and to consider what may be achievable in relation to the regulation of jurisdiction. It would be premature to express a view on the likely scope of that work, let alone to predict its outcome. But I cannot resist proffering three suggestions that are designed to maximise the prospects of success of this work:

- the starting point should be to build consensus by focusing on the topics where agreement can most readily be achieved The scope of the discussions should be expanded to address more complex and more controversial issues only after agreement has been reached on the more tractable core;
- it is important to bear in mind the old adage that the best may be the enemy of the good. If useful steps can be taken towards the objectives identified above, they should be taken even if an ideal outcome cannot be achieved – or at least, cannot be achieved in one step. So for example it may be desirable to have a global judgments convention that extends to all civil and commercial matters: but the challenges of addressing consumer and employment disputes may mean that (following the lead of the Choice of Court Convention) it is more realistic to exclude such matters from the next round of work;
- there is much to be learned from the work that has already been done on the Judgments project, and on the Choice of Court Convention and other Hague

Conference instruments. Other global and regional instruments may also provide useful sources of inspiration. However the challenges of this work are most likely to be met if an open-minded, flexible approach is adopted that builds on, but is not limited by, the experience of the past.

CONCLUDING REMARKS

The brief review in this paper demonstrates that the Judgments Project has already borne significant fruit, both globally and regionally. I am confident that it will continue to do so, and that when the Hague Conference looks back ten years from now on what has been achieved as a result of the Judgments Project, the list will be longer still. The Hague Conference, and its Secretary-General, can be justifiably proud of what has been, and continues to be, built on these foundations.

BUILDING AN INTERNATIONAL COOPERATION SYSTEM FOR THE CIVIL PROTECTION OF CHILDREN

Ignacio Goicoechea
Liaison Legal Officer for Latin America
Hague Conference on Private International Law

Florencia Castro
Legal Assistant to the Liaison Legal Officer for Latin America
Hague Conference on Private International Law

1. WHY SHOULD AN INTERNATIONAL COOPERATION SYSTEM FOR THE CIVIL PROTECTION OF CHILDREN BE BUILT?

A. BACKGROUND

The phenomenon of globalisation has led to an exponential increase in migration and a rise in cases of vulnerable children whose needs cannot be met by a single child protection system. In turn, distance, language and cultural differences and economic constraints often place hurdles in the way of effective access to justice for children and families abroad.

Today, there are countless situations which require the coordinated action of two national child protection systems in order to ensure the effective protection of children. We can mention, *inter alia*, the following:

> International family disputes (custody, contact, relocation abroad, child abduction, parent-child relationships, child support)

In all these situations, it is important to determine which country's child protection system should deal with the dispute; which law should be applied to the case; where necessary, how evidence should be obtained abroad; what sort of cooperation could be expected from the other child protection system (*e.g.*, the recognition of an interim order or the recognition and enforcement of a protective order). It is also important to prevent conflicting court orders being made in two different jurisdictions (*e.g.*, regarding the custody of a child), because, if court orders differ, difficult situations may arise. For example, if two jurisdictions grant physical custody of a child to different persons, contact rights between the parent who does not live with the child and the child might be blocked in practice since, if the child were sent for visitation abroad, the other parent might not return the child and would have a court decision – a custody order – that would entitle him to do so. In turn, if relocation abroad with a child were granted to a parent wishing to relocate, together with contact rights to the non-relocating parent, the non-recognition of such contact rights abroad might hinder the original relocation order. These situations might inadvertently encourage child abductions.

Children found abroad (out of their country of origin or habitual residence) – victims of abandonment, domestic violence, sexual exploitation and sale; non-accompanied, deported, institutionalised, etc.

There are currently many international conventions in criminal matters that deal with the trafficking, sale and sexual exploitation of children. However, children who fall victim to these crimes are quite often simply treated as illegal immigrants and deported. Instead, the child protection system of the country where they have been found should provide them with the immediate necessary protection and then arrange their reintegration into their family or community, in cooperation with the child protection system of their country of origin (or habitual residence). Appropriate assistance to victims of such offences should be ensured, including the adoption of such measures as may be necessary for their social reintegration and their full physical and psychological recovery (as prescribed by the *"Optional Protocol to the Convention on the Rights of the Child on the sale of children, child prostitution and child pornography"*, Article 9, para. 3).

Another example is the situation of children institutionalised abroad in circumstances where their relatives have been denied, for different reasons, their right of access to justice to attempt to recover their children and where the children have been denied their right to be raised by their family or community of origin. In some cases, these children may even be given up for adoption in the country where they have been found, without a proper investigation of the whereabouts of their families and the due consideration of their possible reintegration into their country of origin (*e.g.*, children of deported parents or parents deprived of their liberty).

Placement of children abroad and intercountry adoption

In order to place children for care or adoption abroad, there is a need for effective coordination between the two relevant child protection systems; otherwise, children might be placed in a vulnerable position (*e.g.*, if guardians do not meet the conditions laid down by the authority who placed the child under their care or refuse to return the child; intercountry adoptions which are not recognised in the country of residence of adoptive parents, or children who are abandoned or discriminated against in the country to which they have been taken by their adoptive parents).

B. LIMITATIONS OF NATIONAL CHILD PROTECTION SYSTEMS

We should ask ourselves why national child protection systems cannot deal with the situations described above properly. The answer to this question has to do with different limitations that they have, some of which will be briefly described below:

(i) *Procedural limitations*: in some cases, child protection authorities do not have international jurisdiction to take action. In other situations, due process cannot be granted to all the parties, in particular to those that reside abroad, or the recognition and enforcement of protective orders cannot be granted in the foreign jurisdiction relevant to the case.

(ii) *Lack of co-operation from the relevant operators of the foreign child protection system*: in many cases, there is a need to rely on the co-operation of the foreign child protection system in order to provide effective protection to the child. However, the mechanisms necessary to implement such co-operation are not in place (*e.g.*, to locate the child, produce evidence, implement protective measures, secure access to justice, provide social assistance, etc.).

(iii) *Lack of knowledge of operators:* in many cases, the operators of the child protection system are not cognisant of the proper application of international conventions or such other tools as may help them to address international child protection situations (*e.g.*, to secure co-operation from another child protection system).

(iv) *Lack of resources:* in the child protection field, it is quite common to find institutions which are overburdened with work and lack the necessary human and material resources for the proper operation of the national child protection system. Naturally, this lack of resources has a negative impact on the time taken to address international child protection situations (*e.g.*, long delays due to the lack of human resources and/or suitable means of communication, language barriers, etc.).

C. THE MANDATE OF THE UNITED NATIONS CONVENTION ON THE RIGHTS OF THE CHILD ("CRC" OR "CONVENTION")

The CRC establishes that States are responsible for securing the rights recognised by the Convention and that they must put in place all such cooperation instruments and mechanisms as may be deemed necessary in order to safeguard those rights. The key role of international co-operation for the international protection of children has been highlighted in the very Preamble of the Convention. This co-operation requires coordinated action among the child protection systems of the States involved and, where necessary, the conclusion of agreements in the context of different situations and cross-border disputes.

The need to develop international co-operation for the protection of children can be observed in countless situations enshrined in the CRC. For example, there could be situations linked with compliance with jurisdictional rules, rights of defence and due process. These are the situations which may arise under Articles 9, 10, and 11 of the CRC, where the separation of a child from his parents should only be ordered by "competent" authorities, subject not only to judicial review, but also to the rules of due process. In an international child abduction case, the judge seized to decide on the return might lose sight of his/her field of competence and decide on the merits of a custody case, a matter which falls within the jurisdiction of the Court of the State of habitual residence of the child. In this case, there might be two conflicting custody decisions, which could also jeopardise the exercise of access rights. In these circumstances, we should also be aware of the risk of falling into "parochial" interpretations, in particular, in relation to the interpretation of the notion of the best interests of the child, which calls for a responsible attitude on the part of the systems involved.

In custody, *patria potestas*, relocation or contact cases, the national systems involved should be developed so as to secure due process for the parties and to prevent the existence of detrimental decisions abroad. In particular, where parents do not reside in the same State, this factor should be taken into account and measures should be taken to secure the effective implementation of the order concerning the upbringing of the child (custody, contact, relocation, etc.) in both countries.

In the case provided for under Article 19 of the CRC (protection from all forms of abuse), co-ordination among the relevant child protection systems is required in order to prevent such situations and to provide necessary support for the child and for those who have care of the child.

Migrant children should be protected despite their nationality or migratory status. In turn, when taking protective measures for these children, as appropriate, due consideration should be given to any family available to care for them in their country of origin, for which purpose the coordinated action of the relevant competent authorities of both States involved in the case will be necessary.

In the case of unaccompanied children (refugees, asylum seekers, displaced children or fugitives) or children abandoned abroad, the relevant child protection systems involved should strive to find family who can care for the child in the country of origin and contribute to their safe reintegration into such a country.

Addressing the scourge of sexual exploitation and abuse, and the sale and trafficking of children, calls for the effective co-operation of child protection systems (as is also required by the "*Optional Protocol to the Convention on the Rights of the Child on the sale of children, child prostitution and child pornography*" (Article 10, para. 2)).

Intercountry adoption and the recovery of child support abroad are other clear examples of situations where the co-ordination among child protection systems and the conclusion of international agreements are needed to secure the effective protection of children. As we will discuss below, these situations have already been regulated by the relevant international instruments prepared within the framework of the Hague Conference on Private International Law.

All the different situations described above are just some examples of the multiple occasions where the coordinated action of the different child protection systems involved may be needed in order to secure the international protection of children. Such co-ordination may be required at the administrative or judicial level or simultaneously at both levels.

Furthermore, in addition to the general coordination of the operation of child protection systems, there are specific situations where the CRC mandates States to promote the conclusion of bilateral or multilateral agreements or accession to existing agreements as an effective means to protect children in specific situations (*e.g.*, international child abduction (Article 11), intercountry adoption (Article 21), international recovery of child support (Article 27), abuse and sexual exploitation (Article 34) and kidnapping, sale and trafficking of children (Article 35)). Fortunately, these situations have already been addressed by several international instruments which have developed specific international legal co-operation mechanisms between child protection systems. The ratification of or the accession to these instruments has been recommended by the Committee on the Rights of the Child, through General Comment No 5 (2003) on "*General*

Measures of Implementation for the CRC" (i.e., the 1980 *Hague Convention on the Civil Aspects of International Child Abduction*, the 1993 *Hague Convention on the Protection of Children and Co-operation in Respect of Intercountry Adoption*, and the 1996 *Hague Convention on Jurisdiction, Applicable Law, Recognition, Enforcement and Co-operation in Respect of Parental Responsibility and Measures for the Protection of Children*); and General Comment No 6 (2005) on *"Treatment of unaccompanied and separated children outside their country of origin"* (i.e., the 1993 *Hague Convention on the Protection of Children and Co-operation in Respect of Intercountry Adoption*, and the 1996 *Hague Convention on Jurisdiction, Applicable Law, Recognition, Enforcement and Co-operation in Respect of Parental Responsibility and Measures for the Protection of Children*).

In light of the foregoing considerations, we can conclude that both the text of the CRC and its practical implementation mandate the development by States of international legal co-operation schemes as a means to secure the effective international protection of children. Consequently, States should bear this in mind when considering developing the necessary implementing measures which need to be taken to secure the effective implementation of the Convention.

2. "INTERNATIONAL LEGAL COOPERATION" AS A BASIS FOR AN "INTERNATIONAL COOPERATION SYSTEM FOR THE CIVIL PROTECTION OF CHILDREN"

A. INTERNATIONAL LEGAL COOPERATION AND INTERNATIONAL CHILD PROTECTION CONVENTIONS

In order to provide effective protection to children in situations which require the participation of more than one national protection system, it is necessary to put in place efficient cooperation mechanisms between the different protection systems involved in the case. Basically, we should determine when, and to what extent, a national protection system should participate in a case and how it is supplemented or assisted by the other protection system involved.

This framework should be developed within the scope of the so-called "International Legal Cooperation", which refers to the procedures or mechanisms available to facilitate the force and effect of legal acts or proceedings that must be pursued in a foreign jurisdiction.

In this regard, we consider that the international instruments of legal cooperation intended to facilitate coordination among the different national child protection systems, with the purpose of providing children with effective protection in international situations, are the ones that will constitute the basis of a true "International Cooperation System for Child Protection".

Following the previous terminological clarifications, we can now go on to analyse how this "International Cooperation System for the Protection of Children" is being developed.

First of all, it is worth taking into account that international legal cooperation takes place primarily through international agreements, at the global, regional, sub-regional or bilateral levels. With regard to the international protection of children, international agreements on diverse topics have been developed in different fora. In Latin America, there are several international instruments in force in this field which have been adopted by the United Nations (New York Convention on the Recovery Abroad of Maintenance), the Hague Conference on Private International Law (*Hague Convention of 25 October 1980 on the Civil Aspects of International Child Abduction; Hague Convention of 29 May 1993 on Protection of Children and Co-operation in Respect of Intercountry Adoption; Hague Convention of 19 October 1996 on Jurisdiction, Applicable Law, Recognition, Enforcement and Co-operation in Respect of Parental Responsibility and Measures for the Protection of Children; and Hague Convention of 23 November 2007 on the International Recovery of Child Support and Other Forms of Family Maintenance*), and the Organisation of American States (*Inter-American Convention on the Return of Children, Inter-American Convention on Support Obligations, Inter-American Convention on International Traffic in Minors*). Moreover, some States have developed bilateral agreements in order to address specific topics for the protection of children (*Convention on International Return of Children between the Oriental Republic of Uruguay and the Chile Republic (1982), Convention on International Protection of Children between the Oriental Republic of Uruguay and the Argentine Republic (1982), Convention on international return of children between the government of the Oriental Republic of Uruguay and the Peru Republic (1989)*). All these international instruments constitute the basis of the International Cooperation System for the Protection of Children.

In addition to the texts of the above-mentioned Conventions, a second level of tools for international cooperation, such as handbooks, guides to good practice, and networks of Central Authorities, Judges and contact points, have been developed in a progressive and sustained manner during the past few decades, with the aim of facilitating the effective development of legal cooperation, and consequently, the operation of the International Cooperation System for the Protection of Children.

This second level of tools, mainly networking, facilitates the development of legal cooperation for the international protection of children, both on a horizontal level between the same actors in different States (e.g., Central authorities with

Central Authorities and Judges with Judges), as well as between different actors within the same State (e.g., Central Authorities with Judges and other contact points or actors within the system).

B. THE 1996 HAGUE CONVENTION ON INTERNATIONAL CHILD PROTECTION: GENERAL ARTICULATING MECHANISM

Among the instruments mentioned above, it is worth making special reference to the 1996 Hague Convention on the Protection of Children, owing to its general and broad scope. This instrument was drafted with the aim of providing a practical mechanism of cooperation among States to secure the effective protection of children internationally and, more specifically, to avert conflicts of jurisdiction and applicable law, and to facilitate cooperation and the recognition and enforcement of protective orders among the legal systems involved in situations of international child protection.

The Convention on International Child Protection in a way constitutes the main basis of the International Cooperation System for the Protection of Children and applies to a wide array of situations, such as, *inter alia*, cross-border disputes on custody rights, contact, relocation and parental responsibility; international trafficking in children, child abuse, civil protection of child victims of sale and sexual exploitation; children without parental care (unaccompanied children or children separated from their parents); and the placement of children in institutional or foster care abroad.

The Convention also acts as a supplement to the 1980 Hague Convention on Child Abduction and the 1989 Inter-American Convention on the international return of children, as well as a supplement to the 1993 Hague Convention on Intercountry Adoption.

The rules on jurisdiction included in the Convention provide, as a general principle, that the courts of the country of habitual residence of the child have jurisdiction to take measures directed to the protection of the child's person or property. However, the Convention establishes some exceptions to this principle, such as: in cases of urgency, jurisdiction based on the place where the child or property belonging to the child is present; in cases of wrongful removal or retention of a child, the temporary retention of the jurisdiction of the State in which the child was habitually resident before the wrongful removal or retention; if certain conditions are fulfilled, the jurisdiction of the authorities of the State deciding on an application for divorce; or, by way of exception, the possibility of a transfer of jurisdiction to a court that is better placed to hear the case. All of these exceptions have been established with a view to the paramount consideration of the best interests of the child, which should be assessed by the authority with jurisdiction to order the protective measure in relation to the child.

Furthermore, the Convention also determines the law applicable to the case at issue, adopting as a general principle the application of the *lex fori*. This is clearly convenient as it simplifies the task of operators who will apply their own law rather than a foreign law in order to protect the child. As in the case of jurisdiction, there are certain exceptions to the general principle, all of which are aimed at the more effective protection of the child.

The cooperation mechanism set forth in the Convention focuses on the action of Central Authorities, who are in charge of cooperating – in the broadest sense – with the national authorities with jurisdiction in relation to child protection matters, as well as with the Central Authorities of the other State Parties involved.

Lastly, the Convention establishes a method of recognising and enforcing the measures of protection taken under the Convention. This involves the recognition of measures of protection taken in one Contracting State in all other Contracting States by operation of law. This enables effective coordination to take place between the different protection systems involved.

The advantages of the 1996 Convention have been recognised in different international fora, which have recommended the ratification thereof or accession thereto (the Committee on the Rights of the Child, under General Comments No 5 and 6 mentioned *supra*; the "United Nations Guidelines for the Alternative Care of Children" (para. 138); and the Special Commissions of the Hague Conference on the 1980 Hague Convention on Child Abduction and the 1993 Hague Convention on Intercountry Adoption, which recommend it as a supplement to the instruments mentioned above).

3. CHALLENGES FACING THE BUILDING OF AN INTERNATIONAL COOPERATION SYSTEM FOR THE PROTECTION OF CHILDREN

As has been previously stated, nowadays there are a variety of international instruments on child protection which cover a wide range of dangerous situations for children. This could lead us to conclude that we already have an International Cooperation System for the Protection of Children. However, we believe that we are still at an early stage and, although some of the international instruments on child protection have gradually penetrated into national systems, there are still important challenges to overcome in order to achieve efficient coordination between the different national systems of protection so that the effective protection of children at risk can be ensured.

The different challenges identified could be classified as: (i) policy challenges, related to the development and implementation of conventions or to the creation of such mechanisms as may be necessary for cooperation to be promoted, and (ii) operative challenges, related to the actual operation of the international protection system (this refers to the coordinated operation of national protection systems in international cases).

i. Policy challenges

First, the challenge might appear in the process of selecting the topics that need to be addressed by an international convention or in the drafting stage, which might take years of discussions and analysis. What is more, the process of incorporating a particular Convention into the different national legal systems and its implementation might also constitute a great challenge to the international community.

In order to face the first challenge, both States and international organizations should be mindful of the needs constantly emerging from reality. Communications and migration movements have certainly given rise to new issues in matters related to children which have gradually been addressed by the international legal community. In this regard, a thorough analysis of the new issues arising in the field of international child protection will lead us to determine whether there is a need to develop new instruments of protection in different areas of the protection of children.

The process of State incorporation of an international Convention must be analyzed from different standpoints. On the one hand, there is an international community willing to afford additional protection to their children; on the other hand, practice shows us that it takes years or decades to incorporate and implement international conventions on child protection in national legal systems. Accordingly, the promotion of International Conventions is of utmost importance and can undoubtedly facilitate a State's process of ratifying or acceding to a treaty. The active participation of those who operate the system, who can visualize more clearly the benefits of the new tool, as well as the participation of the academics who might carry out the scientific analyses necessary for the study and implementation stages, constitutes a best practice that has proved to be really useful to facilitate and speed up this process. In effect, the authority having jurisdiction to analyze a convention (generally, the Ministry of Foreign Affairs) is not usually the authority responsible for the protection of children in a given country. In addition, this authority is generally overburdened with work and urgencies to be dealt with on a daily basis, which makes it postpone the analysis of child protection conventions until quieter times that will probably never come. That is why having the assistance of the operators of the child protection system and academia could be extremely useful to facilitate the process of incorporating new International Conventions into the local legal system (*e.g.*, drafting of reports on the legal relevance of the convention, explanation of the importance of ratifying or acceding to a convention to members of Parliament, etc.).

Furthermore, it should be noted that political commitment to becoming a Party to a treaty is not enough. The interested State should also undertake to duly implement the treaty so as to ensure its effective operation. Only then will its status as Party to the Convention make sense. This task may require the adoption of local regulations, the coordination of actions among the different operators of the child protection system and, particularly, solid promotional work and training for both those who will operate the mechanism and those who might provide assistance to users, as well as to the users themselves.

ii. Operative challenges

Not only should States incorporate and implement conventions, but they should also implement them correctly, so that their objectives can be realized.

The first hurdle to overcome in this regard is cultural barriers. For instance, some operators of the child protection system might believe that they can address any situation of a vulnerable child and that they do not need the assistance of any other protection system. Judges may sometimes be an example of this. As they are used to working alone, they may find it difficult to comprehend and accept that there are judges and operators of the other protection system engaged in children issues who are willing to assist them in order to protect children in an effective manner. Sometimes it is necessary to ask the other jurisdiction for information; in other situations, it is simply a matter of accepting that the other protection system has competence to address and determine a particular situation.

In addition, there are preconceptions about other cultures or child protection systems which often lead us to believe that our system is better than others and that our way of analyzing and addressing a problem is the only one possible or the best. When interpreting international conventions, operators tend to rely on their cultural background, running the risk of turning an international case into a local one, which would be contrary to the objectives and premise of the international instrument applicable to the case.

Becoming aware of the international dimension of the cases covered by the conventions and developing trust among the different national protection systems are key factors to the effective operation of the International Cooperation System for the Protection of Children.

One of the main achievements over the past few years in connection with the operation of Child Protection Conventions and the promotion of trust among different legal systems might be the development of networking among the key operators of the conventions, that is to say, Central Authorities and Judges.

The establishment of the International Hague Network of Judges has simplified the development of such trust. These judges are experts trained both to act as role models to their own colleagues in their own countries and to assist their colleagues abroad. In particular, the development of direct judicial communications has added another excellent tool to facilitate legal cooperation for the effective protection of children.

Consequently, we may conclude that the development and use of these Networks of Judges and Central Authorities is a further challenge to be addressed by the operators of the national protection systems in the coming years.

On the other hand, it is essential that States provide the operators of the child protection system with the necessary material and human resources to fulfil the objectives of the Conventions. It might seem obvious but, unfortunately, this is not often the case and sometimes results in non-compliance with the convention by the State involved and the ensuing lack of protection for children whose rights should be guaranteed by that very instrument in force and effect.

4. CONCLUSION

In light of the ideas expressed above, we may conclude that it is necessary to continue working on the development of an International Cooperation System for the Protection of Children which allows the coordinated and efficient participation of the different national child protection systems. For such a purpose, we should not only promote the accession to or ratification of the existing Child Protection Conventions which constitute the basis of that protection system, but we should also be mindful of the new issues which may arise in connection with the international protection of children in order to address them properly.

Furthermore, we should work towards ensuring the effective application of the Conventions in force in the different States, since only the correct implementation of the existing instruments will afford real protection to all children. To that end, intense and thorough work regarding coordination, training and promotion of the Conventions should be undertaken by all the operators engaged in the international protection of children.

The political commitment of every State involved will be of utmost importance in order to achieve the cooperation required by the Conventions, to promote further accessions to or ratifications of the Conventions, as well as to ensure the proper implementation of the Conventions. In particular, the active participation of the relevant operators of the child protection system will also be important so as to overcome the different challenges resulting from the processes of creation, accession / ratification and implementation of the Conventions.

We consider that although we have come a long way in the field of the international protection of children, we still have a long way to go. To this end, the incorporation and implementation of the 1996 Hague Convention in a considerable number of States will entail an unprecedented development as it will lay a solid foundation for the operation of an International Cooperation System for the Protection of Children. Many international operators seek to protect the rights of the child in international situations. However, it is only through the coordinated commitment and work of these operators (administrative authorities and courts, non-governmental organizations and international bodies) that we will be able to build an effective International Cooperation System for the Civil Protection of Children.

THE CAPE TOWN CONVENTION AND PROTOCOLS AND THE CONFLICT OF LAWS

Roy Goode QC
Emeritus Professor of Law in the University of Oxford
Emeritus Fellow of St John's College, Oxford

It is both a pleasure and a privilege to be invited to contribute to a Liber Amicorum for Dr Hans van Loon, though I do so with considerable trepidation as a general commercial lawyer whose ignorance of private international law is about to be revealed and who accepted the invitation only in the knowledge of the generosity of private international lawyers to outsiders wandering on to their patch. Like the great 17th-century mapmaker John Speed "I have put my sickle into other mens corne."

As Secretary General of the Hague Conference on Private International Law for 16 years, Hans has guided it with humour, skill and commitment through sometimes choppy waters, greatly enhancing the influence of the Conference and its Permanent Bureau, negotiating the accession of the European Community, steering the Conference's work on a wide range of conflict of laws conventions on which he has published widely and lectured extensively around the world and, most recently, setting up the Conference's Asia Pacific Regional Office in Hong Kong. Despite the pressures of work Hans always managed to appear relaxed, offering afternoon tea and a congenial chat to visitors who like myself dropped in without appointment, as if he had all the time in the world. He has achieved much and will be greatly missed.

The increasing international harmonisation of commercial law has from time to time led to speculation that in this area at least the role of private international law will be seriously diminished. That has not proved to be the case. Private international law continues to flourish, and one of the reasons is that no international convention can cover the entire field related to its subject-matter. There will always be an important role for the conflict of laws in international lawmaking. What is interesting is the interplay between a convention's substantive provisions and the conflict of laws, an issue which the present paper examines in the context of the 2001 Cape Town Convention on international interests in mobile equipment and its associated Aircraft Protocol, this being a complex pair of instruments which entered into force on 1 March 2006 and are rich in conflict of laws issues. The Convention has already secured 55 ratifications and the Aircraft Protocol 49 ratifications, with more in train and promises to be one of the most important private commercial law conventions ever to be concluded. The Luxembourg Protocol, concluded in February 2007 and devoted to railway rolling stock, will not be discussed. Brief reference will, however, be made to some special features of the Space Protocol, concluded in March 2012.

INTRODUCING THE CAPE TOWN CONVENTION

The international harmonisation of commercial law can take one of two forms: the harmonisation of substantive law or the less ambitious and more readily attainable harmonisation of conflict of laws rules. The purpose of the latter is to ensure that in whatever Contracting State proceedings are brought the same choice of law rules will be applied. This helps to avoid that form of forum shopping which seeks to have proceedings brought in the State whose conflict of laws rules lead to the application of the law most favourable to the claimant. For claims involving proprietary rights the law almost universally applied by the conflict of laws is the location of the object in question at the time of the relevant dealing, that is the *lex situs*, or *lex rei sitae*.[1] This works well enough as a conflicts rule for assets that typically remain in one place but is unsuited to high value tangible movables that typically cross national borders in everyday use, in particular aircraft and railway rolling stock. But even if a suitable conflicts rule could be devised for such assets there would remain the serious disadvantage that the substantive law varies from State to State or, in the case of space assets when no longer on Earth, is not governed by any readily determinable rules of private law. In some States the creditor is given strong protection, in others the law is debtor-oriented, while in relation to priorities there is not even an agreed conflicts rule, so that priorities will depend on the applicable law selected by the *lex fori* and are likely to vary from State to State. The resulting uncertainties create risk for creditors and may lead either to the refusal of credit or to an increase in the cost.

It was these considerations that led to the adoption of the Cape Town Convention on international interests in mobile equipment and its associated Protocols. The purpose of the Convention is to introduce a set of uniform rules

1 It will be observed that English law (and the writer is an English lawyer) differs from civil law systems not only in its law but also in its Latin!

governing the creation, registration and priority of competing security and related interests in such mobile equipment and thereby to reduce uncertainty and consequential risk, open capital markets to financing that would otherwise be unavailable and lower borrowing costs and fees for credit insurance. It has been estimated that in relation to aircraft objects implementation of the Convention with a particular set of declarations under it could save billions of dollars a year, and for several years a significant Cape Town discount from credit exposure fees has been able to be provided throughout the OECD, whilst in States that have a bankruptcy-immune provision under or comparable to what is provided by Alternative A of Article 11 of the Aircraft Protocol companies are often able to raise money in the capital markets against the issue of enhanced equipment trust certificates on terms significantly cheaper than are available for bank loans.

The Convention covers three categories of equipment: aircraft objects (that is, airframes, aircraft engines and helicopters), railway rolling stock and space assets (spacecraft, payloads and parts thereof). The Convention provisions are equipment-neutral but for each category of equipment there is a separate Protocol, which not only supplements the Convention but, unusually, controls its entry into force and adapts it to meet the specific needs of the relevant industry sector. The Convention establishes a unique type of interest, the international interest, defined as the interest of the chargee under a security agreement or the interest vested in a person who is the conditional seller under a title reservation agreement or a lessor under a leasing agreement. Compliance with the relatively simple formalities for an agreement establishes the international interest, which can then be registered in the International Registry for the type of equipment in question.

The Convention provides a set of basic default remedies which must be made available in each Contracting State and contains a set of simple priority rules based on the order of registration in the International Registry. With certain exceptions an international interest has priority over any other interest subsequently registered and over an unregistered interest, whether or not capable of registration. Registration is against the object, not the debtor, and is therefore available only for uniquely identified objects.[2] One effect of these provisions is that though they do not preclude the grant of interests under national law these will usually be overridden by a registered international interest even if earlier in time. Also provided by the Convention are rules governing the creation and priority

2 In the case of aircraft objects the identification criteria are the manufacturer's name, generic model and serial number. These must be satisfied not only for registration but for the constitution of the international interest, whereas in the other two Protocols requirements for the latter are very flexible.

of assignments of "associated rights" (rights to payment and other performance under the agreement).

Both the Aircraft Protocol and the Space Protocol extend the registration and priority provisions of the Convention to outright sales and supplement or modify the Convention in other ways, most notably by providing strong creditor protection in the event of the debtor's insolvency.[3]

SPHERE OF APPLICATION

Some international Conventions are bounded by the conflict of laws in that they do not apply in a Contracting State unless the rules of private international law of the forum State lead to their application. Examples are the 1980 Vienna Convention on Contracts for the International Sale of Goods where applicable by virtue of Article 1(1)(b) of the Convention[4] and the 2009 UNIDROIT Convention on substantive rules for intermediated securities. The Cape Town Convention is not of this kind. Once incorporated into the law of a Contracting State it takes effect according to its own terms and the fact that such State's rules of private international law would otherwise lead the issue to be governed by a foreign law is irrelevant. All that is required to trigger the application of the Convention and Aircraft Protocol is that the parties have entered into an agreement falling within one of the three categories referred to above and relating to a uniquely identifiable aircraft object, that the agreement is duly constituted under Article 7 of the Convention and that the requisite connecting factor exists, namely situation of the debtor in a Contracting State or, in the case of aircraft objects, registration of the aircraft in the nationality register of a Contracting State, at the time of the agreement. A court in a non-Contracting State could also apply the Convention if its conflict of laws rules lead to the application of the law of a Contracting State and the other conditions for the application of the Convention are satisfied.

---

3 For a comprehensive analysis of the Convention and Aircraft Protocol, see Roy Goode, Official Commentary on the Convention on International Interests in Mobile Equipment and the Protocol thereto on Matters Specific to Aircraft Equipment (Revised Edition 2008). The third edition of this Official Commentary will be published in the summer of 2013.

4 The effect of which is that the Convention applies to contracts of sale between parties whose places of business are in different States when the rules of private international law lead to the application of the law of a Contracting State. The scope of Article 1(1)(b) when read with Article 95 remains controversial.

THE CONVENTION TREATMENT OF THE CONFLICT OF LAWS

The Convention and Aircraft Protocol treat conflict of laws rules in a variety of ways:

(1) Occasionally they prescribe a positive conflicts rule. So under Article 5(4), where a State comprises several territorial units, each of which has its own rule of law in respect of the matter to be decided, and where there is no indication of the relevant territorial unit, it is for the law of that State to decide which is the territorial unit whose laws are to govern, or in the absence of any such rule, the law of the territorial unit with which the case is most closely connected. Again, Article VIII of the Aircraft Protocol allows the parties to an agreement or a contract of sale to choose the law which is to govern their contractual rights and obligations, wholly or in part. I shall return to this Article a little later.
(2) More commonly the Convention and the Aircraft Protocol make a reference to the applicable law in specific provisions without specifying how that law is to be determined. References to the applicable law are to the domestic rules of the law applicable by virtue of the rules of private international law of the forum State (Article 5(4)). In other words, *renvoi* is excluded. In at least one case the applicable law could, unusually, be the Convention itself.
(3) The two instruments contain several apparently simple but in reality quite complex provisions on jurisdiction which are not discussed here.
(4) Where the Convention makes no reference to the applicable law, it may nevertheless apply by virtue of Article 5(2), which prescribes the applicable law as the residual rule to determine matters governed by the Convention which are not expressly settled in it and are not deducible from the general principles on which it is based.

NATURE AND CONSTITUTION OF THE INTERNATIONAL INTEREST

The international interest established by the Convention is an autonomous *sui generis* interest the characteristics of which derive solely from the Convention itself, not from national law. Further, it is constituted as such where the agreement creating or providing for it is in writing, relates to an object of which the chargor, conditional seller or lessor has power to dispose, enables the object to be identified in accordance with the Protocol and, in the case of a security agreement, enables the secured obligations to be determined, but without the need to state a sum or maximum sum secured (Article 7). An international interest so constituted is effective under the Convention whether or not it is an interest of a kind recognised by the applicable law and whether or not it conforms to the formal requirements of the applicable law. This is not to say that the applicable law is entirely irrelevant to the creation of an international interest. Matters of substantive validity, such as the existence of a *consensus ad idem* or the impact of illegality, are governed by the applicable law. This is nowhere expressly stated in the Convention but is implicit in the requirement that there be an agreement. The applicable law may also confer the requisite power of disposal, though the Convention itself implies a power of disposal on the part of a debtor by virtue of its registration requirements, which would otherwise not be necessary to preserve priority against a subsequent international interest wrongfully granted by the debtor.

CHARACTERISATION

As stated above, the Convention applies to three types of agreement: a security agreement, a title reservation agreement and a leasing agreement. There is an important distinction between a security agreement and the other two agreements in that the default remedies available to a secured creditor are set out more extensively than for a conditional seller or lessor, reflecting the traditional view in many legal systems that the conditional seller or lessor is the owner and on termination of the agreement for default and repossession should be free to deal with the repossessed object as it pleases. However, in the United States, Canada, New Zealand, Australia and certain other American jurisdictions a conditional sale agreement and certain types of leasing agreement are characterised as security agreements. So, sensibly, the Convention leaves characterisation to be dealt with by the applicable law.

> "Article 2 — The international interest
> 1. This Convention provides for the constitution and effects of an international interest in certain categories of mobile equipment and associated rights.
> 2. For the purposes of this Convention, an international interest in mobile equipment is an interest, constituted under Article 7, in a uniquely identifiable object of a category of such objects listed in paragraph 3 and designated in the Protocol:
>   (a) granted by the chargor under a security agreement;
>   (b) vested in a person who is the conditional seller under a title reservation agreement; or
>   (c) vested in a person who is the lessor under a leasing agreement.
>
>   An interest falling within sub-paragraph (a) does not also fall within sub-paragraph (b) or (c).

3. The categories referred to in the preceding paragraphs are:
   (a) airframes, aircraft engines and helicopters;
   (b) railway rolling stock; and
   (c) space assets.
4. The applicable law determines whether an interest to which paragraph 2 applies falls within subparagraph (a), (b) or (c) of that paragraph.
5. An international interest in an object extends to proceeds of that object."

It is important to note that Article 2(4) goes only to characterisation, not to the sphere of application. So the effect is not to subject to the Convention all interests that constitute security interests under the applicable law but simply to leave it to the applicable law to characterise an agreement which falls within the Convention definition of a security agreement, a title reservation agreement or a leasing agreement. For example, while a consignment agreement structured in a particular way may constitute a security agreement under Article 9 of the Uniform Commercial Code it does not fall within any of the above Convention definitions, so that the Convention does not apply.

PARTY CHOICE OF LAW

In international commercial contracts a high degree of autonomy is given to the parties in choosing the law which is to govern their contractual relations. The limits on this vary from jurisdiction to jurisdiction. But if one leaves on one side for the moment mandatory rules of a legal system which cannot be excluded by agreement but are applicable only if the contract is governed by the legal system and can therefore be excluded by a choice of foreign law, and overriding (super-mandatory) rules which are of such policy importance that they apply regardless of the otherwise applicable law, the constraints on choice of law are quite limited. Article VIII of the Aircraft Protocol, which applies only where a Contracting State makes a declaration under Article XXX(1) opting into it, includes the following provision:

> "The parties to an agreement or a contract of sale, or a related guarantee or subordination agreement, may agree on the law which is to govern their contractual rights and obligations, wholly or in part."

The questions for consideration are what Article VIII(2) adds to the general principle of party autonomy and what constraints remain. The conflict of laws rules of some States limit party choice by requiring that the chosen law has some connection with the parties or the transaction or by restricting the power of choice to agreements with an international element, thus excluding party choice in the case of purely domestic agreements in which all the elements of the situation are based in one State. In a Contracting State opting into Article VIII such limits on party choice cannot be imposed. The parties are, of course, bound by any applicable mandatory and overriding rules but these do not limit party choice, they merely impose themselves on the transaction, leaving the law selected by the parties to govern other matters. Member States of the European Community (now the European Union) are precluded from making a declaration under Article XXX(1) applying Article VIII, since the EC has declared that it will make no declaration under Article XXX(1), leaving Member States bound by the Rome regulation on the law applicable to contractual obligations (Rome I).

MATTERS REFERRED TO THE APPLICABLE LAW

The Convention expressly leaves it to the applicable law to determine a whole range of matters, only a few of which can be examined here. Several of the items, particularly those dealing with remedies, the installation on and removal from an object of an item which is not itself an object but may be an accession, defences and rights of set-off against an assignee, are capable of ready resolution by reference to well-established conflict of laws principles. But there are some that cause more difficulty, because it is not immediately clear how a well-known principle is to be applied to the facts or because they raise the question whether the issue is to be resolved by reference to the language of the Convention and the principles on which it is based or by the applicable law, or because the question relates to priority issues falling outside the provisions of the Convention or the relevant Protocol. Space allows only a few of these to be examined here.

INSOLVENCY AND THE APPLICABLE LAW

Unusually for a private commercial law convention the Cape Town Convention intrudes on insolvency law, an area previously regarded as taboo. Article 30(1) provides that an international interest registered in conformity with the Convention prior to the commencement of the insolvency proceedings is effective in those proceedings, that is, it must be recognised by the insolvency administrator as having proprietary effects. But under Article 30(2) nothing in Article 30 impairs the effectiveness of an (unregistered) international interest in the insolvency proceedings where that interest is effective under the applicable law. Since the international interest is the creation of the Convention, not of national law, the reference to "international interest" must be construed as referring to the national equivalent, namely a security interest or interest held by a conditional seller under a title reservation agreement or a lessor under a leasing agreement.

The applicable law will depend on the conflict of laws rules of the forum, which will typically be the rules of the *lex concursus* itself but could be those of another State in which proceedings are brought, *e.g.*, for recovery of the aircraft object where it is situated outside the insolvency State. In most jurisdictions the law to be applied to property claims in the first instance is the *lex situs* of the object at the time of the relevant dealing, though this may be displaced (a) by a subsequent dealing when the object is in a different *situs*, in which case it is for the law of that *situs* to determine the impact of that dealing on any prior rights, and (b) by special avoidance provisions of insolvency law. This is straightforward as regards security interests, where one applies the law of the place of the object at the time of the grant of the security interest, but the analysis requires some refinement as regards title reservation and leasing agreements, because the title of the conditional seller or lessor derives not from the agreement but from an antecedent manufacture or acquisition by the conditional seller or lessor. Nevertheless the international interest, and thus its national law equivalent, is created by entry into the title reservation agreement or leasing agreement, and it is therefore the *lex situs* at the time of that agreement that is the applicable law.

Under Article 30(3)(a) nothing in Article 30 affects any rules of insolvency law applicable in insolvency proceedings relating to the avoidance of a transaction as a preference or a transfer in fraud of creditors, though no other grounds of avoidance in insolvency may be asserted against a registered international interest. Nor does the Convention affect any rules of procedure relating to the enforcement of rights to property under the control or supervision of an insolvency administrator, *e.g.*, for the purpose of a restructuring of the debtor or an arrangement with creditors.

ASSIGNMENT AND NOVATION

The Convention provides for the assignment of associated rights (that is, rights to payment or other performance under the agreement) and such an assignment carries with it the related international interest unless the parties so agree. An assignment of the international interest is registrable in the International Registry under Article 16(1)(b). "Assignment" is defined by Article 1(b) as a "a contract which, whether by way of security or otherwise, confers on the assignee associated rights with or without a transfer of the related international interest." Sometimes transactions by which a new party acquires the creditor's rights take a form which some legal systems would regard as a new agreement (novation), not an assignment, and if, as I at one time believed, the characterisation of the transaction were governed by the applicable law this could lead to the need for a fresh registration with a new priority point. But given the wide variety of approaches in national legal systems to the distinction between assignment and novation, and the need for predictability as well as the protection of third parties, I have concluded that "assignment" has an autonomous meaning under the Convention and that national law characterisations do not come into play. On this basis an assignment which, for example, also involves the assumption by the assignee of the assignor's accrued and/or accruing liability to the debtor is to be treated as an assignment so far as it involves the transfer of the creditor's rights and a novation to the extent that the transfer of obligations is treated as such by the applicable law.

SUBROGATION

Article 38(1) provides that nothing in the Convention affects the acquisition of associated rights and the related international interest by legal or contractual subrogation under the applicable law, and such acquisitions too are registrable in the International Registry under Article 16(1)(c). Of course the reference to the applicable law is primarily to non-Convention law. However, Article 9(4) provides that a person who, after the debtor's default under a security agreement, discharges the secured debt becomes subrogated to the rights of the chargee. There seems no reason why this right of subrogation should not be treated as arising under "the applicable law" even though it is the law embodied in the Convention itself.

PRE-EXISTING RIGHTS OR INTERESTS

Article 60(1) provides as follows:

> "Unless otherwise declared by a Contracting State at any time, the Convention does not apply to a pre-existing right or interest, which retains the priority it enjoyed under the applicable law before the effective date of this Convention."

By a pre-existing right or interest is meant one of any kind in or over an object created or arising before the effective date of the Convention, which is the time the Convention enters into force or the time when the State in which the debtor is situated becomes a Contracting State, whichever is the later. The pre-existing right or interest need not be of a kind equivalent to an international interest. It could be a right or interest arising under a different kind of contract or, indeed, a right or interest arising by operation of law, such as a non-consensual lien. Of all the Articles in the Convention Article 60 is the most difficult, because various elements necessary to make it work are not made explicit. By "the applicable law" is meant the domestic rules of law applicable by virtue of the rules of private international law of the forum State (Article 5(3)). As stated earlier, conflict rules will usually lead to the application of the law of the situation of the asset at the time of the agreement. Again, the applicable law in a State which was not a Contracting State at the time the pre-existing right or interest arose will have no concept of an international interest, so that the priority contest is between the pre-existing right or interest and an interest equivalent to an international interest where the conditions of priority (*e.g.*, registration) under the applicable law have been satisfied.

It is open to a Contracting State to make a declaration applying the Convention to pre-existing rights or interests arising under an agreement (that is, a security agreement, title reservation agreement or leasing agreement) as from a date not earlier than three years after the declaration becomes effective, so that during the period allowed by the declaration the holder of a pre-existing right or interest which is of a registrable kind can preserve its interest by registration. Article 60 is silent on the question who is entitled to make the declaration but it seems clear that it can be made only by the Contracting State where the debtor was situated at the time of conclusion of the agreement under which the pre-existing right or interest arose, which is the same connecting factor as that governing the application of the Convention as a whole under Article 3(1).

THE SPACE PROTOCOL

The secured financing of satellites and other space assets gives rise to distinctive problems of private international law which the Space Protocol is designed to alleviate. In the first place, though the normal rules on the law applicable to contracts apply, matters are more difficult when it comes to property rights between private parties. That is because for a long time space activity was the prerogative of governments, so that all international treaties in this area deal with matters of public international law concerning the rights and responsibilities of States and the State regulation of space activity, so that there have been no uniform private law rules in the area. There has been at least one court case[5] in which it was contended that a security interest in a satellite in outer space, even if validly perfected under the applicable law (which was disputed), was not subject to the priority rules of any determinable national law, so that secured and unsecured creditors were to be treated a ranking *pari passu*. Secondly, the value of a satellite

[5] *In Re ProtoStar Ltd.*, Case No. 09-12659 (MFW), US Bankruptcy Court for the District of Delaware. The case was eventually settled.

as collateral is limited because of the obvious practical difficulties in enforcing the security, so that financiers attach much greater value to the debtor's receivables derived from the grant of licences and lease capacity which can be assigned to the creditor as additional collateral. In other words, satellite finance is seen as more in the nature of project finance than asset-based finance.

It was thus considered essential to bring the assignment of these "debtor's rights" into the Space Protocol and to provide a means of securing their priority. The initial suggestion to permit their registration as international interests in themselves was discarded, since the whole Convention and registry system is based on uniquely identifiable physical assets. The solution was to provide for recording of debtor's rights against the registration of the related international interest granted by the debtor, so that there would always be a searchable association between the registered international interest and the assignment of debtor's rights. This aspect of the Space Protocol has generally been under-estimated, but it solves a serious problem in receivables financing in that there are not only uniform rules governing the priority of successive assignments of receivables but there is not even an agreed conflicts rule, though both aspects are addressed in some detail in the UNCITRAL Legislative Guide on Secured Transactions. It is true that the UN Convention on the assignment of receivables in international trade contains a conflicts rule in Article 30(1) applying the law of the assignor's location to the priority of competing claimants, together with an Annex in different sections by any of which a State can declare itself bound and dealing with priority on the alternative bases of registration and absence of registration, but so far only one State, Liberia, has ratified the Convention. So for satellite financing the Space Protocol fills a major gap.

THE LAW APPLICABLE IN RELATION TO SPACE ASSETS

Most of the proprietary aspects of dealings in space assets, whether pre-launch or post-launch, are covered by the substantive rules of the Convention and the Space Protocol. This is fortunate because the space law treaties are concerned essentially with public law rights and duties, not with concepts of property in private law. Moreover, space assets receive little or no mention in our otherwise admirable textbooks on private international law. Reference to the *lex situs* as the applicable law is unhelpful if by *situs* one means the physical location of a space asset which has reached Earth orbit, because there is no *lex* in space.

Since the rationale of the *lex situs* rule is that the law governing property rights should be that of the jurisdiction which has control of the asset, the concept of control should replace that of physical location in the case of assets in space, and

Article VIII of the 1967 Outer Space Treaty gives control to the State which is the State of registry of the object under the 1975 Registration Treaty. So for registered objects the appropriate law to govern dealings is the *lex registri*. However, space objects are not registrable until they are at Earth orbit or beyond. Moreover, not all registrable objects are registered. This is not a significant problem as regards the pre-launch phase, in which most of the financing is provided, because the Convention, in combination with the Space Protocol, applies to pre-launch as well as post-launch agreements and its provisions cover most of the property issues likely to arise. There are two principal exceptions. The first is the acquisition of an international interest by legal or contractual subrogation, as where a surety pays the amount necessary to discharge the debtor's obligations under a security agreement. Article 38 of the Convention preserves such rights of subrogation, and Article 16(1)(c) provides for their registration in the International Registry. The second relates to pre-existing rights or interests. Both of these involve resort to the applicable law. But it is highly unlikely that subrogation will occur before the asset is in space, so that leaves only the treatment of assets in space but unregistered and pre-existing rights or interests, For these assets the most appropriate law would seem to be the law of the State which has international responsibility for space activities in relation to the space asset under Article VI of the Outer Space Treaty.

THE LAW APPLICABLE TO DEBTOR'S RIGHTS

The Space Protocol governs the formalities, effects and priority of an assignment of debtor's rights to the creditor and for the most part its provisions avoid the need to resort to national law. But there remains some issues left to be determined by the applicable law, including the extent to which a transfer of debtor's rights to the creditor is permitted (Article X(1)) and the availability of defences and rights of set-off against the creditor as assignee (Article X(2)). Questions of transferability are most likely to arise where the agreement under which the debtor's rights arise contains a prohibition against assignment. Most legal systems give effect to this at least to the point of laying down that the debtor does not have to recognise the title of the assignee, but some override the prohibition in the interests of protecting the free flow of receivables in the stream of trade. The applicable law will usually be that governing the assigned obligation, as exemplified by Article 14(2) of Rome I. Where this is the law of a State that has ratified the 1988 Unidroit Convention on International Factoring the assignment of debtor's rights will have effect notwithstanding any prohibition against assignment (Factoring Convention, Article 6(1)) unless at the time of conclusion of the contract of sale of goods under which the debts arise the debtor has its place of business in a Contracting State which has made a declaration under Article 18 (Article 6(2)). Defences and rights of set-off will typically be governed by the law applicable to the claim against which the defence or right of set-off is asserted. See, for example, Rome I, Articles 12 and 17.

CONCLUSION

The application of the conflict of laws rules under the Cape Town Convention and Protocols is at certain points not free from difficulty. But the extensive references to the applicable law[6] vividly illustrate the continuing importance of conflict of laws in international instruments dealing with the substantive harmonisation of private law. Also of interest is the need to resort to instruments of public international law, such as the Outer Space Treaties, in order to determine the applicable law concerning international interests relating to space assets. So private international law continues to flourish and with it the Hague Conference and the Permanent Bureau. Long may that continue!

6 There are approximately 20 provisions of the Convention and Aircraft Protocol referring to the applicable law.

THE USE OF PRIVATE INTERNATIONAL LAW ESCAPE DEVICES TO MANAGE THE MEDIATE APPLICATION OF (FOREIGN) HUMAN RIGHTS IN CIVIL AND COMMERCIAL DISPUTES IN AUSTRALIA[1, 2]

Thomas JOHN ACIArb
Head of the Private International Law Section at the Access to Justice Division, Australian Government Attorney-General's Department

Lukas DELAHAYE
German Referendar in the Private International Law Section of the Australian Government Attorney-General's Department

I. INTRODUCTION

Traditionally, the relationship between public and private law has been characterised by a sharp separation along the public/private law divide. This divide exists domestically, but it is equally present in international law. As Professor Mills has observed:

> In the study in international law, a sharp distinction is usually drawn between public international law, concerned with the rights of other states and individuals,

---

1 The views expressed in this paper are those of the authors and they should not be attributed to the Commonwealth of Australia, its Government or any of its agencies.

2 We express our deep gratitude to Ms Louise Glanville, First Assistant Secretary, Access to Justice Division, Australian Government Attorney-General's Department, for her tremendous support in the completion of this paper. We also thank the members of that Department's Private International Law Section: Nastassja Jardim, William Brydie-Watson, Heidi Austin and Rishi Gulati, who provided useful comments on drafts of this paper.

and private international law, concerned with issues of jurisdiction, applicable law and the recognition and enforcement of foreign judgments in international private law disputes before national courts.[3]

However, this sharp distinction blurs and the schism between the two areas narrows.

There is a growing body of scholarly debate that traces this narrowing, with commentators increasingly zooming in on the so-called "horizontal effect" of human rights on private law, that is, the effect these rights have on the relationships between private parties that are governed by private law.[4] And there is clear evidence that this horizontal effect is increasingly the basis for litigation. The most recent example is the matter *Esther Kiobel v Royal Dutch Petroleum Co*,[5] heard in the U.S. Supreme Court in February and October 2012. This case tests the application of the USA's Alien Tort Statute (ATS) to alleged conduct by several oil corporations where the conduct is said to amount to abetting the Nigerian government in violating international human rights. It is only the most recent, and arguably one of the most significant, examples of a class of civil litigation cases that have at their heart the violation of human rights through private actors.[6]

This paper seeks to contribute to this debate from an Australian perspective. It does so by focusing on a particular aspect of the horizontal effect: the mediate application of human rights on private relationships as the result of the operation of Australian choice of law rules. More specifically, the paper seeks to identify how Australian courts may deal with circumstances in which this mediate application would lead to results that are difficult to reconcile with the domestic understanding of similar rights or where the foreign human right is unknown in Australia.

Two German cases were the genesis for this paper. The first concerned the validity of a bank guarantee given by an inexperienced and impecunious young person to secure loans for her parents.[7] The second concerned the validity of a will that purported to apply Egyptian law, which significantly favoured the heirs of the deceased husband.[8] In both instances, the German courts assessed the

3 A Mills, *The Confluence of Public and Private International Law: Justice, Pluralism and Subsidiarity in the International Constitutional Ordering of Private Law* (Cambridge University Press, 2009), 1.

4 O O Cherednychenko, "Fundamental rights and private law: a relationship of subordination or complementarity?" (2007) 3(2) *Utrecht Law Review* 1, 1.

5 *Esther Kiobel v Royal Dutch Petroleum Co*, US Supreme Court, No. 10–1491.

6 For example *Baumann v DaimlerChrysler Corp.* (2011) 644 F.3d 909.

7 Decision of the Federal Constitutional Court (*Bundesverfassungsgericht*) of 19 October 1993, BVerfGE 89, 214.

8 Decision of the Supreme Court of Frankfurt, (*Oberlandesgericht Frankfurt*) of 10 May 2010, ErbR 2011, 29.

respective private transactions against a range of human rights as entrenched in, and developed under, the German *Grundgesetz*. As a result the courts voided each transaction as being incompatible with German basic law: the guarantee on the basis of the principles of party autonomy and social justice and the welfare state (Articles 2(1) and 20(1), 28(1) of the German Constitution);[9] the will on the basis of the equal treatment of man and woman and the prohibition of discrimination on the basis of gender, faith, political or religious views (Articles 3(2) and (3) of the German Constitution).

Of course, these cases are part of German domestic law. They have no immediate application in Australia. However, they may find mediate application in Australia where Australian choice of law rules lead to the application of German law to cross-border civil and commercial relationships. In these instances, Australian courts would pick up and apply German human rights principles in Australia – or they would use an escape device to avoid their application.

Part II of this paper considers the application of human rights in Australia. While all attempts have been made to provide an accurate reflection of the rich tapestry of judicial consideration and legislative and executive intervention, which characterise the manner in which human rights are protected and guaranteed in Australia, this paper does not purport to address this area exhaustively and in all its nuances. Part III then examines how foreign law applies in cross-border civil and commercial relationships and disputes. Part IV considers which private international law escape devices may be suited to avoiding the application of foreign law, advancing several arguments why the most suitable and appropriate one is public policy or *ordre public*.

II. HUMAN RIGHTS AS PART OF AUSTRALIA'S LEGAL ORDER

To provide context to the key themes of this paper, it is necessary to start by examining how human rights are, or become, part of Australia's domestic legal order by looking at various possible sources for human rights.

9 J Isensee "Vertragsfreiheit im Griff der Grundrechte: Inhaltskontrolle von Verträgen am Maßstab der Verfassung" in U Hübner, B Grossfeld, W Ebke (eds), *Festschrift für Bernhard Grossfeld* (Verlag Recht und Wirtschaft, Heidelberg, 1999), 498.

1. THE AUSTRALIAN CONSTITUTION

The Australian Constitution entrenches a limited number of constitutional rights. The majority of these rights are not positive rights of individuals exercisable and effective against the whole world; rather, these rights operate as constraints on legislative powers and government. Some have been expressly included in the Constitution, including the right to a trial by jury (s80 of the Constitution) or the freedom of religion (s116 of the Constitution).[10] Others have been implied from the text and structure of the Constitution because they are said to be instrumental to ensuring that the institutional mechanisms set forth in the Constitution are not compromised. Such implied rights include the freedom of political communication.[11] While there remain ongoing discussions concerning whether the Constitution actually contains human rights,[12] it seems that it is an increasingly accepted proposition that it contains a range of rights which are at least akin to such rights.

2. INTERNATIONAL HUMAN RIGHTS

International human rights include those that have developed as part of customary international law and those that are now embodied in international treaties. They are, as Giannini and Farbstein have observed, part of an international legal system which:

> … [first,] establishes acceptable norms of conduct, such as prohibitions on torture, extrajudicial killing, and war crimes; and second, [which] provides, when possible and desirable, enforcement mechanisms that supplement and support domestic enforcement of the established norms.[13]

Rights that arise from these norms of conduct are the focus of this paper. However, readers should keep in mind that this paper offers only a Commonwealth or federal perspective. It is beyond the scope of this paper to consider any issues that are the result of any jurisdictional interactions within the Australian federation

---

10 *Cheng v R* (2000) 74 ALJR 1482 (right to trial by jury). *Williams v Commonwealth of Australia* [2012] HCA 23 (freedom of religion).

11 *ACTV v The Commonwealth* (1992) 177 CLR 106. *Wotton v Queensland* (2012) 285 ALR 1.

12 C Saunders, "The Australian Constitution and Our Rights" (2010) Future Justice 117, 117.

13 T Giannini, S Farbstein, "Corporate Accountability in Conflict Zones: How *Kiobel* Undermines the Nuremberg Legacy and Modern Human Rights", (2010) 52 *Harvard International Law Journal Online* 119, 124.

that have a bearing on this area (such as any effects state or territory human rights legislation may have at federal level).[14]

The initial question that arises then is whether, and if so, how, international human rights are, or can become, part of Australia's legal order. It appears that, based on orthodox methodology, there are three possible options: (1) by direct application; (2) by ancillary application; and (3) by assessment of domestic bills and legislation against a human rights framework. In turn, each of these options will be dealt with below.

a. The direct application of international human rights in Australia

International human rights may either be treaty-based, that is they are agreed between nations, or they are part of customary international law. The following discussion briefly examines whether international human rights derived from either source are part of Australia's domestic legal system by direct application.

i. Treaty-based international human rights

Australia follows the dualist theory. This theory views international and domestic legal systems as two distinct spheres. As a result, international human rights are not considered part of Australia's domestic legal system. This is even so in cases in which Australia ratifies an international agreement but does not take implementing steps.[15] Such implementing steps, in the form of domestic legislation, are required to transform the content of treaties into domestic rights and obligations. Without them, the international agreement does not form part of Australian law.[16] The acceptance of the dualist theory, and the need for transformative steps, is justified by doctrine of the separation of powers.[17] The importance of this doctrine in relation to the direct application of international human rights was also highlighted by Justice Brennan in *Re Citizen Limbo*. Drawing a clear distinction between "lofty aspirations", such as international human rights, and "the rules of law which courts are capable and fitted to enforce",[18] His Honour noted that:

> It is essential that there be no mistake between the functions that are performed by the respective branches of government. It is essential to understand that courts perform one function and the political branches of government perform another.

14 *Momcilovic v The Queen* (2011) 280 ALR 221.
15 *Polites v The Commonwealth* (1945) 70 CLR 60.
16 *R v Keyn* (1876) 2 Ex D 63. *Teoh Minister for Immigration and Ethnic Affairs v Teoh* (1995) 183 CLR 273, 287.
17 *Minister for Immigration and Ethnic Affairs v Teoh* (1995) 183 CLR 273, 287–8.
18 *Re Limbo* (1989) 92 ALR 81, 82.

> ... [I]t would be a mistake for one branch of government to assume the functions of another in the hope that thereby what is perceived to be an injustice can be corrected. Unless one observes the separation of powers and unless the courts are restricted to the application of the domestic law of this country, there would be a state of confusion and chaos which would be antipathetic not only to the aspirations of peace but to the aspirations of the enforcement of any human rights.[19]

Incorporation into domestic law of rights and obligations as they arise under international agreements and treaties occurs directly by way of legislation and is thus, as noted above, a matter for the Parliament, not the courts. Importantly, under s51(xxix) of the Constitution, the Commonwealth (i.e. federal) Parliament is given a particular power to make laws with respect to the implementation of international obligations. This power seeks to bridge any power gap the Commonwealth may have to make laws with respect to international human rights and allows Australia to be a polity with an international personality.[20]

ii. Human rights based on customary international law

A separate question is whether rules of customary international law, including human rights that are considered part of customary international law, are part of Australian domestic law. It is suggested that in Australia, this question, which has been the "subject of only limited judicial consideration",[21] is far from settled.

Of course, the two cases on point, *Chow Hung Ching*[22] and *Nulyarimma*,[23] have followed dualist doctrine, championing the view that customary international law, too, does not apply directly in Australia, and that legislative action is required before customary international law could create rights and obligations domestically. However, both decisions fail to offer conclusive views on the issue. Particularly unhelpful appears to be the decision in *Nulyarimma*, which offers three separate approaches. Justice Merkel found that customary international law may, in appropriate circumstances, supply offences that the common law receives. Justice Whitlam flatly rejected this proposition, holding that customary international law rules cannot be received domestically without further transformation. Justice Wilcox agreed with Justice Whitlam in relation to offences purportedly derived from customary international law concerning the

19 *Re Limbo* (1989) 92 ALR 81, 82–3.
20 *Victoria v The Commonwealth* (1996) CLR 416, 477–8.
21 R French, 'International Law and Australian Domestic Law', paper, *Supreme Court of New South Wales Annual Conference*, 21 August 2009.
22 *Chow Hung Ching v The King* (1949) 77 CLR 449.
23 *Nulyarimma v Thompson* (1999) 96 FCR 153.

criminal sphere. However, His Honour considered whether, assuming that there is a difference between criminal and civil customary international law rules, the latter may possibly become more readily part of domestic law.

b. The ancillary application of international human rights

While, as seen above, international human rights will not apply immediately unless they are implemented in Australia domestically, it is possible that they apply through ancillary means. It must be said at once that the term "ancillary" in this context is not used to refer to the influence international human rights have in the development of the common law. That it can, has of course been noted by Justice Brennan in *Mabo*:

> [T]he common law does not necessarily conform with international law, but international law is a legitimate and important influence on the development of the common law, especially when international law declares the existence of universal human rights.[24]

It is also not used to explain that the use of international human rights in support of judicial argument such as in *Gutnick*, where Justice Kirby referred to the ICCPR's rights to freedom of expression and reputation in support of his reasons.[25]

Rather, "ancillary" is used to denote the application of international human rights through the interpretation of domestic statutes and the construction of the Australian Constitution. It has been suggested that the use of ancillary means allows for the domestic application of international human rights through "the backdoor".[26]

i. Statutory construction, gap filling and ambiguities

Courts have used international human rights to interpret, and fill gaps and resolve ambiguities in, primary legislation. Courts use the canon that no law is to be construed as to abrogate or curtail fundamental rights and freedoms, unless there is a clear statutory language that it was Parliament's intention to do so.[27] These rights include certain "human rights or freedoms (of which personal liberty is the most basic)…"[28] or fundamental liberties and values as protected by

24 *Mabo v Queensland [No 2]* (1992) 175 CLR 1, 42.
25 *Dow Jones and Co, Inc v Gutnick* (2002) 210 CLR 575, 626–7.
26 *Minister for Immigration and Ethnic Affairs v Teoh* (1995) 183 CLR 273, 288.
27 *Bropho v State of Western Australia* (1990) 171 CLR 1, 18. *Coco v R* (1994) 179 CLR 427, 437.
28 *Al-Kateb v Godwin* (2004) 219 CLR 562.

common law.[29] Similar approaches have been taken by courts to fill legislative gaps and resolve ambiguities in laws. However, they will only resort to international human rights to fill gaps or resolve ambiguities if the legislation does not show a clear legislative intent to override or contradict international law.[30]

ii. Interpreting the Constitution

There is a debate whether ambiguities within the Australian Constitution should be resolved by reading the instrument as being subject to international law, including international human rights.[31] Traceable in judicial exegesis for some time,[32] the high watermark of the debate is, and remains, the High Court's decision in *Al-Kateb*.[33] In this case, former Justices McHugh and Kirby advanced arguments in favour and against conforming the Australian Constitution to international law. Still, it appears currently a settled principle that the Australian Constitution is not read subject to, or conforming with, international law.[34] This, however, must be distinguished from the situation where the High Court has used international law, including international human rights law, to provide context to the consideration of the Constitution.[35]

Other examples in which the High Court has, or at least some justices of that court have, used international human rights in that way include decisions concerning the retrospective application of criminal legislation,[36] the free speech cases of the mid-1990's,[37] and cases in which the High Court drew on jurisprudence of the European Court of Human Rights to examine some of the characteristics of a "court" for the purpose of Chapter III of the Constitution (which deals with the judicial power of the Commonwealth).[38]

However, it must be pointed out that the ancillary application of international human rights as described above is still not settled and remains, in parts, controversial. To date, it is difficult to find indications of systematic and principled approaches to the ancillary application of international human rights in Australia.

29 *Minister for Immigration & Citizenship v Haneef* [2007] FCAFC 203, [113].
30 *Polites v Commonwealth* (1945) 70 CLR 60, 73, 77–8.
31 K Walker, "International Law as a Tool of Constitutional Interpretation" (2002) 28 *Monash University Law Review* 85, 95.
32 *Polites v Commonwealth* (1945) 70 CLR 60, 78.
33 *Al-Kateb v Godwin* (2004) 219 CLR 562.
34 *AMS v AIF* (1999) 199 CLR 160, 180. *Western Australia v Ward* (2002) 213 CLR 1, 390–1.
35 *Singh v Commonwealth* (2004) 222 CLR 322, 358, 360–1.
36 *Polyukhovich v Commonwealth* (1991) 172 CLR 501, 611–12.
37 *ACTV v The Commonwealth* 1992) 177 CLR 106, 140, 154–5, 211. *Theophanous v Herald and Weekly Times Ltd* (1994) 182 CLR 104, 162–3.
38 *Forge v Australian Securities and Investments Commission* (2006) 228 CLR 45.

3. THE APPLICATION OF AUSTRALIA'S HUMAN RIGHTS FRAMEWORK

Finally, Australia's Human Rights Framework contains a range of key measures, which aim to further protect and promote human rights in Australia via legislation and/or policy initiatives. This Framework is marked by three relevant key measures.

The first measure is the development, in cooperation with Australian states and territories, of a new National Human Rights Action Plan. This Plan outlines future action for the promotion and protection of human rights. The second measure is the review of existing legislation, policies and practices for compliance with the seven core UN human rights treaties to which Australia is a party. This includes the plan to consolidate federal anti-discrimination laws to remove unnecessary regulatory overlap, to address inconsistencies across laws and to make the system more user-friendly. The third measure has been the enactment of the *Human Rights (Parliamentary Scrutiny) Act 2011* (Cth). Under this Act, all new laws that are introduced into Parliament, must be accompanied by statements of compatibility with Australia's core international human rights obligations.

The establishment of a Parliamentary Joint Committee on Human Rights seeks to further amplify the success of this framework. This Committee now scrutinises bills and legislative instruments for consistency with the seven core UN human rights treaties.

4. A BRIEF CONCLUSION TO PART II

Following dualist tradition, treaty-based international human rights do not apply automatically in Australia. Before they have force domestically, implementation action must be taken. There are many examples for the domestic implementation of international human rights, and it is clear they may govern civil and commercial relationships. Examples include the *Racial Discrimination Act 1975* (Cth) which applies, for example, to employment contracts. In addition, international human rights can also have an ancillary application in Australia, including through constitutional and statutory interpretation, as part of customary international law and, far less controversially, through Australia's Human Rights Framework. These are the orthodox ways in which human rights find application in Australia. Overall, despite the absence of a bill of rights at the federal level, it can be said that Australia has a robust mechanism to ensure and guarantee human rights.

III. HUMAN RIGHTS AND AUSTRALIAN PRIVATE INTERNATIONAL LAW

The orthodox approach to the domestic application of human rights fails to take into account a further possible way in which human rights may find application domestically: the mediate application of human rights that are part of a foreign legal system (foreign human rights) as the result of Australia's choice of law rules and principles.

As Mills observed, choice of law rules and principles operate as an "allocation of regulatory authority" over private matters.[39] The allocation of regulatory authority is important in cross-border contexts where more than one jurisdiction could relevantly supply the law to govern a transaction or dispute: the choice of law rules and principles then ensure that only the laws of one possible jurisdiction will apply, thus promoting legal certainty and transparency. The allocation may be the result of parties' express choices, for example, where they expressly select a foreign law to govern their cross-border contract. Alternatively, courts have developed choice of law rules and principles to resolve allocative questions. For example, parties seeking compensation in cross-border tort cases are, in Australia, bound by the *lex loci delicti* rule, that is, the law of the jurisdiction in which the tort occurred governs the dispute. There are currently no private international law rules or principles that concern the application of human rights.

Australian courts are well versed in applying choice of law rules and principles and, as a result, they regularly apply foreign law domestically. The foreign law is received as evidence of the "actual status", "status quo" or "as-is condition" of the foreign law as provided by experts versed in the foreign law.[40] Thus, the foreign law is applied "as is", courts are not permitted to adjudge the foreign law directly.[41] However, there are instances in which domestic courts do not apply foreign law domestically, even though the *prima facie* relevant choice of law rule or principle required its application. These instances include where the foreign law is so different when compared with the domestic law, that it becomes too different and thus incompatible.

---

39 A Mills, *Confluence of Public and Private International Law* (Cambridge University Press, 2009) at 18.

40 H Dörner, "Bürgenhaftung und ordre public" in O Sandrock, K P Berger, *Festschrift für Otto Sandrock zum 70. Geburtstag* (Verlag Recht und Wirtschaft, Heidelberg, 2000), 207.

41 Bundesgerichtshof IX ZB 2/98, published in *ZIP* 12/99, 483, 484.

1. "HOW DIFFERENT IS TOO DIFFERENT"? – WHEN DIFFERENCE BECOMES INCOMPATIBILITY

The differences between the foreign and domestic law are the result of a number of circumstances. The respective legal traditions, constitutional settings, approaches of the judiciary and domestic legal frameworks, all contribute to those differences. The differences span any aspect of the law, including, and it is almost trite to state, human rights law.

Importantly, the mere fact that foreign law is different is not a reason for not applying it domestically. As Judge Cardozo remarked: "*[w]e are not so provincial as to say that every solution of a problem is wrong because we deal with it otherwise at home.*"[42] However, when applying differing foreign and domestic law, domestic courts will engage in a level of comparative analysis and evaluation that seeks to establish whether the effect of the foreign law is broadly compatible with the values that underlie the domestic legal system. If the effects are not compatible, courts will search for an escape mechanism or device that will allow them to avoid the application of the foreign law and to revert back to the application of purely domestic legal rules and principles. Knop, Michaels and Riles recently suggest that, when engaging in this comparative analysis and evaluation, courts:

> … [M]ust run up against the same "how different is too different" question that confronts feminists – the ethical moment at which some feminists will decide that gender equality cannot give way to some compromise with tolerance of cultural difference ends. Indeed, under the so-called public policy exception to choice-of-law rules, a court will not apply a foreign law if that law is offensive to fundamental values of its own legal system.[43]

It is suggested that the resolution of such cases via the application of the public policy exception is the correct approach. However, it is submitted that Australian courts have used, or, in the right circumstances, would use, other private international law escape devices to make the choice where the mediate application of foreign human rights law has effects that are incompatible with values that underlie the Australian legal system. The following part seeks to identify such devices.

42 *Loucks v Standard Oil Co of New York* (1918) 224 N.Y. 99, 111.

43 K Knop, R Michaels, A Riles, "From Multiculturalism to technique: feminism, culture and the conflict of laws style" (2012) 64(3) *Stanford Law Review* 1, 6.

2. ESCAPE DEVICES TO AVOID THE APPLICATION OF FOREIGN LAW

It is now appropriate to recall the two German cases that were the genesis for this paper. The first case concerned the validity of a bank guarantee given by an inexperienced and impecunious young person to secure loans for her parents, the second the validity of a will that purported to apply Egyptian law, which significantly favoured the heirs of the deceased husband. In both instances, German human rights law had a profound impact on, and shaped, German private law.

It becomes apparent at once that it is conceivable that in relation to a cross-border transaction or dispute relating to bank guarantees or wills, Australian courts may be required to apply German law. If so, the courts would be required to apply – mediately – German human rights law.

It is not intended to offer any views as to whether the effects of the German law – the voiding of private legal instruments as agreed to between private parties by applying human rights laws – would be incompatible with the values underpinning the Australian legal system. Rather, the examples are recalled to give some context to the question of which escape device a court may use to avoid the mediate application of foreign human rights. It is proposed to conduct the following discussion at a suitably abstract level.

The range of possible escape devices available to courts is quite considerable. Any established method that enables a court to avoid the application of foreign law would be available. For example, the doctrine of *forum non conveniens*,[44] the re-characterisation of subject matters or so-called *dépeçage*, all could be used to avoid the mediate application of foreign human rights domestically. A detailed consideration of all devices would go beyond the scope of this paper. Therefore, it is proposed to focus on three particular devices, namely (a) the dichotomy of procedural and substantive law, (b) *renvoi*, and (c) the public policy exception.

---

44 This device has been applied successfully in the Chevron/Ecuador litigation to block claims of human rights violations brought under the ATS. However, its application as an escape device is controversial. C A Whytock, C Burke Robertson, "Forum Non Conveniens and the Enforcement of Foreign Judgments" (2011) 111 *Colum. L. Rev.* 1444. R A Brand, "Tinkering with Private International Law as a Response to Alleged Human Rights Violations", Letters Blogatory, http://lettersblogatory.com/2012/05/30/tinkering-with-private-international-law-as-a-response-to-alleged-human-rights-violations/ [last accessed 11 December 2012]. See also R A Brand, "Access-To-Justice Analysis On A Due Process Platform", (2012) 112 *Colum. L. Rev.* 76.

a. Procedural v substantive law

In the cause of identifying the *lex causa*, the question arises whether the particular issue is procedural or substantive in nature. The basic rule is that aspects of a dispute, which can be characterised as procedural in nature, will be governed by the law of the forum hearing the matter: the universally accepted private international law rule *lex fori regit*. Conversely, if the subject matter is characterised as one of substance, then a choice of law rule is used to determine which law applies. It has been suggested that the procedural/substantive dichotomy would find its roots in a number of notions, including convenience to the parties and procedural efficiency, the provision of natural justice, increased transparency and predictability of process and sovereignty.[45]

In private international law, this dichotomy is of fundamental importance. However, so far, there appears to be no clearly established test to identify procedural over substantive issues. One approach is the assessment on a case-by-case basis,[46] but current "Australian" approaches have been summarised[47] as (1) a "mode" or "conduct of court proceedings" approach, focussing particularly on procedural convenience and the deterrence of forum shopping;[48] (2) an "outcome determinative" approach that considers matters which affect the existence, the extent or enforceability of rights or duties as substantive in nature;[49] and (3) a "modified outcome determinative" approach which seeks to identify whether the selection of the forum would produce an advantageous outcome when compared to selecting the other forum.[50]

In developing these tests, courts have continuously narrowed the scope for procedural issues, finding, for example, that limitation periods, evidentiary questions and the kind and amount of damages are all substantive in nature. They therefore attract the application of private international law rules and principles and with that, in the right circumstances, the mediate application of foreign human rights.[51] Still, and despite the narrowing of its scope, it seems at least feasible that, in appropriate circumstances, courts may choose this escape device to avoid the mediate application of foreign law by characterising the issue as procedural, thus attracting, through the application of the *lex fori regit* rule, domestic law.

---

45 R Garnett, *Substance and Procedure in Private International Law* (Oxford University Press, 2011), 10–5.

46 *Boys v Chaplin* [1971] 1 AC 356; *Re Fuld's Estate (No 2)* [1968] P 675, 695.

47 The terminology chosen here reflects the terminology coined by R Garnett, *Substance and Procedure in Private International Law* (Oxford University Press, 2011), 18–23, 25.

48 *McKain v Millar* (1991) 174 CLR 1.

49 *Pfeiffer v Rogerson* (2000) 203 CLR 503.

50 *Neilson v Overseas Project Corporation of Vic* (2005) 223 CLR 331.

51 Certain jurisdictions characterize, for example, limitation questions as human rights issues.

b. *Renvoi*

A *renvoi* arises where a forum court selects and applies choice of law rules which point towards the entire foreign law, that is, the foreign law including both the foreign law's choice of law rules and its substantive legal rules and principles. Due to the application of the foreign choice of law rules, it is *prima facie* unclear which law will ultimately apply – domestic law, foreign law or the law of a third jurisdiction. To resolve this uncertainty, it is necessary to ascertain the content of the foreign conflict rules that would apply in relation to the case at hand.[52]

There are three conceivable outcomes. First, the application of the foreign conflict rules results in the foreign law being applicable to the matter. In other words, the domestic court will need to apply the foreign law. Second, the foreign conflict rules points back to the domestic jurisdiction. In this circumstance, the domestic court would apply domestic law.[53] The third possible scenario would be that the foreign conflict rules refer to a third jurisdiction, requiring the domestic court to apply the foreign law of that jurisdiction.[54]

Until the High Court's decision in *Neilson* in 2005,[55] *renvoi* was not thought to be part of the Australian domestic legal system. In this case, the plaintiff sought damages for injuries sustained whilst living in China. Under Australian law, the application of the *lex loci delicti* would have meant, first, that Chinese law was applicable to the matter, and second, that the plaintiff was time barred because according to the applicable Chinese statute of limitation, the period in which the claim could have been brought, had expired. However, by finding that the *lex loci delicti* rule referred to the entire Chinese law, including its private international law rules, and by ascertaining that those rules referred back to Australian law, the High Court was able to avoid the application of shorter Chinese limitation periods, availing the plaintiff of the more favourable, longer periods under Australian law.

It is submitted that after the decision in *Neilson*, which has attracted considerable criticism, including for the introduction of *renvoi* into Australian domestic law, Australian courts may consider to use this escape device to avoid

---

52 This will require characterising the dispute within the foreign legal system which may lead to a different finding and, based on this re-characterisation of the dispute, the application of different conflict rules.

53 This considers the situation where the foreign conflict rules only refer to the domestic law excluding private international law rules. It does not consider a possible reference of the foreign rules to the entire domestic law, including domestic conflict rules, which could lead, without a circuit breaker, to infinite remissions.

54 In cases where the foreign law refers to the entire law of a third jurisdiction, it is at least conceivable that this would lead to further transmissions or remissions.

55 *Neilson v Overseas Projects Corporation of Victoria Ltd* (2005) 223 CLR 331.

the mediate application of foreign human rights that are incompatible with values that underpin the Australian legal order.

c. The public policy exception

Finally, Australian courts may choose to conduct a comparison between the effects of legal systems in the context of the public policy exception. In Australia, the public policy exception is an inherent or reserve power of the courts. However, in one way or another, the exception is part of all legal systems regardless of their respective legal tradition.[56] The exception, which is available to ensure certain minimum standards of morality and social conduct, can operate "negatively", for example, to secure domestic law against implications of applicable foreign law that are incompatible with such standards. It can also be used "positively", that is, to guarantee the application of mandatory domestic rules.[57]

It is most likely that due to increased cross-border activities, the public policy exception will gain importance in resolving incompatibilities between foreign and domestic law.[58] However, unlike their civil law counterparts, common law courts are more conservative in using the exception, applying it with caution and only in serious cases. Importantly, common law courts use the public policy exception to refuse the application of foreign law on the basis that its application would constitute a grave infringement of fundamental rights. For example, in *Sykes v Cleary*, the High Court noted that:

> There is nothing novel in the proposition that a municipal court may, on grounds of public policy, refuse to apply the law of another country, even in cases where, according to the municipal law, the matter in issue is governed by the law of that other country.[59]

Referring to Lord Cross of Chelsea's speech in *Oppenheimer vs. Cattermole*, the High Court went on to note that the application of foreign law could be refused where the application would result in gross human rights violations .[60] Similarly,

---

[56] A Davies, A Bell, P LG Brereton, *Nygh's Conflict of laws in Australia* (LexisNexis Butterworths, Sydney, 2010), 376.

[57] This paper does not weigh into the ongoing debate whether the strict mandatory application of mandatory domestic laws is a subcategory of the public policy exception. However, the decision to make a law mandatory in application can be characterised as a public policy decision of the legislator.

[58] B von Hoffmann, K Thorn, *Internationales Privatrecht*, (C H Beck, München, 9th ed., 2007), 273.

[59] *Sykes v Cleary* (1992) 176 CLR 77. *Habib v Commonwealth of Australia* [2010] FCAFC 12, [77].

[60] *Sykes v Cleary* (1992) 176 CLR 77. The court referred to the House of Lords' decision in *Oppenheimer v Cattermole*. There, the House of Lords considered whether, after German law

commentators have observed that it has long been recognised that "breaches of internationally recognised basic standards of human rights and morality" occasioned by foreign law would not be received domestically.[61] It is submitted that this exception should not only apply in very narrowly defined circumstances of gross or grave direct violations, but that the public policy exception should be applied equally – and exclusively – in cases in which the mediate application of foreign human rights would be incompatible with domestic ones.

3. THE EXCLUSIVE USE OF THE PUBLIC POLICY EXCEPTION

At first glance, the flexibility of a suit of escape devices that can deal with the mediate application of foreign human rights seems attractive. They represent a significant toolkit from which courts can choose the most appropriate one for each case. However, it is suggested that the resulting hotchpotch of doctrinal uncertainty is deeply unsatisfactory.

By contrast, despite its generally more restrictive application, it seems that in cases in which the mediate application of foreign human rights would produce domestically incompatible results, the sole application of the public policy exception is best suited to avoid such incompatibility. This is so for the following reasons.

First, to perform the comparison between the foreign and the domestic law, courts would consider the outcome of a specific case. To use an effect or outcome-specific approach is not unknown under Australian law As Justice Brennan noted in *Attorney-General (UK) v Heinemann Publishers Australia Pty Ltd*:

> Every legal system which permits or commands its courts to apply foreign law must make reservations, reservations attaching not so much to the recognition or application of foreign institutions or rules in abstracto as to the effect which their application, recognition or enforcement would have in the case before the court.[62]

---

was found to be applicable in this matter, the court should give effect to a German decree of 1941, according to which German citizens of Jewish faith were deprived of their German nationality if they were living abroad. In that decision Lord Cross of Chelsea commented that "a law of this sort constitutes so grave an infringement of human rights that the courts of this country ought to refuse to recognise it as a law at all." See *Oppenheimer v Cattermole (Inspector of Taxes)* [1976] A.C. 249, 277–8. See also Lord Salmon's speech at 282–3. See also *Kuwait Airways Corp v Iraqi Airways Co* [1998] All ER (D) 149.

61 A Davies, A Bell, P LG Brereton, *Nygh's Conflict of laws in Australia* (LexisNexis Butterworths, Sydney, 2010), 379.

62 *Attorney-General (UK) v Heinemann Publishers Australia Pty Ltd* (1988) 165 CLR 30, 50.

Similarly, the discussion relating to the substance-procedure dichotomy has shown that courts readily engage in this approach, although, it is not suggested that the dichotomy should be used interchangeably to avoid the mediate application of foreign human rights. As Garnett observed recently, when compared with each other:

> [...] public policy is often a more transparent and principled basis for applying forum law than the traditional procedural characterization, which can mask unarticulated policy concerns. Public policy is also a more precise tool to, allowing for calibration to the facts of an individual case, compared to the all or nothing blanket procedural approach.[63]

Second, the sole use of the public policy exception would provide a singular gateway that limits the uncertainty as to which device courts would use to resolve incompatibilities caused by mediate application of foreign human rights. It also limits the risk that courts create unwanted consequences that are the result of resolving such incompatibilities using the other mechanisms. The various criticisms expressed by commentators in response to the High Court's introduction of the doctrine of *renvoi* into Australian domestic law in *Neilson* are evidence of the possibility of such unwanted consequences.

Third, as a direct consequence of using the public order exception as the singular gateway, the law relating to conducting such comparisons would develop only under the public policy exception. The assessment of foreign human rights "as they are" would be performed against a robust domestic mechanism as described in Part II above. A gradual development of Australian jurisprudence will likely result in a sophisticated, powerful device that controls the application of foreign human rights domestically. Commentators have already attempted to group cases into categories which then serve as starting points for the development of the law in this area by way of analogy or extension.[64]

Finally, the sole use of the public order exception would better align Australia with other jurisdictions, including most civil law countries. These jurisdictions resolve cases in which the mediate application of foreign human rights is an issue, exclusively by applying a public policy exception. Considering that the majority of Australia's trading partners, especially with the Asia-Pacific region, are of civil law tradition, this development would further Australia's global and regional legal integration.

---

63 R Garnett, *Substance and Procedure in Private International Law* (Oxford University Press, 2011), 339.

64 M Tilbury, G Davis, B Opeskin, *Conflict of Laws in Australia* (Oxford University Press, Oxford, 2002), 393.

IV. CONCLUSION

Australia possesses a robust mechanism for ensuring human rights, and incorporates international human rights via varying means. Orthodox sources include domestic implementation of internationally recognised human rights, the use of such rights to interpret the Australian Constitution and domestic laws as well as the recently announced Human Rights Framework. However, due to growing cross-border engagement, Australian courts will be increasingly confronted with a fourth way in which human rights may find application domestically: through the application of Australian choice of law rules and principles. This mediate application of foreign human rights raises its own issues, one of which is the escape devices that should be used in order to avoid their application where the foreign human right is incompatible with values underpinning Australia's domestic legal order. This paper advances several arguments, suggesting that this issue should be resolved solely by resorting to the public policy exception. The sole use of this exception would improve doctrinal certainty and further Australia's legal international integration, thus strengthening Australia's role as a global and regional transactional hub. As to what would be the precise boundaries of this exception, it is suggested that careful analysis needs to be carried out to answer the various difficult questions that arise given the breath of human rights issues that Australian courts presently do, and will continue to confront in the future.

LE DIALOGUE DES JUGES DANS LE CONTENTIEUX PRIVÉ INTERNATIONAL

Catherine KESSEDJIAN
Professeur, Directeur adjoint, Collège européen de Paris

Au moment de choisir un sujet pour honorer le dédicataire de ce livre, nous avons retrouvé dans nos archives une note interne au Bureau Permanent, en date du 27 mars 1997, adressée par l'auteur de ces lignes à H. van Loon, M. Pelichet et A. Dyer[1], les informant des résultats d'une réunion tenue à Bruxelles quelques jours auparavant au cours de laquelle avait été émise l'idée que le Bureau Permanent pourrait organiser des séminaires de « sensibilisation » à destination des juges. L'idée ayant été bien reçue par les représentants de la Commission européenne, il avait même été suggéré que le Bureau Permanent pourrait demander un financement au titre du programme Grotius[2]. Ce qui sera connu ensuite comme le « séminaire de de Ruwenberg » de 1998[3] était né. Il est l'origine de ce qu'il est convenu d'appeler désormais « le dialogue des juges ».

Le contentieux privé international devient de plus en plus complexe, au fur et à mesure de l'évolution de la mondialisation qui, en faisant fi des frontières physiques pour les activités de toute nature engendrant des conséquences sur les hommes où qu'ils soient situés, s'accommode mal des frontières juridiques et procédurales qui demeurent la règle encore au début du XXIe siècle.

Les dernières lignes directrices en date, adoptées par la Conférence de La Haye en juillet 2012, correspondent à un développement important des relations indispensables que les juges, à travers les frontières, doivent désormais entretenir pour améliorer la bonne administration de la justice dans le contentieux

1 Telle était, à l'époque, la composition du Bureau Permanent de la Conférence de La Haye de droit international privé.

2 C'est également à l'occasion du même projet qu'un fond optionnel a été créé, permettant aux Etats intéressés de participer financièrement à un projet dédié, de manière volontaire, indépendamment du budget général de la Conférence.

3 Information disponible sur le site de la Conférence (www.hcch.net).

international. Elles portent un titre extrêmement long[4] qui dénote peut-être une frilosité encore ressentie par certains Etats et certains juges à pleinement se prêter à un véritable dialogue transfrontière. Ce document se présente en trois parties : 1) Des lignes directrices émergentes relatives au développement du réseau de juges de La Haye ; 2) Des principes relatifs aux communications judiciaires générales ; 3) Des principes relatifs aux communications judiciaires directes dans des affaires particulières et les garanties communément acceptées.

Dans cette brève contribution, nous nous proposons de répondre à deux questions : 1) Pour permettre le dialogue, est-il nécessaire que les juges agissent dans des affaires précisément circonscrites, dans une branche du droit limitée ? 2) Quelles sont les limites procédurales qui demeurent pour permettre un véritable dialogue transfrontière ?

1. LE CADRE SUBSTANTIEL DANS LEQUEL LE DIALOGUE INTERVIENT

Pour que le dialogue des juges réussisse est-il nécessaire que les questions posées aux juges soient encadrées par les mêmes normes juridiques ? En d'autres termes, le succès du réseau international des juges de la Haye est-il dû au fait qu'ils doivent appliquer les mêmes normes, celles issues de la Convention Enlèvement d'enfants ? Ou bien peut-on envisager d'étendre le mécanisme à toutes sortes de contentieux, y compris lorsque le droit applicable n'est pas harmonisé entre les Etats dont relèvent les juges qui dialoguent ?

Il ne fait guère de doute que le dialogue des juges sera grandement facilité s'ils doivent appliquer les mêmes normes substantielles, comme c'est le cas au sein du réseau de La Haye. Toutefois, il ne s'agit pas là d'une condition *sine qua non* et l'on peut parfaitement étendre le dialogue à des juges qui appliqueraient leur droit national au fond du litige. L'identité des normes juridiques applicables n'est pas nécessaire au bon fonctionnement d'un système de dialogue transfrontière.

Un premier exemple peut être tiré de l'affaire West Carribean. L'affaire est désormais bien connue. Elle met en cause une société américaine (établie en Floride), Newvac Corp., affréteur d'un aéronef exploité par une compagnie colombienne West Carribean Airways et des ayants droit des victimes d'un crash aérien. Le vol en cause, en provenance de Panama City et à destination

[4] Lignes de conduite émergentes relatives au développement du réseau international de juges de La Haye et principes généraux relatifs aux communications judiciaires, y compris les garanties communément acceptées pour les communications judiciaires directes dans des affaires particulières, dans le contexte du réseau international de juges de La Haye. Doc. prél. 3 A, révisé, à l'intention de la Commission spéciale de juin 2011 sur le fonctionnement pratique de la Convention Enlèvement d'enfants.

de Fort-de-France, s'est écrasé au Venezuela, tuant tous les passagers originaires de Martinique et les membres d'équipage de Colombie. Des ayants droit ayant agi en Floride, les tribunaux de cet Etat ont appliqué la théorie du *forum non conveniens* pour décliner l'exercice de la compétence, les incitant à entreprendre leur action en Martinique. Insatisfaits de cette décision, ils se sont pourvus devant le tribunal de grande instance de Fort-de-France, mais pour lui demander de se déclarer incompétent. L'action était audacieuse. Mais elle était la seule à même, pour les demandeurs, de tenter de contrer la décision de *forum non conveniens.* Il convient de préciser à ce stade que, au regard de la Convention de Montréal du 28 mai 1999, applicable à l'affaire[5], les demandeurs bénéficient d'une option de compétence, qu'ils sont les seuls à pouvoir exercer. Les juridictions de Floride, domicile de l'un des défendeurs à l'action, font partie des compétences prévues par la liste limitative de la Convention. Or, la Convention ne prévoit pas la possibilité d'appliquer la théorie du *forum non conveniens.* Cette affaire était donc idéale pour que juges français et juges américains se parlent et décident ensemble de la conduite à tenir pour statuer sur la compétence. Ils devaient tous appliquer les mêmes textes et devaient pouvoir s'entendre pour en faire une application coordonnée afin d'améliorer l'administration de la justice. Au lieu de cela, ils se sont superbement ignorés et les demandeurs sont ainsi dans l'impasse après avoir déjà dépensé des sommes probablement importantes, uniquement pour trouver le juge compétent. En effet, le 7 décembre 2011[6], la Cour de cassation française a confirmé l'option de compétence de la Convention de Montréal et a jugé que rien ne permet d'aller à l'encontre du choix effectué par les demandeurs entre deux juridictions également compétentes au titre de la Convention. Le bras de fer entre les juges français et américains, par parties interposées, ne donne pas une bonne image du droit international (deux interprétations opposées des mêmes normes de base) ni du fonctionnement de la justice étatique dans un contentieux privé international. Certes, ce n'est pas la première fois que de telles contradictions se font jour[7], mais c'est probablement la première fois qu'une telle impasse est atteinte. Il est cependant probable que si les juges avaient pris la peine de se parler, ils seraient parvenus à une interprétation commune des règles applicables. Le résultat insatisfaisant, pour dire le moins, résulte du défaut de dialogue.

Un second exemple peut être pris dans un domaine où, au contraire, on manque de normes techniques harmonisées. Il existe de nombreux sujets pour

---

5 La France et les Etats-Unis d'Amérique sont parties à la Convention.

6 Civ. 1, 7 déc. 2011, pourvoi n°10-30919, *JDI* 2012.1384, note S. Clavel, *RCDIP* 2012.138, Rapport A. Maitrepierre, *D.* 2012.254, note Ph. Delebecque et 1237, obs. Jault-Seseke, *RTDCiv* 2012.367, note Ph. Théry.

7 Des exemples nombreux sont donnés par les actions de groupe transnationales dans lesquelles des européens avaient souhaité saisir les tribunaux américains avec des succès mitigés selon les affaires.

lesquels les juges auraient avantage à coordonner leurs décisions alors même qu'ils appliquent des normes juridiques différentes. Il faut cependant qu'ils partagent les valeurs de base, sous-jacentes aux affaires dont ils sont saisis. Ainsi pour les actions civiles en matière de droits de l'homme. Le droit international ne prévoit rien sur ces actions, même si le rapport de John Ruggie pour les Nations Unies encourage tous les moyens à la disposition des parties pour faire respecter les droits de l'homme. Mais, pour le moment, la matière est essentiellement fondée sur le droit national, sans harmonisation de ces normes. Toutefois, il est suffisant que les juges partagent les mêmes valeurs pour qu'ils puissent coordonner entre eux les procédures dont ils sont saisis. En d'autres termes, peu importent les règles techniques qu'ils doivent appliquer dans chacune des procédures, il suffit que les juges tendent vers les mêmes objectifs. C'est d'ailleurs pourquoi le Comité sur le contentieux international dans l'intérêt du public, au sein de l'*International Law Association*, dans la résolution adoptée à Sofia en août 2012[8], a prévu à nouveau des règles de coordination et de coopération transfrontières entre les juges. Cette coordination était déjà présente dans la résolution adoptée à Rio de Janeiro sur les actions de groupe transnationales[9], comme elle l'était, mais de manière moins développée, dans les travaux du Comité prédécesseur sur le contentieux international en matière civile et commerciale de la même société savante[10]. On notera la progression de la pensée des membres de ces Comités. En 1996, pour les mesures provisoires, il est seulement dit que, si les Etats donnent leur autorisation, les juges peuvent dialoguer entre eux, par delà les frontières. C'est la seule remarque qui sera faite dans ce rapport. En 2012, les règles sont beaucoup plus détaillées et les lignes directrices pour les juges sont plus précises. Par ailleurs, les membres du Comité ont considéré que l'autorisation des Etats n'était pas nécessaire, à partir du moment où les règles de protection des droits de la défense sont respectées.

2. LES LIMITES AU DIALOGUE DES JUGES

Les Lignes de conduite de La Haye, dans la troisième partie portant sur les affaires particulières, prévoient tout d'abord que le dialogue des juges ne peut

8 La résolution et le rapport, portant sur les questions de droit international privé en matière d'actions civiles pour violation des droits de l'homme, sont disponibles sur le site de l'ILA, www.ila-hq.org. L'auteur de ces lignes était le Président du Comité lors de la préparation et de l'adoption de la résolution.

9 ILA, *Report of the Seventy-Third Conference*, 2008, Resolution 1/2008, p.17 et le rapport p.534.

10 V. notamment, ILA, *Report of the Sixty-Seventh Conference*, Helsinki 1996, p. 203 ; ILA, *Report of the Sixty-Ninth Conference*, London 2000, p.137 ; ILA, *Report of the Seventieth Conference*, New Delhi 2002, p.412.

pas servir à l'obtention des preuves. Cela se comprend aisément, dans la mesure où la Conférence de La Haye a adopté une convention en matière d'obtention des preuves à l'étranger, que cette convention donne compétence à l'autorité centrale de chacun des pays concernés pour mener à bien le processus d'obtention des preuves. Cela n'est pas dit ainsi, mais quand les Lignes de conduite affirment : « l'obtention des preuves doit suivre les voies prévues par la loi », on peut penser que, pour les pays qui ont ratifié la Convention de La Haye de 1970, c'est bien ce que les rédacteurs avaient en tête.

Par ailleurs, il est à nouveau préciser, plus avant dans le texte, que « tout juge intervenant dans une communication judiciaire directe doit respecter la loi de son pays »[11]. Cela va sans dire, mais si les rédacteurs ont jugé bon de rappeler ce principe, c'est probablement pour la même raison déjà évoquée à propos de l'intitulé des Lignes de conduite, à savoir la réticence de certains Etats.

Deux points sont consacrés à la préservation de l'indépendance des juges qui participent au processus de communication transfrontière[12]. Le premier point s'adresse au juge participant lui-même qui doit s'assurer que son indépendance est pleine et entière dans sa prise de décision, malgré le processus de dialogue dans lequel il est engagé. Le second point est de nature plus générale et pose un principe cardinal selon lequel aucune communication ne doit compromettre l'indépendance des juges dans leur prise de décision. On peut penser que ce second point qui, à première vue, paraît redondant avec le premier, s'adresse lui plutôt aux parties et aux tiers, de manière à ce qu'ils ne soient pas tentés d'interférer dans la prise de décision.

Etonnamment, la partie la plus faible des Lignes de conduite concerne les garanties procédurales dues aux parties. Certes, sur certains aspects, elles ont été améliorées par rapport à une version antérieure mentionnée en note infra paginale 4. Mais il ne nous paraît pas que l'équilibre le meilleur ait encore été atteint. Le premier point de la section 6.4 mentionne que « sauf circonstances spéciales, les parties doivent recevoir une notification de la nature de la communication envisagée ». Nous avons beau chercher des hypothèses concrètes qui seraient couvertes par ces « circonstances spéciales », nous ne parvenons pas à en trouver. Il nous semble que, quelles que soient les circonstances, les parties doivent toujours être informées qu'une communication entre juges va avoir lieu et les points sur lesquels cette communication va porter. Il est possible, ensuite, ainsi que le précise le 4ème point que la participation des avocats ou des parties ne soit pas nécessaire, ou utile, ou souhaitée. Mais cela est différent. En effet, on peut imaginer que dans un cas extrêmement conflictuel et pour amorcer

[11] Et en note, il est à nouveau donné l'exemple de l'obtention des preuves déjà mentionné précédemment.

[12] Points 6.2 et 6.3.

une première ébauche de solution ou lancer des pistes possibles d'orientation du dossier, les juges doivent être seuls, dans un premier temps. Mais les parties doivent être informées. Si elles ne le sont pas, alors on ne comprend pas pourquoi il faut conserver, sans exception, trace des communications judiciaires et qu'elles doivent pouvoir être consultées par les parties (2ème point). Il semble donc qu'il existe une certaine contradiction entre le 1er et le 2ème point de la section 6.4.

Mais, même à supposer qu'il existât effectivement des circonstances dans lesquelles les parties ne devraient pas être informées, à tout le moins, les Lignes de conduite devrait donner des exemples de ces circonstances afin que les règles soient plus prévisibles pour elles et qu'elles puissent adapter leur conduite en conséquence. Laisser complètement ouverte, à la seule discrétion du juge, la décision de savoir si les parties seront informées ou non, ne semble pas conforme aux principes de bonne administration de la justice et de respect des droits de la défense.

Quant au point 6.5, il ne laisse pas d'étonner. Qu'un juge puisse suivre des règles de droit interne « offrant plus de latitude », passe encore. On peut supposer en effet que, s'agissant de règles de l'Etat dans lequel le juge concerné siège, elles sont connues des parties et de leurs conseils qui ne seront donc pas pris par surprise. En revanche, que les Lignes de conduite permettent au juge d'appliquer des « pratiques » plus souples, sans plus de détail que cela, est particulièrement surprenant. Rien n'indique en quoi peuvent consister ces « pratiques ». Où le juge les trouvera-t-il ? Qui les aura validées ? Comment les parties connaîtront-elles ces « pratiques » ? Soit, il est possible de répondre à ces questions, et les Lignes de conduite doivent être plus précises. Soit, en l'état actuel du développement du droit, aucune précision ne peut encore être donnée, et il ne semble pas que l'on puisse maintenir une telle liberté donnée au juge.

Mises à part les réserves exprimées dans les derniers développements de ce bref hommage, nous voudrions, pour finir, saluer la vision du dédicataire des ces lignes qui a su, tout au long de ces années depuis 1998 et le premier séminaire de de Ruwenberg, tenir la barre sans fléchir, malgré les nombreux sceptiques, et mener à bien un projet qui se révélera, à n'en pas douter, comme l'un des outils majeurs du contentieux privé international au XXIe siècle.

LA PROPOSITION DE LA COMMISSION EUROPÉENNE POUR UN « DROIT COMMUN EUROPÉEN DE LA VENTE » VUE SOUS L'ANGLE DES CONFLITS DE LOIS

Christian Kohler
Directeur général honoraire à la Cour de justice de l'Union européenne
Honorarprofessor à l'Europa-Institut de l'Université de la Sarre

Les relations entre le droit matériel uniforme et le droit international privé ont, de tout temps, été complexes et symbiotiques, le premier ne pouvant se passer du second. En effet, que ce soit pour définir le champ d'application du droit uniforme ou pour combler les lacunes laissées par celui-ci, l'intervention des règles de conflits de lois est souvent nécessaire et parfois expressément prévue. Ces règles influant directement sur l'application du droit uniforme, leur unification mérite d'être poursuivie avec la même persévérance que l'élaboration du droit uniforme. Les travaux de la Conférence de La Haye visant à l'adoption de « Principes » sur le choix de la loi applicable en matière de contrats internationaux[1] s'inscrivent dans cette ligne. Quant à l'unification du droit matériel, le projet de l'Union européenne pour un droit « européen » de la vente s'est concrétisé dans une récente proposition de la Commission. Les relations entre le droit uniforme et les règles de conflits de lois y sont articulées dans une perspective originale, et le présent *Liber amicorum* pour Hans van Loon offre une occasion bienvenue pour regarder de plus près la proposition sous cet angle de vue[2].

---

1 En novembre 2012, dans la perspective de l'adoption d'un instrument non contraignant en la matière, une Commission spéciale a approuvé le texte des « Principes » sur la base de la version finale présentée en juin 2011 par le Groupe de travail chargé par la Conférence.

2 La présente contribution se fonde sur une communication de l'auteur lors de la 22ième réunion du Groupe européen de droit international privé, tenue en septembre 2012 à La Haye sur invitation de Hans van Loon et Teun Struycken.

I. LA PROPOSITION DE LA COMMISSION

1. Le 11.10.2011, la Commission européenne a présenté sa proposition de règlement « relatif à un droit commun européen de la vente »[3]. Le règlement proposé a pour objet, aux termes de son article 1er, « de favoriser les conditions d'établissement et de fonctionnement du marché intérieur par la création d'un corps uniforme de règles en matière contractuelle », nommé « droit commun européen de la vente » (ci-après DCEV), qui figure à l'annexe I du texte. Ces règles peuvent être utilisées « dans le cadre de transactions transfrontières » portant notamment sur la vente de biens, « lorsque les parties contractantes conviennent de les appliquer » et que le vendeur est un professionnel. Lorsque toutes les parties sont des professionnels, le DCEV peut être appliqué si au moins l'une des parties est une petite ou moyenne entreprise.

2. Tout comme ses antécédents, la proposition de la Commission a donné lieu à un débat mouvementé sur les fondements ainsi que l'opportunité de l'initiative, l'utilité d'introduire un tel régime facultatif étant au centre des discussions. Les premières réactions provenant des parlements nationaux étaient pour le moins réservées, quatre parlements ayant même introduit des avis motivés pour non-conformité de la proposition avec le principe de subsidiarité[4]. Le Conseil a, lors de sa réunion de décembre 2011, identifié un certain nombre d'aspects nécessitant une discussion approfondie parmi lesquels figurent, outre les questions visant les règles matérielles proposées, « the personal, material and territorial scope of the proposal » ainsi que « the complexity of linking the proposal with the different legal systems »[5].

3. Il n'est pas de notre propos de contribuer à la discussion sur le *fond* de la proposition[6]. En revanche, il paraît utile d'évoquer les aspects de droit international

[3] COM(2011) 636.

[4] Voir l'article 6 du protocole (n° 2) sur l'application des principes de subsidiarité et de proportionnalité, tels que visés à l'article 5, par. 3 et 4, TUE. Les avis motivés émanent des parlements de l'Autriche, de la Belgique, de l'Allemagne et du Royaume-Uni (cf., par exemple, la motivation développée par le Deutscher Bundestag, Drucksache 17/8000 du 30.11.2011). Si la Commission est obligée d'en tenir compte, elle n'est pas tenue de procéder à un « réexamen » formel de la proposition, le seuil requis à cet effet par l'article 7 du protocole (un tiers des voix attribuées) n'étant pas atteint.

[5] Voir le communiqué de presse (doc. 18498/11, p. 25). En juin 2012, un débat sur la base juridique ainsi que sur la nécessité de la proposition a révélé des divergences de vue qui, selon le Conseil, « ne devraient cependant pas empêcher que l'on commence à examiner l'annexe » de la proposition (voir doc. 10760/11, p. 20).

[6] Voir dernièrement les rapports et discussions du colloque « Europäisches Vertragsrecht auf dem Verordnungsweg ? » (Würzburg, avril 2012), publiés à la *Zeitschrift für Europäisches Privatrecht (ZEuP)* 2012, p. 705-939.

privé mentionnés par le Conseil, à savoir les conditions d'application du DCEV, et plus particulièrement l'articulation du « droit commun » avec les règles de conflits de lois existantes. Une réflexion sur ces aspects est d'autant plus nécessaire que, pour la Commission, les modalités proposées de cette articulation justifient le recours à la base juridique envisagée, à savoir l'article 114 TFUE concernant le « rapprochement » des droits des États membres[7].

II. CARACTÉRISTIQUES DU « DROIT COMMUN EUROPÉEN DE LA VENTE »

4. Pour bien situer le débat sur les liens entre le DCEV et les conflits de lois, il importe de rappeler les caractéristiques essentielles du régime proposé. Pour la Commission, il ne s'agit pas d'offrir aux parties d'un contrat international la possibilité de choisir des règles matérielles qui ne remplaceraient que les dispositions *supplétives* de la *lex contractus* normalement applicable. La proposition vise au contraire à introduire « un corps *complet* de règles contractuelles » qui constituerait un « second régime » de droit des contrats « commun à l'ensemble de l'Union »[8]. Ce régime doit régler « des questions de droit des contrats revêtant une importance pratique au cours du cycle de vie d'un contrat transfrontière »[9]. A cet effet, il comporte, notamment pour les contrats entre un professionnel et un consommateur (« B2C »), une série de dispositions auxquelles les parties ne peuvent pas déroger par contrat[10].

5. Les effets du choix de ce « second régime » sont précisés à l'article 11 du règlement proposé : lorsque les parties sont convenues d'appliquer le DCEV, « seul ce droit régit les matières relevant de ses dispositions »[11]. Cette exclusivité est encore précisée à l'article 4 du DCEV (Annexe I du règlement) concernant l'interprétation du « droit commun » : après avoir stipulé que celui-ci doit être interprété « de façon autonome » (par. 1), la disposition ajoute que les questions

---

7 Voir *infra*, V.

8 Voir la communication de la Commission « Un droit commun européen de la vente pour faciliter les transactions transfrontières sur le marché unique » (COM(2011) 635), pt. 2.1, p. 8 s. ; c'est nous qui soulignons.

9 *Loc. cit.*, p. 10. Malgré cette ambition, une série de matières de nature contractuelle ne relèvent pas du DCEV, telle notamment la nullité du contrat pour illégalité ou immoralité ainsi que d'autres questions fréquemment rencontrées (pluralité de débiteurs ou de créanciers, cession, compensation ou fusion, cumul d'actions, etc.). Toutes ces matières sont régies « par les dispositions préexistantes du droit national » applicable en vertu du règlement Rome I.

10 Cf. COM(2011) 635, p. 7 ainsi que le considérant 30 du règlement proposé.

11 Il régit également « le respect des obligations d'information précontractuelle et les moyens d'action ouverts en cas de manquement à celles-ci ».

qui relèvent du champ d'application du DCEV mais qui ne sont pas expressément réglées par celui-ci « doivent l'être conformément aux objectifs et aux principes qui lui sont sous-jacents (...), sans qu'il soit recouru au droit national applicable en l'absence d'une convention relative à l'utilisation du DCEV, ou à tout autre droit » (par. 2)[12].

III. LE RÉGIME D'APPLICABILITÉ DU « DROIT COMMUN »

6. Le DCEV se présente ainsi comme un corps de règles qui, pour les matières qu'il régit, se veut complet et auto-suffisant et démontre les caractéristiques d'un instrument de droit international uniforme. Aussi serait-il concevable de régler son applicabilité dans les États membres indépendamment des règles de conflits de lois normalement applicables, à l'instar de la méthode suivie, entre autres, par la Convention de Vienne sur les contrats de vente internationale de marchandises (CVIM). Ce n'est pas la voie choisie par la Commission. En effet, celle-ci propose, ainsi qu'il ressort du considérant 10 du règlement, que la convention d'application du DCEV « devrait être un choix opéré au sein du droit national » applicable soit en vertu des règlements sur la loi applicable aux obligations contractuelles (Rome I) ou extracontractuelles (Rome II), soit en vertu « de toute autre règle de conflit pertinente ». Le considérant poursuit que la convention entre les parties

> « ne devrait donc pas revenir à choisir le droit applicable au sens des règles de conflit de lois, ni être confondue avec cette formalité, et elle ne devrait pas remettre ces règles en cause. Le présent règlement ne touchera donc nullement aux règles de conflits de lois existantes ».

IV. EXAMEN DU RÉGIME PROPOSÉ

7. Les réactions de la doctrine au régime d'applicabilité proposé par la Commission ont été généralement réservées, voire critiques en raison (1) de la complexité de la démarche et (2) des conflits qu'elle suscite avec le système du règlement Rome I en matière de protection des consommateurs[13]. S'y ajoute une analyse des motifs

12 Par ce degré d'exclusivité, le DCEV se distingue même des conventions de droit uniforme qui admettent le recours à la loi normalement applicable pour les questions concernant les matières régies par la convention mais « qui ne sont pas expressément tranchées par elle », cf. l'article 7, par. 2, de la CVIM.

13 Voir p. ex. J. Basedow, « Das fakultative Unionsprivatrecht und das internationale Privatrecht », *in* H. Kronke/K. Thorn (ed.), *Grenzen überwinden – Prinzipien bewahren. Festschrift für*

qui, paraît-il, ont guidé la Commission dans son choix et qui concernent la base juridique pour le règlement proposé. Ces interrogations conduisent à la question de savoir si une solution différente pour les règles d'applicabilité ne devrait pas être préférée.

1. COMPLEXITÉ DE LA DÉMARCHE

8. La réglementation proposée oblige le juge (et tout opérateur du droit) à procéder par deux étapes. Dans un premier temps, il doit rechercher la loi applicable en vertu des règles de conflits de lois pertinentes, cette loi pouvant être, dans l'hypothèse des règlements Rome I ou Rome II, soit celle choisie par les parties, soit celle applicable à défaut de choix. Dans l'un ou l'autre cas, la détermination du droit applicable peut, faut-il le rappeler, se révéler difficile. En outre, la loi applicable ainsi déterminée peut être celle d'un État tiers, ce qui soulève la question, controversée, de savoir si l'applicabilité du DCEV peut être convenue dans un tel cas. Ensuite, il est également possible que, à la place d'une loi nationale, une convention de droit uniforme s'applique en vertu de ses propres règles d'applicabilité, lesquelles ne sont pas affectées par les règlements communautaires précités (cf. notamment art. 25 Rome I). Ainsi, un contrat entre professionnels établis dans des États contractants de la CVIM est-il en principe régi par cette convention.

2. CONFLITS SUSCITÉS PAR L'ARTICLE 6 DU RÈGLEMENT ROME I

9. Lorsque la loi applicable a été établie, le juge doit vérifier, dans un second temps, si les parties sont convenues, au sens de l'article 8 du règlement proposé, de l'application du DCEV. Si tel est le cas, la loi applicable est écartée au profit du « droit commun européen »[14] et ne subsiste, s'agissant notamment de ses dispositions impératives, en principe que pour les matières *non* régies par le

Bernd von Hoffmann, 2011, p. 50 s. ; S. Corneloup, « Der Anwendungsbereich des Optionalen Instruments, die Voraussetzungen seiner Wahl und das Verhältnis zur Rom I-VO », *ZEuP* 2012, p. 705 s., et la réaction de A. Flessner, « Der Status des Gemeinsamen Europäischen Kaufrechts – Kommentar zu *Sabine Corneloup* », *ZEuP* 2012, p. 726 s. ; H. Eidenmüller/N. Jansen/E.-M. Kieninger/G. Wagner/R. Zimmermann, « Der Vorschlag für eine Verordnung über ein Gemeinsames Europäisches Kaufrecht », *Juristenzeitung* 2012, p. 269 s.

14 Le considérant 25 du règlement relève que le choix du DCEV implique l'exclusion de l'application de la CVIM en vertu de l'article 6 de celle-ci. Or, il s'agit là d'une question d'interprétation d'une convention internationale qui ne peut être fixée par le législateur de l'Union.

DCEV[15]. Toutefois, s'il est vrai que l'exclusivité de ce dernier résout la plupart des problèmes des contrats entre professionnels, la situation est différente pour les contrats conclus avec des consommateurs. En effet, il résulte de l'article 6, par. 1 et 2, du règlement Rome I que le consommateur ne peut être privé de la protection que lui assurent les dispositions impératives de la loi du pays de sa résidence habituelle, c'est-à-dire les dispositions « auxquelles il ne peut être dérogé par accord ». Or, dans le contexte du DCEV, l'application de l'article 6 rencontre des difficultés lorsque le consommateur a sa résidence habituelle dans un État membre en raison de la coexistence de deux régimes contractuels dont chacun comporte des dispositions impératives. Lorsque les parties sont convenues d'appliquer le DCEV, y a-t-il encore lieu de comparer les dispositions impératives de celui-ci avec celles du droit matériel normalement applicable ? En d'autres termes, le niveau de protection exigé par l'article 6 est-il celui du « premier régime » ou celui du « second régime » ? Dans la perspective du règlement Rome I, la réponse paraît s'imposer : l'objectif de protection poursuivi par l'article 6 ayant toujours été compris comme garantissant au consommateur l'application des dispositions les plus favorables[16], il conviendrait de vérifier le niveau de protection du DCEV à l'égard de celui du premier régime. Par conséquent, sur la base de la rédaction actuelle de l'article 6, et à moins de définir autrement la relation entre la loi nationale la plus favorable et le DCEV, le « droit commun européen » ne l'emporterait sur le premier régime que si ses dispositions de protection sont au moins équivalentes à cette loi, ce qui doit être vérifié dans chaque cas.

10. Il n'est pas possible d'échapper à cette vérification, comme le voudrait le considérant 12 du règlement proposé, au motif qu'il n'y aurait « aucune disparité entre les législations des États membres (…) lorsque les parties ont choisi d'appliquer » le DCEV puisque celui-ci comprendrait « un corps complet de règles impératives et totalement harmonisées protégeant les consommateurs »[17]. En effet, cette affirmation part d'une pétition de principe puisque, ainsi que le voudrait la proposition de la Commission, la convention sur l'application du « droit commun européen » n'intervient que dans un deuxième temps, après l'identification du premier régime. C'est à ce moment que la vérification de l'équivalence de protection des dispositions concernées est exigée par le *ratio* de

[15] Voir cependant sur l'application des lois de police dans les conditions prévues à l'article 9 Rome I et l'article 16 Rome II, S. Corneloup, *supra*, note 14, p. 717 s.

[16] Il est constant que si la loi choisie par les parties conformément à l'article 3 du règlement Rome I est plus favorable au consommateur, elle prévaut sur la loi de la résidence habituelle.

[17] Cf. considérant 12 du règlement, où il est encore dit qu'en conséquence, l'article 6, par. 2, Rome I « n'a aucune importance pratique pour les matières régies par le DCEV ».

l'article 6. Les disparités qui, en dépit des mesures d'harmonisation[18], continuent à exister entre les législations nationales, ne rendent cette vérification pas obsolète et, en fait, l'exercice peut être assez complexe[19]. S'il est vrai que la proposition de la Commission voudrait éviter de telles démarches complexes, celles-ci paraissent inéluctables lorsque l'applicabilité du DCEV doit passer par les règles de conflits de lois[20].

11. Au demeurant, le raisonnement figurant au considérant 12 du règlement proposé ne s'applique, en toute hypothèse, que si le consommateur a sa résidence habituelle dans un État membre. Lorsqu'il réside dans un État tiers, c'est la loi de cet État qui, dans l'optique du règlement Rome I, est applicable à défaut de choix. La question de savoir si les parties peuvent convenir de l'application du DCEV même dans un tel cas est controversée en doctrine, plusieurs auteurs estimant qu'une telle convention suppose que la *lex contractus* soit la loi d'un État membre[21]. D'aucuns seraient même disposés à voir dans la convention d'application du DCEV un *choix tacite* de la loi de l'État membre concerné qui écarterait la loi de l'État tiers objectivement applicable[22]. Même si l'on partageait ce point de vue, tant le choix de la loi applicable que l'accord des parties d'appliquer le DCEV devraient néanmoins être vérifiés, s'agissant de la protection du consommateur, à l'égard de la loi de l'État tiers. Toutefois, ce raisonnement paraît assez artificiel, et il suffit à cet égard de songer à l'hypothèse d'un contrat conclu par un consommateur résidant en Suisse avec un professionnel établi en Allemagne et prévoyant l'application

[18] En effet, le niveau de protection peut être supérieur à celui prévu par les directives. L'affirmation de la Commission selon laquelle le degré de protection assuré par les dispositions impératives du DCEV « est égal ou supérieur à celui de l'acquis actuel », n'y change rien. Voir dernièrement le règlement 2011/83, *infra*, note 30.

[19] Lorsqu'un contrat conclu entre un professionnel établi en France et un consommateur résidant en Allemagne prévoit l'application du DCEV, la protection du consommateur y prévue doit être comparée à celle assurée par le droit national allemand. Lorsque les parties, conformément à l'article 3 du règlement Rome I, ont soumis leur contrat à la loi française, il convient de comparer d'abord la protection offerte par cette loi par rapport à celle assurée par le droit allemand ; à supposer que la loi française soit plus favorable au consommateur que la loi allemande (et donc en principe applicable), une convention d'application du DCEV devrait être vérifiée à l'égard du niveau de protection assuré par la loi française.

[20] En revanche, si l'on voulait que le choix du DCEV soit toujours possible, il faudrait accepter que celui-ci l'emporterait le cas échéant sur les droits nationaux offrant un niveau de protection supérieur aux consommateurs.

[21] Cf. S. Corneloup, *supra* note 14, p. 713 s. ; M. Fornasier, « "28." versus "2. Regime" – Kollisionsrechtliche Aspekte eines optionalen europäischen Vertragsrechts », *RabelsZ* 76 (2012), p. 401 s.

[22] Cf. la discussion de cette problématique chez H.-P. Mansel, Der Verordnungsvorschlag für ein Gemeinsames Europäisches Kaufrecht, *WM Zeitschrift für Wirtschafts- und Bankrecht* 2012, p. 1253 s., 1261, 1263. Il est vrai que la rédaction peu claire du considérant 14 peut prêter à une telle interprétation : aux termes de celui-ci, la convention d'appliquer le DCEV impliquerait pour les consommateurs « de pays tiers (...) le choix d'un droit étranger pour eux [et] devrait être soumise aux règles applicables en matière de conflits de lois ».

du DCEV : on voit mal comment un juge allemand, à supposer que l'affaire soit portée devant lui, arriverait à voir dans cette stipulation, dans un premier temps, un choix tacite de la loi allemande, les parties n'ayant ni la conscience ni l'intention de choisir une loi nationale quelconque[23] ; la construction apparaît encore moins convaincante si l'on adopte le point de vue du droit international privé suisse, l'article 120 LDIP excluant l'élection de droit en matière de contrat de consommation.

V. RÉGIME D'APPLICABILITÉ ET BASE JURIDIQUE DU RÈGLEMENT PROPOSÉ

12. Face aux difficultés et incertitudes qu'implique la méthode qui passe par le droit national applicable, on est conduit à s'interroger pourquoi la Commission ne propose pas *l'application de plein droit* du DCEV sur la base des conditions précisées dans l'instrument lui-même, à l'instar du nombre de conventions internationales de droit uniforme. En fait, la réponse à cette question passe par la recherche de la compétence de l'Union pour adopter un acte comme celui qui est proposé. Les visas de ce dernier citent comme base juridique l'article 114 TFUE (ex-article 95 CE) lequel confère à l'Union la compétence pour arrêter « les mesures relatives au rapprochement des dispositions législatives (...) des États membres qui ont pour objet l'établissement et le fonctionnement du marché intérieur ». Or, ce n'est pas la seule source de compétence concevable, deux autres bases juridiques entrant en compétition avec l'article 114 TFUE[24]. Il s'agit, d'abord, de l'article 81 TFUE (ex-article 65 CE) lequel prévoit l'adoption de mesures de coopération judiciaire « dans les matières civiles ayant une incidence transfrontière ». Ensuite, au cas où ni l'article 81 ni l'article 114 ne seraient considérés comme base suffisamment solide, il pourrait être recouru à l'article 352 TFUE (ex-article 308 CE), qui attribue une compétence « résiduelle » pour adopter les dispositions appropriées lorsque « une action de l'Union paraît nécessaire (...) pour atteindre l'un des objectifs visés par les traités, sans que les traités n'aient prévu les pouvoirs d'action requis à cet effet ». Les différences essentielles entre les trois bases juridiques consistent dans la procédure législative, s'agissant notamment des majorités requises au Conseil pour l'adoption des mesures en question. Si les actes tant de coopération judiciaire que de rapprochement des législations sont adoptés, dans la procédure législative ordinaire[25], à la majorité qualifiée au Conseil, celui-ci statue à

[23] Il leur manque le « kollisionsrechtliche Erklärungsbewusstsein ».
[24] Cf. J. Basedow, « Art. 114 AEUV als Rechtsgrundlage eines optionalen EU-Kaufrechts : Eine List der Kommission ? », *EuZW* 2012, p.1.
[25] Art. 294 TFUE.

l'unanimité lorsqu'il arrête les dispositions sur la base de l'article 352 TFUE. Pour la Commission, cette exigence condamnait, politiquement, le recours à l'article 352. Ensuite, le choix de l'article 81 TFUE ne se recommandait guère en raison, entre autres, de la position particulière du Danemark, de l'Irlande et du Royaume-Uni. Aussi, seule la compétence conférée par l'article 114 TFUE pouvait-elle, dans l'optique de la Commission, servir comme base juridique de la mesure envisagée. Or, le règlement proposé concerne-t-il le « rapprochement » des droits des États membres alors qu'il a pour objet « la création d'un corps uniforme de règles en matière contractuelle » (art. 1) qui s'appliquerait *à la place* du droit national ? Si l'on répond par la négative, seul l'article 352 TFUE pourrait fournir une base juridique pour le règlement proposé.

13. La problématique n'est pas sans précédent. Elle a fait l'objet d'une affaire devant la CJUE suite à l'adoption par le Conseil du règlement n° 1435/2003, relatif au statut de la société coopérative européenne (SEC). S'écartant de la proposition de la Commission, qui, soutenue par le Parlement, avait voulu faire adopter le règlement comme mesure de rapprochement basée sur l'article 95 CE, le Conseil avait fondé l'acte sur l'article 308 CE. La Cour lui donna raison[26]. Rejetant le recours du Parlement, elle soulignait que

> « le règlement vise à mettre en place une forme juridique nouvelle se superposant aux formes nationales de sociétés coopératives, la SEC devant être considérée comme une forme juridique européenne, de nature spécifique et communautaire, de sociétés coopératives. (…) De surcroît, la forme de la société coopérative européenne coexiste avec celle des sociétés coopératives de droit national.
>
> Dans ces conditions, ce règlement, qui laisse inchangés les différents droits nationaux existants, ne saurait être regardé comme ayant pour objet de rapprocher les droits des États membres applicables aux sociétés coopératives. Par conséquent, l'article 95 CE ne pouvait constituer une base juridique appropriée pour l'adoption dudit règlement, qui a ainsi été adopté à bon droit sur le fondement de l'article 308 CE. »[27]

14. Consciente de l'arrêt *SEC*, la Commission justifie le recours à l'article 114 TFUE en soulignant que le DCEV constituerait « un second régime de droit contractuel au sein du droit *national* de chaque État membre »[28]. Toutefois, cette

[26] CJCE 2.05.2006, aff. C-436/03, Parlement européen c. Conseil.

[27] Cf. le sommaire de l'arrêt, basé sur les points 38 s. du texte. Se référant à cet arrêt, la Commission a proposé, en février 2012, de fonder le règlement sur la « fondation européenne » sur l'article 352, cf. COM(2012) 35, p. 5.

[28] COM(2011) 635, p. 9 (souligné par nous). En fait, il s'agit d'un jeu de mots lorsqu'il est dit ensuite que la convention d'application de DCEV ne constituerait pas un choix du droit

affirmation est contredite par les caractéristiques susmentionnées de ce régime[29], notamment le fait que celui-ci, au lieu de rapprocher les droits nationaux, les laisse intactes et coexiste avec eux, comme c'était le cas avec la SEC dans les rapports avec les régimes nationaux de sociétés coopératives. Dans ce contexte, deux éléments excluant le recours à l'article 114 TFUE méritent d'être relevés. D'une part, le « second régime » est conçu comme un droit spécial pour des transactions transfrontalières[30], alors que l'article 114 TFUE vise principalement à l'harmonisation des situations internes. D'autre part, pour les transactions concernées en premier lieu par le « second régime », à savoir les contrats conclus avec des consommateurs, les droits nationaux sont déjà harmonisés par des mesures prises sur la base de l'article 114 TFUE (ou ses prédécesseurs), dernièrement par la directive 2011/83 relative aux droits des consommateurs[31]. On voit mal comment un règlement permettant aux parties d'un contrat de droit privé d'écarter le droit national harmonisé en vertu de l'article 114 TFUE au profit d'un corps de règles *uniformes et autonomes* pourrait être qualifié de mesure de rapprochement des droits *nationaux* au sens dudit article. Il en résulte que, comme dans le cas de la *SEC*, le règlement DCEV ne peut être fondé que sur l'article 352 TFUE[32].

VI. SOLUTION ALTERNATIVE

15. La compétence de l'Union pour adopter le règlement proposé ne pouvant être basée sur l'article 114 TFUE, la construction élaborée dans la proposition de la Commission, c'est-à-dire le passage obligé par le droit national applicable en vertu des règles de conflits de lois, perd sa raison d'être et son utilité politique. Ceci ouvre la possibilité de concevoir des règles d'applicabilité qui correspondent à la vraie nature du « droit commun » tel que proposé. Ainsi qu'il a été évoqué plus haut, le DCEV constitue un corps de règles complet et auto-suffisant et présente les caractéristiques d'un instrument de droit international uniforme. Aussi serait-il cohérent de définir son applicabilité dans les États membres indépendamment

applicable au sens du droit international privé mais en réalité « un choix opéré au sein du droit national applicable ».

29 Voir *supra*, II.

30 L'article 13, sous a), du règlement proposé permet aux États membres de prévoir l'application du DCEV lorsque les parties sont établies ou résident dans le même État membre.

31 Du 25 octobre 2011, *JO* L 304 du 22 novembre 2011, p. 64. Cette directive modifie les directives 93/13 (clauses abusives) et 1999/44 (vente des biens de consommation) et abroge les directives 85/577 (contrats négociés en dehors des établissements commerciaux) et 97/7 (contrats à distance).

32 On rappellera que s'agissant du droit des marques, la directive 89/104 visant à l'harmonisation des droits nationaux est basée sur un prédécesseur de l'article 114 TFUE (art. 100a CEE), tandis que la base juridique du règlement (CE) n° 40/94 sur la marque communautaire est l'article 235 CE, devenu l'article 352 TFUE.

des règles de conflits de lois normalement applicables. Dès maintenant, les dispositions « opérationnelles » du règlement proposé peuvent, par ailleurs, être comprises dans la perspective d'une applicabilité « de plein droit » du régime optionnel[33]. En effet, rien dans les articles 3 à 7 n'impose la conclusion que l'applicabilité du DCEV doit passer par le droit national applicable, cette construction ne ressortant que des considérants du règlement. À supposer qu'un régime d'applicabilité de plein droit soit envisagé, il sera certes nécessaire de réfléchir si les conditions prévues aux articles 4 à 7 conviennent entièrement à cet égard ou s'il ne faudrait pas préciser les hypothèses où une des parties (ou même les deux) sont établies dans un pays tiers. Sans vouloir mener cette réflexion dans le cadre de la présente contribution[34], il est possible de s'orienter à la méthode suivie à l'article 1, par. 1, sous b) CVIM. Si cette méthode est transposée, *mutatis mutandis*, au DCEV, le régime optionnel serait applicable, outre dans l'hypothèse où les parties contractantes ont leur résidence habituelle dans différents États membres, lorsque les règles de droit international privé du juge saisi mènent à l'application du droit d'un État membre. Le passage par les règles de conflits de lois ne serait pourtant obligé que dans les cas où au moins une des parties réside habituellement dans un État tiers.

VII. REMARQUE FINALE

17. Compte tenu des considérations qui précèdent, quelles peuvent être les perspectives pour le projet du règlement créant le DCEV ? Lors de sa réunion des 7 et 8 juin 2012, le Conseil a constaté que « les divergences de vues sur la question de la base juridique ne devraient pas empêcher que l'on commence à examiner l'annexe », c'est-à-dire le DCEV proprement dit, et que « la position finale sur la base juridique ne pourra être arrêtée que lorsque la structure et le champ d'application définitifs de la proposition auront été définis »[35]. Or, à moins de changer radicalement le caractère de l'acte proposé afin de pouvoir le fonder sur l'article 114 TFUE, on voit mal comment le Conseil pourra échapper à la conclusion que seul l'article 352 TFUE fournit une base juridique suffisamment solide. Puisqu'il est peu probable de parvenir au sein du Conseil à l'unanimité

[33] A. Flessner, *supra* note 13, s'est notamment prononcé en faveur d'une telle solution, ses arguments s'appuyant notamment sur le droit primaire de l'Union.

[34] En tout état de cause, il sera nécessaire de régler les relations du DCEV avec les règles de conflits de lois normalement applicables, notamment les règlements Rome I et Rome II. Les règles d'applicabilité devraient être qualifiées de *lex specialis* par rapport aux dispositions de ces règlements. Il serait également judicieux de clarifier les rapports avec l'acquis communautaire en matière de protection des consommateurs.

[35] Doc. 10760/12, p. 20.

requise par cet article[36], il reste à voir si le projet de la Commission convainc un nombre suffisant d'États membres pour déclencher la procédure visant à instaurer une « coopération renforcée » au sens des articles 20 TUE et 326 s. TFUE[37].

[36] Cet élément distingue la situation du projet DCEV de l'affaire *SEC* où le règlement litigieux avait déjà été adopté à l'unanimité.

[37] Aux termes de l'article 20 TUE, les coopérations renforcées visent à favoriser la réalisation des objectifs de l'Union, à préserver ses intérêts et à renforcer son processus d'intégration. La décision autorisant une coopération renforcée est adoptée par le Conseil en dernier ressort, lorsqu'il établit que les objectifs recherchés par cette coopération ne peuvent pas être atteints dans un délai raisonnable par l'Union dans son ensemble. Le règlement (UE) n° 1259/2010 sur la loi applicable au divorce a été adopté, par 14 États membres, dans le cadre d'une telle coopération, l'unanimité au Conseil, requise par l'article 81, par. 3, al. 1, TFUE pour l'adoption du règlement dans la procédure législative spéciale ne pouvant être atteinte. Cf. en outre, sur la légalité de la décision du Conseil autorisant une coopération renforcée dans le domaine du brevet unitaire, les conclusions de l'avocat général Y. Bot dans les affaires jointes C-274/11 et C-295/11, *Espagne et Italie/Conseil*, actuellement pendantes devant la CJUE.

INNOVATIVE FEATURES OF THE HAGUE SECURITIES CONVENTION

Karl Kreuzer
professor emeritus University of Würzburg (Germany)

INTRODUCTION

Hans van Loon's long and fruitful service as Secretary General to the Hague Conference can be characterized as a period of innovation. Innovative are also many features of the Hague Securities Convention, adopted during his service. Therefore it may be appropriate to highlight those features in a contribution to the Liber Amicorum presented to *Hans van Loon*.

Over the last decades, transnational transactions of securities have become an issue of immense numerous and economic importance. In order to cope with the crucial legal problems engendered by this evolution of the transnational financial markets three major international legal organisations have sponsored pertinent international instruments. On the level of substantive law the *Sixth Inter-American Specialized Conference on Private International Law* (CIDIP-VI), held in Washington DC in 2002, has adopted the *Model Inter-American Law on Secured Transactions*, which covers security interests over, *inter alia*, incorporeal items (cf. Article 2). More specifically, the *Convention on Substantive Rules for Intermediated Securities*, adopted in Geneva on 9 October 2009 (*Geneva Securities Convention*) under the auspices of the International Institute for the Unification of Private Law (Unidroit), aims at harmonizing the national legal frameworks for modern intermediated securities holding systems. By harmonizing substantive rules regarding intermediated securities, this Convention intends to strengthen the stability of national financial markets and especially to alleviate cross-border transactions. By making diverging national systems compatible, the *Geneva Securities Convention* substantially complements the *Convention on the Law Applicable to Certain Rights in Respect of Securities held with an Intermediary* of 5 July 2006 sponsored by the Hague Conference on Private International Law, (in the following: "the Convention", "Securities Convention") which aims at the worldwide unification of conflict of laws rules regarding securities held with an intermediary. While this convention has already been generally described by numerous authors,[1] the following contribution will focus on main innovative features of the said Convention. "Innovative" means original in comparison with earlier Hague and other Conflict of laws Conventions and, in that way, means dissociation from traditional conflict of laws standards. As the Securities Convention is the first Hague Convention in the field of business law, a comparison with other Hague Conventions is forcibly restricted to general and formal issues. Also, in principle, "innovation" is understood here as a describing, not as an evaluating term.

1. GENERAL INNOVATIVE FEATURES

1.1. SUBJECT AND GENESIS OF THE CONVENTION

The Convention is innovative with regard to its subject as it is the first international conflict of laws instrument ever in the area of property aspects of securities.

Furthermore, the Convention is innovative as regards its mode of generation: The genesis of the Convention is characterised by a new method of developing international instruments, a "fast track procedure" which can be described as an intensive, continuous, completely transparent, multilaterally interactive discussion process among all interested individuals and institutions, steered by a Drafting Group acting as a kind of task force in close co-operation with the Hague Conference's Permanent Bureau, especially *Christophe Bernasconi*, who was in fact the *spiritus rector* and general manager of this innovative procedure.

From my experience as a member of the drafting group and as one of the three reporters, such a fast track procedure is ambivalent: It has obvious advantages but also considerable disadvantages. The most obvious advantage is the comparatively very short period of less than two years between the start of the formal procedure and the final step, i.e. the diplomatic conference adopting the convention. However, such a successful short track procedure necessitates a comprehensive and thorough preparation as it has been done by the report elaborated by *Christophe Bernasconi* for the Securities Convention.[2] Disadvantages of a fast track procedure are time pressure and various negative consequences thereof: enormous stress-time for the core team; meetings of the drafting committee lasting largely beyond midnight with subsequent translating sessions for the

---

1 Cf. the Bibliography on the website of the Hague Conference at www.hcch.net.

2 Cf. Preliminary Document No 1 (2000): Report on the Law Applicable to Dispositions of Securities Held through Indirect Holding Systems, prepared by *Christophe Bernasconi*; all documents are available on the website of the Hague Conference.

French version of the draft; formally or/and substantially immature innovative provisions and moreover inconsistencies of wordings inserted at different points of time into the text[3] or diverging versions of the official English/French convention texts,[4] causing considerable interpretation problems. Due to time pressure, some mayor problems could not be discussed in depth at the Diplomatic Conference. Especially, it was unfortunate that the primary rule was changed only during the Diplomatic Conference from a purely objective approach (PRIMA) to a mixed approach with party autonomy as primary rule. Thus, some consequential rules could be worked out only after that major change and therefore under extreme time pressure (e.g. Article 7, partly Article 12). Consequently, some adopted rules may not be as mature as desirable. From these experiences one can learn that a fast track procedure should not go to be a model for *any* future Convention but it should rather be decided, on a case by case basis, which working method to follow. The same cautious approach should be chosen for official reports: if I'm right, the Securities Convention is the first Hague Convention with three joint rapporteurs for the Official Commentary and also the first Convention for which the States were given the opportunity to comment on the draft commentary. Plural rapporteurs may produce a more balanced commentary but may also trigger time consuming discussions delaying the completion of the commentary. And States may take the opportunity of commenting the draft for demanding modifications of the text incompatible with what has been decided by the Diplomatic Conference.

1.2. RULE MAKING STYLE OF THE CONVENTION

The Convention is, in part, innovative with regard to its rule making style. Due to the intensive participation of leading representatives of the Anglo-American financial industry and because of the existence of a modern model for conflict rules on indirectly held securities in section 9 of the UCC (1994), the style of quite a number of rules in the Securities Convention is much stronger influenced by a common law style that traditional Hague Conventions do not adhere to. In my opinion, the results of this influence are in part positive, in part negative. A positive effect of the influence is, for instance, the introduction of a comprehensive list of definitions in Article 1, unknown to earlier Hague Conventions (cf. *infra* 1.4). Clearly unfortunate is the retention of the so called blacklists containing irrelevant issues (cf. Articles 2(3); 6). Blacklists make sense only in connection with general clauses where they exclude possible but undesired results of interpretation. This

---

3 E.g. the Preamble still refers to the abandoned so called PRIMA approach, see section 2.2.

4 Cf. for instance Article 2(2): "in relation to a *disposition of* or *an interest* in securities"/"concernant un *transfert de titres* ou d'un droit sur ces titres".

was the case for Article 1(2) of the Securities Convention so long as the scope of the Convention was determined by the vague general term "*proprietary rights*".[5] However, the blacklist went to be superfluous when the term "*proprietary rights*" was replaced, in Article 2(1) of the November 2001 draft,[6] with a *conclusive* white list enumerating positively the issues to which the Convention applied. Likewise redundant is the blacklist in article 6 because there is no need to define the issues which do *not* trigger the legal effects of a rule where the requirements for triggering the legal effects of the rule are positively and *conclusively* stated (here in Articles 4 and 5). Such a "black list" has no normative content ("non-rule"). Article 6 is an example for an unnecessary provision, adopted as part of a political compromise between European delegations and the US-delegation.

1.3. PARTIES TO THE CONVENTION

The Convention is innovative by enabling, in Article 18, for the first time, Regional Economic Integration Organisations to become parties to a Hague Convention so far the Organisation has competence over matters covered by the Convention. This is vital for the participation of both the European Union and its Member States because the Union has exclusive competence to conclude international agreements that affect legal instruments enacted by the Community. And in fact, several European instruments were already in force in the area of the Securities Convention at the end of 2002.[7] Thus, without Article 18, none of the Member States of the European Union would be in a position to become a party to the Securities Convention. The provision closely follows Article 48 of the UNIDROIT Cape Town Convention of 2001 on International Interests in Mobile Equipment.[8]

---

5 See Article 1(2) Annotated July 2001 draft (Prel. Doc. No 3).

6 Prel. Doc. No 6.

7 Cf. Directive 98/26/EC ... on settlement finality in payment and securities settlement systems, OJ L 166/45; Directive 2001/24/EC ... on the reorganisation and winding up of credit institutions, OJ L 125/15; Directive 2002/47/EC ... on financial collateral arrangements, OJ L 168/43.

8 On 15 December 2003 the EU-Commission submitted to the Council a proposal for a Decision concerning the signing of the 2002 Hague Securities Convention (COM(2003) 783). On 23 June 2005, the Council asked the Commission to assess four legal issues namely: (1) scope of application, (2) extent of third-party rights, (3) consequences for substantive and public law, and (4) impact of the diversity of laws on settlement systems and prudential regimes (10339/05 JUSTCIV 112). The legal assessment of the Commission was submitted on 3 July 2006 (SEC (2006) 910) and discussed by the EU Council on 20 December 2006 without taking a decision (15464/06 JUSTCIV 250).

1.4. DEFINITIONS

The Securities Convention is the first Hague Convention to introduce a *comprehensive* list of definitions of terms used in the instrument (Article 1). This innovation is to be welcomed *in casu* because many of the terms used in the Convention are new in the field of conflict of laws but of common use in substantive national laws, though possibly with diverging meaning from jurisdiction to jurisdiction. So, the autonomous definitions in the Convention prevent national courts from interpreting Convention terms as if they were national terms.

1.5. SCOPE ISSUES

According to its heading ("Scope of the Convention and of the applicable law") Article 2 of the Securities Convention determines the scope of both the Convention and the Convention law, i.e. the national (substantive) law applicable by virtue of the conflict rules of the Convention (*lex causae*). In contrast, earlier drafts of the Convention distinguished clearly between the scope of the *Convention* and that of the *applicable law*. The scope of the *Convention* was substantially circumscribed by the terms "proprietary aspects"[9] or "proprietary rights".[10] On the other hand, the scope of the applicable law was determined, in a separate article, by a positive list of specific issues.[11] However, as the generic term "proprietary rights", solo, seemed to be too imprecise to define the scope of the Convention, Article 1(2) of the annotated July 2001 draft introduced a blacklist of those issues which were *not* covered by "proprietary rights" and hence not covered by the Convention.[12] Even so, this blacklist, again, appeared not sufficient to define the term "proprietary". Therefore, in the November 2001 draft,[13] the positive list circumscribing in the earlier drafts the scope of the *applicable law* was moved to the provision on the scope of the *Convention* replacing there the term "proprietary". And in the heading of the provision on the scope of the *Convention* the words "and of the

9 January 2001 draft (Prel. Doc. No 2, June 2001): Article 1: "Scope of the Convention (1) This Convention determines the law governing the proprietary aspects of dealings in securities ..."; similar: February 2001 draft, Article 1 (*ibid.*).

10 Annotated July 2001 draft (Prel. Doc. No 3, July 2001): Article 1 "Purpose of the Convention (1) This Convention determines the law governing proprietary rights in respect of securities ...".

11 January and February 2001 drafts (Prel. Doc. No 2, June 2001): Article 5 "Scope of the applicable law"; annotated July 2001 draft (Prel. Doc. No 3 July 2001): Article 4 "Determination and scope of the applicable law".

12 Prel. Doc. No 3: Article 1 "Purpose of the Convention ... (2) This Convention does not determine the law applicable to ... non-proprietary aspects of rights or duties in respect of securities ... , and in particular: ...".

13 Prel. Doc. No 6: Article 2 "Scope of the Convention and of the applicable law".

applicable law" were added. Thus, the formerly separate rules on the scope of the Convention and of the Convention determined law were merged into one single scope provision. At the same time, the term "proprietary rights", in the title of the Securities Convention, was replaced with "certain rights". The negative blacklist of the former provision on the scope of the Convention (Article 1(2) July 2001 draft) was retained as new Article 2(2) in spite of the fact that, in view of the *positive* list of issues circumscribing the scope of the Convention, the black list was no more needed for the interpretation of the deleted generic term "proprietary rights". The merged scope provision was maintained in the following drafts[14] and in the Convention itself.

The Securities Convention is the first Hague Convention merging these two issues. To my knowledge, all earlier Hague Conventions are starting with a Chapter on and restricted to "Scope of the Convention". Some, but not all of the earlier conventions also provide for a section on "Scope of the applicable law"[15] or at least for an article, defining the issues governed by the convention-determined law,[16] annexed to the rules determining the applicable law. This traditional approach had also been observed in the earlier drafts of the Securities Convention (of January, February and July 2001) containing different rules as to the scopes of the Convention and of the applicable law. In my view, this merger, in the Securities Convention, of the provisions on the scope of the Convention and of the *lex causae* is unfortunate. I would have preferred keeping the traditional differentiation between scope of the Convention and scope of the Convention law. Thus, presumably, many debates on the interpretation of Article 2 of the Convention could have been prevented. In fact, one can argue, that Article 2 does not really deal with the scope of the Convention but solely with the domain of the *Convention law* whereas the (material and international) scope of the *Convention* is determined on the basis of the definition in Article 1 for securities held with an intermediary and of the internationality element in Article 3. Therefore the provision on the scope of the Convention could have simply read: "The rules of this Convention shall apply to securities held with an intermediary in any situation involving a choice between the laws of different countries." (cf.

14 December 2001 draft (Prel. Doc. No 7); January 2002 draft (Prel. Doc. No 8); April 2002 draft (Prel. Doc. No 10); June 2002 draft (Prel. Doc. No 15).

15 Convention of 22 December 1986 on the Law Applicable to Contracts for the International Sale of Goods, Chapter II – Applicable Law, Section 2 Scope of the applicable law (Articles 12 and 13).

16 See e.g. Article 7 Convention of 1 August 1989 on the Law Applicable to Succession to the Estates of Deceased Persons; Article 8 Convention of 1 July 1985 on the Law Applicable to Trusts and on their Recognition; Article 10 Convention of 2 October 1973 on the Law Applicable to Maintenance Obligations; article 8 Convention of 2 October 1973 on the Law Applicable to Products Liability; article 8 Convention of 4 May 1971 on the Law Applicable to Traffic Accidents.

Article 1(1) of the Convention on the Law Applicable to Contractual Obligations 1980 – Rome Convention). Consequently, the title of the Convention could have been: "Convention on the law applicable to securities held with an intermediary". In my opinion, the genesis and analysis of as well as the debates regarding the Securities Convention show that the traditional differentiation between the scope of a Convention and of the law designated by the conflict rules of that Convention, or, better, between the requirements for the applicability of a Convention and the domain of the law determined by the conflict rules of the same Convention, should be maintained.

Moreover, the Convention innovates insofar as it does not define the type of internationality required for triggering the applicability of the Convention (Article 3). This innovation deviates from the tradition of the Hague conventions but is in conformity with the Rome convention. Akin to that convention it suffices that the situation involves a choice between the laws of different States. This lack of concretization reflects the globalisation of capital markets where it is difficult or even impossible to definitely distinguish between internal and cross border situations. In fact, it seems hardly possible to state in the moment of entering a securities transaction whether it will finally turn out as a domestic or a transnational one.

2. THE PRIMARY CONFLICT RULE AS MAYOR INVENTIVE FEATURE

Among all the provisions of the Securities Convention the primary rule for the determination of the applicable law (Article 4) constitutes without any doubt the most innovative one.[17] It replaces the mandatory *situs* rule with the principle of party autonomy. Of course, this rule of the Securities Convention does not revolutionise the whole world of conflict of laws, but it does so as far as the law of property is concerned by abandoning for a specific sector, but on a worldwide basis, a century old mandatory conflict of laws rule.

In the following I'll substantiate why the primary conflict rule of the Securities Convention constitutes a revolution in the field of conflict of laws and why this revolution is necessary. In order to fully understand the weight of this provision we shall look at its background (2.1) and genesis (2.2).

---

17 The Convention contains various other – general (e.g. Article 11 (3)) or securities-bound (Articles 5 to 8; 12) – innovative provisions which, however, are of minor importance and cannot be discussed here.

2.1. THE BACKGROUND: DYSFUNCTION OF THE *SITUS* RULE IN CASE OF INDIRECTLY HELD SECURITIES

The huge mass of daily high value securities transactions across borders urgently necessitates conflict rules enabling market participants (investors and credit providers) to determine with certainty in advance the applicable law and thereby to ascertain whether and how they can acquire ownership of or interests in securities. Predictability regarding the applicable law is vital for securities transactions across borders.[18] However, in this area, the current traditional conflict rules, together with diverging national substantive laws, result in severe legal uncertainty in the market place all over the world.

What are the reasons for this unfortunate situation? Let me start with a personal experience. When I was a freshman at the law faculty of the University of Freiburg/Germany, more than fifty years ago, I spent a month in the local office of *Deutsche Bank* in order to get an inside view of banking practice. One of my tasks was to cut off bonds' coupons at the occasion of a rent-day. So I held physical securities in my hands and it was evident for me that every holder could take home the certificates like other movables, books or apples for instance. Therefore, I easily understood that certificated bearer securities representing rights were to be treated, under both substantive and conflict law, as movables. Thus, the traditional *lex rei (cartae) sitae* rule was applicable to (directly held) securities in relation to property issues. Hence, any transfer of securities (whether outright or by way of security) and any grant of security interests in securities (whether possessory or non-possessory) was governed by the law in force at the place where the securities, i.e. the representational certificates, were physically located at the time of the transaction. Accordingly, up to the middle of the 20th century leading text books, at least in Europe, did not even mention the problem of determining the law applicable to securities[19] or did, in case of bearer securities,[20] simply refer to the *lex situs cartae*. In the 1960s of the last century the factual situation changed radically. The rapid growth of the volume of securities transactions within national markets made the delivery of certificated physical securities to buyers or collateral takers more and more impossible. The so called

[18] Cf. Group of Thirty Study Group Report. *Global Clearing and Settlement: A Plan of Action* (2003), Recommendation 15 (Advance legal certainty over rights to securities, cash. or collateral): "Market participants must be able to determine, with certainty and reasonable cost and effort, what law defines and governs their rights to securities, cash, or collateral in a clearing and settlement system or other intermediary, what those rights are, and how to perfect and enforce them." Available at www.group30.org/home.php.

[19] See e.g. M. Wolff, *Private International Law*, 2nd edition, 1950.

[20] See e.g. H. Batiffol, *Traité élémentaire de droit international privé*, 2nd edn., 1955, no. 552; G. Kegel, *Internationales Privatrecht*, 1960, p. 229.

"paperwork crisis"[21] in New York and elsewhere compelled national legislators to cope with this new mass phenomenon. Three main instruments were used to address the paperwork problem for bonds and shares: (1) immobilisation of the physical certificated securities of an entire issue at (national) Central Securities Depositories (CSDs); (2) partial dematerialisation of securities by means of the replacement of individual physical certificates with global (physical) certificates representing an entire issue, compellingly deposited with a (national) CSD[22] and (3) dematerialisation of securities by replacing any paper bound securities with securities represented solely by entries in a CSD[23] or in the books of the issuer ("book securities"). This happened, for instance, generally in France and in part, i.e. limited to treasury bonds, in Germany. All these instruments are replacing directly held securities with a system of indirect (intermediated) holding of securities. Actually, the vast majority of securities around the world are held in (domestic or transnational) indirect holding systems: holding, transferring and pledging of securities by means of book-entries to securities accounts maintained by one or several intermediaries.

Three points are important in this context: (1) The paperwork problem was dealt with only by national legislators for their national markets; and the national solutions were often not in harmony but at variance. (2) The national provisions relating to the paperwork crisis were not accompanied by appropriate conflict rules replacing the traditional *lex cartae sitae* rule. (3) The substitution of direct with indirect holding systems immobilises all securities at the place of the relevant deposit or registry. In this way, securities are turned into *immovables*, whatever legal shape this immobilisation may have: a pool of fungible certificated securities or a deposit of global certificates with a CSD, or a registry with an issuer or a CSD. One may argue that, in all the cases just mentioned, there is still a "location" of the securities either at the place of the CSD or at the place of the issuer – not a traditional location of tangible paper securities that could be seen and touched, but a "sublimated location" of an electronic book-entry reflecting the issuance of non-tangible securities. Therefore, at first sight, such an immobilisation of securities seems to be irrelevant under conflict of laws aspects, because the

---

21 In 1968 the average daily trading volume at the New York Stock Exchange was 13 million shares (cf. Securities Industry Study, Report of the Subcommittee on Commerce and Finance of the Committee on Interstate and Foreign Commerce, House of Representatives, 1972, pp. 1, 3). In 1999 the daily average volume was 809 million shares: cf. http://nyse.com/pdfs/activity99.pdf.

22 Germany, for instance, replaced individual certificates by global (jumbo) certificates in 1972 for bonds (§ 9a DepotG) and in 1994 for shares (§ 10 (5) AktG). So, today, virtually no individual certificated securities exist anymore in Germany and thus no freshman could repeat my exercise of cutting off coupons.

23 Cf. e.g. K. Kreuzer (ed.), *Abschied vom Wertpapier? – Dokumentelose Wertbewegungen im Effekten-, Gütertransport- und Zahlungsverkehr*, 1988.

situs-rule applies to both movables and immovables. Accordingly, the *situs* rule seems to be appropriate even for "immaterialized" securities. But this reasoning is valid only where the *situs* rule designates for *all* securities, involved in a single transaction, the same location (or at least locations within the same jurisdiction) and thus the same *lex causae*. However, this will rarely be the case because in the context of securities held with an intermediary the meaning of the connecting factor "location" may vary from jurisdiction to jurisdiction.[24] Thus, in our context of indirectly held securities, the uniformity of the traditional *situs*-rule may turn out to be only fictitious. And when a national interpretation of the *situs*-rule has made clear how the *situs* has to be understood (e.g. as physical location of certificates), the market participants have to find out, in order to determine the applicable law, where the securities are located (deposited or registered). However, due to the varying techniques to represent and deposit securities, the "location" of securities may often be doubtful. There exists no world-wide binding obligation for securities to be deposited or registered once and forever in the same depository or registry (e.g. with a CSD), for instance in the home country of the issuer. And the issuers may be free not only to choose the depositary or depositories but may also not be bound to publicly make known the location of securities. In addition, the access to the information necessary may be difficult or even in some cases impossible,[25] due to the fact that in indirect holding systems investors typically are not recorded at the location of the securities but only in the books of the intermediary with whom the investor has a direct relationship. Thus, securities of a specific issue may be spread all over the globe.[26] And, even if the *situs* rule points clearly to the location of a specific institution (CSD, International CSD or any other depository or registry), the institution may not easily be identifiable with a single location when its functions are dispersed over offices located in different jurisdictions. But the main problem resides in the lack of homogeneity of portfolios: Nowadays, many portfolios (accounts) contain securities issued in different jurisdictions (mixed portfolios or accounts). In today's market practice, such portfolios are very often granted *entirely* as collateral (fiduciary transfer or pledge). In order to gain legal certainty and to exclude any legal risk in these cases, parties are compelled, on the basis of the *situs* rule, to determine the *lex cartae sitae* for every single kind of securities and to comply with the perfection

24 Location of the (individual or global) security certificates (if any)? Of the registry (if any)? Of the immediate or highest-tier intermediary? Or of the issuer?

25 Cf. Pöch, „Die Regelung des internationalen Wertpapierverkehrs ist in Bewegung – aber wohin?", [Austrian] *Bankarchiv* 2004, p. 507 (at p. 514 and fn. 66).

26 Even France, where securities are completely dematerialised, allows the creation of certificates for securities to be traded abroad; cf. Witz, "Die Entmaterialisierung des Effektenwesens in Frankreich", in Kreuzer, *ibid.* (fn. 23) p. 47 et seq.; see also Girsberger, "Revolution des Internationalen Wertpapier-Sachenrechts? – Dynamik der Rechtsvereinheitlichung durch die Haager Konferenz", in *Festgabe für Anton K. Schnyder zum 50. Geburtstag*, 2002, p. 77 (at 78).

requirements of the respective domestic laws. As a result, a multitude of different laws may govern a single transaction. Thus, the *situs* rule produces a splitting of the law governing an undivided transaction. It is evident that the research activities described are extremely time consuming, expensive, and risky. And this difficult task to determine and comply with number of foreign laws is permanent, when a portfolio is not a static but a dynamic one, for instance, when new securities are added to a pledged account (portfolio) from time to time or even constantly, maybe even on a daily or hourly basis. In fact, in such cases an updating of the pledged portfolio is simply not manageable. So, participants can hardly be sure about the exact extent of their rights and especially to what extent these rights would be recognised in cases of emergency.

Therefore, in the real world of indirectly held securities, possibly dispersed over depositories and registries all over the globe, the location of securities lacks the certainty necessary to serve as an appropriate connecting factor for determining the law applicable to securities. Changing circumstances, i.e. the dematerialization of securities, the replacement of direct with indirect holding of securities and the substitution of national securities' markets with a single global securities' market, has made the spontaneous internationally uniform conflict of laws in the form of the *situs* rule dysfunctional for securities.

2.2. THE GENESIS OF THE PRIMARY CONFLICT RULE ADMITTING PARTY AUTONOMY

The crucial law splitting triggered by the traditional *lex rei sitae* approach in case of inhomogeneous securities portfolios can only be averted by determining the law of a single jurisdiction to govern all securities covered by one single transaction. To reach this objective the so called "PRIMA" approach has been proposed prior to and during the Diplomatic Conference in The Hague. This approach chooses, for designating the law governing property issues for securities, exclusively the **P**lace of the **R**elevant **I**nter**M**ediary as connecting factor. PRIMA focuses on the location of the office of the investor's immediate intermediary maintaining the account to which the securities of the investor are credited. By determining the applicable law independently of any physical location of the securities PRIMA prevents the law splitting in case of inhomogeneous portfolios. Therefore, PRIMA has been already implemented by § 8-110 US-UCC and some European States[27]

[27] For Belgium and Luxembourg see Bernasconi/Potok/Morton, in Potok (ed.), *Cross border collateral: legal risk and the conflict of laws* (2002), no. 2.112; for France: Article 29 Loi Nr. 83-1 of 3 January 1983, which unilaterally declares French law applicable to pledges of (even foreign) securities when the relevant account is maintained by an intermediary located in France.

but also by two EU directives[28] and consequently by the legislation of Member States of the European Community transposing these directives in their internal law.[29] While PRIMA dominated the beginning of the negotiations on the Hague Securities Convention, it turned out during the debates in the Hague that, especially due to the advanced information technology allowing the flexible outsourcing of activities relating to the maintenance of security accounts,[30] it was extremely difficult to exactly determine *the*, i.e. a single place of the intermediary maintaining the securities account, respectively to determine the location of that account. In fact, it was not possible to find a *globally acceptable criterion* to precisely indicate this place.

2.3. PARTY AUTONOMY AS PRIMARY RULE

Rebus sic stantibus, it was clear that the Convention had to go beyond PRIMA in order to guarantee the necessary ex ante-legal certainty and predictability with regard to the applicable law. In this respect, the decisive step forward was initiated by a proposal of the Permanent Bureau of the Hague Conference in May 2002,[31] i.e. only a few months before the Diplomatic Conference, putting forward a redraft of the core provisions of the future Convention, i.e., of the primary rule and the fall-back rules to determine the applicable law. In particular, the proposal suggested, for designating the applicable law, no longer to primarily focus on the concept of locating securities accounts or offices maintaining such accounts. Instead, the paper proposed to allow the account holder and the relevant intermediary to agree, under specific conditions, on the applicable law. Eventually, this approach was unanimously adopted by the Diplomatic Conference as primary conflict rule in Article 4.[32] This shift, in property matters, from an "objective" connecting factor to party autonomy was an unorthodox and pioneering step which few would have predicted at the beginning of the proceedings. The choice of law by the parties was recognised to be the only conceivable connecting factor appropriate to reach both ex ante-legal certainty and a single law governing all securities covered by a

---

28 Article 9(2) Directive 98/26/EC; Article 9 Directive 2002/47/EC (both *supra* fn. 7).

29 Cf. e.g. for Belgium: Devos/Servaes, in Potok (fn. 27) n° 6.6; for Germany: § 17a DepotG; for Austria: § 33a PIL-Act (BGBl. I n° 117/2003); see also Schefold, *IPRax* 2000, 468 (473–476) with references concerning the transposition in other states in fn. 77 and 79.

30 Such activities (delivery of documents, call centres, administration of dividends, giving advice, monitoring, back-up, etc.) are often dispersed among offices in different jurisdictions.

31 Proposal for a redraft of Articles 4 and 4*bis* (Prel. Doc. No 13).

32 Article 4: "Primary rule (1) The law applicable to all the issues specified in Article 2(1) is the law in force in the State expressly agreed in the account agreement as the State whose law governs the account agreement or, if the account agreement expressly provides that another law is applicable to all such issues, that other law. …".

single transaction in case of inhomogeneous portfolios. This novel rule of choice of law stands in sharp contrast to the traditional choice of law rule in property matters, i.e., the *mandatory situs* rule. The admission of party autonomy is the most important innovation of the Securities Convention, the weight of which cannot be overestimated.

Party autonomy as primary rule in the Convention is, at the end, not really restricted by the so called reality test in Article 4(1) phrase 2, which has been adopted by way of compromise in order to satisfy the advocates of the traditional *situs* rule. This test requires, for the effectiveness of the choice of law agreement, that the intermediary has, at the time of the agreement on governing law, an office maintaining securities accounts in the selected State ("Qualifying Office"). This rather ineffectual requirement unnecessarily complicates the conflict rules regime and should not have been adopted. *Unqualified* party autonomy as primary rule would have been better.

Party autonomy in Article 4 is primarily designed and necessary for inter-individual securities transactions in the framework of business (outright or fiduciary transfer of ownership, pledging arrangements), especially for high value capital market transactions. Whether party autonomy and the fall back rules in Articles 5 and 6 are appropriate for anonymous stock-exchange securities transactions ("consumer transactions") has not been considered during the Diplomatic conference. Likewise the question which parties should be in a position to choose the applicable law – the parties to a specific transaction or those to the account agreement (between account holder and intermediary) – has not really been discussed despite the fact that the project started with the aim to adopt a Convention "on the law applicable to *dispositions* of securities held through indirect holding systems".[33] The reason for this silence may be found in the facts (1) that the agreement of the parties envisaged by the Conference was focusing on the relationship between the account holder and the intermediary (account agreement) and no more on the parties of a disposition (disposition agreement) and (2) that the choice of law agreement was determining not only the law applicable to a disposition but also to all the other issues listed in article 2 of the Convention.

2.4. CONSEQUENTIAL RULES

For lack of space, I have to restrict myself to a few remarks on consequential rules, resulting from the admittance of party autonomy.

[33] See *supra* fn. 2.

2.4.1. *Fall-back rules (Articles 5, 6[34])*

In consequence of the introduction of party autonomy as primary conflicts rule in Article 4(1), the "objective" conflicts rules in Article 5 came to be subsidiary provisions (fall-back rules) applicable only where the *lex causae* is not determined under Article 4(1). The first fall-back rule in Article 5(1) constitutes a novel rule among the subsidiary provisions, bound to the specificity of securities: If there is a written account agreement which "expressly and unambiguously" states that the relevant intermediary entered the account agreement through a particular office, then the applicable law is the law in force at the location of that office, provided that the "Qualifying Office" requirement is fulfilled. The remaining fall back rules (Article 5(2) and (3)) do not bring about new solutions, as they designate the law of the place of incorporation or organisation of the relevant intermediary. Like the primary conflict of laws rule, the fall back rules are conceived for inter-individual business transactions in the capital market. They are not designed for anonymous (consumer) stock-exchange securities transactions. As the location of securities of indirectly held securities is uncertain one could have chosen as connecting factor in such (consumer) cases the intermediary operating the transaction (PRIMA) or, probably better, the place of the stock exchange. Unfortunately, there is no universally valid identification criterion, comparable with the BIC (Bank Identifier Code), for every intermediary maintaining securities accounts by way of which it would be possible to designate in the account agreement, with absolute certainty, the jurisdiction where the relevant intermediary is located.

2.4.2. *Protection of third parties' rights in case of change of the applicable law (Article 7)*

Under Article 4, the account holder and its intermediary are able to change the applicable law at any time without the consent of third parties. This novel rule generated the need to protect third parties who often will have no knowledge of the change or may not be in a position to preserve their position. The convention protects third parties by maintaining the applicability of the old law with respect to interests in securities that were acquired before the change of law occurred (Article 7(4)). In other words: Well acquainted rights are not impaired by a mere change of law agreed by third parties.

[34] As to Article 6 see section 1.2.

2.4.3. *"Federal clause" (Article 12)*

Article 12 sets forth several interpretative and substantive provisions relating to the application of the Convention with regard to Multi-unit States. In the past, such so called "Federal clauses" were relatively short, as it was also true for the first draft of the Securities Convention.[35] However, the subsequent discussions proved that the "Federal Clause" must substantially depend on the solution found for the choice of law rules. Consequently, the drafts for the provision, finally named "Determination of the applicable law for Multi-unit States", changed with every new draft for the conflict rules. So, the final wording of Article 12 is closely connected with the final version of the conflict rules in Articles 4 and 5. In addition, article 12 takes into account relevant particularities of contracting States' legal systems. Thus, the lesson taught by this experience is that the "Federal Clause" in international Conventions cannot be taken as a standard general clause, like, e.g., public order, but heavily depends on the shaping of the conflict rules and on the legal environment in contracting States.

3. CONCLUDING REMARKS

The Hague Securities Convention represents a major effort to cope with the problem of transnational securities transactions. Its practical importance can hardly be overestimated. The Convention stands for a new generation of Hague Conventions: It differs from earlier Hague Conventions by a new matter, a new method, a (partly) new rule-making style, innovative general and securities-bound conflict rules, especially a fundamentally new approach in international property law by introducing party autonomy as connecting factor. Insofar as the latter innovation is concerned, the Hague Securities' Convention constitutes, in spite of some deficiencies, a revolutionary and necessary step at least as far as inter-individual securities business transactions across borders are concerned.

---

[35] Article 11, January 2001 draft (Prel. Doc. No 2).

INSTRUMENT OPTIONNEL INTERNATIONAL ET DROIT INTERNATIONAL PRIVÉ – SUBORDINATION OU INDÉPENDANCE ?

Paul Lagarde
Professeur émérite de l'Université de Paris I
Membre de l'Institut de droit international

1. Le sujet de cet article, rédigé en signe d'amitié et de gratitude envers Hans van Loon et l'institution qu'il a su, en grand capitaine, piloter par grand vent pendant près de vingt ans, n'est pas nouveau. Le problème des rapports entre droit uniforme et droit international privé est aussi vieux que les premières lois uniformes. Il avait fait l'objet en 1965 d'un cours très novateur de Malintoppi[1] et, à la même époque, de quelques autres études[2]. Il en résultait qu'une distinction devait être faite entre conventions unifiantes, faisant coexister, pour les situations internationales, des règles uniformes conventionnelles avec les droits nationaux, et lois uniformes, destinées à se substituer dans chaque Etat contractant aux dispositions nationales qui y étaient en vigueur.

Pour les conventions unifiantes, illustrées principalement par les conventions en matière de transports[3], le problème à résoudre était celui de la délimitation du domaine respectif de la convention et du droit national applicable et l'accord était réalisé sur le principe qu'il fallait consulter les règles d'application de

[1] Malintoppi, « Les rapports entre droit uniforme et droit international privé », *Rec. Cours La Haye*, 1965 III, p. 1-87.

[2] V. en France : Bauer, « Les traités et les règles de droit international privé matériel », *Rev. crit. DIP* 1966.537 ; Malaurie, « Loi uniforme et conflit de lois », *Travaux du Com. fr. de DIP*, 1964-1966, p. 83 et s. ; Lagarde, « Le champ d'application dans l'espace des règles uniformes de droit privé matériel", *Etudes de droit contemporain,Travaux et recherches de l'Institut de droit comparé de Paris, VIIIème Congrès international de droit comparé*, 1970, p. 149-158.

[3] Notamment Berne, 25 octobre 1952, C.I.M. et C.I.V. ; Genève, 19 mai 1956, C.M.R. ; Bruxelles, 29 avril 1961, transports de passagers par mer ; Varsovie, 12 octobre 1929, transport aérien, et les textes subséquents.

la convention avant de se référer aux règles nationales de conflit de lois. La loi française du 18 juin 1966 sur le transport maritime en tirait la conséquence et se déclarait applicable exclusivement aux transports « qui ne sont pas soumis à une convention internationale à laquelle la France est partie et en tout cas aux opérations de transport qui sont hors du champ d'application d'une telle convention » (art. 16). La convention de Vienne du 11 avril 1980 sur les contrats de vente internationale de marchandises se rattache à ce schéma. Selon son article 1er, et sauf si les parties l'ont écartée (art. 6), elle s'applique lorsque les parties ont leur établissement dans des Etats différents (définition de l'internationalité) et que ces Etats sont des Etats contractants ou que les règles de droit international privé mènent à l'application de la loi d'un tel Etat (définition du rattachement à un Etat contractant). *A contrario*, et comme pour le transport maritime, le droit national de l'Etat désigné par la règle de conflit du for saisi s'applique dans les autres situations.

Pour les lois uniformes, après les conventions du 7 juin 1930 portant respectivement loi uniforme sur la lettre de change et règlement de certains conflits de lois en la matière, l'attention s'était portée sur les lois uniformes issues des deux conventions signées à La Haye le 1er juillet 1964, portant respectivement sur la vente internationale, dite LUVI, et sur la formation des contrats de vente internationale, destinées à être introduites dans le droit des Etats contractants pour se substituer aux règles existantes. Il s'agissait alors de savoir si leur application était subordonnée au jeu des règles de conflit de lois ou si elles s'appliquaient directement dès lors que la situation était internationale au sens de leur article 1er, sans le détour de la règle de conflit. Le choix par ces conventions de la seconde solution[4] avait été diversement apprécié[5] et a pu expliquer l'échec de ces lois uniformes.

La première convention du 1er juillet 1964 permettait en outre à chaque Etat contractant de subordonner l'application de la loi uniforme à un choix des parties (art. V)[6], ce qui avait pour conséquence qu'un tel choix était une incorporation de la loi uniforme dans le contrat, toujours soumis aux dispositions impératives de la loi objectivement applicable, et non un choix de droit international privé (art. 4 de la loi uniforme)[7].

---

[4] Art. 2 LUVI : « Les règles de droit international privé sont exclues pour l'application de la présente loi, sauf dans les cas où celle-ci en dispose autrement ». Même disposition à l'art. 1 § 8 loi uniforme sur la formation des contrats de vente.

[5] V. par exemple, pour la France, en plus des références citées note 2, la discussion ayant suivi la communication précitée de Malaurie au Comité français de droit international privé.

[6] Art. V : « Chaque Etat peut [...] déclarer qu'il n'appliquera la loi uniforme qu'aux contrats dont les parties ont, en vertu de l'article 4 de la loi uniforme, choisi cette loi comme régissant le contrat ».

[7] Article 4 : « La présente loi est également applicable lorsqu'elle a été choisie comme loi du contrat par les parties, que celles-ci aient ou non leur établissement ou leur résidence habituelle sur le

2. Cette idée d'un instrument optionnel connaît de nos jours un succès remarquable, particulièrement dans l'Union européenne. Déjà, dans sa communication du 11 juillet 2001 (COM(2001) 398 final) concernant le droit européen des contrats, la Commission européenne envisageait comme solution possible l'élaboration d' un « modèle purement optionnel qui doit être choisi par les parties » (n° 66). Reprise et développée un peu plus tard par le livre vert du 1er juillet 2010 relatif aux actions envisageables en vue de la création d'un droit européen des contrats pour les consommateurs et les entreprises, cette idée a trouvé corps dans la proposition de la Commission du 11 octobre 2011 de règlement relatif à un droit commun européen de la vente[8]. Soucieuse de remédier aux entraves au fonctionnement du marché intérieur résultant des divergences entre les droits nationaux des contrats, la proposition de règlement :

> « instaure un droit commun européen de la vente qui harmonise les droits des contrats des États membres non pas en imposant la modification de leur législation nationale en vigueur en la matière mais en créant au sein de cette dernière un second régime de droit contractuel pour les contrats relevant de son champ d'application »[9].

Ce second régime ne serait applicable que lorsque les parties décideraient ensemble de l'appliquer.

Ce procédé de l'instrument optionnel a trouvé une autre application, moins attendue, en matière de régimes matrimoniaux. L'Allemagne et la France ont en effet pris l'initiative de rapprocher leur droit des régimes matrimoniaux et de créer un régime matrimonial commun offert au choix des parties et destiné à prendre place aux côtés des autres régimes matrimoniaux en vigueur dans le droit national des deux Etats[10]. L'accord entre les deux Etats, ouvert à l'adhésion de tout autre Etat membre de l'Union européenne, a été signé le 4 février 2010 et il est en cours de ratification.

Le recours ainsi fait à la méthode de l'instrument optionnel, sans périmer les questions rencontrées dans l'application des conventions unifiantes et des lois

territoire d'Etats différents et que ces Etats soient ou non des Etats parties à la convention du 1er juillet 1964 portant loi uniforme sur la vente internationale d'objets mobiliers corporels, dans la mesure où elle ne porte pas atteinte dispositions impératives qui auraient été applicables, si les parties n'avaient pas choisi la loi uniforme ».

[8] SEC(2011) 1165 final et SEC(2011) 1166 final. Sur ce texte, v. déjà C. Aubert de Vincelles, *JCP G* 2011.1376 ; B. Fauvarque-Cosson, *D.* 2012.34 ; A.-S. Choné-Grimaldi, *Contrats, Concurrence,* Consommation, n° 4, avril 2012, étude 6 ; G. Paisant, *JCP G* 2012.560 ; V. Heuzé, *JCP G* 2012.750.

[9] Point 9 du préambule du projet de règlement.

[10] Sur cet accord, v. Ph. Simler, *Droit de la famille*, n° 5, mai 2010, étude 8.

uniformes plus anciennes, en a fait naître de nouvelles[11]. Ces instruments étant appelés à devenir des régimes optionnels au sein des droits nationaux des Etats parties, leur application est-elle subordonnée à la désignation du droit de l'un de ces Etats par les règles de conflit de lois du tribunal saisi (I) ? Cette application dépendant en toute hypothèse d'un accord des parties, le régime de cet accord est-il lui aussi déterminé – et dans quelle mesure – par le droit international privé (II) ?

I. L'APPLICATION D'UN INSTRUMENT OPTIONNEL EST-ELLE SUBORDONNÉE À LA DÉSIGNATION DU DROIT D'UN ETAT PARTIE PAR LES RÈGLES DE DROIT INTERNATIONAL PRIVÉ ?

La réponse de principe est affirmative (A), mais elle soulève quelques difficultés d'application dans les deux instruments étudiés (B).

A. LA RÉPONSE DE PRINCIPE

3. Par hypothèse, un instrument optionnel n'est applicable que si les parties l'ont désigné. Il s'agit d'une désignation positive (*opt in*) et non d'une faculté d'exclusion (*opt out*) non exercée, comme dans la convention de Vienne.

L'accord franco-allemand instituant un régime matrimonial optionnel prévoit que les époux qui pourront le choisir sont ceux « dont la loi applicable au régime matrimonial est celle d'un Etat contractant » (art. 1er).

La proposition de règlement relatif à un droit commun européen de la vente est moins claire. Le point 10 de son préambule est sur la même ligne que l'accord franco-allemand :

> « La convention d'application du droit commun européen de la vente devrait être un choix opéré au sein du droit national qui est applicable en vertu du règlement

[11] V. notamment, en France, Puig, « L'avènement des sources optionnelles du Droit », *Rev. trim. dr. civ.*, 2012.493 ; Béhar-Touchais, « Relation d'un instrument optionnel avec les lois nationales », note pour le Parlement européen, accessible sur le site www.europarl.europa.eu/webnp/webdav/site/myjahiasite/users/emartinezdealosmoner/public/Behar-Touchais%20FR.pdf; Fauvarque-Cosson et Béhar-Touchais, *Mise en œuvre des instruments optionnels européens en droit privé*, Société de législation comparée, coll. Trans Europe Experts, 2012, vol. 6. En Allemagne, Fornassier, « 28. versus 2. Regime. – Kollisionsrechtliche Aspekte eines optionalen europäischen Vertragsrechts », *RabelsZ* 76 (2012) 401.

> (CE) n° 593/2008 ou, pour les obligations d'information précontractuelle, du règlement (CE) n° 864/2007 du Parlement Européen et du Conseil du 11 juillet 2007 sur la loi applicable aux obligations non contractuelles [...], ou de toute autre règle de conflits de lois pertinente. Cette convention entre les parties ne devrait donc pas revenir à choisir le droit applicable au sens des règles de conflit de lois, ni être confondue avec cette formalité, et elle ne devrait pas remettre ces règles en cause. Le présent règlement ne touchera donc nullement aux règles de conflits de lois existantes ».

En revanche, le texte même de la proposition de règlement est muet sur la question. Son article 3, intitulé « Caractère facultatif du droit commun européen de la vente », n'exige que le caractère transfrontière de la vente :

> « Les parties peuvent convenir de soumettre au droit commun européen de la vente leurs contrats transfrontières portant sur la vente de biens [...], dans le cadre du champ d'application territorial, matériel et personnel défini aux articles 4 à 7 ».

Et, selon son article 4, un contrat est transfrontière lorsque les parties ont leur résidence habituelle dans différents pays dont l'un au moins est un Etat membre.

Le caractère transfrontière ainsi défini paraît bien être une condition du choix de l'instrument optionnel[12]. Est-il une condition suffisante ? Le respect du droit international privé, affiché par le préambule, suggère que le contrat doive en outre être régi par le droit d'un Etat membre pour que les parties puissent, à l'intérieur de ce droit, choisir l'instrument optionnel. A défaut, elles pourraient quand même le faire – comment les en empêcher ? – mais la portée de leur choix ne serait pas la même que si ces conditions étaient remplies (v. *infra*, II, A).

4. La subordination de l'instrument optionnel au droit international privé comporte deux aspects qu'il faut bien distinguer. Le premier concerne la possibilité de choisir l'instrument optionnel. Le choix ne produit son plein effet que si la relation est régie par le droit d'un Etat contractant. Le second a trait à la détermination, au sein des Etats contractants, de celui dont le droit régira la relation. Cette question n'est pas anodine. Les instruments optionnels ne sont pas des textes complets. Ainsi l'accord franco-allemand instituant un régime matrimonial commun se réfère à plusieurs reprises à la loi applicable au régime matrimonial. Il en est ainsi à l'article 1er, pour définir le champ d'application du régime optionnel et à l'article 3 § 2 pour les règles applicables à la forme du choix dudit régime. Le rapport explicatif renvoie également à la loi du régime pour ce

---

12 Cette condition est d'ailleurs discutable, car on ne voit pas pourquoi l'instrument optionnel, paré de tant de vertus, ne pourrait pas être choisi par des parties à un contrat transfrontière, établies dans des Etats tiers et ayant soumis leur contrat à la loi d'un Etat membre.

qui concerne le changement de régime matrimonial et la nullité de certains actes juridiques conclus en contravention de ses dispositions. De même, bien que le futur droit européen commun de la vente doive en principe « comprendre un corps complet de règles impératives et totalement harmonisées protégeant les consommateurs »[13], l'article 10 de la proposition de règlement confie aux Etats membres le soin de prévoir des sanctions en cas de manquement à des obligations spécifiques. Et le point 27 du préambule énumère un certain nombre de « matières de nature contractuelle ou non » ne relevant pas du droit commun européen de la vente et qu'il renvoie au droit national applicable en vertu des règlements Rome I et Rome II.

La réponse à ces deux séries de questions n'est pas identique dans les deux instruments optionnels examinés dans cette étude.

B. PROBLÈMES SPÉCIFIQUES À CES DEUX INSTRUMENTS

1° Le régime matrimonial franco-allemand

5. Le régime matrimonial franco-allemand est une bonne illustration de la première difficulté. Le choix de l'instrument optionnel suppose applicable le droit de l'un des Etats contractants (deux actuellement, peut-être davantage ultérieurement[14]). Une telle règle, pour bien fonctionner, suppose une harmonisation préalable des règles de conflit de lois des Etats concernés. Il faut que dans les deux Etats la loi applicable au régime soit celle de l'un d'entre eux.

Au jour où ces pages sont écrites, le règlement européen relatif à la compétence, la loi applicable, la reconnaissance et l'exécution des décisions en matière de régimes matrimoniaux est encore en cours de négociation et les règles de conflit en la matière ne sont pas les mêmes en France et en Allemagne. Cette divergence fait obstacle à l'uniformité recherchée. Un exemple suffit à le montrer. Si deux époux portugais ayant leur résidence habituelle en France choisissent sans autre précision le régime optionnel de la participation aux acquêts, la loi applicable au régime est actuellement, selon la règle de conflit française (convention de La Haye du 14 mars 1978, art. 4), la loi française et, selon la règle de conflit allemande (art. 15 EGBGB renvoyant à l'art. 14 § 1), la loi portugaise, qui accepte sa compétence (art. 52, 2° c. civ.). Le prochain règlement européen sur les régimes matrimoniaux

[13] Préambule de la proposition de règlement, points 11 et 12.
[14] V. art. 21 sur les adhésions d'autres Etats.

fera disparaître cette distorsion franco-allemande. La loi applicable au régime matrimonial de ce couple sera la loi française[15].

Certains problèmes subsisteront cependant. Considérons maintenant un couple français résidant habituellement au Luxembourg et faisant choix du régime optionnel. Le droit applicable objectivement à leur régime est actuellement[16] et restera le droit luxembourgeois, mais possibilité est donnée aux époux de choisir la loi française. Encore faut-il qu'ils le fassent pour pouvoir choisir le régime franco-allemand de participation aux acquêts.

Il se peut aussi que les règles de conflit des deux Etats (ou que le futur règlement sur les régimes matrimoniaux) concordent pour désigner la loi d'un Etat tiers, sans permettre le choix de la loi allemande ou de la loi française. On peut imaginer qu'un couple portugais vivant à New York ou même au Portugal choisisse sans autre précision le régime optionnel franco-allemand. La loi applicable objectivement à leur régime sera la loi portugaise ou la loi de New York. Il se peut que ces époux aient pris soin de choisir en même temps pour leur régime matrimonial la loi française ou la loi allemande, mais ce choix ne sera pas valable, en l'état des règles de conflit française et allemande et de la proposition européenne, puisque le choix est limité à la loi de la nationalité ou de la résidence habituelle de l'un ou l'autre des époux. Et même si la loi de ces époux (nationalité ou résidence habituelle) permettait un choix illimité[17], ce choix ne lierait pas les tribunaux français ou allemands s'ils venaient à être saisis.

Dans un système qui soumet l'instrument optionnel au droit international privé, le choix d'un tel instrument en dehors de ce cadre ne peut être qu'un choix d'incorporation. Le régime matrimonial est régi par sa loi propre et c'est à cette loi de dire jusqu'où elle admet ce choix. En droit comparé, certains Etats limitent l'autonomie de la volonté en la matière et n'admettent pas le choix d'un régime étranger si la règle de conflit désigne leur propre droit comme applicable[18].

---

15 V. la proposition de la Commission, art. 17.

16 En France par application de la convention de La Haye, en Allemagne par renvoi de la loi française à la loi luxembourgeoise.

17 Comme c'était le cas en France avant l'entrée en vigueur de la convention de La Haye du 14 mars 1978 sur la loi applicable aux régimes matrimoniaux.

18 V. en ce sens, art. 53 C. civ. portugais, sur lequel v. *Régimes matrimoniaux, Successions et Libéralités*, Union internationale du Notariat latin, sous la direction de M. Verwilghen, Bruxelles, Bruylant, 2003, ch. XV, Portugal, n° 41, p. 2109. De même, pour la Slovénie, art. 39 LDIP, *ibid.*, ch. XVIII, Slovénie, n° 16, p. 2327 et pour le Maroc, art. 14 dahir du 12 août sur la condition civile des étrangers : « La validité intrinsèque d'un contrat de mariage et ses effets sont régis par la loi nationale du mari au moment de la célébration du mariage ou, s'il a été conclu au cours du mariage, par la loi nationale des époux au moment du contrat. La même loi décide si, et dans quelle mesure, les époux ont la liberté de se référer à une autre loi. Lorsqu'ils s'y sont référés, c'est cette dernière loi qui détermine les effets du contrat de mariage. »

2° *Le droit commun européen de la vente*

6. Les mêmes difficultés se poseront pour l'instrument optionnel européen en matière de vente. Si, comme l'indique le préambule, le règlement ne touchera nullement aux règles de conflit existantes et si le choix de l'instrument optionnel est un choix au sein du droit national applicable en vertu des règlements Rome I et Rome II, c'est bien que cet instrument optionnel ne pourra s'appliquer pleinement que si la loi applicable au contrat est celle d'un Etat de l'Union. Et comme tous ces Etats (sauf le Danemark et le Royaume-Uni) sont liés par le règlement Rome I (pour s'en tenir à celui-ci), la difficulté signalée pour le régime matrimonial franco-allemand de règles de conflit divergentes paraît résolue.

Ce n'est cependant pas tout à fait vrai, en raison du maintien en vigueur par le règlement Rome I (art. 28) de la convention de La Haye du 15 juin 1955 sur la loi applicable aux ventes à caractère international d'objets mobiliers corporels, encore en vigueur dans cinq Etats de l'Union européenne, dont la France. Cette convention, comme le règlement Rome I, admet le libre choix de la loi applicable au contrat, donc le choix de la loi d'un Etat membre de l'Union. Si les parties n'ont pas choisi de loi applicable et ont seulement fait choix de l'instrument optionnel, il faut examiner les règles de rattachement objectif prévues par ces textes pour déterminer si la loi applicable est celle d'un Etat de l'Union. Comme ces règles ne sont pas les mêmes dans les deux instruments, il se peut que, pour les Etats parties à la convention la loi applicable à la vente soit celle d'un Etat tiers et pour les autres celle d'un Etat membre, et inversement. Si le directeur d'une entreprise française désireuse de vendre ses produits à une entreprise marocaine se déplace au Maroc et y reçoit la commande, le droit applicable au contrat, à défaut de choix, sera la loi marocaine selon la convention (art. 3 § 2), mais la loi française selon le règlement (art. 4, § 1,a) . La solution variera donc selon que le litige sera soumis à un tribunal français ou à un tribunal belge[19]. Et, même lorsque les deux textes conduisent l'un et l'autre à la loi du vendeur (vente sans déplacement du vendeur), le choix simple de l'instrument optionnel fera problème si le vendeur est établi dans un Etat tiers, car la loi du contrat ne sera pas celle d'un Etat de l'Union. Dans une telle situation, ce choix ne sera, comme pour le régime franco-allemand, qu'un choix d'incorporation soumis aux aléas des lois impératives de la loi normalement applicable, par exemple pour les contrats de consommation.

Si la relation pour laquelle un instrument optionnel a été choisi par les parties peut se rattacher à la loi d'un Etat contractant, il faut encore déterminer quelle est cette loi. La réponse est à chercher dans les règles de droit international privé, auxquelles les deux instruments optionnels prétendent ne pas porter atteinte. Là encore, du fait de la convention de La Haye du 15 juin 1955, il se pourra que, pour

[19] La Belgique a en effet dénoncé la convention.

le rattachement objectif, les règles de conflit divergentes désignent le droit de deux Etats membres différents[20]. Heureusement, s'agissant de matières dans lesquelles les parties peuvent généralement disposer de leurs droits, les parties pourront désigner le droit applicable à leur contrat et il pourrait même être opportun d'exiger des parties qu'elles choisissent la loi d'un Etat membre.

Le choix de l'instrument optionnel, tant pour le régime matrimonial que pour la vente, est ainsi appelé à coexister ou à se confondre avec le choix de droit international privé. Ce choix pose des problèmes spécifiques.

II. LA CONVENTION DE CHOIX DU RÉGIME OPTIONNEL EST-ELLE SOUMISE AU DROIT INTERNATIONAL PRIVÉ ?

La première et principale question que pose le choix de l'instrument optionnel est de savoir si ce choix est ou non un choix de droit international privé. De la réponse à cette question dépendra le régime de la convention de choix.

A. LE CHOIX DE L'INSTRUMENT OPTIONNEL EST-IL UN CHOIX DE DROIT INTERNATIONAL PRIVÉ ?

7. Il faut ici rappeler les discussions qui ont précédé l'adoption du règlement Rome I et précisément de son article 3. Alors que la convention de Rome du 19 juin 1980 n'envisageait et ne permettait que le choix d'un droit étatique, la proposition de règlement Rome I donnait au contraire aux parties la possibilité de choisir des « principes et règles de droit matériel des contrats, reconnus au niveau international ou communautaire », mais cette avancée n'a pas été conservée dans le texte définitif du règlement. Sur ce point, le préambule du règlement Rome I admet la possibilité d'un choix d'incorporation de tels principes (point 13), ce qui va de soi puisque par hypothèse un tel choix devrait respecter les règles impératives du droit normalement applicable, mais le préambule ajoute que : « si la Communauté adoptait dans un instrument juridique approprié des règles de droit matériel des contrats, y compris des clauses et des conditions-types, cet instrument pourrait prévoir que les parties puissent choisir d'appliquer ces règles » (point 14). Le futur règlement relatif à un droit européen de la vente crée cet « instrument juridique approprié », lequel pourra donc être choisi dans le

[20] Par exemple dans le cas d'une vente d'Allemagne en France avec déplacement du vendeur en France.

cadre de l'article 3 du règlement Rome I. C'est à partir de là que les difficultés commencent.

En effet, puisque l'instrument optionnel comprend notamment les contrats de vente conclus par les consommateurs, il semblerait logique de ne permettre le choix dudit instrument que dans les limites permises par l'article 6 du règlement Rome I. Si toutefois l'intention est d'affranchir l'instrument optionnel des contraintes de toute loi étatique, il faudrait que le règlement introductif de l'instrument optionnel précise clairement que ce dernier peut être choisi par dérogation aux articles 3 et 6 du règlement Rome I[21].

8. La proposition de la Commission du 11 octobre 2011, en prétendant créer au sein de la législation nationale des Etats membres un second régime de droit contractuel de la vente, élude la difficulté et court-circuite l'application du règlement Rome I. Si par exemple le consommateur a sa résidence habituelle dans un Etat membre, le choix de l'instrument optionnel ne portera pas atteinte aux règles de cet Etat protectrices du consommateur, puisque par hypothèse cet instrument fera déjà partie de son propre droit[22]. Selon une terminologie un peu hermétique, le choix ne sera pas entre 28 régimes (celui des 27 Etats membres + celui de l'instrument optionnel), mais entre 2 régimes coexistant dans l'Etat membre dont le droit est applicable, celui de son droit commun et celui constitué par l'instrument optionnel. Dans cette logique, certains auteurs[23] souhaitent même l'extension de cette possibilité de choix aux contrats internes à un Etat membre[24].

Ce système « 2 versus 28 » ne vaut que dans les relations intracommunautaires. Si le consommateur a sa résidence habituelle dans un Etat tiers, le choix de l'instrument optionnel pourra être soumis à des restrictions de la part du droit de cet Etat tiers[25]. Pour les Etats membres, si aucune des parties n'est établie dans un Etat membre ou si la loi d'un tel Etat n'est pas applicable à leur contrat, le choix de l'instrument optionnel s'apparente à une clause *paramount*. Il liera les

21 V. nos observations in Schulze et Schulte-Nölke (dir.), *European Private Law - Current Status and Perspectives*, Sellier, 2011, p. 277.

22 L'instrument garantit un niveau élevé de protection du consommateur (préambule, points 11 et 12), ce qui limiterait les risques de conflit, mais on ne peut exclure des différences à la marge (v. Choné-Grimaldi, [préc. note 8], n° 10, citant les délais de prescription) ni la possibilité pour un Etat membre d'augmenter le niveau de protection.

23 V. Fornasier [préc. note 11], p. 410.

24 L'instrument optionnel est réservé aux contrats transfrontières (art. 4 de la proposition), mais l'article 13 prévoit la possibilité pour tout Etat membre de permettre d'appliquer le droit commun européen de la vente à un contrat interne à cet Etat membre ou à un contrat entre professionnels.

25 V. les exemples construits par Fornasier [préc. note 11], p. 426.

parties même dans ses dispositions impératives, mais seulement dans les limites permises par le droit de l'Etat régissant le contrat[26].

9. Ces considérations sont transposables au régime matrimonial franco-allemand. Ce régime est un régime nouveau introduit dans la législation nationale des deux Etats contractants. Si la loi objectivement applicable est la loi française ou la loi allemande, le choix de ce régime est un choix de droit interne. Si le régime matrimonial est rattaché objectivement à une tierce loi, le choix du régime franco-allemand sera un choix de droit international privé s'il s'accompagne du choix de la loi de l'un des deux Etats contractants, sinon un choix d'incorporation.

L'autonomie de l'instrument optionnel par rapport au droit international privé ne peut donc être complète. La convention de choix de cet instrument n'a pas la même valeur selon la loi objectivement applicable à la relation en cause. Il faut donc examiner son régime juridique.

B. LE RÉGIME DE LA CONVENTION DE CHOIX

10. Il résulte de l'insertion de ces deux instruments optionnels dans la législation nationale de chacun des Etats concernés que le choix d'un tel instrument n'est pas assimilable à un choix de droit international privé, par lequel les parties choisissent le droit d'un Etat donné pour régir leur relation. Si le droit applicable objectivement est celui d'un des Etats parties à l'instrument, le choix de l'instrument optionnel est un choix de droit interne. Dans le cas contraire, il doit être accompagné du choix du droit de l'un des Etats parties pour produire son plein effet.

Cela dit, on aurait pu concevoir que ces deux conventions de choix, dont l'objet est différent, soient néanmoins soumises à des règles voisines, analogues à celles figurant dans le règlement Rome I[27] ou dans la proposition de la Commission sur les régimes matrimoniaux. L'option inverse a été retenue et les règles adoptées s'efforcent à juste titre d'être appropriées à la matière considérée.

Ces règles spécifiques sont assez succinctes. L'accord franco-allemand indique seulement que le choix du régime optionnel se fait par contrat de mariage (art. 3 § 1), mais il faudra bien se référer au futur règlement sur les régimes matrimoniaux pour déterminer la loi applicable aux modalités formelles du choix de la loi applicable et du contrat de mariage (art. 19 et 20 de la proposition). L'autonomie du contrat de choix par rapport au droit international privé est bien plus marquée

---

26 Sur l'effet de la clause *paramount*, v. en France Com. 4 fév. 1992, *Rev.crit. DIP*, 1992.495, note Lagarde, *DMF* 1993.90, note Bonassies.

27 V. sur le régime du contrat de choix les considérations – écrites après le livre vert de la Commission mais avant la publication de sa proposition – de Martine Behar-Touchais [préc. note 11], § 1.2.

dans le projet de règlement relatif à un droit commun européen de la vente. L'article 8 de ce projet requiert une « convention des parties à cet effet », avec, mais seulement pour les contrats entre professionnels et consommateurs, l'exigence que le consentement du consommateur soit donné par une déclaration expresse distincte de celle exprimant son accord pour la conclusion du contrat. Pour déterminer les conditions d'existence et de validité d'une telle convention, le même article 8 renvoie aux dispositions pertinentes de l'instrument optionnel et celui-ci dispose qu'il doit être interprété de façon autonome, « sans qu'il soit recouru au droit national qui serait applicable en l'absence d'une convention relative à l'utilisation du droit commun européen de la vente, ou à tout autre droit » (art. 4).

11. En conclusion, il apparaît bien que l'intégration dans le droit national des Etats parties des deux instruments optionnels examinés dans cette étude a pour effet que leur choix ne peut produire son plein effet que si le droit de l'un de ces Etats est applicable en vertu des règles du droit international privé. Si c'est le droit d'un autre Etat qui est applicable, les dispositions de ces instruments peuvent seulement être incorporées dans le contrat, dans les limites prévues par cet autre droit. La convention de choix de ces instruments est distincte de celle de choix du droit d'un Etat partie et obéit à un régime propre, déterminé par l'instrument optionnel lui-même ou par le droit national auquel celui-ci pourrait renvoyer. Ainsi est assurée une coordination praticable de ces instruments avec le droit international privé.

Décembre 2012

THE DRAFT HAGUE PRINCIPLES ON THE CHOICE OF LAW IN INTERNATIONAL CONTRACTS AND ROME I[1]

Ole LANDO
Professor emeritus of comparative law, Copenhagen Business School
President of the former Commission on European Contract Law

The Hague Conference on Private International law was established in 1893, at a time when private international law was becoming more and more in fashion among jurists. Those who established the Conference must have seen that private international law serves its purpose best when it is made uniform. They were no doubt also fascinated by the subject and wished to have a forum to exchange their profound and subtle thoughts. Many academic lawyers were and still are enthusiastic for private international law. They probably agree with Thomas Baty that "there is a sweep and range in it, which is almost lyric in its completeness. It is the fugal music of law."[2]

This may explain why the Hague Conference on Private International law attracts brilliant lawyers to its Permanent Bureau. The Bureau's comparative studies on private international law and its other documents are of a high scholarly standing. Its present Secretary General, Hans van Loon, is also a true scholar.

The Hague Conference is presently preparing Principles on the Parties' Choice of Law in International Contracts (hereinafter the Principles), a project

1 I am grateful to Mrs Sophie Pineau of the Permanent Bureau and to professor Bénédicte Fauvarque-Cosson for helping me in procuring documents available on the sessions of the Hague Conference, and to Professors Fauvarque- Cosson, Marielle Koppenol-Laforce, Thomas Michael Kadner Graziano, Simeon Simeonides, Neil Cohen and Daniel Girsberger for useful information on the texts. In addition I have had a very rewarding exchange of views with professor Kadner.

2 Thomas Baty, *Polarized Law* (1914) p. 5, here quoted from Arthur Nussbaum, *Principles of Private International Law*, New York 1943, Introduction VII.

that originated in 2006. The latest session of the Special Commission preparing the Principles was held from 12 to 15 November 2012, and a Working Group on the same subject is scheduled to be held in June 2013.[3]

This article is about the Principles and their relationship with the EC Regulation of 17 June 2008 on the law applicable to contractual obligations (Rome I) and the soft laws, notably the Unidroit Principles of International Commercial Contracts (PICC) published by Unidroit in Rome in 2011, the Principles of European Contract Law (PECL) prepared by the Commission on European Contract Law and published in 2000 and 2003[4] and the Draft Common Frame of Reference of 2009[5] (DCFR) prepared by the Study Group on a European Civil Code.

Unless otherwise indicated, the articles referred to are those of the Principles in *Rec Com*, and the Comments to the Principles those in Prel. Doc No. 1, see footnote 3.

I admit that it would have been better to prepare this article when the work at the Principles was finished, but I want to make a contribution relating to the work of Hans van Loon.

The criticism to be passed on the Principles in the following should not overshadow the fact that I highly appreciate the work that is being done.

---

3 I base the article on the following documents issued by the Permanent Bureau:
Feasibility Study on the Choice of Law in International Contracts – Overview and Analysis of Existing Instruments
Note prepared by Thalia Kruger for the Permanent Bureau, Preliminary Document No 22 B of March 2007 for the attention of the Council of April 2007 on General Affairs and Policy of the Conference.
- Minutes of the Meetings of the Special Commission on Choice of Law in International Contracts (12–16 November 2012) Nos 1–8.
- Development Process of the Draft Instrument, Drawn *up by the Permanent Bureau*, Prel. Doc. No 6, February 2011.
- Consolidated Version of Preparatory Work Leading to the Draft Hague Principles on the Choice of Law in International Contracts, Drawn up by the Permanent Bureau. Prel Doc No 1, hereinafter *Prel. Doc 1.*
- Draft Hague Principles as Approved by the November 2012 Special Commission Meeting on Choice of Law in International Contracts and Recommendations for the Commentary, hereinafter *Rec com.*

4 Part I & II edited by Ole Lando and Hugh Beale, and published by Kluwer 2003, Part III edited by Ole Lando, Eric Clive, André Prum, and Reinhard Zimmermann and published by Kluwer 2003.

5 *Principles, Definitions and Model Rulers of European Private Law Draft Common Frame of Reference (DCFR)* edited by Christian von Bar and Eric Clive Full Edition Vol. 1–6 Sellier 2009.

I. PARTY AUTONOMY

The Principles affirm party autonomy. Party autonomy is already part of the law of many legal systems. It is provided in Rome I and is thereby the law of 27 European countries.[6] It is affirmed in most of the laws of the 50 United States of America. Statutes on the private international law of Russia and China have embodied the principle and so have the laws of many other countries. One may therefore ask why the Hague Conference undertakes to prepare principles on the parties' choice of law in international contracts.

In preparing the Principles, the Permanent Bureau of the Hague Conference made comparative law studies and launched an inquiry by means of a questionnaire addressed to the Members of the Conference the International Chamber of Commerce, and arbitration centres and bodies active on an international scale. The Bureau found that there are countries, notably in South America, that do not accept party autonomy or only do so to a limited extent. Therefore, promoting party autonomy in the area of international contracts, not only on a domestic and regional scale, but also worldwide, is a genuine need of the actors in international trade. The consultations have confirmed the importance of a growing recognition of the choice of law in international contracts.

II. WHY NOT PREPARE PRINCIPLES ON THE LAW APPLICABLE IN THE ABSENCE OF CHOICE OF LAW BY THE PARTIES?

The Principles are intended to be a companion of the *Hague Convention of 30 June 2005 on Choice of Court Agreements*. After abortive attempts to agree on a convention on jurisdiction and recognition and enforcement of judgments, the Members of the Hague Conference agreed to prepare a Convention covering the Choice of Court Agreements only.

The Principles have a similar limited scope of application covering the parties' choice of law only, and not the law applicable when the parties have not made a choice of law.

The latter situation still occurs very often, and in March 2009 the Permanent Bureau recommended that the future instrument should cover the conflicts of law rules on the law applicable, when the parties have not made a choice of law. This recommendation was supported by the majority of the Working Group on Choice

6 Denmark still adheres to the former Rome Convention on the law applicable to contractual obligations of June 1980 which provides almost the same rules on the parties' choice of law as does Rome I.

of Law in International Contracts at its meeting on 21 and 22 January 2010. However "it was also considered that a discussion on subsidiary rules should be dealt with subsequent to the development of choice of law rules on applicable law. That is to say, the first tranche of work undertaken by the Working Group is to define rules concerning choice of law agreements (without however excluding the Working Group from considering the interrelationship between choice of law and subsidiary rules[7])." In its Conclusions and Recommendations of 7–9 April 2010, the Council on General Affairs and Policy of the Hague Conference noted that there was support in the Working Group for a comprehensive draft instrument also including rules applicable in the absence of choice. The Council, however, found that priority should be given to the development of rules for cases where a choice of law has been made. The Council may have been convinced by the fact that many States, already bound by a regional instrument, did not feel the need to invest their efforts in a project of international proportions. They felt that some specific substantive law conventions are sufficient to regulate any problems that may arise.[8]

During the last decades, the world has seen an approximation of the conflict of law rules respecting contracts. The rules of Rome I, of the Swiss act on private international law of 1987, and the laws of China of 2010,[9] Russia of 2002,[10] and Ukraine of 2005[11] are similar. Furthermore, they do not differ radically from the Inter American Convention on the law applicable to contracts of 1994 which is in force in Mexico and Venezuela. They all follow the leading principle that in the absence of a choice of law by the parties, a contract shall be governed by the law of the country with which it has its closest connection. Rome I provides specific rules that give expression to this principle. They are "strong" rules, which only give way to the law of another country to which the contract is manifestly more closely connected. Others, for instance the Russian and the Swiss statutes, provide specific rules of presumptions which apply unless the contract is more closely connected with another country. It need not be manifestly more closely connected. Among the specific rules, the one providing that the contract is to be governed by the law of the habitual residence of the party required to affect the characteristic performance of the contract plays an important role.

7 I am grateful to Professor Neil Cohen for this information on the report of a Working Group meeting.

8 Prel. Doc No 7 para 24.

9 The Law of the People's Republic of China of 28 October 2010 "on the application of the law on civil law relationships with contacts abroad" came into force on 1 April 2011.

10 As laid down in Articles 1186(3) and 1211 in Part 3, Section IV of the Civil Code of the Russian Federation of 2002 see Civil Code of the Russian Federation. Third Part (English and Russian Edition). Infotropic Media; 2nd edition, 2010, Moscow – Berlin.

11 As provided in §44 of the Ukrainian Law of 23/6 2005.

Some countries still adhere to antiquated conflict rules,[12] but in some of them a reform is on the way. All in all the ongoing approximation is an encouraging signal for an attempt at unification.

The debates in the Hague Conference would then show whether the difficulties of reaching an agreement are as insurmountable as those which a jurisdiction convention faced. However, even if some countries back out, an Instrument covering this subject may be of great value for many other countries.

I have asked some of the participants of the Special Commissions meeting in November 2012 for their views on the matter. There does not seem to be any feeling among them to take this subject on board, at least not now. As one said, "I don't think that anyone has the stomach to tackle this at the international level."

That, in my view, is a pity. It is submitted that comparative law studies on the laws relating to the conflicts of law rules on the applicable law, when the parties have not made a choice of law, will reveal a greater need of international trade for uniform rules than for promoting party autonomy. It would be useful if contracts between parties from States that are bound by a regional instrument and parties from other States, and among them the emerging economies, China, South Korea, India and Brazil, were governed by such uniform rules.

Certainly Hague Principles, which also cover conflicts of law rules on the applicable law, when the parties have not made a choice of law, will not have the company of a Hague Convention on jurisdiction, but is this company a necessity?

III. WHY PRINCIPLES AND NOT A CONVENTION?

The Instrument is drafted as *Principles* and not as *Convention*. It appears from Prel. Doc No 1[13] that the term Principles was preferred to Convention because the Conference wishes the black letter rules *and* the comments and illustrations to be part of the Instrument.

In order to enhance a uniform application of the Rome Convention of 19 June 1980 on the law applicable to contractual obligations, Professors Giuliano and Lagarde supplied an explanatory report to it.[14] Although the report was not binding, it was very useful and still gives guidance on the rules of Rome I that are the same or similar to those of the Convention. The American Uniform

[12] This applies to the laws of the Latin American countries that have adopted the treaties of Montevideo of 12 February 1889 and of 19 March 1940 and the Bustamente Code of Private International Law of 20 February 1928.

[13] See Prel. Doc No 1, Introduction no 7 at p 5.

[14] Report on the Convention on the law applicable to contractual obligations by Mario Giuliano, Professor, University of Milan, and Paul Lagarde, Professor, University of Paris I, *OJ C 282, 31/10/1980 P. 0001–0050 (hereinafter the Giuliano-Lagarde Report).*

Commercial Code is published with comments. They are not binding, but they are often referred to by the courts. The Hague Conference should perhaps consider also supplying an explanatory report or comments to its future Instruments, be they Principles or Conventions.

IV. WILL THE PRINCIPLES BE ENACTED AS AN OPT-IN INSTRUMENT?

The Preamble of the draft Principles provides:

1. This instrument sets forth general principles concerning choice of law in international commercial contracts. They affirm the principle of party autonomy with limited exceptions.
2. They may be used as a model for national, regional, supranational or international instruments.
3. They may be used to interpret, supplement and develop rules of private international law.
4. They may be applied by courts and by arbitral tribunals

Are the Principles intended to be an opt-in instrument?

Prel. Doc No 1, paragraph 7 states that "the Council expressed its initial preference for a non-binding instrument", and that "the method used is that within UNIDROIT for the development and revision of the UNIDROIT Principles of International Commercial Contracts,"(the PICC). This could indicate that, like the PICC, the Principles will only apply when the parties choose them, so that it will be an opt-in instrument

This does not appear clearly from the Principles and the Comments so far available. I have, however, been informed that the issue was not definitely resolved at the November 2012 meeting of the Special Commission. It was intentionally left open to allow the greatest possible flexibility.

In Member States, which today do not allow or set limits to the parties' choice of law, and which will introduce the opt-in solution, the parties must also agree to have the Principles apply to their choice of law. This means that Peter from X country and John from Y country, who agree to have their contract governed by the law of Y country, must also agree to have the Principles apply. Why require this double choice? What happens to parties who chose the law, but not the Principles? Is their choice ineffective or invalid?

For States that already allow the parties' choice of law, the opt-in solution will bring about two systems for the parties' choice of law. That appears to be pointless.

I find it difficult to see the purpose of an opt-in model for an instrument that promotes the parties' choice of law.

V. THE PRINCIPLES AND ROME I

1. The Preamble, paragraph 2 provides that the Principles are to be used as "a model for national, regional and, supranational or international instruments", and paragraph 3, that they "may be used to interpret, supplement and develop rules of private international law." The Comment in Prel. Doc No 1,[15] paragraph 12 states that "the emphasis is on the Hague Principles as a model for legislation: the legislators in charge of reforming rules relating to the choice of law in international contracts may be encouraged to use the future instrument for inspiration or for support." In addition, it is stated that "it may be legitimately expected that the future instrument will be used as a source of inspiration for the gradual development of uniform rules relating to the law applicable to international contracts, by avoiding any risk of conflict of norms with the range of instruments laying down the principle of party autonomy at the regional level."

However, the Comments in Prel. Doc. No 1 paragraph 13 state that "there will be no direct interference with the Rome I Regulation." What that means is not clear to me, since paragraph 13 also states that it is "clear that the solutions used in the future instrument may influence the evaluation and eventual reform of the Rome I Regulation."[16]

Will they?

2. Article 3 of the Draft Principles on *rules of law* provides that a reference to law includes rules of law that are generally accepted on an international, supranational or regional level as a neutral and balanced set of rules, *unless the law of the forum provides otherwise. Rules of law* include soft law instruments like the PICC, the PECL and the DCFR.

States that allow the parties to choose soft law rules will give effect to the parties' choice of one of these instruments. They will accept it as a genuine *choice of law* (in German *kollisionsrechtliche Parteiverweisung*). Then, the soft law rules of PICC or PECL will apply, and its provisions, for instance on validity, will replace the corresponding mandatory rules of the otherwise applicable law.[17]

---

15 Prel. Doc No 1 (see note 3).

16 Prel. Doc No 1 (see note 3).

17 However, the overriding mandatory rules of the forum and its public policy will apply; see Article 11, paragraph 1 of the Draft Principles. Paragraph 2 provides that the law of the forum determines when a court may or must apply or take into account overriding mandatory provisions of another law.

There are advantages attached to this choice. Parties who choose one of these instruments do not have to debate whether to select the law of one State over another. They select neutral principles and avoid that the party whose state law is chosen gets the advantage of "playing at home" and that the other party gets the often serious handicap of "playing away." To choose one of these instruments is also an advantage for parties whose legal systems are not fully developed or which contain "ancient relics of a dead past".

The former Article 2(1) in Prel. Doc No 1 provided that a reference to law includes rules of law. As Article 3, which replaces Article 2(1), is now drafted, parties who envisage a litigation in court may not select soft law rules when the law of the forum prohibits it.

It follows implicitly from recitals 13 and 14 of the Preamble to Rome I, that Rome I does not allow parties to choose soft law rules as a genuine *choice of law* (*kollisionsrechtliche Parteiverweisung*), but only as an *incorporation* (*materielrechtliche Parteiverweisung*) in the contract. Then the rules of law will replace the non-mandatory, but not the mandatory, rules of the law applicable to the contract.

It would be advisable for the countries of the European Union to change Rome I on this point.

In international arbitration practice, it is widely accepted that that parties may choose rules of law to govern their contract as a genuine choice of law.[18]

3. On the parties' agreement on the choice of law Article 6 of the Draft Principles provides:

1. Subject to paragraph 2,
   a) Whether the parties have agreed to a choice of law is determined by the law that was purportedly agreed to;
   b) If the parties have used standard terms designating different laws and under both of these laws the same standard terms prevail, the law designated in those terms applies; if under these laws different standard terms prevail, or if no standard terms prevail, there is no choice of law.
2. The law of the State in which a party has its establishment determines whether that party has consented to the choice of law if, under the circumstances, it

[18] See, *e.g.*, Article 28(1) of the UNCITRAL Model Law on International Commercial Arbitration, with amendments as adopted in 2006, Article 17 of the ICC Rules of Arbitration, London Court of International Arbitration Rules, Article 22(3), Article 1496(1) of the French Code of Civil Procedure, Article 1051 of the German Code of Civil Procedure, Article 36 of the Arbitration Law of Japan (2003), Article 187(1) of the Swiss Federal Act on Private International Law of 18 December 1987 and the Danish Arbitration Act of 24 June 2005 § 28.

would not be reasonable to make that determination under the law specified in paragraph 1.

As for consent, paragraphs 1(a) and 2 are in substance identical with Article 10 of Rome I, which also covers validity. Validity includes the so-called defects in consent (*vices de consentement*) such as mistake and misrepresentation. The expression in paragraph 1(a) "whether the parties have agreed to a choice of law" may cover the meeting of the minds only, but may also include defects in consent. This might be clarified in the comments.

Paragraph 1(b) provides that "if the parties have used standard terms designating different laws and under both of these laws the same standard terms prevail, the law designated in those terms applies; if under these laws different standard terms prevail, or if no standard terms prevail, there is no choice of law".

The explanation given to me by Professor Thomas Kadner, who participated in the work, is the following.

Let us take the example that in his offer Peter has referred to the law of X and in his answer John has referred to the law of Y.

If the parties have used standard terms designating different laws, the crucial question under Article 6(1)(b) then is whether "under both of these laws the same standard terms prevail." We would thus need to know if the substantive law of country X and the substantive law of country Y reach the same solution as to the battle of forms issue (*e.g.*, both apply first shot rules or both apply last shot rules to the present case).[19]

The scenario does not contain this information. Let us thus work with two hypothetical situations:

(1) If, *e.g.*, law X and law Y both apply last shot rules, the law of country Y will indeed apply.
(2) If, on the contrary, law of country X provides a last shot rule but law of country Y a first shot or a knock-out rule, the result under Article 6(1)(b) is that "under these laws (*i.e.*, under the laws chosen in the standard terms used by Peter and John) different standard terms prevail ... (and) there is no choice of law."

Professor Kadner has also explained that "the idea of Art. 6(1)(b) is to maintain party autonomy as much as possible. The starting point is the observation that

19 Under the first shot rule, the terms of the party who fired the first shot, for instance the terms of the offer, wins the battle, under the last shot rule the terms of the party who fired the last shot, for instance the acceptance, wins the battle. Under the knock-out rule the conflicting terms knock each other out, and the contract is concluded on the basis of those terms that are common in substance.

choices of law clauses are often included in standard terms. If the standard terms used by the parties provide for the application of different laws, one might be inclined to ignore the choice of law in the standard terms and use objective connecting factors instead (the argument being that the parties have not agreed on the applicable law). Art. 6 suggests a different approach, the aim of which is to uphold party autonomy as much as possible. Art. 6 thus helps to respect party autonomy as to the applicable law in situations where there is only a 'false conflict,' *i.e.*, the outcome under both laws chosen would be the same as to the applicable law."[20]

My first reaction to these explanations is that Article 6(1)(b) does *not* respect party autonomy. Freedom of *contract* presupposes that the parties agree. The first shot and the last shot rule do not express agreement, but solve a disagreement.

I understand that Professor Kadner is of the opinion that the Principles' knock-out rule, *i.e.*, Article 6(1)(b) 'in fine' (no standard terms prevail) will govern "if the situation is as unclear as it is under the CISG."

In England, the last shot rule is supported by Treitel[21] "with modifications"[22] and the English cases do not give a clear picture. In a sales contract governed by the US Uniform Commercial Code § 2:207, the first shot rule applies to contracts when the terms of the acceptance materially alter the terms of the offer, and the last shot rule if they do not;[23] in most cases a choice of law clause is considered to be a material term.

I understand that the last shot rule governs in the other common law countries.

A survey of CISG and 17 legal systems of the European Union shows that in CISG[24] and in eight of them the law is unsettled,[25] the knock-out rule governs in

[20] This explanation is in substance supported by Professor Neil Cohen, who also participated in the work.

[21] Treitel, *Law of Contract* 11th ed. 2001, 20 f, and *British Road Services Ltd. v Arthur Crutchley & Co.Ltd (No.1)*[1967] 2 All ER 285.287 but see Cheshire, *Fifoot and Furmstone's Law of Contract* 2001, 178, who does not seem to support that solution.

[22] See *Butler Machine Tool Co. v. Ex-Cell-O Corp. Ltd* [1979] 1 WLR 401,817 CA.

[23] However, it follows from UCC Article 2:207(3) that when conduct by both parties recognizes the existence of a contract for sale although the writings of the parties do not otherwise establish a contract the knock-out rule governs.

[24] German courts reported in the Unilex (CISG Article 19) tend to apply the knock-out rule, see BGH 9 January 2002 and OLG Köln 24 May 2006. The Dutch *Gerechtshof Hertogenbosch* 19 November 1996 seems to apply the last shot rule. The doctrine is divided. Farnsworth in Bianca & Bonell. *Commentary on the International Sales Law* (1987) Article 19, 2.3 supports the last shot rule; Lookofsky, *Understanding the CISG in Scandinavia* 2nd ed 2002 § 3.8 favours the knock-out rule.

[25] The survey of the laws of the EU Member States on the battle of forms in the Draft Common Frame of Reference (supra note 5) Volume I p 333 lists the laws of Spain, Portugal, Italy, the Czech Republic, Sweden, Finland, Denmark and Slovakia as unsettled.

six,[26] the first shot rule in one (the Netherlands) and the last shot in two systems (*semble* in England and in Scotland). One must presume that among the laws outside of the European Union there are several that are unsettled or unclear.

A rule that relies on the substantive laws on the battle of forms is problematic, when the laws of so many countries are unsettled or unclear.

Instead of the rule in Article 6(1)(b) I would prefer the knock-out rule: ignore the choice of law in the conflicting standard terms, and use objective connecting factors. This solution will make it easier for the parties, especially in those cases where the law on the battle of forms of a country is unclear or unsettled.

Under Rome I, the rules of the forum would probably determine the battle of forms when the parties have used standard terms designating different laws.[27] The courts of those countries whose laws are unsettled may find guidance in the knock-out rule provided in PICC Article 2.1.22, PECL Article 2:209 and II 4:209 of the DCFR.

Since so many laws are unsettled it would be preferable to apply the knock-out solution to this problem as suggested above. This is one of the few point on which an amendment to the Rome I may be considered.

VI. WILL THE PRINCIPLES PROMPT AMENDMENTS TO ROME I?

Article 27 of Rome I provides that by 17 June 2013 the EU Commission shall submit to the European Parliament, the Council and the European Economic and Social Committee a report on the application of Rome I, that applies to contracts that have been concluded after 17 December 2009. If appropriate, the report shall be accompanied by proposals to amend Rome I.

I have mentioned a few points – rules of law and battle of forms, see sections V 2 and 3 above, where, in my view, the Principles may give rise to consider a revision of Rome I. I wonder, however, whether they are important enough to set the whole revision machinery working. If, however, revision machinery is started under Article 27, they may of course be considered.

Apart from that, I do not think that the Principles, as they appear after the November 2012 meeting of the Special Commission, may prompt amendments to Rome I.

---

26 According to the Draft Common Frame of Reference (supra note 5) Volume I p 332 Germany, Austria, France, Belgium, Poland and Estonia.

27 See Magnus in *von Staudinger's Commentary to EGBG* (the Act introducing the BGB) 2002 Article 31 no 32, which, in accordance with German law, maintains that the conflicting terms "knock each other out", so that there is no choice of law. The German authors to whom Magnus refers are of the same opinion.

VII. CONCLUSION

As said above, I regret that the Hague Conference did not decide to prepare rules that cover the law applicable in the absence of a choice of law by the parties together with the rules on the parties' choice of law, and I fail to appreciate the choice of the opt-in model. I would have preferred that the Special Commission not put the limitation in Article 3 upon the parties' choice of rules of law. Finally, the rule in Article 6(1)(b) should be replaced by the more simple rule that there is no choice of law if the parties have used standard terms designating different laws.

However, as the Principles were approved at the November 2012 meeting, they hold several provisions of considerable value. The basic idea, to have uniform rules on the subject, will be an advantage for all the Member States, especially for those whose rules are not up to date. It will be a great help for the users to have Principles, which include both black letter rules and comments.

THE NEED FOR A GLOBAL COOPERATION NETWORK TO PROTECT FOREIGN TOURISTS/CONSUMERS AND THE COMEBACK OF PRIVATE INTERNATIONAL LAW

Claudia LIMA MARQUES
Professor of Private International Law of the Federal University of Rio Grande do Sul, Porto Alegre, Brazil
President of ASADIP – Associación Americana de Derecho Internacional Privado, Assunción, Paraguay

INTRODUCTION

Amicus means friend. Hans van Loon received in Lima, Peru, the highest honors (*Homenaje*) from the ASADIP ("*Asociación Americana de Derecho Internacional Privado*") not only because he is a friend of our region, of our people and specially, of our children, but also because of his great contribution for the development of Private International Law in the three Americas. His qualities and kindness as a human being, as well as his recognized competence and vision, are known by all that had the pleasure to be with him. I had the honor to work as his assistant at the 100th Year Session of the Hague Conference, in 1993, to assist with the participation of non-member States of Latin America in the future Convention on cooperation in international adoption of children. Since then he became a role model for me, leading me to believe that Private International Law can help to improve the lives of individuals in all parts of the world. Therefore it is a great pleasure to participate in this *Liber Amicorum*.

To honor this belief of a more 'multi-dimensional' Private International Law, I will use this article to summarize my work[1] in a traditional theme of this

1 See C. Lima Marques, "Towards a global approach to protect foreign tourists", in A. Sierralta, C. Lima Marques and J.A. Moreno Rodríguez, *Derecho Internacional, Mundialización y*

discipline: the protection of foreign tourists. According to the World Tourism Organization (UNWTO),[2] the tourist is the visitor or traveler who stays longer than 24 hours (an overnight stay) and that remains for less than one year in the country or place visited. The main purpose of the visit can be business, leisure or other personal purpose (such as educational, religious, family visits, cultural and linguistic exchanges) other than to be employed by a resident entity in the country or place visited.[3] It is also to be noted that the type of visa that this individual has received (tourist visa, student or short business visa) is not decisive to characterize someone as a tourist. During this stay or travel, the tourist is also a consumer.

In my opinion, the protection of foreign tourists – normally made *ex post* at the country of the domicile of the tourist – has a chance to be more effective if made *ex ante* and at the country visited, preventing cross-border litigations and assuring better access to justice with basic legal assistance in foreign languages. Due to the current development of an international dimension of consumer law[4] and to a currently more substantive/political view of the role of conflicts of law rules,[5] this article will argue that it is possible to use both these disciplines to assure a more effective worldwide protection of foreign tourists (I). The second part of this article will analyze if it is possible to build, with the help of Private International Law tools, a global cooperation network using the well-established consumer protection agencies and the national consumer protection system to protect foreign tourists in the country visited (II).

Gobernanza, CEDEP (2012), 449–455. See also C. Lima Marques, „Der Schutz der Verbraucher in einer globalisierten Welt", in K. Sonntag (Hg.), *Heidelberg Profile – Studium General*, Winter (2012), 111–155.

2 See "Global Code of Ethics for Tourism", in http://ethics.unwto.org/en/content/global-code-ethics-tourism.

3 See http://unstats.un.org/unsd/statcom/doc08/BG-TourismStats.pdf, paragraph 2.9.

4 G. Howells, I. Ramsay and T. Wilhelmsson, "Consumer law and its international dimension", in G. Howells, I. Ramsay and T. Wilhelmsson, *Handbook of Research on International Consumer Law*, Elgar (2010), 1.

5 E. Jayme, "Identité culturelle et intégration: le droit internationale privé postmoderne", *Recueil des cours* 251, Kluwer (1995), 259 and A. Bucher, "La dimension sociale du droit international privé", in *Recueil des Cours* 341, Kluwer (2010), 202.

I. THE INSUFFICIENCY OF EXISTING BINDING RULES IN THE PROTECTION OF TOURISTS AT THE GLOBAL LEVEL: THE COMEBACK OF PRIVATE INTERNATIONAL LAW

As Hans van Loon wrote, globalization "*denotes the process of growing interdependence of societies and people worldwide, in practically all areas of life: economy and finance, politics and culture, [...]. It goes beyond the mere linking of discrete societies and markets – the background of traditional private international law – and leads to transnational fusion of societies and markets.*"[6]

In this globalized world, consumers are the key players,[7] but it is not so easy to create binding rules for the protection of consumers in the global level.[8] The rules on consumer protection remain national[9] (and in some contracts, supranational).[10] Besides the conventions on international carriage,[11] the only worldwide instruments on the subject are the UNIDROIT Convention on travel contracts (1970),[12] which achieved limited success,[13] and soft law regulations, such as the UN Guidelines for Consumer Protection from 1985/1999.

Scholars[14] used to classify consumers either as active (those who travel from one country to another with the purpose of consumption) or as passive consumers (those who receive the information or contract in their country of habitual residence, with no physical moving, for example, in e-commerce or in the case of consumers invited to travel abroad for a special event to consume). This distinction between passive and active consumers with the delocalization made by the use of new technologies is presently being challenged.[15] Nevertheless,

6 J. H. van Loon, "Unification of private international law in a multi-forum context", in E.-M. Kieninger (Ed.), *Denationalisierung des Privatrechts?* Mohr (2005), 33.

7 R. Iain, "Consumer protection in the Era of Informational Capitalism", in T. Wilhelmsson et al. (ed.), *Consumer Law in the Information Society*, Kluwer (2001), 45.

8 C. Twigg-Flesner & H. Micklitz, "Think global – Towards International Consumer Law" 203 *Journal of Consumer Policy* 33, 3 (2010).

9 D. Fernández Arroyo, "General Report", in D. Fernández Arroyo (Ed.), *Consumer Protection in International Private Relationships*, CEDEP (2010), 659.

10 See E. Poillot, *Droit européen de la consommation et uniformisation du droit des contrats*, LGDJ (2006), 87ff. See also T. Bourgoignie (Ed.), *L'intégration économique et la protection du consommateur*, Blais (2009), 9ff.

11 K. Tonner, "Electronic Commerce and Travel Law", in T. Wilhelmsson et al. (note 7), 207.

12 The 1970 Convention was ratified only by six countries, but two countries have denounced it, Belgium and Argentina: www.unidroit.org/english/implement/i-70.pdf.

13 M. P. Garcia Rubio, *La responsabilidad contractual de las agencias de viaje*, Montecorvo (1999), 29.

14 E. Jayme and C. Kohler, "Europäisches Kollisionsrecht 1999", in *IPRax* 404 (1999).

15 N. Reich, "Minimal to full to 'half' harmonization", in J. Devenney and M. Kenny (Ed.), *European Consumer Protection*, Cambridge (2012), 5.

the distinction is still used in Private International Law to focus the protective rules of conflicts of law only on the passive consumers; as for example in the 1980 Rome Convention on the law applicable to contractual obligations and the Rome I Regulation No. 593/2008.[16]

A. CHANGES IN THE GLOBAL MASS TOURISM AND CHALLENGES TO CONSUMER LAW

According to the UNWTO, the number of international arrivals has reached one billion persons in 2012 for the first time in modern history.[17] If in 1950 tourism destinations were concentrated in industrialized countries in Europe and North America, presently 45% of tourism in the world has developing countries as a destination. This new decentralized mass tourism to developing countries has shown that these countries are less prepared for the influx of visitors.

The decentralization of tourism is followed by a fragmentation of mass tourism, considered no longer restricted to an elite but rather a cross-class phenomenon. We can also speak about a specialization: there are today, besides leisure and cultural tourism, conference tourism, adventure tourism, youth tourism, religion tourism, educational tourism etc. Scholars highlight that there was a cultural change in tourism in the 21st century,[18] to include activities that were previously not considered consumption, such as tourism for conferences, professional or religious training. They warn that long-term students who travel beyond one year are not considered tourists or migrants, but consumers.[19]

Indeed, in our postmodern times[20] international consumption has also become more and more common.[21] The desire to connect with other cultures and to be active on the global market[22] is an important trend of our times.[23] Since the 90s, Zygmunt Baumann alerts that the consumer of the future will be a tourist,[24]

16 H. Micklitz, J. Stuyck, E. Terryn, *Consumer Law*, Hart: London (2010), 563.

17 World Tourism Barometer. In https://s3-eu-west-1.amazonaws.com/storageapi/sites/all/files/docpdf/unwtohighlights12enlr_1.pdf.

18 J. Tudela, "Madurez y insuficiencia del derecho del turismo español: su presente y sus incertidumbres", in J. Facal (Org.), *Derecho del Turismo*, FCU (2006), 256ff.

19 E. D Busto, "Marco Regulatorio del turismo estudiantil en la República Argentina", in J. Facal (note 18), 282ff.

20 E. Jayme (note 5), 60.

21 C. Lima Marques, "A proteção do consumidor: aspectos de direito privado regional e geral", in *XXVII Curso de Derecho Internacional* – OEA/CIJ, Washington (2001), 657ff.

22 C. Madrid Martinez, "El derecho internacional privado venezuelano y su respuesta frente al consumidor internacional", in C. Lima Marques and D. Fernández Arroyo, *The global financial crisis and the need for consumer regulation*, Orchestra (2012), 255ff.

23 C. Lima Marques, "Brésil – Rapport national" in: D.P. Fernández Arroyo (note 9), 47ff.

24 Z. Bauman, *Globalização: As consequências humanas*, Rio de Janeiro: Zahar (1999), 85ff.

but changes at the global mass tourism could be calling for the help of Private International Law solutions.[25]

Consumer law scholars[26] also call attention to the challenges presented to the law by the international mass tourism. These challenges for the law do not derive only from technological progress (electronic booking, maps and information about tourism services in foreign places, reservation at distance), from the complexities and diversity range of the current tourism contracts (package tours, time-sharing, adventure tourism, youth educational tourism, tourism for conferences, professional, language and religious training, etc.), but are also connected with changes to the tourist's profile. Next to mass tourism to all social classes, a new elite tourism industry is blooming and there are changes in the tourism industry (global network alliances of the transport industry, new commercial agreements to 'code sharing' and global chains of travel packages/ tours expertise, specialization of national travel agencies etc.).

The legal doctrine calls for a "renewal of international instruments on tourism".[27] One of the changes in mass tourism is the decrease in the use of travel agencies and organizers. Brazilian research data shows that many tourists no longer use travel agencies or travel organizers,[28] but rather hire the services directly in the country of destination: today 65.4% of the foreign tourists visiting Brazil have no travel agency at their home State.[29]

These challenges on mass tourism can no longer be answered only with changes in national law and have been responded by supranational laws in the context of economic integration processes, like those from the European Union (EU)[30] and MERCOSUR,[31] and by more than hundreds of bilateral and trilateral agreements on the protection of tourists.[32]

25 C. Lima Marques, "Consumer Protection in Private International Law Rules: the need for an Interamerican Convention on the law applicable to some consumer contracts and consumer transactions", in T. Bourgoignie (Dir.), *Regards croisés sur les enjeux contemporains du droit de la consommation*, Blais (2006), 145ff.

26 K. Tonner (note 11), 205.

27 See J. Tudela, "Madurez y insuficiencia del derecho del turismo español: su presente y sus incertidumbres", in *Derecho del Turismo*, J. Facal (note 18), 251.

28 L. R. Atheniense, *A responsabilidade jurídica das agências de viagens*, Del Rey, (2002), 17ff.

29 Www.turismo.gov.br/export/sites/default/turismo/o_ministerio/publicacoes/downloads_publicacoes/Documento_Referencial_Turismo_no_Brasil_2011-2014.pdf.

30 K. Tonner (note 11), 207.

31 See A. Soares, "A tutela internacional do consumidor turista", *Revista de Direito do Consumidor* 82 (2012), 113ff.

32 China has more than 146 bilateral agreements, see W. Dan, "A Protecção do Turista através do Direito do Consumidor", *Revista de Direito do Consumidor* 83 (2012), 40. Some of these Bilateral Agreements have a special clause to facilitate the access of Chinese tourists to national enforcement agencies of consumer protection and linguistic help, see Brazil-China and EU-China Memorandum of Understanding.

Today the UNWTO recognizes "the insufficiency of binding rules at the global level governing rights and obligations of tourists and of tourist service providers",[33] especially in the "context of increasing diversification of destinations and generating countries".

B. THE EFFORTS OF THE UNWTO TOWARDS SUBSTANTIAL UNIFORM RULES AND THE NEED FOR PRIVATE INTERNATIONAL LAW RULES TO COMPLEMENT THE SYSTEM OF GLOBAL PROTECTION

The UNWTO "desiring the achievement of a high level of tourist protection" has recognized "the need to establish uniform provisions relating to the protection of tourists" in case of "*force majeure*" (emergency situations and bankruptcy of the travel agency or travel package provider).[34] After incidents such as the Iceland volcano case, tsunamis and nuclear disasters, the UNWTO recognized the necessity "for greater protection for travelers in the event of disasters in all parts of the world"[35] and has decided to create a Working Group[36] to elaborate an international legal instrument[37] for the protection of national and international tourists.

In 2011, the Working Group on the protection of tourists/consumers reached a consensus "on the need to elaborate a legal document which can provide guidelines" and substantive norms addressing the key issues of "providing assistance", ensuring "repatriation of consumers", supplying "information to tourists including in terms of the handling of bankruptcy situations of the travel organizers" and "accommodations."

In 2012, an unofficial draft was made available in the Internet, but its scope of application is restricted to tourists travelling with travel packages.[38] A tourist is for this purpose only "a person who concludes a travel package contract with a travel organizer" (Annex I, Chapter 1 of the draft).

There are no conflicts of law rules in the draft of a "UNWTO Convention on the protection of tourists and tourism service providers", because its main purpose is to clarify the responsibilities of the host country, the country of origin

[33] UNWTO, CE/94/3 I e.

[34] Www2.unwto.org/en/event/workshop-protection-touristsconsumers-and-travel-organizers.

[35] UNWTO CE/88/2 and CE/DEC/2(LXXXVIII).

[36] UNWTO CE/89/8 and CE/DEC/11(LXXXIX).

[37] UNWTO CE/93/4(a).

[38] Www.elementis.hr/uhpa/docs/files/U1012047%20draft%20ECTAA%20UNWTO%20convention.pdf.

of the tourist, the country of the origin of the travel organizer and the travel organizer itself in case of catastrophes or emergencies. Tourists not covered by the Convention, and all tourists raising other problems than those covered by the Convention would need to resort to national law.

However, to achieve a high level of protection and to increase "the confidence of tourists in tourism service providers", as the Preamble of the future UNWTO Convention stipulates, much more is needed.

II. POSSIBLE ROLE OF PRIVATE INTERNATIONAL LAW IN THE PROTECTION OF GLOBAL TOURISTS: A SUGGESTION

This state of the art presents an opportunity to create new Private International Law rules. Let us analyze the current models and the possible role of this discipline in the protection of foreign tourists.

A. MODELS OF PROTECTION OF TOURISTS IN PRIVATE INTERNATIONAL LAW

It is noteworthy that some 'evolutions' in Private International Law began with tourists. They have changed the method and the policy of this discipline, but this has not always resulted in the creation of special conflicts of law rules to protect tourists.

The first example is the so-called "American Revolution on conflicts of law". This 'evolution' on conflicts of law began with the famous case of a car accident in Ontario (Canada) caused by a tourist from New York (*Babcock v. Jackson*)[39] and the decision stressed that substantial policies of legal rules should be the starting point for choice-of-law solutions.[40]

In Europe, the case of the contracts concluded by German tourists in Spain has lead to a change in the traditional approach and promoted the emergence of consumer law directives with horizontal effect, now including special rules on conflicts of law to protect these tourists as consumers.[41] The time-sharing cases and the cases of tourists in Turkey have also impacted on the new rule of the

39 S. Symeonides, *The American Choice-of-Law Revolution*, Nijhoff (2006), 101ff.

40 E. Jayme, "The American Conflicts Revolution and its Impact on European Private International Law", in E. Jayme, *Gesammelte Schriften*, Vol. 4, Müller (2009), 293.

41 E. Jayme, *Zur mittelbar horizontalen Drittwirkung von EG-Richtlinien über das IPR* (note 41), 344.

Rome I Regulation on consumer protection,[42] and can be given as some examples of the so-called 'European Revolution' on conflicts of law.

From the EU comes an interesting model to protect tourists as consumers, which could be very useful: the network of European Consumer Centers. The *ECC-Net* offers free consumer help and advice, not only by giving information (travel advice and buyers' guide for European consumers), but also by helping to avoid problems and, if necessary, makes available an expert who provides free services to help in settling complaints against an EU-based foreign trader.[43] This system and the Regulation No. 2006/2004 on Consumer Protection Cooperation have proved to be very useful at the Olympic Games of 2012 and represent a gateway to the European Small Claims Procedure, facilitating access to justice for consumers in Europe.[44]

Some authors consider the ongoing process of the OAS on an Inter-American Convention on consumer protection as a new revolution on current conflicts of law in the Americas.[45] Anyway, the 2012 MERCOSUR Draft Agreement on the law applicable to consumer contracts has its roots not only in the negotiations of the CIDIP VII, but also in the time-sharing problems in Uruguay with tourists from Brazil, Argentina and Paraguay.[46] It is to be noted that MERCOSUR has a successful experience with administrative agreements of cooperation for the protection of visitors (2005 Inter-Institutional Letter of Understanding among the agencies of consumer protection of MERCOSUR Member States for the protection of consumers-visitors) and the Technical Chambers of discussion and assessment between the tourism sectors and these bodies.

In Brazil, the need to include conflicts of law rules on the Consumer Code (Senate Bill 281/2012) began with the Panasonic case: a Brazilian tourist that bought in Miami a video camera with a 'global warranty' and could not enforce the warranty in Brazil because the Brazilian Panasonic subsidiary did not recognize the warranty given by the parent company in Japan.[47] As a result, the Superior Court used all rules of the Consumer Code as overriding mandatory rules, calling for special rules on the international protection of consumers.[48]

We can say that there are currently four models of tourist protection in Private International Law: 1. Indirectly, by the establishment of substantial special uniform rules for contracts of interest to the sector, such as the UNIDROIT

[42] E. Jayme, *Europäische Kollisionsrecht: Neue Aufgaben, neuen Techniken* (note 41), 375.
[43] Http://ec.europa.eu/consumers/ecc/index_en.htm.
[44] Https://e-justice.europa.eu/content_small_claims-42-en.do.
[45] A. Perez, "Consumer Protection in the Americas: A Second Wave of American Revolutions?" 5 *U. St. Thomas L.J.* (Spring 2008), 699.
[46] C. Lima Marques, "Consumer Protection Policy in MERCOSUR", in M. Franca Filho, L. Lixinski and M. Giupponi, *The Law of Mercosur*, Hart (2010), 331ff.
[47] C. Lima Marques (note 21), 657ff.
[48] See E. Klausner, *Direito Internacional do Consumidor*, Renovar (2012), 141ss.

Convention on Travel Contracts, the conventions on carriage by air of the Warsaw system or the Draft of UNWTO; 2. Directly, by the creation of special conflict rules to protect the consumers, applicable – sometimes – also to tourists, such as the Regulation No. 593/2008 on the law applicable to contractual obligations (Rome I) of the EU;[49] 3. By the establishment of channels of administrative cooperation to expedite conciliation, such as the MERCOSUR Agreement on consumer visitors of 2005, or of small claims courts and administrative assistance, as established in the Regulation No. 2006/2004; 4. Guarantee of privileged access to the forum of domicile of the consumer, even when the consumer is a tourist, through the use of consumer law as overriding mandatory rules. These cross-border claims are very costly and difficult to enforce, also because of the small amount of the claim and the existence of "*forum non conveniens*".

In other words, the foreign tourist as a consumer has sometimes a *forum actoris* privilege, but no special connecting factor in conflicts of law rules. This can be seen as an incentive to expensive and ineffective cross-border litigation in the country of origin of the tourists. The rationale behind the existent different regimes on the international protection of tourists as consumers was the acceptance of the internationality of the relation, allowing the use of the common connecting factors, like party autonomy or the *lex loci celebrationis*. More effective protection could be achieved in the country visited by avoiding demands against the transport service or against the travel organizer for redress.

My thesis is that the role of Private International Law has changed in the matter of international tourist protection: it is now more political and focused on increasing confidence of tourists and on developing tourism as an economically and socially positive phenomenon.

B. THE CREATION OF A GLOBAL COOPERATION NETWORK USING THE EXISTENT CONSUMER AGENCIES SYSTEM: A PRAGMATIC TASK OF PRIVATE INTERNATIONAL LAW

The first concern of conflicts of law was the harmony of national and foreign decisions. It results in the application of the law of the country of destination: *the lex loci delicti commissi* for torts against tourists and the *lex loci executiones* for contracts performed at the country visited. These neutral connecting factors also help to avoid discrimination between national and foreign tourists in the national market visited. With the evolution of consumer protection law, nationally and supranationally, the characterization of the tourists as consumers has allowed the

49 R.A.M. Paiva, *Direito, Turismo e Consumo*, Renovar (2012), 236.

consumer to sue the travel agency, the tour organizer, the transport industry or the hotels in the country of origin, opened new possibilities of procedural discussions (*forum non conveniens*, anti-suit injunctions, unfair binding consumer arbitration clauses, *ex ante* binding conciliation etc.). It shifted the connecting factor to the *lex loci celebrationis*.

To build more confidence on an effective international protection of tourists, innovative methods of Private International Law are needed. Because the new role of this discipline is more political – it is to prevent 'conflicts', it is necessary to promote international cooperation and the creation of really global administrative and judicial nets, that should include small claims courts, also using the consumer law system already in place!

This *ex ante* protection may use the national consumer rules as a minimum (substantive) protection tool, assuring international cooperation and mutual assistance to allow the solution of the majority of the cases and consumer problems in the country of destination of the tourist, avoiding *ex post facto* cross-borders litigations.

MERCOSUR has used the administrative cooperation agreement and multilingual questionnaires to allow for more than 80% of the problems to be solved with the simple intervention of the national enforcement authorities by phone, assuring information to foreign tourists and to the tourism industry about the rights of consumers, and also encouraging the consumer movement and the national agencies to act on behalf of foreign tourists. Since 2007 the EU has established a network of national consumer enforcement authorities with similar investigation and enforcement powers with similar success EU-wide.

In my opinion this political role of Private International Law can be successfully achieved if a global forum, such as the Hague Conference on Private International Law, is willing to build a worldwide cooperation network using the well-established consumer protection agencies, the existent small claim tribunals and judicial authorities.

The tourist should be protected as consumer, regardless of the kind of visa held. Problems in contracts and services appear already in the country of destination of tourists, but they are not addressed in this country due to the inexistence of fast and efficient channels for these visitors. On the other hand, there is a great demand for litigation in the tourists' countries of residence.[50] These are fairly inefficient and expensive cross-border litigation cases, or litigation with the trip organizers (even if, with electronic means, hiring these services is increasingly done directly), litigation that could be avoided with better information, more administrative cooperation for the prevention and creation of conciliatory and urgent measures.

---

50 See D. Benitez, "Informe del Derecho del turismo en Argentina", in J. Facal (note 18), 232–233.

The ASADIP members, in Brazil (23 March 2012), manifested their full support to add to the agenda of the Hague Conference Work Program the topic of tourist protection, with an emphasis on international administrative cooperation (*Carta do Rio de Janeiro*).[51] The Brazilian Government supports the suggestion, thus, I was asked to draft a suggestion on a "Convention on Co-Operation in Respect of the Protection of Tourists and Visitors Abroad".

At the current stage the Draft has only nine articles, divided in Chapter I (Objective and Scope of Application) and II (Mutual Assistance and Legal Aid). Article 1 lays down the objectives.[52] Article 2 defines the notions of "Tourist and visitor abroad", "Central Authority", "Competent Authority", "Seller or supplier", "Consumer complain"). Article 3 allows the application of the Convention also in case of emergencies, complementing the UNWTO Convention.

Under the Article 4, each Contracting State should indicate a Central Authority to organize the cooperation efforts, in order that the Central Authority in the receiving State shall provide advice, information and assistance to tourists, using the established channels of mediation and of enforcement of consumer rights and the small claims tribunals available in the country as partners and also distance procedure and enforcement agreements, if these are available. The Central Authority in the State of the habitual residence of the tourist can be connected to provide assistance and legal counseling to the tourist and to the other Central Authorities, and will provide to the tourist a copy of its data, when the tourist returns to the country of origin, using all established channels of mutual assistance, receipt of evidence, distance procedure and facilitated enforcement, available at this time in the country to help this tourist. The Central Authority of both countries may share data, formularies and evidences to facilitate to process the tourist claim.

---

51 Http://asadip.files.wordpress.com/2012/04/carta-de-rio-de-janeiro8asadip230312en-espac3b1ol-y-portviii.pdf.

52 "*Article 1 – Objective:* 1. This Convention lays down the conditions under which the Central Authority and the competent authorities in the Contracting States should cooperate with each other and facilitate the access to justice and to administrative help for foreign tourists. 2. This Convention establishes a network of authorities responsible for monitoring and enforcing the application of legislation concerning consumer and tourist protection, aiming to ensure compliance with the legislation of the visited State ("the receiving State") and to facilitate the solution of a breach or infringement of the legislation in the receiving State and the access to justice of foreign tourists also for small claims in this State, so as the use of the documents produce for administrative complaints made in other Contracting States. 3. This Convention also lays down the conditions under which the competent authorities in the Contracting States designated as responsible for the enforcement of the laws that protect consumers' interests shall also cooperate with each other in order to ensure compliance with those laws, with international tourist protection standards and special regional and international legal instruments in order to enhance the protection of consumers' and tourists' economic and safety interests."

According to Article 5 each Contracting State should also designate the competent authorities responsible for the enforcement of the laws that protect consumers' interests and then shall cooperate with each other and the Central Authority, without prejudice to any bilateral or multilateral agreement. Article 6 establishes the obligations of the receiving State[53] and Article 7 sets the obligations of the State of origin.[54] Article 8 regulates the exchange of information upon request and the limits of information sharing and Article 9 entitles the tourists to legal aid in a non-discriminatory way. The suggestion has a MERCOSUR similar multilingual formulary to help the tourist to explain the problems to the enforcement agency. An optional set of conflicts of law rules to protect tourists could complement this suggestion.

CONCLUDING REMARKS

Foreign tourists and visitors as consumers contribute to strengthening the tourism sectors and to promoting the economic development in all States, and at the current state of Private International Law foreign tourists should not be discriminated and should have access to justice and to administrative assistance in both their country of origin and destination as to be able to upheld their private rights. It seems clear that a foreign tourist may need special information and help in foreign languages about legal issues and about consumer law in the country visited, but cooperation between administrative consumer agencies and small claim courts can provide that. A new global judicial and administrative

---

53 "*Article 6 – Obligations of the Receiving State.* 1. The Contracting State visited or the State where the tourist is located at the moment of the infringement of consumer rights, problem or accident ("the receiving State") shall consider the tourist as a consumer, without any kind of discrimination and provide, under its law, the tourist or visitor with any help available in its administrative and judicial system. 2. To assure mutual assistance, accessibility and recognition of all complaints and claims in the contracting States, the receiving State shall co-operate [...] as follows: I – taking all measures possible to inform and counsel the tourists, directly or indirectly, about their rights and possibilities to take legal measures during the stay in this country, using the forms suggested at the Annex; II – indicating the competent authorities in the region to advise and address complaints to under the laws of this country; III – putting the tourist in contact with the enforcement authorities to consumer protection, small claims tribunals or free legal services and network that can assist in the situation; IV – register the case, keeping all data for five years and cooperate with the Central Authority and competent authorities designated as responsible for the enforcement of the laws that protect consumers' interests of the other Contracting States. V – maintain and develop the formulary suggested in Annex I in its own languages and inform all Central Authorities of the main changes of the law that can have impact on the protection of tourists or consumers."

54 "*Article 7 – Obligations of the State of Origin.* [...] I – mutual information about the legal rights of consumers and tourists; [...]; VI – joint efforts to prepare written material and training for the enforcement authorities or Central Authorities of other countries about the legal regime in the country [...]."

cooperation network can ensure that these foreign tourists will be able to benefit of the already in place consumer protection system and access to justice in all States and regions, avoiding inefficient cross-border litigations in consumer issues. A pragmatic comeback to Private International Law…

THE MISSING LINK BETWEEN DETERMINING THE LAW APPLICABLE AND THE APPLICATION OF FOREIGN LAW

BUILDING ON THE RESULTS OF THE JOINT CONFERENCE ON ACCESS TO FOREIGN LAW IN CIVIL AND COMMERCIAL MATTERS

(Brussels, 15–17 February 2012)

Philippe LORTIE
First Secretary

Maja GROFF
*Senior Legal Officer, Permanent Bureau of the Hague Conference on Private International Law**

INTRODUCTION AND BACKGROUND

Since its founding in 1893, the Hague Conference on Private International Law has developed a range of international instruments which determine applicable law in a given area of law or otherwise require the ascertainment of aspects of foreign law.[1] As a result, judges and other officials in States Parties to Hague Conventions

* The views expressed in this article are those of the authors and cannot be attributed to the Hague Conference.

1 A full list of Hague Conventions can be found on the Hague Conference website, www.hcch.net, under "Conventions".

regularly, within the scope of the operation of these Conventions, have to apply or know foreign law (in addition to national and regional conflict of law rules which provide for the application of foreign law). However, the Hague Conference has never developed a complete instrument to facilitate access to foreign law. Rather, one finds snippets of a solution in various instruments, such as in Articles 14 and 15 of the Hague *Convention of 25 October 1980 on the Civil Aspects of International Child Abduction* (the "1980 Hague Child Abduction Convention"), Article 30(2) of the Hague *Convention of 19 October 1996 on Jurisdiction, Applicable Law, Recognition, Enforcement and Co-operation in Respect of Parental Responsibility and Measures for the Protection of Children* (the "1996 Hague Child Protection Convention"), and Article 57 of the Hague *Convention of 23 November 2007 on the International Recovery of Child Support and Other Forms of Family Maintenance* (the "2007 Hague Child Support Convention").

Access to law nationally and, in addition, access to foreign law – given the contemporary globalised, international society – are at the heart of notions of respect for human rights, access to justice, the rule of law and the proper administration of justice: all subjects dear to Hans van Loon. In his speech of 15 February 2012 in Brussels at the opening of the Joint Conference of the European Commission and the Hague Conference on Access to Foreign Law in Civil and Commercial Matters (hereinafter the "Joint Conference"),[2] Hans van Loon noted that "while access to foreign law is of particular interest to specialists in private international law, the theme is, in reality, at the intersection of several disciplines, including that of the proper administration of justice – a responsibility and obligation fundamental to the rule of law – and access to justice – a fundamental and complementary right of the citizen." Representing this multidisciplinary perspective, experts in private international law, comparative law, constitutional law, human rights law, information technology, electronic legal tools, and library science were gathered at the Joint Conference. Also reflecting a multidimensional approach dear to Hans van Loon, legal professionals from diverse backgrounds, including governmental officials, judges, arbitrators, lawyers, notaries and academics, were present at and contributed to the Joint Conference. The international meeting provided a unique opportunity to further assess, within the mandate of the Hague Conference, the need for and feasibility of a potential new global instrument facilitating access to foreign law.

In 2006, the Permanent Bureau of the Hague Conference was invited by the then Special Commission on General Affairs and Policy to "prepare a feasibility study on the development of a new instrument for cross-border co-

[2] The Conclusions and Recommendations of the Joint Conference, generously funded by the European Commission, can be found on Hague Conference website, www.hcch.net, under "Work in progress," then "General Affairs," then "Info Doc. No 10 of April 2012."

operation concerning the *treatment* of foreign law." In 2007 an international experts group on this topic was convened. The group concluded that it was not advisable to "attempt to comprehensively harmonise the different approaches to the treatment of foreign law, as there [was] no need or likelihood of success for such harmonisation." However, the experts agreed that there was "clearly a need to facilitate access to foreign law."[3]

The Permanent Bureau was subsequently mandated to develop a Questionnaire for Members of the Hague Conference "with a view to identifying practical difficulties in accessing the content of foreign law and determining the areas of foreign law for which information is required, [and inviting] Members to comment on the models suggested [for an international instrument or mechanisms] and their possible implementation." In Questionnaire responses, Member opinion was divided as to whether and/or how to move forward with any new international instrument or mechanisms in this area,[4] but the responses evidenced a number of significant trends for accessing the content of foreign law, including the use of Internet sources. In the light of this latter trend, a second international experts group was convened in 2008 on "Global Co-operation on the Provision of Online Legal Information on National Laws." Experts at that meeting suggested that while access to law via the Internet was a low-cost and crucial part of any efficient, modern approach to access to foreign law, administrative and/ or judicial cooperation, and networks of experts and expert institutes were also important features of any new instrument or mechanisms.

The Joint Conference of 2012, attended by more than 130 experts from 35 States, nine international or regional organisations, and ten other professional or expert organisations from every region of the world,[5] produced a range of useful results supplementary to Hague Conference work carried out in previous years. It confirmed a number of findings of background studies and experts groups, and provided a set of elaborated ideas and parameters for the possible development of a future instrument.

The Joint Conference confirmed the existence of an increasing need in practice to facilitate access to foreign law as a result, among other things, of globalisation and the cross-border movement of persons, goods, services and

3 The 2007 expert meeting report and all preliminary documents on this topic are available on the Hague Conference website, www.hcch.net, under "Work in progress," then "General Affairs."

4 For a full summary of Questionnaire responses, see "Feasibility study on the treatment of foreign law – Summary of the responses to the Questionnaire," prepared by the Permanent Bureau, Prel. Doc. No 9A of March 2008 for the attention of the Council of April 2008 on General Affairs and Policy of the Conference, available on the Hague Conference website, www.hcch.net, under "Work in progress," then "General Affairs."

5 See the Joint Conference's Conclusions and Recommendations preamble, *supra*, note 2.

investments.[6] It also confirmed the need to facilitate access to foreign law in many areas of the law, and in particular such areas as family law, the law of succession and commercial law.[7] The meeting confirmed an earlier finding of the 2007 Hague Conference experts group that any global instrument in this field should focus on the facilitation of access to foreign law and should not attempt to harmonise the status of foreign law in national procedures.[8]

Another important Conclusion and Recommendation of the Joint Conference was that any future instrument "should contemplate a range of mechanisms to cater to the needs of various actors of different means and resources who are seeking access to foreign law, including judges, legal practitioners, notaries, government officials and the general public, in a variety of circumstances, and should be operational in different legal systems and traditions, and address language barriers [...] [c]ircumstances may include cross-border litigation and non-contentious matters such as contractual negotiations, estate planning, and family arrangements."[9]

This approach, sensitive to the needs of a range of legal actors, is an important evolution in comparison with the 1968 London Convention[10] which is limited to access to information on foreign law by judicial authorities in the context of court proceedings only. Limiting such mechanisms to courts has, among other things, created an imbalance with respect to reciprocal services rendered between some States of a common law tradition and States of a civil law tradition. Because foreign law is predominantly treated as fact in a number of common law jurisdictions,[11] the common law judge has traditionally had little or no *ex officio* role in assessing the foreign law of other States, and thus would make limited use of legal co-operation mechanisms in this area. It is hoped that a new instrument, carefully designed to benefit a wide array of users, would attract States from a diversity of legal traditions including those of the common law tradition.

The balance of this paper, in the limited space available, will sketch a variety of mechanisms which could be included in a modern international instrument on access to foreign law in the light of the valuable information shared at the Joint

---

6 Conclusion and Recommendation No 1, *ibid.*

7 *Ibid.*

8 Conclusion and Recommendation No 4, *ibid.*

9 Conclusion and Recommendation No 6, *ibid.*

10 The *European Convention of 7 June 1968 on Information on Foreign Law* (the "London Convention"). The *Inter-American Convention of 8 May 1979 on Proof of and Information on Foreign Law* (the "Montevideo Convention") also focuses on judges and courts as the principal users of that Convention (see Art. 4).

11 It is important to note that not all common law jurisdictions treat foreign law as a question of fact rather than law. For example, under federal law of the United States of America and the law of most of its states, a determination of foreign law is considered to be a question of law and judges have *ex officio* powers to independently research that law.

Conference. First, we will address possible mechanisms to provide general access to legal information; that is, access to the "black letter law." The paper will then address possible mechanisms to obtain, depending on circumstances, "tailored" foreign legal information (*e.g.*, legal information applied to facts and/or with interpretative added value).

There was recognition at the Joint Conference that most of the mechanisms presented below should find their way into a *binding* international instrument (*i.e.*, a new Hague Convention) for several reasons. As a number of the envisioned mechanisms are co-operative in nature, their use could be conditional on being made reciprocally available among Contracting States. In order to be effective at a global level, some of these mechanisms would have to follow – or progressively strive to follow – a number of important principles or provisions enshrined in a binding instrument.

As mentioned above, it was agreed during the Joint Conference that any future instrument on access to foreign law should be flexible and include various options for States to choose from. In the light of the experience of the Hague Conference, the management of such options, which would create in most circumstances obligations upon States Parties, would seem to be better addressed in the context of a binding instrument.

It was also recommended at the Joint Conference that where possible, deadlines to respond to requests should be included in a new, effective instrument (improving upon older instruments). Finally, the meeting also recognised that "tailored" foreign legal information does not necessarily have to be provided without cost to users, and that indeed, practically speaking, the provision of such services at a cost may enable better services.[12]

I. GENERAL ACCESS TO FOREIGN LAW – ACCESS TO BLACK LETTER LAW

A. ACCESS TO BLACK LETTER LAW VIA THE INTERNET

A primary tool to provide general access to foreign legal information at present, given information technology (IT) developments over the last 20 years, is online legal resources available via the Internet. The Joint Conference underlined "the opportunity offered by advances in information technology for the facilitation of effective, cost-efficient and prompt access to foreign law,"[13] noted the importance

[12] Conclusion and Recommendation No 14, *supra*, note 2.
[13] Conclusion and Recommendation No 7, *ibid*.

of cost-free access to online national legal information, and acknowledged general principles on the topic developed at the 2008 Hague Conference experts meeting, the "Guiding Principles to be Considered in Developing a Future Instrument,"[14] which provide as follows:

GUIDING PRINCIPLES TO BE CONSIDERED IN DEVELOPING A FUTURE INSTRUMENT

Free access

1. State Parties shall ensure that their legal materials, in particular legislation, court and administrative tribunal decisions and international agreements, are available for free access in an electronic form by any persons, including those in foreign jurisdictions.
2. State Parties are also encouraged to make available for free access relevant historical materials, including preparatory work and legislation that has been amended or repealed, as well as relevant explanatory materials.

Reproducing and re-use

3. State Parties are encouraged to permit and facilitate the reproduction and re-use of legal materials, as referred to in paragraphs 1 and 2, by other bodies, in particular for the purpose of securing free public access to the materials, and to remove any impediments to such reproduction and re-use.

Integrity and authoritativeness

4. State Parties are encouraged to make available authoritative versions of their legal materials provided in electronic form.
5. State Parties are encouraged to take all reasonable measures available to them to ensure that authoritative legal materials can be reproduced or re-used by other bodies with clear indications of their origins and integrity (authoritativeness).
6. State Parties are encouraged to remove obstacles to the admissibility of these materials in their courts.

Preservation

7. State Parties are encouraged to ensure long-term preservation and accessibility of their legal materials referred to in paragraphs 1 and 2 above.

Open formats, metadata and knowledge-based systems

8. State Parties are encouraged to make their legal materials available in open and re-usable formats and with such metadata as available.
9. States Parties are encouraged to cooperate in the development of common standards for metadata applicable to legal materials, particularly those intended to enable and encourage interchange.
10. Where State Parties provide knowledge-based systems assisting in the application or interpretation of their legal materials, they are encouraged to make such systems available for free public access, reproducing and re-use.

14 Conclusion and Recommendation No 8, *ibid.*

Protection of personal data

11. Online publication of court and administrative tribunal decisions and related material should be in accordance with protection of personal data laws of the State of origin. Where names of parties to decisions need to be protected, the texts of such decisions and related material can be anonymized in order to make them available for free access.

Citations

12. State Parties are encouraged to adopt neutral methods of citation of their legal materials, including methods that are medium-neutral, provider-neutral and internationally consistent.

Translations

13. State Parties are encouraged, where possible, to provide translations of their legislation and other materials, in other languages.
14. Where State Parties do provide such translations, they are encouraged to allow them to be reproduced or re-used by other parties, particularly for free public access.
15. State Parties are encouraged to develop multi-lingual access capacities and to co operate in the development of such capacities.

Support and co-operation

16. State Parties and re-publishers of their legal materials are encouraged to make those legal materials more accessible through various means of interoperability and networking.
17. State Parties are encouraged to assist in sustaining those organisations that fulfil the above objectives and to assist other State Parties in fulfilling their obligations.
18. State Parties are encouraged to co-operate in fulfilling these obligations.

The Guiding Principles generally do not set out "hard" obligations for States. Rather, the bulk of the Guiding Principles are aspirational, so as to take account of the disparate levels of technological development and resource availability in diverse jurisdictions, and to promote incremental improvements in this area over time. It should be noted that the Guiding Principles have already been influential in a number of legislative endeavours and expert venues.[15] The Guiding Principles enshrine a range of non-controversial good practices in the provision of electronic / online legal information, shared across a number of leading jurisdictions in this field. Many States have embraced online provision of legal information as a low-cost solution to facilitate access to an array of legal information (including legislation, case law, doctrine and official commentary), made accessible, via the

[15] For instance, the Guiding Principles were cited a number of times in comments to the recent *Uniform Electronic Legal Material Act* (2011) of the National Conference of Commissioners on Uniform State Laws (the Uniform Law Commission) of the United States of America. See also G. Greenleaf, A. Mowbray, and P. Chung, "The Meaning of 'Free Access to Legal Information': A Twenty Year Evolution" (October 6, 2012), Law via Internet Conference, 2012 (available at SSRN: http://ssrn.com/abstract=2158868 or http://dx.doi.org/10.2139/ssrn.2158868).

Internet, to a very wide-range of national and foreign users, such as judges, legal practitioners, notaries, government officials, academics, business people and the general public. Moreover, States and international organisations have recognised that making legal information easily available online promotes transparency, the rule of law, and economic activity.

As more and more States put their national legal information online, there is a need to co-ordinate these efforts at the international level to ensure that there is a progressive endeavour to make certain that this information meets basic standards of quality and international accessibility, such as those set out in the Guiding Principles. To this end, a new instrument on access to foreign law could contain several provisions on online legal information, drawing from or inspired by the Guiding Principles.

Further, it would be important that any new instrument be generally "medium neutral,"[16] and that cost-effective IT solutions for any of the co-operation mechanisms described below be considered (for example, electronic communications systems for judges and other professionals, electronic forms and "Country Profiles" on national law and other information, etc.).

B. ACCESS TO THE BLACK LETTER LAW / GENERAL INFORMATION ON NATIONAL LAW WHERE NOT AVAILABLE ON THE INTERNET – CENTRAL AUTHORITIES, JUDICIAL NETWORKS AND NETWORKS OF PROFESSIONALS

A number of other co-operation mechanisms could also be included in an international instrument to provide access to general information on the law, filling any gaps in legal information available online for a given State, where online information is insufficient in its coverage, or online translations are lacking. Thus, as more quality information on national law becomes available via the Internet, the mechanisms described in this section would be used less frequently to gain only general information on the law.[17] In any case, unlike the above-described

---

16 For instance, Art. 13 of the 2007 Hague Child Support Convention was included in order to help ensure that this Convention might gradually be able to operate in a medium-neutral environment, allowing for electronic communications and electronic documentation for applications under the Convention.

17 From the perspective of judicial experience with the London Convention, it has been noted that a significant proportion of requests for information on foreign law under the London Convention could be eliminated if more accessible online information on national law were provided (see von Richter Dr. Serge-Daniel Jastrow, Berlin, "Zur Ermittlung ausländischen Rechts: Was Leistet das Londoner Auskunftsübereinkommen in der Praxis?", *IPRax* 2004, Heft 5, p. 402).

provision of online legal information – which would be publically available and accessible to a theoretically unlimited range of users – the co-operation mechanisms described below would by necessity be limited to certain sets of users, and in some circumstances could be subject to a fee.

A number of bodies in a given State will be in a position to provide access to general information on the law when not available on the Internet, but these resources will generally not be known to foreigners. In most cases, language will be a barrier to locate the most appropriate body to obtain the required information. To be useful, access and contact information should be centralised and made available in a number of languages accessible to the international community. This information could be collected and presented, for example, by the Permanent Bureau of the Hague Conference and/or by a Central Authority in each participating State. The Joint Conference highlighted "the value of establishing or improving mechanisms to identify qualified experts or expert institutes to assist with accessing the content of and interpreting foreign law."[18]

Central Authority

An international Central Authority co-operation system has been a key feature of a range of successful modern Hague Conventions. Such a specialised and dedicated authority in each State, however small, could have as one of its specified duties the obligation to provide general information on national law, including legislation, case law, and general doctrine or *travaux préparatoires*, as appropriate. Information could be provided directly by a Central Authority, responding to a request (subsequent to any necessary consultations), as is done under the European Judicial Network (the "EJN") with its national contact point system.[19] Alternatively, the Central Authority could ask a specialised body such as a specific government department, an association of legal professionals or a specialised legal institute to respond on its behalf.[20] The request could alternatively be sent directly to a specialised body previously identified and designated by the State bearing the obligation to respond to such requests.

Users of this mechanism could include judges and government officials (and possibly legal practitioners and notaries), and would likely be free of cost as much

18 Conclusion and Recommendation No 13, *supra*, note 2.

19 Decision No 568/2009/EC adopted jointly by the European Parliament and the Council of 18 June 2009 amending Council Decision 2001/470/EC establishing a European Judicial Network in civil and commercial matters, OJ 30 June 2009, L. 168/35.

20 Art. 6 of the London Convention allows the "receiving agency" of a State Party to reply itself to a request for information, to transmit the request to another official governmental body, or to a private body or lawyer (in the latter case it must transmit to the requesting authority an estimate of costs for the private service, and request the authority's permission to proceed).

as possible. Regarding language and translation issues, a rationalised approach to cost-apportionment would have to be designed for the written requests and responses, supported by any language capacities of officials staffing Central Authorities.[21]

Judicial Network

States may also wish to contemplate enabling the formation of "closed" judicial networks (*i.e.*, a network composed of and open to judicial authorities only), perhaps modelled on the EJN[22] or the International Hague Network of Judges (IHNJ) specialising in family matters (developed under the auspices of the Hague Conference),[23] available to members of the judiciary at no charge and on the basis of reciprocity.[24] Judges could be enabled to quickly access general information on foreign law, supplementary to materials available online, from their peers in other jurisdictions. In such communications, the overcoming of language barriers could be aided based on knowledge of languages of the communicating judges.

Networks of Professionals

Finally, general information on foreign law could also be provided by both "closed" and open networks of legal professionals, for the benefit of lawyers and other non-judicial legal practitioners, such as notaries.[25] Much can be learned in this respect from the experience of the World Notaries Network established by the International Union of Notaries (*Union internationale du notariat latin*) which links 80 national associations of notaries around the world through an Internet-based system. Each association is represented in the Network by a correspondent who will respond to a request, either directly or with the assistance of the relevant expert in the jurisdiction, at no charge, based on reciprocity. Additionally or alternatively, the Hague Conference could keep a user-friendly web database, accessible to the public, listing bar associations – and their websites / directories, as available – to in effect establish an "open network" of foreign lawyers.

21 Art. 14 of the London Convention provides that the request and the reply be in an official language of the requested State.

22 *Supra*, note 19. Users of the EJN have noted its strength due to the relative informality of communications and the non-binding information exchanged between judges and other authorities.

23 See "Members of the International Hague Network of Judges" available on the Hague Conference website at www.hcch.net under "Child Abduction Section".

24 The Joint Conference noted "initiatives in different States and regions establishing and promoting networks for legal professionals, including judges, which facilitate co-operation and enhance access to foreign law", see Conclusion and Recommendation No 12, *supra*, note 2.

25 *Ibid.*

Contracting States to a new instrument could have the obligation to inform the Permanent Bureau of appropriate associations of legal professionals within their State, and to keep this information up-to-date.[26] States could similarly be required to provide contact and other information as to the existence and services offered by expert institutes in their jurisdiction.[27]

The provision of legal information through such an open network of individual experts and expert institutions could be subject to a schedule of fees for service or be left to market-based or nationally determined fees. As with judicial networks, oral communications based on knowledge of languages of the individual lawyers or other experts would assist in overcoming language barriers.

C. ACCESS TO A CERTIFIED COPY OF THE LAW

Central Authorities could also offer the service of providing, possibly at a fee, officially certified copies of national law, including historical materials or law previously in force at a given date. Such a certified copy of foreign law may be useful for various purposes including litigation, and for a range of actors, including judges, legal practitioners, notaries, government officials and possibly the general public. This might be an important service to provide for some jurisdictions whose courts require certified copies of the foreign law at issue. Such a Central Authority service or function could be gradually replaced, at least in part, by online authenticated legal materials, whereby authoritative versions of law are available online.[28]

II. TAILORED FOREIGN LEGAL INFORMATION

In addition to a need to have access to the black letter of the law, there is a need for access to expertise to interpret and apply the law. The Joint Conference "recognis[ed] that additional mechanisms are needed to obtain tailored foreign legal information, for example, the application of the information to specific facts, which may require the interpretation of the relevant law by judges, government

26 See for example Art. 2 of the Decision establishing the EJN, which requires States to determine national professional associations, and representatives thereof, to participate in the network (*supra*, note 19).

27 For example, the Swiss Institute of Comparative Law (*Institut suisse de droit comparé*), the Max Planck Institute for Comparative and International Private Law (*Max-Planck-Institut für ausländisches und internationales Privatrecht*) and the Hellenic Institute of International and Foreign Law. See Conclusion and Recommendation Nos 9 and 13, *supra*, note 2.

28 For example, countries such as France and Austria have official and authenticated national legislation online.

officials, foreign law experts or expert institutes."[29] Furthermore, the Joint Conference noted "initiatives among courts of different States to facilitate the requesting and the receiving of opinions or decisions on foreign law in particular cases."[30]

There are many circumstances where access to "tailored" foreign legal information may be required. These circumstances include cross-border litigation, arbitration and other dispute settlement, and general non-contentious matters, such as contractual negotiations, estate planning, starting a business, and making family legal arrangements. Thus, the range of beneficiaries who could make use of tailored foreign legal information is equally broad as for general information on foreign law. It includes judges, lawyers, notaries, government officials, professionals of different kinds, members of the business community, and the general public. Finally, depending on the circumstances and the beneficiary, different degrees of complexity of information and analysis may be required. At a minimum, it may include contextualized general information about the law, such as an explanation or tailored summary of the law in a particular area. It could also include an authoritative opinion or an interpretation of the law against a set of facts. Finally, it could include a binding decision concerning the interpretation or application of the law against a set of facts.

A. CONTEXTUALIZED INFORMATION ABOUT THE LAW / SUMMARIES

A contextualized general explanation or summary of the law, possibly in connection with a set of actual or hypothetical facts, could be provided by a number of bodies in a given State. It could be provided by a Central Authority / appropriate governmental bodies, or forwarded to private bodies in a fashion parallel to that described above for Central Authorities providing information on black letter law.

Over the course of time, Central Authorities or other bodies could provide readily available tailored foreign legal information in the form of thematic summaries or Questions and Answers, to be posted online, as desired. To reach this level of sophistication, statistics concerning requests for information would have to be compiled. One could borrow from both the experience of the EJN in relation to the development of factsheets in a broad range of areas of the law and from the Hague Conference with regard to the establishment of "Country Profiles" under specific Conventions.

29 Conclusion and Recommendation No 9, *supra*, note 2.
30 Conclusion and Recommendation No 10, *ibid.*

One could also envisage the development of closed specialised networks with a view to obtaining contextualised general explanations or summaries of the law such as the World Notaries Network established by the International Union of Notaries (*Union internationale du notariat latin*), described above. The IHNJ, also described above, could either be expanded to cover additional areas of the law or serve as an example for the development of additional judicial networks specialised in other areas of the law. Guidance regarding the development of judicial networks and general principles for judicial communications have emerged from the experience of the IHNJ,[31] and these principles could be reflected in an international instrument on access to foreign law.

B. AUTHORITATIVE OPINION OR INTERPRETATION OF THE LAW AGAINST A SET OF FACTS

Tailored foreign legal information in the form of authoritative opinions or interpretations of the law against a concrete set of facts (*e.g.*, in the context of litigation) could also be provided through a system of Central Authorities either responding directly to requests or through identified or designated specialised bodies, as described above. In this context, one could contemplate providing these services at a cost with a view to enabling better services, given the expert intervention involved. However, in the context of closed networks of associations of professionals one could consider the provision of free services, especially if the number of incoming and outgoing requests for information were comparable.

With regard to courts or parties to court proceedings seeking authoritative opinions or interpretations of the law against a set of facts, the Joint Conference noted a number of initiatives among courts of different States to facilitate the requesting and the receiving of such information. Some of these mechanisms, or a version thereof, could be replicated in an international instrument.

For example, in New South Wales (NSW), Australia, the Supreme Court may order, on the application of a party and with the consent of all parties, that "proceedings be commenced in a foreign court to answer questions as to the principles of foreign law or as to their application."[32] A reciprocal provision

---

[31] See "Emerging Guidance regarding the development of the International Hague Network of Judges and General Principles for Judicial Communications, including commonly accepted safeguards for direct judicial communications in specific cases, within the context of the International Hague Network of Judges", draw up by the Permanent Bureau, Prel. Doc. No 3A – Revised as of July 2012, for the attention of the Special Commission of June 2011 on the practical operation of the 1980 Hague Child Abduction Convention and the 1996 Hague Child Protection Convention.

[32] Uniform Civil Procedure Rules 2005 (NSW), r. 6.44(1).

allows parties in foreign proceedings, where questions of Australian law arise, to seek "authoritative pronouncements" on Australian law from the NSW Supreme Court.[33]

Another example from Australia is the possibility for the NSW Supreme Court, on the application of one or more of the parties, or on its own motion, to order that a question of foreign law be answered by a referee.[34] This rule mirrors an already-established mechanism for the reference of a question for inquiry, report and adoption of a referee's report by a court.[35] A designated referee could, in this context, be a retired judge from the relevant foreign jurisdiction.

In addition to the these developments in the Uniform Civil Procedure Rules, the Chief Justice of the NSW Supreme Court has negotiated and concluded arrangements with foreign jurisdictions that allow for questions of foreign law to be determined in those jurisdictions.[36] Rules found in these arrangements could serve as inspiration for the establishment of mechanisms within a multilateral instrument.

In the context of authoritative opinions or interpretations of the law against a set of facts, experience under the London Convention shows that the request must clearly state both the question of foreign law to be answered and the facts or assumptions upon which the answer is to be determined. Furthermore, experience shows that the body answering the request may require additional information or may seek amendments to the question asked or clarification of the facts / assumptions stated, with a view to better answering the question. Valuable experience gathered under the London Convention could inform a new international instrument providing for such requests, allowing for rapid co-operation mechanisms to facilitate two-way exchange of information and dialogue, and the development of specialised model forms for making and responding to such requests.

---

[33] P.L.G. Brereton, "Proof of Foreign Law: Problems and Initiatives", (2011) 85 *A.L.J.* 1, at p. 7. Uniform Civil Procedure Rules 2005 (NSW), r. 6.45.

[34] Uniform Civil Procedure Rules 2005 (NSW), r. 6.44(2).

[35] Brereton, *supra*, note 33.

[36] *Ibid.* See the *Memorandum of Understanding between the Supreme Court of Singapore and the Supreme Court of New South Wales on References of Questions of Law* and *Memorandum of Understanding between the Chief Justice of New South Wales and the Chief Judge of the State of New York on Questions of Law.*

C. BINDING DECISION CONCERNING THE INTERPRETATION OR APPLICATION OF THE LAW AGAINST A SET OF FACTS

Circumstances upon which a binding decision concerning the interpretation or application of the law against a set of facts would most likely be limited to cross-border litigation[37] and requested either by courts or parties to court proceedings, depending on the *ex officio* role of the judge and how foreign law is treated by the forum.

During the Joint Conference, the *Uniform Certification of Questions of Law [Act] [Rule] (1995)*[38] and similar mechanisms of certification found in state laws, were brought to the attention of participants. The Uniform Act / Rule provides a relatively simple and efficient means by which federal and state courts in the United States of America can obtain binding answers (*i.e.* with "precedential effect") on unsettled questions of state law, in general from the highest appellate court of the state whose law is in question. The Act / Rule also provides the possibility to send and receive certified questions of foreign law to and from Mexican and Canadian courts. One could contemplate the inclusion of such mechanisms in a future international instrument.

Finally, another mechanism worth exploring would be the possibility to proceed to a transfer of proceeding or part of a proceeding to a more appropriate forum on a question of interpretation or application of foreign law. The *Uniform Court Jurisdiction and Proceedings Transfer Act* (UCJPTA) developed by the Uniform Law Conference of Canada could provide inspiration in this respect, as may Articles 8 and 9 of the 1996 Hague Child Protection Convention.[39]

In the context of these latter authoritative or binding solutions, the Joint Conference "recognis[ed] that where in the context of adjudication involving foreign law, an opinion or a decision on the application of that law from a foreign court is requested, procedures should assure the due process rights of the parties".[40]

---

37 One could also contemplate this possibility in the context of arbitration proceedings if parties to the proceedings were to agree.

38 Information on the Act is available on the website of the Uniform Law Commission of the United States of America, at www.uniformlaws.org/Act.aspx?title=Certification Of Questions of Law (1995).

39 However, it is important to note that the transfer may only be able to take place on the condition of the receiving court having a jurisdictional link. It is interesting to note that the UCJPTA includes a rule that an order to transfer proceeding or parts thereof can provide for the return of the proceeding to the original court on the occurrence of "specified events" (see Article 15(2)(d)).

40 Conclusion and Recommendation No 11, *supra*, note 2.

CONCLUSION

In summary, a new instrument in this area could set standards as to the quality of the legal information to be available in a range of circumstances, offer a number of optional administrative and judicial co-operation mechanisms to obtain foreign legal information, and allow for the identification of international networks of professional associations, individual experts and expert institutes and judges.[41]

The development of an internationally binding instrument on access to foreign law could benefit from a number of post-Convention services provided by the Hague Conference: *inter alia*, a specialised website, development of Guides to Good Practice, development of Country Profiles, development of standard forms, monitoring of Convention operation, meetings of experts focusing on specific topics, establishment of networks, Special Commission meetings to review the practical operation of the Convention, and expertise in effectively managing multilingual environments.

It is important to note that the Joint Conference recommended that "[a]ny future instrument in this field should not be exclusive in nature, but rather should be complementary to existing and future mechanisms that also facilitate access to and the treatment and application of foreign law".[42] Thus, a new instrument should supplement and add, in a non-constraining way, to any existing methods of ascertaining foreign law, including established regional or national systems.

In the final analysis, what is at stake is the quality of the application and understanding of foreign law applied, with a view to having a satisfactory legal result, from the perspective of the proper administration of justice.[43] Judges around the world are, by virtue of their national conflict of law rules and other

---

41 In its preliminary work, the Hague Conference had suggested a sketch of a potential three-part instrument: (a) facilitating access to online legal information; (b) enabling cross-border administrative and/or judicial cooperation; and, (c) establishing a global network of experts and expert institutions. See "Accessing the content of foreign law and the need for the development of a global instrument in this area – a possible way ahead", a note drawn up by the Permanent Bureau, Prel. Doc. No 11A of March 2009 for the attention of the Council of March / April 2009 on General Affairs and Policy of the Conference, available on the Hague Conference website, www.hcch.net, under "Work in progress," then "General Affairs."

42 Conclusion and Recommendation No 5, *supra*, note 2.

43 A number of prominent common law judges have recently noted the insufficiency of the traditional common law practice of relying upon conflicting expert opinions as a basis for effectively ascertaining foreign law at issue before a court (*e.g.*, Judge R. Posner of the U.S. Court of Appeals, 7th Circuit, in *Bodum United States Inc v La Cafetiere Inc* (2010) 621 F.3d 624 (7th Cir (US)), J.J. Spigelman, former Chief Justice of the Supreme Court of New South Wales, in "Proof of Foreign Law by Reference to the Foreign Court", *L.Q.R.* 2011, 127(APR), 208–216, and Justice P.L.G. Brereton of the Supreme Court of New South Wales, in *supra*, note 33). Moreover, participants at the Joint Conference raised concerns about the current "amateur" application of foreign law and/or the avoidance of application of foreign law (at times despite legal obligations to the contrary), given the present lack of effective mechanisms to ascertain foreign law.

rules of private international law found in Hague Conventions and in other instruments, regularly called upon to ascertain and apply foreign law in a given case. Commercial actors (including small and medium-sized businesses), families and individuals also regularly must ascertain the content of foreign law in non-contentious settings. Given intensifying globalisation and trans-border activity, this raises the question as to whether the global *system* of private international law can operate and be administered adequately in the absence of a comprehensive and effective solution in this area.

THE 1993 HAGUE INTERCOUNTRY ADOPTION CONVENTION AND SUBSIDIARITY: IS THE SUBSIDIARITY PRINCIPLE STILL "FIT FOR PURPOSE"?[1]

Laura Martínez-Mora
Principal Legal Officer, Hague Conference on Private International Law

Hannah Baker
Senior Legal Officer, Hague Conference on Private International Law

Emmanuelle Harang
Legal Officer / Co-ordinator of the Intercountry Adoption Technical Assistance Programme (ICATAP), Hague Conference on Private International Law

I. INTRODUCTION

The "principle of subsidiarity of intercountry adoption" is one of the key pillars of the *Hague Convention of 29 May 1993 on Protection of Children and Co-operation in Respect of Intercountry Adoption* (the "1993 Convention"). However, it is a much-debated concept. Indeed, its interpretation and implementation have been challenging and rarely straightforward. According to this principle, a child should be raised by his or her family of origin or extended family whenever possible. If this is not possible, other forms of permanent family care in the country of origin should be examined. Only after due consideration has been given to national solutions should intercountry adoption be considered, and then only if it is in the

1 The authors would like to thank Doctor Isabelle Lammerant and Professor William Duncan (former Deputy Secretary General of the Hague Conference) for reading an earlier draft of this paper and providing comments.

child's best interests. The principle has provoked passionate commentary, with some arguing that it is a key principle for upholding children's rights and best interests, whilst others decry the principle for "ruining" intercountry adoption and depriving many children of a permanent family.

As the 1993 Convention approaches its twentieth anniversary, it is therefore perhaps an appropriate moment to take a detailed look at this principle and to consider whether the concept is still "fit for purpose": is the application of the principle, in practice, achieving the goal the authors of the Convention intended? And perhaps, more fundamentally, are the aims of subsidiarity still valid some twenty years on, in particular, in an ever-more globalised world in which the understanding of children's rights has evolved? In this article, we attempt to address these questions. We first examine why the principle was included within the Convention. We then turn to some of the main arguments made by some commentators as to why the subsidiarity principle may not now be considered "fit for purpose". Thirdly, we look at how some States are implementing and applying the principle and consider what impact the principle may have had in practice. Lastly, in light of the previous analysis, we explore the question of whether there is a need for a re-consideration of this key pillar of the 1993 Convention.

As many will know, Hans van Loon is the "father" of the 1993 Convention: it was his vision and deep understanding of the subject which drove the drafting of this instrument. This analysis of the subsidiarity principle is therefore carried out in the spirit which he so passionately embodies and which we all admire: that of continued reflection and debate to ensure that we are never complacent and are always considering how we can better protect the world's children and, in this particular case, to ensure that children are raised in permanent families, wherever possible, rather than languishing in institutions or being raised in other forms of alternative care which are not in their best interests.

II. WHAT IS THE "SUBSIDIARITY PRINCIPLE" AND WHY WAS IT INCLUDED WITHIN THE 1993 CONVENTION?

As Doctor Isabelle Lammerant has described, the "subsidiarity principle" could be named the "double[2] subsidiarity" principle as there are, in fact, two "levels" inherent within it. At the *first level* of subsidiarity (see the Preamble to the 1993 Convention), alternative domestic permanent family placements should be considered subsidiary to a child being raised in his / her own (nuclear or extended)

2 I. Lammerant, *L'adoption et les droits de l'homme en droit comparé*, Bruylant, 2001, pp. 666 and 705.

family of origin. At the *second level* of subsidiarity, once it has been identified that alternative care outside the family of origin is in a child's best interests, there is an obligation upon States to give "due consideration" to placement of the child within the State of origin (preferably permanent family care), before looking to *intercountry* adoption (Preamble and Article 4 *b)*).

When considering the rationale behind the inclusion of the "subsidiarity principle" in the 1993 Convention, the reason for the first 'level' of subsidiarity is not hard to identify. Indeed, the primary importance of the family of origin to the protection and well-being of children has been reaffirmed many times during the past century in international legislation and policy.[3] It is also a consistent theme in the *1989 UN Convention on the Rights of the Child* ("UNCRC").[4] There has, therefore, long been an acknowledgement that the laws and policies of States concerning children should, first and foremost, support and preserve families.[5] A placement of a child away from his / her family of origin should only take place following a carefully conducted assessment of the needs and best interests of the particular child.[6] Further, where alternative care for a child is required, priority should be given to "family-type alternative care".[7]

At the second 'level' of subsidiarity, the idea that *domestic* family outcomes must be given "due consideration" before *intercountry* adoption can be determined to be in a child's best interests, is perhaps less universally accepted. Looking to the Convention's background material, the 1990 van Loon Report[8] makes clear that, at the time of the drafting of the 1993 Convention, there was "growing worldwide agreement that in the continuum of child care services ... before intercountry adoption is chosen, sufficient consideration should be given to possible alternative plans for the child in his or her own country in view of the difficulties in transplanting a child from one society and culture to another."[9] Indeed, based on this rationale, the subsidiarity principle had, by 1990, already

3 *E.g., 1959 UN Declaration of the Rights of the Child*, the *1986 UN Declaration on Social and Legal Principles relating to the Protection and Welfare of Children, with Special Reference to Foster Placement and Adoption Nationally and Internationally.*

4 See UNCRC Preamble and Articles 7–9, 16 and 20–22.

5 In this regard, the Committee on the Rights of the Child in its Report following the "Day of General Discussion on Children without Parental Care" (2005), recommended "that States Parties develop, adopt and implement, in collaboration with civil society ... a comprehensive national policy on families and children which supports and strengthens families" (para. 645).

6 By a competent and appropriate multi-disciplinary group of experts. This assessment should include short and long-term planning for the child and regular reviews of the placement. See the *2009 UN Guidelines for the Alternative Care of Children.*

7 *Supra*, note 5, para. 666, "[i]n order to avoid long-term placement of children in institutions that do not provide the type of setting children need, not only for survival, but also for development...".

8 J.H.A van Loon, "Report on Intercountry Adoption," Hague Conference on Private International Law, *Proceedings of the Seventeenth Session (1993)*, at p. 11.

9 *Ibid.* para. 86. See also paras 70 *et seq.*

been included in other international instruments.[10] The van Loon Report also provided specific examples of the attempts of several individual States to prioritise 'in-country' outcomes for children in need of alternative care over intercountry solutions.[11] International consensus at that time was therefore that *domestic* alternative permanent family solutions, in general, were to be preferred, *for child welfare reasons*, to similar *intercountry* solutions. As a result, there was a need for intercountry adoption to be placed appropriately within the hierarchy of alternative family care options available to children so that the response to children in need of such care remained child-focused and did not continue to be, or become, 'market' (or adult) driven.

III. THE CHALLENGES OF SUBSIDIARITY

Some commentators have argued that the "subsidiarity principle", rather than promoting child welfare, actually hinders the ability of many children in need to find a family of their own. In this section, we consider some of their arguments and we provide our response to each "argument".

ARGUMENT 1: IMPLEMENTING SUBSIDIARITY RESULTS IN INTERCOUNTRY ADOPTION BECOMING A MEASURE OF "LAST RESORT"

A common misconception of the subsidiarity principle, as set out in the 1993 Convention, is that the principle obliges States Parties to consider intercountry adoption as a measure of "last resort": *i.e.*, to consider that all other domestic outcomes must have been exhausted before intercountry adoption can be considered. If interpreted in this way, subsidiarity can become a justification for the very care of children which the 1993 Convention seeks to avoid: the institutionalisation of children, even where a suitable and eligible family abroad may be willing to care for the child. In fact, to the contrary, the 1993 Convention insists that, "the placement of a child in a family, including in intercountry adoption, is the best option among all forms of alternative care, in particular to be preferred over institutionalisation".[12] The Convention asks States Parties to give "due consideration" to *domestic* family options before deciding that *intercountry*

10 The 1986 UN Declaration (supra, note 3) and the UNCRC.
11 *Supra*, note 8, paras 46 *et seq.*
12 G. Parra-Aranguren, Explanatory Report to the 1993 Hague Convention, Hague Conference on Private International Law, *Proceedings of the Seventeenth Session (1993)*, paras 45–46.

adoption is in the best interests of a child, for the child welfare reasons outlined in the previous section.

This confusion concerning the interpretation of subsidiarity often arises in the context of discussion concerning the principle as espoused within the UNCRC. Article 21 *b* of the UNCRC is worded in a slightly different manner to Article 4 *b* of the 1993 Convention. Article 21 *b* states that intercountry adoption may only be considered, "if the child cannot *in any suitable manner* be cared for in the child's country of origin" [emphasis added]. However, as Hans van Loon commented "the difference [between the instruments] ... may be more apparent than real".[13] Indeed, Article 21 *b* of the UNCRC does not exclude an interpretation to the effect that, it "sees [institutional care] ... as less preferable than adoption". This flows from the wording of Article 20(3) of the UNCRC, which refers to alternative child care including adoption, "or *if necessary* placement in suitable institutions for the care of children" [emphasis added]. This wording suggests that, if anything, institutionalisation is the "last resort" for children. Furthermore, UNICEF's 2010 statement indicates that, "[w]hen ... a child's family is unavailable, unable or unwilling to care for her/him, then appropriate and permanent family-based solutions should be sought."[14]

In the African context, this debate can be more challenging to resolve since Article 24 *b* of the African Charter on the Rights and Welfare of the Child ("ACRWC") specifically states that intercountry adoption "may, *as the last resort*, be considered as an alternative means of a child's care" [emphasis added]. On the contrary, in practice, in some States in Africa (as elsewhere) intercountry adoption is or has been, the "first" and only resort, and this has led to abuses. There has also been, on occasion, a perception that intercountry adoption is a form of neo-colonialism. All this has led some African countries to strictly apply the "last resort" principle of the ACRWC and prohibit, or severely restrict, intercountry adoption.

The reality in these countries, however, may be that there is a high number of children deprived of suitable alternative care: e.g., institutionalised or living on the street. It is true that intercountry adoption, when permitted by domestic law,[15] is not a solution for all these children as many of them may not be adoptable and increased efforts must be made to support their families, prevent abandonment

[13] J.H.A. van Loon, "International Co-operation and Protection of Children with regard to Intercountry Adoption", *Recueil des cours* (1993-VII, vol. 244).

[14] UNICEF's 2010 Press Release concerning intercountry adoption.

[15] In some States with legal systems based fully or partly on Sharia law, adoption is prohibited. These States have alternative institutions for providing children in need with alternative permanent family care (*e.g.*, the institution of *kafala*, which provides for the care of the child in another family but does not sever the child's legal ties with his/her family of origin). Cross-border *kafala* arrangements are not within the scope of the 1993 Convention but are within the scope of the 1996 Hague Child Protection Convention.

and to find domestic, family-based permanent alternative care solutions. However, if the "last resort" becomes really the "exception", one could then legitimately ask whether this is in the best interests of the children in need of alternative care. Indeed, it would be extremely interesting to listen to the views of adults who were raised mainly in institutions and who have grown up with no family.

As Doctor Benyam Mezmur has explained,[16] the solution, in the African context as well as generally, is that an individualistic response, including permanency planning, should always be adopted and this must be based on a 'best interests' analysis of the particular child. This is the response which is in accordance with *all* international instruments. Whilst certain forms of institutional alternative care will always be required (*e.g.*, for temporary care) and, in certain situations, may play a vital role in child protection, in many (perhaps most) cases, institutional care should not be the preferred option when a permanent family solution is available for a child.[17] As Professor William Duncan, has explained: "The principle of subsidiarity, while of central importance, should not be applied in an inflexible manner ... It is important that the idea of subsidiarity be always interpreted and applied in the context of the 'best interests' principle."[18]

ARGUMENT 2: IMPLEMENTING SUBSIDIARITY CAUSES UNNECESSARY DELAYS

Another argument against the subsidiarity principle is that the attempts it requires to support the family of origin and, if applicable, the efforts required to find *domestic* alternative care solutions, take considerable time and delay matters for children (sometimes leaving children in temporary institutional or foster care for lengthy periods). Moreover, as a result, when a decision is finally taken to place a child for intercountry adoption, the child is older and therefore the chance of him/her being adopted has diminished.

The response to this argument is that it is a matter of establishing good practices when implementing and operating the subsidiarity principle, as well as allocating the necessary resources. As the Guide to Good Practice No. 1 on the 1993 Convention makes clear, whilst "[t]he Convention refers to [giving due consideration to] "possibilities" for the placement of a child in the State of

---

16 B. Mezmur, "Intercountry Adoption as a measure of last resort in Africa: advancing the rights of a child rather than a right to a child", *International Journal on Human Rights*, June 2009.

17 *Supra*, note 6, paras 20–22.

18 W. Duncan, "Intercountry Adoption: Some Issues in Implementing and Supplementing the 1993 Hague Convention on Protection of Children and Co-operation in Respect of Intercountry Adoption", in *Children on the Move, How to Implement their Right to Family Life*, Eds J. Doek, H. van Loon and P. Vlaardingerbroek, 1996, p. 78.

origin ...[,] [i]t does not require that all possibilities be exhausted. This would be unrealistic; it would place an unnecessary burden on authorities; and it may delay indefinitely the possibility of finding a permanent home abroad for a child". Further, "States should guarantee permanency planning in the shortest possible time for each child deprived of his / her parents".[19]

ARGUMENT 3: SUBSIDIARITY 'LEGITIMISES' DOMESTIC ALTERNATIVE FAMILY SOLUTIONS WHICH MAY HAVE FEWER SAFEGUARDS THAN CONVENTION-COMPLIANT INTERCOUNTRY ADOPTIONS

Some States do not have the necessary resources to properly implement domestic alternative family solutions: *i.e.*, whilst domestic adoption, for example, may be available, it may have far fewer safeguards for children than an adoption carried out under the 1993 Convention. For example, in some States there are difficulties in terms of the information, counselling, assessment and support provided to prospective adoptive parents and adoptive families. Without such safeguards, there is a real risk that the placement could result in an outcome detrimental to the child's best interests. In other cases, the family solutions provided domestically are temporary and therefore do not provide the permanence widely accepted as in children's best interests. In addition, in some cases, the types of placement available domestically do not create a permanent parent-child relationship, unlike adoption.

The response to this argument is that, in application of the principle of non-discrimination, States should, as a minimum, apply the 1993 Convention safeguards to domestic adoption procedures and, wherever possible, promote permanent family solutions for children, with appropriate safeguards.

ARGUMENT 4: IN AN INCREASINGLY GLOBALISED WORLD, THE RATIONALE UPON WHICH SUBSIDIARITY IS BASED NEEDS TO BE RE-CONSIDERED

In addition to the points above, there is an argument against "level two" of subsidiarity which is perhaps less frequently discussed. This goes to the heart of the rationale for the principle and asks whether, if we live in an increasingly

[19] Hague Conference on Private International Law, *The Implementation and Operation of the 1993 Hague Intercountry Adoption Convention – Guide to Good Practice*, Guide No 1, Family Law (Jordan Publishing Ltd), 2008, paras 48 and 50.

globalised world, it is still the case that, twenty years on from the conception of the Convention, there remain "difficulties in transplanting a child from one society and culture to another"? Could it be the case that cultural differences are not so stark today due to the fact that the movement of persons is so much more commonplace and we all live in a "melting pot" of cultures and societies?[20] If so, it is argued, perhaps it should not be the case, in child welfare terms, that *domestic* family outcomes are any more privileged in the hierarchy of alternative care options for children than international family outcomes? Proponents of this argument state that most adopted persons are doing well in their new country and culture and there have been no "systemic" problems of adaptation for intercountry adoptees. Moreover, what happens in the case of in-family intercountry adoptions, or adoptions by persons with the same nationality and culture as a child but who, for various reasons, habitually reside in another country: is subsidiarity applicable to these situations?[21]

In relation to the cultural 'transplantation' point, the experiences of intercountry adoptees should be at the heart of this debate (since only they can say if they found being "transplanted" from one culture to another difficult). In this regard, further studies need to be carried out before ready conclusions can be drawn. One can imagine, however, that the experiences of intercountry adoptees will likely vary tremendously based upon a whole host of factors, such as: the age when they were adopted, the two particular countries and cultures involved in the adoption, the nationality and/or culture of the adoptive family, as well as factors such as the preparation which they, as children, and their prospective adoptive parents received. It may therefore be extremely hard to draw any generalised conclusions from further studies.

As regards the application of subsidiarity to in-family intercountry adoptions, it should be recalled that "it is not subsidiarity itself which is the overriding principle of this Convention but the child's best interests".[22] The subsidiarity principle therefore has to be implemented and interpreted flexibly, in an individualised manner and "in most cases the child's interests may be best served by growing up with the biologically-related family abroad."[23] However, the question of how subsidiarity should be applied to the situation of intercountry adoptions by unrelated persons, but those with the same nationality/culture as the child, is more complicated. It is clear that when applying "level two" of subsidiarity and searching for the best family abroad for a specific child, an analysis of the particular child's best interests may result in priority being given

20 Although, on the contrary, globalisation in some cases can exacerbate cultural identities.

21 For a detailed discussion on this issue, see *Guide to Good Practice*, *supra*, note 19, chapters 2.1 and 8.6.

22 *Ibid.* at para. 52.

23 *Ibid.*

to families with the same nationality/culture as the child (over other families which have no link with the State of origin). However, adopting a generalised policy which, as a matter of course, always gives priority to nationals habitually resident in another State, in particular without studying the possibility for the child of adoption in the State of origin, would clearly fail to respect the principle of subsidiarity and the Convention.

IV. SUBSIDIARITY "IN PRACTICE"

In addition to the arguments set out above, another consideration when determining whether the subsidiarity principle remains "fit for purpose" is to examine the impact the principle has had "in practice" in the past twenty years in States of origin and receiving States. Has the principle led to any specific changes in law or policy in these States which have promoted children's rights or interests? This section seeks to examine this issue and argues that, whilst challenges in relation to implementation remain, positive developments have taken place which can be traced back to the subsidiarity principle.

STATES OF ORIGIN

The subsidiarity principle has had positive effects in many States of origin which are Parties to the 1993 Convention, in particular those with basic child protection systems. Indeed, one of the great achievements of subsidiarity is that it has led to developments and improvements concerning child protection in general in some States. For example, it is easy to see the results of the implementation of the "second level" of subsidiarity in some countries, as there has been a sharp increase in domestic adoptions (or other domestic permanent family solutions) due to, amongst other reasons, the development of active policies at the domestic level to promote adoption, including, in some countries, policies to break-down taboos regarding adoption. This has been the case, for example, in Chile (between 1988 and 1999, there were 1,372 domestic adoptions and between 2000 and 2011, 5,516), China and India (from 2,409 domestic adoptions in 2006, to 5,693 in 2010). In many cases, this increase in domestic adoption has been accompanied by a decrease in intercountry adoptions: *e.g.*, in Chile (between 1988 and 1999, there were 4,812 intercountry adoptions and between 2000 and 2011, 1,055), China (from 11,227 in 2003 to 4,405 in 2011) and India (from 1,173 in 2003, to 628 in 2011). Further, it has also often been accompanied by the creation of specific programs for the adoption of children with "special needs" (*e.g.*, in Chile and China (the "green channel" programme)).[24]

The aim of the 1993 Convention is neither to increase nor to decrease intercountry adoptions. It is instead for intercountry adoptions to take place where they are needed by children and to ensure that those intercountry adoptions which do take place are in the best interests of the particular children involved. However, if intercountry adoptions are decreasing because steps have been taken by States of origin to promote permanent domestic alternative care outcomes *within* the country, this is a very positive outcome of the Convention (provided the appropriate safeguards are in place for children – see argument 3 above). As Professor Duncan said in 1995, "hopefully, the Convention will provide further impetus for the development of … [placing agencies in the country of origin which have the capacity to explore alternatives to intercountry adoption], and may indirectly thereby reduce the need for intercountry adoption."[25]

Unfortunately, however, a reduced global "need" for intercountry adoption is unlikely to be the main reason for the overall decline in the number of intercountry adoptions. In fact, in many cases, the decline in numbers is linked to the closures and moratoriums put in place to stop systemic abuses, including, sometimes, the sale of children. This has been the case in countries which, prior to the closures, were principal "sending countries" (*e.g.*, Cambodia, Guatemala and Romania). Where the 1993 Convention is in force in such countries, it is a tool to fight these abuses and helps to establish a proper legal framework for adoptions. In such cases, the Convention is not the reason for the decline in the number of intercountry adoptions, as it is only a tool to stop those abuses. Therefore, as Professor Smolin has highlighted, to blame the 1993 Convention for the decline in intercountry adoptions would be an overly-simplistic analysis of the situation and a misunderstanding of the goal of the Convention.

Regarding the "first level" of subsidiarity, in countries with transition economies, specific programmes to preserve families of origin and prevent family separation have been developed and have contributed to the decrease in intercountry adoptions mentioned above (as less families of origin abandon their children). However, there are still challenges in this respect, particularly in States where there is a large gap between the rich and poor and no middle class. In the case of Brazil, for example, there are policies concerning prevention

[24] Sources of statistics: Chilean Central Authority (SENAME), Indian Central Authority (CARA) and P. Selman (2012), Key Tables for Intercountry Adoption (available upon request from the author (pfselman@yahoo.co.uk)).

[25] Emphasis added. See W. Duncan, "The Hague Convention on the Protection of Children and Co-operation in respect of intercountry adoption 1993. Some issues of special relevance to sending countries" in *Intercountry Adoptions: Laws and Perspectives of "Sending" Countries*, Ed. E.D. Jaffe, p. 217, at p. 222.

of abandonment and family reintegration (*e.g. National Plan for the Promotion, Protection and Defence of the Rights of Children and Adolescents to a Family and Community life*), but child institutionalisation remains a challenge and poverty remains the main cause of child institutional placement. In addition, in some cases, the procedures to declare the adoptability of the child can be extremely lengthy, often as a result of a desire by the State to comply with family preservation.

In other States, there remain many challenges in implementing subsidiarity at *both* "levels" due to extreme poverty and therefore often under-developed national child protection systems and/or taboos regarding adoption. Many of these States are well aware of the subsidiarity principle and understand its rationale, but the lack of resources and domestic infrastructure make it extremely difficult to apply. In these countries, in practice, as stated above, intercountry adoption becomes the "first resort", in addition to the institutionalisation of children. Indeed, finding out how to preserve families in States of origin where extreme poverty is a cause of relinquishment is a key issue in the intercountry adoption debate. It is a concern which must be confronted if intercountry adoption is to be seen as an ethical, child welfare practice. Professor Smolin has stated that, "[i]ntercountry adoption as a response to extreme poverty in developing nations creates an intercountry adoption system in service of the desire of persons in rich countries for children, rather than a genuinely humanitarian response to the best interests of children." Indeed, in some States of origin, it has been, and continues to be the case that intercountry adoption outcomes are preferred to domestic adoptions, not because of the particular child's welfare but because of the monetary benefits intercountry adoption brings or the financial support it provides to the child welfare system.[26]

Another challenge may also be that traditional structures for the care of children are not working anymore in these countries due to complex factors such as extreme poverty, urbanisation and the HIV/AIDS pandemic. In some countries, there may also be challenges regarding public awareness of alternative care options generally and a need for public education: *e.g.*, there may be ignorance concerning the existence of domestic adoption, or misunderstandings concerning the legal implications of the institution.

Whilst it is apparent therefore that the implementation of the subsidiarity principle has prompted some important and positive developments in certain States of origin, there is clearly a significant need for further improvement, both at the level of family preservation, as well as in terms of developing domestic alternative family outcomes for children in need.

[26] D. Smolin, "Abduction, sale and traffic in children in the context of intercountry adoption", *Info Doc.* No 1, Special Commission of June 2010.

RECEIVING STATES

In many traditional receiving States there has long been a strong focus on family preservation. In many of these countries, economic support is more readily available to families. Children are therefore separated from their family of origin, in principle, only in exceptional cases.[27] Moreover, even in cases where children are separated from their family, there is often legislation and policy which attempts to ensure that, where in the child's best interests, all efforts are made to reunify the child with his/her family.[28]

However, whilst efforts at family preservation are commendable, the paradox for some of these States is that, in certain circumstances, these attempts to preserve families of origin may actually be hindering the possibility, for some children, of living in a permanent family. This situation may arise in States where the desire to preserve biological ties is so strong that it prevents child protection "actors" within the State from considering (early enough, or at all) domestic alternative permanent care options for children, such as domestic adoption. Instead, children may be left languishing in State care (e.g., foster homes or residential care), whilst efforts are continued to re-engage the biological parent(s) or to reunify the family.[29] For example, in France, a 2008 Report on adoption stated that too often the culture surrounding child protection was such that the "actors" involved, such as the social workers and judges, viewed the domestic adoption of a child as a 'failure' by the State to maintain links with the child's family of origin, rather than as a positive child protection measure.[30]

In a similar vein, in receiving States where the number of "in-coming" intercountry adoptions is high but there are also many children in the country waiting to be adopted (e.g., in the U.S. – where, in 2009, there were 114,556 children waiting to be adopted and 12,735 "in-coming" intercountry adoptions by U.S. resident adoptive parents),[31] questions have been asked as to whether more could, and should, be done for the children in need of alternative care *within* the country. It has even been suggested by some that an obligation should be placed

27 *E.g.*, due to child neglect, abuse, parental death or illness. On the other hand, certain States, such as the UK, are criticized because children are separated from their family of origin too quickly.

28 *E.g.*, in the U.S., the *Adoption and Safe Families Act* of 1997 was enacted to promote expedited timeframes within which to place children in permanent homes through reunification, adoption or guardianship.

29 *E.g.*, the Civil Code (Articles 347, 350) is relatively restrictive in terms of the children who may be considered in need of adoption: where parents maintain some contact with their children, it appears very unlikely that the child will be declared adoptable.

30 J.M. Colombani, *Rapport sur l'adoption*, 2008, pp. 49–50.

31 U.S. Central Authority (Department of State).

on prospective adoptive parents to apply for domestic adoption first, before an application for intercountry adoption will be accepted.[32]

Whilst there is a need for further, clearer statistics on the number and profile of children in need of adoption in some of these States (since a child being in an institution or in the care of the State does not mean the child is, or should be, "adoptable"), several States have recognised the issue and are taking steps to attempt to address this and the high number of children in State care. For example, in the U.S., in 2008, the *Fostering Connections to Success and Increasing Adoptions Act* was introduced, establishing innovative mechanisms to promote domestic care solutions and adoptions, such as assistance being provided to members of the child's extended family, financial support for adoptive families and the promotion of adoption for those with special needs.[33] In a similar way, in 2009, Spain established a committee to analyse foster care and domestic adoption due to the fact that more than 30,000 children are in the State care system; Denmark made amendments to the Danish Act on Social services with the aim of promoting domestic adoption in 2009; and Quebec diversified the choices of care provision so that there is a varied array of both transitory and permanent child care options for children in need (2006 Child Protection Law).

Whilst the subsidiarity principle is a legal obligation placed upon States of origin under the Convention, there is certainly more that could, and should, be done by some receiving States in terms of "good practices" to ensure that the children habitually resident in their State also have every chance of growing up in a loving family. Moreover, in application of the principle of the "co-responsibility of States", one could argue that receiving States should verify with States of origin whether there is a need for intercountry adoption for children in that State *before* sending any requests for intercountry adoption: where this is not the case, requests should not be sent.

V. CONCLUSION: IS THE SUBSIDIARITY PRINCIPLE STILL "FIT FOR PURPOSE"?

Unfortunately, we do not yet live in a world (and are unlikely to for the foreseeable future) where all States are able to rely on strong and effective national child protection systems: this is very much a "work in progress". Whilst this remains the case, countries which permit intercountry adoption should ensure that it is safe, principled and ethical. The "subsidiarity principle" has been widely

32 International Social Service Monthly Review, *Special Edition on the Principle of Subsidiarity*, March-April 2009.

33 *Ibid.*

supported over the years as it has been shown that, if well implemented, it can work to support this end. As a result, in our view, the main challenge is not to re-consider the principle itself but to consider how to *interpret* and *implement* it in the best interests of children.

Practice has shown us that, in some States, *interpretations* of subsidiarity can be extreme and, in some cases, politically motivated for reasons unconnected with children's welfare. Such interpretations of subsidiarity are not in the best interests of children. The rights and interests of children demand a more balanced and nuanced approach which does not bow to generalisations, but permits an individual analysis of each child's circumstances and best interests.

There is also room for improvement in relation to the *implementation* of the subsidiarity principle. In particular, governments should allocate sufficient resources to child protection systems so that authorities can take decisions regarding alternative care in a timely manner, without unnecessary delays and bureaucracy, and ensure that domestic alternative care outcomes apply, as a minimum, the same standards as the Convention.

As the 1993 Convention reminds us when interpreting and implementing subsidiarity, as when applying the Convention generally, the goal must always be for every child "to grow up in a family environment, in an atmosphere of happiness, love and understanding".[34]

[34] Preamble.

THE RIGHT TO A FAIR TRIAL, *FORUM NON CONVENIENS* AND THE LIMITS OF THE POSSIBLE

David McClean*
Emeritus Professor of Law, University of Sheffield

A PREAMBLE

On hearing of the loss of Calais, the last remnant of the once-extensive English dominions in mainland France, Queen Mary I observed that when she died the word 'Calais' would be found written on her heart. Perhaps Hans van Loon's heart will be found to bear the phrase 'Judgments Project', for that endeavour was such a major feature of the work of the Hague Conference during 'the van Loon years'. Ideally, room would also be found for the word 'globalisation': Hans van Loon has overseen major efforts not only to secure the globalisation of the existing Hague Conventions[1] but also the globalisation of the Conference itself with, for example, the major initiative to promote the work of the Conference in Latin America.

As the work on the Judgments Project showed very clearly, globalisation comes at a price. The growing number of member States, and the increased number (and in some cases the greater activity) of delegations attending Special Commissions and Diplomatic Sessions of the Conference, causes problems for the practical working of those bodies.[2] The greater the number of national legal systems of which account has to be taken, the harder it is to produce substantive agreement on the texts of new Conventions.

* Hans van Loon and I once worked out that my association with the Conference, almost always as a representative of the Commonwealth Secretariat, began one year before he joined the Permanent Bureau; so I take particular pleasure in contributing to this book.

1 See S Detrick and P Vlaardingerbroek (eds), *Globalization of Child Law: the Role of the Hague Conventions* (Martinus Nijhoff, 1999).

2 I examined some of these consequences of enlargement in J Fawcett (ed), *Reform and Development of Private International Law* (OUP, 2002) at 267–8.

That last statement calls for some closer analysis. Anyone at all familiar with the work of the Hague Conference recognises that the broad legal 'families' or traditions have their own mind-sets, and dialogue between those families requires some 'thinking outside the box' of familiar thought-patterns on the part of each participant. Some negotiations run into 'constitutional' red lines: if a particular rule of law has, for whatever reason, a constitutional basis in a given legal system (for example the Due Process Clause of the U.S. Constitution) room for manoeuvre may be drastically limited.

But there is another phenomenon which is a source of difficulty. One of the fascinations of comparative law is that even within a given legal tradition, say that of the common law, particular ideas have come to be expressed in rather different language in different legal systems. The variations in language may have a basis in the structure of the given national system, but often they are simply the result of the preferences of a legislative drafter, a senior judge's choice of words in what comes to be regarded as a leading case, the 'accidents of litigation' and of the Parliamentary process.[3] There may be no issue of principle as between different formulations, but for that very reason the representatives of a particular State may resist a proposal which adopts a formulation not its own.

There must be yet one more preambular clause to this paper. Lawyers are adept at finding forms of words which 'paper over the cracks', which give an appearance of agreement that vanishes on close examination. It is notorious that the welfare, or 'best interests', of a child is something which all can agree is the best criterion for decisions as to a child's future; and that ideas as what that criterion means in actual practice differ widely. I would suggest that 'fair trial' is another example. English observers are horrified at the use of juries in many U.S. jurisdictions to set the (often very high) level of exemplary damages; American observers may be shocked at the disappearance of the jury in English civil trials and increasingly from all but the most serious criminal trials (and not even always then[4]) and at the absence of extensive and intrusive pre-trial discovery in the English system. Both systems may be entirely fair, but the point is that agreement on the need for a fair trial does not carry with it any agreement about the merits of different forms of civil procedure. A cynic would say that procedures are only seen as fair by the successful party.

3 The same may of course happen in international negotiations. It is not unknown for delegates at The Hague to welcome a Working Paper which offers a solution to the issue under discussion, not noticing that the paper uses language, not directly on that point, varying from an earlier text. The use of two languages and differing translations exacerbates the problem.

4 See sections 44 to 50 of Part 7 of the Criminal Justice Act 2003 dealing with cases in which jury tampering has occurred or is suspected.

A FAIR TRIAL?

The European Convention on Human Rights and comparable documents guarantee the right to a fair trial. So Article 6(1) of the ECHR provides: 'In the determination of his civil rights and obligations or of any criminal charge against him, everyone is entitled to a fair and public hearing within a reasonable time by an independent and impartial tribunal established by law.'[5] The text is silent on private international law issues: where is this tribunal to sit; under what law is it to be established? The text, like a great deal of legal debate, assumes a single-State set of issues.

It could be argued that if a plaintiff begins proceedings in the courts of State A, the courts of that State are obliged by Article 6 to hear those proceedings and give judgment within a reasonable time. A lawyer in the civil law tradition would want to qualify that to deal with cases of '*litispendence*' or '*lis alibi pendens*', where the issue is already before a court in another State. The common lawyer would add the doctrine of *forum non conveniens*.[6] That latter issue is a notably divisive one; it took many hours in the discussions of the Judgments Project and a compromise solution seemed to be within reach.

There is an important threshold issue. It is arguable that the practice of *forum non conveniens* is contrary to international law as expressed in the human rights instruments. In the celebrated case of *Owusu v Jackson*[7] (which held that the English practice was incompatible with the Brussels Convention of 1968 on jurisdiction and the recognition and enforcement of judgments in civil and commercial matters) the Opinion of Advocate General Léger contains a passage notable for its hostility to the English practice.[8] He declared that the suspension of proceedings brought about by a stay, which might operate *sine die* was 'inherently unsatisfactory in terms of legal certainty'. The *forum non conveniens* doctrine was liable to undermine legal protection for people, especially claimants, established in the Community. He continued:

> 'Finally, in the event of the claimant not succeeding in producing the evidence in question to oppose a stay of proceedings (which could be pronounced *sine die*) or to recommence proceedings already suspended, the only possibility that would remain if he sought to pursue his claims would be to take all the steps needed to

5 See, for example, the Charter of Fundamental Rights of the EU, Article 47 (OJ C364/1, 18.12.2000); American Convention on Human Rights, Article 8; Constitution of Barbados, Article 18 (and similar provisions in the constitutions of many former UK colonies).

6 It is odd that there is no generally accepted English word or phrase for either concept. I cannot in this paper address the wider issue of *lis alibi* nor the successful work on choice of court clauses.

7 Case C-281/02 *Owusu v Jackson (t/a Villa Holidays Bal Inn Villas)* [2005] ECR I-1383.

8 Paragraphs 266 to 270.

> commence a new suit before the foreign court. It goes without saying that those steps have a cost and are likely considerably to prolong the time spent in the conduct of proceedings before the claimant finally has his case heard. Moreover, in that respect, the mechanism associated with the *forum non conveniens* doctrine could be regarded as incompatible with the requirements of Article 6 of the European Convention on the protection of human rights and fundamental freedoms.'

This is not the place for a detailed examination of all the Advocate General's assertions but the final observation is of especial interest. It is certainly true that *forum non conveniens* proceedings may take a deal of time (and expense) and they have been criticised as mere litigation about litigation. But the notion of a 'fair trial' has to be viewed from the standpoint of *both* parties, not just that of the claimant. *Forum non conveniens* can be seen as a means of balancing the great advantage a claimant may enjoy in the choice of venue.

The relevance of Article 6 had in fact already been addressed by the House of Lords in a case[9] in which a plea of *forum non conveniens* failed, for requiring the case to be heard in South Africa would, because of the lack of funding and legal representation in that country, deny the plaintiffs a fair trial on terms of litigious equality with the defendant. That was a decision applying common law principles and Lord Bingham of Cornhill was surely right to say that, at least in that context, Article 6 added nothing to the principles applied by the English courts.[10] In a case concerning anti-suit injunctions,[11] Aikens J observed:

> 'Article 6 of the ECHR does not provide that a person is to have an unfettered choice of tribunal in which to pursue or defend his civil rights. ... Article 6 of the ECHR does not deal at all with where the right to a "fair and public hearing before an independent and impartial tribunal established by law" is to be exercised by a litigant. The crucial point is that civil rights must be determined somewhere by a hearing and before a tribunal in accordance with the provisions of Article 6.'

That suggests that a distinction might be drawn between cases in which the alternative forum is a State party to the ECHR (so that there is some guarantee of a fair trial in a reasonable time) and those in which it is not. Such a distinction would involve an exercise of judicial creativity and opinions will naturally differ as to the desirability of judge-made law in this context.

---

9 *Lubbe v Cape plc* [2000] 1 WLR 1545.

10 At p. 1561. See, however, the discussion in J Fawcett, "The Impact of Article 6(1) of the ECHR on Private International Law" (2007) 54 *ICLQ* 1 at 9–11.

11 *OT Africa Line Ltd v Hijazy (The Kribi)* [2001] 1 Lloyd's Rep 76 at [42].

BUT WHAT ARE WE TALKING ABOUT?

Those familiar with the Hague Convention on the Taking of Evidence Abroad will recall the trouble that has been created by the reference in Article 23 of that Convention to 'pre-trial discovery of documents as known in Common Law countries'. The authors of the Convention failed to note that 'pre-trial discovery' has no uniform meaning within the common law tradition; it is notoriously far more extensive, and burdensome to defendants, in United States practice than in most other common law countries. There is a danger that the same mistake might be made about *forum non conveniens*.

The core idea of *forum non conveniens* is that a court with jurisdiction to hear a claim may decline to exercise that jurisdiction if it is persuaded that some other court is a more suitable forum.[12] As Wendy Kennett observed in a perceptive article,[13] '[t]he development of the doctrine of forum non conveniens is seen by English lawyers as a significant improvement in the rules of jurisdiction: a sophisticated device for ensuring international harmony of decision-making and a proper allocation of resources',[14] but it is viewed with hostility by civilians (as the passage from Advocate General Léger's Opinion already referred to illustrates very well). She analysed some of the underlying reasons for that hostility:

> 'The lack of any legislative framework may lead foreign lawyers to conclude that the doctrine operates in a more arbitrary manner than is in fact the case. Opinions may legitimately differ as to the predictability of decision-making in *forum non conveniens* cases, but the general structure within which the courts must operate is clear and well-established.'[15]

There is a broad discretion exercised by the judge, and such discretion is alien to some legal traditions; but it is a discretion to be exercised judicially and there is an abundance of case law to guide its exercise.

She identified another fear that had been expressed, that *forum non conveniens* could lead to a denial of justice if the English court stayed its proceedings in favour of another court and the latter then concluded that it lacked jurisdiction. But, she argued, if it emerged that the action could not be heard in the allegedly more appropriate forum, an application could be made to continue the English proceedings: there would not, after all, be a more appropriate forum available.

---

12 The English practice is authoritatively set out in *Spiliada Maritime Corpn v Cansulex Ltd* [1987] AC 460.

13 "Forum Conveniens in Europe" (1995) 53 *CLJ* 552.

14 At p. 553.

15 At p. 555.

Kennett also suggests that some civilian writers think that the court acts of its own motion in deciding whether or not to retain the case:

> 'In civil law systems the judicial process is court-directed and often closely identified with state sovereignty so that such an approach is plausible. In contrast, decisions about jurisdiction in England are largely concerned with the private interest of the parties. Only rarely do public interest factors or questions of sovereignty arise'.[16]

IS THE ENGLISH APPROACH FOLLOWED EVERYWHERE?

For good or ill, the answer is 'no'. The practice in *forum non conveniens* cases differs, and the differences seem to be growing.[17] Some of Wendy Kennett's arguments, true of the English practice, do not apply universally.

The assertion that the plaintiff can never be denied a forum by the operation of the *forum non conveniens* doctrine does assume a certain co-operation between States, a degree of comity that was notably lacking in a series of cases in the United States and France which can be referred to collectively as 'the West Caribbean saga'. In 2005 a West Caribbean Airways aircraft crashed in Venezuela while en route from Panama to Martinique (which is of course an overseas *département* of France). Almost all the deceased passengers and those claiming as successors were residents of Martinique; the airline was a Colombian corporation. Proceedings were begun in the courts of Florida, which had jurisdiction as some of the other defendants were Florida corporations. The defendants pleaded *forum non conveniens*, arguing that Martinique was an available and more appropriate forum.[18] The plea was successful and the Florida proceedings were stayed.[19]

Proceedings then took place in Martinique and the courts there held that they had, and would exercise, jurisdiction. These decisions were reversed by the French Cour de Cassation. It declared the *indisposibilité* (unavailability) of the French forum. That was a surprising, and in some respects a novel decision, but one that

---

16 At p. 556.

17 Some of the divergent factors are examined in RA Brand and SR Jablonski, Forum Non Conveniens – *History, Global Practice, and Future Under the Hague Convention on Choice of Court Agreements* (OUP 2007); but the process has continued.

18 The case was governed by the Montreal Convention 1999 and the Florida and French courts took different views as to the availability of the plea of *forum non conveniens* under that Convention.

19 *Re West Caribbean Airways SA* 619 F Supp 2d 1299 (SD Fla, 2009) and on appeal *See Pierre-Louis v Newvac* 584 F 3d 1052 (11th Cir. 2009), cert den sub nom *Bapte v. West Caribbean Airways*, 130 *SCt* 3387 (2010).

plainly challenged the decision of the Florida court. Those who had resisted the *forum non conveniens* plea in Florida could now say that Martinique was not an 'available' alternative forum.

Some of the plaintiffs therefore sought to have the original decision of the Florida court set aside. It refused to change its earlier decision, in a regrettably bad-tempered judgment: 'Where a *forum non conveniens* dismissal is concerned, American courts do not blindly accept the jurisdictional rulings or laws of foreign jurisdictions that purport to render their *forum* unavailable'.[20] The result is that proceedings could not continue either in Florida or Martinique.

That may prove to be a 'one-off', but there are not unrelated practices in the United States courts which cause some concern. Quite properly a court may grant a stay on *forum non conveniens* grounds and impose conditions to protect the interests of the parties. One such condition, which seems to have been imposed in a number of cases in which the alternative forum was a State in South America, is that the United States court will not consider resuming consideration of the case unless it is determined by the highest court in the alternative forum that that State will not exercise jurisdiction.[21] The stipulation that the case must be taken to the highest court, and a ruling obtained from that court, imposes a considerable burden on the claimant: it might be costly, or for procedural reasons impossible, to obtain such a ruling. Other conditions are designed to protect the interests of the claimant; some, like the waiver of any applicable statute of limitations in the alternative forum, are used in many countries, but the condition that the defendant comply with the discovery practices that a U.S. court would follow seems to be an example of imposing the procedural rules of one State on matters being tried elsewhere.

There are other and well-established features of United States practice that differ from that followed in England.[22] One concerns the 'public interest'. In England, Lord Bingham could say that

> 'public interest considerations not related to the private interests of the parties and the ends of justice have no bearing on the decision which the court has to make. … In applying this principle questions of judicial *amour propre* and political interest or responsibility have no part to play'.[23]

---

20 *Re West Caribbean Airways* (SD Fla, 2012; not yet reported).

21 See the recent case of *Palacios v The Coca-Cola Co* (2nd Cir, 2012) and earlier decisions such as *Aguinda v Texaco Inc* 303 F 3d 470 (2nd Cir, 2002).

22 As always it is necessary to recall that individual States have their own practices. So, for example, the Texas courts abolished *forum non conveniens* (*Dow Chemical Co v Castro-Alfaro* 786 SW 2d 674 (Tex, 1990)) and it was later reinstated by legislative action but only in respect of foreign claimants; the treatment of foreign claimants in the US generally is noted below.

23 *Lubbe v Cape plc* [2000] 1 WLR 1545 at 1561.

But in the United States 'public interest factors' play an important part in *forum non conveniens* decisions.[24] Public-interest factors include having localised controversies decided in the local forum, administrative concerns, including the congestion of court dockets, and the imposition of jury duty upon residents of a county or state with little connection to the litigation. One senses that congestion of court lists is a major factor, compounded by the attractiveness of U.S. fora. A claimant has many advantages when suing in the United States which may be unavailable elsewhere: for example, broad discovery powers and possibly exemplary damages if successful.

Another feature of United States practice is the different treatment accorded to foreign as opposed to U.S. claimants. In Koster v American Lumbermens Mutual Casualty Co[25] the U.S. Supreme Court held that 'greater deference' was to be given to a choice of the 'home forum' by a plaintiff. In general, the standard of deference for a U.S. plaintiff's choice of a home forum permits dismissal on *forum non conveniens* grounds only when the defendant 'establish[es] such oppressiveness and vexation to a defendant as to be out of all proportion to plaintiff's convenience, which may be shown to be slight or nonexistent'.[26]

This was reasserted by the Supreme Court in *Piper Aircraft Co v Reyno*:[27]

> 'In *Koster*, the Court indicated that a plaintiff's choice of forum is entitled to greater deference when the plaintiff has chosen the home forum. When the home forum has been chosen, it is reasonable to assume that this choice is convenient. When the plaintiff is foreign, however, this assumption is much less reasonable. Because the central purpose of any *forum non conveniens* inquiry is to ensure that the trial is convenient, a foreign plaintiff's choice deserves less deference.'

As a Circuit Court of Appeals observed:[28]

> 'When a foreign plaintiff chooses a US forum ... a plausible likelihood exists that the selection was made for forum-shopping reasons, such as the perception that United States courts award higher damages than are common in other countries. Even if the US district was not chosen for such forum-shopping reasons, there is nonetheless little reason to assume that it is convenient for a foreign plaintiff.'

---

24 This is established in two leading Supreme Court cases: *Gulf Oil Corp v Gilbert* 330 US 501 (1947); *Piper Aircraft Co v Reyno* 454 US 235 (1981).

25 330 US 518 (1947).

26 At p 524.

27 454 US 235 (1981).

28 *Iragorri v. United Technologies Corp* 274 F.3d 65 (2nd Cir. 2001). See, for illustrative examples: *SAS Institute Inc v World Programming Ltd* 468 Fed Appx 264 (4th Cir, 2012); *Duha v Agrium Inc* 448 F 3d 867 (6th Cir, 2006).

Notwithstanding the justifications advanced, the practice appears to an outside observer to be frankly discriminatory.

It now seems that Canadian law is moving closer to that of the United States in respect of 'public interests'.[29] The Uniform Court Jurisdiction and Proceedings Transfer Act, drafted by the Uniform Law Conference of Canada in 1994, is gradually being adopted by the various Canadian jurisdictions. This Act formulates the *forum non conveniens* doctrine in statutory language and one of the considerations that courts are directed to have in mind is 'the fair and efficient working of the Canadian legal system as a whole'.[30] Court decisions have offered various suggestions as to what this means, with no clear consensus yet emerging.

Case law development has also produced an Australian variant of the *forum non conveniens* doctrine.[31] The development was accomplished partly in England where a finding that the continuance of the case in the English courts would work an injustice because it would be 'vexatious or oppressive' to the defendant was at one time an essential requirement for the grant of a stay on *forum non conveniens* grounds; this approach was approved by the English Court of Appeal in *St Pierre v South American Stores (Gath and Chaves) Ltd.*[32] The language of vexation and oppression has no place in the modern English test. As Lord Goff stated it in *Spiliada Maritime Corpn v Cansulex Ltd*[33]

> 'The basic principle is that a stay will only be granted on the ground of *forum non conveniens* where the court is satisfied that there is some other available forum, having competent jurisdiction, which is the appropriate forum for the trial of the action, *i.e.*, in which the case may be tried more suitably for the interests of all the parties and the ends of justice.'

This requires the court to conduct a balancing exercise in judging which forum is more appropriate.

The Australian courts' earlier approach was similar to that in *St Pierre v South American Stores (Gath and Chaves) Ltd.* After the developments in English law culminating in the new statement of the test in the *Spiliada* case, the Australian High Court had to reconsider the matter. In *Voth v Manildra Flour Mills Pty Ltd*[34] the majority thought that mere reliance on vexation or oppression was

29 See S G A Pitel, "The Canadian Codification of *Forum Non Conveniens*" (2011) 7 *J Priv I L* 251.
30 Uniform Act, s 11(2)(f).
31 See A Gray, "*Forum non conveniens* in Australia: a Comparative Survey" (2009) *CLWR* 38 3 (207).
32 [1936] 1 KB 382 (CA).
33 [1987] AC 460.
34 (1990) 171 CLR 538 (considering the earlier case of *Oceanic Sun Line Special Shipping Co Inc v Fay* (1988) 165 CLR 197, where the High Court was divided).

unsatisfactory; in particular it did not enable the court to respond to inappropriate 'forum-shopping' by a plaintiff. There seemed to be a choice between following the 'balancing act' approach of *Spiliada* or adopting a test which asked whether the choice of an Australian forum was 'clearly inappropriate'. The latter test was adopted:

> 'From an abstract (and international) standpoint there is much to be said for the "more appropriate forum" test. It is designed to ensure that the cause of action is litigated in the natural or more appropriate available forum and litigation in that forum will generally reflect the balance of convenience between the parties. The justification for the selected forum declining to exercise its jurisdiction is that it defers to the exercise of jurisdiction by another available and more appropriate forum.
>
> But it is important to recognise that the actual question posed for decision by *Spiliada* is: what is the natural and appropriate forum in the sense already discussed? In the light of all the potential factors which may be relevant to the resolution of that question, it is in some cases a question by no means easy to answer, particularly at an interlocutory stage of proceedings. Indeed, it is desirable to discourage the litigation of such a difficult issue as an interlocutory question by means of what has been described as a war of affidavits. The complexity of modern transnational transactions and relationships between parties is such as to indicate that in a significant number of cases there is more than one forum with an arguable claim to be the natural forum, that is, the forum with which the action has the most real and substantial connection.
>
> The "clearly inappropriate forum" test is similar and, for that reason, is likely to yield the same result as the "more appropriate forum" test in the majority of cases. The difference between the two tests will be of critical significance only in those cases — probably rare — in which it is held that an available foreign tribunal is the natural or more appropriate forum but in which it cannot be said that the local tribunal is a clearly inappropriate one. But the question which the former test presents is slightly different in that it focuses on the advantages and disadvantages arising from a continuation of the proceedings in the selected forum rather than on the need to make a comparative judgment between the two forums. That is not to deny that considerations relating to the suitability of the alternative forum are relevant to the examination of the appropriateness or inappropriateness of the selected forum. The important point is that, in those cases in which the ascertainment of the natural forum is a complex and finely balanced question, the court may more readily conclude that it is not a clearly inappropriate forum.'[35]

[35] At p 558.

This test still involves examining the choice of that forum for elements of vexation or oppression in the sense of productive of serious and unjustified trouble and harassment.[36]

There is a further complication in the Australian situation in that some of the rules of court in the various State Supreme Courts use language which does not reflect the High Court rulings.[37]

THE HAGUE CONFERENCE'S TASK

Many would say that in the present context the issue that faced the Hague Conference in the course of the Judgments Project debates was essentially whether the civil lawyers would accept some, no doubt carefully regulated, form of *forum non conveniens*.[38] That is correct, but it begs an important question: which version of *forum non conveniens* are we talking about? Is it that found in England (which has changed over the years, and continues to undergo subtle changes[39]) or in Australia or Canada or the United States? It would be necessary not only to secure the goodwill of the civilians but also to secure agreement among the common lawyers. That might involve regulation of the conditions that could be imposed on a stay, and an obligation to resume consideration of a case were the foreign court to decline jurisdiction. The more detail is included the less likely are some States to agree; and there are echoes there of the earlier Judgments Project experience.

The Conference's resumed work on judgments is to look at the rules of indirect jurisdiction, or jurisdictional filters as they are now to be called. If that includes matters of *lis alibi pendens*, the common lawyer would expect *forum non conveniens* to be included too. At least to the common law mind, there is no real difference between the case in which an issue is already being litigated in another forum and that in which it could be so litigated.

36 *Henry v Henry* (1996) 185 CLR 571; *Régie Nationale des Usines Renault SA v Zhang* [2002] HCA 10, (2003) 210 CLR 491.

37 Eg, the Victoria Supreme Court (General Civil Procedure) Rules 2005, r 7.05(2)(b) allowing the court to set aside service on a defendant outside Australia on the ground that "Victoria is not a convenient forum for the trial of the proceeding".

38 See P D Trooboff, "On Finding Solutions to Tough Issues" in *E Pluribus Unum: Liber amicorum Georges A L Droz* (Martinus Nijhoff, 1996).

39 See the discussion of the English courts' greater willingness in recent years to hear direct criticism of the foreign court in Dicey, Morris and Collins, *The Conflict of Laws* (15th edn, 2012, Lord Collins of Mapesbury (ed)) at para 12-040ff.

WHAT HAS BEEN ACCOMPLISHED THUS FAR

The Special Commission working on the Judgments Project adopted a Preliminary Draft Convention in October 1999. Article 22 of that text, entitled 'Exceptional circumstances for declining jurisdiction'[40] survived largely unchanged in the Interim Text produced by the abortive 19th Session of the Conference in 2001 but with significant disagreement as to the circumstances in which the Article would apply.

The key provisions are as follows:

> '1. In exceptional circumstances, when the jurisdiction of the court seised is not founded on an exclusive choice of court agreement valid under Article 4, or on Article 7, 8 or 12, the court may, on application by a party, suspend its proceedings if in that case it is clearly inappropriate for that court to exercise jurisdiction and if a court of another State has jurisdiction and is clearly more appropriate to resolve the dispute. Such application must be made no later than at the time of the first defence on the merits.
>
> 2. The court shall take into account, in particular –
>
> *a)* any inconvenience to the parties in view of their habitual residence;
>
> *b)* the nature and location of the evidence, including documents and witnesses, and the procedures for obtaining such evidence;
>
> *c)* applicable limitation or prescription periods;
>
> *d)* the possibility of obtaining recognition and enforcement of any decision on the merits.
>
> 3. In deciding whether to suspend the proceedings, a court shall not discriminate on the basis of the nationality or habitual residence of the parties.'

It will be seen that paragraph 1 combines the language of the Australian test (that the chosen forum is 'clearly inappropriate') with the more common balancing approach asking if the alternative forum is 'clearly more appropriate'. However, this is not a compromise. The Explanatory Report makes it clear that:

> 'The three conditions must ... be looked at separately. Thus, the fact that another forum may be "clearly more appropriate" does not necessarily mean that the forum seised is itself "clearly inappropriate".'

[40] In addition to the official Explanatory Report, see P Nygh, "Declining Jurisdiction under the Brussels I Regulation 2001 and the Preliminary Draft Hague Judgments Convention: a Comparison" in J Fawcett (ed), *Reform and Development of Private International Law* (OUP, 2002) at p. 302; see especially pp. 327–30 on the Leuven-London Principles which influenced the Hague text.

This suggests that the proposed, cumulative, test is actually stricter than any of the existing formulations.

Paragraph 3, as an anti-discrimination provision, seems unexceptionable; no-one favours discrimination. But is it compatible with the approach of the United States courts in giving 'greater deference' to the forum choice of 'home' claimants? That approach can be encompassed in a broad understanding of 'inconvenience to the parties', but this is a matter on which clarity really is essential if there is to be genuine agreement and not merely acceptance of a form of words that could be interpreted in different ways.

And nowhere in the text is there any reference to 'public interest' factors, or in the Canadian formulation 'the fair and efficient working of the legal system as a whole'. Does this silence permit or prohibit reliance on such considerations, given that paragraph 2 opens with the words 'The Court shall take into account, *in particular*' [my italics] and so does not offer an exclusive list of relevant factors?

Although Article 22 has been regarded as a significant achievement, there is actually a deal of work still to be done if genuine agreement is to be reached.

A CAUTIOUS CONCLUSION

The unsurprising lesson of the Judgments Project is that there are some areas in which the aim of the Hague Conference, the progressive unification of the rules of private international law, cannot be achieved. Great success has attended the work of the Conference in addressing relatively 'new' areas of law, such as international child abduction. But it is much harder to agree, and even harder to secure the acceptance back home, of changes in entrenched practices and understandings. International negotiation in private international law, like politics, is the 'art of the possible', and that art has its limits.

THE 1996 HAGUE CONVENTION AND THE EUROPEAN UNION: CONNECTION AND DISCONNECTION

Peter McEleavy
Professor of International Family Law, University of Dundee
Barrister, 1 Garden Court, Family Law Chambers, London

Contributing to this *Liber Amicorum* in honour of Hans van Loon, whom I have known, worked with and admired since 1996, is a great pleasure. Our first encounters were when I served as a recording secretary at the Eighteenth Session of the Hague Conference in 1996 and thereafter through my work on the Hague Conference's International Child Abduction Database, INCADAT. Over the course of these seventeen years, Hans van Loon has navigated the Hague Conference through a period of unprecedented change. The world of private international law, traditionally somewhat rarefied, with legislative initiatives agreed and implemented over the course of many, often too many, years has evolved into a much more politicised domain, one very much subject to the challenges and burdensome expectations which characterise 21st-century life.

A central element in this transformation has been the acquisition by the European Community, now the European Union, of competence to legislate in matters of private international law. The latter development has presented enormous challenges and opportunities for the Hague Conference in equal measure, and no instrument has been as exposed to this maelstrom as that adopted at the Eighteenth Session, the Hague Convention of 19 October 1996 on Jurisdiction, Applicable Law, Recognition, Enforcement and Co-Operation in Respect of Parental Responsibility and Measures for the Protection of Children.

CONNECTION

Throughout its existence, and even during the negotiation stage, the Hague Convention on the Protection of Children has been inextricably linked to the

Europeanization of private international law. Indeed, as the Lagarde Explanatory Report notes, at paragraph 172, a disconnection clause was included at Article 52(2) specifically to deal with the treaty which the then European Union States were in the process of negotiating. When concluded in 1998 the latter instrument, known as the Brussels II Convention,[1] would scarcely have been regarded as a rival to the all encompassing Hague Convention, given that its scope in matters of parental responsibility extended only to a small subset of the potential civil proceedings which might arise, namely those concerning children of both spouses where the children were habitually resident in a Member State and which arose on the occasion of the matrimonial proceedings with which the Convention was primarily concerned. That situation changed with the Treaty of Amsterdam and the European Community's acquisition of competence in private international law, for after the transformation of Brussels II into a Council Regulation,[2] and even before it became directly applicable, work began to extend its material scope in respect of parental responsibility matters.

The possibility of 1996 Hague Convention, which all the then EC Member States had been involved in negotiating, being promoted as a common European instrument, had of course evaporated by the start of the 21st century. In the new world of Community private international law the Commission was determined to further its own agenda and acquire new fields of competence. And so during the negotiation of what ultimately became the Brussels IIa Regulation,[3] the 1996 Hague Convention was merely a rival text, albeit one which the Commission was content to plunder to build a more advanced and rigorous Community regime for the free movement of judgments and to deal with intra-EU cases of child abduction.

It was only once the future of the revised Brussels II Regulation was secure, and as part of the fraught compromise on the issue of child abduction,[4] that formal European engagement with the Convention was sanctioned, with a Council Decision issued authorizing Member States to sign the Convention in the interests of the Community.[5] This was necessary for in adopting the original

1 Convention drawn up on the basis of Article K.3 of the Treaty on European Union, on Jurisdiction, Recognition and Enforcement of Judgments in Matrimonial Matters, OJ 1998 C221, 1–26.

2 *Council Regulation (EC) No 1347/2000 of 29 May 2000 on Jurisdiction and the Recognition and Enforcement of Judgments in Matrimonial Matters and in Matters of Parental Responsibility for Children of both Spouses* OJ 2000 L160, 19–29.

3 Council Regulation (EC) 2201/2003 of 27 November 2003 Concerning Jurisdiction and the Recognition and Enforcement of Judgments in Matrimonial Matters and the Matters of Parental Responsibility, Repealing Regulation (EC) no. 1347/2000, OJ 2003 L 338/1.

4 P McEleavy 'The New Child Abduction Regime In The European Union: Symbiotic Relationship or Forced Partnership? [2005] *J Priv Int L* 5.

5 OJ 2003 L048/1–2. The then Member States signed the Convention on 1 April 2003, except for the Netherlands, which had already signed on 1 September 1997.

Brussels II Regulation the Community had acquired external competence over certain aspects of the 1996 Convention and thereby deprived Member States of the authority to ratify or accede to the instrument independently.[6]

The achievement of the Council Decision, driven by those EC Member States having a more internationalist perspective, whereby the Hague Convention could follow in the slipstream of the Brussels IIa Regulation, might be regarded as modest. Certainly it cannot mask the central political and inter-institutional message of the revision of Brussels II, that the Community wanted its own texts to dominate in Europe and had little concern for the global dimension of child protection, but, it opened the door to the EC States becoming party en masse to the 1996 instrument and thereby could create the momentum so crucial to the success of a global convention.

That process was not, however, a simple one, for progress towards all Member States becoming party to the Hague Convention was initially blocked by Spain which fell into dispute with the United Kingdom over the operation of mixed competence conventions[7] with regard to Gibraltar. The impasse was only broken in late 2007 with the creation of a post-box system for communications between the Spanish and Gibraltarian authorities, although not for communications between the authorities of other States and Gibraltar. Thereafter, steps were immediately taken to authorise ratification. In this, Council Decision of 5 June 2008[8] provided that Member States not already party, should ratify, or accede to, the Hague Convention in the interest of the European Community. Under Article 3(1) of the Decision Member States were to take the necessary steps to deposit simultaneously their instruments of ratification or accession with the Ministry of Foreign Affairs of the Kingdom of the Netherlands, if possible before 5 June 2010. This date was not uniformly respected, but by 1 February 2013 all but two of the twenty-seven European Union States (Belgium and Italy) had become parties to the 1996 Hague Convention, thereby ensuring that the instrument now has a firm European foundation, with thirty-nine States Parties in total.

DISCONNECTION

The history and early years of the 1996 Hague Convention may have been closely intertwined with the Brussels IIa Regulation, but of course if the global instrument is to flourish in what is currently its core constituency, the two must

6 Both the Netherlands and Ireland were restrained from completing their ratification process.

7 The other being the Unidroit Convention on International Interests in Mobile Equipment, 2001, UNTS I-41143.

8 OJ 2008 L 151/36–38.

be disconnected. It is a weakness of the European Regime, that the disconnection is not as clear or as precise as it could be.

In terms of basic structure, both instruments contain rules on jurisdiction, the recognition and enforcement of judgments and co-operation. There are, though no choice of law provisions in Brussels IIa. Chapter V of Brussels IIa deals with relations with other instruments. Two provisions are of particular relevance, the specific disconnection clause concerned with the 1996 Convention in Article 61, and Article 62. In the Hague Convention the relevant provision is Article 52. Applying these provisions and disentangling the two instruments is not always straightforward or indeed satisfactory.

The task of users is though facilitated as a result of an effective commonality as regards the material scope of the instruments. Insofar as the core issue of measures for the protection of the person or property of the child is concerned, it may be noted that there is no reference in the Hague Convention to "civil matters", such as appears in Article 1 of the Brussels IIa Regulation. However, the impact of that requirement has been minimised in recent European Court case law confirming that Brussels IIa covers not only situations where children are placed in care,[9] but placements which involve the deprivation of a child's liberty.[10] In these decisions Advocate-General Kokott has been keen to ensure a parallelism between the Convention and Brussels IIa.[11] In Case C-435/06 *C* she stated:

> *"in as regards relations between the Member States, within its scope of application Regulation 2201/2003 takes precedence over international conventions (see Articles 60 and 61 of the Regulation). However, international instruments continue to apply between Member States and third countries. For that reason, the provisions of the Regulation and corresponding provisions in other conventions ought, so far as possible, to be interpreted in the same way, in order to avoid different results according to whether a case concerns another Member State or a third country."*

The disconnection of the instruments as between each of the four aspects of private international law covered is now considered in turn.[12]

9 Case C-435/06 *C* [2007] E.C.R. I–10141; Case C-523/07 *Proceedings Brought by A* [2009] E.C.R. I–2805.

10 Case C-92/12 PPU *Health Service Executive v SC and AC.*

11 Opinion, para. 50.

12 See generally *1996 Hague Convention Practice Guide*, United Kingdom Ministry of Justice, 2013, of which the present author is principal author, and from which the examples cited below come.

JURISDICTION

The disconnection between the Convention and Brussels IIa, in matters of jurisdiction is for certain categories of case somewhat ambiguous. Reference must first be made to Article 52(1) of the Convention which provides that "*This Convention does not affect any international instrument to which Contracting States are Parties and which contains provisions on matters governed by the Convention, unless a contrary declaration is made by the States Parties to such instrument.*" This would leave the jurisdiction regime of Brussels IIa untouched as between Member States. However, Article 61(a) of Brussels IIa specifies that, as between the two instruments, Brussels IIa shall apply: "*where the child concerned has his or her habitual residence on the territory of a Member State*". In such circumstances, which will be most cases, it is the jurisdiction rules of Brussels IIa which have to be applied. Equally, it is clear that where a child is habitually resident in a non-Regulation, Contracting State the jurisdictional framework of the Convention will be applied.

However, where a child is neither habitually resident in a Brussels IIa State nor a Convention State there are further complexities and some uncertainty. Where a child has no habitual residence anywhere, but is present in the jurisdiction, both Brussels IIa and the Convention could apply. It may be that jurisdiction should be taken under both, in the alternative. Where a child is present in the jurisdiction but habitually resident in a third State the geographical scope of the Convention is not engaged. Brussels IIa could apply in such situations under the prorogation mechanism of Article 12, but as to whether Article 13 (presence) could be applicable depends on the interpretation and scope of that provision (i.e. whether it implies a child have no habitual residence anywhere, or simply no habitual residence in an EU Member State). Where neither Brussels IIa nor the Convention is applicable, the door can be opened to the application of residual rules on jurisdiction.

Child Abduction

Reference must be made at this juncture to the issue of international child abduction. The role of the 1980 Hague Convention in this matter is well known, in that it provides a mechanism for the summary return of a child wrongfully removed to, or retained in, another 1980 Contracting State. The 1996 Convention complements, but does not in any way replace, the operation of the 1980 Convention. Of particular note is Article 7 of the 1996 Convention, which provides an additional jurisdictional rule to bolster the effectiveness of the 1980 Convention where the abduction takes place between Contracting States to the 1996 Convention. The rule operates to ensure that the abductor does not gain an advantage by abducting the child to another Contracting State and then claiming that the child has gained a new habitual residence, so that it is the courts of the country to which the abduction has been made which now have jurisdiction. The rule provides that jurisdiction remains with the state of the child's original habitual residence until either the removal/retention has been acquiesced in by those with rights of custody under the terms of the 1980 Convention, or the child has lived in the new state for at least a year after the person, institution or other body having rights of custody has or should have had knowledge of the whereabouts of the child, no request for return under the 1980 Convention is outstanding, and the child is settled in his or her new environment.

Article 7 has certain similarities to Article 10 of Brussels IIa, which governs the attribution of jurisdiction where an abduction takes place as between Regulation States. However, Article 7 is less strict in preserving the jurisdiction of the original State of habitual residence. This can be seen from the following explanation:

> "*if return proceedings conclude without an order to send the child back, the child has been in the new State for more than 12 months since the left behind parent has had or should have had knowledge of his or her whereabouts, and the child has become habitually resident and settled there, then the courts of that place will have jurisdiction. Under Brussels IIa a transfer can only occur in such situations where a left behind parent has acquiesced in the abduction or has lost or given up in proceedings in the original State of habitual residence; the passage of time combined with a non-return order in 1980 Convention proceedings will not bring about a transfer.*"[13]

The attribution of jurisdiction following a wrongful removal or retention can therefore be presented in the following terms:

1 Where a child habitually resident in a European Union Regulation State is wrongfully removed to or retained in a Convention State, which is not a Regulation State, then the application of Article 7 by such a State should preserve the jurisdiction of the courts of the original EU Regulation State in which the child was habitually resident, in accordance with its terms.
2 Where a child habitually resident in European Union Regulation State is wrongfully removed to or retained in a different Regulation State, then Article 10 Brussels IIa will preserve the jurisdiction of the courts of the original EU Regulation State in which the child was habitually resident, in accordance with its terms.

[13] P. McEleavy (2010) *International & Comparative Law Quarterly*, pp. 505–519, at 510.

3 Where a child habitually resident in a European Union Regulation State is wrongfully removed to or retained in a Convention State, which is not a Regulation State, the control of jurisdiction as between *EU Regulation* States is unclear.

The lack of clarity expressed in Point 3 can be explained as follows. First, the child abduction rules in Brussels IIa are focused on wrongful removals and retentions as between Regulation States. This can also be seen in the structure of Article 10, Brussels IIa which seeks to preserve the jurisdiction of the original Regulation State of habitual residence where the child is abducted to another Regulation State.

What is not clear is how Regulation States should treat the jurisdiction of the original Regulation State of habitual residence where the child is abducted to a Convention State (e.g. a child habitually resident in Ireland is abducted to Australia; sometime thereafter the child relocates to England; would the High Court in London have jurisdiction in such circumstances; would the High Court have to defer to the jurisdiction of the Irish Courts; which regime regulates jurisdiction as between the UK and Ireland in such circumstances?).

There is no express guidance as to whether Article 10, Brussels IIa could or should apply as between Regulation States in a situation where a child is wrongfully removed to or retained in a Convention State.

If it were accepted that Article 10, Brussels IIa does not apply in such circumstances, the alternative would be for Article 7, 1996 Hague Convention to apply as between Regulation States. But this option too is not free from doubt. It will be recalled that Brussels IIa must be applied where a child is habitually resident in a Regulation State, however, it is unclear whether the terms of Article 61(a), Brussels IIa mean that Article 7 of the Convention cannot be relied upon in other Regulation States where a child habitually resident in a Regulation State is wrongfully removed to or retained in a Convention State. If such cases are regarded as falling outside the scope of Brussels IIa (since Article 10 of Brussels IIa does not address the position if the abduction is from a Regulation State to a non-Regulation State), Article 7 of the Convention could apply, and so preserve, even if not indefinitely, the jurisdiction of the original, Regulation State in which the child was habitually resident.

The following example illustrates how these issues could arise in practice:

Following the entry into force of the 1996 Hague Convention, child A, habitually resident in England, is unilaterally removed by his Danish father to Copenhagen (Denmark is not subject to Brussels IIa). The British mother issues return proceedings under the 1980 Hague Convention in Denmark. The Danish court finds the removal to be wrongful but declines to make a return order on the basis of the child's objections. This ruling is upheld on appeal.

Jurisdiction in Denmark as regards the child will be controlled by Article 7, 1996 Hague Convention.

3 months after the appeal ruling is handed down, and 14 months after the removal, the father wishes to bring custody proceedings in Copenhagen. It is entirely feasible that the elements of Article 7, to allow substantive jurisdiction over the child to be taken by Denmark, could be satisfied.

The Danish court considers that it has jurisdiction and it makes a residence order in favour of the father. Several months later the father moves to Germany to take up a new job and the child moves with him. The relocation of the child is legal under Danish law. Father and child quickly become settled in Germany.

The previous discussion on the application of Article 10, Brussels IIa and Article 7, 1996 Hague Convention is relevant to determining how jurisdiction should be attributed as between the United Kingdom and Germany in circumstances such as these.

If Brussels IIa States should apply Article 7 between each other where a child is abducted to a non-Regulation, Convention State, then the transfer of jurisdiction from the UK to Denmark should be respected by Brussels IIa States. This would in turn mean that the legality of the relocation of the child from Denmark to Germany should be accepted, allowing the child to become habitually resident in Germany and the German courts to acquire jurisdiction under Article 8, Brussels IIa. Jurisdiction would not be retained by the English courts.

However, if Art 10, Brussels IIa were deemed to be activated once the child arrived in a Brussels IIa State (or always to have been applicable as between Brussels IIa States), that could lead to jurisdiction being retained by the English courts, vis-à-vis other Brussels IIa States.

APPLICABLE LAW

Brussels IIa, as noted, does not contain rules on applicable law. It was always intended that the Convention would provide the applicable law rules to be applied by Regulation States, and the applicable law rules of the Convention will apply between Regulation States who are Contracting States to the Convention, as well as in their relations with non-Regulation Contracting States.[14] Nevertheless there is still a significant issue of compatibility as between the two instruments which was overlooked in the drafting of the Brussels IIa Regulation.

14 See Article 62 of Brussels IIa. That this was the intention of the European legislator is demonstrated, for example, by the Commission of the European Union's *Practice Guide for the Application of the New Brussels II Regulation*, Chapter XI.

This relates to the general choice of law rule in Article 15. The opening clause of Article 15(1) is explicit in providing that the provision operates where the authorities of Contracting States are "*exercising their jurisdiction under the provisions of Chapter II* [of the Convention]". As has been previously explained, jurisdiction will only actually be exercised under Chapter II in very limited situations, because of the primacy of Brussels IIa over the Convention. In England and Wales, to avoid Article 15 being deprived of meaningful effect, the accompanying domestic Regulations have addressed this issue through the inclusion of a clause to the effect that: "*The reference to Chapter II of the Convention in Article 15(1) of the Convention is to be read as including a reference to Chapter II of the Council Regulation.*"[15]

RECOGNITION AND ENFORCEMENT

Insofar as recognition and enforcement is concerned there is certainty. Article 61(b) provides clarity in specifying that Brussels IIa applies to the recognition and enforcement of: "*a judgment given in a court of a Member State on the territory of another Member State, even if the child concerned has his or her habitual residence on the territory of a third State which is a contracting Party to the said Convention.*" Therefore it is clear that as between Regulation States, recognition and enforcement of a judgment given in one Regulation State in another Regulation State will always be governed by Brussels IIa.

CO-OPERATION

Finally, the Convention contains a variety of rules on co-operation. Many of these are discretionary, but the detailed and specific nature of the rules means that they have much greater potential than the more general provisions contained in the Regulation. That being so it must be asked whether the Convention rules could be applied as between Regulation States. A clear answer cannot be given. If a child is habitually resident on the territory of a Regulation State Article 61(a) of Brussels IIa provides that that Regulation should apply, and it has of course its own co-operation provisions and the Member States could, in negotiating Brussels IIa, have chosen to include identical provisions to those in the Hague Convention. However, Article 62 states that "*agreements and conventions referred to in Articles 59(1), 60 and 61 shall continue to have effect in relation to matters not governed by this Regulation.*" The interpretation of "matters not governed by

[15] SI 2010/1898 reg.7.

this Regulation" is key, does this refer to general areas, such as choice of law, or, can it be interpreted at a micro level to refer to specific provisions which feature within an instrument like the Convention, but not in the corresponding Chapter of Brussels IIa? If the latter view were to be accepted then those provisions within the Convention's co-operation chapter, which do not appear in Brussels IIa, could be applied as between Regulation States.

CONCLUSION

For all their shared history and the significant overlap in material scope, it might have been anticipated that the disconnection between the 1996 Hague Convention and the Brussels IIa Regulation would have been watertight. The uncertainties which exist may of course be addressed during the forthcoming revision of the latter instrument but the fact they exist at all says much about the manner in which the European Community/Union engaged with global family law issues and the Hague Conference in the early years of its private international law competence. It must be hoped that for the review process lessons have been learnt from recent shared experiences on maintenance obligations, which were characterised more by collaboration than competition. If coordinated and viable solutions are to be found to contemporary international family law problems, then as between all law and policy makers there must be connection, not disconnection.

THE LUGANO CONVENTION AND THE INTERNATIONAL COURT OF JUSTICE

Justice Gustaf MÖLLER
Former Member of the Supreme Court of Finland
Of Counsel, Krogerus Attorneys Ltd.

1. THE CASE BEFORE THE ICJ

The case "Jurisdiction and Enforcement of Judgments in Civil and Commercial Matters (*Belgium v. Switzerland*)" relates to the Lugano Convention of 16 September 1988 on jurisdiction and the enforcement of judgments in civil and commercial matters (hereinafter the "Lugano Convention"). The case was filed in the Registry of the International Court of Justice (hereinafter the "ICJ") on 21 December 2009. By the application, Belgium instituted proceedings against Switzerland in respect of a dispute concerning

> "the interpretation and application of the Lugano Convention of 16 September 1988 on jurisdiction and the enforcement of judgments in civil and commercial matters ..., as well as the application of the rules of general international law governing the exercise of State authority, in particular in judicial matters ...[, and relating] to the decision by Swiss courts not to recognize a judgment of the Belgian courts and not to stay proceedings which were later initiated in Switzerland on the subject of the same dispute"

In its application Belgium stated the dispute "has arisen out of pursuit of parallel judicial proceedings in Belgium and Switzerland" regarding the civil and commercial dispute between "the main shareholders in Sabena, the former Belgian national airline now in bankruptcy". The Swiss shareholders concerned were the SAirGroup (formerly Swissair) and its subsidiary SAirLines; the Belgian shareholders were the Belgian State and three Belgian companies in which it directly or indirectly holds all of the shares.

Further, Belgium submitted that "[i]n connection with the Swiss companies' acquisition of equity in Sabena in 1995 and with their partnership with the Belgian shareholders, contracts were entered into, between 1995 and 2001, for among other things the financing and joint management of Sabena" and that this set of contracts "provided for the exclusive jurisdiction of the Brussels courts in the event of dispute and for the application of Belgian law".

According to the application, the Belgian shareholders considered that the Swiss shareholders had breached their contractual commitments and non-contractual duties thereby causing injury to the Belgian shareholders. Therefore, the Belgian shareholders had on 3 July 2001 sued the Swiss shareholders in the Commercial Court of Brussels, seeking damages to compensate for, among other things, the amount lost on investments made on the basis of representations by the Swiss shareholders and for the expenses incurred by the Belgian shareholders as a result of the defaults by the Swiss shareholders.

On 20 November 2003, the Commercial Court of Brussels found that it had jurisdiction over the contractual and non-contractual claims pursuant to Articles 17 and 5(3) of the Lugano Convention; these provide, respectively, in matters relating to a contract for the exclusive jurisdiction of the courts chosen by the parties in their contract, and in matters of non-contractual liability for the jurisdiction of the courts for the place where the harmful event occurred. On the merits, the Court, applying Belgian law, found various instances of misconduct on the part of the Swiss shareholders but rejected the Belgian shareholders' claims for damages. Both the Belgian and Swiss shareholders appealed against this decision to the Court of Appeal of Brussels, which, by partial judgment of 19 May 2005, upheld the Belgian courts' jurisdiction over the dispute on the basis of the Lugano Convention. The proceedings on the merits remained pending before that Court.

Belgium stated that in various proceedings concerning the application for a debt-restructuring moratorium (*sursis concordataire*) submitted by the Swiss companies to the Zurich courts, the Belgian shareholders had sought to declare their claims against the Swiss companies. It asserted, however, that the Swiss courts, including in particular the Federal Supreme Court, had refused to recognise the future Belgian decisions on the civil liability of the Swiss shareholders, or to stay their proceedings pending the outcome of the Belgian proceedings. Belgium contended that these refusals violated various provisions of the Lugano Convention and the "rules of general international law governing the exercise by States of their authority, in particular in judicial matters".

To found the jurisdiction of the ICJ, Belgium invoked in its application solely the unilateral declarations recognising the compulsory jurisdiction of the ICJ made by the Parties pursuant to Article 36, paragraph 2, of the Statute of the ICJ on 17 June 1958 (Belgium) and 28 July 1948 (Switzerland). Moreover, Belgium noted that there was no dispute resolution clause in the Lugano Convention placing conditions on recourse to the ICJ and that the Court of Justice of the European Communities (hereinafter the "ECJ") was without jurisdiction in the area.

At the end of its application, Belgium requested the ICJ to adjudge and declare, *inter alia*, that Switzerland had by virtue of the decision of its courts to hold that the future judgment in Belgium on the contractual and non-contractual liability of SAirGroup and SAirLines to the Belgian State and to the Belgian companies will not be recognised in Switzerland in the SAirGroup and SAirLines debt-scheduling proceedings, is breaching the Lugano Convention, in particular Articles 1, second paragraph, provision (2); 16(5); 26, first paragraph; and 28, thereof; and that Switzerland, by virtue of the refusal by its judicial authorities to stay the proceedings in the dispute between, on the one hand, the Belgian State and the Belgian companies and, on the other, the liquidation estates of SAirGroup and SAirLines, companies in debt-restructuring liquidation, pending the conclusion of the proceedings currently taking place in the Belgian courts concerning the contractual liability of SAirGroup and SAirLines to the Belgian State and the Belgian companies, is violating the Lugano Convention, in particular Articles 1, second paragraph, provision (2); 17; 21; and 22, thereof; as well as Article 1 of Protocol No. 2 on the uniform interpretation of the Lugano Convention (hereinafter "Protocol No. 2").

On 18 February 2011, Switzerland submitted preliminary objections to the jurisdiction of the ICJ and the admissibility of the application. Thereafter, further to a request to such effect from Belgium dated 21 March 2011 and received in the Registry of the ICJ on the same day, the ICJ, by order dated 5 April 2011, removed the case from the list before Switzerland had submitted any Counter Memorial on the Merits.[1]

2. QUESTIONS RAISED BY THE CASE

Despite the fact that the case was removed from the list, the case raises several interesting questions. The Lugano Convention of 1988, which was concluded between the Member States of the European Communities and the European Free Trade Association (hereinafter "EFTA") Member States, is formally a multilateral convention under international law. However, the Lugano

1 The arguments submitted in Belgium's application in support of the contention that Switzerland had breached the Lugano Convention have been thoroughly analysed and discussed in an expert opinion that Professor Christian Kohler had prepared in August 2010 at the request of Switzerland. This expert opinion has been published in *RSDIE (Revue Suisse de droit international et européen)*, 22e année (2012) pp. 441–485.

Convention corresponds very closely to the Brussels Convention of 27 September 1968 on jurisdiction and the enforcement of judgments in civil and commercial matters (hereinafter the "Brussels Convention"), which was concluded between the six original Community Member States and adopted consequent upon the accession of new Member States to the Community. The Brussels Convention is a Community instrument subject to the Protocol of 3 June 2001, which entrusted the ECJ with the power to interpret the Convention. In fact, Belgium was a Contracting Party to the Lugano Convention of 1988. However, this Convention had meanwhile been replaced by the new Lugano Convention of 2007, which was not concluded by the Member States of the European Community, but by the Community which then had exclusive competence in the matter. Having regard to these particularities, both the question of whether Belgium as a matter of European Union (EU) laws is entitled to institute proceedings concerning the Lugano Convention of 1988 before the ICJ and the question whether the ICJ had jurisdiction were open to doubt. The first mentioned issue was dealt with in an expert opinion submitted by Switzerland.[2]

In my capacity as co-author (together with Mr P. Jenard) of the Report on the Lugano Convention 1988,[3] I was asked by Professor Monique Jametti Greiner of the Swiss Federal Office of Justice to prepare an expert report for the ICJ on the issue whether the ICJ had jurisdiction as to the interpretation of the Lugano Convention. My terms of reference were received from her. This article is based on that opinion, to which Switzerland referred to in the proceedings,[4] and reflects the views expressed therein.

3. ABSENCE OF JUDICIAL MECHANISM IN THE LUGANO CONVENTION

One of the reasons why the EFTA Member States could not, instead of negotiating a new convention, accede to the Brussels Convention was that the Brussels Convention was subject to the Protocol of 3 June 1971 to the Brussels Convention, which entrusted the ECJ with the power to interpret the Convention. The ECJ could not be assigned jurisdiction to interpret the Lugano Convention, which is not a source of community law. Furthermore, the EFTA Member States could not have accepted a solution according to which an institution of the Communities

2 The Expert Opinion on EU law was provided by Sir Francis Jacobs, former Advocate General at the European Court of Justice. See Exceptions préliminaires, no. 202.

3 Report by Mr. P. Jenard and Mr. G. Möller on the Convention on jurisdiction and the enforcement of judgments in civil and commercial matters done at Lugano on 16 September 1988 (90/C189/07) (hereinafter referred to as the "Report").

4 Exceptions préliminaires no. 167.

would, as court of last resort, rule on the Lugano Convention. Ensuring an interpretation as uniform as possible of the Lugano Convention, while taking account of the powers of the ECJ with regard to the interpretation of the Brussels Convention, many of the provisions of which were reproduced in the Lugano Convention, had therefore to be achieved by other means. The solution adopted is based on the principle of information and consultation and not judicial hierarchy.

Already before the working party of governmental experts from the Member States of the European Communities and experts appointed by the EFTA Member States for the negotiations leading to the Lugano Convention was set up, it was suggested in the Swiss initiative to what at that time was called the "Parallel Convention" (to the Brussels Convention): that judges from the ECJ and the highest courts of the various EC and EFTA Member States, parties to the convention, should meet regularly to discuss possible conflicts on the interpretation of the Lugano Convention and possibly issue recommendations relating to the interpretation of the Convention.[5]

The working party agreed that it was necessary that representatives appointed by each signatory or acceding State meet to exchange views on the functioning of the Lugano Convention. To this end, Article 3 of Protocol No. 2 provides that a Standing Committee composed by representatives appointed by each signatory or acceding State shall be set up. This Standing Committee was not intended to be a bureaucratic body but rather a forum where national experts could exchange their views on the functioning of the Convention and, in particular, on the case law as it develops in the various Contracting States, with the aim of fostering in that manner, as far as possible, uniformity in the interpretation of the Convention.

However, divergent views were expressed as to whether the Standing Committee should be composed of judges or civil servants. This was due to the fact that in some states the interpretation of an international convention was eventually a matter for the Government and not for the courts. Therefore, it was decided that it was for each State to appoint its representative on the Committee.[6]

Regarding the role of the ICJ, it was never suggested that the ICJ should have any competence at all regarding the Lugano Convention, let alone a similar jurisdiction to rule on the interpretation of the Lugano Convention as the ECJ had to rule on the interpretation of the Brussels Convention.

As noted in the Report, the ECJ could not be assigned jurisdiction to interpret the Lugano Convention, which is not a source of Community law and more importantly even:

---

5 See Lugano Convention on Jurisdiction and the Enforcement of Judgments in Civil and Commercial Matters done at Lugano on 16 September 1988 II "travaux préparatoires". Publications de l'Institut suisse de droit comparé (Zürich 1991), p. 38.

6 The Report at para. 118.

> "Nor was it conceivable to assign such jurisdiction to *any other international court* [italics added] or to create any new court since, *inter alia*, the Court of Justice of the European Communities already had jurisdiction under the 1971 Protocol to rule on the interpretation of the Brussels Convention and conflicts of jurisdiction between international courts had at all events to be avoided."[7]

To give the ICJ the power to interpret the Lugano Convention would not have been consistent with the aims of the Convention. The term "*any other international court*" also includes the ICJ. At the diplomatic conference, which adopted the Lugano Convention, no delegation raised the question whether the ICJ may under public international law in some circumstances have jurisdiction to interpret the Lugano Convention. Neither was this question raised in the working party. That solution seemed clearly undesirable and no Contracting Party expressed the need of a formal exclusion of the ICJ's jurisdiction in the language of the Lugano Convention.

The creation of a new court was never seriously considered either and the above quoted sentence in the Report was entirely uncontroversial. The fundamental concern was that "conflicts of jurisdiction between international courts had at all events to be avoided". Therefore, there was consensus that a situation, where the ECJ would have jurisdiction to rule on the interpretation of the Brussels Convention and another international court would have such jurisdiction to rule on the interpretation of the Lugano Convention, would be untenable since the provisions of the two Conventions are to a large extent even literally identical.

No delegation voiced the need to compensate for the lack of an internationally binding judicial mechanism since Protocol No. 2 was supposed to fill this gap. There was a common understanding that neither the ICJ nor any other international court would on the basis of the Lugano Convention have jurisdiction to rule on the interpretation of the Lugano Convention in the same or similar way as the ECJ has jurisdiction to rule on the interpretation of the Brussels Convention. Having regard to the fact that the scope of application *ratione materiae* (Title I), the provisions on jurisdiction (Title II), on recognition and enforcement (Title III), on authentic instruments and court settlements (Title IV), and the general provisions (Title V) are with a few exceptions even literally identical, it would hardly be appropriate if *one* international court, i.e. the ECJ, would have jurisdiction to rule on the interpretation of the Brussels Convention and *another* international court, i.e. the ICJ would have a similar jurisdiction to rule on the interpretation of the Lugano Convention.

Consistent with the decision not to provide for internationally binding adjudication under the Lugano Convention, the competence to interpret the

[7] The Report at para. 110.

Lugano Convention was specifically left with the national jurisdictions and an interpretation as uniform as possible was intended to be ensured by means of consultations between experts from the Contracting States and not by means of a solution based on judicial hierarchy. By so excluding all international jurisdictions, the Contracting States specifically renounced the concept of a unified interpretation of the Lugano Convention by the means of an international court. By leaving the ultimate authority to adjudicate disputes on the interpretation and application of the Lugano Convention with their domestic courts, the Contracting States were fully conscious of and took into account the possibility of diverging interpretations in national case law. Therefore, in the context of Protocol No. 2, the Report states:

> "The intention was to arrive at as uniform as possible an interpretation where the provisions in question were identical in the two Conventions."[8]

4. CONCLUSIONS

The genesis of the Lugano Convention in its European context demonstrates that the final adjudication of Lugano Convention issues was never intended to be a matter for an international court. A situation, where the ECJ would have had jurisdiction to rule on the interpretation of the Brussels Convention and another international court would have had such jurisdiction to rule on the interpretation of the Lugano Convention, would have been untenable since the provisions of the two Conventions are to a large extent literally identical. The competence to interpret the Lugano Convention was specifically left with the national jurisdictions. Having renounced the concept of a unified interpretation of the Lugano Convention by the means of a solution based on judicial hierarchy, the Contracting States consciously took into account the possibility of diverging interpretations in national case law. An interpretation as uniform as possible was to be ensured by means of consultations (i.e. a mechanism of exchange of information and a Standing Committee).

8 The Report at para. 112.

SUBSTANCE AND PROCEDURE: ASPECTS OF DAMAGES IN TORT IN THE CONFLICT OF LAWS

Robin MORSE
Professor of Law, King's College London

INTRODUCTION

The dichotomy between substance and procedure in the conflict of laws has always been murky. Each category may be classified in different ways in different countries and, perhaps, also, in the same country. This problem is illustrated, vividly, in the context of torts in the conflict of laws and, more specifically, in the context of damages in tort. Back in 1896, Dicey wrote that English lawyers gave "[...] the widest possible extension to the meaning of the term 'procedure'".[1] In the context of assessment of damages in England it was held in 2007 that such questions were "procedural" and governed, thus, by the law of the forum.[2] In contrast, the High Court of Australia held in relation to a tort committed within Australia, that "procedure" should be confined to rules "governing or regulating the mode or conduct of court proceedings".[3] It is sometimes said more generally that classifying a foreign rule as procedural relieves the forum of having to apply a rule of foreign law with which it has no familiarity,[4] or which it would be unduly inconvenient to apply' but this is often a counsel of despair.[5]

1 Dicey, *Conflict of Laws* (1896), p. 712.
2 *Harding v Wealands* [2006] UKHL 32, [2007] 2 A.C. 1.
3 *John Pfeiffer Pty Ltd v Rogerson* (2002) 203 C.L.R. 503, 543–544. *Cf. Régie Nationale des Usines Renault SA v Zhang* (2002) 210 C.L.R. 491, 520, leaving open the question of whether this statement applied to foreign torts as opposed to torts committed within Australia.
4 Dicey, Morris and Collins, *The Conflict of Laws* (15th ed, 2012), p.204.
5 *Cf. Phrantzes v Argenti* [1960] 2 Q.B.19.

INTERNATIONAL INSTRUMENTS

International instruments, at least those concerning the law applicable to obligations, have never sought, generally, to determine the distinction between substance and procedure – a task which – inevitably, would be impossible to accomplish in a practical way. This is usually because such instruments tend to state the scope of the law applicable to an obligation, though not always with clarity. The Hague Conventions on the Law Applicable to Traffic Accidents and Product Liability contain no general provision on the distinction but there are specific provisions which bear upon it. The "Rome" contributions are somewhat more varied. The Rome Convention on the Law Applicable to Contractual Obligations, the Rome I Regulation and the Rome II Regulation all state that the instruments do not apply to "evidence and procedure" subject to a limited exception in regard to the burden of proof,[6] but there are also in these instruments specific rules on the scope of the applicable law which impact on this distinction in the national law of some countries. This produces a degree of ambiguity, some of which will be explored in what follows, mainly in the context of damages in tort.

AMBIGUITY IN THE HAGUE CONVENTIONS

Article 8 of the Hague Convention on the Law Applicable to Traffic Accidents provides that the applicable law shall determine "in particular" "the existence and kinds of injury or damage which may have to be compensated (Article 8(3)) and "the kinds and extent of damages" (Article 8(4)). In contrast, Article 8 of the Hague Convention on the Law Applicable to Products Liability provides that the applicable law shall determine "in particular" "the kinds of damage for which compensation may be due" (Article 8(3)) and "the form of compensation and its extent" (Article 8(4). The French text of Article 8(4) of each Convention is identical, but that of Article 8(3) is different. The provisions, whether deliberately differently drafted or not, leave many questions of scope open. For example does the applicable law govern assessment of damages? Does "form" include, for example, whether damages can be awarded in the form of periodical payments or a lump sum? How does the expression "in particular" relate to questions such as this (and indeed other questions)?

---

6 Rome Convention, Article 1(2)(h); Rome I, Article 1(3); Rome II, Article 1(3).

THE ROME CONTRIBUTIONS: A "CONTRACTUAL INTERLUDE"

By way of a "contractual interlude", it can first be noted that the Rome Convention on the Law Applicable to Contractual Obligations provided in Article 10(1)(c) that the law applicable to the contract should govern "in particular" "within the limits of the powers conferred on the court by its procedural law, the consequences of breach, including the assessment of damages in so far as it is governed by rules of law". This provision is largely replicated in Article 12(1)(c) of the Rome I Regulation, except that "consequences of breach" is replaced by "the consequences of total or partial breach of obligations".[7] These provisions indicate a limitation on the scope of procedure when it comes to dealing with questions of remedy and damages at the European level.[8]

THE POSITION IN ROME II: TORT/DELICT

In contract cases, how damages are assessed is often governed by specific rules or, by assessing within the limit of what is recoverable, the factual loss that the aggrieved party has incurred. This means that the court has to decide whether a particular item of loss is recoverable at all and then has to decide on its value.[9] In tort cases it is different. There may be economic losses which can be assessed by arithmetical calculation, but there may also be losses which are more intangible and related specifically to the person who suffers them in a physical sense, but which also causes financial loss, in consequence. There may also be future financial losses which need to be assessed. Thus, the question of damages in tort involves inherent difficulties even in the context of Rome II. Some of these are examined below but before embarking on that, the question will be analysed by reference to English law, apart from the Rome II Regulation. It is helpful to keep in mind that Article 15(c) of Rome II, however, provides that the law applicable to non-contractual obligations (in this paper we are only concerned with such obligations which are characterised as sounding in tort/delict) shall govern "the existence, the nature and the assessment of damage or the remedy claimed." A matter falling within this proposition cannot therefore be held to be a matter of evidence or procedure for the purposes of Rome II, but the scope of the proposition needs to be elucidated, as also examined below.

---

7 This makes no substantial difference to the matter discussed in this contribution.

8 See, *e.g.*, *Chitty on Contracts* (31st ed.) 2011, paras 30–337, *et seq.*

9 This will be a matter of "evidence" governed by the law of the forum, but evidence in this context means proof of loss.

"AN ENGLISH LAW INTERLUDE"

As pointed out above, historically, English conflict of laws has accorded a wide scope to the category of procedure, particularly when it comes to the remedy and its quantification, available to the claimant. This is true of the common law and, in one case, where the common law has been, in part changed by statute, which statute has also been thought to preserve, in part the common law, in the interpretation of the statute. The statute to be examined here is the Private International Law (Miscellaneous Provisions) Act 1995, Part III (hereafter "the 1995 Act" or "the Act") which is concerned with choice of law in tort. Although the Act has largely been superseded by Rome II,[10] there are matters which might be covered by the Act even after Rome II. Thus Article 1(1) of Rome II provides that the Regulation shall not apply "to the liability of the State for acts and omissions in the exercise of State authority (*acta iure imperii*). There are, arguably, examples of cases falling within this category which will probably continue to be governed by the Act rather than by Rome II.[11] Section 14(3)(b) of the 1995 Act provides that the choice of law rules contained in the Act do not affect "any rules of evidence, pleading or practice or authorises questions of procedure in any proceedings to be determined otherwise than in accordance with the law of the forum." In *Harding v Wealands*[12] it was necessary to consider the scope of this provision in the context of damages. Here it was held that the liability in tort was governed by the law of New South Wales, Australia, but the other question was whether a "cap" on damages for non-pecuniary loss imposed by the law of New South Wales should be applied. The Court of Appeal, by a majority, held that it should.[13] The House of Lords held that it should not, on the basis that the question related to the quantification of damages, unaffected by the Act because of section 14 (3)(b). The question of quantification of damages was a matter of procedure, governed by English law as the law of the forum, and what was procedural had to be determined in accordance with English law as it was understood in the common law in 1995.

The question of damages is, of course more nuanced, and the House of Lords recognised that to be the case. English courts have distinguished "between the kind of *damage* which constitutes an actionable injury and the assessment of

10 Neither the Act nor Rome II apply to defamation and related claims. See 1995 Act, s. 13; Rome II, Article 1(2)(g).

11 See *e.g., Sharp v. Ministry of Defence* [2007] EWHC 224 (QB); *R. (on the application of Al-Jedda) v Ministry of Defence* [2008] UKHL 58, [2008] 1 A.C. 332. See also *Bici v Ministry of Defence* [2004] EWHC 786 (QB).

12 [2006] UKHL 32, [2007] 2 A.C. 1.

13 [2004] EWCA Civ 1735, [2005] 1 W.L.R. 539.

compensation (*i.e., damages*) for the injury which has been held to be actionable".[14] It follows from this that: questions as to whether damage is, or is not, too remote to be recoverable as a matter of law is substantive and thus depends on the applicable law; questions as to what heads of damage (*e.g.*, pain and suffering) should be similarly characterised and submitted to the applicable law;[15] and also the question of whether the claimant is under a duty to mitigate any damage initially suffered.

The issues in *Harding v Wealands*[16] were further explored by the Court of Appeal in *Cox v Ergo Versicherung AG*,[17] in which the husband of the claimant was killed while riding a bicycle near the barracks in Germany at which he was stationed. It was not disputed that liability was governed by German law under the 1995 Act. The claimant alleged, however, that assessment of damages was governed entirely by the provisions of the English Fatal Accidents Act 1976, whereas the defendant claimed that this issue was governed by relevant provisions of the German Civil Code which provisions would produce substantially less compensation for the claimant than would English law.

In short, relevant provisions of German law enabled the claimant to be compensated for loss of "maintenance", including future maintenance, (*e.g.*, by a new partner). whereas under the English Act compensation is payable for loss of "financial dependency", consequent on the death of the deceased. These were regarded as fundamentally different. Nonetheless, the provision of German law provided the relevant head of damage and the question remained as to how this should be quantified, as a matter for the *lex fori*, given that the German head of damage, a matter of substantive law governed by the German applicable law, was unknown to the law of the forum. Here it appears to have been held that assessment, as a matter of English law, was to be determined "on principles and in a manner analogous to that applicable under German law"[18] to a claim under the relevant provision of German law. This, perhaps, shows the limitations on the English law approach to damages in that foreign law is being applied under the guise of English law.

ROME II AND DAMAGES IN TORT

Although English law regards questions of remoteness of damage and heads of damage as a matter of substance governed by the applicable law, its approach

[14] [2005] 1 W.L.R. 539, at [25], citing *Boys v Chaplin* [1971 A.C. 356, a case on the common law.
[15] *E.g.*, *Boys v Chaplin*, above.
[16] Above.
[17] [2012] EWCA Civ 854.
[18] At [66].

to assessment of recoverable damage is rather more blunt. Such questions are exclusively governed by the law of the forum both at common law and under the 1995 Act (by way of transformation from the former to the latter).[19] In contrast, Rome II provides that the law applicable to the tort governs "the existence, the nature and the assessment of damage or the remedy claimed".[20] As regards matters of remoteness and heads of damage, it would seem that no change is made but as regards assessment, there is a fundamental change since assessment is now to be carried out according to the applicable law.

There is, however, a certain convenience with the English law approach. This is because many tort cases involving personal injuries, where England is the contemplated forum are, dealt with by insurers (often English), with a view to settlement, and, thus it is convenient for them to have English law in mind rather than having to engage in research on foreign law. Be that as it may, the primary consideration from a claimant's perspective is to obtain the largest award possible. If the claimant has a choice of *fora* in which to proceed which may well be the case under national and European jurisdictional rules, the claimant will choose to proceed in the forum which gives the best monetary result. This would be antithetical to one of the objectives of Rome II which is aimed at producing conflict rules which designate the same national law as applicable irrespective of the country of the court in which an action is brought.[21] Furthermore the national law of Member States may not speak the same voice on the difficult matter of assessment.[22] There is thus a need for uniformity of treatment. Article 15(c) provides uniformity in terms of words, but whether it will do so in terms of actual practice is more unclear.

In relation to actual pecuniary losses consequent on a tort, assuming they are recoverable under the applicable law, as will usually be the case, there should be no difficulty since this will normally be an arithmetical calculation. More difficulty may emerge in quantifying general damages for non-pecuniary loss (*e.g.*, pain and suffering, loss of amenity) and future financial loss, assuming these are recoverable under the applicable law. Here, quantification is more imprecise and is unlikely to be governed by strict rules of law.[23] As regards general damages, it has been suggested that the applicable law should be interpreted in a broad sense to include judicial conventions, practices, tariffs, guidelines or formulae as

---

[19] *Harding v Wealands*, above.

[20] Article 15(c).

[21] Rome II, Recital (6).

[22] See Plender and Wilderspin, *The European Private International law of Obligations* (3rd ed), p. 448.

[23] "Caps" on damages (see *Harding v Wealands*, above) are an exception. It would seem that under Rome II, a court would have to give effect to the cap, subject perhaps to public policy principles. If there are more general rules of law dealing with the issue of assessment these rules will have to be applied.

well as the approach to calculating awards in individual cases and the relevance of specific facts, *e.g.*, the social and economic conditions in a particular country which may be used by foreign judges in calculating awards.[24] Such factors may not be easy to establish in many countries. There may be no adequate records of previous cases and even if there are it may not be straightforward for lawyers or insurers involved in cases proceeding in a different country to gain access to them. This difficulty will persist whether the forum requires proof of foreign law by the parties or whether it is for the forum judge to decide the question *ex officio*. The difficulty may be exacerbated by the fact that in some legal systems damages are assessed by a jury (usually subject to directions from the court) whereas in other systems quantification is for the court alone. The latter systems cannot be expected to empanel a jury: this is a procedural question.[25] But if a forum is to attempt to produce a result which is consistent with the result which would be reached by a jury in the country of the applicable law, it may be faced with a range of awards to choose from and these awards may not always be consistent with each other.

Although Rome II is consistent with the principles and aims of the Regulation, there are "wrinkles" in the Recitals. Thus by virtue of Recital (33) to Rome II, "According to the current national rules on compensation awarded to victims of road traffic accidents, when quantifying damages for personal injury in cases in which the accident takes place in a State other than that of the habitual residence of the victim, the court seised should take into account all the relevant actual circumstances of the specific victim, including in particular the actual losses and costs of after-care and medical attention." The precise meaning and effect of this statement is most unclear. It does not change the terms of Article 15(c), but perhaps may lead to a degree of flexibility in its interpretation.[26]

In principle Article 15(c) could lead to an award of exemplary or punitive damages if such damages are permitted under the applicable law. Recital (32) to Rome II suggests, however, caution in this respect when it states that "the application of a provision of the law designated by this Regulation which would have the effect of causing non-compensatory exemplary or punitive damages of an excessive nature to be awarded may, depending on the circumstances of the

---

24 Dickinson, *The Rome II Regulation* (2008), pp. 575–576. This may well be of importance in relation to future economic losses, *e.g*,, future loss of earnings by the victim. As to discount rates, see Dickinson, above, p. 575; Rushworth and Scott [2008] LMCLQ 274.

25 See Article 15(d) of Rome II. And see *e.g.*, *Re T & N Ltd* [2005] EWHC 2990 (Ch) (no question of an English court empanelling a jury to assess damages in accordance with foreign law).

26 For some views, see Symeonides (2008) AJCL 173; Dickinson, above, pp. 580–581. Note also the Commission Statement appended to Rome II which appears to be concerned with the problems of the substantive law of assessment rather than the application of conflict of laws rules on that issue.

case and the legal order of the Member State of the court seised, be regarded as being contrary to the public policy (*ordre public*) of the forum."

Lastly Article 15(c) combined with Article 15(d) suggests (the matter is not entirely clear) that if the applicable law requires damages to be paid in the form of periodical payments whereas under the law of the forum they are payable once and for all as a lump sum, the forum need not apply the rule of the applicable law if it is not within the "limits of the powers conferred on the court by its procedural law."[27] Essentially, this should be seen, to that extent, to be a procedural question.

CONCLUSION

The dichotomy between substance and procedure in the context of damages in tort has given rise to differences and difficulties in the past. Rome II, laudably, attempts to achieve uniformity on what is a vital question in the conflict of laws in tort. However, as can be seen from the foregoing, in this regard, Rome II itself is not free from difficulty. Its application by the national courts of Member States is likely to provide challenges in the years ahead.

27 Article 15(d). See Plender and Wilderspin, above, pp. 452–453.

L'ARBITRAGE ÉTRANGER ET LA RECONNAISSANCE DES SENTENCES ARBITRALES ÉTRANGÈRES DANS LE NOUVEAU DROIT PORTUGAIS DE L'ARBITRAGE

Rui Manuel MOURA RAMOS
Professeur à la Faculté de Droit de l'Université de Coimbra
Membre de l'Institut de Droit International
Ancien Juge au Tribunal Général de l'Union européenne
Président émérite de la Cour Constitutionnelle portugaise

1. Le 14 mars 2012, une nouvelle loi sur l'arbitrage[1] est entrée en vigueur au Portugal, prenant inspiration de la Loi-Type de la CNUDCI sur l'Arbitrage Commercial International de 1985.[2] Cette loi abroge[3], à l'exception d'une seule de ses dispositions qui demeure partiellement en vigueur[4], la loi n° 31/86, du 29 août, en vigueur depuis le 29 novembre 1986, qui, ayant considéré le modèle constitué par la Loi-Type de la CNUDCI, s'en était écartée sciemment en des points importants. Au contraire, le législateur de 2011 a pris la direction opposée, s'alignant d'une façon expresse sur ce dernier modèle.[5]

---

1. Voir la loi n° 63/2011 du 14 décembre, dont l'article 1er, n° 1, approuve la Loi sur l'Arbitrage Volontaire publiée en annexe à ladite loi et qui en fait partie intégrante.
2. Cet instrument a été adopté par la Commission des Nations Unies pour le droit du commerce international (CNUDCI) lors de sa dix-huitième session, le 21 juin 1985.
3. Voir son article 5, n° 1.
4. En effet, la disposition citée à la note précédente maintient en vigueur l'article 1er, n° 1 de la loi n° 31/86 pour ce qui concerne l'arbitrage en matière de droit du travail.
5. Un tel alignement est visible soit par rapport au texte initial de la Loi-Type, soit en ce qui concerne les amendements dont il a fait l'objet en 2006 (voir, à ce propos, la résolution n° 61/33 de l'Assemblée Générale des Nations Unies du 3 décembre 2006).

Comme le diplôme qu'elle vient remplacer, la nouvelle loi s'adresse notamment à l'arbitrage interne, tout en s'occupant également de l'arbitrage international.[6] Elle s'éloigne cependant de ce dernier texte dans la mesure où, tout en suivant également la Loi-Type de la CNUDCI[7], d'une part, elle règle également la question de la reconnaissance et de l'exécution des sentences arbitrales étrangères, et, d'autre part, elle pose certaines règles qui s'adressent aux arbitrages étrangers. Ce sont ces deux ensembles de règles, nouveaux dans le droit portugais commun de l'arbitrage, que nous considérerons dans cette étude. Cependant, pour y arriver, il est nécessaire de préciser la notion d'arbitrage étranger, ou mieux, pour employer la terminologie que la nouvelle loi a adoptée, celle d'arbitrage localisé à l'étranger.[8]

2. On ne rencontrera, dans la nouvelle loi comme dans celle qu'elle est venue remplacer, aucune définition directe de ce qu'on doit comprendre par arbitrage étranger.[9] Mais la notion apparait très clairement identifiée à l'arbitrage localisé à l'étranger, à l'article 61 de la loi, où il est question de la définition du champ d'application dans l'espace de la nouvelle loi. Cet article, qui s'occupe également du champ d'application matériel de la loi, correspond, à la différence que la disposition y contenue ne réglait que le champ d'application dans l'espace de cette loi, à l'article 37 de la loi n° 31/86, qui, pour sa part, faisait application du même critère prévu, à des fins similaires, à l'article 1er, n° 2 de la Loi-Type. Nous laisserons de côté la définition du champ d'application matériel de la nouvelle loi, dont l'unique intérêt réside dans le fait que les diplômes qui l'avaient précédée

[6] Cette approche méthodologique n'est pas la seule. Certains systèmes s'adressent simplement à l'arbitrage, sans faire de distinction entre l'arbitrage interne et l'arbitrage international, tout en appliquant, dans les deux situations, le même système de règles, et en faisant donc l'économie de la définition d'arbitrage international – c'est le cas, au Brésil, de la loi 9307 du 23 novembre 1996. D'autres systèmes, comme celui de l'*Arbitration Act* anglais (1996), arrivent au même résultat, parce qu'ayant prévu au début des dispositions spéciales (les articles 85 à 87) pour l'arbitrage interne, ces règles ont très tôt été considérées contraires au droit européen et par la suite abrogées ; et il en va de même avec la récente loi écossaise, qui contient également une codification complète et intégrée de l'arbitrage interne et international. Dans la majorité des cas, cependant, les législations s'adressent à l'arbitrage interne, tout en prévoyant des dispositions pour l'arbitrage international. Le système allemand (loi du 22 décembre 1997, qui porte réforme, en la matière, du Code de Procédure Civile) en constitue une variante. S'adressant aux arbitrages dont le lieu (tel que défini dans la loi-même) est situé en Allemagne, il y est prévu que certaines de ses dispositions (les articles 1032, 1033 et 1050, relatifs aux rapports avec les tribunaux étatiques) s'appliquent également aux arbitrages dont le siège se trouve à l'étranger.

[7] Voir le chapitre VIII de cette loi.

[8] Voir les articles 55, 56, 58, 59, n° 1, al. h, et 61 de la loi. Tout en se rapportant à la même réalité, l'article 57 parle cependant simplement de sentence arbitrale étrangère.

[9] Contrairement à ce qui arrive, par exemple, avec la loi espagnole (loi 60/2003, du 23 décembre) qui dispose, à l'article 46, n. 1, qu' « on comprend par décision étrangère celle prononcée en dehors du territoire espagnol ».

ne réglaient pas la reconnaissance des sentences arbitrales étrangères[10], et ne prendrons en considération que la partie de la disposition qui s'adresse à la définition du champ d'application dans l'espace de la loi. Il y est dit, à ce propos, qu'elle s'applique à tous les arbitrages prenant lieu en territoire portugais.

Le nouveau régime se présente donc comme une réglementation complète de la matière de l'arbitrage, s'adressant à l'arbitrage interne (compris comme celui qui ne présente point d'éléments d'extranéité) et à l'arbitrage international, pourvu que, dans un cas comme dans l'autre, le lieu de l'arbitrage soit situé sur le territoire portugais. On fait ici recours à l'idée de siège de l'arbitrage[11], qui apparait comme s'imposant naturellement dans les arbitrages internes mais qui se recommande également dans ceux présentant un caractère international[12], compte tenu de l'importance des tribunaux étatiques dans l'exercice de certaines fonctions d'assistance et de contrôle dans le cadre de l'arbitrage.[13] L'importance d'une telle précision apparait de prime abord, si l'on constate le besoin de résoudre les conflits de juridictions, notamment ceux de nature positive, qui pourraient facilement se présenter dans la détermination des ordres juridictionnels qui auraient des fonctions à exercer dans le contrôle de l'arbitrage (notamment international).

La loi portugaise se borne à une référence au siège[14], sans d'autres précisions[15], mais on devra tenir compte, pour la désignation de celui-ci, de l'article 31 de la loi, d'après lequel les parties peuvent fixer librement le lieu de l'arbitrage, une telle fixation étant dévolue au tribunal arbitral lui-même, compte tenu des circonstances du cas, y compris les convenances des parties, si celles-ci ne se mettent pas d'accord à ce propos. On peut donc conclure que la notion de siège demeure, comme il arrive dans d'autres systèmes juridiques[16], un concept juridique qui consacre

---

10 Voir *supra*, n° 1, *in fine*. Par contre, la Loi-Type règle également la reconnaissance et l'exécution des sentences (articles 35 et 36), tout en précisant (article 35, n° 1) qu'elle a en vue à ce propos toute sentence arbitrale « quel que soit le pays où elle a été rendue ».

11 Cette référence au siège comme critère d'application dans l'espace des lois nationales en matière d'arbitrage est devenue, pour une certaine doctrine, indiscutable (dans ce sens Andreas Bucher, *Le nouvel arbitrage international en Suisse*, Bâle, 1988, Helbing et Lichtenhahn, p. 25), ayant eu la faveur de la plupart des conventions internationales et des législations nationales.

12 En particulier pour la défense de ce critère dans le cadre de l'arbitrage international, voir Georgios Petrochilos, *Procedural Law in International Arbitration*, Oxford, 2004, Oxford University Press, p. 65.

13 Voir l'article 6 de la Loi-Type de la CNUDCI, citée *supra*, note 2.

14 L'arbitrage doit avoir lieu en territoire portugais.

15 Contrairement à ce qui arrive, par exemple, avec la loi fédérale suisse sur le droit international privé, dont l'article 176, n° 1, exige encore, cumulativement, pour son application, qu'au moins l'une des parties n'ait, au moment de la conclusion d'arbitrage, ni son domicile ni sa résidence habituelle en Suisse.

16 Voir *l'Arbitration Act* anglais, dont la troisième section définit « le siège de l'arbitrage » comme le siège juridique de l'arbitrage, qui peut être soit désigné par les parties dans la convention d'arbitrage, par un arbitre ou par une autre institution ou personne à laquelle les parties ont donné des pouvoirs à cet égard, ou par le tribunal arbitral, dûment autorisé par les parties, soit

notamment la primauté de l'autonomie des parties à cet égard et qui empêche l'application purement mécanique d'un critère géographique qui écarterait le rôle de la volonté des parties. Un tel concept traduit donc un lien juridique, pas simplement géographique, entre l'arbitrage et un ordre juridique donné, qui n'est pas mis à l'écart du seul fait que les opérations matérielles par lesquelles l'arbitrage prend corps, même la rédaction de la sentence, ont physiquement lieu dans un autre pays.[17]

L'arbitrage lié d'une telle façon à l'ordre juridique portugais étant donc soumis à ce système, tout autre arbitrage doit, par rapport à ce système[18], être considéré comme étranger, sa réglementation lui échappant en principe.[19] Cela est naturellement vrai pour les arbitrages présentant un lien juridique donné avec un ordre juridique étranger. Mais la solution adoptée et la conception qui la soutient n'impliquent cependant pas l'idée qu'un arbitrage « étranger » *hoc sensu* doive nécessairement présenter un lien juridique quelconque avec un ordre juridique donné. La question se pose, naturellement, au moment de la reconnaissance de la décision issue d'un tel arbitrage, le problème étant celui de savoir s'il y a lieu de reconnaitre ou non des décisions arbitrales délocalisées (*non domestic*, *homeless*, *statelessness*), dans le sens qu'elles ne présentent aucun point d'ancrage avec un système de droit donné.[20]

3. À la suite de ce qui est prévu par la Loi-Type de la CNUDCI sur l'arbitrage commercial international[21] la loi portugaise prévoit désormais tout un chapitre dédié aux mesures provisoires et ordonnances préliminaires (articles 20 à 29). C'est dans l'ensemble de ces dispositions qu'on rencontre des règles s'appliquant à (ou ayant une incidence sur) des procédures d'arbitrage étrangères.

La première de ces règles est celle contenue au numéro 1 de l'article 27 de la loi, où, s'agissant de la reconnaissance ou de l'exécution des mesures provisoires, il est statué que les mesures provisoires prononcées par un tribunal arbitral sont reconnues comme ayant force obligatoire et, sauf indication contraire du tribunal arbitral, sont exécutées sur demande adressée au tribunal compétent, quel que soit

---

déterminé, en l'absence d'une telle désignation, compte tenu de l'accord des parties et de toutes les circonstances pertinentes.

17 Dans ce même sens, Georgios Petrochilos (*loc. cit.* note 12), p. 68.

18 La notion d'arbitrage étranger est donc une notion relative, dans la mesure où elle implique toujours qu'on ait en tête une référence à un ordre juridique donné.

19 En principe, parce que la loi portugaise prévoit elle-même une certaine réglementation (ou, mieux, une certaine prise en compte) de l'arbitrage « étranger ». Voir *infra*, n° 3.

20 La question a été surtout discutée à l'égard du domaine matériel d'application de la Convention de New York du 10 juin 1958.

21 Il s'agit du chapitre IV A, où l'on trouve les nouveaux articles 17 à 17 J.

le pays où elles ont été prononcées, sous réserve des dispositions de l'article 28.[22] Cette disposition renforce donc l'importance de la procédure d'arbitrage, en prévoyant la reconnaissance et l'exécution des mesures provisoires prononcées par tout tribunal arbitral, même par un tribunal arbitral siégeant à l'étranger[23], et en conduisant donc à inclure dans sa prévision des procédures d'arbitrage ne relevant pas de l'ordre juridique portugais (au sens de notre loi, des arbitrages étrangers). On pose donc le principe de la reconnaissance des mesures provisoires prononcées par un tribunal arbitral dans le cadre d'une procédure d'arbitrage étrangère.

S'agissant maintenant des motifs de refus de la reconnaissance ou de l'exécution, il est prévu à l'article 28, n° 1, alinéa a, iii, que la reconnaissance ou l'exécution d'une mesure provisoire peut être refusée par un tribunal étatique portugais, à la demande de la partie contre laquelle cette mesure est invoquée, si le tribunal a la conviction que la mesure provisoire a été rétractée ou suspendue par le tribunal arbitral ou, lorsqu'il y est habilité, annulée ou suspendue par le tribunal de l'État étranger dans lequel a lieu l'arbitrage ou conformément à la loi duquel cette mesure a été accordée.[24] Cette disposition reconnait d'abord la compétence du tribunal arbitral, même un tribunal arbitral siégeant hors du territoire portugais et ne présentant donc aucun lien juridique avec l'ordre juridique portugais, pour rétracter ou suspendre des mesures provisoires qu'il aurait précédemment prononcées. Et elle reconnait également, dans la mesure où un tel tribunal aurait été compétent à ce propos, la compétence des tribunaux étatiques étrangers (ceux de l'Etat où a lieu l'arbitrage et ceux de l'Etat conformément à la loi duquel une mesure provisoire a été accordée) au même effet. De ce fait, les décisions qu'ils auront prises dans un tel sens empêcheront la reconnaissance et l'exécution des mesures provisoires que le tribunal arbitral aurait prononcées. Encore une fois nous sommes devant des arbitrages étrangers, ne présentant aucun lien juridique avec le territoire ou l'ordre juridique portugais, et notre droit commande la non-reconnaissance de certaines mesures prononcées par le tribunal arbitral, qui en principe seraient reconnues, du fait de sa suspension ou rétractation par le tribunal arbitral lui-même ou par un tribunal étatique (celui du lieu de l'arbitrage ou celui conformément à la loi duquel la mesure provisoire avait été accordée). On règle donc les conditions de l'efficacité au Portugal de mesures prononcées dans le cadre d'arbitrages étrangers. Et on reconnait à cet égard l'effet préclusif de décisions de tribunaux (soit arbitraux soit étatiques) ne présentant aucun lien juridique avec le territoire ou l'ordre juridique portugais. La reconnaissance d'un

---

22 Cet article énonce les motifs de refus de la reconnaissance de ces mesures, tout en reproduisant l'article 17 I de la Loi-Type.

23 Au sens défini *supra*, au n° 2.

24 Voir l'article 17 I, n° 1, al. a, iii de la Loi-Type.

tel effet préclusif (et la non reconnaissance de la mesure provisoire prononcée par le tribunal arbitral, qui en est la conséquence) semblent découler de l'autonomie de la procédure arbitrale (étrangère, dans le cas d'espèce), qui s'impose donc à l'ordre juridique du for, en soi-même et dans les liaisons qu'elle présente avec d'autres ordres juridiques étatiques.

Encore en matière de mesures provisoires, l'article 29 de notre loi[25] reconnait également la compétence des tribunaux étatiques (dans ce cas des tribunaux portugais) pour prononcer des mesures provisoires en relation avec des procédures d'arbitrage, qu'elles aient ou non leur lieu en territoire portugais, l'étendue d'une telle compétence étant la même que celle dont ils disposent en relation avec des procédures judiciaires. La règle fait le contrepoint avec celles des articles 20, n° 1 (où on reconnait la compétence des tribunaux arbitraux siégeant en territoire portugais pour prononcer des mesures provisoires) et 27, n° 1 (où on reconnait la force obligatoire et la possibilité d'exécution des mesures provisoires prononcées par un tribunal arbitral, même si l'arbitrage est un arbitrage étranger), et celle de l'article 28, n° 1, alinéa a, iii (où il est question de l'effet neutralisateur de décisions en matière de mesures provisoires prononcées par un tribunal arbitral ou par un tribunal étatique, soit celui de l'Etat du lieu de l'arbitrage soit celui conformément à la loi duquel la mesure avait été accordée), reconnaissant maintenant la compétence directe des tribunaux (étatiques) portugais pour prononcer des mesures provisoires en relation avec une procédure d'arbitrage. Il y est spécifié que ce pouvoir n'est pas limité aux arbitrages dont le siège[26] se trouve en territoire portugais, mais qu'il s'étend, au contraire, également aux arbitrages étrangers, que son étendue est la même que celle dont dispose ce tribunal dans des procédures judiciaires (article 29, n° 1), et qu'il est exercé conformément à ses propres procédures, en tenant compte des particularités d'un arbitrage international (article 29, n° 2).[27]

Enfin, et maintenant en matière d'assistance des tribunaux (étatiques) pour l'obtention de preuves, l'article 38, n° 1, prévoit, au cas où la preuve à produire dépendrait de la volonté d'une des parties ou d'un tiers et dès qu'ils refusent sa collaboration, qu'une partie, avec l'approbation du tribunal arbitral, peut demander au tribunal étatique (portugais) compétent que la preuve soit produite devant lui, ses résultats devant être renvoyés au tribunal arbitral.[28] Et on ajoute au numéro 2 de cet article que ce qui est dit au numéro précédent s'applique

---

25 En reproduisant maintenant l'article 17 J de la Loi-Type.

26 Au sens précisé *supra*, au n° 2.

27 Voir, exactement dans le même sens, l'article 17 J de la Loi-Type.

28 La disposition suit l'article 17 J de la Loi-Type, même si l'assistance des tribunaux (étatiques) en matière d'obtention de preuves y est prévue en des termes plus larges. Cet article précise, en outre, que le tribunal peut satisfaire à cette demande, dans les limites de sa compétence et conformément aux règles relatives à l'obtention de preuves.

également aux demandes d'obtention de preuves adressées à un tribunal étatique portugais dans le cadre d'arbitrages dont le lieu se trouve à l'étranger (arbitrage étranger).

Il est bien clair que les dispositions citées révèlent l'importance que la loi portugaise attache aux mesures provisoires prononcées par le tribunal arbitral, une telle importance découlant de la reconnaissance de leur force obligatoire et de la possibilité de leur exécution. Cependant, le fait qu'une telle reconnaissance soit ouverte aux décisions de tout tribunal arbitral, quel que soit le siège de l'arbitrage, place l'arbitrage étranger au même plan de l'arbitrage dont le statut est constitué par l'ordre juridique portugais, en contribuant de la sorte à minimiser l'importance d'un tel statut. Le fait que les décisions ayant trait à de telles mesures, prises par le tribunal arbitral lui-même ou par des tribunaux étatiques étrangers, soit de celui de l'Etat du siège de l'arbitrage soit de celui conformément à la loi duquel la mesure a été accordée, doivent être prises en compte par les tribunaux portugais lors de la reconnaissance des mesures provisoires prononcées par un tribunal arbitral rend le tribunal portugais responsable de l'exécution du statut de l'arbitrage étranger, dans une mesure semblable à celle où il se trouve par rapport à l'arbitrage de statut portugais, c'est-à-dire, celui dont le lieu de l'arbitrage se trouve localisé en territoire portugais.[29] Et ce même rôle dévolu aux tribunaux portugais apparait également à l'article 29, où ces instances judiciaires se voient reconnaitre le pouvoir de prononcer des mesures provisoires en relation avec une procédure d'arbitrage, qu'elle ait ou non son lieu en territoire portugais, et à l'article 38, où il est admis que les tribunaux portugais peuvent satisfaire à des demandes d'obtention de preuves, formulées dans le cadre de procédures d'arbitrage dont le lieu se trouve en territoire portugais ou bien ailleurs. En plaçant le tribunal portugais dans la même position, à l'égard de procédures d'arbitrage se déroulant ou non en territoire portugais, et en concevant ses compétences de la même façon qu'elles sont comprises lors de l'exercice de compétences semblables dans des procédures arbitrales régies par la loi portugaise, les dispositions citées arrivent donc soit à réduire l'importance du caractère étranger d'un arbitrage, soit à affaiblir la distance qui écarte cette procédure de l'exercice de la juridiction étatique.

4. Malgré les considérations qui précèdent, il ne demeure pas moins vrai qu'il y a encore lieu, à l'égard de l'ordre juridique portugais, à une différence nette entre arbitrage réglé par la loi portugaise (pour ainsi dire, « national ») et arbitrage étranger. La preuve d'une telle différence réside dans le fait que si à la décision arbitrale prononcée dans une procédure ayant lieu en territoire portugais[30] et qui

[29] Toujours au sens précisé plus haut, au n° 2, *supra*.

[30] Et, de ce fait, réglée par la loi approuvée par la loi n° 63/2011.

n'a pas fait l'objet de recours ou de modification[31] est reconnue la même force obligatoire que celle dont jouissent les décisions judiciaires définitives et la même force exécutoire que celle des sentences des tribunaux étatiques[32], les décisions prononcées dans des arbitrages dont le lieu se trouve à l'étranger ne produisent d'effet au Portugal[33], quelle que soit la nationalité des parties, que si elles sont reconnues par le tribunal étatique portugais compétent (article 55). Le lieu de l'arbitrage, dont le relief avait été réduit par les dispositions citées au numéro précédent, apparait donc dans toute son importance.[34]

On soulignera, tout d'abord, que c'est la première fois que cette question (celle de la reconnaissance et de l'exécution des sentences arbitrales) apparait réglée dans les actes législatifs qui se sont occupés de l'arbitrage au Portugal. En effet, les régimes précédents avaient laissé la question en suspens. Il fallait donc se référer au Code de Procédure Civile[35], où cette question était réglée dans les mêmes termes, soit pour les décisions judiciaires étrangères soit pour les décisions prononcées par des arbitres à l'étranger.[36] La préoccupation du législateur, en matière d'arbitrage, étant d'assimiler la décision arbitrale à une décision judiciaire, il est apparu comme naturel que les décisions arbitrales étrangères suivent le sort des décisions judiciaires du même type.[37]

Pour ce qui est, maintenant, de la solution elle-même, on rappellera que le droit portugais suit, en effet, depuis longtemps, en matière de reconnaissance de décisions étrangères, le système de la reconnaissance sous contrôle préalable, ce

---

31 À titre de rectification, de sentence interprétative ou de sentence additionnelle, dans la mesure où ces instruments ont leur place. Voir l'article 45 de la loi portugaise et l'article 33 de la Loi-Type.

32 Dans ce sens, l'article 42, n° 7, de la loi.

33 Sous réserve de ce qui est impérativement statué par la Convention de New York de 1958 sur la reconnaissance et l'exécution des décisions arbitrales étrangères ou par d'autres traités ou conventions liant l'Etat Portugais. Voir le même article 55.

34 On retrouvera la solution contraire à l'article 35, n. 1 de la Loi-Type, qui établit que « la sentence arbitrale, quel que soit le pays où elle a été rendue, est reconnue comme ayant force obligatoire et, sur requête adressée par écrit au tribunal compétent, est exécutée sous réserve des dispositions du présent article et de l'article 36 ».

35 L'article 1094, n° 1 de ce diplôme disposait, en effet, que, « sans préjudice des dispositions contenues dans les traités et dans les lois spéciales, une décision touchant des droits privés prise par un tribunal étranger, ou par des arbitres à l'étranger, ne produit aucun effet au Portugal, quelle que soit la nationalité des parties, si elle n'est pas révisée et confirmée ».

36 À la suite de la décision législative (prise par la loi n° 63/2011) de concentrer tout le régime de l'arbitrage dans cette même loi, l'article 1094, n° 1, du Code de Procédure Civile ne s'adresse, désormais, qu'aux seules reconnaissance et exécution des sentences prononcées par des tribunaux judiciaires étrangers. Voir la modification apportée à cette disposition par l'article 2 de la loi n° 63/2011.

37 On aurait pu, au contraire, concevoir, pour la reconnaissance de ces décisions, un régime, comme celui de la Convention de New York du 10 juin 1958, qui aurait en vue sa nature spécifique.

qui implique que la sentence étrangère ne pourra produire d'effet au Portugal[38] qu'après avoir fait l'objet d'un contrôle (dit révision) par un tribunal portugais. Cette orientation, d'après laquelle il faut une décision nationale permettant à la décision étrangère d'opérer dorénavant dans l'ordre juridique du for les effets qui lui reviennent, conformément à la loi de l'État d'origine, n'a jamais été vraiment mise en cause dans le droit commun de la procédure civile internationale portugais. Son extension aux décisions arbitrales ne saurait donc surprendre, si on se rappelle que l'idée de base de notre législateur a toujours été de réduire l'écart entre les décisions judiciaires et les décisions arbitrales.

5. Si le législateur s'est limité jusqu'à présent à concentrer dans un même diplôme toutes les questions se rapportant à l'arbitrage, sans modifier le système de contrôle préalable de la décision arbitrale étrangère précédemment consacrée, il en va tout autrement des termes et conditions de ce contrôle. En effet, à ce propos, l'article 56 de la loi énonce maintenant, d'une façon limitative, les seuls fondements pouvant amener au refus de la reconnaissance et de l'exécution de la sentence arbitrale étrangère[39], soit sur demande de la partie contre laquelle la sentence a été invoquée, soit à la suite d'une vérification du tribunal compétent.[40] On peut donc conclure que la reconnaissance sera la règle, les exceptions étant limitativement énoncées, mais surtout, que, contrairement à ce qui était le cas auparavant[41], le régime de la reconnaissance et de l'exécution est énoncé de façon autonome à la loi[42], ne faisant plus l'objet d'un renvoi à celui prévu pour les décisions judiciaires étrangères.

Concernant maintenant les conditions de refus de la reconnaissance, on reconnaîtra très aisément l'influence de la Loi-Type, dont l'article 36 a pratiquement été reproduit à l'article 56, n° 1 de la nouvelle loi. S'alignant également sur la Loi-Type, le numéro 2 de l'article 56 prévoit aussi que si une demande d'annulation

---

38 Nous parlons, évidemment, de l'autorité de chose jugée et de la force exécutoire. Pour ce qui est des effets latéraux des jugements (effets secondaires rattachés à un jugement pour des règles de droit matériel) ou de l'effet du jugement comme moyen de preuve, la règle n'a plus sa place. L'article 1094, n° 2 du Code de Procédure Civile précise, d'ailleurs, que « la révision n'est pas nécessaire quand, dans un procès en cours devant les tribunaux portugais, la décision [étrangère] est invoquée comme simple moyen de preuve sujet à l'appréciation de celui qui doit juger la cause ».

39 Aux termes de la loi, « sentence arbitrale prononcée dans un arbitrage localisé à l'étranger ».

40 Alinéas a et b du n° 1 de l'article 56 de la loi.

41 En effet, avant l'entrée en vigueur de la loi n° 63/2011 l'article 1097 du Code de Procédure Civile prévoyait que « les dispositions de l'article précédent [l'article 1096, où étaient énoncées les conditions dont dépendait la confirmation d'une décision judiciaire étrangère] s'appliquent aux sentences arbitrales dans la mesure du possible ». Cet article 1097 a donc fait l'objet d'une abrogation expresse par l'article 5, n° 3 de la loi n° 63/2011.

42 La même option a été prise au Brésil, par la loi n° 9.307 du 23 septembre 1996 (voir les articles 34 à 40), et en Italie, par la loi n° 69 du 18 juin 2009, qui a modifié les articles 806 à 840 du Codice di Procedura Civile.

ou de suspension d'une sentence a été présentée à un tribunal visé au sous-alinéa v) de l'alinéa a) du numéro 1 du même article, le tribunal portugais auquel est demandée la reconnaissance ou l'exécution peut, s'il le juge approprié, surseoir à statuer et peut aussi, à la requête de la partie demandant la reconnaissance ou l'exécution de la sentence, ordonner à l'autre partie de fournir des sûretés convenables.

Enfin, l'article 57, n° 1 de la loi dispose, en reprenant l'article 35, n. 2 de la Loi-Type, que la partie qui prétend la reconnaissance d'une sentence arbitrale étrangère, notamment en vue de son exécution au Portugal, doit en fournir l'original dûment authentifié ou une copie certifiée conforme, ainsi que l'original de la convention d'arbitrage ou une copie certifiée conforme. Et que, au cas où ladite sentence ou ladite convention n'est pas rédigée en langue portugaise, la partie en produira une traduction dûment certifiée dans cette langue. Pour ce qui est, maintenant, de la procédure, il est prévu qu'une fois la requête de reconnaissance présentée, avec les documents mentionnés ci-dessus, la partie contraire est citée pour signifier son opposition dans un délai de 15 jours (n° 2), qu'une fois les mémoires terminés et les diligences considérées indispensables par le rapporteur réalisées, l'examen du procès est permis, aux fins des allégations, aux parties et au Ministère Public, dans un délai de 15 jours (n° 3), et qu'on procèdera au jugement d'après les règles propres à l'appel (n° 4).

6. Pour ce qui a trait aux motifs de non-reconnaissance de la décision arbitrale, on doit souligner qu'ils ont été limités à des vices extrêmes de la convention d'arbitrage (l'affectant en tant qu'acte juridique, en raison des parties ou de l'objet), de la procédure arbitrale ou de la sentence arbitrale elle-même, qui font l'objet d'une énumération au numéro 1 de l'article 56. Pour ce qui est de la convention d'arbitrage en tant qu'acte juridique, la reconnaissance pourra être mise en cause du fait de son invalidité, à l'égard, naturellement, de la loi la régissant (la loi à laquelle les parties l'ont subordonnée ou, à défaut, la loi du pays où la sentence a été rendue) (deuxième partie du sous-alinéa i de l'alinéa a) ; à propos des parties à la convention, le même peut résulter de son incapacité (première partie du sous-alinéa i de l'alinéa a) ; enfin, en ce qui concerne l'objet, il faut que le différend sur lequel elle porte soit susceptible d'être réglé par arbitrage conformément à la loi portugaise (sous-alinéa i de l'alinéa b).[43] Concernant maintenant la procédure arbitrale, la reconnaissance pourra être refusée si la preuve est apportée du fait que la constitution du tribunal arbitral ou la procédure n'a pas été conforme à la convention des parties ou, à défaut d'une telle convention, à la loi du pays où l'arbitrage a lieu (sous-alinéa iv de l'alinéa a) ou du fait que la partie contre

[43] Rappelons que ce motif de non-reconnaissance n'a pas besoin d'être invoqué et prouvé par la partie contre laquelle la sentence est invoquée.

laquelle la sentence est invoquée n'a pas été dûment informée de la désignation d'un arbitre ou de la procédure arbitrale, ou qu'il lui a été impossible pour une autre raison de faire valoir ses droits (sous-alinéa ii de l'alinéa a). À l'égard de la sentence arbitrale, dernièrement, le refus de la reconnaissance découlera tout d'abord du fait de sa contrariété à l'ordre public international de l'État Portugais (sous-alinéa ii de l'alinéa b)[44], mais pourra résulter également du fait qu'elle n'est pas encore devenue obligatoire pour les parties ou a été annulée ou suspendue par un tribunal du pays dans lequel, ou en vertu de la loi duquel elle a été rendue (sous-alinéa v de l'alinéa a)[45], ou du fait qu'elle porte sur un différend non visé dans la convention d'arbitrage ou qu'elle contient des décisions qui en dépassent les termes (sous-alinéa iii de l'alinéa a)[46]

Le fait que ces motifs de non-reconnaissance coïncident[47], à l'exception d'un seul cas, manifestement non applicable à cet égard[48], avec des fondements d'annulation de la sentence arbitrale rendue en territoire portugais[49] témoigne du rapprochement fait par la loi entre la sentence arbitrale rendue au Portugal et celle étrangère et, ramenant les motifs de non-reconnaissance de la décision étrangère à des circonstances ayant trait à l'arbitrage au sens large, renforce donc nettement le profil reconnu à cette institution par notre droit.

On peut donc conclure qu'en matière de fondements de reconnaissance des sentences arbitrales étrangères, l'élimination du renvoi précédemment fait au régime de la reconnaissance des décisions judiciaires n'a pas eu une simple portée formelle, vu que le système qui l'a remplacé n'a rien à voir avec les décisions de ce type, tout en ayant été bâti, comme nous venons de le voir, sur des particularités propres à l'arbitrage lui-même.

7. Il est maintenant temps de conclure cette réflexion sur le régime consacré par la récente loi portugaise de l'arbitrage aux arbitrages étrangers, soit au cours de la procédure arbitrale elle-même soit au moment où sa reconnaissance est demandée au Portugal.

On soulignera d'abord la nouveauté absolue de l'entreprise, si nous nous en tenons au sein du droit portugais commun, vu que si le premier aspect de la question était absolument inconnu, le deuxième n'était considéré qu'au moyen

44 On devra rappeler ici, également, la remarque faite à la note précédente.
45 Sur cette question, Georges Petrochilos (*loc. cit.* note 12), p. 299-337.
46 Étant entendu toutefois que, si les dispositions de la sentence qui ont trait à des questions soumises à l'arbitrage peuvent être dissociées de celles qui ont trait à des questions non soumises à l'arbitrage, seule la partie de la sentence contenant des décisions sur les questions soumises à l'arbitrage pourra être reconnue et exécutée.
47 Voir les sous-alinéas i à iv de l'alinéa a et l'alinéa b du n° 3 de l'article 46 de la loi.
48 Voir l'hypothèse prévue au sous-alinéa v de l'alinéa a du n° 1 de l'article 56.
49 Coïncidence que l'on remarquera également à la Loi-Type. Voir les articles 34, n° 2, et 36, n° 1, de cet instrument.

d'un renvoi à un régime structurellement différent, qui serait d'application « dans la mesure du possible ».

Par la suite, on reconnaîtra qu'une même idée peut être considérée sous-jacente au traitement donné aux deux questions. Ainsi, en posant des règles[50] dont l'application aura lieu au cours d'une procédure arbitrale étrangère, le législateur portugais s'oriente dans le sens d'étendre à ces procédures les mêmes dispositifs légaux qu'il prévoit pour les arbitrages dont le siège se trouve au Portugal, tout en assimilant donc les premières procédures à ces dernières. D'autre part, dans le domaine de la reconnaissance des décisions arbitrales étrangères, il est question d'une autre forme d'assimilation. Pour ce qui est de la neutralisation des effets d'une sentence arbitrale étrangère, on prévoit à ce titre l'application du même cadre légal que celui auquel on ferait référence s'il était question de l'annulation d'une décision arbitrale rendue au Portugal, l'arbitrage étranger étant donc traité[51], aux fins de la production de ses effets au Portugal, comme l'arbitrage dont le siège se trouve au Portugal.

Au delà de la modernisation des solutions dont notre droit fait l'objet à ce propos, on reconnaîtra donc dans les aspects de l'initiative législative que nous commentons la présence du même objectif de renforcement de l'institution arbitrale qui a caractérisé la réforme du régime de l'arbitrage dans son ensemble. Un renforcement qui a à sa base la reconnaissance de l'autonomie de l'instance arbitrale, autonomie qui explique donc, à la fois, soit le rapprochement entre l'arbitrage étranger et l'arbitrage « national », soit la construction d'un régime propre pour la reconnaissance des décisions arbitrales étrangères.

---

50 Celles dont on parle *supra*, au n° 3.

51 En dehors du fait (d'une certaine forme essentiel) qu'il y a lieu dans ce cas à un contrôle préalable (par une instance judiciaire) de la décision arbitrale étrangère. Mais les fondements qui peuvent amener l'organe de contrôle à refuser la reconnaissance sont les mêmes, comme nous l'avons vu, que ceux qui pourraient être à la base de l'annulation d'une décision arbitrale rendue au Portugal.

EXCLUSIVE CHOICE OF COURT AGREEMENTS AND PARALLEL PROCEEDINGS

Peter Arnt NIELSEN*
Professor, Head of the Law Department, Copenhagen Business School

1. CHOICE OF COURT AGREEMENTS

For businesses, choice of court agreements are of manifest importance in international matters. A choice of court agreement stipulates, for the purpose of deciding disputes that have arisen or may arise in connection with a particular legal relationship, the courts of a State or one or more specific courts of a State that shall have jurisdiction to the exclusion of the jurisdiction of any other courts. However, a choice of court agreement may also stipulate that courts of two or more States are to have jurisdiction, and other combinations can be envisaged, e.g. an asymmetric agreement, which is exclusive as regards proceedings brought by one party, but not as regards proceedings brought by the other party.

The purpose of choice of court agreements is to provide predictability as to the State in which litigation can be instituted. Furthermore, such agreements usually protect the parties against forum shopping, because proceedings instituted in a State other than the chosen one will be dismissed due to lack of jurisdiction.

One problem of significant importance arises where the parties have entered into a choice of court agreement providing for exclusive jurisdiction in one State and one of them initiates proceedings in another State (parallel or concurrent

* The author was member of the Danish delegations to the EU for negotiations on *the New Brussels I* in 2011–2012, negotiations on *Brussels I* in 1999–2000, and the revision of the *Brussels Convention* in 1998–1999. He was also a member of the Danish delegations to the Hague Conference on Private International Law for negotiations on *A Global Judgments Convention* in 1997–2001, and *the Choice of Court Convention* in 2002–2005. The author admires Hans van Loon for his immense knowledge of and contribution to private international law and for his fantastic personality.

proceedings). Which court should decide on the validity of the choice of court agreement? The court first seized? The chosen court? Or both courts?

The global Hague Convention on Choice of Court Agreements (*the Hague Convention*) of 2005 addresses this issue.[1] It has also been dealt with during negotiations in 2011 and 2012 on the recast of the EU Regulation on Jurisdiction and Recognition and Enforcement of Judgments in Civil and Commercial Matters (*Brussels I*).[2] The Regulation applies to all Member States of the European Union. The negotiations resulted in *the New Brussels I* adopted on 12 December 2012. It will apply from 10 January 2015.[3]

2. THE HAGUE CONVENTION

The Hague Convention is of paramount interest to global businesses. It applies to exclusive choice of court agreements in civil and commercial matters (see Article 1). However, consumer and employment contracts and other specific subject matters are excluded (see Article 2).

The purpose of *the Hague Convention* is to promote international trade and investment through enhanced judicial co-operation by enhancing uniform rules on jurisdiction and on recognition and enforcement of foreign judgments. In particular, the Convention provides certainty and ensures the effectiveness of exclusive choice of court agreements between parties to commercial transactions.

The Hague Convention has not yet entered into force, but it has been signed by the US and the EU and ratified by Mexico. Both signatories have indicated an intention to ratify the Convention as soon as possible. Argentina, Australia, Canada, Costa Rica and New Zealand are among the other States that have expressed a continuing interest in joining the Convention.

Article 3 of *the Hague Convention* defines an exclusive choice of court agreement as "an agreement concluded by two or more parties that [...] designates, for the purpose of deciding disputes which have arisen or may arise in connection with a particular legal relationship, the courts of one Contracting State or one or more specific courts of one Contracting State to the exclusion of the jurisdiction

1 Convention of 30 June 2005 on Choice of Court Agreements.

2 Regulation 44/2001 of 22 December 2000 on Jurisdiction and the Recognition and Enforcement of Judgments in Civil and Commercial Matters. See, for instance, U. Magnus and P. Mankowski, *Brussels I Regulation*, 2nd ed. 2012, H. Gaudemet-Tallon, *Compétence et exécution des jugements en Europe*, 4th ed. 2010, and B. Hess, *Europäisches Zivilprocessrecht*, 2010.

3 *The New Brussels I*, Article 81. The new Regulation, 1215/2012 of 12 December 2012, was published in the *Official Journal of the European Union* on 20 December 2012 (L 351).

of any other courts". Such an agreement is deemed exclusive "unless the parties have expressly provided otherwise."

Article 3 also set up formal conditions for a choice of court agreement. Such an agreement must be concluded or documented in writing or by any other means of communication, which renders information accessible so as to be usable for subsequent reference. Finally, the provision establishes the doctrine of separability; an exclusive choice of court agreement that forms part of a contract shall be treated as an agreement independent of the other terms of the contract. The validity of the exclusive choice of court agreement cannot be contested solely on the ground that the contract is not valid.

As far as the operative provisions on jurisdiction of the Convention are concerned, Article 5 determine the obligations of the chosen court or courts, and Article 6 determines the obligations of other courts, that is to say any court not designated in the choice of court agreement.

According to Article 5, the court or courts of a Contracting State designated in an exclusive choice of court agreement shall have jurisdiction to decide a dispute to which the agreement applies, unless the agreement is null and void under the law of that State. The reference to "the law of that State" includes the choice of law rules of the forum State.[4]

According to Article 5(2), a court that has jurisdiction under paragraph 1 shall not decline to exercise jurisdiction on the ground that the dispute should be decided in a court of another State. This provision precludes resort to the doctrines of forum non conveniens and *lis pendens*.[5]

A court of a Contracting State other than that of the chosen court shall suspend or dismiss proceedings to which an exclusive choice of court agreement applies (see Article 6). However, that court may nevertheless take the case, if: (a) the agreement is null and void under the law of the State of the chosen court; (b) a party lacked the capacity to conclude the agreement under the law of the State of the court seized; (c) giving effect to the agreement would lead to a manifest injustice or would be manifestly contrary to the public policy of the State of the court seized; (d) for exceptional reasons beyond the control of the parties, the agreement cannot reasonably be performed; or (e) the chosen court has decided not to hear the case.

The Hague Convention contains neither a *lis pendens* nor a forum non conveniens provision, because there are no alternative grounds of jurisdiction under it. Consequently, under the Convention, any court seized of proceedings

4 T. Hartley and M. Dogauchi, *Explanatory Report on the 2005 Hague Choice of Court Agreements Convention* (2007) 43 (*The Hague Explanatory Report*). See also R.A. Brand and P.M. Herrup, *The 2005 Hague Convention on Choice of Court Agreements. Commentary and Documents* (2008).

5 *The Hague Explanatory Report* 44.

is entitled to determine the validity of an exclusive choice of court agreement. It can be the court first seized regardless whether this court was designated in the agreement or not. In the former case, Article 5 applies, in the latter, Article 6.

Furthermore, in case of concurrent proceedings, the Convention does not provide a mechanism for determining which of the courts seized should have, if any, priority to determine the validity of the choice of court agreement. Consequently, parallel proceedings, both involving the question of the validity of the exclusive choice of court agreement, may exist in two Contracting States.

Judgments given by courts designated in an exclusive choice of court agreement shall be recognised and enforced under *the Hague Convention*, see Article 8. Recognition and enforcement are subject to some exceptions listed in Article 9. In this context, Article 9(a), (b), (f) and (g) are relevant.

According to Article 9(a), recognition or enforcement may be refused if the agreement was null and void under the law of the State of the chosen court, unless the chosen court has determined that the agreement is valid. The last part of the provision means that the court addressed may not substitute its judgment for that of the chosen court. The purpose of this is to avoid conflicting rulings on the validity of the agreement among different Contracting States: they are all required to apply the law of the State of the chosen court, and they must respect any ruling on point by that court.[6]

Under Article 9(b), recognition or enforcement may be refused if a party lacked capacity to conclude the exclusive choice of court agreement under the law of the State of recognition and enforcement.

According to Article 9(f), the judgment may also be refused recognition or enforcement if it is inconsistent with a judgment given in the requested State in a dispute between the same parties.

Finally, Article 9(g) provides that the judgment may also be refused recognition or enforcement if it is inconsistent with an earlier judgment given in another State between the same parties on the same cause of action, provided that the earlier judgment fulfils the conditions necessary for its recognition in the requested State.

These provisions rest on the assumption that parallel or concurrent proceedings are possible under *the Hague Convention*. Consequently, conflicting judgments may follow even if one of the courts derived its jurisdiction from an exclusive choice of court agreement it considered valid.

6 *The Hague Explanatory Report* 54.

3. BRUSSELS I

In the European Union, *Brussels I* is the successor to the Brussels Convention from 1968 (*the Brussels Convention*), and it rests upon the revision of the Convention that took place in 1998/99.[7] It is a cornerstone of EU Law within the area of Justice and Home Affairs. These instruments have created free movement of judgments within the EU and harmonised the rules of international jurisdiction in cases where the defendant is domiciled in a Member State. They also contain provisions on choice of court agreements and concurrent proceedings.

On the other hand, Member States apply their national rules of international jurisdiction where the defendant is domiciled in a non-Member State, and they apply national law in respect of recognition and enforcement of judgments from such States.

Brussels I is in force in all Member States, including the United Kingdom, Ireland and Denmark, because the United Kingdom and Ireland decided to participate in *Brussels I* and special arrangements have been made in respect of Denmark.[8]

Generally, *Brussels I* works well. However, during 2004–2009, the European Commission conducted surveys of its application in the Member States.[9] Following these surveys, in 2009 the Commission adopted a Green Paper on the review of *Brussels I*. And, on 14 December 2010, it published a proposal for a review of the Regulation (*the Proposal*).[10]

The overall objective of *the Proposal* was to abolish the exequatur procedure. However, the Commission also took up other important issues; one of them was the issue of the efficiency of exclusive choice of court agreements and concurrent proceedings. During the recast negotiations, Member States agreed to adopt a new provision dealing with this question. However, in order to understand the new solution, it is necessary to examine the law as it is at present, that is *Brussels I*,

---

7 For the 1998/99 Revision, see P.A. Nielsen, "Behind and Beyond Brussels I. An Insider's View", in P. Demaret, I. Govaere and D. Hanf (eds) *30 Years of European Legal Studies at the College of Europe. Liber Professorum 1973/74–2003/04*. College of Europe (2005) 241–261.

8 A "Parallel" Agreement of 19 October 2005 and *Brussels I* is in force between the EU and Denmark as from 1 July 2007, see Statute No 1563 of 20 December 2006. See also P.A. Nielsen, "Brussels I and Denmark", *IPRax* (2007) 506–509.

9 B. Hess, T. Pfeiffer and P. Schlosser, Study JLS/C4/2005/03, *Report on the Application of Regulation Brussels I*, (2007) (*the Heidelberg Report*). See also A. Nuyts, *Study on Residual Jurisdiction* (2007) and Groupe europêen de droit international privé (GEDIP), "Proposed Amendment of Regulation 44/2000 in order to apply it to External Situations", *IPRax* (2009) 283–284.

10 Proposal for a Regulation of the European Parliament and of the Council on Jurisdiction and the Recognition and Enforcement of Judgments in Civil and Commercial Matters of 14 December 2010, COM (2010) 748 final/2. The Green Paper on the review of Council Regulation (EC) No 44/2000 on Jurisdiction and the Recognition and Enforcement of Judgments in Civil and Commercial Matters, COM (2009) 175 final.

Article 23 on choice of court agreements, Article 27 on *lis pendens*, and the Gasser judgment of the European Court of Justice (ECJ) that drew attention to the issue.

3.1. BRUSSELS I, CHOICE OF COURT AGREEMENTS AND LIS PENDENS

Article 23 of *Brussels I* is the key provision for choice of court agreements. According to this provision, where the parties, one or more of whom is domiciled in a Member State, have agreed that a court or the courts of a Member State are to have jurisdiction to settle any disputes which have arisen or which may arise in connection with a particular legal relationship, that court or those courts shall have jurisdiction. Such jurisdiction shall be exclusive unless the parties have agreed otherwise.

Furthermore, formal requirements are set out in Article 23, which provides that the agreement conferring jurisdiction shall be either: (a) in writing or evidenced in writing; or (b) in a form which accords with practices which the parties have established between themselves; or (c) in international trade or commerce, in a form which accords with a usage of which the parties are or ought to have been aware and which in such trade or commerce is widely known to, and regularly observed by, parties to contracts of the type involved in the particular trade or commerce concerned. Finally, any communication by electronic means, which provides a durable record of the agreement, shall be equivalent to "writing".

Contrary to *the Hague Convention*, *Brussels I* provides for alternative grounds of jurisdiction, for instance for contracts in Article 5(1) and for tort and delict in Article 5(3). Consequently, in order to avoid parallel proceedings and conflicting judgments, *Brussels I* has a *lis pendens* provision dealing with the situation where proceedings involving the same cause of action and between the same parties are brought in the courts of different Member States.

For such cases *Brussels I*, Article 27, provides that any other court than the one first seized, shall of its motion stay its proceedings until such time as the jurisdiction of the court first seized is established. Where the jurisdiction of the court first seized is established, any other court shall decline jurisdiction in favour of that court.

The relationship between Articles 23 and 27 is crucial for the efficiency of exclusive choice of court agreements. The relationship was settled in 2003 when the ECJ delivered the Gasser judgment.

3.2. THE GASSER JUDGMENT

For years, the Gasser judgment has been meet with significant criticism.[11] A contract had been concluded between an Austrian party, Gasser, and an Italian party, Misat. The contract provided, inter alia, that the Austrian courts should have exclusive jurisdiction to determine any dispute between the parties. However, Misat instituted proceedings against Gasser in Italy under Article 5(3) of *Brussels I* claiming that the exclusive choice of court agreement was invalid. Subsequently, Gasser instituted proceedings in Austria relying on the choice of court agreement, but Misat claimed that the Austrian court should stay its proceedings until such time as the Italian court, having been seized first, had decided whether the choice of court agreement were invalid, and, in the affirmative, whether the court had jurisdiction under Article 5(3).

The ECJ ruled that the Austrian court should stay its proceedings and wait for the decision of the Italian court on its jurisdiction. The ECJ referred to the fact that the proceedings in Italy were instituted first. Due to the inefficiency of the Italian court system, it would probably take years for the Italian court to reach a decision on its jurisdiction. Meanwhile, proceedings in other Member States should be put on hold due to the applicability of Article 27.

The Gasser judgment created the phenomenon of "Italian Torpedoes" meaning that a party can obtain de facto immunity from court proceedings in the Member States of the EU for years, provided that party wanting immunity manages to institute proceedings first in Italy.[12] This is an unacceptable situation, especially where the parties have entered into a choice of court agreement. Consequently, in its *Proposal*, the Commission stated:[13]

> "The efficiency of choice of court agreements needs to be improved. Currently, the Regulation obliges the court designated by the parties in a choice of court agreement to stay proceedings if another court has been seised first. This rule enables litigants acting in bad faith to delay the resolution of the dispute in the

---

[11] Case C-116/02 (Gasser). For strong criticism, see T. Hartley, "Le droit international privé: esprit et methods", in *Mélanges en l'honneur de Paul Lagarde* (2005) 322–335, and R. Fentiman "Case Note on Case C-116/02 (Erich Gasser GmbH v. Misat Srl)", *Common Market Law Review* (2005) 241–259.

[12] Italian Torpedoes were invented by M. Franzosi, "Worldwide Patent Litigation and the Italian Torpedo", *European Intellectual Property Review* (1997) 382. See also *The Heidelberg Report*, 159 and 194–201, characterising the problem as "serious", M. Bogdan, "The Brussels/Lugano Lis Pendens Rule and the "Italian Torpedo", *Scandinavian Studies in Law* (2007) 89, J. Fawcett, "The Impact of Article 6(1) of the ECHR on Private International Law", *International and Comparative Law Quarterly* (2007) 1, and L. Merret, "The Enforcement of Jurisdiction Agreements within the Brussels Regime", *International and Comparative Law Quarterly* (2006) 315.

[13] *The Proposal* 3.

agreed forum by first seizing a non-competent court. This possibility creates additional costs and delays and undermines the legal certainty and predictability of dispute resolution which choice of court agreements should bring about."

3.3. THE NEW SOLUTION

Consultations prior to the recast negotiations in 2011 and 2012 showed large support from stakeholders and Member States to improve the efficiency of choice of court agreements under *Brussels I*. Among the various ways to achieve that objective, preference was expressed for granting priority to the chosen court to decide on its jurisdiction. Such a mechanism would largely accord with the system established in *the Hague Convention*, Article 5(1), thus ensuring a coherent approach within the European Union and at the international level were the Union to conclude the Hague Convention in the future.[14] Consequently, the Commission proposed the following provision at Article 32(2) of *the Proposal*:

> 2. With the exception of agreements governed by Sections 3, 4 and 5 of this Chapter, where an agreement referred to in paragraph 1 confers exclusive jurisdiction to a court or the courts of a Member State, the courts of other Member States shall have no jurisdiction over the dispute until such time as the court or courts designated in the agreement decline their jurisdiction.

The Commission's proposal was basically sound. Consequently, it was adopted, but with a number of clarifications and improvements, see *the New Brussels I*, Article 31(2)-(4):

> 2. Without prejudice to Article 25, where a court of a Member State on which an agreement as referred to in Article 25 confers exclusive jurisdiction is seised, any court of another Member State shall stay the proceedings until such time as the court seised on the basis of the agreement declares that it has no jurisdiction under the agreement.
>
> 3. Where the court designated in the agreement has established jurisdiction in accordance with the agreement, any court of another Member State shall decline jurisdiction in favour of that court.
>
> 4. Paragraphs 2 and 3 shall not apply to matters referred to in Sections 3, 4 or 5 where the policyholder, the insured, a beneficiary of the insurance contract, the injured party, the consumer or the employee is the claimant and the agreement is not valid under a provision contained within those Sections.

---

14 *The Proposal* 8.

The adopted provision is a new *lis pendens* mechanism that ensures that the agreed court and only the agreed court can determine the validity of the choice of court agreement if proceedings are initiated before that court. Thus, *the New Brussels I*, Article 31(2) and (3) is an exception to the general *lis pendens* provision in Article 29 of the new Regulation.

The purpose of the new provision is to "enhance the effectiveness of exclusive choice-of-court agreements and to avoid abusive litigation tactics", see *the New Brussels I*, Recital 22. The provision "ensure[s] that [...] the designated court has priority to decide on the validity of the agreement and on the extent to which the agreement applies to the dispute pending before it." It also follows from Recital 22, that the designated court should be able to proceed irrespectively of whether or not the non-designated court has already decided on the stay of proceedings.

The new provision only applies to exclusive choice of court agreements. Consequently, it will not apply where the parties have entered into conflicting exclusive choice of court agreements or entered into a non-exclusive choice of court agreement. Finally, the provision will not apply if a court designated in an exclusive choice of court agreement has been seized first. In such cases, Article 29, the general *lis pendens* provision, applies and gives the designated court priority to decide the validity of the choice of court agreement. Thus, the new *lis pendens* provision only applies where the designated court has been seized after proceedings have been initiated in a non-designated court.

The new *lis pendens* provision will not come into play in two instances.

First, it only applies "subject to Article 26" of *the New Brussels I*. Consequently, if the defendant in the proceedings instituted before a court not designated in the choice of court agreement does not contest the court's jurisdiction, he has in accordance with Article 26 implicitly accepted the court's jurisdiction and waived the express choice of court agreement.

Second, if the defendant in the proceedings instituted before a court not designated in the choice of court agreement does not institute proceedings before the designated court, the latter court is not given priority to decide on the validity of the choice of court agreement. It is not sufficient for the defendant to invoke the exclusive choice of court agreement before the court not designated in the agreement.

Furthermore, the new *lis pendens* provision only applies where the chosen court establishes jurisdiction on the basis of the choice of court agreement. The new mechanism will not apply where the chosen court sets the choice of court agreement aside, but assumes jurisdiction, for instance, under Article 5(1). In this case, Article 29, the ordinary *lis pendens* mechanism, will apply. Finally, the new *lis pendens* mechanism will not apply to cases involving weak parties under *the New Brussels I*, Chapter II, Section 3, 4 and 5; that is, insurance, consumer and employment cases, where the weak party is the claimant and the agreement is not valid under Arts. 15, 19 and 23.

The solution in Article 32(2) and (3) is partly inspired by the doctrine of "competence over the competence", which is well known and well functioning in international commercial arbitration; see, for instance, Article 8 and Article 16 of the Model Law on International Commercial Arbitration.[15]

In the Gasser case, the new Article 32(2) and (3) would have led to the result that the Austrian courts would have exclusive jurisdiction to determine the validity of the choice of court agreement, provided that proceedings were instituted before that court in accordance with the choice of court agreement. Furthermore, the Italian court would be obliged to stay the proceedings before it at the time proceedings were instituted in Austria. Finally, the Italian court would be obliged to decline jurisdiction if the Austrian court established jurisdiction in accordance with the agreement. If the Austrian court came to the conclusion that it did not have jurisdiction in accordance with the agreement, the Italian court could continue with the case.

3.4. CHOICE OF LAW AND SEPARABILITY

Brussels I does not have a provision on choice of law for choice of court agreements. However, it has a uniform standard for formal validity in Article 23, see section 3.1. During the recast negotiations, the Commission proposed a choice of law rule on the substantive validity of choice of court agreements; see *the Proposal* Article 23(1). According to this proposal, this issue is governed by "the law of the Member State", whose courts are granted jurisdiction under the choice of court agreement.

The Commission's proposal was adopted. It is based on the similar solution in *the Hague Convention*, in which a chosen court shall determine the validity of a choice of court agreement under "the law of that State".[16] However, the reference in the Convention to "the law of that State" includes the choice of law rules of the forum State.[17] It was not very clear from the Commission's proposal whether the reference to "the law of that Member State" included the choice of law rules or not, but the intention was that it should be the case. Therefore, *the New Brussels I*, Recital 20 makes it clear that the reference to "the law of that Member State", like *the Hague Convention*, includes the choice of law rules of that Member State.

15 UNCITRAL's Model Law on International Commercial Arbitration, as adopted by the United Nations Commission on International Trade Law on 21 June 1985 and amended on 4 December 2006.

16 *The Proposal* 9.

17 *The Hague Explanatory Report* 43.

The Commission's proposal was presented as "a harmonised conflict of law rule on the substantive validity of choice of court agreements, thus ensuring a similar outcome on this matter whatever the court seised".[18] However, this is not the case, because the adopted rule does nothing but codifying the status quo. At present, each Member State applies its own choice of law rules in respect of substantive validity of choice of court agreements. The reason for this is that neither the Rome Convention nor the Rome I Regulation on choice of law for contractual obligations cover choice of court agreements; see Article 1(2)(d) of these instruments.[19] Consequently, choice of law for substantive validity of choice of court agreements is decided differently in the Member States. Some apply *lex fori*, others apply *lex contractus* and others a combination of these two laws.

In 2006–2008, during the negotiations on the Rome I Regulation, this issue could have been resolved, but it was never really on the agenda.[20] Therefore, the recast negotiations on *Brussels I* were an obvious occasion to adopt a real uniform choice of law rule for all Member States. Considering the overall intention of the recast procedure in respect of choice of court agreements, enhancing the efficiency of choice of court agreements, a choice of law rule based on the principle of alternative validity should have been adopted. This principle, well known in the Rome Convention and the Rome I Regulation for choice of law for formal validity of contractual obligations, would entail that the choice of court agreement should be upheld, provided it was valid in substance under either the law of the Member State in which the chosen court was (*lex fori*), or the law that governed the dispute (*lex causae*).[21]

The Commission did not propose to codify the doctrine of separability for choice of court agreements. The doctrine has been recognised by the ECJ.[22] However, during the recast negotiations on *Brussels I*, it was agreed to adopt this doctrine, see *the New Brussels I*, Article 25(5). As mentioned in Section 2, the doctrine is also applied in *the Hague Convention*, Article 3(d).

---

18 *The Proposal* 9.

19 Convention of 19 June 1980 on the Law Applicable to Contractual Obligations, and Regulation No 593/2008 on the same subject matter. The Regulation is in force in all Member States except Denmark.

20 See O. Lando and P.A. Nielsen, "The Rome I Regulation", *Common Market Law Review* (2008) 1687–1725 and O. Lando and P.A. Nielsen, "The Rome I Proposal", *Journal of Private International Law* (2007) 29–51.

21 The Convention, Article 9, and the Regulation, Article 11.

22 Case C-269/95 *(Benincasa)*.

4. CONCLUSION

Both *the Hague Convention* and *the New Brussels I* address the issue of parallel proceedings with regard to disputes covered by an exclusive choice of court agreement.

On the one hand, they have a lot in common. Both instruments accept the doctrine of separability for choice of court agreements, and they also provide that the court or courts chosen in the agreement shall determine the substantive validity of the agreement under its own law, including its choice of law rules. Furthermore, both instruments contain form standards for such agreements.

On the other hand, the two instruments differ significantly on *lis pendens* in respect of exclusive choice of court agreements, that is to say where parallel proceedings are pending in different States in spite of the exclusive choice of court agreement. Whereas *the Hague Convention* does not regulate the question of which court should have priority to determine the validity of the agreement, *the New Brussels I* give strict priority to the agreed court if proceedings are instituted before it. The difference can be explained by the fact that Regulation, unlike the Convention, has a much broader scope and alternative bases of jurisdiction. However, the new European solution could, in principle, be adopted in *the Hague Convention*, should it be revised.

THE RELATIONSHIPS BETWEEN LATIN AMERICA AND THE HAGUE CONFERENCE REGARDING THE RECENT DEVELOPMENTS OF PRIVATE INTERNATIONAL LAW

Didier OPERTTI BADÁN
Professor of Private International Law in Uruguay
Member of the Uruguayan Institute of Private International Law
Member of the Governing Council of UNIDROIT
Former Uruguayan Minister of Foreign Affairs
Former Secretary General of LAFTA

I. GENERAL APPRAISAL

It is a remarkable honour for me to participate in this Liber Amicorum dedicated to Hans van Loon, a highly justified homage than in our particular case requires both an institutional and a personal recognition for his permanent relationship with Latin American countries and particularly with Uruguay. In 1996 I participated under similar conditions in the Liber Amicorum dedicated to Georges A.L. Droz.[1] On that occasion I also did it under the spell of personal and institutional testimonies fully justified by the cooperation initiated by Droz in 1975 (CIDIP-I, Panama)[2] and that of Mr. van Loon afterwards made deeper by tightening the ties between the Hague's universal organization and the Inter American codification.

1 OPERTTI BADÁN, Didier, "L'œuvre de la CIDIP dans le contexte du Droit International Privé Actuel", in *Liber Amicorum Georges A.L. Droz*; A. BORRÁS *et al.* (eds.), *E Pluribus Unum*, 269–286, 1996 Kluwer Law International, Printed in the Netherlands.

2 CIDIP stands for Inter-American Specialized Conference of Private International Law.

The time has come now to examine to what extent is this regionalism alive and how much of that possibility is linked to the results that the Hague Conference may reach in the works that it is nowadays carrying out.

Both the universal and the regional approach have, in my opinion, wide acceptance in this shared undertaking of regulating private legal relationships through legal rules. The former are each day more frequent and complex, and they require legal answers that are suitable for subjects and provide them with legal certainty and predictability, like Mr. van Loon has been doing as the Secretary General of the Conference. In this sense, he has deepened this relationship by creating permanent coordination activities with States and public organizations (Unidroit and UNCITRAL) and private ones (ASADIP – American Association of Private International Law, in our region). That enables us nowadays to follow closely The Hague works and, as far as possible, to participate effectively either as delegates or as experts, though regretfully not always in person, as we would desire. All the preceding explains that in 2013 we can continue the reciprocal cooperation through distinguished Latin American jurists or regional academic associations and national institutes, *e.g.*, Mexican Academy of Private International and Comparative Law and Uruguayan Institute of Private International Law. The permanent and synchronized connection through an active and efficient Latin American expert[3] has contributed to that purpose. This is the case of the Uruguayan Institute of Private International Law, which has answered the questionnaires and provided its proposals in several subjects of The Hague's agenda, supporting the working method and trying to contribute to it with a positive vision that seeks avoiding lack of communication.

There is no doubt that this coordination can be deepened in our region with the leading participation of the Organization of American States (OAS), which role through the several CIDIP has been very relevant in the past. We should remember the role of the Inter American Children's Institute, with Ubaldino Calvento and its central office in Montevideo, in The Hague's and CIDIP's codification work in family law. These contacts were updated with lively interest by Hans van Loon.

In the light of these initial appraisals and assuming the understanding of the organizers, which I take for granted, Professor Cecilia Fresnedo de Aguirre is beside me in this work.[4]

---

3 Mr. Ignacio Goicoechea.

4 She is the Academic Secretary of the Uruguayan Institute of Private International Law and is responsible in great measure of the permanent communication with the work of The Hague. She has also participated personally in the latter's working sessions with a positive contribution to the proposed solutions. She has published specialized articles about different Private International Law matters in Europe.

Finally, it is worth pointing out that when we refer to Latin America we are choosing the above-mentioned process conducted by CIDIP – which also include other countries, *e.g.*, USA and Canada –, as far as it represents a *communis opinio* attributable to an important number of countries (19) in the region.

Besides, it is not the purpose of this article to examine the different conventions of The Hague and CIDIP but to get closer to the subject from a global personal perspective that tries to identify the connecting points between both codification exercises, showing objectives and trends.

II. UNAVOIDABLE HISTORICAL PRECEDENTS

Since 1824, as Tatiana B. de Maekelt[5] reminds us, a motion was filed at the Panama Congress convened by Simon Bolivar for the "prompt beginning of the codification works on Private International Law." To confirm that foundational impulse in the region, we cite here the 1878 Lima Congress, unfortunately interrupted by the Pacific War, and the 1888–1889 Montevideo Congress, both preceded by proposals of great jurists: that of Antonio Arena – with the influence of Pradier Foderé – in 1878 and that of Gonzalo Ramírez in 1887. The latter points out in a letter signed in Buenos Aires in June 21 of that year and addressed to the Uruguayan Minister of Foreign Affairs, Mr Julio Herrera y Obes, the need to enter into a treaty "that includes all the subjects that are the object of the science that is known in *ius gentium* as Private International Law".[6] We must add that the Ramírez' proposal was approved by Sáenz Peña in Argentina.

The details of CIDIP's historical process have been synthesized in CIDIP-VI' documents[7] and we refer to them.

The First Hague Conference was held, by the impulse of Tobias M. Asser, who took back Mancini's initiative, on September 1893. Fragmentary treaties with

5 Maekelt, Tatiana B. de, "La codificación Interamericana desde la Perspectiva de la Codificación Estatal de Derecho Internacional Privado", in *El futuro de la codificación del Derecho Internacional Privado en América. De la CIDIP VI a la CIDIP VII*, Córdoba, Argentina, Alveroni Ediciones, 2005, pp. 27–51, p. 28.

6 Ramírez, Gonzalo, *Proyecto de Código de Derecho Internacional Privado y su Comentario,* Buenos Aires, Félix Lajouane, Editor, M DCCC LXXXVIII, p. 3. See also Acts of CIDIP-I, 1975, Vol. II, p. 318–320, where M. Droz manifested: "dicen en Europa que la Conferencia de La Haya es una vieja dama del Derecho Internacional, porque nació en 1893, pero que en la Conferencia de La Haya, se sabe bien que tiene una hermana mayor, la Conferencia Panamericana, que fue la primera en promover la codificación del Derecho Internacional Privado. Por eso puedo asegurar que la Conferencia seguirá todos los esfuerzos con mucho interés y mucha atención." (p. 318).

7 Document prepared by the Secretary General, entitled "The history of the CIDIP Process", in *CIDIP-VI, Documents*, Vol. II, Washington D.C., 2002, p. 11 *et seq.*

limited scope and of difficult application, with an exaggerated casuistic concern,[8] where approved though without linking effects.

A great number of States incorporated to The Hague, which created close connections with other organizations. Consequently, The Hague acquired an "unquestionable universality".[9]

III. UNIVERSALISM AND REGIONALISM: A RENOVATED DEBATE

This contribution aims neither at reproducing nor at reviving overcome contradictory or self-excluding schemes of universalism and regionalism, as opposing political and legal terms, but to respect each other's scopes of functioning in the quest for a common interest. The Hague performs at the international level a very important task, very well received by States, doctrine and private agents. On the part of CIDIP – the most recent stage of the regional codification (1975 to date) – is playing its own role with the impulse of the Inter American Juridical Committee, of the legal area of the Secretary General of the OAS and with the collaboration of experts. Both codification exercises are equally valid in its own scope and the results they reached, though diverse, contribute to this process of compromise of the States with Private International Law when they approve the various Conventions, which in the case of CIDIP are twenty two in force and being applied – open to the adhesion of third States, except, *e.g.*, the 1981 Caracas Convention on Extradition –, as well as other instruments and Declarations. In the case of The Hague, since 1893 to date, there are twenty-eight Conventions in force; this intergovernmental organization keeps on producing its fruits. This parallelism does not intend to assimilate both processes but to underline its common objectives, without prejudice of the differences.

The work of CIDIP has had a strong influence in the national codification of private international law of several countries, *i.e.*, Peru, Venezuela and Uruguay, among others.[10]

---

8 Alfonsín, Quintín, *Teoría del Derecho Privado Internacional*, Montevideo, Idea, 1984, p. 293.

9 Van Loon, Hans, "Quelques Aspects de la Mondialisation dans le domaine des conflits de juridictions", in *Travaux du Comité Français de Droit International Privé, Années 2004–2006*, Paris, Ed. A. Pedone, 2008, pp. 227–243, p. 227–228.

10 See Opertti, Didier & Fresnedo, Cecilia, "The latest trends in Latin American Private International Law: The Uruguayan 2009 General Law on Private International Law", in *Yearbook of Private International Law*, Vol. XI, 2009, Munich, sellier.elp, 2010, pp. 305–337 (the referred Law is still under parliamentary consideration).

The Hague offers in some cases solutions that are not included in regional legal developments:[11] testamentary dispositions, succession of estates of deceased persons, protection of adults, among others. That is why, before trying our own codification it is unavoidable to consider the merit of these solutions to determine whether they serve to the interests of our region's civil and commercial private agents. To that purpose we must keep on working on the fact that both the conflict of laws system and that of the substantive rules shape current answers both from the theoretical and positive point of view. It suffices to remember here the ancient 1889 Montevideo Treaties, which in spite of its limited 1940 revision are still in force. Thus, far from being dogmatic approach, this one takes into account the use and convenience of international instruments in terms of complementarity when this is possible, or respecting each other's scopes of application. The formulas adopted by each forum correspond to a specified frame of legal relationships and to the particular needs of the covered scope.[12]

The Hague and CIDIP share the main objective of providing solutions to the conflict of laws and jurisdictions regarding concrete and differentiated legal relationships, and appeal, when that is possible, to substantive or direct rules.[13]

The doctrine has discussed vigorously the possibilities of harmonizing the two codification efforts referred, rather prematurely and even with certain prejudices from ones and the others, which were overcome due to maturity and good offices of friends who are also relevant jurists. That is how we find, during the last decades, debates that challenge the justification of the regional codification, which has been qualified of rhetoric, not without certain lightness. This means lack of knowledge and misunderstanding of the scientific community's consensus in qualifying The Hague, from Latin America, as the lighthouse illuminating our Private International Law. From the starting point of the asymmetry between The Hague and CIDIP regarding their organization and available material resources, we assume the task of technical interchange without any prejudice and convinced that this is the best way.

It must be borne in mind that CIDIP is an organ of the OAS (Article 52, paragraph g of the Charter), which has 34 active Member States – Cuba is

[11] We refer here to the subjects dealt with in CIDIP. Besides, the 1928 Bustamante Code and the 1889 and 1940 Montevideo Treaties – all of them in force – deal with most of the subjects ruled in The Hague.

[12] See Opertti Badán, Didier, "La Codificación del Derecho Internacional Privado: Análisis Comparativo de la Labor Realizada por la Conferencia de Derecho Internacional Privado de La Haya y por la CIDIP", in *España y la codificación internacional del Derecho internacional privado. Terceras jornadas de Derecho internacional privado,* San Lorenzo de El Escorial, 13 y 14 de diciembre de 1991, Madrid, Eurolex, 1993, pp. 261–283.

[13] See, for example, Inter-American Convention on Domicile of Natural Persons in Private International Law (CIDIP-II, Montevideo, 1979), Hague Convention of 5 October 1961 Abolishing the Requirement of Legalisation for Foreign Public Documents, among others.

suspended since 1962 –, called "Inter American Specialized Conference", which is convened periodically by the General Assembly, the maximum organ of the system. Its technical support come from the Inter American Juridical Committee and the Secretary of Legal Issues of the Secretary General, without prejudice of the Expert Meetings and specialists' works. The Conference itself gathers delegates from the Member States – the only ones enabled to vote –, some of which do not include experts. Under these conditions its members are tempted to use concepts of sovereignty that are very much rooted and strong traditions both in the drafting of projects and in the diplomatic process of approval.

In spite of the latter, I can state from my experience that the CIDIP has functioned without political influences and obeying prevailing technical criteria, due to the active participation of some delegates.

Even when two great legal systems coexist in CIDIP – common law and civil law – it is very difficult to harmonize them at a regional level, even more after the incorporation of the Caribbean States in the OAS. However, in order to avoid breaking the unity of the system, formulas of both legal families has been combined, as far as possible, though with different results – *e.g.* the 1979 Convention on General Rules, particularly underlying policies and substantive justice- and even though a very scarce ratification from the United States of America is obtained – only two Conventions – and none from Canada.

In this scenario a very strange phenomenon occurs because on the one hand there is an active negotiation with the common law countries, exhausting creativity in the selection of connections and transactional substantive solutions, but on the other hand the aim of a wide adhesion is not reached.

The aforementioned difficulties seem more typical of the regional codification, but in our opinion it is not about confronting The Hague and CIDIP, but to recognize to the former its universality and to CIDIP's private International Law not a divisive and autonomous role that might hinder harmony. On the contrary, certain nexus *ratione materiae* are evident and show common objectives.[14]

We must point out that both in The Hague and in CIDIP there are Latin American States with a strong activism, like for example Argentina, Brazil, Mexico, Paraguay, Uruguay and Venezuela, with a relevant participation in both spheres.

A full centralization by means of a universal international codification could only be based on the participation of Latin American States as peers. At the lack of that solution, the region's adhesion to international solutions becomes more complex and uses to leave the debate to non technical grounds, which put the focus not in the product's quality but in its gestation. It is worth to point out

[14] *E.g.*, Child Abduction and maintenance.

the formula of the Inter American Convention on International Child Abduction (CIDIP-IV, Montevideo, 1989), Article 34.

IV. CIDIP: INTER AMERICAN OR LATIN AMERICAN?

Very well known authors specialized in the matter like Jurgen Samtleben[15] and Diego Fernández Arroyo[16] have formulated the question in the title with a strictly technical approach and suggested that in fact the work of CIDIP has not reached an Inter American scope, because of the lack of accession of the United States, Canada and the Anglophone Caribbean States to its conventions. After recognizing this fact we think that we must distinguish between the institutional competence of the Conference (CIDIP) within the framework of the OAS and therefore including all the Member States, and their effective participation in the Conventions' negotiations and forward accession to them.

The question might lead to suppose a certain exclusivism, a non confirmed approach because of the approval of CIDIP Conventions that register a strong influence from the common law. We can quote, for example, the 1975 Panama Convention on Arbitration, the 1979 Montevideo Convention on General Rules, the 1994 Mexico Convention on contracts, the 2002 Washington model law on secured transactions, which have included solutions proposed by representatives of the common law. It is also very clear that Latin American States, due to its common source – civil law –, are more prone to reach agreements.

However, all the previous statements mean that CIDIP offers a scenario open to different formulas both regarding codifying methods and its solutions, which tries to avoid possible conflicts of repeating or interfering with The Hague's solutions, to which it approximates.

---

15 Samtleben, Jurgen, "Los resultados de la labor codificadora de la CIDIP desde la perspectiva europea", in *España y la codificación internacional del Derecho internacional privado. Terceras jornadas de Derecho internacional privado,* San Lorenzo de El Escorial, 13 y 14 de diciembre de 1991, Madrid, Eurolex, 1993, pp. 293–302.

16 Fernández Arroyo, Diego P., "La reglamentación de las relaciones de tráfico privado externo entre España e Iberoamérica: elementos para la definición de una actitud española", in *España y la codificación internacional del Derecho internacional privado. Terceras jornadas de Derecho internacional privado,* San Lorenzo de El Escorial, 13 y 14 de diciembre de 1991, Madrid, Eurolex, 1993, pp. 303–322 and "¿Qué CIDIP para cuál América?", in *Avances del Derecho Internacional Privado en América Latina, Liber Amicorum* Jürgen Samtleben, Coordinadores: Jan Kleinheisterkamp y Gonzalo A. Lorenzo Idiarte, Max Planck Institut, Montevideo, FCU, 1ª ed., January 2002, pp. 31–54. Besides, Fernández Arroyo is the author of a must-have book on the codification work of CIDIP: *La Codificación del Derecho Internacional Privado en América Latina. Ámbitos de producción jurídica y orientaciones metodológicas*, Madrid, Eurolex, 1994.

I must also state that a major inclusion of the countries in the region with a developed economy at a world level would lead them to global scenarios and in the light of their solutions, to meet afterwards the regional solutions. That is the case of the United States. However, and as a counter face of this statement, it is important to verify that two Latin American States that appear as the ten first economies in the world – Mexico and Brazil – are an active party in CIDIP, and in the case of Brazil, its recent accession to several Conventions of CIDIP shows the dynamic of the codification process and the changes of perspective of the States regarding this process. In our opinion, there is a positive element to point out here when it comes to make balances about the utility or convenience of the work of CIDIP.

V. PRESENT AND FUTURE OF THE RELATIONSHIP BETWEEN CIDIP AND THE HAGUE

From a realistic perspective of its present situation, we can state that while The Hague offers a permanent functioning framework, which ensures the continuity of its working process, CIDIP goes through latent periods of variable duration, which is typical of its nature: it is a periodical meeting convened by a political organ, the General Assembly of the OAS. OAS Member States do not consider those themes without a tangible political interest a priority. Thus, Private International Law and the mobilization of CIDIP require an institutional political effort which is absolutely different from that of The Hague. That is why those Latin American States that are interested in Private International Law development, like Uruguay, must keep on participating actively in both scenarios, without excluding UNCITRAL, Unidroit and others developed by the regional integration mechanisms, like MERCOSUR. Whatever the case, they should not accept a legal homogenization in which we do not believe.

Likewise, those Latin American states which are members of The Hague, even outside CIDIP, would be able to submit at the former these propositions with the support of the Inter American system on subjects that are not exclusively regional and give an answer to issues of an undoubtedly general interest, *e.g.*, transboundary movements and migration of people, electronic commerce, international investment contracts, consumer protection, among others. The approach should be ecumenical and not parochial.

We must analyse the link between The Hague and experts' private organizations, like ASADIP. The main authorities of The Hague, and certainly among them the honoured Hans van Loon, have actively participated in some of ASADIP's meetings, which have enabled the sharing of concepts and opinions regarding the points of the agenda. We can say that a truly strategic alliance has been consolidated between both institutions.

By requiring through questionnaires the opinion of specialists and Institutes from the region on its agenda's subjects, The Hague could reach a technical representation and its Diplomatic Conference could opportunely profit from it.[17]

As a part of the present as well as of The Hague's future influence, we can refer here to the more recent works of the Conference to draft optional rules, particularly the Convention of 30 June 2005 on choice of court agreements and the present works on the draft Principles on the choice of law in international contracts.[18]

The drafting of an optional rule – of a non-State nature – would show the difficulties The Hague experiences to reach the approval of its Conventions by the States, as it was made evident with the intent of revision of the Brussels Convention on jurisdiction, as well as with the formula on choice of court agreements in commercial matters.[19]

Both subjects have a particular interest because they correspond to an approach that opens bigger spaces to the parties' private will within the

[17] For example, the Answer of the Uruguayan Institute of Private International Law (IUDIPr) to the Questionnaires sent by the American Association of Private International Law (ASADIP) in February 2011. The Report was drafted by the Institute's authorities (Profs. Drs. Eduardo Tellechea Bergman and Cecilia Fresnedo de Aguirre, with the participation of Prof. Dr. Didier Opertti Badán) and approved by the Institute's Plenary in its session of 23 March 2011. The Questionnaire was addressed by The President of the Inter-American Juridical Committee, João Grandino Rodas, to the Member States, academics, members of the Bar Associations and other entities specialized in Private International Law.

[18] See: van Loon, Hans, (Travaux); Usunier, Laurence, "La Convention de La Haye du 30 juin 2005 sur les accords d'élection de for. Beaucoup de bruit pour rien?", *Rev. crit. DIP*, 99 (1) janvier-mars 2010, pp. 37–81; Bureau Permanent de la Conférence de La Haye de droit international privé, "Choix de la loi applicable aux contrats du commerce international: Des Principes de La Haye?", *Rev. crit. DIP*, 99 (1) janvier-mars 2010, pp. 83–102; Moreno Rodríguez, José, "Los contratos y La Haya: ¿ancla al pasado o puente al futuro?, J. Basedow / D.P. Fernández Arroyo / J. Moreno Rodríguez (coordinadores), *¿Cómo se codifica hoy el derecho comercial internacional?*, Asunción, CEDEP / Thomson Reuters / La Ley Paraguaya, 2010, pp. 245–339, and "Contracts and Non-State Law in Latin America", *Rev. dr. Unif.* 2011–4, pp. 877–889; Fresnedo De Aguirre, Cecilia, "La autonomía de la voluntad, ¿un cheque en blanco? Los Principios de la Conferencia de La Haya", in *El derecho internacional privado en los procesos de integración regional,* Diego P. Fernández Arroyo / Juan José Obando Peralta (Coordinadores), Jornadas de la ASADIP 2011, San José, Costa Rica, 24–26 de noviembre, ASADIP / Editorial Jurídica Continental, 2011, pp. 67–92), and "Party autonomy, a blank cheque?", *Uniform Law Review* – en edición – (updated version of "La autonomía de la voluntad, ¿un cheque en blanco?", in *El derecho internacional privado en los procesos de integración regional,* Diego P. Fernández Arroyo / Juan José Obando Peralta (Coordinadores), Jornadas de la ASADIP 2011, San José, Costa Rica, 24–26 de noviembre, ASADIP / Editorial Jurídica Continental, 2011, pp. 67–92).

[19] See Van Loon, Hans, (*op. cit.* note 9).

framework of a globalized society, abided by limits that guarantee and preserve the unavoidable and final role of the States.

There is no doubt that this issue is not beyond the regional interest, with independence of the formal scope in which it is dealt with. It is worth remembering that in the ASADIP session held in Asunción in the year 2010, we exchanged ideas with José Moreno Rodríguez – Paraguayan delegate to the Working Group on the aforementioned draft Hague Principles on contracts – with the objective of reaching certain technical consensus that could be afterwards reflected during the discussion of the subject.

From all the previous commentaries we can deduce the importance of the common undertaking of The Hague and the regional system towards the progressive development and codification of Private International Law. In the context of a tight cooperation relationship, shown by The Hague when the designation of a contact officer for Latin America[20] whose performance has a wide approval.

Finally, it is unimaginable to separate the activities of The Hague from those held in the region in the field of PIL, as well as to leave aside the doctrinal developments provided by The Hague's Academy's courses, which put in tune the universal thinking with the regional approaches linked by a set of shared values mainly represented in the juridical expression. Particularly regarding the future of CIDIP, which should be cleared, we repeat that "CIDIP is a historical process that is not extinguished, that should help the region to do well in the global space, a bit 'unifying and comprising' not only in the areas of international commerce, where there is an 'hyperactivity' of private subjects, but also and specially in those where the State's initiative should be wider".[21]

The close connection between the agendas of The Hague and CIDIP has produced highly positive results, as we can see in the field of family law, v. gr. maintenance, child abduction and adoption, perhaps because widely consented values predominate there, beyond legislative differences originated in legal systems with a strong religious dependency. We cannot find a similar situation in other subjects, which respond to strong opposing interests at stake that make more difficult to reach a balance between purely individual and collective values.

---

20 See note 3.

21 Opertti Badán, Didier y Fresnedo De Aguirre, Cecilia, "El pasado y el futuro del Derecho Internacional Privado en la Organización de Estados Americanos. Reflexiones para suscitar un debate", Derecho Internacional, Mundialización y Gobernanza. Jornadas de la ASADIP, Lima, Noviembre de 2012 (Organizadores: Aníbal Sierralta – CIAC –, Claudia Lima Márques – ASADIP – y José A. Moreno Rodríguez – CEDEP), Asunción, CEDEP-ASADIP, 2012, pp. 55–69, p. 63.

VI. THE HAGUE AND THE REGIONAL SYSTEM IN GLOBALIZATION

It has been said that the real world lacks and governance that meets its emerging needs, the role of corporations, especially economic ones, the movement of persons and emigration without pause – regular or irregular –, the creation of new legal subjects, like the NGO, among others. This typical phenomenon of the 20th century, which sometimes acts as a simple pretext to explain the imbalances of economic international relationships, is in our opinion a situation to which Private International Law cannot be indifferent. We remember here Horatia Muir-Watt's eloquent expression[22] in her Course at the Academy, when she talks about the "epistemological shakings that accompany the architecture of the international order as an effect of the globalization phenomenon". She afterwards refers to "the interconnection of the markets with ruling competence that identify on the one hand the public interest, and on the other a private field given to the will".

The Hague Conference with its essentially conflict of laws method, UNCITRAL with specific solutions to international commerce, UNIDROIT with the drafting of substantive rules and general principles, and CIDIP through the methodological pluralism deal with certain specific categories in a pragmatic way. All these organizations participate in the quest for ruling formulas that fit with the technological change and the community's permanent values. This is undoubtedly a contribution to that *governance* of the international community which is still uncompleted. Although in the political aspects it counts on organizations like the United Nations, and commercial ones such as the World Trade Organization, it does not achieve – due to the mediation of the States – full effects in the application of its instruments. This obliges us to accept the problems' progressive solution as a reality.

On the grounds of the aforementioned we can identify a space for Private International Law, for neither individuals nor States or international organizations could ignore globalization. The Hague Conference has opened wide and crowded avenues regarding these subjects and it will have to cope, as Basedow[23] proposes,

---

22 MUIR-WATT, Horatia, "Aspects économiques du droit international privé (Réflexions sur l'impact de la globalisation économique sur les fondements des conflits de lois et de jurisdictions)", *Recueil des cours*, Vol. 307 (2004), pp. 25–384, especially pp. 47 *et seq.* Free translation by the author.

23 BASEDOW, Jurgen, "El derecho privado estatal y la economía: el derecho comercial como una amalgama de legislación pública y privada", in *¿Cómo se codifica hoy el derecho comercial internacional? Biblioteca de Derecho de la Globalización* (Coordinadores: J. Basedow, D.P. Fernández Arroyo, J.A. Moreno Rodríguez), Asunción, La Ley Paraguaya / CEDEP / Thomson Reuters, 2010, pp. 5–27. Free translation by the author. See also: BASEDOW, Jurgen, "Global Life, Local Life? – About the Globalization of Law and policy-Making" in *Liber*

with the task of drafting international rules that reinforce the juridical scenario in a 'private-public' amalgam – an expression of the own Basedow –, referring to commercial law, that is located at the very centre of the game of the different associations and interest groups.

The statements above are without prejudice of The Hague's compromise with the subjects related with the individual and his family, a Civil Law area which is unavoidable. The Hague has counted on Mr. van Loon as a true leader of a global agenda that though recognizing priorities has been able to keep all the big themes of the contemporary juridical society.

I could not end this contribution without thanking, in my name and in that of my collaborator, the personal manner in which Mr. van Loon has treated us as equals, in a dialog without geographical or institutional differences.

Amicorum en homenaje al Profesor Dr. Didier Opertti Badán, FCU, Montevideo, FCU, 2005, p. 817.

APPLICATION OF THE 1961 *APOSTILLE* CONVENTION IN VENEZUELAN *EXEQUATUR* PROCEEDINGS

Gonzalo PARRA-ARANGUREN
Former Judge of the International Court of Justice

I. INTRODUCTION

1. It is a great pleasure to participate in the *Liber Amicorum* dedicated to a dear friend, Hans van Loon, who has conducted in a remarkable way the work of the Hague Conference on Private International Law for several decades. My contribution deals with the *1961 Hague Convention Abolishing the Requirement of Legalization for Foreign Public Documents* (hereinafter, 1961 Hague Convention), acceded by Venezuela and in force as of 16 March 1999. However, the analysis undertaken examines only, not in an exhaustive manner, its application in *exequatur* contentious proceedings before the Venezuelan Supreme Tribunal until December 2012, inclusive, based on the judgments available on the website of the Supreme Tribunal (www.tsj.gov.ve).

2. Traditionally, the Political-Administrative Chamber of the Supreme Tribunal (hereinafter, Political-Administrative Chamber) had been competent to decide on the recognition and enforcement of foreign judgments in Venezuela, but the 2004 Organic Law of the Supreme Tribunal assigned this faculty to its Civil Cassation Chamber (hereinafter, Civil Cassation Chamber). The 2010 Law, actually in force, permits *exequatur* applications to be presented either to the Civil Cassation Chamber or to the Political-Administrative Chamber.

3. The Organic Law of the Supreme Tribunal prescribes that the President of the competent Chamber is to designate one of its Magistrates (*Ponente*) to prepare the Judgment's Draft, which is submitted to vote; decisions shall be adopted by majority, concurrent or dissenting opinions being permitted. Therefore the decision is a judgment of the Chamber, even though it is prepared by a Drafter, because it has to be examined and approved by the majority of its Magistrates. In this respect, it should be borne in mind that a substantial number of persons (experts, lawyers, legal advisers, technicians) are assigned to help each Judge in his eventual legal research, even though they are not identified by name in the web page of the Supreme Tribunal.

II. PREFERENTIAL APPLICATION OF TREATIES

4. Article 1 of the Venezuelan Private International Law Act, in force as of 6 February 1999, prescribes that cases with foreign elements, *i.e. exequatur* of decisions rendered abroad, are to be decided, in the first place, by rules of Public International Law on the matter, in particular by treaties in force between Venezuela and their State of Origin.

5. Venezuela deposited on 28 February 1985 the instrument of ratification of the *Inter-American Convention on Extraterritorial Validity of Foreign Judgments and Arbitral Awards (CIDIP-II, Montevideo 1979)* (hereinafter, 1979 Inter-American Convention). The same action was undertaken by Argentina (12 January 1983), Bolivia (10 August 1998), Brazil (27 November 1995), Colombia (10 September 1981), Ecuador (1 June 1982), Mexico (12 June 1987, only in respect to patrimonial matters), Paraguay (16 August 1985), Peru (15 May 1980) and Uruguay (15 May 1980) (www.oas.org).

6. Article 2(c) of the 1989 Inter-American Convention expressly requires that documents coming from Contracting States are to be presented with legalization.

7. *Exequatur* proceedings for judgments coming from Contracting States have been usually decided in accordance with the 1979 Inter-American Convention. However, the Political-Administrative Chamber applied it to judgments coming from Chile, which is not a Contracting State, as it is evidenced by way of example in decisions 02215 of 28 November 2000, drafted by *Carlos Escarrá Malavé*, 00795 of 4 March 2001, drafted by *Hadel Mostafá Paolini*, 02581 of 5 May 2005, and 00741 of 22 March 2006, the last two drafted by *Levis Ignacio Zerpa.*

8. The 1961 Hague Convention entered into force for Argentina (18 February 1988), Colombia (30 January 2001), Ecuador (2 April 2005), Mexico (14 August 1995), Peru (30 September 2010), Uruguay (14 October 2012) and Venezuela (16 March 1999), all of them Contracting States to the 1979 Inter-American Convention.

9. Article 8 of the 1961 Hague Convention prescribes that it shall be given preferential application over the 1979 Inter-American Convention. This conclusion is indisputable not only because it is a specialized treaty regulating formalities of documents but also a posterior treaty to all its Contracting States. Therefore documents coming from any of them should bring an *apostille* and not legalization as required by its Article 2(c).

10. It is self-evident that *apostilles* cannot be required for documents coming from non-Contracting States to the 1961 Hague Convention. This obvious conclusion was recently stated in Exeq. 00162 of 20 May 2010, drafted by *Antonio Ramírez Jiménez*, indicating that the judgment was produced with legalization and not with *apostille*, because it came from Uruguay, not a Contracting State to the 1961 Hague Convention (its accession came into force on 14 October 2012).

11. Notwithstanding fundamental principles of the Law of Treaties, the Civil Cassation Chamber has requested on several occasions the production with *apostille* of documents coming from non-Contracting States to the 1961 Hague Convention.

12. Decision Exeq. 00214 of 3 May 2005, drafted by *Luis Antonio Ortiz Hernández*, in the fist place indicates that Arab States are not Contracting States to the 1961 Hague Convention. However, it ordered the presentation with an *apostille* of the judgment rendered in the Republic of Lebanon, adding the mistake that it had to be signed by the Venezuelan Embassy; in the judgment on the merits of the same proceeding, Exeq. 00777 of 15 November 2005, surprisingly stated that the petitioner complied with the request.

13. The Civil Cassation Chamber has also requested production of documents with *apostille* from the Dominican Republic, at the time not a Contracting State to the 1961 Hague Convention (its accession, not objected by Venezuela, came into force on 30 August 2009). As examples may be mentioned decisions Exeq. 00233 of 29 March 2007, Exeq. 00713 of 10 August 2007, Exeq. 00430 of 20 June 2007, drafted by Iris *Armenda Péña Espinoza*, and Exeq. 00374 of 30 May 2007, drafted by *Luis Antonio Ortiz Hernández*. Moreover, because such presentation was not made, decisions Exeq. 00713 of 10 August 2007 and 00198 of 10 April 2008, drafted by Iris *Armenia Péña Espinoza*, and Exeq.01014 of 19 December 2007, drafted by *Luis Antonio Ortiz Hernández*, declared inadmissible the applications, even though not precluding the interested party from presenting a new petition accompanying the requested document.

14. Article 852 of the Venezuelan Civil Procedure Code requires presentation of documents with legalization, to be stamped by the Venezuelan Diplomatic or Consular agents accredited in their State of Origin (Article 11, paragraph 29 of Consular Service Law). However, this rule only applies to documents coming from non-Contracting States to the 1961 Hague Convention, because the preferential application of treaties is prescribed in Article 1 of the Private International Law Act.

15. Therefore, decision Exeq. 00018 of 25 January 2008, drafted by *Iris Armenia Peña Espinoza*, did not accept a document coming from Colombian without *apostille* because it was legalized by a Colombian Vice-consul accredited in Venezuela.

16. Decision Exeq. 00118 of 28 February 2012, drafted by *Carlos Oberto Vélez*, declared inadmissible the application to obtain *exequatur* for a judgment rendered by the Palestine National Authority because it was legalized by the Palestinian Embassy in Venezuela and not by the Venezuelan Consulate in Palestine.

17. However, the Civil Cassation Chamber accepted documents legalized by both, the Foreign Affairs Ministries of Cuba and of Venezuela, presented in the proceedings decided in Exeq.00558 of 24 November 2011 and Exeq. 00670 of 5 December 2011, both drafted by *Isbelia Pérez Velázquez*.

III. REGULATION OF THE 1961 HAGUE CONVENTION

18. Article 2 of the 1961 Hague Convention provides that documents to be produced in the territory of Contracting States shall be exempted from legalization; legalization defined as the formality by which the diplomatic or consular agents of the country in which the document has to be produced certify the authenticity of the signature, the capacity in which the person signing the document has acted and, where appropriate, the identity of seal or stamp which it bears. However Article 3 permits them to require, as only formality, an "Apostille" placed on the document itself or on an "allonge", in the form of the model attached to the Convention, stamped by the competent authority designated by the State of origin, in accordance with its Article 6; Contracting States are obliged to give the pertinent information to the Foreign Affairs Ministry of the Netherlands.

19. Competent authorities are also allowed to issue *apostilles* in electronic form and to maintain electronic Registers of Apostilles, as suggested by the *e-APP* *(electronic Apostille Program)*; program which has not yet been adopted by Venezuela.

20. Therefore, Legalization and *Apostille* are different formalities.

21. Exeq. 00469 of 29 October 2010, drafted by *Luis Antonio Ortiz Hernández*, accepted the *apostille* issued by the Foreign Relations Ministry of Colombia after its verification via its webpage. Notwithstanding, in a preposterous way it added that the judgment complied "with the formalities required for its validity in Colombia, because if that were not the case it could not had been legalized by the Venezuelan Embassy in Colombia".

22. In compliance with Article 6 of the 1961 Hague Convention, Venezuela designated the Ministry of Foreign Affairs as competent authority to issue *apostilles*, as it may easily be evidenced in the website of the Hague Conference on Private International Law (www.hcch.net) and in the website of the Venezuelan Ministry of Foreign Affairs (www.mre.gov.ve). Obviously this designation is for Venezuelan documents to be produced abroad.

23. The website of the Hague Conference on Private International Law informs that Ecuador designated its *Ministerio de Relaciones Exteriores, Director-General de Legalizaciones* as competent authority to issue *apostilles*. However, decision Exeq.00647 of 13 October 2008, drafted by *Carlos Oberto Vélez*, accepted the *apostille* placed by the *Presidente Subrogante de la Corte Superior de Guayaquil*.

24. The Civil Cassation Chamber has indicated in some opportunities that Article 1(2)(b) of the 1961 Hague Convention modifies Article 600 of the *Ley de Enjuiciamiento Civil*. As example may be mentioned following decisions, drafted by *Iris Armenia Peña Espinoza*: Exeq. 00233 of 29 March 2007, Exeq. 00430 of 20 July 2007, Exeq. 00399 of 17 July 2009, Exeq. 00469 of 29 October 2010, and Exeq. 00425 of 12 August 2011. Such statement does not make any sense because Venezuela has not enacted any *Ley de Enjuiciamiento Civil* but a *Código de Procedimiento Civil*, its Article 600 not regulating formalities of documents. Negligence may explain the error incurred in the first of the above-mentioned decisions because of copying a reference valid for Spain; later judgments reproduced the statement without noticing the mistake. This copy and paste method was clearly used in Exeq. 00425 of 12 August 2011, drafted by *Iris Armenia Peña Espinoza*, copying the erroneous paragraph from decision Exeq. 00430; and it also seems to have been used in Exeq. 00399 of 17 July 2009 and in Exeq. 00469 of 29 October 2010, drafted by *Luis Antonio Ortiz Hernández*. However, for unknown reasons, the mistaken statement was not included in decisions Exeq.00018 of 25 January 2008 and Exeq. 00450 of 21 July 2008, both drafted by *Iris Armenia Peña Espinoza*.

IV. PREFERENTIAL APPLICATION OF THE 1961 HAGUE CONVENTION

25. The preferential application of the 1961 Hague Convention was clearly explained by the Civil Cassation Chamber in Exeq. 00387 of 31 May 2007, drafted by *Isbelia Pérez Velásquez*. It recalled that Colombia and Venezuela are Contracting States therefore undertaking the obligation to exempt legalization for foreign public documents, and for this reason when coming from Colombia they are to be presented with *apostille* issued by its Foreign Relations Ministry.

26. Same statement was recently repeated in Exeq. 00726 of 20 February 2012, drafted by *Carlos Oberto Vélez*, also in respect to a document coming from Colombia. Based on Article 1 of Venezuelan Private International Law Act and recalling that the 1961 Hague Convention was prepared to facilitate international circulation of documents, exempting them from legalization, the Civil Cassation Chamber concluded that Colombian documents presented with *apostille* complied with Article 2(c) of the 1979 Inter-American Convention requiring legalization.

27. The Civil Cassation Chamber, in other cases, has accepted documents with *apostille* coming from Contracting States to the 1979 Inter-American Convention, without expressly stating the preferential application of the 1961 Hague Convention. It proceeded in this way, by example in decision Exeq. 00025 of 30 January 2008, drafted by *Iris Armenia Peña Espinoza*, in case of documents coming from Argentina; recently Exeq. 00131 of 1 March 2012, drafted by *Isbelia Pérez Velásquez*, indicates that Colombian documents were produced with *apostille*, guaranteeing therefore their authenticity and legality.

28. Based on the clear text of the 1961 Hague Convention the Civil Cassation Chamber specified in Exeq. 00387 of 31 May 2007, drafted by *Isbelia Pérez Velásquez*, that Venezuelan Diplomatic and Consular Agents are not entitled to place *apostille* to a Colombian document because that faculty belongs to the competent authority designated by Colombia, *i.e.* its Ministry of Foreign Affairs.

29. However, Exeq. 00203 of 11 April 2008 requested the production of document with *apostille* placed by Venezuelan Embassy in Colombia; decision Exeq. 00835 of 9 December 2008, drafted by *Iris Armenia Peña Espinoza*, declaring inadmissible the petition because not presented.

30. Similarly, Exeq. 00178 of 15 April 2009, drafted by *Luis Antonio Ortiz Hernández* required presentation of a document with *apostille* stamped by the Venezuelan Embassy in Colombia. However, deciding on the merits the *exequatur* was granted in decision Exeq. 00026 of 10 February 2010 because it had been presented with the *apostille* issued by the Colombian Ministry of Foreign Affairs.

31. Exeq. 00450 of 21 July 2008 requested presentation with *apostille* of a document coming from Massachusetts, United States of America, indicating that Venezuelan Diplomatic or Consular Agents have no faculty to do it. However, in a preposterous way, decision Exeq. 00836 of 9 December 2008, drafted by *Iris Armenia Peña Espinoza*, declared inadmissible the application, among other reasons, because the applicant had not presented the document with apostille "issued by the respective consular authority".

32. The Civil Cassation Chamber has frequently requested the presentation documents with legalization, even though they come from Contracting States to the 1961 Hague Convention.

33. It would be a long list to indicate all of them. As examples may be mentioned decisions Exeq. 00046 of 1 February 2008, drafted by *Luis Antonio Ortiz Hernández*, requesting presentation with legalization of documents coming from Florida, United States of America; Exeq. 00168 of 2 April 2008, drafted by *Isbelia Pérez Veláquez*, in respect of a judgment rendered in New York; Exeq. 00418 of 29 July 2009 deciding on the merits the application to be inadmissible because it was not produced; and Exeq. 00094 of 22 February 2008, drafted by *Isbelia Pérez Velásquez* declaring inadmissible the *exequatur* because documents coming from Spain had not been presented with legalization as required by Article 852 of the Venezuelan Code of Civil Procedure. However, a later application to obtain *exequatur* of the same Spanish Judgment was granted in Exeq. 00130 of 1 May 2012, drafted by *Isbelia Pérez Velásquez*, not mentioning the formalities complied with by the documents presented.

34. Admission of documents with legalization coming from Contracting States to the 1961 Hague Convention is seldom explained.

35. However, the Political-Administrative, not in *exequatur* proceedings, indicated in Judgment 01732 of 6 July 2006, drafted by *Emilio García Rosas*, that the document was accepted because the interested party had obtained the legalization from the Venezuelan Consul in Florida, United States of America, therefore guaranteeing its authenticity, even though such formality was to be exempted in accordance with the 1961 Hague Convention.

36. Acceptance of documents with legalization has been recently explained by the Civil Cassation Chamber in its decision Exeq. 00795 of 16 December 2009, drafted by *Carlos Oberto Vélez*. In the first place it was pointed out that the 1961 Hague Convention, in force in Colombia and Venezuela, aimed via the *apostille* to facilitate international circulation of documents, avoiding therefore the heavy and expensive formality of legalization, adding that it has to be applied preferentially in accordance with Article 1 of the Venezuelan Private International Law Act. However, documents without *apostille* were accepted because of the legalization stamped by the Venezuelan Consul in Barranquilla, consequently guaranteeing their authenticity, but the Civil Cassation Chamber considered it necessary to call the attention in general terms to all *exequatur* petitioners that documents should be presented with *apostille*, not requesting legalization from Venezuelan Consuls in Colombia.

V. FINAL COMMENTS

37. The judgments rendered in *exequatur* proceedings examined above demonstrate that the Political-Administrative and the Civil Cassation Chamber have frequently accepted documents with legalization and not with *apostille*, even though they come from Contracting States to the 1961 Hague Convention.

38. Therefore the accession by Venezuela to the 1961 Hague Convention has not in practice exempted legalization of documents, as it was already remarked by the present writer some years ago.[1]

39. The Organic Law of the Supreme Tribunal gives competence to its Constitutional Chamber to revise judgments rendered by other Chambers when they violate fundamental principles sanctioned in treaties in force in Venezuela. However, no revision has been undertaken yet of any judgment applying incorrectly the 1961 Hague Convention, *i.e.* to documents from non-Contracting states or requesting presentation with *apostille* stamped by Venezuelan Diplomatic or Consular Agent to documents coming from Contracting States, even though the fact has been publicly acknowledged by the President of the Constitutional Chamber, *Luisa Estella Morales Lamuño*.[2]

1 "El tratamiento de la apostilla en el juicio venezolano del *exequátur*", *Revista de la Facultad de Ciencias Jurídicas y Políticas de la Universidad Central de Venezuela* (No. 131, Caracas, 2008, pp. 77–178.

2 *Tratamiento del Foro venezolano a la Extradición, Ejecución de sentencias penales, Exequátur, Exhortos y Arbitraje*. Tribunal Supremo de Justicia, Serie Eventos, número 32, Caracas, Venezuela, 2010, pp. 23–24.

40. The Constitutional Chamber has not acted *ex officio*, the President of the Republic has not given instructions to do it and not even the interested parties have applied for revision.

41. Most of the mistakes incurred by the Political-Administrative Chamber and by the Cassation Civil Chamber may be easily avoided by doing some research via the Internet to obtain the necessary information.

42. This recommendation does not appear to be very complicated, because the Civil Cassation Chamber has based some decisions on investigation made in webpages, not even verifying the accuracy of the information obtained, as it has been the case among others in Exeq. 00469 of 29 October 2010, drafted by *Luis Antonio Ortiz Hernández*, to confirm the authenticity of an electronic *apostille* issued in Colombia (www.minrelext.gov.co/Apostilla); in Exeq. 00065 of 18 February 2011, drafted by *Carlos Oberto Vélez*, to determine Swedish legislation on the webpage of the European Commission (http://ec.europa.eu/civiljustice/parental_resp/parental_resp_swe_es.htm) and in the official page of the Government of Sweden (www.sweden.gov.se/sb/d/3288/a/19570) and in Exeq. 00429 of 12 August 2012, drafted by *Carlos Oberto Vélez*, where information was obtained on the webpage (texaslawhelp.org, Texas Divorce Brochure)

43. It may also be recalled that the Civil Cassation Chamber has called by telephone the Venezuelan Ministry of Foreign Relations to obtain information, as indicated in Exeq. 00118 of 28 February 2012, drafted by *Carlos Oberto Vélez*, in respect to the address of the Venezuelan Consul in Palestine.

44. Similar actions may be undertaken for the correct application of the 1961 Hague Convention in Venezuela. Consultation of the website of the Hague Conference on Private International Law (www.hcch.net) is advisable to determine and understand the requirements imposed by the convention. A very easy explanation is found in two documents, available on the above-mentioned website, entitled: "*The ABCs of Apostilles: How to ensure that your public documents will be recognised abroad*" and the *Brief Implementation Guide: "How to join and implement the Hague Apostille Convention."*

45. It does not seem to be asking a great effort to the Magistrates and their assigned personnel.

Caracas, Yuletide 2012

LA CONFÉRENCE DE LA HAYE DE DROIT INTERNATIONAL PRIVÉ : VERS UNE COOPÉRATION JUDICIAIRE DANS LES MATIÈRES CIVILES ET COMMERCIALES À L'ÉCHELLE UNIVERSELLE[1]

Fernando PAULINO PEREIRA
Responsable de la coopération judiciaire civile au Secrétariat général du Conseil de l'Union européenne
Président du groupe de travail du Conseil e-Law dans les deux formations : e-Justice et e-Law

I. INTRODUCTION

La Conférence de La Haye de droit international privé œuvre depuis 1893 à l'unification progressive du droit international privé. Treize États européens ont participé à la première session de la Conférence, réunie par le Gouvernement des Pays-Bas. Cependant, elle agit comme organisation internationale depuis 1955, suite à l'adoption du Statut de la Conférence.

Le travail effectué par la Conférence de La Haye (ci-après HCCH) constitue certainement le fondement d'un nouvel ordre juridique international qui est de grande importance pour l'établissement d'un espace de prévisibilité et de sécurité juridique pour les citoyens et pour les entreprises dans des situations transfrontalières. Déjà au moment de la création de la HCCH, le mouvement accru des personnes et des entreprises au-delà des frontières engendrait le besoin de trouver des solutions juridiques permettant de régler les problèmes qui se posaient.

L'objectif de la HCCH est noble puisqu'il consiste à faciliter la vie des gens qui vivent un conflit en situation transfrontalière. Établir des mécanismes pour donner une réponse au déplacement ou au non-retour illicite d'un enfant, ou pour

[1] Les opinions émises dans cet article n'engagent que son auteur.

assurer le recouvrement international des aliments destinés aux enfants constitue un exemple de l'importance du travail de la HCCH. Ce travail est également de première importance pour les entreprises qui cherchent à régler leurs différends dans le cadre de procédures judiciaires transfrontalières. C'est certainement dans cette perspective que, il y a un peu plus de cent ans, Tobias M.C. Asser recevait le Prix Nobel de la paix pour l'œuvre lancée par la Conférence dans le domaine du droit international privé.

On constate une nette évolution de l'intérêt que les États dans le monde apportent aux instruments et aux valeurs de la HCCH. Avec 72 États membres provenant des quatre coins du monde et avec un nombre considérable d'autres États qui sont parties à certaines conventions, même s'ils ne sont pas membres de la Conférence, les instruments de La Haye sont appliqués quotidiennement dans un nombre considérable de cas. Il suffit de penser à la convention de 1961 supprimant l'exigence de la légalisation des actes publics étrangers. À cela s'ajoute le fait que la HCCH a établi de nouveaux moyens de coopération entre États membres de la Conférence et États tiers, qui visent à promouvoir l'entente et la concertation par des moyens autres que par l'application d'instruments internationaux. Tel est le cas par exemple du processus de Malte.

L'Union européenne est particulièrement attentive aux travaux de la Conférence de La Haye. Très vite après l'entrée en vigueur du Traité d'Amsterdam, par lequel l'Union européenne (à l'époque, la Communauté européenne) a acquis de nouvelles compétences dans le cadre des traités constitutifs, l'Union a démontré son intérêt à devenir membre de la Conférence de La Haye. À cet effet, il a été nécessaire de modifier le Statut de la Conférence, un processus dans lequel le Secrétaire général a joué un rôle déterminant concernant l'évolution des travaux, une évolution qui a été acceptée à l'époque par tous les États membres de la Conférence de La Haye. Devenant la première organisation internationale membre de la HCCH, l'Union européenne a clairement voulu démontrer l'importance de la HCCH dans la construction du droit international privé à l'échelle mondiale.

Le présent article vise à décrire les efforts qui ont été effectués, d'une part, par la HCCH et, d'autre part, par l'Union européenne pour œuvrer en commun dans la voie de la construction d'une coopération judiciaire dans les matières civiles et commerciales au sein de la Conférence de La Haye à l'échelle universelle.

II. LES EFFORTS DANS LE CADRE DE LA HCCH

Au début des années 90, tous les États membres de l'Union européenne étaient également des États membres de la HCCH. En outre, il convient de rappeler que beaucoup d'entre eux avaient soutenu depuis longtemps les travaux effectués dans le cadre de la Conférence de La Haye. À l'époque, les délégations auprès de la HCCH étaient normalement représentées par des professeurs éminents des États membres qui avaient le grand mérite de préparer le texte des conventions pratiquement en pleine autonomie et sans l'intervention des pouvoirs gouvernementaux des États membres. Il n'était nécessaire de prévoir la participation des autorités publiques nationales que dans un deuxième temps, afin de procéder à la signature, à la ratification ou à l'acceptation d'une convention conclue au niveau de la HCCH.

À cette époque-là, des représentants des institutions de l'Union européenne ont commencé à participer, comme observateurs passifs, à certains travaux de la HCCH. Cela a été le cas des travaux préparatoires de ce qui est devenu, en fin de parcours, après beaucoup d'années de négociations, la convention de La Haye de 2005 sur les accords d'élection de for.

Ce n'est toutefois qu'après 1994 que l'Union européenne a été clairement présente dans les travaux menés dans le cadre de la Conférence de La Haye. Ceci résultait surtout de deux facteurs.

Le premier était l'entrée en vigueur du Traité de Maastricht, lequel a octroyé de nouvelles compétences à l'Union européenne, notamment dans le domaine de la coopération judiciaire dans les matières civiles et commerciales.

Le deuxième était le fait que la HCCH était en train de négocier une convention qui est devenue la convention de La Haye de 1996 concernant la compétence, la loi applicable, la reconnaissance, l'exécution et la coopération en matière de responsabilité parentale et de mesures de protection des enfants. Or, cet instrument couvrait certains aspects touchant à la responsabilité parentale, lesquels étaient négociés en parallèle par les États membres au sein de l'Union européenne, dans le cadre d'une convention qui est devenue le règlement dit « Bruxelles II ».

C'est d'ailleurs pourquoi la convention de 1996 prévoit un article 10 qui touche à la question de la compétence pour connaître d'une demande en divorce ou en séparation de corps des parents d'un enfant résidant habituellement dans un État membre contractant à la convention, ou en annulation de leur mariage. En outre, l'article 52 prévoit une clause de déconnexion qui permet aux États membres de l'Union européenne d'appliquer des instruments internationaux auxquels ils sont parties contractantes et qui contiennent des dispositions sur les matières réglées par la convention.

L'Union a également entamé un processus de négociation à l'égard d'autres instruments négociés à La Haye. Cela a été le cas de la convention de 2006 sur la loi applicable à certains droits sur des titres détenus auprès d'un intermédiaire et de la convention de 2005 sur les accords d'élection de for.

L'adoption et l'entrée en vigueur du Traité d'Amsterdam ont constitué une étape fondamentale dans la création de nouvelles compétences au niveau de l'Union européenne et d'une nouvelle phase de coopération, plus ferme, plus interdépendante, entre l'Union européenne et la Conférence de La Haye.

C'est dans ce contexte que l'Union européenne a démontré sa volonté de devenir membre de la HCCH. En effet, l'Union était habilitée à adopter des mesures qui coïncidaient, partiellement ou totalement, avec les domaines d'activité de la HCCH. Une telle participation lui donnerait le statut pour exercer ses compétences externes en participant comme membre de plein droit à la négociation des conventions au sein de la HCCH dans les domaines qui relèveraient de sa compétence.

À cet effet, le Conseil de l'Union européenne a décidé d'autoriser la Commission européenne à négocier les conditions et les modalités d'adhésion. Par lettre commune de la Présidence, pour le compte du Conseil et de la Commission, adressée à la HCCH le 19 décembre 2002, la Communauté a présenté sa demande d'adhésion à la HCCH et a sollicité l'ouverture des négociations.

Cette volonté se confrontait cependant à un problème majeur de technique juridique, étant donné que la HCCH, conformément à son Statut adopté en 1955, ne permettait que l'adhésion d'États souverains. Il n'était donc pas prévu d'accepter des organisations internationales, telles que l'Union européenne, comme membres de la HCCH.

Cette situation impliquait le besoin de procéder à un ajustement du Statut de la HCCH. Un besoin qui coïncidait avec un moment où la HCCH prenait un poids croissant dans un contexte de mondialisation et d'intégration régionale. La Conférence de La Haye comptait alors parmi ses membres un nombre considérable d'États de plusieurs continents comme c'était le cas des États membres de l'Union européenne, des États-Unis d'Amérique, du Canada, du Japon, de la Russie, de la Chine, de l'Australie ou de la Nouvelle Zélande. En outre, des contacts étaient en cours avec d'autres États qui, par la suite, sont devenus des États membres de la Conférence.

Tout s'est déroulé d'une façon constructive. Le Conseil de l'Union européenne a adopté le 5 octobre 2006[2] la décision d'adhérer à la HCCH, le nouveau Statut de la HCCH est entré en vigueur le 1er janvier 2007, et le 3 avril 2007, l'Union européenne a accepté le nouveau Statut. Par lettre du Président du Conseil de l'Union européenne, l'Union européenne a accepté formellement et sans réserve les obligations découlant de son admission à la Conférence.

La révision du Statut a aussi permis de moderniser le fonctionnement des institutions propres à la HCCH, lui donnant des mécanismes de fonctionnement et des structures encore plus aptes à répondre aux attentes pour que la HCCH devienne un centre de gravité dans la construction de la coopération judiciaire civile et commerciale à l'échelle universelle.

---

2 JO L 297 du 26 octobre 2006, p. 1.

Par la suite, l'Union européenne a pleinement participé aux travaux de la Conférence sur la négociation de nouveaux instruments. Il convient de signaler en particulier la négociation de la convention de 2007 sur le recouvrement international des aliments destinés aux enfants et à d'autres membres de la famille ainsi que de son protocole sur la loi applicable.

III. LES TRAVAUX AU SEIN DE L'UNION

Par ailleurs, l'Union européenne a tout mis en œuvre afin de devenir partie contractante aux instruments établis au sein de la HCCH dans la mesure où les matières traitées relèvent de la compétence exclusive de l'Union européenne.

A. ASPECTS GÉNÉRAUX

La volonté de participer aux travaux de la HCCH n'a jamais posé de problèmes pour les institutions de l'Union ou pour les États membres. En particulier, il convient de souligner que le Conseil de l'Union européenne avait adopté, en premier lieu en 2006, en plein accord avec la Commission de l'Union européenne, une stratégie pour les relations extérieures dans le domaine de la coopération judiciaire en matière civile et commerciale. En particulier, il a été clairement mis en évidence que la HCCH constituait une organisation internationale qui renforçait la prévisibilité et la sécurité juridique à l'échelle mondiale dans le domaine qui est le sien et qu'il conviendrait de soutenir son rôle dans une perspective universelle.

B. LES INSTRUMENTS SPÉCIFIQUES

Ceci étant, l'adoption de certaines conventions de La Haye par l'Union a exigé un travail laborieux au sein des instances de l'Union. Elle a exigé l'application, dans certaines situations, de procédures novatrices. Ces solutions ont dû être utilisées pour deux raisons principales : la première, c'est que certaines conventions de La Haye ne prévoyaient pas la participation d'organisations internationales ; la deuxième, c'est qu'il fallait trouver des solutions compatibles avec le droit de l'Union européenne en matière de relations extérieures.

La convention de La Haye de 1996

La question de l'adoption de la convention de La Haye de 1996 par l'Union européenne posait trois problèmes de nature juridique : un premier résultait du fait que cette convention ne prévoit pas la possibilité de la signature ou de la ratification par des organisations internationales. Il en résulte que l'Union européenne (la Communauté européenne à l'époque), en tant que telle, n'était pas en mesure de ratifier ou d'adhérer à la convention. Le deuxième, c'est que la convention couvre à la fois des compétences exclusives de l'Union européenne, dans la mesure où certaines de ces dispositions affectent le droit dérivé de l'Union européenne, et des compétences qui relèvent de la seule compétence nationale. Le troisième, c'est que certains États qui sont devenus entre-temps États membres de l'Union avaient déjà signé et ratifié la convention. Il a donc fallu trouver une solution novatrice susceptible de donner une réponse à ces questions.

Dans ce sens, le Conseil, suite à une proposition de la Commission, a décidé d'autoriser certains États membres[3] à signer[4] puis à ratifier[5] la convention de La Haye de 1996. De cette façon, il a été possible de s'assurer que, à terme, les règles de la convention soient applicables dans tout l'ordre juridique de l'Union, dans le plein respect des principes de son droit, tout particulièrement dans le domaine des relations extérieures.

La convention de La Haye de 2005

La convention sur les accords d'élection de for contribue à favoriser l'autonomie des parties dans les opérations commerciales internationales et à accroître la prévisibilité des solutions judiciaires dans le cadre de ces opérations.

Il est clair que la convention aura une incidence sur le droit communautaire dans la mesure où ses dispositions affectent le régime fondé sur le choix des parties réglé en particulier à l'époque par le règlement (CE) 44/2001, règlement qui vient d'être révisé.

Le Conseil de l'Union européenne, suite à une proposition de la Commission, a décidé de signer la convention par décision du 26 février 2009[6]. Le Conseil doit attendre une proposition de la Commission avant de procéder à l'adoption de l'instrument. Ceci étant, il convient de rappeler qu'il a été jugé préférable par plusieurs États membres de l'Union européenne d'attendre la conclusion des travaux de révision du règlement (CE) 44/2001 avant de procéder à l'adoption de la convention.

---

3 Tous sauf la République tchèque, l'Estonie, la Lituanie, la Hongrie, la Slovénie et la Slovaquie. Vu le protocole annexé aux traités, la décision n'était pas applicable au Danemark.

4 JO L 48, du 1 avril 2004, p. 3.

5 JO L 151, du 11 juin 2008, p. 36.

6 JO L 133, du 29 mai 1999, p. 1.

La convention de La Haye de 2007

La convention de La Haye de 2007 sur le recouvrement international des aliments destinés aux enfants et à d'autres membres de la famille constitue une bonne base pour l'instauration, à l'échelle mondiale, d'un système de coopération en matière d'obligations alimentaires.

Par son article 59, la convention permet aux organisations régionales d'intégration économique telles que l'Union de signer et de ratifier le texte.

Il convient de relever qu'une partie des matières réglées par la convention de 2007 est également couverte par le règlement (CE) 4/2009 relatif à la compétence, la loi applicable, la reconnaissance et l'exécution des décisions et la coopération en matière d'obligations alimentaires. L'acceptation de la convention par l'Union européenne n'affecterait qu'une partie des dispositions du règlement (CE) 4/2009. Il en découle que l'Union ne disposerait de compétences exclusives que pour ces matières. Ceci revient à dire que les autres matières, celles ayant trait à la coopération administrative et à l'aide judiciaire, relèveraient donc de la seule compétence des États membres.

À part ces difficultés de nature juridique sur la portée des compétences au niveau de l'Union européenne, se posait une autre question, de nature pratique. En effet, dans les matières qui ne relèveraient pas de la compétence exclusive de l'Union, il incomberait à chacun des États membres de procéder à la signature et à la ratification de la convention. Cette situation impliquerait que la convention ne serait pas ratifiée par tous les États membres au même moment avec la conséquence possible que certains États membres prennent plus de temps à accepter la convention.

Afin de contourner ces difficultés, l'Union a dû trouver une solution acceptable pour tous les États membres et pour les institutions de l'Union. Par décision du Conseil, l'Union a décidé de signer[7] puis d'approuver[8] seule la convention dans le sens que les États membres sont devenus liés par la convention par l'effet de l'approbation par l'Union.

Cette solution a cependant été adoptée par le Conseil et assortie d'une déclaration conjointe du Conseil et de la Commission au moment de la décision concernant la signature de la convention. Cette déclaration est, bien entendu, applicable *mutatis mutandis* à celle relative à l'approbation de la convention par le Conseil. Cette déclaration précise trois idées fondamentales.

La première c'est qu'en règle générale, les accords entre un État membre et un État tiers en matière de coopération administrative ou d'assistance judiciaire n'affectent pas les règles de l'Union et n'en modifient pas la portée.

---

7 JO L 93 du 7 avril 2011, p. 9.

8 JO L 192 du 22 juillet 2011, p. 39.

Deuxièmement, compte tenu de l'existence du règlement (CE) n° 4/2009, l'Union a décidé, dans le cas précis, d'exercer sa compétence à l'égard de toutes les matières régies par la convention, c'est-à-dire également à l'égard des matières ayant trait à la coopération administrative et à l'assistance judiciaire, et d'adopter seule la convention.

Troisièmement, l'exercice par l'Union de sa compétence à l'égard des matières ayant trait à la coopération administrative et à l'assistance judiciaire dans le cadre de ladite convention n'interdit pas aux États membres de conclure des accords sur ces matières avec des États tiers, pour autant que ces accords n'affectent pas les règles de l'Union et n'en modifient pas la portée conformément à la jurisprudence de la Cour de justice.

Le protocole de La Haye de 2007

Le protocole de 2007 règle la loi applicable aux obligations alimentaires. Lors des travaux au niveau de l'Union européenne sur ce qui est devenu le règlement (CE) n° 4/2009, la question s'était posée de savoir si le règlement devrait régler également des questions relatives à la loi applicable aux obligations alimentaires. Dans ce contexte, il est indispensable de garder à l'esprit que l'article 2 du protocole de 2007 disposait qu'il est applicable même si la loi qu'il désigne est la loi d'un État non contractant. En d'autres termes, il ne serait pas possible de prévoir deux systèmes de loi applicable, l'un pour l'Union européenne et l'autre qui devrait être applicable dans le cadre de la HCCH. Autrement, un régime dérogerait à l'application des règles de l'autre, ce qui poserait des difficultés considérables.

À l'instar de la convention de 2007, le protocole donne la possibilité à l'Union de devenir partie contractante.

L'Union européenne a pris la décision de devenir partie contractante à cet instrument en décidant en outre de l'appliquer à titre provisoire au cas où le protocole ne serait pas entré en vigueur à la date de l'application du règlement (CE) n°4/2209. Non seulement l'Union a décidé de participer pleinement au régime prévu par le protocole mais elle a également décidé de l'appliquer en lieu et place d'un instrument susceptible d'être adopté au niveau de l'Union[9].

[9] Il convient de préciser que cette décision n'est pas applicable au Danemark, en vertu du protocole annexé aux traités, et au Royaume-Uni qui a décidé, conformément au protocole sur la position du Royaume-Uni et de l' Irlande, qu'il ne participerait pas à l'adoption et qu'il n'est donc pas lié par celle-ci ni soumis à son application.

L'e-Justice

Le Conseil de l'Union européenne (Justice et Affaires Intérieures) a adopté en décembre 2008 un plan d'action pluriannuel relatif à l'e-Justice européenne. L'objectif est de faire usage des technologies de l'information et de la communication aux fins de l'e-Justice. L'utilisation de ces nouvelles technologies devrait contribuer à la rationalisation et à la simplification des procédures judiciaires en réduisant les délais de procédure et les coûts de fonctionnement au bénéfice des citoyens, des entreprises, des praticiens du droit et de l'administration de la Justice.

Dans ce sens, le groupe de travail du Conseil « e-Justice » a eu l'opportunité d'accueillir à plusieurs reprises des représentants du Bureau Permanent de la HCCH afin d'échanger des points de vue sur les perspectives de travail dans ce domaine. En particulier, le groupe a eu la possibilité d'être informé sur le projet iChild et sur l'Apostille électronique (e-APP). En effet, les innovations technologiques mises en place par la Conférence de La Haye devraient pouvoir, le moment venu, être pleinement prises en compte dans le cadre de l'e-Justice européenne.

IV. CONCLUSIONS

À l'heure actuelle, il est reconnu qu'il existe une tendance vers une globalisation dans le mouvement des personnes et de l'activité des entreprises au-delà des frontières. Il apparaît donc nécessaire, au nom d'un intérêt collectif universel, de maintenir et de renfoncer les fondements de cet ordre juridique international créé par les conventions établies dans le cadre de la HCCH. Cela permettra d'améliorer la prévisibilité des relations juridiques et la sécurité des personnes et des opérateurs économiques.

Dans ce contexte, il semblerait utile de poursuivre les trois axes fondamentaux suivants au moins dans le cadre des travaux de la HCCH.

Le premier, c'est qu'il conviendrait de faire tous les efforts pour concentrer au sein de la HCCH les travaux qui relèvent de la coopération judicaire dans les matières civiles et commerciales lorsque sont en cause des questions qui ont une portée universelle. Une dispersion des travaux dans plusieurs enceintes internationales n'aurait que pour effet d'éclater une logique qui a été correctement assurée par la HCCH. Des travaux comme ceux qui ont trait à la médiation, aux successions ou à l'accès au droit étranger devraient, autant que possible, être hébergés dans le cadre de la Conférence de La Haye.

Bien entendu, cette logique ne devrait aucunement affecter le besoin de poursuivre la construction, au niveau de l'Union européenne, d'un espace judiciaire européen dans les matières civiles et commerciales.

Le deuxième, c'est qu'il faudrait que le chemin d'expansion qui a été poursuivi d'une façon si habile par l'actuel Secrétaire général de la Conférence de La Haye, Monsieur Hans van Loon, puisse être continué en augmentant dans le futur le nombre d'États membres de la HCCH.

Le troisième concerne les aspects ayant trait à l'e-Justice. Il s'avèrerait utile de poursuivre le dialogue entre l'Union européenne, la HCCH et les États tiers afin de permettre le rapprochement et si possible l'harmonisation des questions techniques horizontales pour autant que cela relève de la mise en œuvre d'instruments adoptés dans le cadre de la HCCH. Ces questions techniques pourraient concerner par exemple la normalisation des échanges d'informations ou des mécanismes d'identification et d'authentification. Seul un tel effort permettra l'interopérabilité entre les systèmes d'e-Justice à créer ou existants au profit de l'efficacité et de la crédibilité dans le domaine de la justice.

En guise de conclusion, il y a lieu de mettre en exergue le respect et l'appréciation qu'il faut apporter à Monsieur Hans van Loon, Secrétaire général de la Conférence de La Haye, qui a réussi à affermir une présence universelle de la Conférence de La Haye de droit international privé dans les matières qui concernent la coopération judiciaire et commerciale.

THE REVOLUTION OF PRIVATE INTERNATIONAL LAW IN THE WORLD AT PRESENT, REGARDING THE MEXICAN CASE

Dr. Leonel PEREZNIETO CASTRO
Honoris Causa Doctorate by the University of Sonora
Professor at UNAM
National Researcher Level III
Counselor of Jáuregui and Navarrete Law Firm, Mexico City

1. INTRODUCTION

The conclusion of the Cold War created a detente in international relations among the great powers of the period, and many politicians and jurists had been of a mind to delimitate structures, areas of influence and in general, relations among states. However, at present, attention is being paid to regulating the juridical life of people and of commercial transactions, in accordance with a new global economic model. This emphasis has changed the parameters for the analysis of international law and PIL in particular, that are at the core of this great transformation, a true Revolution in the analysis of international law and in many spheres of juridical life in general.

This is how this paper will deal with some of the significant topics in this matter, where the depth of the change is notorious (2) to then reflect on the future of this trend (3) and draw some conclusions (4).

2. TOPICS OF CHANGE

In order to limit the scope of this paper, we will only refer to three cases as examples. First, a new demonstration of the impossibility of finding a definition between private law and public law in this case because of investment arbitration.

Second, what has been called the "internationalisation of the contract", which means broadening the domestic juridical categories and finally, the incidence of international juridical traffic on human rights.

2.1. THE IMPOSSIBILITY OF A CLASSIFICATION BETWEEN PUBLIC LAW AND PRIVATE LAW

Until the nineteenth century, attempts were made to classify law into two categories, private law and public law, yet it was never possible to find a full juridical justification because in the nineteenth century itself other different types of law emerged which did not fit within said division, for example, social law. Now, with the development of international law in the field of investment arbitrages, confirmation of the impossibility to classify law in this manner again occurs due to a very important change.

Let us take a quick look at the scene. States sign international bilateral agreements to protect investments; Mexico, for example, has signed twenty eight treaties.[1] Said treaties provide the rules to solve conflicts through international commercial arbitrage.

Our example is the case of a bilateral agreement in which the Mexican government affects the assets of a foreign country with which Mexico has signed an agreement of this type. Some Mexican companies have successfully resorted to this mechanism to claim their rights before other states.

Yet the point I want to emphasize is the following: a bilateral investment agreement, among other things, places the foreign investor at the same level as the State. That is, it turns the individual into a subject of international law. By doing so, the application made by the Arbitrage Court, in addition to applying the principals of international Law, is that it applies internal law and within this, those principles can be from public law, as in the case of expropriations. Consequently, an international tribunal assumes functions that, up until then, were executed by the State exclusively, and on the other hand, that same Court will try private law matters such as the contract and the obligations of the different parties. The award will then be a fine mix of private law, public law and international

[1] 1) Germany (2001); 2) Argentina (1998); 3) Australia (2007); 4) Austria (2001); 5) Belgium/Luxemburg (2003); 6) Belarus (2009); 7) China (2009); 8) Cuba (2002); 9) Korea (2002); 10) Denmark (2000); 11) Slovakia (2009); 12) Spain (2008); 13) Finland (2000); 14) France (2000); 15) Greece (2002); 16) India (2008); 17) Island (2006); 18) Italy (2002); 19) Netherlands (1999); 20) Panama (2006); 21) Portugal (2000); 22) United Kingdom (2000); 23) Czech Republic (2004); 24) Singapore (2011); 25) Sweden (2001); 26) Switzerland (1996); 27) Trinidad and Tobago (2007); 28) Uruguay (2002) Source: Department of Economy, http://200.77.231.70/swb/es/economia/p_APPRIs_Suscritos.

law, when the procedure is of this nature.[2] An Arbitrage Court of this kind, by applying international law principles, bases itself on the precedents of previously-tried cases using this same international system to solve disputes.

Summarizing, in a case such as that of our example, which is frequently repeated all over the world, we can see that the analysis made by international arbiters, whose decision will be internationally acknowledged by national courts, is to apply without any distinction provisions that are classically classified in public law and private law. By doing so, it occurs that what happened in the nineteenth century, before a very accurate classification of the two types of norms (public and private) when social law was born, and contrasted with the classification in fashion in those days. Today the same happens with the indistinct application of this rule by an international court, as in the case of an investment treaty, as we have seen in our example.

Here a change in the analysis works; same that will pervade to other sectors of international juridical life.

Having stated that, let us go to the next example.

2.2. INTERNATIONALIZATION OF THE CONTRACT

What we are dealing with at present is a diminishment or disappearance of the differences between the different juridical systems, under a modern thesis that does not serve political or defense ends, but is merely the confirmation of the difference between internal and international juridical systems. From there we seek to rescue the links between the two types of law that allow them to work in co-ordination for the benefit of international juridical traffic, mainly in the concept of uniformity, as made clear almost fifty years ago by Professor R.Y. Jennings:

> "the first step then ... is to establish a legal bridge between the contract and international law and the relevant municipal law, so that these systems interact."[3]

It is a question of changing the political content of the discussion on dualism[4] to turn it into a juridical discussion which, in its modern sense, is located around the

[2] On this topic, see: Harten Van, Gus, The public private distinction in the international arbitration of individual claims against the State, in: *International and Comparative Corporate Law Quarterly*, No 56 (2) 2007, pp. 371–394 y Gaillard, E. *State Entities in International Arbitration*, AI Series on International Arbitration, No 4, 2008, pp. 31–55.

[3] *Rules Governing Contracts Between States and Foreign Nationals*, Ed. Cambridge, 1965, p. 127.

[4] The theory of "Juridical Dualism" proposed in Germany by Henrich Tripel (*Völkerrecht und Landesrecht.* Leipzig 1899) and in Italy by Dionisio Anzilotti (*Studi Critici di Diritto Internazionale Privato*, No 104, 1898) that postulates an International Law different from domestic law, which was quickly welcomed in Latin America because it unwinds international

contract because this is the most important vehicle of international transactions and of family relationships. In addition to the juridical consequences of the latter, which must maintain continuity and which domestic juridical systems must support, for example, in order to acknowledge a marriage celebrated in a different country or make an international adoption effective or a divorce, etc.[5]

What are the "legal bridges" referred to by Prof. Jennings? They are bridges built by the broad and hard work of many people, by several international organisms and above all, by the political will of the states which are now convinced of the fact that it is through international commerce that wealth that can be distributed internally with jobs and a greater wealth can be distributed in social aid programs.

Therefore, internationally co-ordinated actions have been carried out in order to build these "legal bridges.". A few institutions undertaking this constant work are the Hague Conference on Private International Law, the United Nations Commission for International Trade Law (UNCITRAL), the International Institute for the Unification of Private Law (UNIDROIT), the International Chamber of Commerce (ICC) and the Inter-American Conference on Private International Law (CIDIP).

All of these organisms have objectives defined in the growth of PIL by means of the international conventions which they develop together with model laws and legislative guides that States later approve through their legislatures, as in the case of Mexico, which leads to internally uniform legislation and, through uniformity, an openness to the possibilities of international juridical traffic.

This process enriches national juridical systems, modernises them and enables them to interact internationally.

2.2.1. Within the subject of the internationalisation of a contract, we find thousands of international transactions that are carried out every day all over the world and which PIL studies under the subject Lex Mercatoria.[6]

In effect, these are the hordes of bank and commercial transactions and of those related to services (payments and international transfers, merchandise and service acceptance and delivery, etc.) from one country or continent to another carried

law from internal law. As was the case of many renowned Latin American jurists, such as Carlos Calvo, Gerardo Estrada, Luis María Drago, etc.

5 On this subject, see: Dreyzin de Klor, Adriana, *Los nuevos paradigmas de familia y su reflejo en el Derecho Internacional Privado, Familia, Posmodernidad, Derecho Internacional Privado*, in: *Revista Mexicana de Derecho Internacional Privado y Comparado* May 26, 2010, p. 73 and following.

6 For further information on the subject, see: *Estudios sobre Lex Mercatoria*, Ed. UNAM, 2006 (Jorge Alberto Silva, Coordinator).

out by entities on a global scale. These transactions have increased considerably with electronic communication means and transportation and, at present, the norm regulates that all of these transactions are part of the Corpus Juris of international trade law.[7]

This first means world acknowledgement of the full exercise of the autonomy of the wills that contracting parties shape in their international obligations. As claimed by Walter Biagi, this is "the natural capacity of the person to bring change within the juridical sphere by means of his will."[8]

In this same sense, the customs and habits of each commerce and industrial guild are adopted as compulsory to rule their transactions in a specific sector. The rules (soft law, as we will see further on) issued by non-government organisms such as the International Chamber of Commerce (ICC) and the International Bar Association (IBA) on several subjects including, among others, letters of credit used by banks even above their own local laws (which are outdated) or the rules to assess evidence in international arbitrage, where disputes derived from contracts and the most important transactions are solved.

Together with the analysis above, PIL also studies a series of mechanisms through which international rules are incorporated into the Mexican juridical system, the purpose of which is to build "legal bridges" with foreign countries that are, at present, essential, as is the case with "Mirror Provisions".

2.2.2. "Mirror Image Provisions"

Mexico has resorted to "Mirror Image Provisions" in order to modernize its national juridical system. In effect, in 1986, Mexico adhered to the GATT – now one of the agreements of the World Trade Organization (WOT) and later, in 1994, Mexico signed the NAFTA.[9] Since then, it has signed thirteen additional free trade agreements with other countries.[10] With these instruments, Mexico assumed the

---

7 In this sense, see: Borton, J.H. et al, *The evolution of the trade regime; politics, law and economics of the GATT and the WTO*. Ed. Princeton University, 2008, p. 27.

8 *Rivista di Diritto Civile*, CEDAM, Padua, Vol. 43, núm. 5, 1997, p. 774.

9 On its effect on globalization, see: Montalvo Romero, M. and Viveros Contreras, O. *El efecto jurídico, económico y financiero en el contexto de la globalización*. Ed. Arano, Mexico, 2007, pp. 35 and following. On the topic of international juridical systems such as GATT, see: Kuyper, P.K. The Law of GATT as a special field of international law, in: *Netherlands Yearbook of international law*, Vol. XXV, 1994, Martinus Nijhoff, Holland.

10 1) NAFTA [Mexico, United States and Canada] (1994) 2) Costa Rica (1995) 3) Nicaragua (1998) 4) Chile (1999) 5) TLCUE [European Union] (2000) 6) Israel (2000) 7) Central America North Triangle [El Salvador, Guatemala, Honduras] (2000) 8) European Free Trade Association [Island, Liechtenstein, Norway and Switzerland] (2001) 9) Uruguay (2004) 10) Agreement for Strengthening the Economic Association between Mexico and Japan (2005) 11) Colombia (2011) 12) Peru (2012) 13) Sole FTA between Mexico and Costa Rica, El Salvador, Guatemala, Honduras, Nicaragua (2012) [This renders treaties between Mexico and each one of the

obligation of incorporating "Mirror Image Provisions" within its own legislation that could correspond to the obligations it had assumed with international organisms in order to open its economy and link several of its internal operative sectors to international trade, such as uniform customs mechanisms, tax relief and tariff uniformity, uniformity in trade rules, "dumping" regulation, and compensatory measures, etc. These are "[r]ules agreed on internationally, many of which are reproduced internally to make sure that the behavior of the country in question, at least in trade matters, is carried out in accordance with said rules."[11]

2.2.3. Legislative incorporation of customs and uses

Mexico, with its already open economy, had to develop new rules consistent with its international needs to link its economy to the world, and with this drive it had to multiply dispute rules[12] and direct references to international provisions to incorporate international habits and customs, such as with Art. 71 of the financial institutions law in the matter of Letters of Credit that shows an advanced incorporation system:

> "Article 71, (Paragraph 1): Financial institutions, when issuing Letters of Credit as referred to in sections VIII and XIV of Article 46[13] of this Law, shall comply with that provided for in this article, and as a supplement, to the customs and habits that the parties expressly indicate in each one of them, *without that provided for in the General Law of Negotiable Instruments and Credit Operations in the matter of letters of credit applicable for this operation*" (emphasis added).

In other words, the national state, in this case Mexico, acknowledges the priority of the autonomy of the will of the parties and the incorporation in their contracts of the habits and customs above their internal law on the matter.[14] The above shows that proceeding this way alters, and revolutionizes, the traditional concepts to interpret law that, up until that time, had been followed in a systems

countries separately without effect] Economy Department: http://www.economia.gob.mx/comunidad-negocios/comercio-exterior/tlc-acuerdos.

11 Borton, J.H. Op. cit.

12 Made from the reforms of the Civil Code for the Federal District and the Federal Civil Code and their respective Civil Procedural Codes as from 1988 and later the reforms to the Trade Code in 1994 and 1999.

13 Article 46 of this Law establishes the operations financial institutions can perform related to Letters of Credit: Section XIV. "Issue letters of credit after receiving their amount, make credits effective and make payments to the account of the clients".

14 The Federal Civil Code (1928) sets forth: "against compliance of law disuse, custom or practice in the contrary cannot be alleged" (Article 10 FCC). Now, a special law, in the sphere of its competence (credit) abolishes this general principle.

like that of Mexico, which had been closed to foreign countries for an extended time. Mexican Civil Codes deny that a custom can be above the law.

2.2.4. *"Transplant" or "Cross Fertilization"*

One more source is the so called "Transplant" or "Cross Fertilization" technique[15] of juridical rules from one system to another because of different reasons; for example, the regard people have for a certain juridical system, the performance of which is considered to render the same results if it is "transplanted" to a different juridical system. Also, as is in the case of Mexico, the purpose is to link a previously closed national juridical system to the world by means of more advanced rules which have already proven their efficiency in practice.[16]

The Mexican government should have considered in 1994, or even before that date, if European rules which were more consistent with its codified law system should be "transplanted". Yet, the reality of the magnitude of the trade Mexico has with the United States (80%) should have imposed itself and therefore, it was consistent to "transplant" rules from that country, so that transactions between those two countries could carry on uniformly, and at the same time the Mexican juridical system remain functional to operate with other countries. This was done with rules of complete sectors of the economy, such as telecommunications, environment, business corporations, economic competence, energy, and in general in the fields of economics, agriculture, banks and financial services and many more.[17]

The economy and the juridical system had to concentrate their efforts on obtaining rules to link Mexico to the external world and vice versa.[18] This, to a great extent, explains why Chile and Mexico at present have the most modern systems on foreign trade matters allowing their full opening in trade. With this drive, Mexico is now in the eleventh place on the list of the most important

---

15 On this subject see: Mosquera I.J., Legal transplants and comparative law, in: *International Law, Revista Colombiana de Derecho Internacional* No 2, 2003, Universidad Javeriana.

16 This is a phenomenon that has spread in many Latin American countries. "The most important change for Latin American private law has been to draw away from the European doctrine and approach materials and juridical literature related to the Anglo-Saxon law." Posada Tamayo, J.A. *Una visión desde el Derecho Comparado y el análisis económico del Derecho en la estructura societaria latinoamericana*, in: *Estudios de Derecho* No 146, 2008, pp. 115 and following.

17 On this topic, see: López Ayllon, *Las transformaciones del Sistema Jurídico y los significados sociales del Derecho en México. La encrucijada entre tradición y modernidad.* Ed. Instituto de Investigaciones Jurídicas, UNAM, 1997, p. 183 and following.

18 In this sense, see: Aranda Godoy, A. *Las dificultades de integrar un sistema jurídico de Estado y otro de Mercado Común, en un Acuerdo de Libre Comercio*: *"El TLCUEM"*, in: *Revista Mexicana de Derecho Internacional Privado y Comparado,* 9 March 2001, p. 95 and following.

exporting countries in the world. This is better than many European countries which have traditionally been exporting countries.[19]

2.2.5. Soft Law

This last category deals with the so-called soft law or flexible law issued by the international organisms I mention above.

These are rules that, due to their flexibility, adjust to different situations and reduce the contradiction between systems, leading to uniformity.[20] In addition, these rules help parties in that their contracts can incorporate them and make the rules binding between them.[21]

Let us take a look at an example: rules the parties agree on as compulsory in their contract.

A typical example is that of the International Commercial Terms (INCOTERMS) of the ICC. International quotations for products, in most cases, are done in accordance with these rules (FOB, LAB, etc.) because international trade, especially that of goods, uses as a starting point an offer that includes the quotation and the price of the goods, and if the parties agree on it, transportation.

Once the economic quotation is accepted, the price and all of the terms related to transportation and delivery are accepted, as well as risk transmission, etc. As can be seen, part of the nature of these rules points to the obligations that are agreed upon and which are acquired at a long distance.

After this short trip through the different sources of creation of norms that PIL studies, we can clearly see that this discipline is the motor of change and modernization of modern international law.

Let us now go to the last topic of this paper: human rights motivated by recent Constitutional Reform[22] regarding PIL, which we shall briefly discuss.

---

19 According to available information on the volume and value or exports published by the central Banks of the different countries mentioned in this paper we get the following amounts (in million dollars) Mexico: 349,567,946; Belgium: 344,070,000; Spain: 298,522,532; Austria: 153,925,443; Greece: 25,493,580; Portugal: 53,382,420.

20 Soft Law is the "[d]oor to a more open and complex conception of International Law in accordance with the times of greater world globalization. Toro Huerta, M. *El fenómeno del Soft Law y las nuevas perspectivas del Derecho Internacional*, in: *Anuario Mexicano de Derecho Internacional*. UNAM, vol. VI, 2006, pp. 513 and following.

21 As would be the case for the UNIDROIT principles, in this sense, see: Bonell, M.J. Soft Law and party autonomy the case of UNIDROIT principles, in: *Loyola Law Review*, Vol. 51, summer, 2005, pp. 229 and following.

22 9th. Epoch; T.C.C.; S.J.F. and its Gazette; XXXII, July 2010; p. 2101.

3. HUMAN RIGHTS AND CONSTITUTIONAL REFORM

The subject is presented in the following terms:

International treaties or conventions are elaborated to facilitate international juridical traffic and they raise the level of the rights of those people who domiciled in the countries that sign the treaty. The incorporation[23] of a more favorable right in the internal juridical system, especially in the matter of human rights, must subsist within the system, since the international juridical norm was "nationalized" and integrated into the internal juridical system for the benefit of the people. This point has been sanctioned with the Constitutional Reform with the following terms: "[n]orms related to the human rights acknowledged in this Constitution and with the international treaties on the matter, favoring people at all times, the broadest protection" (Art. 1).[24]

We are certainly before a subject that has not been explored enough, at least from the perspective of PIL.[25] Yet, we begin from the principles of the "broadest protection" of the Constitution and the principle of common good that has been the object of the case law in human rights matters, at least in Latin America.[26] This is a question of the internal legislator subordinating himself to international norms on human rights matters that tend to the common good.

In the case we are analyzing, we will refer to the international norms that have been incorporated to the internal juridical system. In addition, the content of these norms establishes more specific rights, new rights or merely rules that facilitate the scope of said rights. An example will help us analyze this concept.

As provided for in the more important treaties ratified by Mexico,[27] international adoption procedures are provided which are easier and faster

23 By way of Article 133 of the Constitution that establishes: this Constitution, the laws of Congress that proceed from them and all the treaties that agree with same, entered into or that will be entered into by the President of the Republic with the approval of the Senate, shall be the Supreme Law of all the Union. The judges of each one of the States shall follow said Constitution, Laws and Treaties, in spite of provisions on the contrary that might be in the Constitutions or Laws of the States. (reformed through Decree published in the Federal Official Journal on 18 January 1934).

24 Article 1, para. 2 reads as follows: "The Human Rights laws should be interpreted according to the Constitution and according to the international treaties subscribe by Mexico in the Human Rights field, favoring all times to people the broadest protection".

25 An author dealt with this subject, in the seventies: he was Werner Goldschmit, with his Right of Tolerance, in this sense see: *Derecho Internacional Privado*, Ed. El Derecho, Buenos Aires, 1970.

26 On this subject, see: García Ramírez, S. and Morales Sánchez, J. *La reforma constitucional sobre Derechos Humanos* (2009–2011), Ed. Porrúa-UNAM, México, 2011.

27 The Inter-American Convention on the Conflict of Laws in the Matter of the Adoption of Minors of 1984 and the Hague Convention on the Protection of Minors and the Cooperation in the Matter of International Adoption of 1994.

than locally established procedures. With this facilitation, foreigners can adopt Mexican children following a simplified procedure, and thus comply with the common good; that is to say, that a Mexican minor orphan has a family and grows up within it. Yet, when it is the case of a foreigner who comes from a State that has not signed these treaties, he will not be able to adopt a Mexican child using this facilitation regime and therefore cannot comply with the common good of the minor, merely because said State has not signed the international treaty or convention.

The reformed constitutional precept that we have already mentioned tells us that when dealing with these types of rights that the broadest protection must be granted to the person. In this case, the facilitation to exert the right of adoption must be broad as well. Nevertheless, we should be aware that exerting this right is linked to a different topic, which is not less important. An international convention necessarily implies obligations for the States that signed it, as these obligations are indispensable for the convention to function.

The latter can be a weighty argument, but is compensated by an effective supervision structure insofar as the required follow up of the adopted Mexican minor. In international conventions, the obligation of the Contracting State to follow up the care given by adopted parents to adopted children is established during the process of family connection. This is a temporary supervision administrative procedure which can be agreed on by the Mexican authorities with any foreigner who wishes to adopt and who has his domicile in a Contracting State to the Convention. .The adoptive parent informs the Mexican consulate about the family domicile and allows visits from the Mexican consular authorities. This is definitely not a procedure that can be executory to separate an adopted abused minor from its adopted family, and worst of all (and fortunately less frequent now) that the adoption is used to ensnare the minor in a prostitution ring. Really, in order to avoid these mishaps, the judge now has the complete information of any person, including, if applicable, police records, to be able to clearly see that the person who is adopting is adequate for adoption. And this must be the job of the authorities who participate in procedures of this nature. In the case of Mexico, it is the Direction of Family Integrity (DIF). These are the public servants who prepare the files of future adopters.

This example has been obviously stated in a very general way since the subject includes more complex issues, such as double jurisdiction, because it illustrates the way in which a facilitating mechanism to reach the common good of a Mexican minor orphan, should not be subject to a certain State having signed the treaty. The international juridical norm, when incorporated into the Mexican juridical system, when it is "nationalized", must serve all the people within the national territory or who want to adopt a minor, get married or enter into a contract.

An interesting issue linked to the above which can be discussed is the following: is it possible for a national to resort to the facilitation norms of the treaty instead of resorting to the internal norms in the matter of adoption? It could be stated that, in the personal field, the treaty does not include him and consequently he has no option. Nevertheless, it is a procedure that improves the rights of the person, and in that case, human rights, thus we consider it is possible. The treaty has been ratified by Mexico, the international norm was incorporated into national law and this cannot exclude a person whose domicile is in Mexico. In other words, due to the incorporation of the international juridical norm in the internal system, it lost the field of personal application given by the treaty and by being a national norm it applies to all of the people who are within the national territory. Because it favors human rights it must be applied to said person.[28]

It will be a matter of raising the internal norm to the level of the corresponding international norm in the matter of human rights. This will then be the way to reach the common good.

Not all of the cases are as evident as the adoption example. But even when dealing with commercial transactions, there is an important ingredient to equalize rights so that commercial transactions are fair for both parties. Let us take a look at an example. The United Nations Convention on Contracts for the International Sale of Goods[29] establishes rules that define the rights and facilitate their execution. The same question arises: How can they be denied to a person from a country that is not a Contracting State to the treaty? Doing so would be placing the person in a situation of disadvantage, because Mexico decided to incorporate to its juridical system an advanced international purchase-sale system. The juridical system has been modernized in this sector, and it must be for the benefit of everybody.

Only one case could justify the exception to this proposal and it consists of the following.

In the case of commercial, fiscal and other kinds of treaties mutual and permanent interaction is required of the States that have signed the treaty. In addition, they abide by a much-defined international policy. It is only convenient for the Mexican State to grant duty preferences to certain States in exchange for others and it is not convenient to do so with other States. But even in this field, a substantive right linked to the human rights of the person must be extensive for all the others. We cannot find a juridical reason to exclude it.

---

28 A very similar opinion is found in Becerra Ramírez, M. Op. Quote, p. 171 "The Judicial Power, at the request of the party, shall have the faculty to propose a draft law to incorporate any of the provisions of the treaties our country is part of, or of the international custom, that does not have an executor character".

29 On this topic, see: Ferrari, Bruno, *The CISE and Its Impact on National Contract Law Report*, at www.uncitral.org.

4. THE FUTURE OF THIS REVOLUTIONARY TREND

I consider that the world economy will develop in years to come within the scheme of a liberal economy that opens the international juridical currents beyond the national juridical systems. With this drive, international law must focus on the regulation of people and of commercial transactions, including international investment. This projection demands that today's jurist understand the magnitude of the juridical change that is happening internationally, because that will be the world within which he lives. This basic knowledge is given to him mainly by PIL, by showing how institutions are analyzed using a different methodology; thus leading him to think in different ways, and to lift his eyes from national law and see how the world broadens.

5. CONCLUSIONS

It can be concluded that international law at present has emphasised methods of international solution for international juridical traffic both in family matters and in trade matters. By doing so, the application of the international norms and international procedures to solve disputes, among other factors, contributes to revolutionising the traditional juridical approach, especially that which is only limited by the internal juridical categories. Consequently, it is very important to focus modern PIL in that sense, especially in a country like Mexico, which has a merger economy with for more international trade than various European Countries, traditionally exporters.

PROSPECTS FOR THE CONVENTION OF 30 JUNE 2005 ON CHOICE OF COURT AGREEMENTS*

Marta PERTEGÁS
First Secretary at the Permanent Bureau of the Hague Conference on Private International Law
Part-time Professor at the University of Antwerp

Louise Ellen TEITZ
First Secretary at the Permanent Bureau of the Hague Conference on Private International Law
Professor of Law (on leave) from Roger Williams University School of Law

I. INTRODUCTION

In rendering tribute to Hans van Loon's remarkable career and lifelong commitment to private international law, we thought it would be appropriate to reflect on the Convention "that brought us together", the *Convention of 30 June 2005 on Choice of Court Agreements* (hereinafter "the Choice of Court Convention").

During his tenure as Secretary General of the Hague Conference on Private International Law, Hans van Loon bravely faced the stalled negotiations on a comprehensive jurisdiction and enforcement of foreign judgments convention and reoriented the project into a "new direction".[1] Hence, the Permanent Bureau shifted gear to narrow the focus to a more limited convention on choice of court agreements the text of which was eventually submitted to the Diplomatic Session.[2]

---

* The authors gratefully acknowledge the assistance of Mr Carlo Di Nicola, Legal Officer and Ms Cara North, Legal Assistant at the Permanent Bureau, in preparing this article.

1 See *Proceedings of the Twentieth Session (2005)*, Tome III, *Choice of Court*, Antwerp – Oxford – Portland, Intersentia, 2010, Notice to the Reader, p. 5.

2 This new "working route" was facilitated by the work of Andrea Schultz. See, for all, A. Schultz, "Reflection Paper to Assist in the Preparation of a Convention on Jurisdiction and Recognition

The Choice of Court Convention was concluded within a remarkably rapid three year span of time, from the decision in April 2002 to set up an informal working group to facilitate the working process to the conclusion of the Convention by the Diplomatic Session Conference of the Twentieth Session in June 2005. Since then, Hans has consistently presented the Choice of Court Convention not as a mere consolation prize in the context of the Judgments Project, but as an important Convention in its own right. His unwavering faith in the importance of the Convention has proved to be an essential catalyst to the Permanent Bureau's efforts in promoting the Convention (below, II).

Admittedly, the Choice of Court Convention has not yet entered into force, but we dare to hope that it is now only a matter of time before it reaches that crucial milestone. Actually, incorporating the Convention into a key component of the international litigation framework is now primarily in the hands of those States working towards ratification (below, III).

II. LOOKING BACK: PROMISING SIGNS OF SUPPORT

Under Hans van Loon's guidance, the Permanent Bureau has deployed significant efforts in the process of monitoring and promoting existing Hague Conference instruments, both before and after their entry into force. The Choice of Court Convention is of course no exception.[3] For instance, in order to facilitate access to information regarding the Convention, the Permanent Bureau launched a special section on the Hague Conference website that is dedicated to the Choice of Court Convention.[4] The special section includes links to all relevant documentation pertaining to the Convention as well as a comprehensive and up-to-date bibliography listing relevant publications on the Choice of Court Convention.

---

and Enforcement of Foreign Judgments in Civil and Commercial Matters", Prel. Doc. No 19 of August 2002 drawn up for the attention of the meeting of the Informal Working Group of October 2002, see *Proceedings of the Twentieth Session (2005)*, *op.cit.* note 1, pp. 10–35, also available at <www.hcch.net/upload/wop/jdgm_pd19e.pdf>.

[3] For further details, see "Review of the Activities of the Conference in Regard to the Convention on Choice of Court Agreements", drawn up by the Permanent Bureau, Prel. Doc. No 12 of March 2011 for the attention of the Council of April 2011 on General Affairs and Policy of the Conference, available on the Hague Conference website at <www.hcch.net> under "Work in Progress" then "General Affairs" and "Ongoing Work on International Litigation and Possible Continuation of the Judgments Project", drawn up by the Permanent Bureau, Prel. Doc. No 5 of March 2012 for the attention of the Council of April 2012 on General Affairs and Policy of the Conference, available on the Hague Conference website at <www.hcch.net> under "Work in Progress" then "General Affairs", paras 4–7.

[4] Available on the Hague Conference website at <www.hcch.net> under "Specialised sections" then "Choice of Court Section".

In addition, the Permanent Bureau has prepared a publication targeted to the needs of those States considering the Convention, an Implementation Checklist that highlights issues which States may need to consider when preparing to adopt the Convention.[5] Additional efforts spearheaded by the Permanent Bureau include the launching of an electronic discussion group between representatives of interested Members on implementing the Choice of Court Convention. This discussion group provides the opportunity for officials who may wish to exchange information on the steps undertaken in the consideration of the Convention, as well as the issues that have to be addressed in the ratification process. Last but not least, the Permanent Bureau has actively undertaken to present and discuss the Convention at numerous colloquia and seminars, and has in return benefitted from direct comments and feedback on the Convention and its implementation in the jurisdictions concerned.[6]

Most importantly, ratification of the Choice of Court Convention has been encouraged by those who will be its end-users, the international business community. They have acclaimed the Convention as an instrument that responds to real and pressing needs of international businesses for increased certainty and predictability in cross-border transactions and litigation. The International Chamber of Commerce has on two occasions voiced its support for the Convention. In 2007, a first invitation for States to join the Convention was issued and the former Secretary General of the ICC stated that the "Convention should go a long way to reduce the workload of courts and the expense to businesses of long court battles over essentially procedural points".[7] In a 2012 statement, the importance of the Convention in facilitating international trade and commerce was reiterated and governments were once more urged to ratify swiftly the Convention.[8]

The fruits of these collective efforts are readily visible …

Despite not yet having entered into force, the Choice of Court Convention has already exerted an influence on other regional or bilateral legal schemes relating to choice of court clauses. For instance, the Convention's influence is visible in the *Agreement between Australia and New Zealand on Trans-Tasman on Court Proceedings and Regulatory Enforcement* ("Trans-Tasman Agreement").[9] The Trans-Tasman Agreement, which shall enter into force before the end of

5 Available at: <www.hcch.net/upload/checklist37e.pdf>.

6 For an overview, see the sub-section "Recent seminars" at the "Choice of Court Section".

7 See "ICC urges governments to ratify Hague Choice of Court Convention" 18 October 2007, available at: <www.iccwbo.org/News/Articles/2007/ICC-urges-governments-to-ratify-Hague-Choice-of-Court-Convention/>.

8 See "ICC calls on governments to facilitate cross-border litigation", 29 November 2012, available at: <www.iccwbo.org/News/Articles/2012/ICC-calls-on-governments-to-facilitate-cross-border-litigation/>.

9 Available at <www.justice.govt.nz/policy/international-justice/trans-tasman-court-proceed ings/documents/TTCP_signed_treaty.pdf>.

2013, restricts the discretion of courts where there is an exclusive choice of court agreement to which the Hague Choice of Court Convention would apply. Such clauses are to be respected by the parties and the court where proceedings are pending. Similarly, the Convention has had an impact on the "Arrangement on Reciprocal Recognition and Enforcement" that applies between Mainland China and *the Hong Kong Special Administrative Region*.[10]

III. LOOKING AHEAD: A SPEEDY ENTRY INTO FORCE?

The abovementioned signs of support have unfortunately not materialised in the Choice of Court Convention's entry into force. Pursuant to Art. 31(1), the Convention will enter into force following the deposit of the second instrument of ratification, acceptance, approval or accession. To date, only one State – Mexico – has deposited such an instrument. Mexico is thus the first and so far only country to have acceded to the Choice of Court Convention. While the United States of America signed the Convention on 19 January 2009 and the European Union signed it on 1 April 2009, they are both yet to ratify it. The question thus is why has the ratification process stalled since then?

A. SIGNS OF MOVEMENT TOWARDS RATIFICATION IN THE EUROPEAN UNION

In the European Union, the lapse of time between signing and ratifying the Choice of Court Convention appears to be principally linked to the revision of the Brussels I Regulation.[11] It had become apparent that while the Regulation and the Choice of Court Convention shared the common goal of ensuring the efficacy of choice of court agreements, important differences existed as to the application and scope of their respective choice of court regimes. As such, it was felt that the ratification of the Convention by the EU should be postponed until the review of Brussels I was completed and clarity emerged about the new features of the EU

10 *Arrangement on Reciprocal Recognition and Enforcement of Judgments in Civil and Commercial Matters by the Courts of the Mainland and of the Hong Kong Special Administrative Region pursuant to Choice of Court Agreements between Parties Concerned made between the Supreme People's Court of the People's Republic of China and the Government of the Hong Kong Special Administrative Region*, available at: <www.legislation.gov.hk/intracountry/eng/pdf/mainlandrej20060719e.pdf>.

11 Council Regulation (EC) No 44/2001 of 22 December 2000 on jurisdiction and the recognition and enforcement of judgments in civil and commercial matters, OJ 2001, L12, p 1.

choice of court regime, in particular whether review would attempt to align the choice of court provisions under Brussels I with the Choice of Court Convention.[12]

The review process formally commenced in April 2009 with the release of the Commission's Report,[13] which assessed the practical application of the Regulation and the Green Paper,[14] which called for submissions on those issues raised in the report. In December 2010, upon review of the submissions, the European Commission released its proposal,[15] which led to a new Regulation ('Brussels I Recast Regulation') at the end of 2012.[16] From a Hague Conference perspective, two of the changes introduced by the revised section on choice of court agreements in the Brussels I Recast Regulation are particularly significant.

The substantive validity of choice of court agreements is now addressed by the Brussels I Recast Regulation. In contrast, this issue is left silent under Art. 23 of the Brussels I Regulation and as such, its interpretation is left open to the EU courts. While the Court of Justice of the European Union ('CJEU') made clear that there must be precise consent in order for a choice of court agreement to be valid, it remained uncertain under the Regulation which law or rules should govern in circumstances where consent is subject to, for example, duress, mistake, fraud, negligence and incapacity.[17] Consequently, inconsistent decisions were rendered amongst Member States, whereby agreements considered valid in one

12 The European Commission suggested that "a coherent application of the rules of the Convention and those of [Brussels I]..." from the outset. See its *Report to the European Parliament, the Council and European Economic and Social Committee*, on the application of Council Regulation (EC) No 44/2001 on jurisdiction and the recognition and enforcement of judgments in civil and commercial matters, Brussels 21.4.2009 COM (2009) 174 Final, 6 available at http://ec.europa.eu/civiljustice/news/docs/report_judgements_en.pdf.

13 Commission of the European Communities, *Report from the Commission to the European Parliament, the Council and European Economic and Social Committee*, on the application of Council Regulation (EC) No 44/2001 on jurisdiction and the recognition and enforcement of judgments in civil and commercial matters, Brussels 21.4.2009 COM (2009) 174 Final, available at http://ec.europa.eu/civiljustice/news/docs/report_judgements_en.pdf.

14 See, Commission of the European Communities, Green Paper on the review of Council Regulation (EC) No 44/2001 on jurisdiction and the recognition and enforcement of judgments in civil and commercial matters, Brussels 21.4.2009 COM (2009) 175 final, available at http://eurlex.europa.eu/LexUriServ/LexUriServ.do?uri=COM:2009:0175:FIN:EN:PDF.

15 Proposal for a Regulation of the European Parliament and of the Council on jurisdiction and the recognition and enforcement of judgments in civil and commercial matters (Recast), COM (2010) 748 final, available at http://ec.europa.eu/justice/policies/civil/docs/com_2010_748_en.pdf.

16 Regulation (EU) No 1215/2012 of the European Parliament and of the Council of 22 December 2000 on jurisdiction and the recognition and enforcement of judgments in civil and commercial matters (recast) [2012] OJ L 351/1, available on the EU website at < http://europa.eu > under "find legislation".

17 See P. Beaumont and B. Yuksel, "The Validity of Choice of Court Agreements under the Brussels I Regulation and the Hague Choice of Court Agreements Convention", in K. Boele-Woelki, T. Einhorn, D. Girsberger and S. Symeonides (eds.) *Convergence and Divergence in Private International Law Liber Amicorum Kurt Siehr*, Eleven, 2010, p 574; N. Castell and P. de Lapasse, "La révision du règlement Bruxelles I à la suite de la publication du livre vert de la

member state were considered invalid in another.[18] Interestingly, a new recital of the Brussels I Recast Regulation now addresses the issue in line with the solution contained in the Choice of Court Convention.[19]

Another issue identified under the Brussels I Regulation was the priority given to the *lis pendens* rule over the choice of court agreements.[20] Under the Brussels I Regulation, the court first seized is entitled to decide the question of jurisdiction and the chosen court is required to stay its proceedings until a decision as to jurisdiction has been made. This provision provides an avenue for considerable and deliberate delay in proceedings by litigants acting in bad faith and suggests an apparent disregard for the purpose of choice of court agreements. This rule was particularly problematic in instances of related proceedings where, despite the existence of a choice of court agreement, two or more courts were seized. In these circumstances, the chosen court is not required to stay its proceedings until a decision is rendered but rather is given the discretionary power to do so, leading to multiple proceedings being heard and considered simultaneously, resulting in conflicting decisions. During the review process, stakeholders from Member States, as well as other interested parties expressed a preference for the Brussels I Recast Regulation to give priority to the chosen court to decide questions of jurisdiction, regardless of whether it is the first court seized.[21] Accordingly, under

---

Commission", *Gazette du Palais*, 2010, no. 149, p. 26 ; R. Fentiman, *International Commercial Litigation*, Oxford, Oxford University Press, 2010, pp. 68–69.

18 P. Beaumont and B. Yuksel, *ibid* p. 574. See also J. Steinle and E. Vasiliades, "The Enforcement of Jurisdiction Agreements under the Brussels I Regulation: Reconsidering the Principles of Party Autonomy", *Journal of Private International Law,* 2010, Vol 6 No. 3, p 565; See also, B. Hess, T. Pfeiffer & P. Schlosser, The Brussels I – Regulation (EC) No 44/2001, The Heidelberg Report on the Application of Regulation Brussels I in 25 Member States, Munich, Verlag C.H. Beck, 2008 para 326.

19 Recital 20 of Regulation (EU) No 1215/2012 of the European Parliament and of the Council of 12 December 2012 L 351/1 reads as follows: "[w]here a question arises as to whether a choice-of-court agreement in favour of a court or the courts of a Member State is null and void as to its substantive validity, that question should be decided in accordance with the law of the Member State of the court or courts designated in the agreement, including the conflict-of-laws rules of that Member State." Compare with Article 5(1) and 6(a) of the Choice of Court Convention. For extensive commentary, see, F. Villata, *L'attuazione degli accordi di scelta del foro nel regolamento Bruxelles I,* Milan, CEDAM, 2012, pp. 43–122. See also F. Pocar, "Brevi riflessioni in tema di revisione del regolamento Bruxelles I e clausole di scelta del foro", *Diritto del commercio internazionale,* 2012, p 374 and A. Briggs, *Agreements on Jurisdiction and Choice of Law,* Oxford, Oxford University Press, 2008 pp. 530–531.

20 For recent contributions on this particular issue, see *inter alia*, P. Rogerson, "Lis Pendens and Third States: The Commission's Proposed Changes to the Brussels I Regulation" in E. Lein (ed.) *The Brussels I Review Proposal Uncovered,* London, BIICL, 2012, p. 103; See also, L. Fumagalli, "Lis Alibi Pendens: The Rules on Parallel Proceeding in the Reform of the Brussels I Regulation" in F. Pocar, I. Viarengo and F.C. Villata (eds.) *Recasting Brussels I,* Milan, CEDAM, 2012, p 238.

21 See for example, the contributions made in response to the Green Paper, available at http://ec.europa.eu/justice/newsroom/civil/opinion/090630_en.htm.

the new provision all other courts engaged other than the court chosen, under the choice of court agreement, are to "stay [their] proceedings ... until such time as the latter court declares that it has no jurisdiction under the exclusive choice-of-court agreement".[22] This revised rule gives priority to party autonomy and reflects the operation of the Choice of Court Convention.[23]

The alignment of the choice of court provisions under the Brussels I Recast Regulation and the key operational provisions of the Choice of Court Convention provide a clear signal of support by the EU for the Convention. The revisions illustrate an acceptance by the EU of the Convention as an internationally agreed standard at the global level. It is thus essential that the EU urgently turns its attention to the ratification of the Convention.[24] Joining the Convention and inviting its trade partners to follow that path will eventually ensure EU courts and practitioners more legal certainty in situations outside the scope of the Brussels I Recast Regulation.

B. THE VIEW FROM ACROSS THE POND

The lapse in time between signing and ratification in the case of the United States reflects issues connected with the inherent nature of federalism in the United States. The issues surrounding domestic implementation are in strong contrast to the situation in Europe where the Union has competence in this area.[25] In the United States, the recognition and enforcement of foreign judgments is largely a matter of state law, while the treaty power is exclusively in the hands of the federal government. The U.S. State Department, charged with preparing the necessary steps for securing advice and consent from the Senate, also must present a means of domestic implementation of the convention that will insure that the international obligations under the treaty will be met. To that end, the U.S. State Department, Office of Legal Adviser, has worked since the completion of the Convention on June 30, 2005 at building a constituency for the Convention and achieving consensus in the mechanism for domestic implementation. What is essential to recognize is that the U.S. delay in ratification results not from a

22 Recital 22 of Regulation (EU) No 1215/2012 of the European Parliament and of the Council of 12 December 2012 L 351/1.

23 Article 6 of the Choice of Court Convention.

24 Tentatively scheduled for 2012: see Communication from the Commission to the European Parliament, the Council, the European Economic and Social Committee and the Committee of the Regions: Delivering an Area of Freedom, Security and Justice for Europe's Citizens, Action Plan Implementing the Stockholm Programme (COM (2010)) 171 final), p. 28.

25 R. Brand, "The European Magnet and the U.S. Centrifuge: Ten Selected Private International Law Developments of 2008", *ILSA Journal of International and Comparative Law*, 2009, Vol. 15, 367–393.

lack of enthusiasm for the Choice of Court Convention but from "political"[26] and philosophical differences in attitudes about domestic state/federal relations. It is in fact because of this factionalism that the future ability of the United States successfully to negotiate and implement private international law treaties hangs in the balance. While there is no "one size fits all" format for implementation domestically of private international law instruments, there must be the ability to achieve consensus and thus ratification if the U.S. is to continue to participate in further international cooperation and harmonization of law.[27]

1. *The Need for the Convention*

Much has been written, largely by scholars but also by a limited number of practitioners,[28] about the value of the Choice of Court Convention for the United States which is not party to any bilateral or multilateral convention on the recognition and enforcement of civil judgments that would be covered by the Convention. In addition, the U.S. readily recognizes and enforces most incoming

---

26 The reference here is to "political" in a general sense, not a reference to any of the political parties.

27 See, e.g., P. H. Pfund, "Federalism and U.S. Participation in Intergovernmental Efforts to Unify Private Law", *Villanova Law Review*, 2011, Vol. 56, p. 559.

28 *See generally* L. E. Teitz, "The Hague Choice of Court Convention: Validating Party Autonomy and Providing an Alternative to Arbitration", *American Journal of Comparative Law*, 2006, Vol. 53, 543; L.E. Teitz, "Choice of Court Clauses and Third Countries from a US perspective: Challenges to Predictability" in A. Nuyts and N. Watté (eds.) *International Civil Litigation in Europe and Relations with Third States*, Bruxelles, Bruylant, 2005, p. 285; D. P. Stewart, "The 2005 Hague Choice of Court Agreements Convention: A Useful Tool for the Transnational Litigator," in *Foreign Affairs Litigation in United States Courts: The Twenty-Fifth Sokol Colloquium*, 2013; R. Brand, "U.S. Implementation vel non of the 2005 Hague Convention on Choice of Court Agreements", *2010 Yearbook of Private International Law*, 2011, 107–122; R. Brand, "Arbitration or Litigation? Choice of Forum After the 2005 Hague Convention on Choice of Court Agreements", *Belgrade Law Review*, 2009, (Issue No. 3, 2009), 23–35 (available at <www.ius.bg.ac.rs/Anali/Annals%202009/Annals%202009%20p%20023-035.pdf>), also reprinted at *Transnational Dispute Management*, 2010, (Issue 1, April 2010); G. S. Lipe and T. J. Tyler, "The Hague Convention on Choice of Court Agreements: Creating Room for Choice in International Cases", *Houston Journal of International Law*, 2010, Vol. 33, 1; S. B. Burbank, "A Tea Party at The Hague?", *Southwestern Journal of International Law*, 2012, Vol. 18, 101; S. B. Burbank, "Saving the Hague Choice of Court Convention", *University of Pennsylvania Journal of International Law*, 2008, Vol. 29, 657; C. Dubay, "From Forum Non Conveniens to Open Forum: Implementing the Hague Convention on Choice of Court Agreements in the United States", *George Mason Journal of International Commercial Law*, 2011, Vol. 3, 1; *See also* the Report of the Committee on International Commercial Disputes of the Association of the Bar of the City of New York on "The Hague Convention on Choice of Court Agreements," Sept. 8, 2006, available at <www.nycbar.org/pdf/report/DOC182.pdf>; Report and Recommendation of the Section of International Law of the American Bar Association on "The Hague Convention on Choice of Court Agreements," 7–8 August 2006, available at < http://apps.americanbar.org/intlaw/policy/investment/hcca0806.pdf >.

foreign judgments under existing law,[29] as well as enforcing exclusive choice of forum (as they are referred to in the U.S.) clauses.[30] The perception and belief of the majority of practitioners and academics is that U.S. judgments do not fare as well abroad where they are not readily recognized or enforced,[31] especially outside of the common-law world. The Choice of Court Convention, unlike the existing uniform law on recognizing foreign judgments[32] and the American Law Institute (ALI) draft statute,[33] concentrates on the direct *exporting* of U.S. judgments, that is making them enforceable abroad. From a U.S. perspective, it is an essential element of international trade, helping to rectify the current trade imbalance of *importing* more judgments than can be enforced externally. U.S. trading partners, especially those within the European Union, already are able to enforce their judgments both at home and usually in the U.S. in light of the expansive U.S. attitude toward recognition.

The Convention also differs from domestic law in the U.S. on recognition of judgments, as it covers not only the resulting judgment but also the agreement to litigate exclusively in a particular forum.[34] Thus it can be seen as a commercial transaction planning tool, that is providing predictability and certainty, thus increasing cross-border transactions and reinforcing party autonomy. As a dispute resolution mechanism, the Convention is a litigation analogue to the

29 "U.S. law remains remarkably receptive to foreign judgments from around the world." D. P. Stewart, "Recognition and Enforcement of Foreign Judgments in the United States," *Yearbook of Private International Law*, 2010, Vol. XII, 179 at 180.

30 M/S Bremen v. Zapata Off-Shore Co., 407 U.S. 1 (1972).

31 See generally P. Trooboff, "Ten (and Probably More) Difficulties in Negotiating a Worldwide Convention on International Jurisdiction and Enforcement of Judgments: Some Initial Lessons" in J. J. Barcelo & K. M. Clermont (eds.) *A Global Law of Jurisdiction and Judgments: Lessons from The Hague*, The Hague/New York, Kluwer Law, 2002, p. 263. For a study of the relative merits of arbitration and litigation in the international context, see W.W. Park, "The Relative Reliability of Arbitration Agreement and Court Selection Clauses" in J.L. Goldsmith (ed.) *International Dispute Resolution: The Regulation of Forum Selection*, Transnational Publishers, 1997.

32 Uniform Foreign Money-Judgment Recognition Act, 13 U.L.A. 263 (1962), which has been adopted in more than 32 jurisdictions. Although its direct application is only to foreign money judgments, states that have adopted it often look to it for guidance in treating non-money foreign judgments. Of those states adopting the UFMJRA, eight have added a reciprocity requirement, which is discretionary in seven of those states. See National Conference of Commissioners on Uniform State Laws (NCCUSL) (now Uniform Law Commission), available at: < http://www.uniformlaws.org/Act.aspx?title=Foreign Money Judgments Recognition Act >.

33 ALI, *Recognition and Enforcement of Foreign Judgments: Analysis and Proposed Federal Statute*, 2006. Professors Silberman and Lowenfeld, both from the New York University School of Law, were the Reporters. See L. J. Silberman & A. F. Lowenfeld, "A Different Challenge for the ALI: Herein of Foreign Country Judgments, an International Treaty, and an American Statute", *Indiana Law Journal*, 2000, Vol. 75, 635.

34 *See, e.g.* W. W. Heiser, "The Hague Convention on Choice of Court Agreements: The Impact on Forum Non Conveniens, Transfer of Venue, Removal and Recognition of Judgments in United States Courts", *University of Pennsylvania Journal of International Law*, 2010, Vol. 31, 1013.

New York Convention on arbitral awards, which will provide a viable alternative to commercial arbitration in cross-border transactions. Aside from the usual arguments about the costs and time delay in international arbitration, some commercial actors (private and public) prefer the transparency of litigation as well as the possibility for subsequent full appellate review. The implementation of the Choice of Court Convention will not only facilitate cross-border transactions by providing predictability in dispute resolution and enforcement of any resulting judgments, it will provide a foundation for further efforts to increase international trade and certainty through harmonization of the bases for recognition of other categories of judgments.

2. *The Efforts at Implementation*[35]

Although the U.S. began work on implementation as soon as the Report was finalized,[36] earlier efforts at a comprehensive jurisdiction and judgments convention in The Hague[37] had resulted in domestic efforts to prepare federal implementing legislation and subsequently in a proposed statute prepared by the American Law Institute for federalizing the recognition and enforcement of foreign judgments.[38] By the time the Choice of Court Convention was signed, there was also a revised version[39] of the earlier 1962 Uniform Foreign Money-Judgments Recognition Act, which had been adopted by more than 30 states in some

[35] *Ed. LE Teitz*: Although I have been involved in multiple roles and aspects with the Choice of Court Convention (previously member of US delegation, member of US State Dept Study Group, and Co-Reporter on ULC Uniform Law), my primary role, both now as in the past, is as an advocate for the Convention and its ratification by the US through whatever domestic mechanisms will lead to full implementation.

[36] The Report was released in early May 2007: *see* T. Hartley & M. Dogauchi, Explanatory Report on the 2005 Hague Convention on Choice of Court Agreements Convention, *Proceedings of the Twentieth Session (2005)*, Tome III, *Choice of Court*, Antwerp, Intersentia, 2010, pp. 785–863, available at <www.hcch.net/upload/expl37e.pdf>.

[37] There is extensive literature on the Hague jurisdiction and judgments negotiations and drafts. See generally S.P. Baumgartner, *The Proposed Hague Convention on Jurisdiction and Foreign Judgments: Trans-Atlantic Lawmaking for Transnational Litigation*, Tübingen, Mohr Siebeck, 2003; R. A. Brand, "Jurisdictional Common Ground: In Search of a Global Convention" in A.T. von Mehren, J.A.R. Nafziger & S. Symeonides (eds.) *Law and Justice in a Multistate World: Essays in Honor of Arthur T. von Mehren*, Ardsley, N.Y., Transnational Publishers, 2002 at 11; K.M. Clermont, "Jurisdictional Salvation and the Hague Treaty", *Cornell Law Review*, 1999, Vol. 85, 89; L.J. Silberman, "Comparative Jurisdiction in the International Context: Will the Proposed Hague Judgments Convention Be Stalled?", *DePaul Law Review*, 2002, Vol. 52, 319; A.T. von Mehren, "Enforcing Judgments Abroad: Reflections of the Design of Recognition Conventions", 1998, *Brooklyn Journal of International Law*, Vol. 24, 17.

[38] ALI, *Recognition and Enforcement of Foreign Judgments: Analysis and Proposed Federal Statute*, 2006.

[39] The Uniform Foreign-Country Money Judgments Recognition Act was drafted and then approved by the National Conference of Commissioners of Uniform State Laws (now Uniform Law Commission) at its annual conference held between July 21–28, 2005. For full version

version.[40] This tension between federal and state law became more pronounced as the process for implementation continued. To facilitate implementation and reach a compromise that would be in keeping with federalism concepts, the State Department considered an approach of "cooperative federalism" which would involve parallel federal and state legislation, where states could opt out of the federal statute and instead implement the Convention through the adoption of an approved uniform act, the Uniform International Choice of Court Agreements Act, drafted by the Uniform Law Commission. Subsequent efforts focused on aligning the two texts and also addressing issues of federal jurisdiction, applicable law in federal court (the "Erie" issue), the standard for compliance, and some other procedural issues. Following multiple meetings over more than 4 years and efforts to obtain consensus, the result was a stalemate. At that point, in April 2012, the U.S. State Department, Office of Legal Adviser, issued a "White Paper" on a proposed compromise approach.

As part of its ongoing multi-year efforts (from 2005) to move the Convention forward toward securing Senate advice and consent and ratification by the President, the U.S. State Department held an open meeting of the Secretary of State's Advisory Committee on Private International Law (ACPIL) in January 2013. At that meeting, the State Department – without abandoning the cooperative federalism approach – circulated an unofficial draft of federal implementing legislation for consideration, following the model of implementation of the New York Convention. The process continues to be one of reaching out to *all stakeholders* and seeking input from all those who will be end-users of the Convention. The State Department's commitment to seeing the Convention enter into force in the United States remains strong and reflects the U.S. government's continuing active participation in the development of private international law, on the regional and international arenas, as evidenced by its work at the Hague Conference – and for the last 34 years with Hans van Loon.

SOME CONCLUDING REMARKS

Hans van Loon's unwavering support for the Choice of Court Convention is part of his lifelong commitment to bridging different legal systems and traditions while seeking to facilitate cross-border movement. Contrary to many who see the Choice of Court Convention as a "fallback" position and a fragment of the "failed" bigger comprehensive convention, Hans van Loon was able to recognize that the

of the UFCMJRA's text, see <www.uniformlaws.org/shared/docs/foreign%20country%20money%20judgments%20recognition/ufcmjra_final05_notstyled.pdf>.

40 *Supra*, note 32.

Choice of Court Convention was not "rubble" but a needed solid foundation for further expanded work on the recognition and enforcement of judgments.

The Choice of Court Convention, once in force, will serve many purposes as emphasized in the preamble[41] – contract drafting tool, dispute resolution mechanism, and instrument for facilitating trade. It will bridge civil and common law traditions and provide certainty and predictability. That bridge is being built slowly as those on each end strive to build the necessary access roads out of existing domestic law.

[41] Preamble to the 2005 *Convention of 30 June 2005 on Choice of Court Agreements*, *supra* note 1, p. 762.

FEDERALISM AND U.S. IMPLEMENTATION OF PIL CONVENTIONS – IMPLEMENTING THE HAGUE CONVENTION ON CHOICE OF COURT AGREEMENTS

Peter H. PFUND[1]
Assistant Legal Adviser for Private International Law, U.S. Department of State, until 1997

HANS VAN LOON

Hans has been a wonderful colleague and friend since I attended my first session at the Hague Conference in about 1979. Since that time, this remarkable man has moved from junior staff attorney among four to Secretary General of the organization when his three legal colleagues went into retirement about fifteen years ago. During his tenure, the organization has transitioned from crafting largely setting out rules for determining applicable law better to meet current needs through conventions many of which set out substantive law and procedures. The Conference now provides a plethora of activities supporting in particular those Hague Conventions providing for the protection of children and others dealing with legal procedures. The Conference has vastly increased its membership and has become a world organization. It has offered language services in Spanish when that was deemed important to ensure that Spanish-speaking countries would participate in its work and that its Conventions would appeal to Spanish-speaking countries. The Conference's budget has increased to accommodate expanded services for its Member States, and the Conference's staff – much of

[1] The views expressed in this writing are those of the author and not necessarily those of the Department of State. For an earlier article on federalism and PIL treaties, see Pfund, "Federalism and U.S. Participation in Intergovernmental Efforts to Unify Private Law", 56 *Villanova L. Rev.* 559–567 (2011).

it young volunteers – has increased accordingly. Voluntary contributions from Member States have substantially increased, permitting the Permanent Bureau to provide technical assistance to help States implement and become parties to Hague Conventions. Further resourceful initiatives are under way.

During most of Hans' years as Secretary-General, he was very ably assisted by William Duncan as his Deputy. These two dedicated international civil servants were a perfect fit and with the help of the entire staff set the tone for the ambitious work program of the Permanent Bureau and the Conference's Member States.

I feel privileged to have worked with Hans for over 17 years and honored to have been asked to contribute to this Liber Amicorum to celebrate and recognize Hans and his important accomplishments upon his retirement. I am certain that we will continue to benefit from Hans' commitment to the work of the organization and I wish him and Carola all the best as Hans moves on to other tasks.

I hope in this brief piece to help readers understand a problem that now, more than hitherto, confronts the Department of State with regard to implementation of unifying private law. Until recently, obtaining the necessary Senate consent to U.S. ratification of or accession to private international law (PIL) conventions has been difficult and time-consuming enough. However, during the past few years the process has been made all the more difficult through increased sensitivity on the part of the individual states of the United States, and legal organizations representing the states, with regard to the way that law and obligations are imposed on the states by the federal government via international treaty or convention.

Perhaps understanding this renewed sensitivity in the United States and the delicate task it imposes on the federal government will help delegates from other countries to sessions of the Hague Conference better to realize from where U.S. delegates are coming as they participate in those sessions.

FEDERALISM IN THE UNITED STATES AND THE IMPLEMENTATION OF PIL TREATIES

For the United States to be able to become party to an international treaty, there must be a decision of the Executive Branch to submit the treaty to the U.S. Senate, and Senate action to give advice and consent to U.S. ratification of or accession to the treaty. Usually, the Executive Branch will not submit a PIL treaty to the Senate unless there is fair certainty that there is sufficient political support from the private sector for the United States to become a party, that Senate advice and consent will be forthcoming, and that any implementing legislation deemed necessary will be enacted by both houses of Congress. However, even then unforeseen and unforeseeable political forces within Congress may threaten favorable Senate and Congressional action.

The United States has become party to a number of conventions unifying private law or legal procedures because the relevant parts of the private sector, and especially the private legal sector, became convinced that the convention would provide improvements and benefits over the status quo without the convention. In the case of the *Hague Convention of 29 May 1993 on Protection of Children and Co-operation in Respect of Intercountry Adoption*, it took about seven years after the Convention was concluded before the necessary political support of the private sector for U.S. ratification had been marshaled. The support was based largely on the perception of self-interest and what became a moral necessity – that the world's major receiving country of children in adoption could not fail to become a party to a convention crafted by many nations and designed, in the face of serious abuses, to protect the children and birth mothers involved in such adoptions. The preparation of federal implementing legislation and detailed regulations took another seven years.

Most private law in the United States is state law, i.e., it is determined by state legislatures and state courts, and not by the federal government. This is true of family law, commercial law, and law in many other areas. The unification of private law or legal procedures through PIL conventions will therefore have an impact on such state law if the United States is to become a party to them.

The issue to what extent and by what means the federal government could impose changes in the law on the individual states of the United States by a PIL treaty was not a major issue during my PIL years in the State Department ending in 1997. For example, the United States in 1988 became a party to both the 1980 *UN Convention on Contracts for the International Sale of Goods* (CISG) and the *Hague Convention of 25 October 1980 on the Civil Aspects of International Child Abduction* without any major issue arising, notwithstanding that these conventions supplanted state law and imposed new legal obligations. The CISG is implemented in the United States directly by U.S. ratification after Senate advice and consent, without any federal implementing legislation. The 1980 Hague Convention was implemented by enactment of federal legislation – the International Child Abduction Remedies Act (ICARA)[2] – which provided, *inter alia*, for the left-behind parent seeking return of a child from the United States to be able to bring the return action in either the state or federal court of the state where the allegedly abducted child is located. Even the possibility that the parent seeking return could by-pass the state court system, usually charged with family law matters in that state, and bring the return action in the federal court did

[2] Pub. L. No. 100–300, 102 Stat. 437 (1988) (codified as amended at 42 U.S.C. sections 11601–11610 (2006).

not raise any major problems in Congress at that time. In fact, in the apparent belief that federal courts are more likely than state courts effectively to provide for compliance with the treaty obligations imposed by the Convention, a significant number of cases known to the State Department are brought by persons seeking the return of a child from the United States under the Convention in federal courts rather than state courts.

Different mechanisms have been identified for implementing recent Hague Conventions in the U.S. federal system. The *Hague Convention of 23 November 2007 on the International Recovery of Child Support and Other Forms of Family Maintenance* (already approved by the Senate) will be implemented largely through uniform state law – specifically, amendments to the Uniform Interstate Family Support Act (UIFSA). However, the Department of Health and Human Services is expected to be the Central Authority under the Convention, and proposed federal implementing legislation provides that states must adopt the UIFSA amendments or risk the loss of essential federal funding for child support and other purposes.

By contrast, it is proposed that the *Hague Convention of 5 July 2006 on the Law Applicable to Certain Rights in Respect of Securities held with an Intermediary* (an applicable law convention that is currently pending in the Senate) be implemented as a self-executing treaty without implementing legislation. This Convention, which is largely consistent with Articles 8 and 9 of the Uniform Commercial Code, would apply directly to covered transactions.

However, several PIL conventions potentially beneficial and acceptable to the United States have so far not been submitted to the Senate for advice and consent, in part because they are believed to be susceptible to states' rights questions – federalism concerns – that might be seen to outweigh the benefits they promise. I think here of the 1973 UNIDROIT *Convention on the Form of the International Will* and the *1985 Hague Convention on the Law Applicable to Trusts and on their Recognition.*

THE HAGUE CONVENTION ON CHOICE OF COURT AGREEMENTS

The United States has signed the subject *Hague Convention of 30 June 2005 on Choice of Court Agreements* ("Choice of Court Convention"), meaning that it intends to move towards ratification and implementation of the Convention in due course.

The Convention provides for the enforcement of contractual provisions by which the parties to a contract have agreed that a specific court or courts of a particular State will have exclusive jurisdiction to hear and decide on any disputes. The resulting court decision is entitled to recognition and enforcement in all States party to the Convention. Courts in a State party that have not been chosen may not accept the case, and the chosen court may not refuse to adjudicate the dispute.

In the U.S. federal system, there are both federal and state courts in each state of the United States. The Convention does not prescribe jurisdictional rules for States parties. Thus, whether a particular court has subject matter jurisdiction to hear a dispute or to recognize and enforce a judgment is a matter of U.S. law. For federal courts there are specific rules that can limit their jurisdiction. State courts are typically courts of general jurisdiction, but under the Convention, states can decide whether their courts will accept cases that have no connection to the forum.

It is questions surrounding the implementation of the Convention that have aroused in a most specific way the sensitivities of organizations representing the states on an aspect of the imposition of law on the states by treaty and federal legislation. The players in this drama include, on the one hand, bar groups as well as practicing lawyers and academics associated with the American Law Institute. These players generally favor implementing the Choice of Court Convention in the same way that the *New York Convention on the Recognition and Enforcement of Foreign Arbitral Awards* was implemented – exclusively through federal legislation. On the other hand, the Uniform Law Commission (ULC) (formerly the National Conference of Commissioners on Uniform State Law – NCCUSL), representing the interests of the states, favors a "cooperative federalism" approach involving parallel federal and state implementing law. Under this approach, individual U.S. states could choose to enact implementing legislation – the ULC-prepared Uniform Act – that would apply in lieu of the federal legislation for the purpose of implementation of the Convention in that state. Any provision of the state law, and any state court interpretation of the state law, that is not consistent with the full implementation of the Convention in accordance with the federal statute would, however, be preempted by the corresponding provision of the federal law.

The Departments of State and Justice, at meetings held under the auspices of the American Society of International Law (ASIL), and at meetings of the Department of State's Advisory Committee on Private International Law (ACPIL), have sought to bring the parties together and find common ground.

In considering how to implement the Convention, stakeholders have considered – in addition to the threshold question of whether to follow the New York Convention model or a cooperative federalism approach – a basket of difficult issues including the scope of federal court jurisdiction, the availability of removal from state to federal court, the applicable statute of limitations and the mechanism for federal preemption.

Another issue, which arose later in the discussions, is which law federal courts, if charged with a case, would apply – the federal implementing law or, where enacted, the state law that is, in essence and interpretation, to conform to the federal law and its interpretation. Normally, under a 1938 decision of the U.S. Supreme Court, when a case is brought in or removed to a federal court and jurisdiction is based on diversity of the parties, i.e., the parties are from different states or countries, the federal court is to apply state law.

In April 2012, the State Department issued a White Paper[3] that provides for parallel federal and state implementing legislation and sets forth a compromise proposal regarding the unresolved issues. The White Paper begins by listing the following goals that are to help determine how to implement PIL conventions in the United States generally:

- Assurance that the implementation approach taken by the United States will result in U.S. compliance with its international obligations.
- Taking into account the historical allocation of relevant federal and state interests.
- Providing certainty in transactions.
- Promoting transparency.
- Taking into account the views of potential treaty partners regarding implementation.

The White Paper then addresses the most contentious outstanding issues, providing proposals on handling federal diversity jurisdiction, removal to federal court, and statutes of limitation. Those proposals generally favored the interests of the states. In balancing those concessions, the White Paper proposes that, even where federal court jurisdiction is based on diversity, federal courts should apply the federal law rather than state law (if enacted) implementing the Convention in that state.

The White Paper expresses the view that as a matter of principle, when federal law exists for the implementation of a treaty, federal courts should apply it with the straightforward task of construing the federal statute. Uncertainty and confusion would result from the need for the federal court to determine what the state law provides, for preemption purposes whether state law would produce a result different from the result under the federal statute, and thus to what extent the federal law should be applied in lieu of the state law. The White Paper asserts

[3] "Implementation of the Hague Convention on Choice of Court Agreements in the United States", attaching the text of the Hague Convention; the Draft federal implementing legislation, Version #6, February 28, 2012; and the Draft Uniform International Choice of Court Agreements Act, July 2011 (prepared by the ULC).

that the federal approach would be more direct, more transparent, more easily administered and would offer greater appeal to treaty partners and transacting parties.

The White Paper reflects a delicate balance regarding the outstanding issues. It states that while no side would be entirely pleased with this approach, unless a way forward is agreed upon, U.S. ratification of the Convention would not seem possible for many years and the twenty-year effort of negotiating countries to produce the Convention would be lost. Moreover, the White Paper states, U.S. persons would be deprived of the Convention's benefits: the enforcement of choice of court agreements and the recognition and enforcement of U.S. judgments in foreign courts.

A number of stakeholders responded to the White Paper by saying that they could accept its proposals. However, not all stakeholders concurred.

By letter dated May 22, 2012 to the State Department Legal Adviser, Harold Koh, the President of the ULC, Michael Houghton, stated that the ULC could not accept the proposed package because of its objection to the provision on applicable law. The ULC argues that the compromise proposal is

> … troubling, in that it does change the existing federal/state balance by altering a core principle that has governed questions of federal/state jurisdiction since the landmark decision of *Erie v. Tompkins*[4] in 1938 – that when an action is brought in federal court only under diversity jurisdiction, the federal court will apply *state* substantive law in deciding the dispute.

The ULC argues that the alteration in the current balance is not necessary in order to implement the Convention, would facilitate forum shopping, would be unfair to defendants, and would lead to increased uncertainty and unpredictability contrary to the goal of the Convention. The Houghton letter states that uncertainty would also relate to the applicability of other aspects of state law, such as whether there was consent to the choice of court agreement, the validity of the agreement, and whether a party to the agreement lacked capacity or the judgment was obtained by fraud. Finally, the letter states that the approach is unprecedented and does not fit the cooperative federalism model.

In his response letter to ULC President Houghton, dated July 2, 2012, Legal Adviser Koh states that "U.S. policy interests are best served by having federal courts apply federal law in this situation, for several reasons:

> (1) As a matter of principle, where a federal statute has been developed to implement a treaty, federal courts should apply it.

[4] 304 U.S. 64 (1938).

(2) Applying federal law would simplify the task for federal courts, which would not need to interpret state law or analyze whether state law should be preempted.

(3) Applying federal law would promote the development of jurisprudence on interpretation of that law, which is the key to determining whether federal law should preempt state law in a given case. That would promote greater uniformity in treaty interpretation.

(4) Applying federal law would make the implementation process more direct, more transparent, and more attractive to potential treaty partners and foreign litigants.

The Koh letter explains that the position adopted in the White Paper represents a compromise that seeks to reconcile the widely differing views of key constituencies. The Koh letter took issue with what it characterized as incorrect legal objections of the ULC and misplaced concerns about forum shopping, and stated that there appeared to be no reason why other state law issues raised by the ULC would be treated any differently under the federal implementing statute in a state that has chosen to enact the Uniform Act.

The Legal Adviser emphasized that the federal proposal is not unprecedented, and that what is novel is the specific proposal for exclusive use of federal legislation in federal court "in this particular treaty context."

Harold Koh's letter, after thanking the ULC for its commitment to the Convention and in trying to find an agreed basis that would permit proceeding to U.S. ratification, concludes that there appears to be no prospect of agreement in the near term and that further efforts to reach agreement end "for the time being as we assess what might next be done."

The above summaries of the views of the federal government and the ULC do not do justice to the full arguments for each side. The summaries are offered to provide some idea of the considerable work that has been accomplished, the good will of the parties to find an agreed way to implement the Hague Choice of Court Convention, and the difficulty in finding a compromise that would address the various outstanding issues in a manner that would satisfy key constituencies.

At the October 12, 2012 annual meeting of the State Department's Advisory Committee on Private International Law, a panel considered whether a way forward could be found on implementation of the Choice of Court Agreements Convention, but no solution was found.

CONCLUSION

There is clearly agreement in the United States on the merits of the Hague Choice of Court Convention and the benefits it would provide for U.S. interests. Much work by many countries over many years has gone into making the Convention potentially acceptable to the States that participated in its negotiation and to other States as well. In the United States, much work has gone into cooperation on working out the details of implementation in a way that meets the goals for implementation of PIL conventions set out by the Department of State. However, an agreed way forward remains elusive. The parties seem to be at an impasse on this issue but seem to wish for the Convention to move forward. There is awareness that it is important for the success of the Convention, as measured by the number of States that eventually become parties to it, that the United States becomes a party as well.

One must hope that the debate over an implementation mechanism will ultimately be resolved and that the Convention will eventually be sent to the U.S. Senate for advice and consent to U.S. ratification without opposition by any element of the U.S. private sector, given the fragility of PIL conventions in the U.S. political process. However the outstanding issues are addressed in the legislative process, the promise of the benefits that U.S. ratification and implementation of the Convention would provide in the United States and elsewhere should outweigh the concerns of one side or the other with regard to the specific issues of domestic implementation.

In any event, the new level of cooperation between the federal government, the ULC and the practicing bar on implementation of the Choice of Court Convention should become the model for cooperation on implementation of other PIL conventions to which it is hoped the United States may become a party, including perhaps, the *Hague Convention of 1 July 1985 on the Law Applicable to Trusts and on their Recognition* and the 1973 Unidroit *Convention on the Form of an International Will.*

L'AUTONOMIE DE LA VOLONTÉ DANS LES RELATIONS DE FAMILLE INTERNATIONALES : REGARDS SUR LES RÉCENTS INSTRUMENTS INTERNATIONAUX

Mariel REVILLARD*
Docteur en droit

1. Les profondes mutations du droit de la famille au cours du XXe et du début du XXIe siècle sont marquées par la place importante accordée à la volonté individuelle dans le statut personnel, familial et patrimonial prise en compte dans les réformes des législations nationales : choix des formes de couples (mariage, union de fait, partenariat, mariage homosexuel) de séparations et de divorces, de filiations et d'adoptions. L'autonomie de la volonté s'exprime dans le contrat de mariage et la mutabilité du régime matrimonial et dans les successions par des testaments, pactes successoraux, donations et donations-partages.

2. Les liens de famille internationaux se multiplient du fait de la mobilité des personnes. L'autonomie de la volonté dans le statut personnel et familial en droit interne a trouvé sa place dans les relations internationales[1] et plusieurs lois étrangères laissent aux époux le choix de la loi applicable au nom, aux effets du mariage ou du divorce[2]. La voie avait été ouverte pour cette option de législation dans plusieurs conventions de La Haye et règlements communautaires.

---

* Poursuit des activités d'enseignement et de recherche en droit international privé, droit communautaire et droit comparé.

1 P. Courbe, L'influence des réformes du droit de la famille sur le droit international privé, *in Liber Amicorum H. Gaudemet-Tallon*, Dalloz 2000, p. 703.

2 Loi hollandaise du 25 mars 1981, loi allemande du 25 juillet 1986, Loi espagnole du 15 octobre 1990 et 29 septembre 2003, loi belge du 16 juillet 2004.

3. L'introduction de l'autonomie de la volonté dans les relations de famille internationales suppose que soient résolues certaines questions dans sa mise en œuvre, choix de la loi, de la juridiction, sa forme, son moment, le titulaire de ce choix. Leur réponse sera présentée dans le cadre d'instruments internationaux récents sur les régimes matrimoniaux, le divorce, les successions et le mandat d'inaptitude.

RÉGIMES MATRIMONIAUX

4. L'internationalisation du couple[3], soulève la question complexe du régime matrimonial qui se pose pendant toute la durée du mariage et face à un changement de nationalité ou de domicile ou à l'acquisition de biens dans différents pays. La Convention de La Haye sur la loi applicable aux régimes matrimoniaux[4] et les propositions de règlement du Conseil du 16 mars 2011 relatives à la compétence, la loi applicable et l'exécution des décisions, l'une en matière de régimes matrimoniaux, l'autre en matière d'effets patrimoniaux des partenariats enregistrés[5] envisagent l'autonomie de la volonté des époux s'exprimant dans un choix de la loi applicable au régime matrimonial au moment du mariage et pendant le mariage.

5. Au moment du mariage, selon l'article 3 de la Convention de La Haye, les parties ont le choix de la loi applicable à leur régime matrimonial, mais ce choix ne saurait porter sur un nombre illimité de lois . Les époux ne peuvent choisir qu'une loi et en dehors de l'exception de la *lex rei sitae,* ne peuvent se référer à plusieurs lois pour régir leurs relations. Ils peuvent choisir « 1. *La loi d'un Etat dont l'un des époux a la nationalité au moment de la désignation* 2. *La loi de l'Etat sur le territoire duquel l'un des époux a sa résidence habituelle au moment de cette désignation.* 3. *La loi du premier Etat sur le territoire duquel l'un des époux établira une nouvelle résidence habituelle après le mariage* ». La Convention a un caractère universel (art 2) qui élargit le domaine d'application de la Convention en vigueur seulement aux Pays-Bas, au Luxembourg et en France.

6. La loi ainsi désignée s'applique à l'ensemble de leurs biens Si le principe de l'unité du régime matrimonial est retenu, il est écarté par l'article 3 puisqu'il est

---

[3] Sur environ 122 millions de mariages dans l'Union européenne, 16 millions soit 13 % sont internationaux.

[4] G. Droz, *Rép. int. Dalloz* V° régimes matrimoniaux, 2ème éd. 1998, nos 31 et s. ; M. Revillard, *J.cl. dr. int. fasc.* 556 nos 46 et s.

[5] COM (2011) 126 final 2011/0059 (CNS) 16.03.2011 ; COM (2011) 127 final/0060 (CNS) 16.03.2011.

possible de soumettre les immeubles ou certains d'entre eux à la loi du lieu où ces immeubles sont situés ou de prévoir que les immeubles qui seront acquis par la suite seront soumis à la loi de la situation.

7. Cette triple option répond à la plupart des préoccupations des futurs époux[6].

8. L'article 11 prévoit que « *la désignation de la loi applicable doit faire l'objet d'une stipulation expresse ou résulter indubitablement des dispositions au contrat de mariage* ». Les articles 12 et 13 imposent pour tout contrat et pour toute désignation expresse de la loi applicable la nécessité de faire l'objet d'un écrit daté et signé par les deux époux.

9. En plus d'une stipulation expresse résultant d'un écrit ou d'un contrat de mariage, la déclaration des époux peut se faire sur interpellation des époux par l'officier de l'état civil au jour de la célébration du mariage, si la loi du lieu de célébration prévoit cette possibilité[7]. Cette option sera valable en la forme si elle est formulée par écrit dans l'acte de célébration du mariage et datée et signée par les deux époux. En application de ces législations étrangères, on pourra tenir compte du choix de loi applicable et de régime matrimonial mentionné dans l'acte de mariage.

10. La proposition de règlement sur les régimes matrimoniaux du 16 mars 2011 s'inspire largement de la Convention de La Haye[8]. Dans le cadre du rattachement subjectif consacrant l'autonomie de la volonté, on relèvera certaines différences et la présence d'éléments nouveaux. La proposition consacre dans l'article 15 le principe de l'unité de la loi applicable. La loi applicable choisie par les époux ou déterminée à défaut de choix par les autres dispositions de la proposition s'applique à l'ensemble des biens des époux, quelle que soit leur nature, et quelle que soit leur localisation. Le « dépeçage » de la loi applicable au titre de la *lex rei sitae* est exclu.

11. Le choix de la loi applicable au régime matrimonial est limité à l'une des lois suivantes : « a) *la loi de la résidence commune des époux ou futurs époux ou* b) *la loi de l'Etat de la résidence habituelle d'un des époux ou futurs époux au moment de ce choix ou* c) *la loi d'un Etat dont l'un des époux ou futurs époux possède la nationalité au moment de ce choix* ».

---

6 M. Revillard, *Pratique de la Convention de La Haye sur la loi applicable aux régimes matrimoniaux*, commentaires et formules Defrénois 2008, 2ème éd.

7 Italie, Tunisie, Turquie, Mexique, Madagascar, Gabon, Mali, Monaco, Ile Maurice, Sénégal.

8 M. Revillard, Propositions de règlements communautaires sur les régimes matrimoniaux et les effets patrimoniaux des partenariats, *Petites affiches* 6 juillet 2011, n° 133, p. 3.

12. Selon l'article 19, « 1. *Le choix de la loi applicable revêt la forme prescrite pour le contrat de mariage, soit par la loi applicable de l'Etat choisi, soit par la loi de l'Etat du lieu de rédaction de l'acte.* 2. *Nonobstant le paragraphe 1, le choix doit être au moins exprès et formulé par un acte écrit, daté et signé par les deux époux.* 3. *Par ailleurs, si la loi de l'Etat membre dans lequel les deux époux ont leur résidence habituelle commune au moment du choix visé au paragraphe 1 prévoit pour le contrat de mariage des conditions de forme supplémentaires, ces conditions doivent être respectées* ». Ce choix de loi applicable et de régime matrimonial peut être étendu à la forme d'une option pour un régime matrimonial lors de la célébration du mariage devant un officier de l'état civil étranger[9].

13. L'article 20 vise la forme du contrat de mariage qui reprend le contenu des articles 11, 12 et 13 de la Convention de La Haye. Des règles formelles supplémentaires peuvent exister dans un Etat membre où les époux ont leur résidence commune lors de la rédaction du contrat de mariage et ces règles de rédaction ou de publicité devront être respectées.

14. La situation du couple peut évoluer dans le temps et dans l'espace. Les époux peuvent songer à un changement de régime matrimonial ou de loi applicable à leur régime et recourir aux instruments internationaux pour modifier la loi applicable à leur régime matrimonial et en conséquence leur régime. La mutabilité volontaire de la loi applicable introduite par la Convention de La Haye représente un progrès essentiel dans la pratique internationale des régimes matrimoniaux repris dans la proposition de règlement.

15. L'article 6 de la Convention de La Haye prévoit que « *les époux peuvent, au cours du mariage, soumettre leur régime matrimonial à une loi interne autre que celle jusqu'alors applicable* ». Cette option est limitée. Les époux ne peuvent désigner que l'une des lois suivantes. « *La loi d'un Etat dont l'un des époux a la nationalité au moment de la désignation ou la loi de l'Etat sur le territoire duquel l'un des époux a sa résidence habituelle lors de cette désignation ou encore pour tout ou partie des immeubles la loi de leur situation* ». Cette faculté est même offerte aux époux mariés avant l'entrée en vigueur de la Convention le 1er septembre 1992. La loi choisie vise l'ensemble de leurs biens. La loi nouvelle s'applique rétroactivement au jour du mariage sous réserve des intérêts des tiers. Mais les époux peuvent s'opposer expressément à cette rétroactivité.

16. Ce changement de loi applicable s'effectue par déclaration expresse des époux dans un acte passé dans les formes d'un contrat de mariage sans homologation

---

9 *Supra* n° 9.

judiciaire et sans délai. La mutabilité volontaire donne lieu à de nombreuses applications[10].

17. La proposition de règlement admet également le changement volontaire de loi applicable. Aucun changement de loi applicable ne peut intervenir sans manifestation expresse de la volonté des époux. Toute mutabilité automatique de la loi applicable fortement critiquée qui figure à l'article 7 de la Convention de La Haye est exclue.

18. Selon l'article 18, « *les époux peuvent, à tout moment au cours du mariage, soumettre leur régime matrimonial à une loi autre que celle jusqu'alors applicable. Les époux ne peuvent désigner que l'une des lois suivantes : a) la loi de l'Etat de la résidence habituelle d'un des époux au moment de ce choix ; b) la loi d'un Etat dont l'un des époux possède la nationalité au moment de ce choix* ». Le changement de loi applicable au cours du mariage n'a d'effet que pour l'avenir mais les époux peuvent choisir de donner à ce changement de loi applicable un effet rétroactif et cette rétroactivité ne porte pas atteinte à la validité des actes antérieurs conclus sous l'empire de la loi jusque là applicable, ni aux droits des tiers. Par suite de l'unité de la loi applicable, le choix de la loi de situation de l'immeuble n'est pas possible lors d'un changement de loi. Le règlement prévaut à compter de son entrée en application sur la Convention de La Haye (art. 36) et il ne sera plus possible de choisir la loi de situation des immeubles lors d'un changement de loi applicable. Les modalités formelles du changement de loi suivent les stipulations de l'article 19.

19. La proposition de règlement introduit dans l'article 22 l'application de lois de police. Les dispositions du règlement ne pourront porter atteinte à l'application des dispositions impératives dont le respect est jugé crucial par un Etat membre pour le respect de ses intérêts publics. Le statut primaire, non visé dans le règlement de façon générale, trouve ici sa place pour la protection du logement de la famille.

20. La proposition de règlement du conseil du 16 mars 2011 en matière d'effets patrimoniaux des partenariats consacre le choix de la loi de l'Etat de l'enregistrement du partenariat (art. 15). Les partenaires ne peuvent pas choisir une autre loi que celle de l'Etat de l'enregistrement même s'il leur est reconnu

[10] M. Revillard, Pratique de la Convention de La Haye, op. cit., n°s 71 et s. ; Droit international privé et communautaire : pratique notariale, 7ème éd. 2010, Defrénois-Lextenso n° 399.

la faculté de conclure des conventions entre eux. Le texte devrait subir des modifications pour laisser une place à l'autonomie de la volonté des partenaires[11].

21. La proposition de règlement du 16 mars 2011 vise les procédures judiciaires (art. 3 à 14) relatives à la liquidation du régime. Après avoir fixé des règles de compétence propres, l'article 5-2 faisant une part à l'autonomie de la volonté des époux prévoit que « *les époux peuvent convenir que les juridictions d'un Etat membre dont ils ont choisi la loi comme loi applicable à leur régime matrimonial sont compétentes pour statuer sur les questions concernant leur régime matrimonial* ». Selon l'article 4 « *les juridictions d'un Etat membre saisies d'une demande en divorce, séparation de corps ou annulation du mariage des époux, en application du Règlement (CE) n° 2201/2003) sont également compétentes en cas d'un tel accord des époux pour statuer sur les questions de régime matrimonial en relation avec la demande.*

DIVORCES INTERNATIONAUX

22. Les divorces internationaux se développent comme les mariages. Depuis le 21 juin 2012 est applicable le Règlement (UE) 1259/2010 du Conseil du 20 décembre 2010 dit Rome III mettant en œuvre une coopération renforcée dans le domaine de la loi applicable au divorce et à la séparation de corps[12]. En vue d'assurer aux couples internationaux plus de sécurité et de prévisibilité, les articles 5 à 16 du Règlement établissent des règles uniformes sur la loi applicable au divorce et à la séparation de corps[13]. Si les époux sont d'accord, ils pourront choisir la loi applicable à leur divorce ou à leur séparation de corps. Ceci représente l'innovation majeure du Règlement. A défaut de choix par les parties, l'article 8

11 Projet de rapport Alexandra Thein, Commission des affaires juridiques 27 juillet 2012, 2011/0059 CNS.

12 Règl. (UE) n° 1259/2010, 20 décembre 2010 : JO 29 décembre 2010 n° L. 343, p. 10. C'est la première fois dans l'histoire de l'Union européenne que des pays ont recours au mécanisme de la coopération renforcée qui permet à 9 pays ou plus d'adopter une mesure importante qui est bloquée par une faible minorité d'Etats. 14 Etats membres participent à cette coopération renforcée : Allemagne, Autriche, Belgique, Bulgarie, Espagne, France, Hongrie, Italie, Lettonie, Luxembourg, Malte, Portugal, Roumanie et Slovénie.

13 M. Revillard, *Divorce des couples internationaux : choix de la loi applicable*, Defrénois 2011, p. 445 ; P. Hammje, Le Règlement (UE) du Conseil du 20 décembre 2010 n° 1259/2010 mettant en œuvre une coopération renforcée dans le domaine du divorce et de la séparation de corps, *Rev. crit. DIP* 2011, p. 291 ; H. Gaudemet-Tallon, *Le divorce international depuis la communication de Patrick Courbe au Comité français de droit international privé, Mélanges à la mémoire de P. Courbe*, 2011, Dalloz 2012 ; M. Revillard et R. Crône, *Le Règlement Rome III sur les divorces internationaux (analyse et formules)*, Defrénois 2012, p. 560.

du Règlement détermine la loi applicable au divorce. A défaut de choix par les parties, ce rattachement objectif est relégué au rôle de règle subsidiaire.

23. Le Règlement Rome III ne porte que sur la loi applicable au divorce et ne concerne pas la compétence judiciaire régie par le Règlement (CE) n° 2201/2003 du 27 novembre 2003 dit Bruxelles II *bis*[14] relatif à la compétence, la reconnaissance et l'exécution des décisions en matière matrimoniale. Le choix du tribunal compétent pour connaitre du divorce relève du Règlement Bruxelles II *bis* qui permet au couple, sous l'article 3, de saisir le juge qui correspond le mieux aux intérêts des époux ou de l'un d'eux. Ici s'exprime encore l'autonomie de la volonté. Le champ d'application de Rome III est limité à la dissolution ou au relâchement du lien matrimonial. La convention des parties ne porte que sur le choix de la loi applicable au principe du divorce.

24. Les effets du divorce n'étant pas pris en compte par le Règlement (art. 1 § 2), la loi applicable à la prestation compensatoire dépend du Règlement n° 4/2009 CE du Conseil du 18 décembre 2008[15] relatif à la compétence, la loi applicable, la reconnaissance et l'exécution des décisions et la coopération en matière d'obligations alimentaires auxquelles sont assimilées les prestations compensatoires applicables depuis le 18 juin 2011 qui consacre notamment comme loi pouvant être désignée la loi applicable aux relations patrimoniales des parties ou la loi applicable à leur divorce (art. 15 du Règlement du 18 décembre 2008 renvoyant aux articles 7 et 8 du protocole de La Haye du 23 novembre 2007[16] qui permet aux parties de désigner la loi applicable à leurs obligations alimentaires).

25. Le domaine limité du Règlement Rome III, laisse perplexe sur l'intérêt du choix de la loi applicable au divorce qui pourra être désignée en fonction de sa teneur libérale consacrant un droit fondamental au divorce ou loi prohibitive ne connaissant que la séparation de corps. Cette loi peut être la loi d'un Etat membre participant, d'un Etat membre non participant ou d'un Etat tiers Les époux peuvent désigner l'une des lois suivantes (art. 5) : « a) *la loi de l'Etat de la résidence habituelle des époux au moment de la conclusion de la convention, ou* b) *la loi de l'Etat de la dernière résidence habituelle des époux pour autant que l'un d'eux y réside encore au moment de la conclusion de la convention ; ou* c) *la loi de l'Etat de la nationalité de l'un des époux au moment de la conclusion de la convention ; ou* d) *la loi du for* ».

---

[14] Règl. (CE) 2001/2003, 27 novembre 2003, JO 23 décembre 2003, n° L. 338, p. 1 ; E. Galant, *Rép. int. Dalloz* 2ème éd. V° Règlement Bruxelles II *bis*.

[15] Règl. (CE) n° 4.2009, 18 décembre 2008, JO L.7, 10 janvier 2009.

[16] Protocole de La Haye 23 novembre 2007, JO L. 331/19, 16 décembre 2009.

26. Les époux sont libres du moment où ils conviendront de la loi applicable à leur divorce. Cette convention peut être établie au moment du mariage dans leur contrat de mariage. La convention désignant la loi applicable peut être conclue et modifiée à tout moment mais, au plus tard, au moment de la saisine de la juridiction et même au-delà, devant la juridiction au cours de la procédure, sous réserve que la loi du for l'autorise. Ce type d'accord procédural ne sera pas possible devant le juge français, celui-ci n'étant permis que pour les droits dont les parties ont la libre disposition.

27. Le problème du conflit mobile est réglé dans l'article 5 : si les époux choisissent la loi de l'Etat de leur résidence ou la loi de l'Etat de leur nationalité, il s'agit de la résidence habituelle ou de la nationalité au moment de la conclusion de la convention. Tout changement ultérieur de la résidence ou de la nationalité sera sans effet sur la détermination de la loi de l'Etat dont le droit est applicable.

28. Selon l'article 7, la convention de choix de loi applicable doit être formulée par écrit, datée et signée par les deux époux. Si la loi d'un Etat membre participant dans lequel les deux époux ont leur résidence habituelle prévoit des règles formelles supplémentaires, elles doivent être respectées. La garantie de la forme écrite n'est peut-être pas suffisante. D'autres exigences de forme ont été suggérées, acte dressé par un notaire, un greffier ou un avocat et signé par les parties ou établi devant un juge ou devant l'autorité qui prononce le divorce.

29. Cette option de législation doit seulement être formulée par écrit, datée et signée par les deux époux et la forme authentique notariée n'est pas exigée. D'autres juristes tels que les avocats ont compétence pour conseiller cette convention sous la forme d'un acte écrit, daté et signé par les deux époux. Aucune publicité de la convention n'est prévue dans le Règlement. Au moment d'engager une procédure de divorce, il convient d'interroger les époux sur l'existence possible d'une convention qu'ils auraient passée sur le choix de la loi applicable à leur divorce.

30. La portée de cette désignation de la loi applicable au divorce est limitée. L'autonomie de la volonté laissée aux époux ne porte que sur la dissolution du lien conjugal (causes du divorce) et ne vise pas ses effets notamment ses conséquences patrimoniales exclues du Règlement (art. 1er). La loi applicable à la liquidation du régime ne peut pas être différente de la loi régissant le régime lui-même et la loi applicable au divorce ne peut y déroger. A la suite du Règlement Rome III, se développent des contrats prénuptiaux établis par des juristes anglo-saxons visant de multiples aspects du divorce, loi applicable, pension alimentaire, indemnité de rupture, régime des biens, garde des enfants qui n'entrent pas dans le cadre restrictif du Règlement et risquent d'être inopérants.

31. Le Règlement Rome III exclue le renvoi (art. 11). L'article 10 intitulé « application de la loi du for » prévoit que la loi du for s'appliquera lorsque la loi normalement applicable (par choix ou objectivement) « *ne prévoit pas le divorce ou n'accorde pas à l'un des époux, en raison de son appartenance à l'un ou à l'autre sexe, une égalité d'accès au divorce ou à la séparation de corps* ». Il y a peut-être une contradiction car la volonté des époux devrait pouvoir s'exercer en faveur ou non du divorce. Il est de fait interdit aux époux de choisir une loi qui rendrait leur mariage indissoluble et susceptible simplement de relâchement par la séparation de corps. Le Règlement impose aux membres participants le droit au divorce. L'article 10 vise à lutter contre toute loi discriminatoire qui viendrait à porter atteinte à l'égal accès des époux au divorce ou à la séparation de corps en raison de son appartenance à l'un ou l'autre sexe. Une loi étrangère admettant la répudiation se verra écartée.

32. Selon l'article 12 « *l'application d'une disposition de la loi désignée en vertu du Règlement ne peut être écartée que si cette application est manifestement incompatible avec l'ordre public du for* L'intervention de l'ordre public est d'ailleurs amputée par l'existence de l'article 10. Peu importe que la loi applicable soit celle d'un autre Etat de l'Union européenne ou celle d'un Etat tiers. Est visée l'égalité entre époux dans l'accès au divorce. Le divorce va-t-il devenir d'ordre public international[17] ?

33. Les règles uniformes sur la loi applicable au divorce doivent être appliquées strictement au regard du domaine du Règlement. Si le for est celui d'un Etat participant, le règlement s'appliquera même si les époux ne sont pas des nationaux de cet Etat ou n'y résident pas. Lorsque la loi applicable au divorce ou à la séparation de corps n'a pas été désignée par les époux, le juge d'un Etat membre participant à la coopération renforcée compétent pour connaitre du divorce (cette compétence étant fondée sur le Règlement Bruxelles II *bis*) appliquera le Règlement quelle que soit la nationalité ou la résidence des époux. Le juge saisi déterminera la loi applicable au divorce d'un couple international, quelle que soit sa nationalité ou sa résidence, selon l'article 8 du Règlement. Si le for saisi du divorce n'est pas celui d'un Etat participant, le Règlement ne s'appliquera pas et ceci pourra rendre inefficace une convention de choix de loi conclue par les époux même si ceux-ci étaient issus d'un Etat membre participant. Au moment de l'établissement de la convention, il faudra les informer de la nécessité de porter leur divorce dans un Etat membre participant pour que ce choix soit respecté.

---

17 Plusieurs lois nationales étrangères ont déjà organisées un droit au divorce, art. 61 § 3 Loi suisse, Loi italienne 31 § 2, Loi belge 55 § 3 et la jurisprudence allemande.

34. L'exclusion de l'ensemble des conséquences du divorce du domaine du Règlement Rome III nécessitera une combinaison délicate entre la loi applicable au principe du divorce et à la part accordée sur ce point à l'autonomie de la volonté et les lois applicables à ses différents effets. Le Règlement Rome III n'a fait qu'un petit pas dans l'harmonisation du droit international du divorce et souligne les difficultés de coordination des instruments internationaux dans ce domaine.

SUCCESSIONS INTERNATIONALES

35. L'importance des dévolutions successorales transfrontalières[18] et la divergence des systèmes de conflit de lois et de juridictions dans ce domaine ont justifié la recherche d'une harmonisation. La conférence de La Haye de droit international privé a consacré une part importante de son activité à ces questions dans 4 conventions : la Convention du 5 octobre 1961 sur les conflits de lois en matière de forme des dispositions testamentaires, la Convention du 2 octobre 1973 sur l'administration de successions, la Convention du 1er juillet 1985 relative à la loi applicable au trust et à sa reconnaissance et la Convention du 1er août 1989 sur la loi applicable aux successions. Lors de la négociation de ces deux dernières conventions, nous avons pu apprécier les remarquables qualités intellectuelles de Hans van Loon et son humanisme exprimés dans le rôle majeur qu'il a joué dans l'élaboration des conventions de La Haye en matière familiale.

36. Si ces conventions n'ont pas rencontré l'adhésion souhaitée, elles ont inspiré très largement le Règlement sur les successions du 4 juillet 2012[19] qui admet le principe de l'unité successorale et la *professio juris,* instaure un certificat successoral européen et reprend certaines dispositions de la Convention sur la forme des testaments. Le Règlement (UE) n° 650/2012 du Parlement européen et du Conseil du 4 juillet 2012 relatif à la compétence, à la loi applicable et à la reconnaissance et l'exécution des décisions et à l'acceptation et l'exécution des actes authentiques en matière de succession et à la création d'un certificat successoral européen représente le futur droit des successions internationales

---

18 On estime à 450 000 successions internationales par an au sein de l'Union européenne représentant 23,3 milliards d'euros.

19 JO 27 juillet 2012 L.201/107. Ce texte avait été précédé d'une Proposition de règlement du Parlement européen et du Conseil du 14 novembre 2009 COM (2009) 154 final ; M. Revillard, *Premier commentaire sur la proposition de règlement communautaire,* Defrénois 2010, art. 39056, p. 176 ; G. Khairallah et M. Revillard (sous la direction de), *Perspectives du droit des successions européennes et internationales,* Etude de la proposition de règlement du 14 octobre 2009, Defrénois-Lextenson éd. 2010.

de l'Union européenne[20]. Il s'applique aux successions des personnes décédées à compter du 17 août 2015 (art. 83-1).

37. Le rattachement unitaire représente l'innovation majeure du Règlement. Selon l'article 21 « *sauf disposition contraire du Règlement, la loi applicable à l'ensemble d'une succession est celle de l'Etat dans lequel le défunt avait sa résidence habituelle au moment de son décès* ». Cependant, cette solution d'unicité trouve sa limite puisque chaque fois que l'on changera de résidence, il faudra réviser le projet de préparation de sa succession et il convient également de faire une place à la volonté successorale. L'admission de la *professio juris* permettant au futur *de cujus* de choisir la loi applicable à sa succession, est essentielle pour préparer avec fiabilité sa dévolution successorale. Cette option de législation introduite dans le Règlement n'est pas nouvelle[21]. Elle figure sous l'article 5 de la Convention de La Haye sur les successions et admise de manière plus ou moins étendue dans de nombreux Etats d'Europe et au-delà[22].

38. La *professio juris* permet d'assurer la prévisibilité dans la préparation d'une succession internationale. Le critère de rattachement unitaire à la dernière résidence habituelle fondé sur la présomption de l'intégration du défunt dans le pays où il demeure est un critère de rattachement peu stable dans la mesure où le *de cujus* peut avoir maintenu des liens importants avec son pays d'origine où se trouve une partie de son patrimoine ou bien avec une résidence antérieure de plus longue durée. La *professio juris* introduit un élément de souplesse et de sécurité. De plus la majorité des systèmes de conflit des pays de l'Union européenne adopte en matière successorale le facteur de rattachement de la nationalité du défunt et la possibilité pour le futur *de cujus* d'opter pour sa loi nationale rend plus acceptable l'innovation du critère de la dernière résidence qui, pour ces Etats, représente un

---

[20] M. Revillard, Successions internationales : le Règlement du Parlement européen et du Conseil du 4 juillet 2012 en matière de successions, Defrénois 2012, p. 743 ; P. Lagarde, Les principes de base du nouveau Règlement sur les successions, Rev. crit. DIP 2012, p. --- ; M. Goré, La professio juris, Defrénois 2012, p. 762 ; S. Godechot-Patris, Le nouveau droit international privé des successions, entre satisfactions et craintes, D. 2012, p. 2462 ; G. Khairallah et M. Revillard (sous la direction de), Droit européen et international des successions : le Règlement du 4 juillet 2012, Defrénois-Lextenso éd. 2013.

[21] G. Droz, Regards sur le droit international privé comparé, Recueil des Cours tome 229 (1991-IV) p. 240, n°s 249 et s. ; Travaux Comité français de DIP 1966-1969, pp. 337 et s.

[22] LFDIP suisse, art. 87 al. 2, art. 90 al. 2 et 91 al. 2 ; Loi néerlandaise de 1996 sur les conflits de lois en matière de succession qui a intégré dans son droit international privé la Convention de La Haye du 1er août 1989 art. 46 al. 2 de la Loi italienne du 31 mars 1995 ; Allemagne, art. 25 al. 2 de la Loi du 25 juillet 1986 ; Belgique, art. 79 de la Loi du 16 juillet 2004 portant Code de droit international privé belge. Elle est également admise en Arménie, Belarus, Bulgarie, Kazakhstan, Ukraine, Liechtenstein, Burkina-Faso, Québec, Roumanie, Pologne. De façon limitée à la loi du for pour les meubles : New York, Illinois, Floride, New Jersey, Connecticut, Oregon, Utah, Massachussetts.

bouleversement. Mai cette option de législation doit être encadrée et s'établir sous certaines conditions de fond et de forme.

39 Selon l'article 22-1 « *une personne peut choisir comme loi régissant l'ensemble de sa succession, la loi de l'Etat dont elle possède la nationalité au moment où elle fait ce choix ou au moment de son décès* ». Le choix est restreint à la seule loi nationale et porte sur l'ensemble de la succession.

40. L'article 22-1 alinéa 1 prévoit qu' « *une personne ayant plusieurs nationalités peut choisir la loi de tout Etat dont elle possède la nationalité au moment où elle fait ce choix ou au moment de son décès* ». Les différentes nationalités sont mises sur le même plan et sans distinction entre la nationalité d'un Etat membre ou d'un Etat tiers. Quant au moment du choix, cette nationalité est appréciée soit au moment du choix soit au moment du décès. Le Règlement apporte une solution au conflit mobile. Ceci permet de consolider les actes d'anticipation successorale. Le choix de la loi nationale dont le disposant n'aurait plus la nationalité au jour du décès restera valable.

41. Le choix de la loi nationale doit régir l'ensemble de la succession c'est-à-dire l'intégralité des biens composant la succession quelle que soit leur nature et leur situation dans un autre Etat membre ou dans un Etat tiers.

42. Les conditions de forme de la *professio juris* sont prévues à l'article 22-2 « *le choix est formulé de manière expresse dans une déclaration revêtant la forme d'une disposition à cause de mort ou résulte des termes d'une telle disposition* ».

43. Le choix exprès est la solution qui apportera le plus de sécurité à l'anticipation successorale. Ce choix revêt la forme d'une disposition à cause de mort qui selon l'article 3 (d) englobe le testament, le testament conjonctif ou le pacte successoral. Sous l'article 27, le Règlement intègre les solutions de la Convention de La Haye sur la forme des testaments étendue aux pactes successoraux. La Convention contribue à reconnaitre largement la validité en la forme des testaments[23] ***et*** en vigueur dans 41 Etats dont 15 Etats de l'Union européenne. L'article 75-1 alinéa 2 visant les relations avec les conventions internationales existantes prévoit que les Etats membres parties à la Convention de La Haye continueront de l'appliquer au lieu de l'article 27 du Règlement.

44. La *professio juris* peut aussi résulter des « termes d'une disposition à cause de mort ». Le texte n'impose donc pas que le choix soit exprès. Cette seconde

[23] G. Droz et M. Revillard, *J.cl. dr. int. fasc.* 557-20 n°s 42 et s. ; G. Droz, *Rev. crit. DIP* 1968, p. 1.

possibilité de choix « implicite » ou de présomption de choix demande à être explicitée. Selon le considérant 39 « *le choix de la loi applicable pourrait être considéré comme résultant d'une disposition à cause de mort dans le cas où, par exemple, dans sa disposition, le défunt avait fait référence à des dispositions spécifiques de l'Etat de sa nationalité ou dans le cas où il avait mentionné cette loi d'une autre manière* ». Cette possibilité ajoutée à la proposition de 2009 peut donner lieu à interprétation[24].

45. Selon l'article 22-3 « *la validité au fond de l'acte en vertu duquel le choix de loi est effectué est régie par la loi choisie* ». L'existence du consentement, l'interprétation de volonté du *de cujus* et sa validité au fond sont régies par la loi choisie par le disposant. La modification ou la révocation de la *professio juris* relève aussi de la loi choisie par le *de cujus.*

46. La mise en œuvre du rattachement résultant de la *professio juris* conduit à examiner les correctifs pouvant intervenir dans son application. Le renvoi introduit dans l'article 34 du Règlement est expressément exclu dans le cadre de la *professio juris* pour assurer la prévisibilité voulue par le futur *de cujus.*

47. La *professio juris* est soumise à l'article 35 prévoyant que« *l'application d'une disposition de la loi désignée par le présent Règlement ne peut être écartée que si cette application est manifestement incompatible avec l'ordre public* ». La formule remaniée dans sa rédaction de 2009 est générale. L'ordre public peut être interprété différemment selon les Etats et représente un élément à apprécier dans le choix par le *de cujus* de telle loi nationale en cas de plurinationalités. Si la loi successorale choisie comprend des discriminations fondées sur le sexe, la race ou la religion ou la qualité de la filiation légitime ou naturelle, elle sera écartée au nom de l'ordre public. En revanche, si la loi nationale choisie ne connait pas de réserve, l'ordre public viendra-t-il s'opposer à cette loi ? La réserve ne constitue pas une disposition d'ordre public international et le choix d'une loi nationale qui ne connait pas la réserve n'est pas en soi contraire à l'ordre public[25]. La *professio juris* n'est pas l'occasion pour le testateur de profiter de ce choix pour dépouiller ses proches.[26].

---

24 L'article 79-2 du Code de DIP belge ou la Loi italienne (art. 16 al. 2) exigent que le choix de la *professio juris* soit exprès. La doctrine québécoise également, v. J. Talpis, note 25 ; La Loi suisse qui semble admettre un choix tacite prête à jurisprudence.

25 La doctrine française reste partagée sur ce point. Il faut noter que certaines législations autorisant la *professio juris* prévoient que cette option de législation ne peut pas avoir pour effet de priver un héritier de la réserve que leur assure la loi objectivement applicable : Loi belge de 2004 art. 79, Loi italienne du 31 mai 1995 art. 46 § 2. art. 3099 al. 1 du Code civil québécois.

26 G. Droz, *op. cit.* réf. 21, Cours La Haye 1991, n° 251.

48. La *professio juris* permet d'éviter les difficultés d'interprétation de la résidence habituelle du défunt. L'établissement dès maintenant d'une option de législation en faveur de la loi nationale permet d'anticiper l'entrée en application du Règlement. L'article 83-2 prévoit que « *lorsque le défunt avait, avant le 17 août 2015, choisi la loi applicable à sa succession, ce choix est valable s'il remplit les conditions fixées au chapitre III ou s'il est valable en application des règles de droit international privé qui étaient en vigueur, au moment où le choix a été fait, dans l'Etat dans lequel le défunt avait sa résidence habituelle ou dans tout Etat dont il possédait la nationalité* ». Cette disposition permet de valider rétroactivement un choix de loi applicable établi avant le 17 août 2015[27].

49. En plus de la sécurité juridique, la *professio juris* répond à la volonté du défunt de conserver des liens étroits avec son pays d'origine et d'assurer une protection à ses proches qui ne serait pas accordée par la loi de la résidence habituelle. Ce sera le cas de Français domiciliés en Angleterre possédant des biens en Angleterre et en France qui auront opter pour la loi française. De même, des Britanniques, Canadiens, Américains, Australiens faisant une *professio juris* en faveur de la loi de leur nationalité pourront conserver leur système de dévolution de leur succession.

50. Le rôle de l'autonomie de la volonté dans le Règlement se trouve également dans le cadre de la compétence judiciaire. Au titre de la compétence générale, l'article 4 assure la convergence des compétences législatives et juridictionnelles « *sont compétentes pour statuer sur l'ensemble de la succession, les juridictions de l'Etat membre dans lequel le défunt avait sa résidence habituelle au moment de son décès* ». Si la dernière résidence habituelle du défunt se trouve dans un Etat tiers, le Règlement adopte des règles de compétences subsidiaires sous l'article 10 à certaines conditions.

51. Le souci de coïncidence entre tribunal compétent et loi applicable explique les exceptions aux règles posées aux articles 4 et 10. Si le *de cujus* avait choisi la loi de sa nationalité pour régir sa succession (*professio juris*) et qu'il s'agisse de la nationalité d'un Etat membre, on peut déroger à la compétence prévue par les articles 4 et 10 et porter la question successorale devant les tribunaux de l'Etat dont le *de cujus* avait la nationalité (art. 5 à 9). Cette dérogation résulte soit d'un accord d'élection de for (art. 5), soit d'un déclinatoire de compétence (art. 6). L'accord d'élection de for met en évidence, le rôle de l'autonomie de la volonté

[27] Les dispositions transitoires prévues par les articles 83-2 et 83-4 du Règlement pourront donner lieu à des difficultés concrètes d'appréciation, v. M. Goré et M. Revillard, Defrénois *op. cit.* réf. 20.

sous l'article 5 : « *lorsque la loi choisie par le défunt pour régir la succession en vertu de l'article 22 (professio juris) est la loi d'un Etat membre, les parties concernées peuvent convenir que la ou les juridictions de cet Etat membre ont compétence exclusive pour statuer sur cette succession* ». Cet accord doit être conclu par écrit, daté et signé par les parties concernées (art. 5-2).

52. Dans le domaine des successions, on évoquera la Convention de La Haye du 1er juillet 1985 sur la loi applicable au *trust* et à reconnaissance en vigueur dans de nombreux Etats[28]. L'article 6 de la Convention consacre le principe de l'autonomie de la volonté. Le *trust* est régi par la loi choisie par le constituant sous réserve que la législation choisie connaisse l'institution. Le choix doit être exprès ou à défaut résulter de l'acte créant le *trust* ou de l'acte qui en apporte la preuve. S'il n'est pas possible de déterminer ainsi la loi applicable, il convient d'interpréter ces actes à l'aide des circonstances de la cause. Le *trust* est une institution qui répond à un but de bonne gestion et, dans la majorité des cas, les parties prennent le soin de se référer à un statut type de *trust*[29].

53. Nous mentionnerons enfin l'option de législation prévue dans la Convention de La Haye du 13 janvier 2000 sur la protection internationale des adultes[30]. Les dispositions de la Convention sur le mandat d'inaptitude constituent un apport remarquable pour la connaissance de l'institution et pour régler les effets de cette institution lorsque les personnes concernées se déplacent à l'étranger ou y possèdent des biens. A titre de principe, « *le mandat est régi par la loi de l'Etat de la résidence habituelle de l'adulte au moment de l'accord ou de l'acte unilatéral* » *(art.15).* Cependant de nombreuses législations ne connaissent pas encore le mandat d'inaptitude et celui-ci peut être ignoré de la loi de la résidence habituelle. Aussi une faculté de choix de la loi applicable doit être accordée à l'adulte puisqu'il s'agit de pouvoirs résultant d'un acte de volonté. D'autres lois peuvent être choisies par l'adulte qui pourra désigner par écrit une autre loi. Pourra être choisie « *la loi de l'Etat dont l'adulte possède la nationalité, la loi d'une résidence habituelle précédente, la loi de l'Etat dans lequel sont situés les biens de l'adulte pour ce qui concerne ces biens* » *(al. 2)* Plusieurs lois peuvent être choisies pour régir le mandat

28 H. Van Loon, L'actualité de la Convention de La Haye relative au trust et à sa reconnaissance, Liber Amicorum Mariel Revillard 2007, Defrénois p. 323.

29 G. Droz et M. Revillard, *J.cl. dr. int. fasc.* 557-30, n° 74 à 164.

30 P. Lagarde, La Convention de La Haye du 13 janvier 2000 sur la protection internationale des adultes, *Rev. crit. DIP* 2000, p. 159 et s. ; M. Revillard, La Convention de La Haye sur la protection internationale des adultes et la pratique du mandat d'inaptitude, *in Le droit international privé, esprit et méthodes, Mélanges en l'honneur de Paul Lagarde*, Dalloz 2005, p. 725.

d'inaptitude. Cette possibilité de dépeçage peut présenter un intérêt si la personne concernée possède des biens dans des Etats différents.

54. Le développement de conventions d'option de législation dans les relations de famille internationales offertes dans les récents instruments internationaux met en évidence le rôle essentiel de conseil que doivent jouer les praticiens et, en particulier, les notaires Mais pour ne pas rester lettre morte, on pourrait suggérer l'organisation d'une publicité des actes d'option de législation au niveau international inspiré du registre de dispositions testamentaires mise en place au sein des notariats européens.

THE EUROPEAN PRIVATE INTERNATIONAL LAW AND THE CHARTER OF FUNDAMENTAL RIGHTS

Salla SAASTAMOINEN
Head of Unit 'Civil justice policy', Directorate-General Justice, European Commission

INTRODUCTION

The EU policies on the judicial cooperation in civil matters and private international law and on the fundamental rights are of the same age and share the same sources: In both cases, the Tampere summit in 1999 was a significant milestone if not the starting point. The European Council placed the creation of the European area of justice in civil matters, based on the principle on mutual recognition of judicial decisions, on the top of the EU political agenda.[1] In close connection with the area of freedom, security and justice, the European Council agreed also on the method to elaborate a draft EU Charter of Fundamental Rights. Some months earlier, the previous European Council had already concluded that the fundamental rights applicable at the EU level should be consolidated in a charter to give them greater visibility. The policy on judicial cooperation in civil matters, that in practice consists mainly of the private international law instruments, was brought forward with the 2000 Vienna Programme on Mutual Recognition,[2] while the Charter of Fundamental Rights of the European Union ('the Charter')[3] was declared by the EU institutions in December 2000.

The judicial cooperation in civil matters has a clear legal basis in the EU Treaties, today Article 81 (ex-Article 69) of the Treaty on the Functioning of the European Union (TFEU) that enables the EU to take the necessary

1 The Tampere Council Presidency Conclusions, 15/16 October 1999.
2 Draft Programme on measures for implementation of the principle of mutual recognition of decisions in civil and commercial matters, Council 2001/C 12/01, OJ C 12, 15.1.2001.
3 Published in OJ C 83, 2010 C 83/02, as slightly amended and proclaimed a second time in December 2007.

legislative measures using "Community method", ie based on the proposal of the Commission, mostly by qualified majority in the Council and in co-decision with the European Parliament. The Programme on Mutual Recognition has been implemented successfully by adopting, or at least proposing, legislative initiatives for all issues mentioned in the Programme: The EU has adopted so far 15 regulations, three directives and three Council decisions in the area of judicial cooperation in civil matters, some of which have been already subject to full revisions. There are also a number of instruments on international conventions. The first actions, the Regulation on Insolvency proceedings,[4] the Brussels II Regulation on matrimonial matters and matters of parental responsibility[5] and the Regulation on the service of documents[6] were adopted by the Council already in May 2000. The Commission proposals on the Regulations relating to property consequences of marriages and of registered partnerships[7] as well as on the creation of the European Account Preservation Order[8] of 2011, all three currently under negotiation, completed the work to put the Programme into practice.

The Charter sets out in a single text a whole range of civil, political, economic and social rights of European citizens and all persons resident in the EU. These rights are divided into six sections concerning Dignity, Freedoms, Equality, Solidarity, Citizens' rights and Justice. The Charter became part of the binding Union primary law through the Lisbon Treaty, ref. Article 6 of the Treaty on European Union (TEU), in 2009.

This article examines the inter-linkage between the Charter and the development of the legislation on judicial cooperation in civil matters in in the EU. The Charter is addressed first and foremost to the institutions and bodies of the Union (ref. Article 51). They should respect the rights, observe the principles and promote the application thereof, in accordance with their respective powers. The European Commission has the powers and role of preparing the Union legislation; it has indeed the general monopoly of making legislative proposals to the legislators, the European Parliament and the Council. In this work, the Commission is guided by the Charter: The Commission must respect the rights, observe the principles and promote application thereof whenever proposing new legislation. The focus of this article lies on looking at how the Commission has ensured these duties in the area of the civil justice cooperation and private international law.

The Charter is relevant also when the Member States apply the Union legislation on the judicial cooperation: Pursuant Article 51 of the Charter, the

4 Regulation (EC) No 1346/2000, OJ L 160, 30.6.2000, p.1.
5 Regulation (EC) No 1347/2000, OJ L 160, 30.6.2000, p. 19.
6 Regulation (EC) No 1348/2000, OJ L 160, 30.6.2000, p. 37.
7 COM(2011)126 and COM(2011)127.
8 COM(2011)445.

Member States are required to apply the Charter when they are implementing Union law. The Commission, as the guardian of the Treaties, is in charge of the control of correct application of the acquis by the Member States. The Commission must thus pay attention to the respect of the Charter by the Member States when those implement the acquis in any area of the Union law. It could use the measures under the Treaties, like Article 258 TFEU if it considers that a Member State breaches fundamental rights at the implementation stage. The Charter and the Union legislation on private international law are thus linked also on the context of the application of the civil justice acquis. This aspect is however not dealt with further in the present article.

THE COMMISSION'S METHOD TO ENSURE THE RESPECT OF THE CHARTER

The Commission had to reflect how to ensure that the legislative initiatives respect the rights and principles of the Charter and promote its application. This requires analysing the impacts of the future measure. Already 2001, the Commission decided that any proposal for legislation must be scrutinised for compatibility with the Charter.[9] It also decided that the legislative proposals having a specific link to fundamental rights would incorporate a recital as a formal statement of compatibility.

The impacts of the EU legislative proposals have been always assessed in one way or another during the preparatory work in the Commission. This work has nevertheless been much formalised and made transparent by the impact assessment method, which results with a publication of a separate impact assessment report. The Commission has managed a general policy on impact assessments since early 2000. The White Paper on European Governance instructed that "proposals must be prepared on the basis of an effective analysis of whether it is appropriate to intervene at EU level and whether regulatory intervention is needed. If so, the analysis must also assess the potential economic, social and environmental impact."[10] For that purpose, the Commission has adopted internal guidelines on how to run the assessment in 2002, 2005 and most recently in 2009.[11]

The method started with the assessment of above-mentioned socio-economic and environmental impacts but the analysed areas have been extended with the development of the mechanism. In 2005, the Commission established a

9 SEC(2001)380.
10 COM(2001) 428.
11 "Impact Assessment in the Commission – Guidelines' and 'A Handbook for Impact Assessment in the Commission – How to do an Impact Assessment', 2002; Impact Assessment Guidelines, SEC(2005) 791 and SEC(2009) 92.

methodology for systematic and rigorous monitoring of the compliance with the Charter in Commission legislative proposals.[12] Such monitoring is mainstreamed into the impact assessment procedure, which must take the results into account. The fundamental rights scrutiny must also be contained in the explanatory memorandum that is attached to the Commission legislative proposal. The fundamental rights "reflex" was further reinforced by the Communication on Strategy for the effective implementation of the Charter in 2010[13] that introduced a fundamental rights "check-list" to ensure that the fundamental rights are systematically analysed from the initial drafting of the proposal to the checks of the legality of the final text.

INITIATIVES ON JUDICIAL COOPERATION WITH NO FORMALLY REPORTED IMPACT ASSESSMENT INCLUDING THE FUNDAMENTAL RIGHTS ANALYSIS

The Commission started to scrutinize the compatibility of the initiatives on the judicial cooperation in civil matters with the Charter very quickly after the first guidance decisions. The adopted texts carry a proof of the consideration of the fundamental rights aspects that is expressed usually in their recitals:

The Regulation on the European Enforcement Order,[14] proposed in January 2002, is the first instrument in which the explanatory memorandum expressly dealt with the fundamental rights impacts and the proposal referred to the Charter and reaffirmed that it seeks to promote the fundamental rights and takes into account the principles recognised in particular by the Charter. In particular, it sought to ensure full respect for the right to fail trial as recognised in Article 47 of the Charter (see Recital 11).

This was followed fast in the family law side, when the proposal for the Brussels IIa Regulation,[15] of May 2002, took into account the Charter: As the explanatory memorandum states, the objective of Community action was to protect the child's best interests, and in particular, to give concrete expression to the child's fundamental right to maintain contact with both parents, as laid down in Article 24 of the Charter. To this end, the Commission proposed to extend the principle of mutual recognition to all decisions on parental responsibility and to

[12] COM(2005)172.

[13] COM(2010)573.

[14] Regulation (EC) No 805/2004, OJ L 143, 30 .4.2004.

[15] Regulation (EC) No 2201/2003, OJ L 338, 23.12.2003.

abolish exequatur for rights of access, as well as to elaborate a Union solution for the return of the child in cases of child abduction. Thus, the proposal can be seen as a real promotion of fundamental rights, not only as means to respect them. Recital 33 reaffirms that the Regulation recognises the fundamental rights and observes the principles of the Charter. In particular, it seeks to ensure the respect of fundamental rights of the child as set out in Article 24 of the Charter.

The instruments on the access to justice have close link to the fundamental rights, since the right to access to justice is considered as one of them. The Commission considered that the Directive on legal aid in civil matters,[16] proposed in 2002, is actually required because of the Charter and the European Convention on Human Rights (the ECHR): According to the explanatory memorandum, the initiative follows on from the Charter, which provides that legal aid is to be made available to those who lack sufficient resources in so far as such aid is necessary to ensure effective access to justice (Article 47(3)). The ECHR contains Article 6 which provides that everyone is entitled to a fair hearing. This provision primarily concerns the criminal law, but the principle that everyone is entitled to a fair hearing whatever the nature of the procedure was extended to include, in certain circumstances, a right to legal aid in civil matters.[17] The Mediation Directive,[18] proposed in 2004, encourages the use of mediation, and includes a standard recital, Recital 27, on promotion of fundamental recognised by the Charter. There is however no mentioning on specific assessment in the explanatory memorandum to the proposal of the Directive.

The Regulation on the European Payment Order,[19] proposed in 2004, does not include even the standard recital on the Charter. The Commission had proposed such a recital, without explicit assessment in the explanatory memorandum, but it was rejected at the legislative negotiations. In the "sister" Regulation on the Small Claims Procedure,[20] proposed in 2005, the fundamental rights play a role: Recital 9 confirms the Regulation seeks to promote fundamental rights and takes into account the principles recognised in the Charter. It stresses that the courts should respect the right to a fair trial and the principle of adversarial process, in particular when deciding on the necessity of an oral hearing on the means of taking of evidence, and the extent to which evidence is to be taken. This was important because the small claims procedure is in principle a written procedure, and there were concerns on the procedural rights to be respected.

As clarification it can be mentioned that there was no reference to the fundamental rights yet in the proposals dating before 2002, i.e. in those

16 Directive 2003/8/EC, OJ L 174, 31.1.2003.
17 See ECHR, *Airey v Ireland*, judgment given on 9 October 1979.
18 Directive 2008/52/EC, OJ L 136, 4.5.2008.
19 Regulation (EC) No 1896/2006, OJ L 399, 30.12.2006.
20 Regulation (EC) No 863/2007, OJ L 199, 31.7.2007.

concerning the Regulation on Insolvency proceedings, the Brussels II Regulation on matrimonial matters and matters of parental responsibility, the Regulation on the service of documents nor the Brussels I Regulation on jurisdiction and the recognition and enforcement of judgments in civil and commercial matters.[21] All these instruments were based on the preceding international conventions that had been negotiated earlier, before the Charter declaration, which explains the lack of fundamental rights considerations.

There is no mentioning of the fundamental rights in the judicial cooperation instruments either, like in the Regulation on the taking of evidence[22] that had also been proposed in 2000 before the declaration of the Charter. It is however a bit surprising that the 2007 revision of the Regulation on service of documents,[23] proposed in 2005, does not refer to the fundamental rights analysis, since the correct service of documents is elementary for the rights of defence and thus for the fair trial. The fact that the 2007 Regulation is an amendment may explain the matter so that it was considered that no new impact to fundamental rights was brought by it.

In 2003–2008, the Regulations on the applicable law on contractual obligations (Rome I),[24] proposed in 2005, and on non-contractual obligations (Rome II),[25] proposed in 2003, were negotiated in the European Parliament and in the Council. The Commission received strong critics for the lack of published impact assessment reports, in particular for the Regulation Rome I, since there were differing views on the impact of certain provisions, like Article 6 on the conflict of law rules for consumer contracts, on internal market. The Commission had considered that the Regulations has only a limited impact so it had refrained of carrying out a formal assessment procedure. There is no reference to any fundamental rights considerations in the Rome I Regulation. As regards the Rome II Regulation, the Commission had evaluated in particular the compliance of the proposed applicable law rule relating to violations of privacy (in defamation cases) with the Charter rules on respect for privacy and freedom of expression and information, also covering respect for media freedom and pluralism. The proposal aimed at striking a reasonable balance between different rights. Respect for the fundamental principles as regards freedom of the press was to be secured by a specific safeguard clause. The legislators were however not able to agree on inclusion of the proposed rule in the Regulation, so the adopted Rome II does not have even a recital with the Charter reference.

---

21 Regulation (EC) No 44/2001, OJ L 12, 16.1.2001.
22 Regulation (EC) No 1206/2001, OJ L 174, 27.6.2001.
23 Regulation (EC) No 1391/2007, OJ L 324, 10.12.2007.
24 Regulation (EC) No 593/2008, OJ L 177, 4.7.2008.
25 Regulation (EC) No 864/2007, OJ L 199, 31.7.2007.

INITIATIVES ON JUDICIAL COOPERATION WITH THE FUNDAMENTAL RIGHTS ASSESSMENT INCLUDED IN THE IMPACT ASSESSMENT

The first legislative initiative in the area of private international law on which the Commission carried out a methodical impact assessment was the Maintenance Regulation,[26] proposed in 2005. The impact assessment report is very well developed as regards the potential impacts on fundamental rights in area of maintenance obligations. It observes that effective enforcement of maintenance claims would raise standards to the protection of several fundamental rights, most notably, the rights of children and the right to effective remedy of the creditor. According to Article 24 of the Charter, children must have the right to such protection and care as is necessary for their well-being. Moreover, in all actions relating to children, whether taken by public authorities or private institutions, the child's best interests must be a primary consideration. Regarding the right to effective remedy, it is underlined that fair trial (Article 47 of the Charter) includes effective enforcement of the decision. The fair trial aspects had an impact also to formulation of the proposal as regards the debtor's right to a fair trial and hearing. Defendants' rights to notification, time to prepare defence, of audience and right of review had to be safeguarded. Furthermore, enforcement of maintenance claims involves processing of personal data so that Article 8 of the Charter must be respected. The impact assessment report includes a specific table presenting extensively the positive and negative impacts on fundamental rights. The results were summarised in the "Charter-recital" of the proposed Maintenance Regulation; however, this recital was not supported in the legislative negotiations, and the adopted Maintenance Regulation does not make any reference to the fundamental rights.

Since 2005, the Commission has published impact assessment reports concerning its proposals for

- the Regulation on applicable law on divorce (Rome III),[27] in 2008, that was used also when considering and proposing the Regulation implementing the enhanced cooperation;
- the Regulation on successions and on the creation of a European Certificate of Succession[28] in 2009;
- the Regulation on the recast of the Brussels I[29] in 2010;

---

26 Regulation (EC) No 4/2009, OJ L 7, 10.1.2009.
27 Regulation (EC) No 1259/2010, OJ L 343, 29.12.2010.
28 Regulation (EU) No 650/2012, OJ L 201, 27.2.2012.
29 Regulation (EU) No 1215/2012, OJ L 351, 20.12.2012.

- the Regulations relating to property consequences of marriages and of registered partnerships[30] in 2011;
- the Regulation on the European Account Preservation Order[31] in 2011; and
- the Regulation on the revision of the Insolvency Regulation[32] in 2012.

All these impact assessments have scrutinized carefully the compliance of the proposals with the Charter. Next, some observations on common aspects of these assessments, based on the reports, like on the fundamental rights that are often affected by the judicial cooperation and private international law legislation are presented.

THE FUNDAMENTAL RIGHTS OF THE CHARTER THAT ARE OFTEN AFFECTED BY THE PRIVATE INTERNATIONAL LAW LEGISLATION

Most commonly affected by the EU private international law instruments is Article 47 of the Charter on *the right to an effective remedy and to a fair trial.*[33]

According to Article 47(1), everyone whose rights and freedoms guaranteed by the law of the Union are violated has the right to an effective remedy before a tribunal. This provision is crucial to ensure access to justice in the European law context. Access to justice must be effective to fulfil the requirements of the Charter. A formal entitlement to institute proceedings is not enough: to be effective, the right to a remedy before a tribunal requires that practical impediments must not unduly obstruct the exercise of the rights which individuals derive from EU law. The fundamental rights guaranteed by the Charter are not intended to be theoretical and illusory but practical and effective. The exercise of the rights conferred by EU law must not be rendered 'virtually impossible or excessively difficult' by procedural rules.[34] The right to an effective remedy also includes the right of the creditor to recover his claim within a reasonable period of time and on the basis of efficient procedures.[35]

30 COM(2011)126 and COM(2011)127.

31 COM(2011)445.

32 COM(2012)744.

33 All articles of the Charter are explained and analysed in detail in the "Commentary to the Charter of Fundamental Rights", by EU network of Independent Experts on Fundamental Rights, June 2006.

34 ECJ, Case C-312/93, *Pertbroeck v. Belgian State*, [1995] *ECR* I-4599, para. 23; ECJ, Case C-326/96, *Levez*, [1998] *ECR* I-7835, para. 18; ECJ, Case C-120/97, *Upjohn v. Licensing Authority*, [1999] *ECR* I-223, para. 32.

35 ECHR, judgement 19.3 1997, *Hornsby v. Greece*, ECHR-Reports 1997 II 495;11.1.2001, *Lunari v. Italy*, ECHR-Reports 2001.

Article 47(2) stipulates that everyone is entitled to a fair and public hearing within a reasonable time by an independent and impartial tribunal established by law and that everyone shall have the possibility of being advised, defended and represented. For disputes relating to civil law rights and obligations, this guarantee corresponds to Article 6(1) of the ECHR. Inherent in this provision is the right to defence which includes – in the area of civil law – the right to be heard and the right to make known its views on the truth and relevance of the facts, objections and circumstances put forward by the other party.

The Regulation on the European Enforcement Order (EEO) gives an example of the effect of this Charter provision: The Regulation abolished the exequatur for uncontested claims in civil and commercial matters. In order to strengthen the mutual trust between the Member States' legal systems and to ensure the strict observation of the requirements for a fair trial in keeping with Article 47 of the Charter, the Regulation laid down some common minimum procedural standards, in particular with regard to the service of documents covering the admissible methods of service, the time of service enabling the preparation of a defence and the proper information of the debtor.

When recently recasting the Brussels I Regulation,[36] the Commission analysed its fundamental rights effects, and similarly to the EEO Regulation, the question was what would be the impact of the abolishment of the exequatur to the fundamental rights. The Commission concluded that the abolition of exequatur should be accompanied by procedural safeguards which would ensure that a judgment in breach of the right to a fair trial and the right of defence cannot be recognised and enforced. The proposal would then comply with the Charter, in particular its Article 47. The defendant was given three main remedies to his disposal by which he could prevent – in certain circumstances – that a foreign judgment takes effect in a Member State. Since the refusal grounds which can be invoked against the enforcement of the foreign judgment largely correspond to those which can be invoked today in the context of the exequatur procedure, the level of judicial protection for cross-border proceedings remains at least the same as with the status quo, even when the exequatur is abolished.

A second right often mentioned is *the freedom to conduct a business* recognised under Article 16 of the Charter. This right is based on Court of Justice case-law which has recognised freedom to exercise an economic or commercial activity and freedom of contract,[37] and on Article 119(1) and (3) TFEU, which recognises

[36] The recast was adopted in December 2012 as Regulation (EC) No 1215/2012, OJ L 351, 20.12.2012.

[37] See e.g. ECJ case 151/78, *Sukkerfabriken Nykobing*, para. 19, and case C-240/97, *Spain v. Commission*, para 99.

free competition. Arguably, these rights encompass that the legal system gives effect to the will of the parties.

The Regulation on Insolvency proceedings establishes a legal framework for cross-border insolvencies in the EU. The 2012 revision proposal aims, e.g. to extend its scope, to improve jurisdiction rules and to include rules on groups of companies. According to Commission's assessment, such revision would improve the rights of persons involved in cross-border insolvencies like e.g. right to freedom to conduct business and right to engage in work: The EU-wide recognition of personal insolvency schemes through the extension of scope and ensuing debt discharge would impact positively on the freedom to conduct business as it facilitates the possibility of a second chance for debt-discharged entrepreneurs and natural persons. Further the EU-wide recognition of national hybrid and pre-insolvency proceedings would positively affect the freedom to conduct businesses for companies, as these proceedings would be recognised by all their creditors EU-wide.

Next can be mentioned a *right to property*, enshrined in Article 17 of the Charter, that provides that everyone has the right to own, use, dispose of and bequeath his or her lawfully acquired possessions. This includes also e.g. claims which the creditor lawfully pursues against a debtor. The Regulation on successions and on the creation of a European Certificate of Succession obviously is closely linked with the right to property: The Commission designed its proposal so that the right to property would be reinforced. First, testators would enjoy a greater freedom in planning their succession and would have greater security that their intentions would be carried out; secondly, by introducing a faster and more coordinated process, heirs would receive their part of the succession more quickly, and cases of heirs having to give up rights to an inheritance due to legal complexity and pre-emptively high costs would be reduced if not eliminated.

Another example of impacts to right to property was presented at the 2012 revision proposal for the Regulation on Insolvency proceedings: Extension of the scope affects the rights to property of creditors compared to liquidation procedures, because the hybrid, pre-insolvency and personal insolvency schemes are all based on some form of arrangement between the debtor and a majority of creditors. In these schemes, dissenting creditors can be overruled by the majority. The Commission considered this impact on the right to property to be proportionate to the objective of rescuing businesses and saving jobs, since it has been shown that the median recovery rate for creditors may be significantly higher in case of restructuring as compared to liquidation. The reduction in abusive forum-shopping through improved jurisdiction rules, combined with a right for all creditors of judicial review of the jurisdiction, would improve the protection of the creditor's right to property because there would be fewer cases where his claim was due to the shift of his debtor's centre of main interest to another country.

Also the proposals for the Regulations relating to property consequences of marriages and of registered partnerships proposals on property consequences of matrimonial regimes deal with this fundamental right. By extending the jurisdiction of the court dealing with the separation/divorce or with the succession to have also jurisdiction with regard to the liquidation of the matrimonial property regime, and by introducing *lis pendens* rules and rules on automatic recognition and enforcement of decisions, the Regulation would reduce the costs to parties in terms of time delays and administrative procedures (in terms of parallel proceedings and ensuring that the decision is recognised and enforced). The reduction of such costs would therefore allow both parties, both weak and strong, to have a right to access their property.

This would also contribute to respecting another right, the *equality before the law* under Article 20 of the Charter. The Regulation on successions and on the creation of a European Certificate of Succession was evaluated to have a positive impact on the equality before the law, too, as the same law would be applied across the EU regardless of jurisdiction and forum shopping would be avoided.

In the area of private international family law, besides the above, also the rights protected by Articles 21 and 24 of the Charter become important. Article 21 prohibits *the non-discrimination on all grounds*, including on the ground of sexual orientation. For same-sex couples, the Regulation on successions and on the creation of a European Certificate of Succession was found to improve the possibility to dispose of their property to the benefit of their partner regardless of where they have their habitual residence. On the other hand, the private international law instrument are not capable to solve all problems: It is e.g. doubtful that the Regulation leads to positive effects for a child of a non-married couple or of a same-sex couple to have its rights in cross-border successions recognised in other Member States, since preliminary questions concerning who qualifies as an heir (e.g. spouse, children etc.) are not included in the Regulation. The non-discrimination question was also relevant in the assessment of the impacts of the proposals for the Regulations relating to property consequences of marriages and of registered partnerships. The Commission evaluated that the chosen policy options in the proposals respects fundamental rights and observes the principles recognised in the Charter in particular Article 21

Article 24 of the Charter on *the rights of the child* ensures the right for protection and care to the children. Besides the Maintenance Regulation as mentioned above, the impacts on the rights of the child have been assessed in the context of the Regulation on successions and on the creation of a European Certificate of Succession: Children are typically involved in succession cases as heirs rather than deceased or testators. As a consequence, the measures which improve the legal situation of heirs would have at the same time positive impacts on children. The introduction of a right of the testator to choose the law applicable to his succession in cross-border cases may in some cases weaken the legal position of children even if such choice is very limited (nationality or habitual residence), since the rules for reserved portions vary between Member States. However, the Commission measured that the negative impacts of a limited choice of law on children would only occur in rare cases (most Member States recognise a reserved position of children of the deceased), and are outweighed by considerable positive effects in most cases (in particular increase of legal certainty).

Furthermore, there is a number of other fundamental rights of the Charter that may be affected by the private international law acquis; the assessment reports mention e.g. *respect for private and family life* (Article 7) and *protection of personal data* (Article 8) as well as *freedom of religion* (Article 10) and the *right to freedom of expression* (Article 11). Even the *right to respect of human dignity* in Article 1 is of relevance to the civil justice acquis.

CONLUSION

The Charter of Fundamental Rights has had a clear impact both on the working methods of the Commission as well as on the contents of the European legislation on judicial cooperation in civil matters and private international law. The assessment methodology to evaluate the impacts of the legislative proposals to the fundamental right is today well developed. The Commission is very conscious of respect and promotion of fundamental rights, and follows the established strategy for the effective implementation of the Charter carefully. The policy choices in the European private international law legislation do not only respect, but also promote the Charter rights in the EU.

THE ABOLITION OF EXEQUATUR AND STATE LIABILITY FOR HUMAN RIGHTS VIOLATIONS THROUGH THE ENFORCEMENT OF JUDGMENTS IN EUROPEAN FAMILY LAW

Dr Andrea SCHULZ
Director of the German Central Authority for international custody conflicts, Federal Office of Justice, Bonn, Germany

I. INTRODUCTION

In 2001, the European Court of Human Rights pronounced a judgment in the case of *Pellegrini* vs. *Italy*[1] which was highly relevant in the area of international civil procedure. However, the *Pellegrini* judgment – albeit widely discussed in some European jurisdictions – remained largely unnoticed by academia in many others, *e.g.* in Germany. Nonetheless, more than 10 years later, new questions arise from the judgment in light of recent case law of the Court of Justice of the European Union (European Court of Justice, henceforth: ECJ), in particular with regard to State liability and attribution of certain acts to certain States. Therefore, it is worth revisiting the *Pellegrini* judgment (II.1) before looking at the relevant international and regional legislation (II.2) and the case law of the ECJ in this regard (II.3). Lastly, some possible questions arising from the *Pellegrini* judgment and the subsequent EU legislation as interpreted by the ECJ for the EU Member States and in particular their courts will be discussed (III). This article does, however, not purport to provide definite answers.

---

1 ECtHR, judgment of 20 July 2001, application no 30882/96.

II. THE LEGAL CONTEXT

1. THE 2001 *PELLEGRINI* JUDGMENT OF THE ECHR

a. The facts

After 25 years of marriage, in February 1987 Mrs Pellegrini filed an application for judicial separation from her Italian husband with the Rome District Court. The marriage had been contracted in a religious ceremony in 1962 and recognised by the Italian State under a Treaty between Italy and the Holy See. In a judgment dated 2 October 1990 the Rome District Court granted Mrs Pellegrini's petition for judicial separation and ordered her husband to pay her maintenance.

End of November 1987, Mrs Pellegrini was summoned to appear before the Lazio Regional Ecclesiastical Court of the Rome Vicariate on 1 December 1987 "to answer questions in her matrimonial case". She attended that hearing, unassisted by a lawyer and not knowing what it was about. During the hearing she was informed that her husband had sought for the annulment of the marriage on the ground of consanguinity. She stated that she had known of her consanguineous relationship but did not know whether, at the time of her marriage, the priest had requested a special dispensation.

On 10 December 1987, the Ecclesiastical Court annulled the marriage. On 21 December 1987 Mrs Pellegrini lodged an appeal with the ecclesiastical appellate court (the Roman *Rota*). On 10 March 1988 she was informed that the *Rota* would examine her appeal on 13 April 1988 and that she had twenty days in which to submit observations. On 29 March 1988 Mrs Pellegrini, who was still unassisted by a lawyer, submitted her observations, in which she complained, *inter alia*, that she had not had adequate time and facilities for the preparation of her defence.

In a judgment of 13 April 1988, the *Rota* upheld the decision annulling the marriage on the ground of consanguinity. Mrs Pellegrini received only the operative provisions of the judgment, her request for a full copy having been refused.

Under Article 8 § 2 of the Concordat between Italy and the Vatican, as amended by the Agreement of 18 February 1984 revising the Concordat, ratified by Italy under Law No 11 of 25 March 1985, a judgment of the ecclesiastical courts annulling a marriage which has become enforceable by a decision of the superior ecclesiastical review body, may be made enforceable in Italy at the request of one of the parties by a judgment of the relevant court of appeal. The decision of the *Rota* was subsequently referred to the Florence Court of Appeal for a declaration that it could be enforced under Italian law. Mrs Pellegrini requested the Florence Court of Appeal to set aside the judgment of the ecclesiastical court for infringing her defence rights. She elaborated further on this issue and requested that, in the event that the court should declare the judgment enforceable, her ex-husband be ordered to pay her monthly maintenance for the rest of her life.

In a judgment of 8 November 1991, the Florence Court of Appeal declared the judgment of the *Rota* of 13 April 1988 enforceable. The court found that the opportunity given to Mrs Pellegrini at the hearing before the ecclesiastical court of first instance on 1 December 1987 to answer questions had complied with the adversarial principle and that she had had another opportunity to present her case when appealing to the *Rota*. Concerning maintenance, the Florence Court of Appeal declared that it lacked jurisdiction for an order granting lifetime maintenance. With regard to a possible interim maintenance order the court held that the applicant had not sufficiently demonstrated her need.

Mrs Pellegrini filed an appeal on points of law with the Italian Court of Cassation. She submitted that her defence rights had been infringed in the proceedings before the ecclesiastical courts. She submitted, *inter alia*, that the Court of Appeal had omitted to take account of certain features of the proceedings before the ecclesiastical courts: that the parties cannot be represented by a lawyer, that the respondent is not informed of the reasons relied on by the petitioner for having the marriage annulled until he or she is questioned, that the *defensor vinculis*, who acts as the respondent's guardian, is not obliged to appeal, and that she had not been informed of the possibility to be assisted by a lawyer.

In a judgment of 10 March 1995, the Italian Court of Cassation dismissed the appeal. It confirmed the decision of the Court of Appeal and stated that there was case law authority to support the view that the assistance of a lawyer was not forbidden in proceedings under canon law. The applicant could therefore have taken advantage of that possibility. The Court also held that the fact that Mrs Pellegrini had had a very short time in which to prepare her defence in November 1987 did not amount to an infringement of her defence rights because she had not indicated why she had needed more time. The Court of Cassation did not rule on the fact that the case file relating to the proceedings under canon law had not been examined by the Court of Appeal.

b. *The judgment of the ECtHR*

At the outset, the ECtHR made clear that its task was not to examine whether the proceedings before the ecclesiastical courts complied with Article 6 ECHR as the Vatican was not a Party to that Convention. The Court's task rather consisted in examining whether the Italian courts, before authorising enforcement of the ecclesiastical decision annulling the marriage, duly satisfied themselves that the relevant proceedings fulfilled the guarantees of Article 6. The Court stated that "a review of that kind is required where a decision in respect of which enforcement is requested emanates from the courts of a country which does not apply the

Convention. Such a review is especially necessary where the implications of a declaration of enforceability are of capital importance for the parties."

On the merits of the case, the ECtHR considered that the Italian courts had erred in finding that the adversarial principle, which is one of the elements of a fair hearing within the meaning of Article 6 para 1 ECHR, had been respected. The adversarial principle implies that each party to a trial, be it criminal or civil, must in principle have the opportunity to have knowledge of and comment on all evidence adduced or observations filed with a view to influencing the court's decision. The Court held it to be irrelevant that the nullity of the marriage derived from an objective and undisputable fact (namely consanguinity) which the applicant would not have been able to challenge. This was because, in the words of the Court, "what is particularly at stake here is the litigants' confidence in the workings of justice, which is based on, *inter alia*, the knowledge that they have had the opportunity to express their views on every document in the file". In the same vein, the Court held that Article 6 ECHR had been breached by the Italian courts when they found that the ecclesiastical court had not been under an obligation to inform the applicant about the possibility to seek the assistance of a lawyer before she attended the hearing before the ecclesiastical court for questioning.

In sum, the ECtHR held that the Italian courts had breached their duty of satisfying themselves, before authorising enforcement of the Roman *Rota*'s judgment, that the applicant had had a fair trial in the proceedings under canon law.

2. EU LEGISLATION ON THE RECOGNITION AND ENFORCEMENT OF JUDGMENTS FROM OTHER EU MEMBER STATES ENACTED AFTER THE ECtHR'S *PELLEGRINI* JUDGMENT

Since 2001, the European Union has expanded from 16 to 27 Member States. But at the same time, integration within the EU has also deepened. In Tampere (Finland), in 1999 the EC, as it was then called, decided that a programme of measures aiming at gradually abolishing the need for a declaration of enforceability (exequatur) for judgments from other Member States in cases of cross-border enforcement should be adopted.[2] The first instrument implementing this idea went largely unnoticed as many family law academics and practitioners were still struggling with the fact that the EC now appeared as a legislator in their field and did not follow the legislative process closely. In *Regulation (EC)*

[2] See the Draft programme, subsequently published in OJ C 12/2001, p. 1, which was later adopted.

No 2201/2003 concerning jurisdiction and the recognition and enforcement of judgments in matrimonial matters and the matters of parental responsibility,[3] the need for exequatur was abolished for two types of decisions, provided that the court of origin issued a certificate stating that certain procedural rights had been respected. This concerns access / contact orders (Article 41 of the Regulation) and decisions ordering the return / surrender of a child to the left-behind parent which had been abducted to another EU Member State in certain cases (Article 42 of the Regulation). The next instrument in which this principle was applied was *Regulation (EC) No 805/2004 creating a European Enforcement Order for uncontested claims.*[4] Here the abolition of exequatur was much more widely discussed as it was the sole object of the Regulation. This latter instrument in the field of civil and commercial law, however, will not be dealt with in the present article which focuses on family law.

The principle applied in Articles 41 and 42 of the Brussels II a-Regulation is the following: A person who has obtained a judgment and wants to enforce it in another EU Member State can either apply for a declaration of enforceability / registration for enforcement in the State of enforcement and enforce the judgment following the traditional way, or instead turn to the court of origin and ask for a certificate, a model of which is attached to the Regulation. For access / contact orders, the court of origin shall issue the certificate only if all parties concerned were given an opportunity to be heard, the child was equally given such opportunity unless this appeared inappropriate in light of the child's age and maturity, and, if the judgment was given in default, the person in default was served with the document instituting the proceedings in sufficient time and in such a way to enable that person to arrange for his or her defence, or, if the person was served with the document but not in compliance with the provisions just mentioned, if it is otherwise established that that person accepted the decision unequivocally (Article 41 para 2 Brussels II a-Regulation). Article 42 provides for a similar certificate with regard to certain return orders. It applies to cases where a child who was habitually resident in an EU Member State was abducted to another EU Member State and return proceedings pursuant to the *Hague Convention of 25 October 1980 on the Civil Aspects of International Child Abduction* resulted in a refusal to return the child based on Article 13 of that Convention. If subsequently custody proceedings conducted before the court of the State of former habitual residence of the child pursuant to Article 11 paras 6–8 of the Brussels II a-Regulation lead to a decision ordering the return of the child to the left-behind parent, such decision can be made immediately enforceable without exequatur in all EU Member States (Article 11 para 8 of the Regulation) if

[3] OJ L 338/2003, p. 1 (so-called Brussels II a-Regulation).
[4] OJ L 143/2004, p. 15 (European Enforcement Order – EEO).

the court of origin issues a certificate pursuant to Article 42 of the Regulation. The certificate may be issued only if all parties concerned were given an opportunity to be heard, the child was equally given such opportunity unless this appeared inappropriate in light of the child's age and maturity, and the court has taken into account the reasons and underlying evidence for the non-return order made in the Hague return proceedings in the other State.

3. CASE LAW OF THE COURT OF JUSTICE OF THE EUROPEAN UNION REGARDING ARTICLES 41 AND 42 OF REGULATION (EC) NO 2201/2003

The Brussels II a-Regulation became applicable on 1 March 2005. ECJ case law on the provisions relating to children remained scarce, though, because in light of the length of proceedings for a preliminary ruling of the ECJ on the interpretation of certain provisions, family judges seemed to prefer not to refer questions of interpretation to the ECJ. This changed in 2008 when the ECJ introduced the *Procédure préjudicielle d'urgence* (PPU). Soon after introduction of the new urgency procedure, a child abduction case was referred to the ECJ.[5] A child who had been habitually resident in Germany had been wrongfully retained in Lithuania by her mother following access. Return proceedings under the 1980 Hague Child Abduction Convention had led to a first-instance refusal in Lithuania based on Article 13 of the Hague Convention, and that decision had been transmitted to the German court before which custody proceedings were already pending. The German court granted custody to the German father and ordered the return / surrender of the child to the father in Germany. Meanwhile, the Hague return proceedings in Lithuania also continued, and the Lithuanian Court of Appeal ordered the return of the child to Germany. Litigation between the parents at the enforcement stage in Lithuania in the proceedings relating to the Lithuanian Hague return order reached the Lithuanian Supreme Court. Likewise, proceedings brought by the mother in Lithuania for a declaration of non-recognition with regard to the German return order resulting from custody proceedings pursuant to Article 11 paras 6–8 Brussels II a-Regulation reached the Supreme Court of Lithuania which then submitted a number of questions with regard to the recognition and enforcement of the German return order under the Brussels II a-Regulation and the relationship between the two sets of proceedings to the ECJ. The Supreme Court wanted to know, *inter alia*, whether proceedings for a declaration of non-recognition could be brought in Lithuania in spite of the certificate issued by the German court. The ECJ decided that "opposition to

---

5 ECJ, judgment of 11 July 2008, *Rinau*, Case C-195/08 PPU.

the recognition of the decision ordering return is not permitted and it is for the requested court only to declare the enforceability of the certified decision and to allow the immediate return of the child".[6]

Subsequently, other courts in EU Member States continued to have doubts whether to enforce return orders made by courts in the State of former habitual residence of an abducted child once the courts in the State where the child was now present had refused to return the child pursuant to Article 13 of the 1980 Hague Convention, and referred more questions to the ECJ. In another judgment following a request of the Supreme Court of Austria for a preliminary ruling with regard to the enforcement of a return order under Article 11 para 8, Article 42 of the Regulation,[7] the ECJ remained faithful to its opinion that under the regime of the Brussels II a-Regulation, it is only for the courts of the State of (former) habitual residence of the child to decide on any issues concerning the return of the child in proceedings pursuant to Article 11 paras 6–8 of the Regulation provided that Hague return proceedings have been brought in the other State first but have not resulted in the return of the child because of Article 13 of the 1980 Hague Convention. Neither a change of circumstances and a possible resulting danger for the best interests of the child nor a contradicting, more recent domestic decision allows the courts of the requested State to disregard the foreign return order or to refrain from its enforcement. In the *Povse* judgment, the ECJ even broadened the scope of Article 11 para 8 of the Regulation by stating that "a judgment of the court with jurisdiction ordering the return of the child falls within the scope of that provision, even if it is not preceded by a final judgment of that court relating to rights of custody of the child". This means that also provisional measures issued in summary proceedings without a full taking of evidence with regard to the child's best interests could benefit from this regime. In the opinion of the author of this article, this is contrary to the purpose of the provisions[8] but this is not the topic of this article and shall not be further discussed here.

Courts in other Member States were still not convinced, though, that judgments accompanied by a certificate pursuant to Articles 41 or 42 of the Brussels II a-Regulation have to be enforced in all cases. In 2010, a German court referred a set of questions to the ECJ because the court was reluctant to enforce a Spanish return order which had been certified under Article 11 para 8 and Article 42 of the Regulation. The same German court had refused the return of the child two years earlier, based on Article 13 para 2 of the 1980 Hague Convention, because the then nine-year-old girl was strongly opposed to returning to Spain. In the subsequent custody proceedings in Spain, the judge had ordered the appearance

6 No 89 of the *Rinau* judgment.
7 ECJ, judgment of 1 July 2010, *Povse*, Case C-211/10 PPU.
8 See further Schulz, [2004] IFL 22, 25.

and psychological evaluation of the girl but her mother did not allow her to travel to Spain for the hearing because in the meantime the Spanish court had granted sole custody to the Spanish father and she therefore feared not to be able to leave the country with the child after the hearing. The Spanish court refused to grant her safe conduct for the return to Germany with the child. The mother's request to hear the child by video-conference was rejected by the Spanish judge. The judge ordered the return of the child to her father in Spain and issued a certificate pursuant to Article 42 of the Brussels II a-Regulation in which he certified that the child had had the opportunity to be heard. The German court which was asked to enforce the Spanish judgment held this statement in the certificate to be wrong and submitted a number of questions to the ECJ for a preliminary ruling. In particular, the German court was of the opinion that Article 24 of the Charter of Fundamental Rights of the European Union[9] had been violated because the Spanish court had not heard the child in person while the German court had based its decision on the child's will. The ECJ decided that "[i]n circumstances such as those of the main proceedings, the court with jurisdiction in the Member State of enforcement cannot oppose the enforcement of a certified judgment, ordering the return of a child who has been wrongfully removed, on the ground that the court of the Member State of origin which handed down that judgment may have infringed Article 42 of Council Regulation (EC) No 2201/2003 of 27 November 2003 concerning jurisdiction and the recognition and enforcement of judgments in matrimonial matters and the matters of parental responsibility, repealing Regulation (EC) No 1347/2000, interpreted in accordance with Article 24 of the Charter of Fundamental Rights of the European Union, since the assessment of whether there is such an infringement falls exclusively within the jurisdiction of the courts of the Member State of origin".[10]

This means that any challenge against the certificate has to be brought exclusively in the State of origin of the return order and the accompanying certificate. Likewise, any legal challenge for an alleged violation of fundamental rights may only be brought in that State. And, lastly, even a stay of enforcement for the time during which one of the said challenges might be pending has to be requested exclusively in the State of origin of the decision. In view of the ECJ, once the courts of the State of habitual residence have ordered the return of the child to the left-behind parent and issued a certificate pursuant to Article 42 of the Brussels II a-Regulation only litigation about enforcement measures as such may be conducted before the courts of the State where the child is now present.

9 OJ C 364/200, p. 1 (the Charter).
10 ECJ, judgment of 22 December 2010, *Aguirre Zarraga*, Case C-491/10 PPU.

III. CONSEQUENCES OF POSSIBLE HUMAN RIGHTS VIOLATIONS

1. NEITHER NEED NOR PERMISSION FOR COURTS OF REQUESTED STATE TO CARRY OUT HUMAN RIGHTS SCRUTINY ON INCOMING EU JUDGMENTS WITH CERTIFICATE

The *Pellegrini* judgment of the ECtHR says that in proceedings where exequatur is still required (*i.e.* in the normal cross-border cases relating to the recognition and enforcement of foreign judgments), a court in a State bound by the ECHR does not only have to observe the relevant international or domestic law relating to the recognition and enforcement of foreign judgments and exercise the scrutiny regulated there but – in cases where the court of origin of the relevant judgment is not bound by the ECHR because it is located in a State which is not a Party to that Treaty – also check whether the ECHR has been complied with by the court of origin. Before granting recognition and a declaration of enforceability / registration for enforcement to such judgment, the court has to check whether the procedural standards guaranteed by the ECHR have been respected.

As all EU Member States are Parties to the ECHR, under the "pre-Tampere regime" which still required exequatur for all judgments from other EU Member States, courts of EU Member States requested to recognise and enforce such judgments were therefore not obliged by the ECHR as interpreted by the ECtHR[11] in the *Pellegrini* judgment to carry out any Human Rights scrutiny with regard to the foreign judgment.

The Brussels II a-Regulation and the subsequent case law of the ECJ have now abolished the *need* for a formal decision on the recognition of judgments and a declaration of enforceability for many cases as the former comes by operation of law in all cases and often the latter as well, provided that the court of origin has issued the necessary certificate. Moreover, the ECJ denied even the *right* to exercise such scrutiny to the courts of the State where enforcement is sought – unless the applicant him- or herself requests exequatur. So it looks as if the court requested to enforce a return or contact order from another EU Member

[11] Under ECJ case law, however, a breach of Human Rights protected by the ECHR, in particular Article 6 (fair trial), is a well-established ground for refusal of recognition of judgments from other EU Member States under the public policy clause of EU instruments that still require exequatur, *e.g.* the Brussels I-Regulation (*Council Regulation (EC) No 44/2001 of 22 December 2000 on jurisdiction and the recognition and enforcement of judgments in civil and commercial matters*, OJ L 12/2001, p.1), provided that the violation reaches a certain degree of intensity; see, *e.g.*, ECJ, judgment of 28 March 2000, Case C-7/98, *Krombach*; ECJ, judgment of 2 April 2009, Case C-394/07, *Gambazzi*.

State under Articles 11 para 8, 42 or Article 41 of the Brussels II a-Regulation has no further choice but to enforce it because secondary EU law says so and the ECHR as interpreted by the ECtHR does not require any different procedure at a general level.

2. NO PERMISSION FOR COURTS OF REQUESTED STATE TO CARRY OUT HUMAN RIGHTS SCRUTINY ON SECONDARY EU LEGISLATION ABOLISHING EXEQUATUR

This leads to the question whether the relevant secondary EU legislation needs to – or may – be submitted to scrutiny by the courts of the requested State if there are doubts as to its conformity with the Charter or the ECHR. From the author's (German) perspective this will only be discussed very briefly in light of German case law but as the German Federal Constitutional Court is known as one of the most sceptical courts in the Member States with regard to an adequate Human Rights protection by EU law and institutions, this might nonetheless be of interest for readers from other jurisdictions.

In a decision from 1974[12] the German Federal Constitutional Court claimed the right to check the abstract conformity of secondary EU legislation with the German Constitution's fundamental rights catalogue – as long as no comparable catalogue of rights existed in the EU. The ECJ, on the other hand, was of the view that these matters fell into its own exclusive competence. But in a subsequent decision from 1986,[13] the German Federal Constitution Court acknowledged the level of Human Rights protection reached within the EU and declared that it would in the future refrain from scrutinising EU secondary legislation as to its abstract compatibility with the catalogue of fundamental rights as protected by the German Constitution. It is to be assumed that such judicial self-restraint will all the more be exercised now that the Charter has been given binding force by the Lisbon Treaty. Therefore, there will not be any double control, and the ECJ is the only authority to rule on the legal validity of secondary EU legislation.

[12] BVerfG 29 May 1974, BVerfGE 37, 271 – *Solange I* – "As long as …".
[13] BVerfG 22 October 1986, BVerfGE 73, 339 – *Solange II*.

3. CONSEQUENCES OF POSSIBLE HUMAN RIGHTS VIOLATIONS THROUGH JUDGMENTS GIVEN BY COURTS OF EU MEMBER STATES AND THEIR ENFORCEMENT IN OTHER EU MEMBER STATES

Assuming that a certain return or contact order does indeed infringe Human Rights, from the above it is clear that the State where enforcement is sought does not have any legal possibility to refuse enforcement of a judgment from another EU Member State which is accompanied by a certificate as mentioned in the Brussels II a-Regulation unless the courts in the State where the decision was made granted a stay of enforcement.

On the other hand, in recent years, the ECtHR granted a stay of enforcement by interim measure in a few return cases[14] – sometimes even though domestic remedies had not yet been exhausted.[15] But if the ECtHR does not intervene and the person against whom the order was enforced, or the child, or both, subsequently file an application with the ECtHR for violation of their Human Rights, the question arises against whom such application should be directed and which State could be held liable.

The State where enforcement took place used its sovereign powers and applied coercive enforcement measures which can be attributed to that State. On the other hand, under EU law the authorities of this State had no choice but to enforce the order. It seems that not even a reference to the ECJ for a preliminary ruling could resolve that dilemma: The ECJ has made clear that even a stay of enforcement may not be granted by the courts of the State where enforcement is sought – regardless of the purpose of that stay. So it may be assumed that these courts do not have the right either to order a stay of enforcement and submit questions to the ECJ for a preliminary ruling. In any event, such questions may only refer to the interpretation of EU law in general and not to the solution of the individual case. Once the ECJ has answered the questions submitted by a national court the case is referred back to the latter for continuation. So most likely the ECJ itself would not pronounce itself on whether a certain return or contact order does constitute a violation of the Charter.

If the return or contact order as such, either because of its content or because of some defect in the proceedings leading to the order, constitutes a Human Rights violation, the State where the order was made should equally held liable. So it seems that an application in Strasbourg before the ECtHR could be brought against both States. It remains to be seen how the ECtHR will deal with the legal

14 ECtHR, judgment of 6 July 2010, *Neulinger and Shuruk* v. *Switzerland* (application no 41615/07) [2010] ECHR 1053, *Buday* v. *Belgium*, judgment of 10 July 2012 (application no 4320/11).

15 *E.g.* in the *Buday* case.

situation that the requested State (the State where enforcement is sought) does not have any legal possibility not to enforce the judgment. The case of *Deak* v. *Romania and the United Kingdom*[16] might provide some directions in this respect. It concerned a child abduction from Romania to the United Kingdom. The Hague return proceedings before the English court had taken 3 ½ years. This was to a large extent caused by the fact that the English court had decided that it needed a declaration under Article 15 of the 1980 Hague Convention from Romania, stating that the removal of the child had been wrongful in terms of the Convention. Proceedings in Romania to obtain such declaration took two years. The ECHR found that Romania had breached Article 6 ECHR because of the excessive length of proceedings but the United Kingdom was held not to have violated Article 6. The ECtHR accepted that the English judge, within his discretion, had decided that an Article 15 declaration was required, and that the length of the English proceedings had to a large extent been caused by the length of the proceedings in Romania. The resulting violation of Article 6 ECHR could thus not be attributed to the United Kingdom. A possible way to handle applications brought against a State where a return order was made and certified, and against the State where this order was enforced could be to follow this line of reasoning and argue that the Human Rights violation cannot be attributed to the enforcing State because it is bound by EU law to enforce without any further checks, and the ECHR only requires a check from a Human Rights point of view if the State of origin of the decision is not itself bound by the ECHR.

Interesting questions of conflicts of conventions also arise in cases where the ECtHR orders a stay of enforcement or finds that enforcement constitutes a violation of Human Rights while the State where enforcement is sought is under an obligation not only by domestic but by international (treaty) law or supranational (EU) law to enforce the order. The answer to the question which obligation prevails will depend on the hierarchy of norms but the issue is complicated by the fact that this hierarchy of norms is not the same in all States. In some States, the ECHR enjoys constitutional status, ranging above ordinary laws. In other States, *e.g.* in Germany, it enjoys the same status as any international treaty, which means that it is considered to be on a level below the German constitution but – in case of conflict – above ordinary domestic laws. EU law, on the other hand, is considered to be "supranational" rather than international because EU Member States have transferred parts of their sovereign powers (including certain legislative powers) to the EU. It certainly ranges above domestic law and claims precedence over international law but the latter is not universally accepted. Whether duties arising from secondary EU legislation range above or below duties arising from the ECHR may thus be answered differently from one State to another.

[16] ECtHR, judgment of 3 June 2008, application no 19055/05.

The conflict becomes even more obvious if in the very same case the court of the State where enforcement is sought has already referred questions to the ECJ for a preliminary ruling, and the answers given by the ECJ make it clear that in the individual case the court of the requested Member State has to enforce this particular order. So we might not only be faced with a conflict of norms but also with a "clash of jurisdictions" if the two highest courts in Europe come to opposing results. Perhaps the near future will provide an example as the *Povse* case – a case concerning a child abduction from Italy to Austria – which was already decided by the ECJ in the sense just mentioned[17] – has now been brought before the ECtHR, and on 4 December 2012 the ECtHR ordered a stay of enforcement until further notice.[18] To sum up, the interaction between Private International Law and Human Rights still offers numerous interesting questions to be tackled by Hans van Loon in the future.

[17] See *supra* n 7.

[18] *Povse* v. *Austria*, application no 3890/11.

THE EU MAINTENANCE REGULATION AND THE HAGUE MAINTENANCE PROTOCOL OF 2007

Recognition of Foreign Judgments and the Public Policy Defence

Kurt SIEHR
Professor emeritus of the University of Zürich Faculty of Law
Researcher at the Max Planck Institute for Comparative and International Private Law in Hamburg

I. THE MAINTENANCE REGULATION

On 18 June 2011 the *Council Regulation (EC) No 4/2009 of 18 December 2008 on jurisdiction, applicable law, recognition and enforcement of decisions and cooperation in matters relating to maintenance obligations* (Maintenance Regulation = MR) entered into force in all Member States of the European Union (EU).[1] The MR is unique in at least in three respects:

- The MR covers for the first time *all four aspects* of private international law: jurisdiction, applicable law, recognition and enforcement of decisions and international cooperation.
- For the first time the MR itself does *not regulate every matter* but refers to a Hague instrument for legal treatment. According to Article 15 MR

1 OJ 2009, L 7, p. 1. Denmark by a letter of 14 January 2009 notified the Commission of its decision to implement the Regulation, in a limited fashion (see OJ L 149/80 12.6.2009). Denmark will participate in the Regulation only in so far as its provisions amend Regulation (EC) No 44/2001 (the "Brussels I Regulation").

the applicable law is determined in accordance with the *Hague Protocol of 23 November 2007 on the Law Applicable to Maintenance Obligations.*[2]

- If foreign courts of a Member State are bound by the Hague Protocol, their decisions will be recognized by other Member States without any exequatur and without the possibility of refusal to recognize these foreign decisions because of *violation of public policy* of the recognizing Member State.

I shall focus on the last problem and dedicate my paper to Hans van Loon, a friend of mine and a dear colleague for many years.

II. RECOGNITION OF FOREIGN DECISIONS

1. GENERAL SCHEME

The MR regulates recognition, enforceability and enforcement of foreign decisions in three sections comprising Articles 16–43. Section 1 deals with decisions given in a Member State *bound* by the 2007 Hague Protocol (Articles 17–22), section 2 deals with decisions given in a Member State *not* bound by the 2007 Hague Protocol (Articles 23–38), and section 3 provides some common provisions (Articles 39–43).

a. Decisions given by Member States bound by the 2007 Hague Protocol

An enforceable decision on maintenance shall be recognized in another Member State without any special procedure and without any possibility of opposing its recognition (Article 17(1)). If accompanied by the documents required by Article 20 for the purpose of enforcement, the foreign judgment will be enforced unless the defendant asks for a review in the Member State of origin (Article 19) or if he applies for refusal or suspension of enforcement in the Member State of enforcement (Article 21).

(1) Review in the Member State of origin

If the defendant was not served properly and in time or if he was prevented from contesting the maintenance claim by reason of force majeure or due to extraordinary circumstances without any fault on his part, he may ask the competent court in the Member State of origin to review the decision unless he

---

[2] Hague Conference on Private International Law (ed.), *Recueil des Conventions, Collection of Conventions (1951–2009)*, The Hague 2009, No 39.

failed to challenge the decision when it was possible for him to do so, and he applies for review within a certain time limit.

Also, jurisdiction of the court of origin is no ground for refusal of recognition. This requirement for giving a judgment is definitively and finally decided by the court in the Member State of origin, as has already been regulated by Regulation Brussels I (exception in Article 35) and by Regulation Brussels II (Article 24).

(2) Refusal of enforcement in the Member State of enforcement

The enforcement of a decision of a Member State bound by The Hague Protocol can only be refused on two grounds:

- the right to enforce the decision is extinguished by the effect of prescription or the limitation of action, either under the law of the Member State of origin or under the law of the Member State of enforcement, whichever provides the longer limitation period (Article 21(2) subsection1); and
- the decision of the Member State of origin is irreconcilable with a decision given in the Member State of enforcement or with a decision (except a modifying decision on the basis of changed circumstances) given in another Member State or in a third State which fulfils the condition necessary for its recognition in the Member State of enforcement (Article 21(2) subsection 2 and 3).

The enforcement of a decision of a Member State bound by The Hague Protocol may be suspended by reason of two grounds:

- a review of the decision has been asked for in the Member State of origin (Article 21(3) subsection 1); and
- the decision of the Member State of origin has been suspended in that State (Article 21(3) subsection 2).

The recognition of a decision rendered by a Member State cannot be refused because of violation of public policy of the forum State although it has been recognized for many years that the application of the correct law (the 2007 Hague Maintenance Protocol) as well as the trust in Member States have nothing to do with the refusal of a *single* judgment handed down by a judge of a Member State of origin manifestly violating principles of public policy.

b. *Decisions given by Member States not bound by the 2007 Hague Protocol*

Decisions given by a Member State not bound by the 2007 Hague Protocol (Articles 23–38) – according to Article 24 – may be refused on four grounds:

- manifest violation of public policy (not applied to rules relating to jurisdiction);
- insufficient service of documents which instituted the proceedings;
- irreconcilability with a decision given in the Member State of recognition;
- irreconcilability with a decision of another State recognized in the Member State of recognition.

It is interesting that violation of public policy may be raised as a defence.

c. *Application of the Regulation especially of the Enforcement Provisions*

The MR entered into force on 18 June 2011 (Article 76(3)). The 2007 Hague Protocol has been ratified by the European Union but not yet by Serbia, another subscribing State. The Protocol enters into force after the deposit of the second instrument of ratification (Article 25 of the Hague Protocol). The EU, however, has given notice that within the Community, the rules of the Protocol shall provisionally apply from 18 June 2011, even if the Protocol has not yet internationally entered into force on that date.[3]

With respect to recognition of foreign judgments, Article 75(2) MR provides some special rules. According to Article 75(2)(a) MR, sections 2 and 3 of Chapter IV (Articles 23–43 of the MR) shall apply also to decisions given in a Member State *before* the date of application of this MR for which recognition is requested *after* that date. In this case the Hague Protocol was *not* yet binding on the Member State of origin, but the enforcement of the decision is requested after 18 June 2011.

2. SPECIAL PROBLEMS: BGH DECISION OF 26 AUGUST 2009

To test the MR, a special case should be looked at. This case was decided by the German Federal Court for Civil and Criminal Matters (Bundesgerichtshof = BGH) on 26 August 2009.[4]

---

[3] Article 4 of the Council Decision of 30 November 2009 on the conclusion by the European Community of the Hague Protocol of 23 November 2007 on the Law Applicable to Maintenance Obligations, OJ 2009, No. L 331 p. 17–18.

[4] BGH 26 August 2009, *Entscheidungen des BGH in Zivilsachen (BGHZ)* 182, 188 = *Zeitschrift für das gesamte Familienrecht (FamRZ)* 2009, 1816 with note by Dieter Henrich = *European*

a. *Facts of the Case*

A child was born out of wedlock on 1 August 1999 and happily lived with his maternal grandmother in Poland. The grandmother had been appointed custodian because the residence of the child's mother was unknown.

In 2004 a suit was commenced in Poland against a man resident in Germany. The lawsuit sought a declaration of paternity and payment of maintenance to the child. Service of process was made with international legal assistance and the defendant was asked to appoint somebody in Poland authorized to receive service of process and other judicial notifications. The defendant did not appoint an agent and did not take part in the Polish proceedings. In a hearing, arranged by a German court at the request of the Polish court, the defendant testified that he met the child's mother in Cologne and offered her accommodation without having sexual relations with her. He also mentioned that the mother had told him that she worked as a prostitute in Germany. Later she was taken to a German hospital by the defendant for delivering the plaintiff. She took the child to Poland at the age of 16 months. Finally, the defendant was ready to subject himself to a blood or DNA test in order to prove that he was not the child's father.

The Polish court heard the child's grandmother in February 2005. In this hearing she told the court that her daughter had written that she was pregnant, delivered the child in Germany and resolutely had designated the defendant as the child's father. Yes, her daughter worked in Germany. But the grandmother did not know what kind of work her daughter was engaged in, nor in particular work as a prostitute. The court did not accept the defendant's offer for a paternity test and finally decided the case as "clear". The judgment, handed down on 3 February 2005, declared the defendant to be the child's father and obliged him to pay 500 PLN per month. The judgment, delivered orally without any written sentence, became final on 21 February 2005.

It was requested that this Polish judgment be recognized and enforced in Germany. The *Landgericht* (county court) Köln recognized the judgment and the *Oberlandesgericht* (court of appeal) Köln affirmed.[5] The *Bundesgerichtshof* (BGH) was asked for correction of the decision, and the BGH agreed.

b. *Deliberations of the BGH*

Bases for the recognition of the Polish decision are found in three different rules of law. The decision on paternity is to be recognized according to § 328 Code of Civil

Legal Forum 2010, II – 18 = *Die deutsche Rechtsprechung auf dem Gebiete des Internationalen Privatrechts im Jahre 2009* (*IPRspr.* 2009) No 252.

5 OLG Köln 17 September 2007, *FamRZ* 2008, 1763 = *IPRspr.* 2007 No 208.

Procedure (CCP = *Zivilprozessordnung*, ZPO).[6] The sentence on maintenance has to be recognized and enforced according to Article 32 et seq. Brussels I Regulation 44/2001 and according to Article 5 of the *Hague Convention of 1973 on Recognition and Enforcement of Maintenance Obligations*, as this Convention is not excluded by the Brussels I Regulation (Article 71 Brussels I Regulation). All these sources provide that a foreign decision should not be recognized if the public policy of the forum state is violated (§ 328(1) no. 4 CCP; Article 34(1) Brussels I Regulation; Article 5(1) Hague Convention).

(1) Decision on Paternity

The BGH first asks whether there are any obstacles to recognizing the Polish paternity decision. Five arguments were discussed in order to decide that the Polish decision violates German public policy.

(a) Fair Hearing

At the outset the German court had to decide whether the Polish procedure deviates from the "principles of German procedure law to such an extent that it cannot be held as an ordinary procedure of law and justice". In German civil procedure an absent defendant who did not nominate an agent to receive judicial service and documents is served by post (§ 184 CCP) and not – as in Poland – by deposit of notice in the files. The Polish habit of service was discussed at length but not definitely decided as violating German public policy.

(b) Reliance on Testimony

In German law the testimony of the child's mother may be accepted by the court seized of a paternity suit. Also foreign decisions may be recognized if they relied on the mother's testimony if the man named by the mother to be the child's father did not subject himself to a paternity test.[7] But here the defendant offered to undergo a paternity test which was, however, not accepted by the Polish court.

---

6 The Gesetz über das Verfahren in Familiensachen und in den Angelegenheiten der freiwilligen Gerichtsbarkeit (FamFG) of 17 December 2008, which has special rules for recognition of foreign decisions (§§ 107–110 FamFG), entered into force on 1 September 2009. But also § 109(1) no. 4 FamFG excludes recognition if the foreign decision manifestly violates German public policy.

7 BGH 9 April 1986, *BGHWarn* 1986 No. 107 = *NJW* 1986, 2193 = *IPRax* 1987, 247 with note by Peter Winkler von Mohrenfels = *IPRspr.* 1986 No. 95.

(c) Hearsay Evidence

Instead of the absent mother the child's maternal grandmother gave hearsay evidence. She told the Polish court that the defendant had been named by her daughter as the child's father who she lived with while working in Germany, and who brought her to a hospital for delivery. The grandmother did not know what sort of work her daughter did in Germany. This hearsay evidence was not regarded as sufficient for the BGH, especially because the defendant offered to undergo a paternity test.

(d) Offer of Paternity Tests

The paternity test which the defendant offered to undergo was not accepted by the Polish court, although it is easy today to complete a test abroad and send the results or the blood or DNA samples to Poland by way of international legal assistance. The EU Regulation of 2001 on Taking Evidence Abroad and the Hague Convention of 1970 apply to civil and commercial matters and voluntary international legal assistance is rendered between Germany and Poland. There was no reason to decline this offer by the defendant.

(e) Local Remedies

Finally the BGH had to decide whether the defendant did not lose any remedy against the Polish decision because he did not ask a Polish superior court for review of the judgment of the lower court. After hearing the defendant in Germany and after having offered a paternity test, the defendant was not aware that the Polish court would render a judgment without such a test.

Therefore he cannot be blamed of not asking for review of the Polish decision of which he was not informed until the application for enforcement in Germany.

(f) Intermediate Summary

In summary the BGH held that the Polish paternity decision violates German public policy because it is based on hearsay evidence and not on a paternity test offered by the defendant.

(2) Decision on Maintenance

The second branch of the BGH decision is devoted to the Polish decision on maintenance for the child. The deliberations of the court are rather short. They concentrate on the connection necessary under German law between paternity and maintenance obligations. Only if the paternity of the defendant has been properly established is the defendant obliged to pay maintenance payments to the child. In the present case paternity of the defendant had not been established. Therefore any foreign maintenance decision violates German public policy.

3. EVALUATION OF THE MAINTENANCE REGULATION: RECOGNITION OF FOREIGN DECISIONS

The Maintenance Regulation does not provide any rule on the preliminary question of paternity, marriage and any other relationship from which maintenance obligations may arise (Article 15 MR and Article 1(2) Hague Protocol). Therefore these preliminary questions still must be answered by national conflicts law, and the German decision of the BGH would be the same after entry into force of the MR. With respect to the decision on maintenance the German decision may, however, be different.

a. Foreign Maintenance Decisions of Member States not bound by the Hague Protocol

If the Polish decision had been submitted for enforcement in Germany after 18 June 2011, the same could have been decided by the BGH. The MR would be applicable and the provisions of Articles 23 et seq. (decisions given in a Member State not bound by the 2007 Hague Protocol) would apply according to Article 75(2) MR. Under Article 24(1)(a) MR recognition of any decision of such a Member States may be refused if the decision manifestly violates public policy of the Member State in which recognition is sought.

b. Foreign Maintenance Decisions of Member States bound by the Hague Protocol

If the Polish court had handed down the decision after 18 June 2011, Articles 17 et seq. MR would apply. In these Articles public policy is no longer a defence and ground for non-recognition of a foreign judgment. Article 19 MR provides a right to apply for a review in very limited situations. If the defendant was not properly served with the document instituting the proceedings or if he was prevented from contesting the maintenance claim by reason of force majeure or other extraordinary circumstances, the defendant, who did not enter an appearance in the Member State of origin, may apply for a review of the decision before the competent court of that Member State unless he failed to challenge the decision when it was possible for him to do so. In the Polish case such a right to apply for review was not available because the defendant was properly served with the documents instituting the proceedings. The Polish decision would have to be enforced in Germany.

III. REVIEW AFTER FIVE YEARS (ARTICLE 74 MR)

According to Article 74 MR, by five years from 18 June 2011, the Commission shall submit to the European Parliament, the Council and other bodies a report on the application of the Regulation and shall evaluate its functioning. Here are two suggestions for improvement.

1. HAGUE PROTOCOL OF 2007: BOUND AND NOT BOUND BY IT

In the past many national statutes on civil procedure required for the recognition and enforceability of foreign judgments that the foreign court did not deviate, detrimentally to nationals of the recognizing state, from certain local provisions on the law applicable to certain status problems. Section 328(1) no. 3 German Code of Civil Procedure (CPC), original version, may be taken as an example.

> "Recognition of the judgment given in a foreign state is excluded:
>
> ...
>
> 3. if, detrimentally to a German party, the judgment deviated from the rules provided by Article 13(1) and (3) [marriage according to national law of the parties] or Articles 17 [divorce according to the national law of the husband], 18 [filiation according to the national law of the husband], 22 [legitimation according to the national law of the husband] of the Introductory Statute to the Civil Code ..."

Such dependence of recognition of foreign judgments on the law applied by the state of origin has been repeated in Article 27(4) of the Brussels Convention of 1968. This rule read as follows:

> "A judgment shall not be recognized:
>
> ...
>
> 4. if the court of the State of origin, in order to arrive at its judgment, has decided a preliminary question concerning the status or legal capacity of natural persons, rights in property arising out of a matrimonial relationship, wills or succession in a way that conflicts with a rule of the private international law of the State in which

the recognition is sought, unless the same result would have been reached by the application of the rules of private international law of that State."

In the Brussels I Regulation this requirement for recognition has been eliminated, and this change is correct. There is no longer a *revision au fond*, and the only barrier to be overcome is the *ordre public* of the recognizing state.

2. ORDRE PUBLIC

a. Ordre Public in General

The public policy clauses of instruments on recognition of foreign judgments are designed to prevent foreign judgments from being recognized which are "manifestly contrary to public policy in the Member State in which recognition is sought". By such a clause not only foreign decisions are not recognized which violate basic principles of substantive law but also those which deviate from normal and acceptable principles of civil procedure.

In former times, when certain paternity suits were not allowed in Italy, German maintenance judgments for illegitimate children were recognized in a "*delibazione parziale*" proceeding, although the underlying German paternity statements were not recognized.[8] Such limited proceedings were correct because the governing maintenance instruments (the Hague Conventions of 1958 and 1973) provided that, if the decision does not relate solely to maintenance obligations, recognition is only "limited to the parts of the decision which concern maintenance obligations". On the other hand German maintenance judgments for illegitimate children were not recognized in France if the German decisions based the paternity question on the information given by the mother of the child.[9]

But what should be done with respect to the request for recognition and enforcement of the Polish judgment? Should it be recognized although:

[8] Claudio d'Agostino, Sulla dichiarazione di efficacia parziale della sentenza straniera, *Rivista di diritto internazionale privato e processuale* 5 (1969) 341–366; *Andrea Giardina*, L'exequatur partiel en Italie des décisions étrangères en matière de filiation, in *Multitudo legum – ius unum, Mélanges en l'honneur de Wilhelm Wengler*, Berlin 1973, vol. II, 337–355.

[9] Cass. 16.7.1974, *Rev. crit.* 64 (1975) 461 with note by *Georges Wiederkehr*; Cass. 18.5.1976 and 25.1.1977, *Rev. crit.* 67 (1978) 351 with note by Marthe Simon-Depitre/Jacques Foyer; Ernst Mezger, "Anerkennung deutscher Vaterschafts- und Unterhaltsurteile in Frankreich", *IPRax* 1981, 103–106.

- the defendant offered to undergo a DNA test to prove that he was not the father;
- paternity was assumed on third party evidence given by the child's grandmother;
- the absent mother of the child was alleged to be a prostitute.

I think that the German *Bundesgerichtshof* was correct in applying the public policy clause and in declining recognition of the Polish judgment.

b. Ordre Public in European Regulations

The public policy clause in European Regulations has nothing to do with the system itself in which the decision to be recognized was rendered. It does not codify a ground for non-recognition of the New York type codified in § 5304(a)(1) of the Civil Practice Law and Rules.[10] This section reads:

> "§ 5304 Grounds for non-recognition
> (a) No recognition. A foreign country judgment is not conclusive if
> 1. the judgment was rendered under a system which does not provide impartial tribunals or procedures compatible with the requirements of due process of law;
> ...
> (b) Other grounds for non-recognition. A foreign country judgment need not be recognized if:
> ...
> 4. the cause of action on which the judgment is based is repugnant to the public policy of this state;"

Public policy is a very limited defence against the recognition and enforcement of a foreign judgment. It is limited in three respects:

- There must be a *close* connection (*proximité*) to the forum state;
- The *result* of the decision to be recognized has to violate public policy of the forum state;
- This violation must be *manifest* and not acceptable at all.

These requirements do not qualify the foreign state as a state providing no impartial tribunals with procedures lacking due process and a fair trial. These requirements want to eliminate only those few judgments which deviate from normal court decisions and therefore should not be recognized abroad.

10 *McKinney's Consolidated Laws of New York Annotated*, Book 7B, St. Paul/Minn. 1997 and 2011 *Cumulative Pocket Part*, Pocket Part, p. 251.

c. *Public Policy as Safety Valve*

The public policy exception in European Regulations is simply a safety valve which enables the recognizing jurisdiction to eliminate those decisions in which there has been some serious irregularity. Such an exception should not be removed in order to keep the European "area of freedom, security and justice" undisturbed by some unusual and exceptional foreign decisions. Even in daily life nobody would dispense with security devices simply because cases in which safety valves are needed are rare, exceptional or hardly existent. There are security devices everywhere and they should also be present in the field of international civil procedure. As long as judges in all Member States are not reasonably paid and educated, as long as there are no sufficient local remedies against judicial injustice, as long as there are some prejudices that people of Northern and Western Member States are rich and have a lot of money, there should be some sort of barrier against some miscarriages of justice which happen abroad.[11] This exception will still be used only in exceptional cases and is not likely to be treated as a disguised form of review of foreign decisions as to their substance.

IV. SUMMARY

In 2016 the Commission must submit to the European Parliament, the Council and the European Economic and Social Committee a report on the functioning of the Maintenance Regulation. It is strongly recommended that there should be a public policy exception with respect to the recognition and enforcement of all foreign decisions in maintenance obligations.

---

11 As long as we read in serious newspapers and in well-known law review articles that some Member States have problems establishing an independent judiciary which is well paid and immune to corruption and political interference, it is necessary to keep the defense of public policy in order to prevent that the "area of freedom, security and justice" is not turned into an "area of conflict, insecurity and injustice".

THE MANY PERSPECTIVES OF PRIVATE INTERNATIONAL LAW

David P. Stewart
Visiting Professor of Transnational and International Law,
Georgetown University Law Center
Member, Inter-American Juridical Committee
President-Elect, American Branch of the International Law Association
Board of Editors, American Journal of International Law
Executive Council, American Society of International Law
Executive Council, American Bar Association Section of International Law
Formerly, Assistant Legal Adviser, U.S. Department of State

Throughout his extraordinary and distinguished career as an international lawyer, Hans van Loon has focused on the complex relationship between international and domestic law and the vital importance of using that relationship creatively to further the rule of law. Inspired by (and in honor of) his enormous contributions to the development of private international law through his many years of work at the Hague Conference, I offer here some comments on the field to which he has devoted his professional life.

The main point is that the principles, instruments and mechanisms of private international law should not be perceived as relating simply to technical issues arising from the trans-border flow of trade and capital or the disputes which are inevitably generated by that flow. Properly conceived, private international law works more broadly – multi-dimensionally – by contributing to global economic development and by promoting the rule of law. It also has an often-overlooked but increasingly important human dimension, which is vital to advancing the well-being of families and children throughout the world.

CHOICE OF LAW, JURISDICTION AND JUDGMENTS

Regrettably, but all-too-frequently, the term "private international law" is interpreted narrowly. Especially on the American side of the Atlantic Ocean, it is commonly considered a synonym for *conflicts of laws*. In this restrictive conception, it is thought to include those specialized principles and rules of law applied by national courts to determine which of several competing laws applies to disputes involving parties, property or activity in different countries or nationalities, or to transactions crossing national boundaries.

A somewhat broader view, increasingly held by practitioners who have been trained in civil law systems, expands the definition to include the provisions of domestic law governing the *exercise of domestic jurisdiction* over people, property and transactions in trans-border situations, as well as the *enforcement of foreign judgments*. Here, the main questions tend to focus on the permissible scope of a given court's authority to hear disputes involving foreigners and foreign transactions and to recognize and enforce judgments resulting from adjudications in foreign courts.

These three areas (jurisdiction, choice of law, and enforcement of judgments) are important and of course remain at the conceptual heart of most private international law endeavors. In many domestic legal systems, the relevant rules have been codified in discrete private international law statutes. In others, such as the United States, the rules remain decentralized and diffuse. But in either case, private international law is often viewed as relating primarily to the technical legal issues arising in the judicial resolution of transnational disputes about civil and commercial matters.

The current agenda of The Hague Conference illustrates the unquestionable centrality of these issues. One of the more important projects, for example, involves the problems arising from choice of law in international contracts. First taken up in 2006, the project began as a feasibility study by the Permanent Bureau regarding the development of a non-binding instrument concerning choice of law in international business-to-business contracts with a view to promoting party autonomy. This past November, a Special Commission reviewed the draft set of "Principles on Choice of Law in International Commercial Contracts" which had been produced by a Working Group on the topic.[1]

With regard to jurisdiction and judgments, the long history of efforts at the Hague Conference (and elsewhere) to negotiate a multilateral treaty covering both aspects (a so-called "double convention") is well-known and has been told elsewhere.[2] To date, the international community has not been able to reach general agreement about the permissible bases of domestic jurisdiction over civil

[1] Draft Hague Principles as approved by the November 2012 Special Commission Meeting on Choice of Law in International Contracts and Recommendations for the Commentary, available at www.hcch.net/upload/wop/contracts2012principles_e.pdf.

[2] See, e.g., Brand and Herrup, *The 2005 Hague Convention on Choice of Court Agreements: Commentary and Documents* (Cambridge 2008); Louise Ellen Teitz, "The Hague Choice of Court Convention: Validating Party Autonomy and Providing an Alternative to Arbitration," 53 *Am. J. Comp. L.* 543 (2005).

and commercial cases involving foreign parties or transactions or the specific grounds on which foreign judicial judgments will be recognized or enforced in domestic courts.

One of the most significant and encouraging recent developments, however, has been the successful conclusion of the 2005 Hague Convention on Choice of Court Agreements.[3] This treaty provides that States parties must recognize and give effect to "exclusive choice of court agreements" (sometimes called "forum selection clauses"). The Convention sets forth three basic rules to be applied in Contracting States with respect to choice of court agreements falling within its scope: (i) the court chosen by the contracting parties has (and must exercise) jurisdiction to decide a covered dispute, (ii) courts not chosen by the parties do not have jurisdiction and must suspend or dismiss proceedings if brought, and (iii) a judgment from a chosen court rendered in accordance with such an agreement must be recognized and enforced in the courts of other Contracting States. By its terms, the Convention applies only to exclusive choice of court clauses, but States parties have the option of permitting their courts to recognize and enforce judgments of courts of other States party designated in non-exclusive choice of court agreements.

The potential benefits of the Convention for private parties to qualifying transnational contracts are significant. Resting on the principle of party autonomy, it will ensure that the dispute settlement arrangements agreed to by those private contracting parties are honored in the case of domestic court litigation in much the same way as agreements to arbitrate are respected and given effect. Moreover, it will enhance the enforceability of the resulting judgments in the courts of other States parties, helping to redress the "lack of reciprocity" problem which arises when foreign judgments are given more favorable consideration in some national courts than the judgments of those courts receive in foreign courts.

More recently, the broader question of recognizing and enforcing foreign judgments (the "Judgments Project") has again been taken up by The Hague Conference. In 2011, the Member States asked the Permanent Bureau to study the possibility of resuming work on a broader convention (i.e., addressing issues beyond the scope of the 2005 Convention). This past year, the Judgments Project was restored to the active agenda of the Conference.[4] In light of the origins of the Choice of Court Agreements Convention and the slow pace of adherences, one may properly wonder whether this renewed effort has realistic prospects over

[3] For information on the 2005 Hague Convention on Choice of Court Agreements, see www.hcch.net/index_en.php?act=text.display&tid=134.

[4] See the Permanent Bureau's paper entitled "Ongoing Work on International Litigation and Possible Continuation of the Judgments Project," Prel. Rel. Doc. No. 5 (March 2012), available at www.hcch.net/upload/wop/gap12pd05e.pdf.

the short term. But given the importance of the topic, the discussion needs to proceed.

INTERNATIONAL ASSISTANCE AND COOPERATION

A still more inclusive definition of "private international law" (but one still focused on the litigation context) incorporates the increasingly important *procedural mechanisms* for avoiding and overcoming divergent national rules that can impede settlement of disputes in transnational litigation. Here, few would dispute the importance of the contributions made by The Hague Conference through its conventions on service of process, production of evidence, and the simplification of "legalization" requirements.

The 1965 Convention on the Service Abroad of Judicial and Extra-Judicial Documents in Civil and Commercial Matters[5] and the 1970 Hague Convention on the Taking of Evidence Abroad in Civil and Commercial Matters[6] are among the Conference's most widely adopted instruments. As their titles suggest, these treaties are intended to facilitate service of process and evidentiary discovery in foreign countries through agreed mechanisms of "central authorities." Even more widely ratified is the 1961 Hague Convention Abolishing the Requirement of Legalisation for Foreign Public Documents (the "Apostille" Convention), which facilitates the circulation of public documents executed in one State party to the Convention to be accepted and given effect in another State party to the Convention.[7] For parties to transnational litigation, these mechanisms offer important avenues for overcoming obstacles created by differences in national laws and procedures.

Another interesting (but so far unsuccessful) effort important to transnational litigants has centered on the problems which arise in the context of determining the content of foreign law in domestic courts. With increasing frequency, courts and parties alike must struggle to determine foreign law in the absence of any reliable international mechanism or procedure for arriving at an authoritative determination. One notes with interest the set of "Guiding Principles to be

5 The text of the Hague Service Convention, model forms, and additional information can be found at www.hcch.net/index_en.php?act=text.display&tid=44.

6 For information on the Hague Evidence Convention, see http://hcch.e-vision.nl/index_en.php?act=conventions.text&cid=82.

7 For the text of the Apostille Convention, see http://hcch.e-vision.nl/index_en.php?act=conventions.text&cid=41. A Special Commission on the Operation of the Apostille Convention was held in November 2012; see www.hcch.net/index_en.php?act=events.details&year=2012&varevent=288. Information on the innovative and far-reaching electronic apostille ("e-APP") program can be found at www.hcch.net/index_en.php?act=publications.details&pid=4945&dtid=49.

Considered in Developing a Future Instrument" which was developed by an experts group convened by the Permanent Bureau of The Hague Conference in October 2008.[8]

THE ARBITRATION ALTERNATIVE

Remaining within the perspective of dispute settlement in international commercial transactions, many lawyers would include the increasingly important field of international arbitration. Disputes and controversies are inevitable in commercial transactions, and when those transactions cross national borders, parties are unlikely to be comfortable with seeking recourse to the domestic courts of their opponents. International arbitration offers a viable alternative.

Here, the central international structure has been established by the United Nations Commission on International Trade Law (UNCITRAL) and its well-known trio of instruments: the 1958 UN Convention on the Recognition and Enforcement of Foreign Arbitral Awards (the "New York Convention"), the 1976 UNCITRAL Arbitration Rules (designed for ad hoc or non-institutional arbitrations and revised in 2010), and the 1985 UNCITRAL Model Law on International Commercial Arbitration (amended in 2009). These instruments have long served a vital function in promoting arbitration as an effective and reliable dispute settlement mechanism in international trade and commerce.

Taken together, these instruments offer parties to international transactions a viable alternative to domestic litigation for the resolution of disputes arising from their civil and commercial dealings. Given its importance and complexity, international arbitration is today often viewed as discrete field in its own right, but a broad, contemporary conception of private international law would also embrace it.[9]

SUBSTANTIVE ISSUES OF TRADE, COMMERCE AND FINANCE

A dispute-centric conception of private international law is, however, clearly inadequate. In an increasingly inter-connected world, the harmonization and

[8] For a report on this meeting, see www.hcch.net/upload/wop/genaff_pd11b2009e.pdf. See also the Conclusions and Recommendations on Access to Foreign Law in Civil and Commercial Matters of the Joint Meeting of the European Commission and the Hague Conference, held in Brussels in February 2012, available at www.hcch.net/index_en.php?act=events.details&year=2012&varevent=248.

[9] Investor-state arbitration, on the other hand, might not be included because by definition it involves States acting in their own right.

codification functions of private international law assume ever greater practical importance in promoting trade, commerce and economic development. At its core the process of "globalization" results from private activity, not governmental intervention. It is characterized by expanding markets, increasing mobility, quick and reliable financial transactions, and virtually unlimited, instantaneous information exchange through the mass-media and the Internet.

Private international law contributes to these efforts through greater codification and harmonization of the relevant legal norms and principles. The purpose is to provide transacting parties more legal clarity, certainty and predictability in their civil and commercial transactions. By reducing or removing legal obstacles to the flow of international trade, especially those affecting the developing countries, it contributes directly to economic progress and prosperity in developing countries, especially those lacking the legal and transactional infrastructure necessary to participate fully and efficiently in the modern global economy.

Consider, for instance, the following (somewhat arbitrary) list of illustrative examples.

Sale of Goods. For many practitioners (certainly those in the United States), the most familiar instrument for international codification is the 1980 UN Convention on the International Sale of Goods ("CISG"). The treaty governs the formation of contracts of sale of goods as well as the rights and obligations of the buyers and sellers (including their remedies) having their places of business in different countries, provided these countries have adopted the Convention. As a self-executing treaty in the United States, the CISG treaty is binding law with respect to contracts falling within its scope, and it displaces state laws (including those based on the Uniform Commercial Code) to the extent of any inconsistency.

International Contracts. International transactional lawyers are also familiar with UNIDROIT's Principles of International Commercial Contracts, first adopted in 2004 and updated in 2010. While not a binding instrument, the Principles are occasionally described as a "global law of international commercial contracts" and are increasingly used in trans-border commercial dealings and often referred to by tribunals in international commercial arbitration.[10]

Here again, it is important to draw attention to the work of The Hague Conference on the issue of choice of law in international contracts, and to the draft Principles and recommendations which were adopted by the Special Commission in November 2012.

E-Commerce. Today, international commercial transactions are commonly carried out through electronic data interchange and other means of paperless

[10] See www.unidroit.org/english/principles/contracts/main.htm for the text of the Principles (2010).

communication. National legislatures have, on the whole, been slow to adapt domestic law to these technological innovations. Private international law has also made significant contributions in this area. For example, in 1996, UNCITRAL adopted a model law intended to facilitate the use of electronic commerce by States with differing legal, social and economic systems. In 2001, it adopted a second model law, aimed at legitimizing the use of electronic messaging and identification by making "electronic signatures" the functional equivalent of handwritten signatures. In 2005, it adopted the UN Convention on the Use of Electronic Communications in International Contracts, the central premise of which is "functional equivalency" – meaning that information in electronic (data message) form will not be denied legal effect, validity or enforceability solely on the grounds of its electronic nature.

Secured Interests. Access to adequate and affordable credit is unquestionably an essential building block of economic development. In the case of private trade and commercial transactions, that access is frequently a *sine qua non*. Clarifying and standardizing the rules for such transactions is essential to economic development. UNCITRAL's 2001 UN Convention on the Assignment of Receivables in International Trade was among the first international instruments to address these issues. It aimed to provide a comprehensive approach to the rules governing the transfer by agreement of all or part of or an undivided interest in the assignor's contractual right to payment of a monetary sum (the "receivable") from a third person ("the debtor").

In 2007, UNCITRAL prepared a Legislative Guide on Secured Transactions.[11] The Guide is intended to assist States in developing a modern and efficient legal regime for security interests in goods involved in commercial activities, including inventory. By attracting credit from domestic and foreign lenders, such a regime promotes the development and growth of domestic businesses (in particular small and medium-sized enterprises).

Registration of Secured Interests. The Organization of American States has also been active in the field of secured interests. In 2002, it crafted a Model Inter-American Law on Secured Interests, aimed at regulating security interests and securing the performance of any obligations in movable property.[12] States adopting the Model Law undertake to create a "unitary and uniform registration system applicable to all existing movable property security devices in the local legal framework."[13] To supplement the Model Law, a set of Model Registry Regulations was approved in October 2009. These regulations provide solutions

[11] UNCITRAL's Legislative Guide on Secured Interests, together with related information, is available at www.uncitral.org/uncitral/en/uncitral_texts/payments/Guide_securedtrans.html.

[12] The Model Inter-American Law on Secured Transactions is available at www.oas.org/dil/CIDIP-VIRes5-02.htm (providing text of 2002 OAS Model Law).

[13] See Article 1 of the Model Law.

to questions concerning registration and uniformity, and are intended for use in both civil law and common law systems in a cohesive implementation of the Model Law.[14]

Registration is a central feature of the priority structure applicable to security interests in most types of collateral. The primary role of a registry is to provide for public disclosure of security interests. Widely differing approaches in national laws towards security and title reservation rights can drastically inhibit the extension of finance. Standardization promotes competition, provides greater certainty and transparency for transacting parties, reduces transaction costs, and makes credit cheaper – all important elements in the development process.

Mobile Equipment. A key private international law instrument in this area is UNIDROIT's 2001 Convention on International Interests in Mobile Equipment (often referred to as the "Capetown Convention"). Its focus is on secured interests in easily identifiable, high-priced mobile equipment which can readily move across national boundaries. It provides for the creation of a recognized international security interest sufficient to protect the interests of the creditors. Moreover, it establishes the means for the electronic registration of those interests, to provide notice to third parties and enable creditors to preserve their priority against subsequently registered interests, any unregistered interests, and potentially the debtor's insolvency administrator.

Several protocols to the Capetown Convention have been developed. One, adopted at the same time as the Convention itself, addresses the particular issues related to security interests in aircraft equipment. A second, concluded in 2007, covers the financing of railroad rolling stock (such as engines, freight cars, and passenger cars). A third, on "matters specific to space assets," was adopted in March 2012. UNIDROIT expects to turn to a fourth protocol covering mobile agricultural, construction and mining equipment. Clearly, the Capetown system promises to have a positive impact on the prospects for financing many types of commercial dealings.

Carriage of Goods By Sea. It has long been recognized that the international legal framework governing the international carriage of goods by sea, which extends back over 80 years, had become inadequate for modern transport practices such as containerization, door-to-door transport contracts and the use of electronic transport documents.

In 2008 UNCITRAL adopted a new treaty to replace the antiquated rules contained in such earlier agreements as the Hague, Hague-Visby, and Hamburg Rules. The U.N. Convention on Contracts for the International Carriage of Goods Wholly or Partly by Sea (denominated the "Rotterdam Rules")[15] is intended to

---

14 For the model registry regulations, see www.oas.org/DIL/CIDIP-VII_doc_3-09_rev3_model_regulations.pdf.

15 Generally, see www.rotterdamrules2009.com/cms/index.php.

provide both shippers and carriers with a modern and balanced regime covering maritime contracts of carriage (including those involving other modes of transport such as road or rail). It covers the entire contract of carriage, including liability and obligations of the carrier, obligations of the shipper to the carrier, transport documents and electronic transport records, delivery of the goods, rights of the controlling party and transfer of rights, limits of liability, and dispute settlement.

Intermediated Securities. Promoting capital formation and enhancing the stability of financial markets unquestionably contributes to trade and investment in developing countries. Here again, private international efforts seek to clarify and modernize the relevant law.

In modern securities markets, the traditional concept of custody or deposit of physical certificates evidencing the holder's interests is obsolete. Today's investor rarely has custody of a physical certificate, but instead "holds" securities through a chain of intermediaries that are ultimately connected to a central securities depository. Transactions in these securities typically occur with great rapidity across national boundaries. In many countries, however, domestic law has lagged behind these developments, creating uncertainty and unnecessary risk with respect to trans-border transactions.

In 2006, the Hague Conference adopted a Convention on the Law Applicable to Certain Rights in respect of Securities Held with an Intermediary.[16] This instrument harmonizes the choice of law rules regarding securities held by an intermediary within the territories of States Parties. In 2009, UNIDROIT adopted a Convention on Substantive Rules for Intermediated Securities that, in distinction, aims to harmonize the substantive rules governing the holding, transfer and collateralization of securities.[17] In differing ways, these two treaties are intended to establish internationally agreed regimes that reflect the contemporary realities of the securities markets.

Public Procurement. In most states, government procurement constitutes a large portion of public expenditure. Fair, objective and efficient procurement rules and procedures promote economy, efficiency and competition and thus lead to increased economic development. The lack of such rules and procedures invites fraud, waste and corruption.

In 1994 UNCITRAL adopted a Model Law on Procurement of Goods, Construction and Services,[18] setting out "state of the art" legislative provisions to assist governments in revising their existing procurement laws or adopting

---

16 The 2002 Hague Securities Convention is available at http://hcch.e-vision.nl/index_en.php?act=conventions.text&cid=72.

17 For information on the UNIDROIT securities convention, including text, status and background, see www.unidroit.org/english/conventions/2009intermediatedsecurities/main.htm.

18 Regarding a description of UNCITRAL's work on procurement of goods and services, see www.uncitral.org/uncitral/en/uncitral_texts/procurement_infrastructure.html.

such laws where none currently exist. In 2002 it adopted a Legislative Guide on Privately Financed Infrastructure Projects.[19] The Guide was supplemented in 2003 by Model Legislative Provisions drafted to assist domestic legislative bodies in the establishment of the necessary legal framework.[20]

Cross-border Business Insolvency. Economic growth is also inhibited by the lack of effective mechanisms for cross-border cooperation in insolvency proceedings where debtors have assets, subsidiaries or inter-linked corporate entities in more than one state. UNCITRAL has been active in promoting the legal concepts necessary for reorganization and refinance to be available as a means to retain operation of failed businesses, for example through its 1997 Model Law on Cross-Border Insolvency and by its 2004 Legislative Guide on Insolvency Law.[21]

More recently, in 2009, the Commission adopted a Practice Guide on Cross-Border Insolvency Cooperation. Based upon collected experience and practice, this Guide illustrates how to facilitate the resolution of issues and conflicts arising in cross-border insolvency cases through cross-border cooperation, in particular the use of various international agreements.

Properly considered in their larger context, all of these efforts contribute in vital and substantive ways to economic development on a global scale.

THE RULE OF LAW

Beyond dispute settlement and economic development, the institutions in which private international law is developed work actively to promote the rule of law around the world.

Societies that are genuinely based on the rule of law provide their members with fair and reliable norms by which they can organize their affairs, conduct their business, and resolve their disputes fairly, effectively and efficiently. Clearly, the rule of law consists in more than rules and laws. Promoting the rule of law means more than simply establishing functional institutions to administer those rules and laws. The rule of law rests fundamentally on attitudes and expectations, on a sense of confidence and commitment on the part of the individuals concerned, on broad acceptance and participation, and on a belief that reciprocal behavior will lead to orderly and equitable outcomes. These characteristics must be manifested

[19] For the 2000 Legislative Guide, see www.uncitral.org/uncitral/en/uncitral_texts/procurement_infrastructure/2001Guide_PFIP.html.

[20] The Model Legislative Provisions can be retrieved at www.uncitral.org/uncitral/en/uncitral_texts/procurement_infrastructure/2003Model_PFIP.html.

[21] For the 1997 Model Law on Cross-Border Insolvency, as well as UNCITRAL's 2004 Legislative Guide and its 2009 Practice Guide on Cross-Border Insolvency Cooperation, see www.uncitral.org/uncitral/en/uncitral_texts/insolvency.html.

in dealings between private parties as much as in their interaction with the courts, the criminal justice system, and other institutions of the state.

Private international law makes its most significant contribution to the rule of law at this other level, in the context of interactions between private members of the community with each other. The examples given in the preceding discussion above illustrate some of the many ways in which private international law contributes in this way – facilitating settlement of disputes, establishing accepted norms and principles for cross-border commercial transactions, strengthening investor confidence, etc. Two additional examples can also be mentioned, both drawn from recent OAS efforts.

Consumer Protection. For several years, negotiations have been occurring within the specialized private international law conferences of the OAS known as "CIDIP" on how to improve consumer protection within the hemisphere – specifically, through the rapid and efficient resolution of consumer disputes. In 2003, when CIDIP-VII was convened, member states agreed to focus *inter alia* on means of facilitating the effective resolution of disputes in cross-border consumer transactions. The goal was to find a way to provide consumers with effective, expeditious and economical alternatives to lengthy, costly domestic litigation.

Initially, a Working Group considered approaches from a classic private international law perspective. One possibility put forward by Brazil, Argentina and Paraguay contemplated a new multilateral Convention on Consumer Protection and Choice of Law. Alternatively, Canada offered a draft Model Law on Jurisdiction and Choice of Law for consumer contracts. For its part, the United States promoted a Model Law on Consumer Dispute Settlement and Redress establishing a low-cost and "user friendly" procedure for resolving "small claims" in cross-border consumer contracts.

These divergent proposals represented different approaches to solving the problems faced by individual consumers who purchase goods or services transnationally. To date, no consensus has been reached, and the locus of this effort has since shifted to UNCITRAL's Working Group on online dispute resolution.[22]

Access to Information. A key component in any system characterized by the rule of law is guaranteeing citizens access to government information. In a democracy, such access is considered an indispensable political right, allowing the electorate to make informed decisions and to help ensure government accountability and responsiveness to public needs. It also serves to protect individual rights. Lack of access undermines trust, fosters inefficiency and invites corruption.

22 See Secretariat Note, "Online dispute resolution for cross-border electronic commerce transactions: draft procedural rules," A/CN.9/WG.III/WP.117 and Add. 1 (Aug. 31, 2012), available at www.uncitral.org/pdf/english/workinggroups/wg_3/26th_WG_III/wp_117_e.pdf.

The Inter-American Democratic Charter recognizes that transparency in government activities, responsible public administration, respect for social rights, and freedom of expression and of the press are essential components of the exercise of democracy.[23] In 2009, the OAS General Assembly directed the preparation of a draft Model Law on Access to Information, together with an implementation guide, for the consideration of member states. The final versions of both documents were completed in the spring of 2010 and approved by the OAS's Committee on Juridical and Political Affairs.[24]

THE HUMAN FACE

Private international law goes even further. Arguably, the rule of law is most important at those specific junctures where the interests and activities of the state intersect with the most basic needs and interests of the individual. Few such intersections are more sensitive than those involving families. In a world characterized by rapidly increasing transnational contacts and cross-border mobility, international family law has clearly emerged as an area of specialization in its own right – and, at the same time, is properly considered an integral part of the field of private international law broadly construed.

In this area, The Hague Conference has been working actively for many years to bridge gaps, reduce conflicts and provide orderly and efficient mechanisms of dispute resolution. Several multilateral treaties adopted by The Hague Conference constitute the cornerstones of the still emerging international regime of child and family protection.

Abduction. The 1980 Hague Convention on the Civil Aspects of International Child Abduction[25] aims at the protection of children from the harmful effects of parental abduction and retention in violation of the other parent's custodial rights by providing a procedure for their prompt return to the country of its habitual residence.

Adoption. The 1993 Hague Convention on Protection of Children and Co-operation in Respect of Intercountry Adoption[26] is intended to regularize the process of transnational adoptions and to protect children and their families

23 The text of the Inter-American Democratic Charter is available at www.oas.org/charter/docs/resolution1_en_p4.htm.

24 For information on the Model Law on Access to Information and accompanying legislative guide, see www.oas.org/dil/access_to_information_model_law_final.htm.

25 For the text of the 1980 Abduction Convention and related information, including the Guide to Good Practice, see http://hcch.e-vision.nl/index_en.php?act=conventions.text&cid=24.

26 The Convention on the Protection of Children and Co-operation in Respect of Intercountry Adoption, along with the 2008 Guide to Good Practice (Implementation and Operation), can be found at http://hcch.e-vision.nl/index_en.php?act=conventions.text&cid=69.

against the risks of illegal, irregular, premature or ill-prepared adoptions abroad. It seeks to ensure that intercountry adoptions are made in the best interests of the child and with respect for his or her fundamental rights.

Protection of Children. The 1996 Convention on Jurisdiction, Applicable Law, Recognition, Enforcement and Co-operation in Respect of Parental Responsibility and Measures for the Protection of Children[27] provides for civil measures of protection concerning children, such as orders concerning parental responsibility and public measures of protection or care. It specifies uniform rules determining which country's authorities are competent to take the necessary measures of protection, which country's laws are to be applied, and the recognition and enforcement of measures taken in one Contracting State in all other Contracting States.

Child Support and Family Maintenance. In an increasingly globalized world, families frequently span continents; so do family disputes and dissolutions. Some countries address this issue primarily through bilateral and/or regional agreements providing for reciprocal recognition and enforcement of support orders in defined circumstances. Within the OAS, the 1989 Inter-American Convention on Support Obligations has twelve States parties.

In 2007, the Hague Conference adopted the Convention on the International Recovery of Child Support and Other Forms of Family Maintenance.[28] The basic rule is reciprocity: a decision on child maintenance and support made in one Contracting State must be recognized and enforced in other Contracting States if the first state's jurisdiction was based on one of the accepted grounds enumerated in the Convention. The treaty also provides for effective access to cross-border maintenance procedures.

Migration. Also on the agenda of The Hague Conference for the past few years has been consideration of problems related to temporary or circular migration. The notion has been to consider a co-operative mechanism addressing practical problems arising in the areas of social security, mutual recognition of competencies, remittances, licensing and the monitoring of intermediaries involved in facilitating economic (especially labor)migration.

While far from a complete description of the growing list of international family law agreements and projects (others include protection of the elderly and

27 For the text of the 1996 Convention, see www.hcch.net/index_en.php?act=conventions.text&cid=70. The operation of the 1980 and 1996 Hague Conventions was last considered at a Special Commission held in two parts (in June 2011 and January 2012), see www.hcch.net/upload/wop/concl28-34sc6_en.pdf.

28 The text of the Hague Convention on the International Recovery of Child Support and Other Forms of Family Maintenance (November 23, 2007) and related documents can be retrieved at www.hcch.net/index_en.php?act=conventions.text&cid=131. For the Protocol on the Law Applicable to Maintenance Obligations, see www.hcch.net/index_en.php?act=conventions.text&cid=133.

recognition of unmarried couples), this short list illustrates the many ways in which private international works to promote personal (or human) values in the international arena.

CONCLUSION

The aim of this short essay has been to demonstrate that the principles, instruments and mechanisms of private international law, as reflected in its disparate endeavors, contribute directly to (i) the trans-border flow of trade, capital, people and ideas, (ii) the effective settlement of disputes, (iii) the well-being of families and children, and therefore (iv) global economic development and the rule of law. By focusing primarily on the relationship between international and domestic law, private international law adds an essential element to efforts to promote economic progress and the legitimacy of the law internationally as well as domestically.

For these reasons, private international law is a central, indeed critical field for any international law practitioner, and one of growing functional importance. Private international law, the rule of law, and economic development are not three separate endeavors, only tangentially related. To the contrary, each directly supports the other.

Hans van Loon has always looked beyond the current agenda, seeing the larger landscape and envisioning where those of us who are committed to private international law might best invest our efforts. In particular he has had his eye clearly on the human dimension. It is therefore fitting to close by recalling his words on the occasion of the deposit of the United States' instrument of ratification of 1993 Intercountry Adoption Convention:

> What connects and inspires all these Hague instruments is the awareness that cross-border activity and cross-border relationships need the guidance and protection of the law, not just in the abstract but through effective cooperative legal machinery: to serve the real interests of people, families, and children in the face of the legal complexity that arises when multiple countries and legal systems are involved.[29]

[29] See Statement by Hans van Loon, Secretary General, on December 2, 2007, available at http://amsterdam.usconsulate.gov/uploads/images/t97WDxspD0ABXW0Ajhy5IA/The_Hague_Convention_Secretary_General_Van_Loon_Remarks.pdf.

BECAUSE IT TAKES TWO TO TANGO

Frederike E.M. STIKKELBROECK[1]
Advocaat, admitted to the Amsterdam Bar

"The future belongs to those who believe in the beauty of their dreams."[2]

Eleanor Roosevelt

"I believe in an organization which is not afraid to make clear and precise choices, learning from the past without taking the past as a recipe for the future."[3]

Louise E. Fresco

REFLECTIONS ON REFORM – ABOUT LEADING TOWARDS A SUSTAINABLE FUTURE FOR THE HAGUE CONFERENCE & FOLLOWING A DREAM

Many generations have kept the dream of Professor T.M.C. Asser alive for almost 120 years.[4] They contributed brick by brick to the edifice that is the Hague Conference,[5] embodying Asser's enlightening ideas on cross-border co-operation in civil and commercial matters for greater legal security. The Conference became a world organisation that through its 45 multilateral treaties on private

1 Ms Stikkelbroeck was the first Director of the International Centre for Judicial Studies and Technical Assistance (2009–2011) and Attaché to the Secretary General of the Hague Conference (2006–2011).

2 *It seems to me: selected letters of Eleanor Roosevelt*, edited by Leonard C. Schlup and Donald W. Whisenhunt, The University Press of Kentucky, 2001, p. 2.

3 Open resignation letter addressed to the Director General of the Food and Agricultural Organisation, 14 May 2006, *The Guardian*, <www.guardian.co.uk/world/2006/may/14/foodanddrink>.

4 The First Hague Conference (12–25 September 1893).

5 Hague Conference on Private International Law, referred to as Hague Conference or Organisation.

international law[6] built a strong reputation for excellence. To date, more than 140 States[7] have participated in the successes of the Conference and witnessed manifold legal innovations[8] bridging legal and cultural diversity.

The Permanent Bureau[9] is the intellectual driving force behind the high-end treaty development. However, it has also adopted over the last years – in spite of itself – the role of *primus inter pares* with respect to implementation assistance and education on the Hague Conventions for a great number of the 140 plus States.[10] This has become a vital yet inordinate supplementary task for the petite staff that according to the Statute is composed of a Secretary General and (officially) four Secretaries[11] and runs a budget that is less than a few million euro.

With the considerable rise in the number of active States joining the Conference's multilateral instruments, there is a simultaneously growing need for implementation assistance and education of those who will apply these Conventions in practice, particularly in emerging States. For a number of years the Permanent Bureau has continually been flooded with official government requests for assistance. This leads – as service oriented as its dedicated staff is – to an almost natural shift in practical focus and performance. Inevitably, it also further augments budget and human resources constraints.[12] This is particularly true, given that often elaborate requests emanate predominantly from States that do not (yet) contribute mandatorily to the annual working capital necessary to ensure the continued operations of the Permanent Bureau.[13]

This fascinating yet inconvenient truth undeniably prevents the Permanent Bureau from dedicating sufficient time and intellectual resources to its core work. I believe this irreversible evolution should be the impetus for organisational reform. There should be serious consideration given to the aim and objectives,

---

6 The so-called Hague Conventions. A list of these instruments is available on the website of the Organisation <www.hcch.net> under "Conventions".

7 Member States of the Hague Conference, one Regional Economic Integration Organisation (the European Union), and additional States Parties to one or more Hague Conventions.

8 See Hans van Loon, "The Hague Conference on Private International Law: Asser's Vision and an Evolving Mission", in *Hague Yearbook of International Law 2011*, Koninklijke Brill N.V., 2012, pp. 6–7.

9 The Secretariat of the Hague Conference.

10 Not to mention the States that have not yet established an official working relationship with the Conference but expressed an interest in joining one or more Hague Conventions and/or in becoming a Member.

11 Article 5(1) of the *Statute of the Hague Conference on Private International Law*, see <www.hcch.net> under "Conventions".

12 See also PriceWaterhouseCoopers, "The Hague Conference on Private International Law: Resources Deficiencies and Strategic Positioning – An Independent Analysis and Report, with Recommendations for the Future Development of the Organisation and its Secretariat", May 2001, available on the website of the Organisation <www.hcch.net>.

13 Approximately only 50 percent of the 140 plus States are Member States and contribute to the Organisation's regular operating budget.

followed by the identification of (short- and long-term) strategic goals and priorities of both the Organisation as a whole and the Permanent Bureau in particular. The time has come to properly manage the new reality, enhance credibility and transparency, and introduce accountability and controls to respect and engage the numerous direct[14] and indirect[15] stakeholders. In my view, the Hague Conference, like any other multinational organisation, has a (social) responsibility towards its stakeholders for good governance as well as to have the courage to innovate (not only regarding its activities but also its methods). It should attract and keep talent, foster growth opportunities, and be sustainable.

To guarantee its sustainable future, the Hague Conference should be complemented by another entity. This entity optimises the competitive advantages of the Organisation and empowers its unique global role to further the progressive unification of the rules of private international law. The Hague Conference therefore decided to enter a new era by establishing the Centre.[16] The then Secretary General of the Ministry of Foreign Affairs of the Kingdom of the Netherlands (2008–2012) was among the first to believe in the huge potential of the Centre even though the form and governance had not yet entirely crystallised at that time. The Permanent Bureau received a development aid start-up fund for the purpose of developing the Centre within four years into a (financially) self-supporting entity. Its solid work programme should initially focus only on those States listed by the OECD as Official Development Aid recipients (or ODA States), which represent approximately 64 per cent of the total number of 140 plus States[17] in the ambit of the Hague Conference.

The Hague Conference has proven its visionary leadership with the establishment of the Centre. Where the Permanent Bureau would remain specifically mandated under the Statute to carry out upstream (normative) or core work through developing and monitoring new multilateral treaties, the Centre would simply assume responsibility for the downstream work that – as evidenced

[14] Direct stakeholders in continual contact with the Organisation are the Member States, their National Organs and Embassies, the Depositary of the Hague Conventions and the overseas regional offices of the Conference in Argentina and Hong Kong.

[15] To name a few: non-Member States Party to one or more Conventions, Central and competent authorities (over 3000), networks of liaison judges, sister organisations such as UNIDROIT and UNCITRAL and other United Nations entities, non-governmental organisations, municipality of the host city, field experts on the Hague Conventions, scholars, legal practitioners, universities and citizens etc.

[16] International Centre for Judicial Studies and Technical Assistance. See also the *Annual Report of the Hague Conference* (2008, pp. 85–95; 2009, pp. 57–73; 2010, pp. 53–73; 2011, pp. 58–81) on the Organisation's website.

[17] See Annex 1 of the DAC List of ODA Recipients, which shows all countries and territories eligible to receive official development assistance (ODA) under the Statistical Reporting Directives DCD-DAC of the Development Co-operation Directorate of the Organisation for Economic Co-operation and Development. The Annex is available at <www.oecd.org/dac/aidstatistics/48858205.pdf>.

in practice – inevitably comes with it, *i.e.* fostering consistent implementation and application of the Hague Conventions. Having two complementary entities – intertwined but with distinct roles – would resolve resource deficiencies as well as improve the Organisation's strategic positioning and operation.

With respect to financial and human resources, the Centre would through its own business model *inter alia* indirectly improve the working capital of the Organisation.[18] The Centre would assume the necessary fundraising activity with the aim of establishing its own transparent working capital that would be held and managed separately from the Organisation's regular budget.[19] The Centre would have its own independent budget and be primarily focused on assisting emerging States, which would therefore make it an attractive partner for private and government donors, institutional grant programmes,[20] charitable foundations, and human rights and development aid organisations. Several current and potential donating entities or programmes have indicated that if the Centre were to have an independent legal personality (*e.g.* a foundation under Dutch civil law) with good governance, a transparent decision-making structure,[21] accountability and standardised controls, it would be more attractive to donors.[22] Importantly, an independent and transparent governance structure would not preclude the Centre from being an integral part of the Hague Conference.

In the event that staff members of the Permanent Bureau were called upon to serve as experts in the work programme of the Centre, the Permanent Bureau would receive appropriate compensation for the actual time and costs (such as travel) devoted to the programme, or for replacing those staff members for their usual tasks.[23] This approach would foster in various ways[24] the global

18 Currently approximately 70–80 percent of allocated time and travel is spent by the Permanent Bureau on downstream work, *i.e.* implementation and application assistance and education.

19 The annual regular budget consists of mandatory annual contibutions from Member States of the Hague Conference. The Organisation had 71 Member States at the start of 2013.

20 For example, the Centre was successful in obtaining a considerable action grant for an education project, from the Civil Justice Program of the European Commission, Directorate-General Justice. The Ministry of Economic Affairs of the Kingdom of the Netherlands together with the municipality of The Hague and the Centre invested a lot of time and effort in trying to establishing a grant for innovation.

21 Decision making power should preferably reside with the Centre by its having its own budget and reporting responsibilities to its stakeholders and donors.

22 Other factors that would make the Centre a more attactive recipient of donor funds include being designated as a non-profit, tax-exempt organisation (such as a 501(c)(3) organisation according to the United States' Internal Revenue Code); and/or an entity which provides Official Development Assistance (see *infra* note 17). Annex 2 of the Statistical Reporting Directives of the OECD lists the international agency contributions which are reportable as ODA; relevant organisations can apply to be on the list and therefore become eligible for a greater amount of government funds earmarked for that purpose.

23 The Centre introduced time recording through a time registration system.

24 For example, programmes could be developed where by Permanent Bureau staff members or external experts are asked to train trainers, e.g. regional or local expert fieldworkers of

ramifications of expertise on the existing Conventions and expand indirectly the Organisation's workforce by engaging external experts by the Centre on a consultancy basis. The Centre could draw from a roster of experts from a range of backgrounds including private, government and academic sectors experienced in private international law and the Hague Conventions. Over the years, the Permanent Bureau has developed a global network of people skilled in these areas. This would allow the Centre to respond in a structured and diligent way to the many outstanding requests for assistance by governments.

The Hague Conference would, as a consequence, have greater efficiency, diversity and inclusion with respect to its total workforce – and less travel costs – as preferably the experts would be engaged in the region, or even better, locally. The Organisation would no longer need additional permanent staff members for carrying out downstream work that would now be taken over by the Centre. The Centre, in turn, would only need a few efficient permanent staff members to develop the work programme and training modules, coordinate the range of specialised assistance and education, and to manage and report on the budget. It would increase the number of partnerships in the field with other governmental, non-governmental and private sector organisations.

With reference to strategic positioning, the Centre would optimise the competitive advantages of the Organisation (the dynamics between upstream and downstream work), results and performance,[25] as well as its visibility. Ultimately, this would reinforce its credibility, as well as engagement and support from the Member States regarding the (process to establish) Hague Conventions and presumably increase attractiveness of Membership of the Organisation for many more States. Obviously, it is of great importance that the Hague Conventions operate properly to maximise the benefits which they afford for all parties involved. It is a commonly shared belief that the success and effectiveness of the Hague Conventions lie in their value to the communities they seek to address, leading to greater legal security. The importance of legal security can not be overestimated, particularly as the lives of more and more individuals take on some kind of international dimension; not in the least through their enhanced personal and digital mobility. Finally, Asser was right in believing that legal security also encourages economic development, fosters stability and contributes at length to freedom, peace and justice for all citizens of the world.

Leadership, motivation, dedication and a common commitment from Member States as well as the Permanent Bureau, to believe in and contribute to

organisations such as UNICEF. Those who receive training can go out and train others in the field.

[25] For the avoidance of doubt, referring to developing new multilateral instruments (upstream) by the Organisation, as well as fostering consistent implementation and application by giving technical assistance and education (downstream) by the Centre.

the Centre's objectives are crucial factors for its existence and growth. It should be visible in order to attract the funds necessary to respond to requests of those in need, and also to establish indispensable solid coalitions. In those days, a few years ago, the Centre was deliberately announced without much fanfare. The Permanent Bureau preferred to keep the Centre's profile rather low-key at a time when several Member States were confronted with the first signs of changing economic circumstances that would soon after culminate in a world economic crisis. However, the Centre has yet to get a fair chance at completely crystallising its independent governance and form, and at developing as a self-supporting entity and an integral companion to the Permanent Bureau. That is why, unfortunately, its multi annual work programme and fundraising activities have not yet come to full fruition for the benefit of emerging States and others who are in need of assistance to ensure legal security – a human right – for its citizens. Sadly, the Permanent Bureau seemed all these years to have cautiously veiled its potential from Member States and other parties concerned, as Cinderella's stepmother was reluctant in advocating for her undoubtedly sparkling future.

To conclude, I believe the Centre to be the *conditio sine qua non* for the healthy organic growth of its *alma mater*, the Hague Conference. This Organisation and the Centre, with such a large positive impact on society, have an important mission to continue building together on Asser's legacy which has proven to be more pertinent than ever for all States and their citizens.

Your Excellency, *Cher Hans*, I admire your idealism for greater legal security as a human right for all people. As spiritual father of the Centre, and after years of diligence, you continue to believe in its *raison d'être*.[26] I have great respect for your tenacity. It has been an immense honour that you permitted me to contribute a small brick to the Hague Conference and the Centre, and to dream of their future. I am convinced that the Centre will grow strong when the Organisation firmly embraces it as a companion. I will forever gratefully remember the inspiring discussions we had – and surely will continue to have – with the same energy and fidelity, on the promotion of private international law.

---

[26] *Annual Report 2011* (published in 2012), p. 81.

RECONNAISSANCE ET HOMMAGE

A. (Teun) V.M. Struycken
Ancien président de la Commission d'État néerlandaise de droit international privé

Au moment du départ de M. Hans van Loon, Secrétaire général de la Conférence de La Haye de droit international privé, le mot reconnaissance s'impose. Dans cette brève contribution aux Mélanges, c'est l'œuvre de Hans van Loon (ci-après HvL) au sein de la Conférence que j'ai en vue de célébrer.

Mes premiers souvenirs remontent au printemps 1978. J'avais pour mission de mettre au point un rapport pour l'assemblée de l'Association néerlandaise de droit international, devant porter notamment sur la Convention CE de Bruxelles, 1968. À l'époque, HvL, avocat à La Haye depuis 1974, était membre-secrétaire du bureau de cette association. Nos échanges étaient brefs mais efficaces, et marqués par une grande courtoisie de sa part.

Sa carrière internationale a commencé à peu près en même temps. Par décret royal du 26 avril 1978, n° 77, HvL a été nommé secrétaire de la Commission d'État de droit international privé, en remplacement de M. H. van Hoogstraten, et ce à partir du 15 septembre 1978, date du départ de ce dernier en tant que secrétaire général de la Conférence. Il avait rempli jusqu'à cette date une double fonction. Par lettre du 18 septembre 1978, le nouveau secrétaire général, Georges A.L. Droz, a informé les organes nationaux de plusieurs nominations intervenues au sein du Bureau Permanent de la Conférence, dont celle de HvL, nommé « secrétaire du Bureau » à partir du premier octobre 1978.

HvL a mis tous ses talents et toute son énergie au service de ses nouvelles tâches, sept jours sur sept, 24 heures sur 24. J'en ai été témoin d'assez près.

Début 1988, il a été promu premier secrétaire. Plus tard, en 1995, les vétérans du Bureau Permanent prenant leur retraite après de longues années de service – MM. Georges Droz, Michel Pelichet et Adair Dyer –, la question de la succession de Droz au poste de secrétaire général s'est posée. En fait, pas vraiment. Georges Droz et la Commission d'État se sont mis d'accord sans difficulté le 17 juin 1995 sur la proposition à faire au Gouvernement des Pays-Bas.

Le fondement juridique d'un tel décret du gouvernement émanait de l'article 4 de l'ancien Statut de la Conférence, entré en vigueur le 15 juillet 1955 et disposant que : « [les membres du Bureau Permanent] sont nommés par le Gouvernement des Pays-Bas, sur présentation de la Commission d'État » (texte maintenu lors de l'amendement du Statut à partir du premier janvier 2007, article 5 (1)).

Une Commission spéciale sur les affaires générales et la politique de la Conférence s'est réunie du 20 au 23 juin 1995. À l'époque président de la Commission d'État, j'ai profité de cette occasion pour convoquer la réunion à huis clos des dirigeants des délégations pour discuter de la proposition que la Commission d'État pensait devoir soumettre au Gouvernement. Cette réunion avait été annoncée par une lettre du Bureau Permanent du 15 mai 1995. Une dizaine de dirigeants ont souhaité prendre la parole, tous ne tarissant pas d'éloges sur HvL et soutenant sa candidature. Aussi la conclusion de ces vingt-neuf dirigeants de délégation a-t-elle été unanime en sa faveur. (Plusieurs d'entre eux ont même indiqué après la réunion combien ils appréciaient d'avoir été consultés ! Tempora mutantur.)

HvL a été nommé à partir de fin juin 1996, par un décret du ministre des Affaires étrangères, M. Hans van Mierlo, datant du 12 septembre 1995 (pour des motifs peu clairs, on avait renoncé à la forme solennelle, et plus adéquate, du décret royal pour de telles nominations).

Dans la période qui précède cette nomination, HvL s'est distingué à plusieurs égards. Pour ne citer que quelques exemples, on rappellera un projet qui lui a été confié et qu'il a très adroitement mené, en réalisant des études approfondies, en établissant des contacts utiles un peu partout dans le monde, à l'origine d'un réseau de coopération très efficace, et en faisant montre de qualités diplomatiques extraordinaires. Il s'agit du projet autour de l'adoption internationale, qui a abouti à l'élaboration de la « Convention du 29 mai 1993 sur la protection des enfants et la coopération en matière d'adoption internationale ».

L'étude qui l'a inspiré est « le Rapport Van Loon » d'avril 1990[1], une étude très fouillée et convaincante. L'Acte Final de la Seizième Session (20 octobre 1988) l'autorisait implicitement. Selon la partie B de cet Acte, la Session décide d'inscrire à l'ordre du jour des travaux de la prochaine Session l'élaboration d'une convention sur l'adoption d'enfants en provenance de l'étranger et charge le secrétaire général d'entreprendre les travaux préliminaires et de convoquer une commission spéciale. On peut s'imaginer que cette décision est la suite d'une préparation méticuleuse et de sondages multiples. Sans aucun doute, HvL a eu l'inspiration et la ténacité indispensables à la réussite du projet.

[1] Actes et Documents de la Dix-Septième Session, Tome II Adoption – Coopération, Document préliminaire 1, p. 10-119.

En fait, à l'époque, le droit international privé se trouvait dans une impasse en matière d'adoption d'enfants. La Convention de la Haye du 15 novembre 1965 n'avait aucunement connu le succès escompté. L'une des causes était certainement que la grande majorité des enfants adoptables se trouvaient dans des États non membres de la Conférence et que ces pays n'avaient pas pu participer aux négociations, ce qui explique pourquoi la Seizième Session a précisé, en marge de la décision citée, qu'elle estimait que la présence au sein de cette Commission spéciale des États non membres d'où proviennent beaucoup d'enfants était indispensable.

La machine s'est mise en marche. La Commission spéciale s'est réunie, sous la présidence de T.B. (Brad) Smith QC, délégué du Canada. G.(Gonzalo) Parra Arranguren, du Vénézuela, a été désigné rapporteur, K.J.(Jörg) Pirrung a bien voulu s'acquitter de la présidence du comité de rédaction dont la mission était d'autant plus délicate que le nombre de délégués – beaucoup n'étant pas juristes de profession – et de documents de travail était important. Fait impressionnant, un grand nombre de délégués originaires de pays non membres a participé de manière intensive aux travaux, de même que des représentants d'organisations spécialisées dans la matière. HvL n'a cessé, de manière discrète, de les motiver et encourager, d'entendre leurs souhaits et leurs inquiétudes et d'y apporter une réponse.

Enfin est arrivé le jour de l'ouverture de la Dix-Septième Session. Comme d'habitude à la Conférence, on a rediscuté jusqu'au dernier jour prévu à l'ordre du jour, du 3 octobre au 20 octobre inclus, tout ce qui semblait déjà acquis.

L'Acte Final de la Dix-Septième Session de la Conférence a été signé pendant la séance de clôture du 29 mai 1993 qui, avec la permission gracieuse de la Cour Internationale de Justice, s'est déroulée dans la Grande Salle d'audience du Palais de la Paix. M. Jan C. Schultsz, président de la Session, a prononcé un discours. D'ordinaire assez avare d'éloges, il n'a pu s'empêcher de dire : « In particular Mr Hans van Loon, who was the driving and inspiring power behind our Convention, should be congratulated with the success of all his efforts. This day really is a personal triumph for him. Thank you. »[2]. Des propos remarquables, mais ce que ne dit pas le procès-verbal, c'est que ces paroles ont été suivies d'applaudissements retentissants et longuement prolongés de la part de la foule qui a assisté la signature. Il s'agissait non seulement des délégués des États membres mais aussi de ceux, en grand nombre, des États non membres de la Conférence ainsi que des représentants d'organisations intergouvernementales et d'organismes non gouvernementaux. Un souvenir inoubliable pour tous ceux qui étaient présents !

---

[2] Actes et Documents de la Dix-Septième Session, Tome I Matières diverses, p.25.

Ce succès s'est traduit depuis par un nombre très impressionnant de signatures et de ratifications, au total plus de quatre-vingt-dix ! On comprendra que, peu de temps après, la nomination de HvL comme secrétaire général s'est déroulée sans aucun problème.

À l'Académie de droit international de La Haye, l'événement n'était pas passé inaperçu. Dès l'été 1993, HvL a pu dispenser, au Palais de la Paix, un cours intitulé « International Co-operation and Protection of Children with Regard to Intercountry Adoption ». Il a réussi à faire publier ce cours dans les meilleurs délais[3].

Signer et ratifier une convention est une chose, la mettre en œuvre en est une autre. Pour assurer le succès de la convention sur l'adoption internationale, il s'est révélé indispensable de porter assistance aux agences gouvernementales ayant pour mission de faire fonctionner la convention, surtout celles des pays d'origine des enfants adoptables, en majorité des pays du Tiers Monde. Ces agences devraient, d'une part, opérer en conformité avec la Convention et, d'autre part, mettre au point une structure adéquate. Le Bureau Permanent s'est trouvé confronté à une tâche nouvelle, une tâche qui désormais absorbe beaucoup d'énergie et de temps et implique des dépenses supplémentaires ainsi que des subtilités diplomatiques.

Cette extension du mandat du BP ne se limite pas à la convention sur l'adoption internationale. Il faut noter que certains États membres trouvent difficile de l'accepter comme une conséquence inévitable de la mondialisation de la Conférence.

Cela montre que l'ère du nouveau secrétaire général pourrait être substantiellement différente de celle de son prédécesseur. Cette ère de HvL pourrait faire l'objet d'une étude fouillée et dépassant largement cette modeste contribution (l'histoire de la Conférence, tant l'époque de T.M.C. Asser que celle de la refondation après la deuxième guerre mondiale, initiée par M. H. van Hoogstraten, premier secrétaire général de cette période, aussi bien que l'époque qui vient de se clôturer, est toujours restée un peu dans l'ombre).

Cette nouvelle ère se caractérise par plusieurs grandes lignes dont l'extension du domaine de travail de la Communauté européenne, devenue l'Union européenne, l'augmentation du nombre des États membres de la Conférence (avec le risque de voir augmenter les cotisations impayées) et, parallèlement, du nombre de leurs délégués, l'évolution de la nature de la Conférence (de l'entente de professeurs honorables à l'échange de vues entre de hauts ou moins hauts fonctionnaires munis de documents très fouillés fournis par le Bureau Permanent), le fonctionnement de la Conférence elle-même (décision sur la base du consensus et non plus à la majorité des votes exprimés), la communication électronique et la publication de documents sur le site de la Conférence, la gestion

[3] Recueil des cours de l'Académie, tome 244 (1993-VII), p. 191-456.

d'employés de plus en plus nombreux, avec des problématiques financières non négligeables comme celle des pensions de retraite, la nécessité d'un « planning » serré et d'une mise à jour annuelle pour satisfaire aux exigences des responsables financiers auprès des gouvernements, les locaux abritant la Conférence.

Il n'en reste pas moins qu'il faut enregistrer une certaine continuité : soutenir les contacts diplomatiques, à La Haye et ailleurs, encourager les gouvernements à voir d'un bon œil la signature et la ratification des conventions ainsi que les intérêts financiers de la Conférence. De nombreux voyages ont été entrepris à destination du monde entier.

Ci-dessous figurent quelques observations sur certains de ces thèmes.

La Communauté européenne (CE) a connu une importante évolution. L'une des phases a été marquée par l'entrée en vigueur, le premier mai 1999, du Traité d'Amsterdam du 2 octobre 1997. Le nouvel article 65 inséré dans le Traité de Rome confirme que la CE s'intéresse désormais au droit international privé. Certes, il y avait déjà la Convention de Bruxelles de 1968 et la Convention de Rome de 1980, mais l'article 65 fournit une base solide pour que la CE légifère en matière de droit international privé, d'abord avec une certaine limite (« dans la mesure nécessaire au bon fonctionnement du marché intérieur »), mais sans que cette limite constitue un vrai obstacle.

La CE qui, au début de sa présence à la Conférence, a dû se contenter de l'état d'observateur, disposait pourtant de moyens importants pour imposer sa volonté, notamment du fait des relations intérieures de la CE, et n'a pas manqué de se servir de ces moyens. Bruxelles a commencé à jeter ses ombres sur La Haye. C'est à Bruxelles qu'il était décidé du vote des États membres de la CE au sein de la Conférence. Source d'insatisfaction de plus en plus grave pour les États tiers, à savoir les États membres de la Conférence mais non membres de la CE, en premier lieu les Etats-Unis, puisqu'en effet, les États CE déterminaient souvent la majorité. HvL ne pouvait rester sans rien faire.

Pour contrecarrer cette situation, il a déclenché une offensive visant à attirer de nouveaux États membres de la Conférence, ce qui a rencontré un franc succès. Son idée était en même temps d'éviter que la Conférence, organisation internationale, mais d'une signature surtout européenne, ne soit résorbée par la CE, dont la modestie n'était pas évidente. Selon ses propres paroles, il n'est pas facile de se coucher à côté d'un éléphant. Si la Conférence était une organisation vraiment mondiale, ce risque serait éliminé, sinon réduit.

Le Statut de la Conférence, datant de la Septième Session (1951), et où on trouve la griffe de M. H. van Hoogstraten, ne satisfaisant plus, ne serait-ce que parce que seuls des États pourraient aspirer à la qualité de membre, le moment était venu de repenser et de reformuler certains éléments du Statut (plutôt que d'écrire un tout nouveau Statut ; il ne faut pas ignorer l'histoire !). La porte de la Conférence devait s'ouvrir à la CE pour qu'elle puisse en devenir membre à part entière (et, le cas échéant, à des organisations comparables : les « organisations régionales d'intégration économique », en fait, encore inexistantes), ce dans l'espoir qu'un équilibre pourrait se constituer entre la CE, ayant ses propres intérêts légitimes, d'une part, et la Conférence, d'autre part, comme organisation mondiale. La CE pourrait ainsi contribuer substantiellement au travail de la Conférence, en se rendant compte du nombre inégalable de spécialistes de droit international privé en son sein. Cette dernière circonstance devrait peser. La CE porte une responsabilité certaine dans le développement du droit international privé à l'échelle mondiale. Elle comprendra sa mission inévitable.

Enfin, le texte amendé est entré en vigueur le premier janvier 2007, après avoir coûté pas mal de nuits blanches à HvL. Son article 8, paragraphe 2, se lit désormais comme suit : « Les Sessions, le Conseil et les Commissions spéciales fonctionnent, dans toute la mesure du possible, sur la base du consensus. ». Il s'agit d'un compromis dont le manque de réalisme doit être camouflé par l'habileté de la personne à qui est confiée la présidence. L'une des échappatoires éprouvées est la création d'une commission ad hoc et la nomination des protagonistes du débat et quelques autres, si possible provenant de plusieurs continents, avec la mission de trouver une solution acceptable pour tous. L'avantage de la règle du consensus est que la majorité quelle qu'elle soit a perdu sa position confortable. Mais il faut prendre du temps et accepter, le cas échéant, le risque de résultats dilués.

La mondialisation de la Conférence a eu pour effet que la mission du Bureau Permanent a beaucoup évolué. Quand HvL y faisait son entrée en 1978, le BP comptait quatre personnes, le secrétaire général Georges Droz et ses deux camarades Michel Pelichet et Adair Dyer, et HvL remplaçant Mathijs van Hoogstraten. En plus, il y avait deux ou trois secrétaires et un manutentionnaire/Maître Jacques. Cela a vite changé. Le personnel compte maintenant une trentaine de personnes, dont plusieurs stagiaires et plusieurs juristes qualifiés qui assistent les membres du BP en préparant le grand nombre de documents à soumettre chaque année aux experts se rendant à La Haye pour telle ou telle réunion (Conseil, commissions spéciales). Il a fallu mettre au point une organisation bien rodée et bien réglementée. Sa gestion est devenue une tâche non négligeable du BP, et notamment du secrétaire général.

HvL a fait preuve d'un sens aigu des relations humaines.

En outre, sous sa direction, le BP devra se mettre d'accord de manière systématique sur la politique à suivre sur un grand nombre de dossiers.

Il a fallu une adaptation de l'ancien modèle du BP, qui s'est réalisée étape par étape. On pourra imaginer le temps et l'énergie consacrés par HvL pour développer et vérifier des idées et les mettre en œuvre.

Les contacts avec les États membres doivent être maintenus avec le plus grand soin. Ce souci s'est traduit dans les dernières années par un développement inconcevable il y a encore vingt ans, à savoir la création d'un bureau à Buenos

Aires, siège d'un « collaborateur juridique de liaison » pour l'Amérique Latine ainsi que, tout récemment, d'un bureau comparable à Hong Kong.

L'esprit d'ouverture de HvL s'est révélé d'une autre manière encore. Les États de tradition islamique se sont montrés peu enclins à se lier par des conventions de la Conférence, notamment celles en matière de droit de famille. HvL s'est toujours distingué par sa volonté de modifier le destin souvent misérable de dizaines de millions d'enfants dans ce monde. Son engagement pour la convention sur l'adoption internationale n'en est pas la seule preuve. La très importante Convention du 25 octobre 1980 sur les aspects civils de l'enlèvement international d'enfants s'est heurtée à une résistance tenace de la part de ces pays de tradition islamique. Il en va de même pour la Convention du 19 octobre 1996 concernant la compétence, la loi applicable, la reconnaissance, l'exécution et la coopération en matière de responsabilité parentale et de mesures de protection des enfants. Grâce au Bureau Permanent et à la bonne volonté de plusieurs personnes, une tradition s'est progressivement instaurée : l'organisation de colloques annuels entre, d'une part, des représentants, souvent magistrats de haut rang, de pays islamiques et des représentants d'autres pays, en majorité occidentaux. Ces colloques ont eu lieu, en majorité, sur l'Île de Malte, soutenus généreusement par son gouvernement et ses ambassadeurs successifs à La Haye. Il s'agit de déblayer le terrain en vue d'une coopération significative.

À une certaine distance, on pourrait être tenté de penser qu'une fois l'Acte final d'une Session de la Conférence approuvé, la signature et la ratification d'une convention contenue dans un tel Acte Final sont une question d'automatisme, d'une durée plus ou moins longue d'un pays à l'autre, mais quand même. Il n'en est rien !

Plusieurs grands projets, plus ou moins récents et soutenus par les investissements considérables en termes de temps et d'énergie de dizaines sinon de centaines de personnes, ont abouti et les résultats, tous de grande qualité, se trouvent dans les Actes Finaux successifs. Leur genèse a été rendue accessible via les Actes et Documents de la Conférence, mis au point au Bureau Permanent avec la plus grande acribie. On y trouve également le Rapport mis au point par le Rapporteur désigné au cours des négociations. Un tel rapport n'a pas le statut d'un rapport officiel, c'est-à-dire approuvé par la Session, mais, en pratique, il a la même autorité. Le rapporteur s'en rend compte et bénéficie, lors de la rédaction, du concours des membres du Bureau Permanent compétents en la matière. Depuis quelques années, les Actes et Documents peuvent être consultés sur le site de la Conférence.

Le travail accompli est impressionnant. Espérons qu'il portera encore ses fruits.

Une sommité est sur le point de quitter la Conférence, après trente-quatre ans de services très dévoués, prêtés avec un sens des responsabilités extraordinaire.

Toujours actif sur les fronts multiples de sa fonction, toujours courtois et aimable, Hans van Loon, malgré sa grande modestie, ne peut que se rendre compte de ses grands mérites.

THE RELATIVITY OF LEGAL POSITIONS IN CROSS-BORDER SITUATIONS

The foundations of private interregional law, private intra-community law and private international law

Prof. Dr. M.H. TEN WOLDE LL.M

Professor of Private Law, Private International Law and International Transport Law at the University of Groningen, The Netherlands

Director of the Ulrik Huber Institute for Private International Law, Groningen

1. THE HAGUE CONFERENCE AND HANS VAN LOON; A UNIQUE COMBINATION

From 3 to 20 October 1988 I attended the Sixteenth Session of Hague Conference on private international law regarding *Succession to estates – applicable law* as an auditor and young PhD researcher. At the end of the first conference day the views of the various delegates were so divergent that it seemed useless to continue the session. The next morning, however, the differences proved to have completely vanished and the Sixteenth Session continued and was completed successfully. To a large extent, the members of the Permanent Bureau, Hans van Loon in particular, can be credited for this realization. The unique combination of great knowledge of PIL systems in the world and excellent diplomatic skills united in Hans van Loon have therefore provided an important contribution to the success of the Hague Conference and thus to the development of a world PIL. In addition, as Secretary General, Hans van Loon has always maintained contacts with the academic world. Being part of this academic world in this article I will focus on the academic questions regarding the basis and method of PIL. Is there a universal basis? When a national legislature creates (private law) rules it intends to regulate certain matters in accordance with the values existing within its own society. Obviously this counts for every state in the world. In this respect two questions arise. First: what is the geographic scope of the domestic law of a state? Can it claim application beyond its borders? Second: to what extent should a state allow private law rules of a foreign country in its jurisdiction? What forces a state to set limits on its law on the one hand, and on the other hand to apply foreign law within its borders? Under what conditions and in what form should national law yield to foreign law; what is the appropriate method? Does each type of legal conflict require the same method or do certain factors require legal conflicts between countries that have a particular connection to each other, that have a certain link, to be treated differently than where such a connection is non-existent? In other words: to what extent do the basis and methods of private interregional law, private intra-community law and private international law differ from each other?

2. THE CURRENT DUTCH AND EUROPEAN CONFLICT OF LAWS RULES

In the Netherlands and modern Western Europe the question which law should apply to an international legal relationship is primarily based on the conflict of laws model proposed by Friedrich Carl von Savigny in 1849.[1] The theory put forward by Von Savigny does not approach the matter from domestic law, as the Statutists did, but from an abstract legal relationship which is the starting point in the process of determining the applicable law:

> *"Die Aufgabe geht dahin, dass bei jedem Rechtsverhältniss dasjenige Rechtsgebiet aufgesucht werde, welchem dieses Rechtsverhältniss seiner eigenthümlichen Natur nach angehört oder unterworfen ist (wohin dasselbe seinen Sitz hat)."*[2]

1 *System des heutigen Römischen Rechts, Achter Band*, Berlin 1849.

2 *System*, § 348. Von Savigny approached the problem of conflicting laws from an interstate perspective which is quite logical given the fact that Prussia in 1849 consisted of various regions, some not even geographically connected, in which several particular laws were into force. At the same time Prussia was part of a loose confederation of German States. Von Savigny furthermore recognized the (coming into) existence of a German common law (*das gemeine Deutsche Recht*) among the German states. This led him to the conclusion to apply to the conflict of territorial laws of independent states substantially the same principles as those which govern the collision of particular laws in the same state (§ 348).

The common question is to ascertain for every legal relation (case) that law to which, in its proper nature, it belongs or is subject (where it has its seat).[3] Under this approach, the content, nature and the scope of domestic law is irrelevant in determining which law should apply. Whereas the conflict of laws theory of the Statutists is a law of parameters, primarily determining the scope of domestic law, the theory put forward by Savigny is a law of reference and allocation: it refers the international legal relationship to a particular national system of law based on the nature of the legal relationship in question. The conflict rule brings the legal relationship "home." It does not decide substantive questions of law.

According to Von Savigny the legal basis of the conflict of laws is to be found in the "*Völkerrechtliche Gemeinschaft der miteinander verkehrende Nationen*", an international common law of nations operating with each other, *a community of law among independent states.*[4] In this context the conflict of laws has to meet the requirements placed on it by the growing community of states and the private individuals in them.

The problem that the Statutists had with the application of foreign law within another sovereign territory does not feature in the theory put forward by Von Savigny given that in his theory the state plays only a marginal role in determining the question of applicable law. In Von Savigny's view law flows forth from what he described as the "*Volksgeist*", or "the spirit of nations". Under this construction the state is only required to codify the law. Legal concepts such as marriage, property and contract are derived from the *Volkgeist.* Von Savigny's theory therefore did not suffer from any limitation based on the link between state sovereignty and applicable law; the law was no longer bound to national boundaries but could apply across borders. Under this interpretation the importance of the contribution made by Von Savigny becomes clear, as he reversed one of the fundamental beliefs about the role of the conflict of laws, namely, under his theory the question of which legal principles should apply is answered with reference to the legal relationship and the dispute in question, not the national law of any party.[5]

Von Savigny's view differs from the traditional Statutist theory. For the Statutists the primary role of conflict of laws is to create broad parameters for the manner in which the law of different states should be applied, which meant

3 See the English translation: Friedrich Carl von Savigny, *A Treatise on the Conflict of Laws, and the Limits of their Operation in respect of Place and Time*, translated with notes by William Guthrie, 1880, p. 70.

4 Von Savigny expressly rejects the *comity* concept, put forward by the Dutch Statutists, and the suggestion that the legal basis of conflict of laws is to be found in the demarcation of the sovereign rights of individual states.

5 See the in-depth analyses of Von Savigny's theory by L. Strikwerda, *Semipubliekrecht in het conflictenrecht, verkenningen op een kruispunt van methoden*, 1978, p. 112–133.

that the rights and obligations created by the law of these states formed a fundamental consideration. Under this construction the goal was to create the most equitable balance between the interests of states in the application of their law. As mentioned, Von Savigny rejects the proposition that there is a relationship between law and state sovereignty and places the interests of the citizen and the legal purpose of the conflict of laws as central to the determination of legal disputes. Von Savigny does not touch the question of how to reach justice under substantive law. Rather the conflict of laws has its own aim of justice; it should create legal certainty in international legal intercourse by creating what he called "*Entscheidungsharmonie*", decisional harmony.[6]

Indeed, Von Savigny's paradigm became the starting point for the conflict of laws as we understand it today. The principle of the closest connection[7] remains the most important consideration; it is necessary to determine to which legal system the legal relationship in question has the closest link or connection. Nevertheless, the traditional Savignian model has undergone numerous revisions, several reference categories (of certain legal relationships) have been added and a number of criteria have been elaborated. Doctrines such as characterization, acquired rights and public policy have all changed over time. In addition, a number of new legal principles and doctrines have been discovered and developed, such as the doctrine of *renvoi*, the preliminary question, *Näherberechtigung*, the fait accompli exception and overriding mandatory rules. Furthermore, in Dutch and European Conflict Law, alongside the standard Savignian model, other methods and principles have been added such as the principle of protection of weaker parties, the favour principle (favor), and the principle of party autonomy. The current state of Dutch and European PIL therefore is often referred to as one of "methodpluralism" or as the "eclectic method".

According to the prevailing view, private international law is national law and is not founded on international principles of law or an international body of law. The national legislature is accordingly free to define and develop the conflict of law rules of its own state as it sees fit. It is generally accepted that the primary purpose of the conflict laws (and private international law) is to regulate international legal relations in an effective and just manner. Private international law is intended to ensure that such relationships are not handicapped by the differences between legal systems when legal relations are established across national boundaries. Decisional harmony, the creation of uniformity in the determination of applicable

6 See the Hague Academy lecture of Th.M. de Boer, *Facultative Choice of law, The procedural status of choice-of-law rules and foreign law, Recueil des cours*, Volume 257 (1996), p. 283.

7 Even in the recent Chinese codification of conflict rules in the *Law on Law Application for Foreign-related Civil Relations* this principle fulfills an important role. See Huang Jin, *Creation and Perfection of China's Law on Law Application for Foreign-related Civil Relations,* 2011 International forum on Private International Law, Beijing. China, Volume I, p. 15.

law, and the certainty that it offers, is seen as the ultimate purpose of conflict of laws. Von Savigny based this on his *Völkerrechtliche Gemeinschaft*, a community of law among independent states, in terms of which it is no longer a question of in which country a matter is brought before a judge, because any judge would be able to decide based on the nature of the dispute and the legal relationship what the legal system with the closest connection would be. In contemporary Dutch private international law however the harmony of decisions is geared primarily towards preventing forum-shopping, and to prevent limping legal relationships.

3. FURTHER REFLECTIONS ON THE PRINCIPLES AND METHODS OF THE CONFLICTS OF LAWS IN AN INTERREGIONAL, INTRA-EU AND INTERNATIONAL SETTING

According to the prevailing view among Dutch scholars and the view of the Dutch Supreme Court[8] conflicts of laws at interstate level should be treated the same as conflicts of laws at an international level. When solving conflicts questions at an interstate level, between the several countries of the Kingdom of the Netherlands, a Dutch court should take the international conflict of laws rules as a starting point. International conflicts and interstate conflicts are approached in similar ways: a conflict is a conflict whether at interstate or at international level. This means that since international conflict rules in the several countries of the Kingdom of the Netherlands differ, the interstate conflict rules will differ as well.

However, the question arises whether legal conflicts within the Kingdom really are the same as legal conflicts at an international level. Are these conflicts of laws the same as conflicts within the European Union or conflicts with non-EU states? Does the mere fact that all these situations require a choice between different legal systems mean that the fundamental legal consideration is also the same? Should we judge the situation involving the Netherlands and Aruba in the same way as we judge a situation concerning the Netherlands and Germany? Or the Netherlands and China, the Netherlands and Tanzania, the Netherlands and Chili or the Netherlands and Iran?

Is the designation of the applicable law no more than a mechanical addition and the conflict of laws a mechanism where the operation of a lever produces a certain law? In other words, is the connecting rule a cold mechanism that is not influenced by the question which countries are involved or could potentially be involved? For example, does the fact that we exactly know the content of the

---

8 HR 11 July 2008, *NJ* 2009 454.

private law of the overseas countries of the Kingdom play a part? Does the fact that we know that the legislation and case law of these countries is substantively sound play a role? Does the fact that we know that this law is largely based on similar values and conceptions as our own law play a role?[9] Anyone with an understanding of law generally, feels that such data should play a part. The question is how this can be factored into the inter-regional conflict rules, the international conflict rules and the intra-European conflict rules.

It is submitted that the way in which a country is connected to another country affects the way in which the applicable law should be determined. This not only applies to private interregional law, but also to private intra-community law and to private international law. In order to identify the heart of the problem, it is necessary to first consider its origin.

THE "PROBLEM"; LEGAL POSITIONS DEPEND ON TIME AND PLACE

The fact that every country has its own rules of law implies that a single act or event can have different (or similar) legal consequences in different countries. For example, entering into a marriage in country A can create a community of property between the spouses, whereas the laws of country B stipulate that in such a situation only future income will be shared. Thus the death of a person in country A may result in his children only being able to claim their inheritance after the death of the surviving spouse, while the law of country B grants the children the right to assert a claim for their inheritance immediately. Similarly, a marriage, a divorce or an adoption may have no legal consequence in country A but have absolute legal validity in country B.

Another factor is that the rules of law constantly evolve, meaning that time may also be determinative. This leads to the not surprising insight that *legal positions are dependent on time and place*. Therefore the legal reality in country A can be different from that in country B, country X or country Y. This fact raises the question of whether and in what way the differences in legal consequences require coordination.

9 In international situations, the application of conflict rules is a *leap of faith (ein Sprung ins Dunkle)*; in an interregional setting it is not. The same is true in intra-EU cases.

THE BASIS FOR CONFLICT OF LAWS: A NEW DUTCH SCHOOL

What is the legal basis that forces, or at least requires, that in certain circumstances foreign legal provisions should be taken into account? Why should Dutch law yield to foreign law? A number of different views are important: 1) the basis for the conflict of laws is not universal, therefore it is not the same in every country; 2) the basis is not static but changes over time; 3) the basis is dependent on the relationship between states (the dimension) from which that law stems; 4) which in turn logically makes that basis different, each relating to a different dimension, which may exist simultaneously.

The idea behind the basis of conflict of laws starts with the widely accepted principle of state sovereignty. On the basis of sovereignty a state is entitled to organize its own society at its own discretion. This applies to purely domestic but also to international issues. Each state is entitled to organize the international sphere as it sees fit, in the same manner as it does in the domestic setting. No state is obliged to apply foreign law. The basis for the application of foreign law is thus determined by national legal standards. Private international law is national law and therefore the answer to the question whether and under what conditions we should substitute domestic laws for foreign law must be determined based on our own values and representations. Here, two factors play a part. First, it is an obvious fact that domestic law does not intend to create legal consequences for every action or event that occurs anywhere in the world. The Dutch legislature did not intend to regulate the question of whether an agreement between an Englishman and a Chilean, concluded in Uruguay, should have legal consequences. Similarly, there is no such intention in relation to the question of who should inherit from a deceased with two wives and eight children domiciled in an Arab country. It is therefore important to determine the scope of our own legal rules. In this context, it makes sense to distinguish between rules with an overriding mandatory character (public policy) (category I), rules with a mandatory character (category II) and rules with a regulatory character (category III). The second factor is that the scope of our domestic law may find its boundaries in the recognition of claims of a community (society) of law to which we have a certain relation. Whether such claims are justified is once again to be determined by our own national standards. However, the more intense the relationship with a foreign country, the more similarities that exist between the foreign society and our own, the more the values and customs will be shared and consequently the more the values and the legal principles of law will be shared. Where this is the case, the need for a state to always apply its own domestic law is gradually reduced and the incentive is greater to honour the laws of that foreign country. This also depends on the (historical) shaping of the interrelationship between the societies involved. This component does not play a role when a country leads a fairly isolated existence, but it becomes more important as international legal intercourse intensifies. A country that insists on the absolute application of its own laws where it concerns intensive international trade would utilize its autonomy, but would do so contrary to its own interests and the interests of its subjects. In most circumstances, such a policy will be impossible to maintain since it will not be accepted by the other societies involved.

The basis for the application of foreign law therefore is relative and depends in particular on the relationship between the countries involved. The greater the level of interaction between countries and their societies the more the individual legal societies develop into a single "legal society" with the same underlying values and legal principles, and in turn, the less obvious it is that their own laws prevail over the laws of the other country. One can imagine this development as a sliding scale with on the one end of the scale (left) the state absolutely and exclusively applying its own law (because are few international legal transactions), and at the other end of the scale (right) the state that is neutral to the application of both its own and foreign law (because these societies are so intertwined that they assume the same basic values and legal principles).

It is difficult to give examples of countries which are entirely at the left of the scale, although a country such as North Korea would find itself at the very end. A little further to the right are the countries that are party to several private international law treaties on specific subjects. Then come the countries that have entered into certain forms of cooperation, e.g. COMESA, ECOWAS, SADC, EAC, CARICOM, NAFTA, etc., all with an economic background. Even more closely related are the relations within ASEAN, or within the EEC. A strong bond exists between the member states of the European Union, but it is still not at the right end of the scale. The American states, the Canadian provinces, the countries within the United Kingdom, the Spanish "provinces", the countries within the Kingdom of the Netherlands, are all examples of legal systems on the far right end of the scale. Whether they can reciprocally apply a truly neutral conflict of laws is however not only determined by the state system, but also depends on the interconnectedness of these societies. Given the geographical proximity, one can imagine that Spain and the UK have strong mutually connected societies and are thus at the right end of the scale. In this context, one can also question whether the societies of Aruba, Curacao and St. Maarten, societies that are around seven thousand kilometres away from the Netherlands, are connected to the Netherlands in a way that justifies the application of a fully neutral conflict rules. Although the Queen and the Supreme Court *(Hoge Raad)* are shared and the legal codes are largely the same, there are fundamentally different views on various issues of family law. Common ground in this area seems to be non-existent.

THE METHOD OF THE CONFLICT OF LAWS

Under what conditions and in what form should national law yield to foreign law? In the last eight hundred years, several methods have been utilized, that, according to their point of departure can roughly be divided into two groups. In one group, the problem is solved by determining the spatial scope of national and/ or foreign substantive law. Here, one seeks to answer the question of which of the concurrent legal norms is most appropriate based on the validity of the claim. In the other group, one seeks the legal system which is most closely connected to the international legal relationship. The starting point does not lie with concurrent rules or legal systems, as it does in the first group, but with the object of the norm: the legal relationship. The law of the country where the legal relationship has its center of gravity is to apply. In a way, the drifting legal relationship is brought home by the allocation rule. The determination of this center may occur in abstract, as in Von Savigny's *Sitz*-theory, but can also be dependent on the factual circumstances on the basis of which the proper law should be determined. Characteristic for this group is that the content of the law does not play a part in determining the applicable law.

Remarkably, each of the aforementioned methods usually presents itself as the only true method. Does the one method preclude the other? The thought that the method in question may not suit the setting in which the conflict of laws issue occurs usually does not arise. Neither does the idea that one method may be more appropriate within a certain context of countries than the other. In my view, the latter provides part of the answer to the problem. The nature of a state's legal system and the relationship with the countries or regions involved should form part of the consideration in determining which method should be used.

THE METHOD WITHIN THE EU

In the EU, the method of determining the applicable law is strongly connected to the basis for the legal dispute. Whoever is on the left side of the scale can only rely on the (scope of) its own law, whoever is far right on the scale can only be neutral with respect to domestic and foreign law. Mind you, this may differ subject to context and content. It is therefore important to determine the basis per dimension and per subject, and from there choose the appropriate method. So it seems that the neutral Savignian allocation model works well for a group of countries that share the same basic legal values. In such a context, it is not (or less) important whether domestic law or the law of a foreign country applies, because the substantive law of each of those countries, for example, upholds the principle that spouses should be able to divorce each other. Where these principles are shared, a method with which one dispenses a neutral allocation rule is applied. Where national legal views on a subject differ within a group of countries, one should move to a model which explicitly allows for these national views or conclude that a provision on the applicable law is not useful since a *a community of law* among the member states does not exist.

Studies conducted under the establishment of the Rome III Regulation made clear that the divorce law of the Member State could be divided into four categories; 1) divorce on request, 2) in a comparative view liberal grounds for divorce, 3) in a comparative view cautious grounds for divorce, and 4) prohibition of divorce. The contrasts between category 1 and category 4 were so great that value-neutral European conflict rules did not prove feasible. The attempts to push this situation into a neutral Savignian model at any cost have caused unnecessary delays in finding a uniform solution and we are now stuck with a regulation which will not apply to all Member States. In retrospect, it is of course easy to say, but these problems could have been recognized sooner. What this incident has shown is that, at a European level, insufficient attention has been paid to the establishment of a basis for European conflict of laws and the most desirable conflict of laws method.[10] The value-neutral conflict of laws model of Von Savigny is too readily utilized as a suitable base model without taking into account the underlying communal principles of law of the Member States (whether *a community of law – in the area of law involved* – among the Member States exists) and without regard for the particular interrelationship between the Member States. With the latter I mean the fact that intra-Community situations are equated with situations between national and third countries. This is a fallacy which can be traced in almost every regulation. In intra-European situations legal certainty and predictability, especially the prevention of intra-Community forum shopping, play a major part. The same can hardly be said of a request for dissolution made to a Dutch court involving the marriage of an American and a Dutch national, both domiciled in the Netherlands, a marriage between two Americans domiciled in the Netherlands or a Dutch married couple domiciled in the United States. What European interest is served by applying a conflict rule designed for intra-European relations to those situations? The aforementioned examples concern a different "setting" in which the interests of the Dutch State (society), in which *favour divortii* plays an important role, should take precedence. For the time being, this regulation will therefore not enter into force in the Netherlands. However in the latter case, under Article 8 of the Rome III Regulation, the long arm of Dutch divorce law would not able to reach to the United States since under this provision the law of the habitual residence applies and can only be changed by a joint choice of law by the spouses.

[10] When establishing a general EU PIL Regulation this matter should be dealt with first!

With regard to regulations in areas where the Member States have many common points of departure, the inclusion of conflict rules aimed at the relationship with third countries is obvious. Where it concerns relatively value-free areas, this can be achieved by the use of multilateral conflict rules, however, where it concerns subjects in which certain interests should be protected, such as employment contracts or consumer contracts, the use of scope rules is much more evident. The same goes for directives. It is more conscientious to give a specific scope rule upon issuing directives than it is to regard a single provision as an overriding mandatory rule in retrospect.

Besides the fact that it is generally desirable to distinguish between the conflict of laws within the EU and the conflict of laws in relation to third countries, one should take into account the national interest of the Member States in determining the method for intra-communal divorces. This could have easily been achieved by using the Savignian model as a starting point within the EU, with the exception of those Member States that are strongly committed to the application of their own law by determining the scope of the law within the intra communitarian situation through a scope rule.[11] This rule could be based on the *lex fori*, but could also be limited to a state's own nationals.[12]

By pre-determining which values and conceptions are shared by the Member States within a particular area in need of European codification, the most appropriate method can be determined. This also means that predictions can be made about the success of the recently launched draft regulations in the areas of inheritance law, matrimonial property law and partnership law.

THE METHOD WITHIN THE KINGDOM OF THE NETHERLANDS

The neutral Savignian allocation model seems to work well for a group of countries which share the same basic legal values. As noted before, this does not apply to the Kingdom of the Netherlands. Societies that are forced to adhere to the principle of concordance, whilst they are 7000 kilometres away from one another, have different values and conceptions on many key issues, especially in family law. Where they share the same values, uniform conflict rules are to be preferred. Where this is not the case, one should make room for unilateral scope rules securing the interests of the countries of the Kingdom involved.

11 A mixture of Savignian allocation rules on foreign law and scope rules on domestic law is justified because the situation in which underlying values and conceptions are shared does not yet exist.

12 In Dutch divorce proceedings, the dissolution of a marriage of a Dutch couple, habitually residing in Poland, would, for example, always be governed by Dutch law.

THE METHOD FOR INTERNATIONAL SITUATIONS

Where the connection to a foreign country is uncertain, domestic law should be the starting point. Surely, a basis for the equal handling of domestic and unknown foreign law is non-existent. A neutral allocation rule causing us to make a "*Sprung ins Dunkle*" should be rejected. In those cases, our conflict rule should primarily indicate the scope of our own, domestic, law. Where our law does not warrant application, a rule can be formulated from underlying principles of domestic law on the basis of which a determination is made as to which laws are to be given binding force here. This should be further developed. Anyone searching in Book 10 of the Dutch Civil Code[13] will find various provisions which have essentially been formulated in this way; Articles 19 and 20; Articles 30 and 31; Article 40(concealed); Article 56; several provisions in Title 4; etc.

THE HAGUE CONFERENCE ON PRIVATE INTERNATIONAL LAW

How does the Hague Conference fit into this picture? The Hague Conference and the Permanent Bureau have an important role in identifying existing and potential communities of laws between states upon which PIL rules can subsequently be built. Crucial for success is the work of the Bureau in analysing and documenting underlying values and legal principles. Of particular importance is the work of the Bureau to, where necessary, overcome differences between national legal systems in a pragmatic manner and create the conditions for successful meetings of the Hague Conference. The Hague Conference is therefore an indispensable organization on the world stage of PIL.

4. CONCLUSION

The basis for the application of foreign law is relative and depends particularly on the relationship between the countries involved. The greater the level of interaction between countries the more the individual societies develop into a single 'community of laws of States' with the same underlying values and legal principles, and in turn, the less obvious it is that their own laws prevail over the laws of the other country. National governance through law yields more to intra-

---

13 See for the English translation of Book 10 Dutch Civil Code, *Yearbook of Private International Law*, Vol. XIII, Sellier European Law Publishers Munich, 2011, p. 657. See for a commentary on Book 10 the same yearbook, p. 389.

community governance through law the more values and legal principles are shared within such a community of States.

Under what conditions and according to which method should national law yield to foreign law? The method of determining the applicable law is strongly connected to the aforementioned level of interaction between the societies in the community of States in question. Whoever is on the left side of the "scale" cannot but rely on the (scope of) his own law, whoever is far right on the "scale" can only be neutral with respect to domestic and foreign law. This may however differ, subject to context and content. It is therefore important to determine the basis per dimension and per subject, and from there choose the appropriate method.

It is clear that the Hague Conference has an important task to fulfil in identifying existing and potential communities of laws, bridging possible differences and creating corresponding PIL rules. The progressive unification of private international law, topic by topic, to be established through diplomacy and flexibility coupled with scientific rigor, focused on everyday life and at the same time tying together globally shared values and policies,[14] makes the Hague Conference on private international law an indispensable institution.

[14] See the inspiring presentation of Hans van Loon, *The Hague Conference on Private International Law: Asser's vision and an evolving mission*, presented at the Commemorative Conference celebrating the 100th anniversary of the award of the Nobel Peace Prize to T.M.C. Asser, entitled "Inspiration and Innovation in International Law and Politics", held on 9th December 2011 at the Peace Palace in the Hague, The Netherlands, published in *NIPR* 2012, p. 358, and to be published in the *Hague Yearbook of International Law*.

THE EVOLUTION OF TECHNICAL ASSISTANCE PROVIDED BY INTERGOVERNMENTAL ORGANISATIONS

A Comparative Study of the Hague Conference, IMF, WTO, UNIDROIT and UNCITRAL

Micah THORNER
Director, Hague Conference International Centre for Judicial Studies and Technical Assistance

The Hague Conference on Private International Law has reached a turning point in its history, where for the first time since it became a permanent Intergovernmental Organisation in 1955, a greater portion of its resources are used for various post-Convention services, rather than its more traditional work developing normative private international law instruments. The Hague Conference is not alone in this regard, as many similar intergovernmental organisations such as the International Monetary Fund (IMF), World Trade Organisation (WTO), UNIDROIT and UNCITRAL have been forced to consider whether, and to what extent, offering such support is not only feasible in light of limited resources, but consistent with goals and objectives that were developed in an what often seems to be a bygone era – a time during which developing States were simply excluded from many global cooperation initiatives.

It was due in part to the vision of Hans van Loon, who has served as Secretary General of the Hague Conference since 1996,[1] that the Organisation was able to develop a successful technical assistance programme for States, available not only

1 Mr Van Loon joined the Permanent Bureau of the Hague Conference in 1979 and assumed the post of Secretary General in 1996.

to those which were already or Contracting State to one or more Convention, but also those considering whether to join and had yet to become a State Party.

For more than 30 years, post-Convention services, including the promotion and efforts at monitoring the practical operation of Conventions, have been provided by the Permanent Bureau (Secretariat) of the Hague Conference. The shift from treaty development and administration began at the Hague Conference as early as 1977, when the Permanent Bureau organised the first Special Commission on the operation of the Hague Service Convention. This highly successful first Special Commission review meeting was the start of a practice that has become an established feature of the Organisation.[2]

As the monitoring and support activities of the Hague Conference continued to grow, its Member States reviewed the Organisation's long-term strategic goals and adopted a Report entitled "The Hague Conference on Private International Law on the eve of the New Millennium: Some concrete suggestions for strategic action," which had been drawn up by an informal group of Ambassadors ("Ambassadors' Report").[3] This Report cited the desire of Hague Conference Member States to actively expand the Organisation, among other things, in order to broaden the reach and value of the Hague Conventions. In turn, new States would benefit from participating in Hague Conference events and from utilizing Hague instruments as a tool to engage in multilateral transactions and protect vulnerable persons. By doing so, legal certainty regarding applicable law would extend to new jurisdictions and signal to the rest of the world that new Contracting States were willing to agree to internationally-agreed upon rules, opening up new possibilities for international trade and investment, expanding global protection systems and ensuring broader adherence to the rule of law.

The Ambassadors' Report recommended that, among other things, the following steps should be taken by the Hague Conference:

(a) Increase the membership of the Organisation;
(b) Publicise the Conventions and documents of the Conference and organise seminars in co-operation with appropriate regional organisations in order to facilitate good communication, practical working relationships and the development of trust and confidence between different legal systems;

---

2 This first Special Commission was convened and its Conclusions and Recommendations were implemented, absent an explicit reference in the Convention itself. Starting with the 1993 Intercountry Adoption Convention (Article 42), Hague Conventions now provide, as a standard provision, a clause instructing the Secretary General to convene – at regular intervals – a Special Commission to review the practical operation of the Conventions.

3 The Report drawn up in the Fall of 1999 by the Informal Group of Ambassadors, chaired by H.E. Mr H. Reimann, the then Ambassador of Switzerland, also formed part of the Strategic Plan endorsed in 2002 by the Special Commission on General Affairs and Policy of the Conference. See note 5, *infra*.

(c) Develop training programmes for authorities and judges applying the Conventions.[4]

The Ambassadors' Report was followed by the drawing up of a Strategic Plan for the Conference,[5] which was generally supported at the Nineteenth Diplomatic Session (2002).[6]

In response to the adoption of the Ambassadors' Report and the new Strategic Plan, the Permanent Bureau increased its outreach and promotional activities to encourage new States to join the Organisation, or at the very least join one of its Conventions. Around the same time, regional co-operation and globalisation also began having an impact on the Organisation. This led to encouragement by other international organisations, such as UNICEF and the UN Committee on the Rights of the Child, to join the Hague Children's Conventions, in particular the Intercountry Adoption Convention.[7]

As a result, the Hague Conference saw its Membership grow by almost 57% from 1999 to today,[8] a growth rate which is more than double the average annual rate of expansion since the Statute of the Organisation entered into force for the first Hague Conference Member in 1955.

Of these new Members since 1999, all but the European Union, New Zealand and Russia are currently considered eligible Official Development Aid-eligible (ODA) States by the Organisation for Economic Cooperation and Development (OECD).[9] In other words, more than half of the Organisation's new Members (those that joined in the last 14 years) are States which often receive financial and other support from industrialised countries.

---

[4] "The Hague Conference on Private International Law on the Eve of the New Millennium: Some concrete suggestions for strategic action," Proceedings of the Nineteenth Session, Tome I, Miscellaneous matters, pp. 67–76, at para. 3. The Report also suggested the development of some form of regional presence of the Hague Conference. Such a regional presence is particularly meaningful and important in relation to post-Convention services.

[5] See "The Hague Conference on Private International Law – Strategic Plan", drawn up by the Permanent Bureau, Prel. Doc. No 21 B of March 2002 revised, *ibid.*, pp. 165–211.

[6] Final Act, Part B, Proceedings of the Nineteenth Session, note 4, *supra*, at p. 45.

[7] Similarly, the World Bank, through its *Investing Across Border Initiative*, advises States to consider joining the Apostille Convention as a measure to establishing a regulatory environment more conducive to foreign direct investment. In an initial 2010 report, it finds that the Apostille Convention makes is easier for foreign companies to start up business in the host State by simplifying the process of authenticating foreign public documents.

[8] In 1999, the year the Ambassadors' Report was originally adopted, the Organisation had 46 Member States. As of 1 January 2013, there are an additional 26 Members (25 States plus the European Union).

[9] The OECD Development Assistance Committee List of ODA Recipients shows all countries and territories eligible to receive official development assistance (ODA). The DAC List of ODA Recipients for reporting on 2011, 2012 and 2013 assistance is available at http://www.oecd.org/dac/aidstatistics/48858205.pdf.

As a consequence of the sharp rise not only in Membership, but also Members who have limited financial resources, it became apparent that additional post-Convention Services were needed. Demand for widely available tools and guides for persons and entities tasked with implementing and applying Hague Conventions increased, as did the need for the development of global networks and training programmes for authorities and judges applying the Conventions.

All of these, and other post-Convention activities, were undertaken with the support of the Member States, and often also with their involvement in particular activities. However, no specific additional funding was allocated under the Organisation's Regular Budget. Instead, at the suggestion of some Member States, the Permanent Bureau created a Supplementary Budget to receive and manage additional voluntary contributions for these post-Convention activities. Unlike the Regular Budget, the Supplementary Budget was created specifically to fund specific activities / projects rather than general organisational expenses such as salaries and administration costs.

These developments had implications which may not have been fully anticipated when they began. In particular, because most of the new Members and new States Parties to Hague Conventions were developing States or States with an economy in transition, the extent to which the need for implementation assistance would also grow as the number of Members increased was not fully considered when efforts first began to actively promote the Organisation. At the same time, other international organisations such as UNICEF, the UN Committee on the Rights of the Child, the European Union, and professional organisations such as the *Union Internationale des Huissiers de Justice* (UIHJ) also began encouraging States to ratify or accede to instruments which complimented their own objectives or goals.

The increasing diversity and size of the Hague Conference is beneficial in many respects. But in order to preserve the reputation of the Hague Conference and the value of the Hague Conventions, it became necessary to ensure that adequate Convention support and advice was available for States which needed it. The Organisation then began exploring ways in which to respond to the greater demand for guidance and support. At first, a wide range of tools were created to assist States Parties (both Members and non-Members of the Conference) with the implementation and application of the Hague Conventions such as Practical Handbooks on the operation of the Service and Evidence Conventions; Guides to Good Practice for the 1980 Child Abduction, 1993 Intercountry Adoption Convention, and 1996 Child Protection Convention; Country Profiles for the 1980 Child Abduction and 2007 Child Support Conventions; an ABC's of Apostilles (for the *Convention of 5 October 1961 Abolishing the Requirement of Legalisation for Foreign Public Documents*, commonly known as the 1961 Apostille Convention) and a Guide on how to join and implement this Convention; as well as various electronic tools and databases, such as the International Child Abduction Database (INCADAT).

It was the demand for targeted or customised support and advice provided to one or more States, however, for the Hague Conference to question its transformation over the past several years. Such support is often immensely resource-intensive, and demand always exceeds what can be provided. As a subset of post-Convention Services, it was hard to define such work, but the Hague Conference eventually termed these activities as "technical assistance" so as to align its terminology with development aid agencies which engage in similar types of work. Unfortunately, this term seemed somehow inadequate to describe all of the work, particularly when it involved industrialised States.

The increasing complexity and number of requests for technical assistance made it clear that creative new solutions were needed as programmes and recipients continued to evolve. Among many proposals, it was decided to create from within the Permanent Bureau an International Centre for Judicial Studies and Technical Assistance in 2007. While the exact mission and objectives of this new entity were never fully defined, the hope was that it would help Permanent Bureau experts to effectively manage projects, identify and manage funding, and develop a strategic outlook for future technical assistance work.

The Centre was used as a basis to explore various ways in which the Permanent Bureau could continue to provide the customised support, training and advice to States that needed and requested it. Such assistance could consist of one or more of the following activities:

- fact-finding missions to analyse and diagnose issues;
- developing a strategy for implementation and / or recommendations to overcome identified obstacles in the operation of Hague Conventions;
- drafting and review of implementing legislation and / or enforcement mechanisms;
- assistance with the creation and training of effective Central Authorities;
- seminars, conferences and workshops for judges (including continuing education programmes), other government officials and legal practitioners and group training activities for the purpose of facilitating the consistent implementation and interpretation of Hague Conventions.

At the time of its creation, the Centre managed funding and technical assistance activities for the Permanent Bureau. Since that time, the Centre has continued to support efforts by the Hague Conference to provide greater understanding and consistent application of the Hague Conventions by delivering specialized training programmes and customized technical assistance; supporting efforts by the Member States and States Parties to Hague Conventions or interested States, their government officials, judiciary and other practitioners to consistently, effectively and uniformly apply Hague Conventions; formulating fundraising strategies, and tracking donor trends; and exploring additional sources of funding.

In order to evolve and continue operations after its first few years of existence, the Permanent Bureau considered many ways forward. In addition to identifying creative personnel[10] and funding options,[11] governance of the Centre was a source of lengthy debate. Research was done on the possibility of making the Centre semi-autonomous or autonomous through the establishment of a foundation or other non-profit structure with an independent board and standardized reporting requirements.

It remained unclear, however, how such an entity would function in practice. What would its relationship be with the Hague Conference if it became a distinct entity? How would this affect the perceived value of receiving support from a source other than the Permanent Bureau itself? Would donors be willing to fund the same number of projects if staff time were added on to the budget of every activity? How could the Centre report on activities in a way that would appeal most to donors? How would the Hague Conference ensure that all of its external experts provided high quality, objective support? Would States be required, at least in some instances, to pay for the advice and support they sought from the Centre? Would Membership of the Hague Conference continue to play a role in prioritisation of technical assistance requests? What role would the Hague Conference Regional Offices play? These and many other questions presented themselves during the first years of the Centre's operation.

While research was being done on these various questions, it became clear that other international organisations were facing many of the same issues regarding technical assistance and support, some of which are described below.

INTERNATIONAL MONETARY FUND[12]

Technical assistance provided by the International Monetary Fund (IMF) is available only to Members of the organisation. About two-thirds of IMF technical

10 Personnel proposals included a combination of consultants, interns and experts from the Permanent Bureau which would be funded by donors, project funds, through the salaries of Permanent Bureau staff, or a combination of these.

11 Options considered for funding included private donors (individuals and company sponsorships), NGOs, grants from public and private sources, development aid and contributions from States.

12 For more information on the IMF's technical assistance programme, see IMF, "Technical Assistance Factsheet" (17 August 2012) available at http://www.imf.org/external/np/exr/facts/tech.htm.

assistance goes to low- and lower-middle-income countries. Post-conflict countries are also major beneficiaries.

The aim of the IMF's technical assistance programmes are based on premises similar to those considered by the Hague Conference.

Just like the Permanent Bureau, the IMF provides technical assistance to States related to its areas of core expertise and has experienced a growing demand for such support for low-income countries to build capacity to design and implement poverty-reducing and growth programs. The IMF also contributes actively to the Integrated Framework for trade-related technical assistance, which aims to assist low-income countries expand their participation in the global economy.

The IMF delivers technical assistance in various ways. Depending on the nature of the assignment, support is often provided through staff missions of limited duration sent from headquarters, or the placement of experts and/or resident advisors for periods ranging from a few weeks to a few years. Assistance might also be provided "in the form of technical and diagnostic studies, training courses, seminars, workshops, and "online" advice and support."[13]

The IMF has, like the Hague Conference and the other international organisations examined below, also explored the benefits of using a regional approach to the delivery of technical assistance and training. It operates eight regional technical assistance centres – in the Pacific; the Caribbean; East, West, Central, and Southern Africa; the Middle East; and in Central America. The IMF will open in 2013 a second regional centre in West Africa for non-Francophone countries in the region. In addition to training offered at the IMF Institute, the IMF also offers courses, workshops, and seminars for country officials through a network of seven regional training institutes and programmes, as well as in the context of the regional technical assistance centres.

The regional centres are complemented by technical assistance financed through topical trust funds. The first such fund began operations in May 2009, concentrating on building capacity in connection with anti-money laundering and combating the financing of terrorism. Two new trust funds began operating in May 2011. A third trust fund is being prepared while several others continue to be developed, including one for training in Africa.

Technical assistance accounts for about one-quarter of the IMF's operating budget. It is financed by both internal and external resources, the latter comprising funds from both bilateral and multilateral donors. Such cooperation and resource sharing with external donors has distinct advantages: it leverages the internal resources available for technical assistance; helps avoid duplication of advice by different donors; and strengthens collaboration with donors and other technical assistance providers.

13 *Ibid.*

WORLD TRADE ORGANISATION[14]

Within the World Trade Organisation (WTO) Secretariat, technical assistance is coordinated by the Institute for Training and Technical Cooperation (ITTC).

In April 2001, the Technical Cooperation Audit was created by the WTO Secretariat. This function is intended to ensure that the very significant financial and human resources engaged in WTO-administered technical assistance and training programmes are used to optimum effect. It provides feedback to the Members, to the Secretariat (the technical assistance providers), and to donors to WTO's funds for trade-related technical assistance and capacity building.

More recently, this past year, the WTO adopted a Results Based Management (RBM) System for reporting the outcomes of its technical assistance work. The new system provides the basis for structural monitoring and evaluation of the Secretariat's trade capacity-building programmes. A similar reporting mechanism has been suggested for the Hague Conference, but it remains unclear whether such an objective tool would be compatible with the often subjective results of Hague Conference technical assistance work.

The WTO has also recognised the demand-driven nature of technical assistance. In response, consultations were conducted last year (2012) with all stakeholders in various formats, i.e., by region, by the economic development status of a State, or the type of donor. These consultations confirmed an increasing demand for WTO technical assistance specifically focused on the challenges associated with the implementation of WTO agreements, the capacity to make effective use of WTO rights and meet obligations. These consultations were followed by discussions with Members to determine whether adequate financial resources could be made available.

The Secretariat continually attempts to follow the most rational and pragmatic approach in preparing its annual Technical Assistance Plan, to ensure a do-able level of activities and that the demand can be met by the Secretariat. The strengthened function of technical assistance coordination, both internally in the Secretariat, which is performed through a Technical Assistance Coordination Task Force, as well as externally, i.e., with regional bodies, other IGOs and all other stakeholders is of critical importance in the efficient delivery of its trade capacity building programmes and in building synergies. The Secretariat puts a "high premium" on strategies for enhancing its cooperation and relationships with regional institutions and partners.

---

14 For more information on WTO Technical Assistance, see WTO, "Committee on Trade and Development – Biennial technical assistance and training plan: 2012–2013 (Revision)" (3 February, 2013) available at http://www.wto.org/english/tratop_e/devel_e/teccop_e/tct_e.htm under *WTO technical assistance documents*.

As with many of the international organisations examined in this article, the WTO has also experienced funding challenges, particularly in terms of ensuring timely and adequate levels of financial resources. A number of efficiency measures have therefore been incorporated into technical assistance programmes, including increased offers of e-learning in place of face-to-face lectures and seminars; further cost sharing with partners; and review of the duration of some activities as well as the overall levels of attendance and numbers of officials to be funded for the technical assistance activities.

UNIDROIT[15]

As one of the two sister organisations to the Hague Conference, UNIDROIT has also explored its role in providing technical assistance.

Like the Hague Conference, UNIDROIT has developed multiple databases and practical tools, such as Guides to its work. It has also provided technical assistance to both Member and Non-Member States, as well academic institutions and individuals, with special attention given to developing countries and countries in economic transition.

UNIDROIT's status as an international intergovernmental organisation is also listed on its website as one of the reasons that its experts are particularly well suited to provide support and guidance to States which seek objective support and advice. Like the Hague Conference, it also has faced resource issues and considered, back in 1996, the possibility of establishing a foundation intended "to promote activities that UNIDROIT considers to be particularly meritorious, but which it is not in a position to finance out of its budget."[16] For an organisation such as UNIDROIT, the foundation approach was thought to have the advantage of providing a new funding source while maintaining the balance of substantive independence for the organisation and greater ultimate accountability to States parties. It was mainly established to fund a database and a Modern Documentation Centre for Uniform Law. Several years after its creation, however, its ability to serve as a vehicle for additional funding had achieved mixed results.

15 See, e.g., UNIDROIT, "Study LXV – Programme of legal assistance to developing countries: Research Scholarships Programme: Implementation Report for the Financial Year 2009" (2010). A list of each Study LXV (published annually from 1993 to 2009) is available at http://www.unidroit.org/english/studies/study65/main.htm.

16 See UNIDROIT, "The establishment of an Unidroit Foundation" (May 1996) available at http://www.unidroit.org/english/documents/1996/study74/s-74-01-e.pdf at 1.

Currently, beyond cooperation with national or regional institutions and a Research Scholarship Programme[17] for government officials, scholars, and practitioners to use UNIDROIT facilities at its headquarters in Rome, the scope of targeted State support or cooperation is minimal.

UNCITRAL[18]

UNCITRAL, as the other sister organisation to the Hague Conference, is perhaps the most valuable comparative example of how technical assistance programmes have similarly evolved in two different international organisations.

UNCITRAL undertakes a range of technical assistance activities to promote its work and adoption of the legislative and non-legislative texts it has developed to further the progressive harmonisation and unification of private law.

Technical activities undertaken by UNCITRAL include the following:

- organising briefing missions and seminars and participating in conferences to familiarize participants with UNCITRAL texts and their use;
- undertaking law reform assessments to assist governments, legislative organs and other authorities in developing and other countries to review existing legislation and assess their needs for law reform in the commercial field;
- assisting with the drafting of national legislation to implement UNCITRAL texts;
- assisting international development agencies, such as the World Bank, to use UNCITRAL texts in their law reform activities and projects;
- providing advice and assistance to international and other organisations, such as professional associations, organisations of attorneys, chambers of commerce and arbitration centres, on the use of UNCITRAL texts;
- organising group training activities to facilitate the implementation and interpretation of modern commercial legislation based on UNCITRAL texts by judiciaries and legal practitioners;
- preparing teaching and other technical materials for other experts and scholars, such as the Case Law on UNCITRAL Texts system and analytical digests of case law on specific texts, which may be useful in seminars and briefing missions and in the context of university teaching.

---

17 See UNIDROIT, "Research Scholarships Programme" (date unknown) available at http://www.unidroit.org/english/legalcooperation/scholarships.htm.

18 See UNCITRAL, "Technical Assistance to Law Reform" (date unknown) available at http://www.uncitral.org/uncitral/en/tac/technical_assistance.html.

The process for responding to requests for assistance is very similar to that of the Hague Conference. Once the UNCITRAL Secretariat receives a request for technical assistance, it will liaise with the requesting country or organisation to identify the goals of the technical assistance. In light of the nature of the assistance required and the manner in which it can best be provided, UNCITRAL will then decide whether it can respond to the request.

Where the request is from a country, an essential part of that consideration is the provision of information on the country's commercial legal system, including current law reform programs and initiatives and, in particular, those related to UNCITRAL texts. Technical assistance is then organised in consultation with the requesting country or organisation to ensure the identified goals are met.

The demand for UNCITRAL technical assistance has, like with the Hague Conference, grown dramatically in recent years. Because UNCITRAL's regular budget does not include funds for such activities, these activities can only be conducted if funds are obtained from other sources. UNCITRAL established a trust fund in 1993 to facilitate its response to these requests and the Commission and the General Assembly have made repeated appeals for contributions. The Commission receives financial support from States, organisations and individuals. Contributions may be made for general technical assistance activities or for specific projects.

In addition to centralised technical support, UNCITRAL also has a Regional Centre for the Asia Pacific in the Republic of Korea. The main objectives of the Regional Centre are to (a) enhance international trade and development in the Asia Pacific region by promoting certainty in international commercial transactions through the dissemination of international trade norms and standards, in particular those elaborated by UNCITRAL; (b) provide bilateral and multilateral technical assistance to States with respect to the adoption and uniform interpretation of UNCITRAL texts through workshops and seminars; (c) engage in coordination activities with international and regional organisations active in trade law reform projects in the region; and (d) function as a channel of communication between States in the region and UNCITRAL.

Like Hague Conference Regional Offices in Buenos Aires and Hong Kong, the UNCITRAL Regional Centre actively engages in numerous technical assistance activities and promotes the Organisation's work throughout the relevant region.

CONCLUSION

The evolution of the Hague Conference's judicial training and technical assistance programmes and its International Centre in many ways resemble what has occurred in other international organisations, particularly when one examines the challenges other such entities have faced within the past 20 years. While partly due to increasing globalisation, high demand for technical assistance and cooperation will remain inevitable as diverse new States and their unique cultures continue their integration into global networks. As much of the past 20 years brought somewhat unexpected demand for such work, it remains to be seen what the next 20 years will bring.

A WORD OF GRATITUDE

The Rt. Hon. Lord Justice THORPE
Judge of the Court of Appeal, Head of International Family Justice, The Royal Courts of Justice, London

Although I have little scholarship to contribute to any festschrift for Hans I can contribute the voice of a judge, a judge steeped in the common law, a judge who has chosen to specialise in international family justice.

Hans is of course a renowned expert in private international law. Conflict of law was a lively and complex subject for a family lawyer at the outset of my career in the 1960s. Fortunately, some would say, it has faded from the field largely thanks to international instruments which have gained wide support in the thirty-five years of Hans' contribution and leadership.

Over the full span of his career he has made invaluable contribution to Conventions including the Access to Justice Convention in the 1980s, the Trust Convention of 1985 and the 1989 Succession Convention. However in addition Hans has made a lasting contribution to international family law with the creation of the 1993 Inter-Country Adoption Convention. Whether that Convention or the 1980 Abduction Convention is the first foundation of international family justice might be debated.

My close involvement with the Hague Conference and the Permanent Bureau began more or less at the same time as Hans' appointment as Secretary General. Over the ensuing years my regard for Hans has steadily grown. At so many events he has contributed his geniality, his diplomacy and his seriousness of purpose. With great tact, diplomacy and skill he has pursued the objectives of the Conference and has resolutely faced challenges with his style of leadership which is essentially benign paternalism.

Whilst I am grateful to Hans for many kindnesses and great aid I would choose to thank him most profoundly for his acceptance and encouragement of judicial activism in the promotion of the family law Conventions. It is within the years of his leadership that we mark the creation and growth of the Hague International Judicial Network. Within his years of leadership we record the inception and growth of the judicial role at Special Commissions. Hans has to his great credit the 22–25 June 1998 de Ruwenberg Judicial Seminar on the International Protection of Children and the string of Conferences that followed in its wake. At all these Conferences the participation of judges was actively encouraged.

In the same way during the years of Hans' leadership we have seen the development of the use of working groups, often to propose practical solutions to practical problems. To the work of these groups the judicial contribution has been fundamental.

Hans has been particularly successful in developing collaboration between The Hague Conference and the European Commission. The Joint EC-HCCH Conference on Direct Judicial Communications on Family Law Matters and the Development of Judicial Networks held in Brussels from 15 until 16 January 2009 is perhaps the best instance of the fruits of this collaboration.

Finally I must emphasise the debt that we judges owe Hans for presiding over the gestation and delivery of the "Emerging Guidance regarding the development of the International Hague Network of Judges and General Principles for judicial communication, including commonly accepted safeguards for direct judicial communications in specific cases, within the context of the International Hague Network of Judges". He saw that as a guide for judges it had to be the creation of the international judicial community. He required of us patience, commitment and consistency. From our contribution the Permanent Bureau has forged a tool that is modern, practical and of high quality. Those who use it in the future would do well to remember Hans with gratitude. For without him they would not have this highway through otherwise unmapped territory.

BEGINNING TO RETHINK PERSONAL JURISDICTION

Peter D. Trooboff*
Senior Counsel in the Washington office of Covington & Burling LLP

Throughout his long tenure as a member of the Permanent Bureau of the Hague Conference on Private International Law and as its Secretary General, Hans van Loon has grappled with issues of personal jurisdiction. During the initial expert meetings on the Judgments Project in the 1990s, I can well recall Hans raising many questions about how we should address various bases of personal jurisdiction. His probing helped to sharpen understanding of the United States proposal which Professor Arthur von Mehren had developed and shaped. And when Conference Members recognized that the objectives of the initially conceived Judgments Project were too ambitious for political and substantive reasons, Hans joined with his colleagues on the Permanent Bureau in helping to steer the project towards the successfully completed 2005 Hague Convention on Choice of Court Agreements.

Over the over two decades in which I worked with the Conference, Carola and Hans have time and again extended warm hospitality in their home to my wife and me and to members of the American delegations on which I served. We have tried to reciprocate when he visited Washington, often to explain to our Administration and Congress the Conference's future work program and priorities.[1]

* Peter D. Trooboff served as a member of the United States delegation to the Hague Conference throughout its work on the proposed Convention on International Jurisdiction and the Recognition and Enforcement of Judgment and was a member of the U.S. delegation to the diplomatic conference that negotiated and approved the 2005 Hague Convention on Choice of Court Agreements. Mr. Trooboff has subsequently been actively involved in drafting United States implementing legislation for that Convention.

1 Indeed, we had just such a pleasant dinner on the evening of September 10, 2001. It was the next day – 9/11 – during Hans' speech at the U.S. Patent and Trademark Office, then located a few blocks from the Pentagon, that we experienced together the terrible suspension of his remarks, the rapid escape from the building and the subsequent rush to leave the area where the smell of the crashed and burning aircraft from American Airlines Flight 77 was already

I have addressed "Beginning to Rethink Personal Jurisdiction" in this necessarily brief tribute to Hans because I believe that, as we say in the United States, that is where the action is – not only in my country but throughout the common and civil-law world. I am particularly focused on the impact on this subject of two developments – first, globalization of the production and distribution of goods and services in a worldwide market; and, second, the role of Internet in every aspect of today's commercial world. My central point is simple and straight-forward – globalization and the expanding role of the Internet will challenge our traditional thinking about personal jurisdiction. Further, these two forces will require courts, scholars and practitioners, at least, to retune their thinking and in some instances develop rather significant reformulations of either existing rules or how we apply those rules to newly presented factual patterns.

I take my examples from two fields of tort law to illustrate my point – product liability and libel. I have chosen these because, as Professor Horatioa Muir-Watt has said, the simple fact of the structure of the Internet causes cases to become "international automatically." Both of these fields provide ample proof of her point and suggest the difficult new issues that we must address. (I have necessarily summarized cases and limited citations but will be happy to elaborate upon inquiry.)

Let me be clear – this is not a subject only for specialists in private international law. These issues affect every family member, homeowner and citizen. We have all read the cases and listened to the testimony concerning imported products that injure young people and their families or damage their property. These examples range from dangerous toys to defectively designed or manufactured heparin and from drywall in new homes that reek of formaldehyde to adulterated toothpaste. In all these instances, the injured parties have faced extreme difficulty in finding a basis for personal jurisdiction over the responsible party, often the distant manufacturer, in order to adjudicate claims and receive damages. Despite regulations and enforcement, every country has manufacturers who make defective, unsafe products, including my own, for which the law must provide a remedy.

So the problem of finding a basis for personal jurisdiction over those in one nation who cause damage to persons and property in another nation is not concentrated in one country. And the same is surely true about libel, where we have seen how a single news article published through an Internet posting can permanently damage the reputation of a citizen, a business or even a nation. And

heavy in the air. Hans showed great courage during that period when he was forced for many days to remain in the United States and his friends tried to ease his understandable anguish at being present for our national tragedy.

such articles pose especially complex issues view of the broad protection that our First Amendment gives to publication about public figures.

In 2007 Martinus Nijhoff published under the Hague Academy's auspices, *Adjudicatory Authority in Private International Law*, by Professor Arthur von Mehren. This volume revised and updated his Hague Academy general course. Professor von Mehren reviewed succinctly the terminological breakthrough that he and his colleague Professor Donald T. Trautman had made in the 1960s, "Jurisdiction to Adjudicate: A Suggested Analysis", 79 *Harv. L. Rev.* 1121 (1966). They spoke of two kinds of personal jurisdiction or adjudicatory authority that courts, whether common-law or civil-law, have when hearing cases against individuals or legal entities. In their lexicon there is *general* and *specific* jurisdiction. They showed how this terminology was applicable not only to American cases but could be utilized for comparative law purposes in reviewing civil-law cases.

In summary, general jurisdiction defined the situation in which the relationship between the local court and the defendant was such that the court could adjudicate "essentially any kind of controversy involving that person regardless whether the matters in issue derive, or are related to, the circumstances relied upon to establish the authority to adjudicate." General jurisdiction might be established for an individual through, for example, domicile or habitual residence. For a legal entity, general jurisdiction might be the principal place of business or most controversially where the entity is doing business.

The other type of adjudicatory jurisdiction that von Mehren and Trautman discussed is "specific jurisdiction." For specific jurisdiction to exist, the court had to be dealing with a controversy deriving from or closely related to "the very circumstances relied upon to justify the forum's claim of adjudicatory authority." That's easy when an out-of-state driver passing through a community negligently drives an automobile and causes an accident in which a local citizen is injured. The negligence claim for damages clearly arises out of the driving in the jurisdiction and specific jurisdiction exists. But life is never so simple and the requisite relationship can prove elusive.

What policies control in deciding whether to allow particular general or specific jurisdictional bases for multistate jurisdiction? Professor von Mehren suggests that there are four – with the first two being the most important. These are:

- Ease of administration and predictability, which favors objective and relatively inflexible criteria; and
- Litigation fairness to the parties, while favors case-specific analysis of multifaceted criteria, often with a subjective element and based on broad formula such as "minimum contacts".

Two other policies were identified by Professor von Mehren as taken into account in establishing whether a particular jurisdiction should claim adjudicatory authority over a controversy:

- Proportionality, *i.e.*, the jurisdictions that may hear the case should be sufficient in number to allow plaintiff a fair opportunity to bring case but not so many locales as to harass the prospective defendant; and, finally,
- Vindication of important state regulatory policies, *i.e.*, courts should be available to hear claims that concern important governmental policies.

While the von Mehren and Trautman terminology and policy framework worked well for common-law and civil-law thinking about personal jurisdiction, it needs adaptation in situations arising from globalized markets and Internet communications. Professor Ralf Michaels at Duke has reminded us in his fine essay on "Territorial Jurisdiction after territoriality" in the volume titled *Globalisation and Jurisdiction* (eds. P. Slott and M. Bulterman, Kluwer 2004) that "[a]djudicative jurisdiction is an emanation of state sovereignty." He adds that such jurisdiction follows the same criteria as sovereignty which relies heavily on territoriality. However, territoriality starts to lose its meaning in the age of globalization and the Internet. Laurence Usunier puts it well when she emphasizes that "the principal characteristic of the Internet is [its] ubiquity" because all transmitted information is "available immediately to surfers [*internautes*] globally." *La régulation de la compétence juridictionnnelle en droit international privé* ¶ 268 (Economica 2008). In those circumstances, she adds, geographical localization on which private international law depends becomes nearly impossible. Michaels makes a similar point citing John Ruggie for the well documented point that "globalisation leads to an 'unbundling of territoriality' and challenges both the legitimacy and the intelligibility of traditional concepts of territoriality." He argues persuasively for a "re-conceptualization of jurisdiction" because, as he elaborates with three case studies, territoriality no longer gives us an "adequate picture of the world" and, as he shows, falls short as "a theory which yields *legitimate* results." Michaels, *op cit.* at 116. In other words, the tools for localization for jurisdictional purposes no longer function adequately.

With this background, I want to focus on just two fact patterns that will, I think, begin to illustrate how European and American courts are addressing the challenges to thinking about personal jurisdiction raised by two common situations arising from globalization and use of the Internet. In the first paradigm case, a manufacturer located in the United Kingdom ships goods for consumption in another jurisdiction – either another country in the European Union or the United States. The manufacturer also has a local, independent distributor in the country where sales are sought. In addition, the manufacturer's representatives come frequently to various countries to promote sales at trade shows and the like. The product proves to be defective in its manufacture and causes injury to employees of the company that purchases the machine.

How does European law and United States law address such a case? In the case of Europe, the Brussels I Regulation, EC 44/2001 (December 22, 2000), which replaced the 1968 Brussels Convention for the EU states, determines whether courts of the member states of the European Union have jurisdiction in this situation for cases involving those domiciled in other EU countries. Article 5(3) of the Brussels Regulation provides that suit against EU domiciliaries may also be brought, in addition to the domicile of the defendant where general jurisdiction exists, "in matters relating to tort in the courts for the place where the harmful event occurred or may occur." This second ground involves specific jurisdiction with the cause of action arising from such event.

In Case 21/76, *Bier v. Mines de Potasse d'Alsace*, 1976 *E.C.R.* 1735, the Dutch plaintiff alleged that saline discharges in France in the Rhine had damaged down-river Dutch horticulture activities on the Rhine. The European Court of Justice was asked if the case could be heard only where the wrongful conduct originated, *i.e.*, France, or also where the damage manifested itself in the Netherlands. The ECJ looked for a "particularly close connecting factor between the dispute and the court which may be called upon to hear it, with a view to the efficacious conduct of the proceedings." The ECJ determined that Netherlands was also a place "where the damage occurred." It held that, at the option of the Dutch plaintiff, two courts could hear the claim – where the damage originated, France, or where the damage occurred, the Netherlands. In *Bier*, the causing of damage was entirely foreseeable to the French party placing the discharges in the Rhine. In short, the Brussels I Regulation has proved to be well adapted to finding a basis for a court to assert personal jurisdiction over a manufacturer located in one EU or country that fabricates a defective product causing injury within another EU member state.

Turning to the United States, our courts test personal jurisdiction by weighing whether the requirements of the Due Process Clause of the Fifth and Fourteenth Amendment to the Constitution have been satisfied. U.S. courts make that determination by focusing on whether the defendant has "such minimum contacts [with the forum jurisdiction] as does not offend traditional notions of fair play and substantial justice." Under the cases, the courts evaluate not only contacts with the jurisdiction but also the fairness of asserting jurisdiction. In short, as my colleague Professor Ronald Brand has shown in much great depth, (see, *e.g.*, R. Brand, "Tort Jurisdiction in a Multilateral Convention: The Lessons of the Due Process Clause and the Brussels Convention", 24 *Brook. J. Int'l L.* 125, 150 ff. (1998)) and as *Bier* amply demonstrates, civil law courts, in general, focus on the relationship among the activities or transactions that gave rise to the cause of action, and the territory where the courts are located. American courts are constitutionally mandated to focus on the defendant's relationship to the territory for which the court has subject-matter jurisdiction. Professor Hélène van Lith at Erasmus School of Law, relying on Brand among many others, refers usefully to "defendant-specific" jurisdiction of courts of the United States and "claim-specific" jurisdiction of courts in civil-law countries in developing her valuable comparison. (International Jurisdiction and Commercial Litigation: Uniform Rules for Contract Disputes 40 (reviewing restrictive interpretation of special jurisdiction under Article 5) and 328 ff. (T.M.C. Asser Press 2009).)

In an important recent Supreme Court case, a New Jersey company purchased for its use at a Las Vegas trade show a U.K. manufactured scrap metal shear machines. The seller was the exclusive Ohio-based distributor of the machines which was not an affiliate of the manufacturer, although its name resembled that of the U.K. company. Plaintiff worked at the New Jersey company and lost his hand allegedly because of a defect in the machine's manufacture.

Because this was a major case, the court received many *amicus curiae* briefs from trade associations and various interest groups. These included a brief from 17 widely published and cited American law professors in the field urging the Court to affirm the New Jersey court's decision. These law professors argued that "it makes no difference that the Petitioner did not specifically target the individual states" when the foreign manufacturer "purposefully engaged the U.S. distributor" to serve the entire U.S. market for the sale of products that meet U.S. safety standards. If New Jersey could not assert personal jurisdiction over McIntyre UK for injuries caused by its machine in that state, the manufacturer, the law professors point out, could end up not being subject to suit "in any state despite its deliberate efforts to access the entire U.S. market."

The Supreme Court, reversing the New Jersey Supreme Court, held that New Jersey did *not* have jurisdiction over the U.K. manufacturer under the Due Process Clause of the Fourteenth Amendment. Writing for a plurality, Justice Kennedy regrettably rejects "general fairness considerations [as] the touchstone of jurisdiction." Instead, he grounds jurisdiction on discerning defendant's "intention to submit to the power of the sovereign" based on a forum-by-forum analysis of whether the defendant's conduct was "purposefully directed" at a particular state and whether in this case McIntrye UK "purposefully availed itself of the New Jersey market." His opinion forcefully rejects finding such purposeful action in defendant's foresight about where products placed in the "stream of commerce" will be sold or utilized. In this regard, he adopts a far more restrictive view of foreseeability than that advocated by, for example, Mlle. Usunier, who criticizes the American cases as too restrictive in their approach. *Id.* at ¶ 258.

In a strong dissent to the *Nicastro* ruling, which was joined by two other Justices, Justice Ginsberg emphasizes that a majority of the Supreme Court – the dissenters plus Justices Breyer and Alito – reject the "consent" analysis of personal jurisdiction propounded by the four-vote plurality. She explains that McIntyre UK "'purposefully availed itself' … of the United States market nationwide, not a market in a single State or a discrete collection of States." Justice Ginsberg contrasts the heavy burden and cost for Nicastro of pursuing his tort claim in England against the lesser burden for McIntryre UK of defending in New Jersey court "as an incident of its efforts to develop a market for its industrial machines anywhere and everywhere in the United States."

Justice Ginsburg has closely followed global private international law issues since her early work as a civil procedure professor. Her dissent makes the point that "[t]he Court's judgment puts United States plaintiffs at a disadvantage in comparison to similarly situated complainants elsewhere in the world." Noting that McIntyre is based in an EU member state, the United Kingdom, she explains that Article 5 of the Brussels I Regulation permits jurisdiction to be asserted by courts "for the place where the harmful event occurred." She adds, citing *Bier*, that since 1976 the European Court of Justice has interpreted this provision to "authorize jurisdiction either where the harmful act occurred or at the place of injury." Thus, she recognized that in a case similar to *Nicastro* the courts of every EU member state, including the United Kingdom where McIntrye is headquartered, would assert personal jurisdiction over the U.K. manufacturer for the alleged damaged caused by its machine.

Others reacting to the issues raised by the *Nicastro* decision have proposed that anyone sending products subject to government regulation into the United States be required to consent to jurisdiction by appointing an agent for service of process. American industry had severe reservations about that approach and how similar consent requirements might be imposed on them in other countries.

And what guidance does the Supreme Court offer regarding cases like *Nicastro* in which the marketing occurs not only through trade shows but also over the Internet? A leading trade association urged that the Court clarify the law in *Nicastro* by holding, at least, that the accessibility in a forum to an Internet web site for a manufacturer's products does not without more constitute advertising in that forum by the manufacturer and, hence, presence for specific jurisdiction purposes. The Court did not furnish the requested guidance, most probably because the issue was not raised and adjudicated in the lower courts.

To be sure, some find that foreseeability may be an appropriate part of the test whether personal jurisdiction should exist especially in cases involving globalized marketing programs. For example, in the 1999 Hague Draft Convention on International Jurisdiction and the Recognition/Enforcement of Judgments, Article 10 on Torts or Delicts would have allowed in Article 10(1)(b) "A plaintiff to bring an action in tort or delict in the courts of the State … in which the injury arose." But there was a much discussed exception in that same provision. Jurisdiction would not exist if the defendant establishes that the person claimed to be responsible "could not reasonably have foreseen that the act or omission could result in an injury of the same nature in that State." This compromise was intended to take the approach of the Brussels I Regulation and *Biers* but to temper the provision with the Due Process considerations found in American jurisprudence. No consensus existed on how such a provision would operate in practice (*e.g.*, how would the burden of proof be applied) and whether the exception would give rise to even greater uncertainty and complexity especially given the controversy in American courts about the significance of foreseeability.

Turning to issues of libel over the Internet, let us begin with the American cases since they predate the Internet and the jurisprudence of the European Court of Justice. Also they are a useful predicate to reviewing how the ECJ has approach the issues. The two leading Supreme Court decisions date back nearly 30 years, *Calder v. Jones*, 465 U.S. 783 (1984) and *Keeton v. Hustler Magazine,* 465 U.S. 770 (19894). Both were specific jurisdiction cases involving the publication outside the jurisdiction of the forum in which the plaintiff filed suit and both predated the Internet. In *Keeton*, the plaintiff sued in a state with which she had very little relationship. The Supreme Court had no difficulty in finding that the 10–15,000 sales of several magazines to the jurisdiction were sufficient to establish jurisdiction over the defendant. Further, the Court applied a "single publication" rule and allowed *all* damages to be heard in that state. The Court was not impressed by defendant's argument that the state was chosen because of its exceptionally long statute of limitations nor by the plaintiff's limited relationship to the forum. As to this point, the Court had long held that choice of law considerations should not "complicate or distort" the jurisdictional inquiry.

In *Calder*, the Court was concerned with Florida individual defendants who wrote and edited an allegedly libelous article about the plaintiff whose reputation and career were centered in California. The Court held that there was jurisdiction in California. The Court relied on the effects caused in California article which was based on California sources. The Court found that the article was "precisely aimed at California." The employees argued that they should escape jurisdiction because they – unlike their publisher employer – had not acted in California. The Court rejected that argument as well since their conduct, individually evaluated, was focused on California.

Now roll the calendar forward three decades to when the Internet has become a means of communication that impacts reputations. Because the American baseball is reasonably well known globally, I will illustrate with a case involving the great pitcher Roger Clemens. Mr. Clemens is alleged by several major investigations to have used performance-enhancing drugs during a substantial part of his career. Mr. Clemens has denied these charges in Congressional hearings and in the media. In this case, a senior writer for a leading sports Web publication published over the Internet allegedly damaging statements about Mr. Clemens and his use of such substances. Since Mr. Clemens has always lived in Texas, he sued the accuser in federal court in Texas. The federal Court of Appeals for the Fifth Circuit held in a split decision over a strong dissent that the Texas court lacked personal jurisdiction, *Clemens v. McNamee*, 615 F.3d 374 (5th Cir. 2010). Applying the Due Process Clause, the majority said that the "issue narrows to whether these defamatory remarks constituted purposeful availment [of the laws of Texas] such that [defendant] McNamee could have reasonably anticipated being haled into a Texas court as a result of his statements." *Id.* at 379. Relying on *Calder*, the court said that Texas must be the "focal point of the story." But the story referred to the drugs being administered elsewhere and there was an absence of reference to Texas in the story.

To this analysis and reliance on the geographical focus in the content of the story, the dissent responds on two grounds. First, the defendant allegedly travelled to Texas frequently to train Mr. Clemens during his career. That training relationship was allegedly the source of the drug administration even if it did not actually occur in that state. Second, relying on *Calder*, the defendant knew that Clemens lived in Texas and that it was foreseeable that the injury to Clemens would be in Texas. The dissenting judge points out the many ways in which the defendant's conduct satisfied both the traditional minimum conducts test and the "effects" test under *Calder*.

How has the European Court of Justice addressed the issue of libel over the Internet? In several cases the Court has struggled with the same subject. Building on *Bier*, the European Court of Justice in its well-known Case C-68/93, *Shevill v. Press Alliance*, 1995 *E.C.R.* 1, developed the so-called "mosaic principle" for recovery of damages in libel cases. *Shevill* involved the distribution of newspapers in the U.K. containing an allegedly libelous article about the plaintiff's activities while working in France. As Jan-Jaap Kuipers, a lecturer at Radboud Universiteit Nijmegen, explains, *Shevill* "strikes a balance between interests of the publisher and the alleged victim" by creating a second forum for the claim – the place of distribution of the publication provided that the claimant has a reputation there. Kuipers, *Joined Cases C-509/09 & 161/10*, 49 *Com. Mkt. L. Rev.* 1211, 1214 (2012). However, the ECJ limited the damages to those incurred by the plaintiff at that location. If the injured party wanted to collect for reputational damages throughout the world, then the claim had to be brought at the place where the publisher is established (or where the defamatory publication originated if other than the publisher's domicile). This approach limits forum shopping and possibly also reduces the chilling effect that can result from such suits.

Most recently, the Court of Justice of the European Union has confronted how to apply the jurisdictional rule determined in *Shevill* to the situation when the communication has occurred over the Internet. In two companion cases, *eDate Advertising v. X* and *Martinez v. MGM*, C-509/09 and 161/10 (October 25, 2011), the Court of Justice recognized that the Internet, as we have seen, with its ubiquitous quality, is not quite the same as a distributed publication. Where can the plaintiff bring suit for libel in such a case? In both cases, the defendants were publishers established in a country – Austria and the U.K. – other than where – Germany and France, respectively – the plaintiffs sought in court proceedings to have the reports on the Internet permanently barred. Mr. Kuipers explains that digital publication raises a challenge beyond *Shevill* because often the reader accesses a web site to see the publication – there is no distribution. Further, the publication is generally perpetual and global so the actual damage to a reputation may be severe. These same factors raise concerns about the "potential precarious situation" of the Internet publisher who does not necessarily target its audience and in many instances may not be able to foresee where the subject of an article will allege reputational injury has occurred. Kuipers, *op. cit.* at 1220.

The European Court held in *eDate* and *Martinez* that the victim of damage over the Internet to personality rights could sue for all damages in the place where he or she has a center of interests – not, as the Advocate General proposed, where the center of gravity of the dispute is located. While the plaintiff's center of interests will normally be the habitual residence of the plaintiff, the ECJ stated, it could be otherwise for those whose professional career is centered in a place other than where he or she lives, *e.g.*, a French movie actor who chooses to reside with her British husband and U.K.-schooled children in the U.K. but who manages and promotes her acting career from France. From a policy perspective, the Court seems to view the publisher as responsible for knowing the location of the center of interests of those about whom reports are written and, hence, to be able to foresee being sued there.

The analysis in both EU cases mirrors elements of the thinking of the majority and dissenting opinions in *Clemens*. Both the ECJ and the Fifth Circuit panel are struggling to identify a base for personal jurisdiction that takes account of the special circumstances of Internet dissemination of allegedly libelous material. Wisely, I believe that the ECJ's approach relies less on factors that figure in the Fifth Circuit majority decision, *e.g.*, whether the allegedly libelous article included allegations about conduct in the proposed jurisdiction for suit. That is not to say that the two recent ECJ cases are without controversy. For example, Mr. Kuipers explains that the defendant under *eDate* would often have no reason to know where the subject of a publication has a reputation or even where the center of his interests are located if, for example, the article concerns conduct only in another jurisdiction. Further, he adds, the ECJ decision, contrary to considerable precedent, reflects a clear bias in favor of the victim and emphasizes the habitual residence of the plaintiff which may be entirely unforeseeable to the defendant. As you have seen, both majority and dissent in the *Clemens* decision were concerned with not only the extent to which the publication implicated Clemens' reputation in Texas but the foreseeability to the defendant of such damage. As Mr. Kuipers points out, the ECJ now seems to have one rule for print publication and another for Internet publication which is contrary to the technological neutrality that the EU has sought to achieve under the Brussels I Regulation. *Id.* at 1223. In the end, and despite the challenges, the struggle of American courts with the application of fairness considerations seems to this admittedly biased common-law lawyer a less artificial basis for preserving technological neutrality and resolving jurisdictional issues in Internet cases.

How did the Hague Conference propose to address the libel publication situation, hopefully in a way that would cover Internet cases? Article 10(4) of the 1999 draft Convention adopts a more nuanced approach than *Calder* by imposing a gloss on *Shevill* under which the state of injury has jurisdiction only over damages incurred there "unless the injured person has his or her habitual residence in that State." In their report, Professor Nygh and Judge Pocar explain that this enlarged jurisdictional approach avoids multiplying jurisdictions while allowing complete recovery only if plaintiff can show an additional connecting factor – *i.e.*, habitual residence. Even that proposed solution would work less well for globe-trotting artists and executives or lack transparency when the habitual residence itself is unknown, unclear or disputed.

Where does this leave us? It is, in fact, too early to expect a definitive theory or response to all of the questions arising from globalization and Internet commerce. From this brief overview, I see issues of the kind that the Hague Conference needs to address and that, I expect, Hans would want his successors to take up. They require a global solution. It is therefore welcome news that the Hague Conference has decided to begin work on a global recognition and enforcement treaty that would address *solely* indirect bases of jurisdiction. I hope that my good friend Hans would agree that this step-by-step approach to rethinking personal jurisdiction issues seems especially prudent given the Conference's experience with the Judgments Project. Understandably, no consensus exists in the Conference to address direct jurisdictional rules given the many uncertainties reviewed here and the difficulty of reconciling competing policy considerations.

RECOGNITION AND ENFORCEMENT OF FOREIGN CIVIL PROTECTION ORDERS – A TOPIC FOR THE HAGUE CONFERENCE?

Dorothea VAN ITERSON
Former Counsellor of Legislation, Ministry of Justice of the Netherlands

1. INTRODUCTION

On 31 March 2009 I was offered a wonderful reception by Hans and Carola van Loon, marking my retirement. In his address Hans gave the following description of the nature of the international tasks which I had discharged: having a share in developments at the national, regional and global levels, ensuring co-ordination among those levels and making discussion partners aware of the constraints of a sound international legislative policy. My contribution to the Liber Amicorum for Hans is about a subject which, if finally taken on board by the Hague Conference, will again require a high degree of synergy of three levels of regulatory activity.

In 2012 former colleagues of the Ministry of Security and Justice asked me to comment on a Commission proposal for a European Regulation on mutual recognition of protection measures in civil matters. The subject matter was entirely new to me and I was intrigued, not least by the obvious overlap with existing international instruments. In preparing my comments I borrowed useful background information from the note prepared by the Permanent Bureau for the Hague Conference's 2012 Council meeting.[1] A questionnaire was distributed among Member States of the Hague Conference on 30 November 2012. A compilation of responses was not yet available when this contribution was finalized. The views expressed below are my personal views. In the space allotted I can only present a brief analysis.

1 Prel. Doc. No.7, March 2012, www.HCCH.net/work in progress/General Affairs.

2. THE PROBLEM AND RESPONSES TO THE PROBLEM

A leaflet published by the Council of Europe, entitled "Safe from fear, safe from violence"[2] draws attention to the problem in unambiguous terms:

> "Every day in Europe, women are stalked, harassed, raped, mutilated, forced by their family to enter into a marriage, sterilised against their will or psychologically and physically abused in the "safety" of their own homes. The examples of violence against women are endless, its victims countless.(...). Domestic violence is another form of violence that is far too common and that affects not only women, but also men, children and the elderly".

According to information made available on the Dutch government's website on domestic violence in the Netherlands,[3] every year a million of persons are victims of occasional domestic violence in this country. Between 200,000 and 230,000 persons are even faced with serious or repeated domestic violence.

Domestic violence has become a matter for concern at the national and local levels in a large number of countries. Policy makers realize that the problem not only affects people in their private lives, but disrupts society as a whole. This awareness is reflected in increasing legislative activity. Statutes have come into force which attempt to counteract the phenomenon by providing for the issuing of protection orders prohibiting persons causing danger from staying in specified places or from contacting victims or potential victims for a certain period, or imposing criminal sanctions. Parallel to this, several forms of social assistance and rehabilitation have been developed.

3. HUMAN RIGHTS ISSUES

Domestic violence raises important human rights issues. It interferes with a victim's right to privacy or physical integrity. Usually it has an impact on his or her right to respect for family life. It may also restrict other freedoms. Measures of protection, in turn, restrict the perpetrator's right to privacy and to a family life. Reference can be made to case law of the European Court of Human Rights on the failure by authorities to institute criminal proceedings against perpetrators of serious violence.[4] Articles of the European Convention on Human Rights

2 See www.COE.int/human rights/violence against women and domestic violence.
3 Www.rijksoverheid.nl/huiselijk-geweld.
4 Website referred to in footnote 2.

which were found to be violated in a number of cases are Articles 2 (right to life), 3 (prohibition of inhuman or degrading treatment), 8 (right to respect for family life), 13 (right to an effective remedy) and 14 (prohibition of discrimination). One case (no. 71127/01) is interesting because it concerns the interface between criminal law and private law. The applicant, who was a victim of grave physical violence by her husband, had left him with their son. Her requests for interim custody of their child had not been treated as a priority. Custody was awarded to her only when her divorce was pronounced more than a year later. The following year she was again battered by her husband. Her requests for criminal prosecution were then rejected on the ground that it was a "private matter". The Court found a violation of Article 8 (right to respect for family life), given the authorities' failure to adopt the measures necessary to punish and control the applicant's husband. The Court stressed that considering the dispute to be a "private matter" was incompatible with the authorities' obligation to protect the applicant's family life. This case demonstrates that where we are concerned with serious forms of domestic violence, criminal law remedies must be available in addition to remedies in civil law.

4. NATIONAL LEGISLATION IN THE NETHERLANDS – A BRIEF OVERVIEW

A survey of national statutes enacted in the past decade in numerous countries is presented in the Permanent Bureau's note referred to in par. 1. Obviously the national *acquis* should be the starting point for any work to be undertaken at an international level. An overview of legislation in force and policies pursued in the Netherlands may help estimate progress which might be achieved as well as the hurdles to be taken if a global instrument were to be put in place.

a. The *Act instituting a temporary restraining order* (Netherlands Law Gazette 2008, no. 421) came into force on 1 January 2009.[5] It is a tool of administrative law. It grants the burgomaster, or the assistant public prosecutor mandated by him, the power to issue a restraining order to a person if it appears from facts or circumstances that this person's presence in the house presents an immediate serious danger for the security of one or several persons living in the house or staying there more than occasionally, or that there is a severe threat of such violence. A regulation based on the Act sets the criteria to be applied in deciding whether or not to issue an order. The principal aim of the

[5] See J.L.M. Janse, T.C. Borman, "De Wet tijdelijk huisverbod", *Ars Aequi* 2009, pp. 60–67; see also the relevant literature published on www.huisverbod.nl.

temporary restraining order is to prevent further escalation of a conflict that has arisen between partners or within a family and to allow those left behind a cooling-down period in which they can decide if they wish to continue to live with the person causing the danger. For example, a victim may consider obtaining a street injunction in civil proceedings or a divorce. Another aim of the Act is to offer persons concerned proper guidance and assistance. The restraining order is issued for a period of ten days and can be extended to a maximum of four weeks. The Act contains detailed provisions relating to the procedure to be followed before the order is issued. The person who is the subject of the order is not allowed to enter or be present in the house or in its surroundings. He is not allowed to contact any of the occupants mentioned in the order. The injunction does not prevent social workers from liaising between the parties in order to arrange for assistance.

The temporary restraining order in Dutch administrative law was not conceived of as an alternative to criminal prosecution. It was instituted because criminal law provides no instrument for preventive action. In view of its purpose it was preferred to grant the power to issue the order to the burgomaster, and not to the office of the public prosecutor.[6] The burgomaster is in charge of the police as far as it is its duty to assist citizens. The delivery of an administrative restraining order may coincide with criminal proceedings. An interim assessment of the operation of the Act carried out in 2011[7] showed that in a large proportion of cases reviewed there was punishable behaviour and criminal proceedings were actually started. It should be stressed, however, that an administrative restraining order can be issued irrespective of whether the person causing the risk is or will be kept in custody or whether criminal proceedings are instituted or are pending.

The persons concerned (i.e. the person who causes the danger and the persons to whom protection is to be offered) are given prior notice and are heard before the order is issued unless such hearing is inappropriate due to the urgency of the situation. The order states the grounds on which it is based as well as the legal remedy available against it. All those concerned are notified of the order, and of the consequences of non-compliance. The person who is the subject of the order has the right to lodge an appeal directly with the court. In interim relief proceedings he may apply for a provisional order allowing him to return to his home. The police have the duty to assist him in obtaining legal assistance and representation by a solicitor.

---

6 The assistant public prosecutor, who may be mandated by the burgomaster, is not a staff member of the office of the Public Prosecutor. Often he is a police officer.

7 Procesevaluatie Wet tijdelijk huisverbod, 2010, Policy survey commissioned by WODC (Centre for Research and Documentation of the Ministry of Security and Justice).

Whenever the burgomaster issues a restraining order, he informs the local social counselling and assistance services designated by him. These services may already have been contacted by the victim or by persons in the victim's surroundings.[8] Social assistance is provided to both the perpetrator and the victims. If there is a suspicion of maltreatment of children, the child maltreatment hotline is informed. This may trigger a process which leads to measures of child protection such as the appointment of a supervising guardian or placement in care. In principle social assistance should be offered within twenty-four hours. If necessary the victim can be offered accommodation in a refuge centre.

According to the outcome of a survey commissioned by WODC in 2012,[9] 7000 temporary restraining orders were issued in 2011.

b. Dutch *criminal law* offers a wide range of protection measures which can be ordered in conjunction with other sanctions at the various stages of criminal proceedings, either by the criminal court or by the public prosecutor. In the 2012 WODC survey[10] 14 such possibilities are described. The survey questions the need for some of these modalities. The most recent Dutch statute, which provides for a *judicial restraining order* (*Netherlands Law Gazette* 2011, 546), entered into force on 1 April 2012.[11] It offers the criminal court, when sentencing a person, the possibility to impose a restraining order, a no-contact order or a duty to report. Its purpose is to prevent a repetition of punishable offences or of violent behaviour towards victims or witnesses. Its maximum duration is two years. The order is immediately enforceable notwithstanding any appeal.

No statistics were found of restraining orders issued in the context of criminal proceedings.

c. In civil law, a restraining order can be obtained in *interim relief proceedings* in accordance with the relevant provisions of the Dutch Code of Civil Procedure. Proceedings are initiated by summons. The legal basis in civil law for action against domestic violence is tort. The case has to be brought by the victim. The victim must be represented by a solicitor. The person causing the risk may, but need not be represented. The application has to be justified by an urgent interest in obtaining relief. The judge may order any kind of provisional relief which is appropriate in the circumstances. Such relief is

---

8 See par. 6.

9 Centre for Research and Documentation of the Ministry of Security and Justice, survey entitled *Aard, omvang en handhaving van beschermingsbevelen in Nederland* (The nature, the extent and the enforcement of protection orders in the Netherlands), October 2012, with a summary in English. Hereinafter referred to as: 2012 WODC survey.

10 See also parliamentary document *TK* 2010–2011 (32 551) nr. 6, Annexes 1 and 2.

11 See P.W.S. Boer, "Het rechterlijk gebieds- of contactverbod", *Ars Aequi* 2012, pp. 665–668.

without prejudice to any judgment to be rendered in proceedings as to the merits. Since proceedings as to the merits are rarely lodged, the judgment is nearly always definitive. Although there is no statutory maximum duration, usually the order is issued for a specified period. The person against whom an order is issued by default of appearance, may lodge an appeal in fresh interim relief proceedings in which he himself is the plaintiff.

According to the 2012 WODC survey the annual number of protection orders issued in interim relief proceedings is between 450 and 500. There is little case law on such proceedings. The statistics seem to suggest that the administrative approach is a more adequate response to the problem of domestic violence than interim relief in civil law.

5. FACILITATING ACCESS TO LOCAL AUTHORITIES IN THE NETHERLANDS

It has been recognized that domestic violence is not easy to detect. It may take many years before victims decide to report.[12] Victims tend to conceal their problem for reasons of fear, shame, loyalty or dependence. This is why steps have been and are being taken to encourage victims or witnesses to report, so that adequate action can be taken. At the level of the regions, support offices have been set up and a national hotline is available to all those (victims or perpetrators) who wish to report domestic violence or who need help. When the support office is informed of domestic violence, a case manager is appointed. Depending on the circumstances, assistance is provided in various ways. Assistance is intended to help restore relationships within a family, prevent further violence and avoid criminal prosecution. It requires the involvement, not only of the victim, the perpetrator and their family, but possibly also of their social network.[13]

6. MONITORING COMPLIANCE WITH RESTRAINING ORDERS

The monitoring of compliance with criminal or administrative restraining orders primarily rests with the local police. In the case of administrative restraining orders, the police have the power, but are not obliged to do such monitoring. In

---

12 See H. Crum, "Huiselijk geweld samen geweldloos de baas", *Tijdschrift voor Herstelrecht* 2012, p. 50.

13 See J. van Lieshout, "Inzet voor herstel in sociale netwerken", *Tijdschrift voor Herstelrecht* 2012, pp. 32–48; H. Crum, article referred to in footnote 8.

practice police officers depend on the victim's or – to an even greater extent – the social workers' reporting non-compliance. The 2012 WODC survey stresses that a complete record of all occurrences and all the steps taken should be kept and that authorities and bodies involved must keep one another informed. A difficulty lies in the role of the local policemen, which nowadays is reduced to administering local affairs rather than guarding and maintaining contact with citizens. The lack of staff capacity within the police is a true obstacle to adequate action. The monitoring of compliance with restraining orders issued in interim relief proceedings is in the hands of the victim and/or the victim's lawyer.

7. ENFORCING AN ORDER IN THE EVENT OF NON-COMPLIANCE

Apart from the electronic bracelet (which is only used to enforce a criminal sentence) there are hardly any means to effectively enforce an order which prohibits a (potential) perpetrator of violence from being present in certain places. Compliance with a no-contact order – which by definition includes a prohibition from seeking contact by e-mail or telephone – is even more difficult to enforce. It is further complicated when the victim himself contacts the perpetrator. This frequently happens, although such infringement is punishable on the same ground as an infringement by the perpetrator.

As far as the enforcement of civil restraining orders is concerned, the judge may impose a non-compliance payment or determine that the judgment shall be enforced by civil imprisonment. Enforcement requires the services of a bailiff. The victim's lawyer controls the process. According to the 2012 WODC survey, when police assistance is used for the enforcement of civil orders, policemen tend to take their task less strictly than they do when enforcing criminal sentences. Effective enforcement is also hampered by the fact that many perpetrators of violence have no assets on which a non-compliance payment can be recovered. In the case of civil imprisonment, the victim is obliged to pay for the maintenance of the perpetrator during the period of the latter's imprisonment.

8. REGIONAL LEGISLATION

A. COUNCIL OF EUROPE

On 7 April 2011 the Council of Europe adopted a Convention on preventing and combating violence against women and domestic violence. It has so far been ratified by one State and signed by 24 States. It was signed by the Netherlands on

14 November 2012. The Convention imposes on governments of States parties the duty to provide for a comprehensive set of measures meant to help victims or prevent violence. These include setting up a helpline, laying down procedures for informing the police of violence, and granting the police adequate powers to expel perpetrators of violence from the house. The Convention defines a number of criminal offences, for example stalking, sexual harassment and psychological violence.

B. EUROPEAN UNION

In a Communication dated 18 May 2011, bearing the title "Strengthening victims' rights in the EU",[14] the European Commission announced a package of proposals intended to provide relief and support to victims when crimes have been committed against them. The first proposal was for a Directive establishing minimum standards on the rights, support and protection of victims of crime. This Directive was adopted on 4 October 2012 (OJ 14 November 2012, L 315).

Another proposal was for a Regulation on mutual recognition of protection measures in civil matters (COM (2011)276 final).[15] This Regulation is to complement the Directive on the European Protection Order, which was adopted in 2011 (Directive 2011/99/EU of 13 December 2011, OJ 21 December 2011, L 338). The initial proposal for the latter Directive, which was made by a number of Member States, included the recognition and enforcement of measures adopted in both criminal and civil matters. The idea of a combined instrument met with criticism in view of the legal basis chosen.[16] As adopted, the Directive purports to exclude measures adopted in civil matters. Conversely, the future Regulation is to exclude measures adopted in criminal matters, but is likely to specify that for the interpretation of the term "protection measures adopted in civil matters" the criminal, administrative or civil nature of the authority adopting a protection measure should not be relevant. It remains to be seen if the borderline between measures falling under one or the other instrument is clear enough.[17] Moreover, the question arises whether a temporary restraining order issued under the Dutch Act of 2009 (which Act is an instrument of administrative law) can be

14 COM(2011) 274 final.

15 The latest version is on www.consilium.europa.eu, General Approach adopted by the JHA Council on 7 December 2012, doc. 17165/12.

16 See H.-P. Mansel, K. Thorn and R. Wagner, "Europäisches Kollisionsrecht 2011: Gegenläufige Entwicklungen", *IPRax* 2012, pp. 8–9.

17 See Prel. Doc. No.7, par. 41, in particular footnote 106.

characterized as a "protection measure adopted in civil matters". In view of the aim of this statute, it would be desirable to answer this question in the affirmative.[18]

The Regulation will only deal with the recognition and enforcement of protection measures once they have been taken. It will contain no rule of direct jurisdiction. A protection measure ordered in a Member State will be recognized by operation of law on the basis of a certificate to be obtained by the protected person in the Member State of origin. The person causing the risk will, however, have the right to apply for non-recognition or non-enforcement of the protection measure before the courts of the State addressed. The Regulation will contain an exhaustive list of grounds of non-recognition. This solution may delay the process when protection is urgently required. The disadvantage of such delay may outweigh the advantage of enforceability of measures ordered under the new Regulation without the need for an *exequatur.*

The effects of recognition of a protection order will be limited to a six months' period following the issuing of the certificate, even if the duration of the protection measure was longer. Actual enforcement is left to the law of the Member State of enforcement. An open question is whether social assistance is offered in the State addressed and how such assistance is organized if not all the persons concerned are present in the requested State. Such assistance would make it necessary for the bodies concerned in both countries to consult each other and co-operate.

If it is accepted that a temporary restraining order issued by the burgomaster by virtue of the Dutch Act of 2009 is to be characterized as a "protection measure adopted in civil matters" and if further conditions are met, such an order will qualify for recognition or enforcement in another Member State under the future Regulation. A provisional restraining order obtained in interim relief proceedings will also qualify for recognition or enforcement.

9. FURTHER ISSUES OF ARTICULATION AND CLASSIFICATION AT EUROPEAN LEVEL

A. BRUSSELS I, DIVORCE AND CHILD PROTECTION

The articulation of the future Regulation with pre-existing instruments raises some further questions. The Explanatory Memorandum concerning the proposed Regulation explains that this instrument is to become a *lex specialis* in relation to the Brussels I Regulation, so that relevant provisions of the latter Regulation are inapplicable. This is to be welcomed.

[18] Arguments which support this view can be borrowed from EC Court rulings of 27 November 2007, C-435/06 and of 2 April 2009, C-523/07 (two Finnish cases).

Moreover, the Commission considers that a provision should be included to the effect that the future Regulation should not affect the operation of the Brussels II bis Regulation, since the latter's aim is to centralise all proceedings relating to a given divorce or legal separation. However, the question is to what extent Brussels II bis is affected at all. A protection measure ordered against the spouse or ex-spouse of a victim of violence is not within the scope of the Brussels II bis Regulation. It does not interfere with his or her status as a spouse or an ex-spouse. Consequently, protection orders concerning all couples, whether married or not, should be exclusively within the scope of the future Regulation.

The situation is different where orders are intended to protect children from violence by a parent. A restraining order against a parent does interfere with the exercise of the latter's right to contact with his children, as well as his children's right to contact with him. It may even affect the exercise of other elements of parental responsibility, such as the parents' joint obligation to discharge the tasks pertaining to the children's education or health. The Brussels II bis Regulation applies to measures in matters of parental responsibility and child protection. To a certain extent there may be concurrence between the new Regulation and Brussels II bis, unless the new Regulation provides otherwise.

Is it a good idea to exclude measures concerning parental responsibility and child protection altogether from the future Regulation? In practice the spouse and the children of a perpetrator of violence are often designated as protected persons in the same restraining order. Restraining orders may also be aimed to specifically protect a child. For practical reasons it would be appropriate to include all types of restraining orders in the scope of the future Regulation, so that the same regime for recognition and enforcement will apply irrespective of the persons to be protected from violence by one perpetrator. By contrast, any additional "classical" measures of child protection (e.g. the appointment of a supervising guardian, the child's placement in care, etc.) can better remain within the exclusive scope of Brussels II bis. Recognition or enforcement of such further measures in another country would require the involvement of child protection bodies in the country where the child is to reside. Such bodies should be duly authorized by their own authorities to take upon them the relevant tasks.[19] Under the Brussels II bis Regulation and the 1996 Convention, central authorities play a role in facilitating the cross-border "transfer" of tasks and responsibilities. The proposed Regulation as it stands does not set up an infrastructure for administrative co-operation. If classical measures of child protection were to be included in its scope, such complementary arrangements would be indispensable.

Practice so far has shown that there sometimes is a need for speedy action. This also applies to any "classical" measures of child protection to be taken in addition

[19] Explanatory report P. Lagarde to the 1996 Convention, par. 135.

to restraining orders. In view of this need, it may be appropriate to reconsider Article 20 Brussels II bis in the forthcoming review of that instrument. In fact, if a measure of child protection is ordered on the basis of Article 20 Brussels II bis by the courts of the Member State where the child is present (and not habitually resident), Brussels II bis does not afford recognition or enforcement of such a measure in another Member State.[20]

B. PROTECTION OF VULNERABLE ADULTS

Among the Dutch protection orders listed in the 2012 WODC survey are orders issued on the basis of the Act on Compulsory Admissions to Psychiatric Hospitals. If it is accepted that the subject matter of this statute is civil law, orders of this type are within the scope of the 2000 Hague Convention on the international protection of adults (by Council Resolution of 24 October 2008, EU Member States were invited to conclude as soon as possible domestic consultations on accession to the Convention and to begin as quickly as possible or to continue with procedures for its signature and/or ratification). If the future Regulation is to exclude child protection measures from its scope, logically it should also exclude measures of protection in respect of "adults who, by reason of an impairment or insufficiency of their personal faculties, are not in a position to protect their interests" (Article 1 of the Convention). There are, however, good reasons to include restraining orders in respect of such persons in the scope of the Regulation. Such inclusion would make it necessary to set up an infrastructure for international administrative co-operation.

10. A CASE FOR THE HAGUE CONFERENCE?

The likely origin of the Canadian proposal to include the topic of protection orders in the agenda of the Hague Conference is in the ongoing debate on the operation of the Article 13b defence under the 1980 Hague Child Abduction Convention, in the way it is commonly interpreted. Article 11, par. 4 of the Brussels II bis Regulation reflects that interpretation as it stipulates: "A court shall not refuse the return of a child on the basis of Article 13, sub b of the 1980 Hague Convention if it is established that adequate measures have been adopted with a view to ensuring the child's protection after its return". Article 13b mainly refers to measures taken or to be taken by the courts of the country where the child is to be returned (i.e. the country in which the child was habitually resident prior to the wrongful removal).

20 EU Court ruling of 15 July 2012, C-256/09 (*Purrucker*).

In principle there is no issue of recognition or enforcement here. However, there is some room left for the recognition and, as the case may be, enforcement of urgent measures of protection in respect of the child, ordered in the Contracting State where the child has been moved and is present. Such orders may be issued if the left-behind parent has (also) committed acts of violence in the State where the child is being retained. Unlike the provisions of Brussels II bis, the provisions on recognition and enforcement of the 1996 Hague Child Protection Convention apply to such urgent measures. If a specific instrument on civil restraining orders is drafted, there are valid arguments which militate in favour of excluding such orders from the scope of the 1996 Convention, but keeping "classical" measures of child protection within its exclusive scope.

Due attention should be given to further issues of articulation or concurrence with existing instruments, as identified in the case of the draft Regulation.

As explained, at the national level a co-ordinated multidisciplinary approach is taken to the problem of domestic violence. For the effectiveness of a PIL instrument it is important that adequate remedies should be available in criminal law in the States parties, as well as social assistance and counselling.

Moreover, account should be taken of the practical problems which arise in monitoring compliance with protection orders and enforcing them in the event of non-compliance. These problems are likely to be more acute where enforcing authorities are faced with a foreign protection order. In view of this, setting up an infrastructure for cross-border administrative co-operation among States parties may prove indispensable. If no consensus can be reached on the introduction of speedy mechanisms for recognition and enforcement, the added value of an instrument will be small.

Summarizing I would say that, considering the importance of the matter, the topic certainly deserves further consideration, but will have to be examined with the necessary care.

11. CONCLUSION

Without having exchanged views on the subject with Hans, I guess that he personally supports the idea of a Hague instrument in the field of domestic violence. In the thirty years of our very close collaboration, I have always been impressed by his commitment to tasks which, in some way or another, are related to the struggle against social evils. His tireless efforts are reflected in the Hague Conference's outstanding results in terms of "protective" Conventions which were achieved while he was in office and in the successful promotion of work on related topics, even in the remotest areas of the world. I am afraid that it will take Hans some time to settle for a more relaxed life. I warmly wish him a safe landing and many years of happiness.

PUBLIC POLICY IN PRIVATE INTERNATIONAL LAW AND ITS CONTINUING IMPORTANCE

Paul VLAS
Advocate General of the Dutch Supreme Court (Hoge Raad)
Professor of Private International Law and Comparative Law, Vrije Universiteit Amsterdam
President of the Dutch Standing Government Committee on Private International Law

1. INTRODUCTION

When in 1996 Hans van Loon succeeded the famous Georges Droz as Secretary General of the Hague Conference on Private International Law, he took charge of an organization which was more or less regional (European) oriented. Hans van Loon's efforts to transform the Hague Conference into a more global organization have been very successful. His 'marketing offensive'[1] has led to an expansive growth of the Members of the Hague Conference. Currently the Conference has 72 Members: 71 States and one Regional Economic Integration Organization, the European Union. The admittance of a Regional Economic Integration Organization as member of the Conference was made possible in 2005, when the Conference's Statute was revised. It is one of Hans van Loon's merits that at an early stage he realized the importance of the developments within the European Union (then the European Community) and tried to keep the European Union interested and involved in the work of the Hague Conference. By doing so, he acted in the spirit of Tobias Asser, one of the founding fathers of the Hague Conference. At the Commemorative Conference celebrating the 100th anniversary of the award of the Nobel Peace Prize to Tobias Asser, Hans van Loon delivered a

[1] Quote Rolf Wagner, *RabelsZ* (2009), p. 237.

speech on Asser's vision and considered whether the current Hague Conference can be considered to be Asser's legacy.[2] I quote from his contribution (p. 359):

> 'Asser was acutely aware, more than any others, of the continuing contradictions between the '*esprit d'internationalité*' and nationalistic tendencies, the latter of which became stronger during his lifetime. He constantly sought intelligent, pragmatic ways to bring these two forces into harmony'.

This description of Asser fits very well to Hans van Loon himself! Van Loon is always looking for pragmatic ways to harmonize the international spirit, being one of the fundamentals of the Hague Conference, and nationalistic tendencies. Possibly due to the economic crisis which the world is facing today, these tendencies are now more dominant than in 1996 when Hans van Loon took office. In his contribution to the commemoration of Asser's award of the Nobel Prize, Van Loon pointed out that in spite of Asser's efforts, the first Conventions adopted by the Hague Conference did not contain an exception for the fundamental norms and values of each participating State, the exception of public policy (*ordre public*). In my contribution to this Liber Amicorum in honour of Hans van Loon, I will discuss some provisions on public policy in recent international and regional instruments and the question whether there is still a need for such an exception in a globalising world.

2. PUBLIC POLICY IN THE INSTRUMENTS OF THE EUROPEAN UNION

Since 1996 there are an increasing number of instruments of the European Union dealing with aspects of private international law. In the EU instruments dealing with applicable law provisions on public policy can be found, viz. in Article 16 of the Rome I Regulation[3] on contractual obligations – the 'successor' of the 1980 Rome Convention on Contractual Obligations – and in Article 26 of the Rome II Regulation[4] on non-contractual obligations. Provisions on public policy can also be found in EU regulations regarding aspects of procedural law. The most important one in this respect is undoubtedly the Brussels I Regulation, which replaced the 1968 Brussels Convention on Jurisdiction and Enforcement of Judgments (as amended). In both instruments public policy is one of the grounds

---

2 *NIPR* 2012, pp. 358–361.
3 No. 593/2008, OJ 2008, L 177/6.
4 No. 864/2007, OJ 2007 L 199/40.

for refusal of the recognition and enforcement of a judgment given in a Member State.

According to Article 43 of the Brussels I Regulation, the grounds for refusal of recognition and enforcement of a judgment given in another Member State only come into consideration in the appeal proceedings against the decision on the application for a declaration of enforceability. In the first stage of the proceedings for obtaining a declaration of enforceability, the judgment shall be declared enforceable immediately on the completion of the formalities in Article 53 and without any review of the grounds for refusal as mentioned in Articles 34 and 35. Even if the court to which an application for enforceability is submitted is aware of the fact that the judgment which is to be recognized and enforced is manifestly contrary to the public policy of the Member State, the declaration of enforceability cannot be refused as long as the formalities of Article 53 have been met. The principle of mutual trust in the administration of justice of the European Union and its Member States is preponderant in this respect, as emphasized in recital 16 of the Preamble of the Brussels I Regulation, whereas recital 17 states that by virtue of the same principle of mutual trust, the procedure for making enforceable in one Member State a judgment given in another must be efficient and rapid. To that end, the declaration of enforceability should be issued virtually automatically after purely formal checks of the documents supplied, without there being any possibility for the court to raise, of its own motion, any of the grounds for non-enforcement provided for by this Regulation. Where according to the 1968 Brussels Convention public policy is applied by the courts in the stage of recognition and enforcement *ex officio* (see Articles 27 and 34 Brussels Convention), according to the Brussels I Regulation, the party against whom enforcement is sought will have to refer to public policy as a ground for refusal only in the stage of appeal proceedings (Article 45 Brussels I Regulation). Hence, the peculiar situation can exist that a judgment given in a Member State could be manifestly contrary to the public policy of the Member State where recognition and enforcement is sought, but nevertheless be declared enforceable due to the fact that the party against whom enforcement is sought did not lodge an appeal against the declaration of enforceability. Here the strive for an efficient and rapid procedure is more important than the consistency of the legal system where public policy is an instrument which can only be used in exceptional circumstances in order to protect the fundamental norms and values of the State addressed. In my view, public policy should not depend on the conduct of parties in legal proceedings. If a court of a Member State considers a judgment given in another Member State to be manifestly contrary to its public policy, recognition and enforcement of this judgment should be refused irrespective of the question whether the party against whom enforcement is sought would lodge an appeal and apply for this ground for refusal.

In December 2012 a recast of the Brussels I Regulation was accepted by the European Parliament and the Council[5] (hereinafter: Recast). The Recast gives some important changes compared to the present Brussels I Regulation. One of the amendments is the abolition of the enforcement order as provided for in the present Article 38 Brussels I Regulation. According to the Recast not only recognition of a judgment given in a Member State shall take place in the other Member States without any special procedure being required, but also the enforcement of such a judgment. A declaration of enforceability is no longer required (Article 39 Recast). The procedure for the enforcement of judgments given in another Member State shall be governed by the law of the Member State addressed (Article 41(1) Recast). However, according to Article 46 Recast the person against whom enforcement is sought can apply for the refusal of the enforcement in the Member State of enforcement. Enforcement shall be refused on one of the grounds referred to in Article 45 Recast, where mention is made of the refusal of recognition and enforcement 'if such recognition is manifestly contrary to the public policy (*ordre public*) in the Member State addressed'.

Although the Recast emphasizes the importance of mutual trust in the administration of justice of the European Union and therefore the importance of abolition of the enforcement order before the actual enforcement in the Member State addressed (see recital 26 of the Preamble of the Recast), abolishing public policy as a ground for refusal of recognition and enforcement was a bridge too far. Why? If there is a firm belief that the Member States of the European Union belong to the same European 'family' and that a judgment given in Paris should be enforceable in Berlin in the same way as it is enforceable in Marseille, why should there be a need for the exception of public policy? The answer is as simple as the question: because there is still no real mutual trust between the Member States, despite the solemn words used in the Preamble of the Recast. To a large extent this situation can be attributed to the lack of a unified legal system within the (expanding) European Union. As long as there are still important and major differences between the legal systems of the Member States and between the levels of administration of justice of the Member States – and this applies for procedural and substantive law as well – there will be a need for the exception of public policy as *ultimum remedium*, a safety pin in case of emergencies. If there was not any difference in the procedural and substantive law of the Member States of the European Union, this safety pin would no longer be needed. Even in this (utopian) situation, however, public policy might still be needed for particular procedural reasons. According to the case law of the European Court of Justice (ECJ), the Member States remain, in principle, free to determine, according to their own conceptions, what public policy requires. The limits of that conception

[5] No. 1215/2012, OJ 20 December 2012, L 351/1.

are a matter of interpretation, as the ECJ considered in respect of the 1968 Brussels Convention.[6] It is not for the ECJ 'to define the content of public policy of a Contracting State, it is none the less required to review the limits within which courts of a Contracting State may have recourse to that concept for the purpose of refusing recognition to a judgment emanating from a court in another Contracting State' (consideration 23). Therefore, the ECJ expressed that fundamental rights, as laid down in the European Convention on Human Rights, form an integral part of the general principles of law whose observance the ECJ ensures. The ECJ *held* that recourse to the public-policy clause:

> 'can be envisaged only where recognition or enforcement of the judgment delivered in another Contracting State would be at variance to an unacceptable degree with the legal order of the State in which enforcement is sought inasmuch as it infringes a fundamental principle. In order for the prohibition of any review of the foreign judgment as to its substance to be observed, the infringement would have to constitute a manifest breach of a rule of law regarded as essential in the legal order of the State in which enforcement is sought or of a right recognized as being fundamental within that legal order' (consideration 37).

In its judgment of 2 April 2009,[7] the ECJ confirmed what was considered in the *Krombach* judgment. Although these judgments were given under the 1968 Brussels Convention, undoubtedly the decisions will also apply under the Brussels I Regulation, also in view of the continuity existing between the two instruments. Therefore, the notion of public policy under the Recast is the same as set out by the ECJ in its case law.

Where procedural public policy may come into operation from time to time, application of substantive public policy is rare under the Brussels I Regulation. This is not only due to the fact that a difference in the legislation of the Member States cannot be a ground for application of public policy, but is also due to the fact that such an application would be contrary to the fundamental principle of the Brussels I Regulation (as it also was under the 1968 Brussels Convention) that there is no review of the merits of the case (no 'révision au fond' as provided in Article 36 Brussels I Regulation). To my knowledge, substantive public policy has never been used in Dutch case law as a ground for refusal of recognition and enforcement in the context of the Brussels Convention and the Brussels I Regulation. In 1991 Hans van Loon, being then first secretary at the Permanent Bureau, already noticed this situation in his report on the application of the

[6] Case C-7/98, [2000] ECR I-1935 *Krombach v. Bamberski.*
[7] Case C-394/07, [2009] ECR I-2563] *Gambazzi.*

Brussels Convention in the Netherlands.[8] Today, 22 years later nothing has changed in this respect.

3. PUBLIC POLICY IN THE INSTRUMENTS OF THE HAGUE CONFERENCE

Where unification of (private) law is lacking, there is a need for a public policy provision in instruments regarding private international law. After the Second World War it became standard practice that the conventions of the Hague Conference contain a public policy clause. An exception is the Convention on Civil Procedure of 1 March 1954, in which no provision on public policy is to be found, but this omission does not prevent courts of States party to the 1954 Convention applying the exception of public policy if this is determined to be appropriate in the circumstances of the case, as the Dutch Supreme Court (*Hoge Raad*) decided in its judgment of 10 September 1999.[9]

In this case recognition and enforcement of two Argentine judgments was sought in the Netherlands. An Argentine court had fixed a huge amount of money to be paid by a Dutch company to Argentine experts for their work done in Argentine legal proceedings. The Dutch company alleged that it was not informed about the proceedings before the Argentine court or about the judgments rendered. The District Court of Rotterdam allowed recognition and enforcement of the Argentine judgments according to Articles 18 and 19 of the 1954 Convention on Civil Procedure. On appeal in cassation the Dutch company contended that the enforcement of the Argentine judgments would be contrary to the public policy (of the Netherlands), as the company did not know of the proceedings in Argentina. Hence, the fundamental principle of fair trial was violated. According to the Supreme Court, it has to be assumed that Articles 18 and 19 of the 1954 Convention 'do[es] not apply if the foreign judgments concerning legal costs proved to be rendered with obvious disregard of legal principles which are considered fundamental to the legal system of the Contracting State of enforcement'. The Supreme Court quashed the lower court's judgment and decided that the District Court had to verify whether the Dutch company was ignorant of the proceedings in Argentina. The Supreme Court did not specify whether the application of the exception of public policy in the context of the 1954 Convention, in spite of its silence, was consistent with Article 31 of the Vienna Convention on the Law of Treaties. Is it perhaps a matter of 'subsequent practice'

---

8 See his contribution, "L'application pratique de la Convention aux Pays-Bas", *Gazette du Palais* 2 and 3 January 1991.

9 *Nederlandse Jurisprudentie* 2001/41.

within the meaning of Article 31(3)(b) of the Vienna Convention? In my view the inclusion of a provision regarding public policy in conventions of the Hague Conference is now common practice and it is beyond doubt that this exception is applied even if there is a convention (like the 1954 Convention) which does not contain a public policy provision. Such an application is in accordance with the interpretation rules of the Vienna Convention.

In the procedure before the Dutch Supreme Court the Dutch company contended that the amount fixed by the Argentine courts was exorbitant due to the financial measures on 'dollarization' taken in 1991 by the Argentine government to reduce inflation (*Ley de Convertibilidad* 1991) and therefore in violation of Dutch public policy. The Supreme Court did not pay attention to this contention. The question whether a judgment is contrary to the public policy of the State addressed because of the fact that the awarded amount is exorbitant, is closely connected with the merits of the case which cannot be reviewed in the stage of recognition and enforcement of judgments. However, if in the case reported the Argentine courts had informed the Dutch company of the legal proceedings pending in Argentina, should the judgment granting exorbitant costs then be recognized and enforced in the Netherlands? Or should recognition and enforcement be refused on the ground that the money judgment on legal costs is contrary to the public policy, since the exorbitant amount is due to the 'dollarization' of the Argentine peso? I am not convinced that public policy is not at stake in this situation. The same problem arises if a judgment awards punitive damages. Should the recognition and enforcement of such a judgment be refused on the basis of violation of the public policy of the State addressed, or is it also a matter of the merits of the case, which cannot be reviewed? A solution for this problem can be found in the Hague Convention on Choice of Court Agreements of 30 June 2005. Article 11(1) of the 2005 Convention states that recognition and enforcement of a judgment may be refused 'if, and to the extent that, the judgment awards damages, including exemplary or punitive damages, that do not compensate a party for actual loss or harm suffered'.[10] Applying this rule in the analogous situation of the Argentine judgments relating to expert costs, one could contend that recognition and enforcement should take place only to the extent that the costs compensate for the work done by the experts and therefore not for the 'dollarization' of the Argentine peso.

During the last 60 years the provisions on public policy in the conventions of the Hague Conference have evolved. In the 1956 Convention on the Recognition of Foreign Legal Persons public policy is used to set aside the provisions of the Convention (see Article 8: '(...) l'application des dispositions de la présente

10 See on this provision the Hartley/Dogauchi Report, *Actes et Documents*, Twentieth Session (2005), Tome III, p. 835.

Convention peut être écartée pour un motif d'ordre public'). In modern Hague Conventions always the same wording is chosen for the public policy clause, see for example Article 22(a) of the 2007 Hague Convention on the International Recovery of Child Support, stating that recognition and enforcement of a decision may be refused if '(a) recognition and enforcement of the decision is manifestly incompatible with the public policy ("*ordre public*") of the State addressed' and Article 13 of the 2007 Protocol on the Law Applicable to Maintenance Obligations ('The application of the law determined under the Protocol may be refused only to the extent that its effects would be manifestly contrary to the public policy of the forum'). Also the recent Draft Hague Principles as approved by the November 2012 Special Commission Meeting on Choice of Law in International Contracts contain a provision concerning public policy in Article 11(3): 'A court may only exclude application of a provision of the law chosen by the parties if and to the extent that the result of such application would be manifestly incompatible with fundamental notions of public policy (*ordre public*) of the forum'. Perhaps the latter wording is not very accurate, because public policy always concerns fundamental notions of the forum. I would prefer the standard wording as used in most Hague Conventions ('manifestly contrary to the public policy of the forum'), but this is probably a matter of drafting. The 2012 Draft Hague Principles show a common understanding that there is still a need for a public policy provision in global instruments.

It is also common understanding that public policy may only be used in exceptional circumstances as *ultimum remedium* in order to protect the norms and values of the State. However, the notion of public policy differs from State to State and from time to time. What is considered to be acceptable in the legal system of one State, can be unacceptable according to the norms and values of another State. In this respect the acceptance of same sex marriages is a good example. Where certain (European) countries, the Netherlands included, accepted same sex marriages already a decade ago, other countries find these marriages unacceptable and contrary to their public policy. What was unacceptable in the past, can be acceptable in the future. Here the cultural, ethical, religious and economic differences between the various States lead to a difference in the use of the notion of public policy. These differences between legal systems will remain and, hence, the differences in appreciation and application of public policy. However, in most legal systems some common notions of public policy can be found. Notions taken from international conventions on the protection of human rights, such as the European Human Rights Convention and the International Covenant on Civil and Political Rights, can form a common ground for the use of public policy. It is clear that discrimination is unacceptable and that, for instance, a court decision given in violation of the principle of fair trial can be refused by applying the public policy exception. If the decision is rendered in legal proceedings without giving notice to the defendant, recognition and enforcement of this judgment shall be refused for reasons of public policy, as we have seen in the case of the Argentine judgments concerning expert costs. The same applies if the defendant, although given notice of the proceedings, was not given an opportunity to defend his case before the court. These situations are *manifestly* contrary to the public policy.

It is interesting to note that the wording of the public policy provision as used in the Hague Conventions, stood as a model for the wording of the public policy provision in national codifications of private international law. This was, for instance, the case in the Netherlands. In Article 6 of Book 10 of the Dutch Civil Code the provision on public policy can be found regarding the applicable law. Article 6 states that 'foreign law shall not be applied, if its application is manifestly contrary to the public policy'. Book 10 of the Dutch Civil Code[11] came into force on 1 January 2012 and is the end of a long road towards codification of Dutch conflict of laws.

4. CONCLUSION: 'AVEC PATIENCE ET COURAGE'

Public policy can certainly undermine the co-operation between the Parties to a convention. If a State would consider its whole legal system (procedural and substantive law) to consist of public policy, such a State could never be party to any convention. It would always apply its own law and would act against the *'esprit d'internationalité'* which should be prevalent between States. If States want to create a harmonious, peaceful and prosperous world, they have to co-operate and strive for consensus. In the Hague Conference, States are working together to fulfil the aim of the Conference: a progressive unification of the rules of private international law. In this co-operation States have to take into account and respect each other's (legal) views. To some extent public policy is necessary to bridge the differences between the legal systems of the Member States and to make the instruments of the Hague Conference a success. Without public policy as a safety pin, States would be very reluctant to participate in the negotiations and in concluding new conventions. Following his years as Secretary General of the Hague Conference, Hans van Loon knows more than anyone the pitfalls and difficulties in international negotiations. In his work Hans van Loon has, as his illustrious fellow-countryman Tobias Asser, showed courage and patience in striving for a better world and for unification of the rules of private international law.

---

[11] Act of 19 May 2011, *Staatsblad* 2011/272.

THE WORLD WAR II DISTOMO MASSACRE OF GREEK CIVILIANS BY GERMAN ARMED FORCES AND THE RIGHT TO EFFECTIVE JUDICIAL PROTECTION

Prof. em. Dr., Dr.h.c. Spyridon VRELLIS
Director of the Hellenic Institute of International and Foreign Law

I. INTRODUCTION

During the German occupation of Greece in World War II, German armed forces committed, in various parts of the country, brutal massacres involving innocent civilians. Perhaps the most widely known case is that of Distomo, a small village near Delphi.

On 10 June 1944, Gestapo members and the SS of Livadia disguised 20 German soldiers in Greek uniforms and, followed by other German soldiers, started towards Arachova. On their way, they shot and killed every Greek man in their path. At noon they arrived in Distomo, and started to pillage. Afterwards they were directed to the village of Stiri. On their way to Stiri the German soldiers disguised as Greeks and their Greek guides were ambushed by Greek partisans, who killed 18 Germans and one of the Greek guides. In order to take revenge, the Germans returned to Distomo, surrounded the village, executed 12 civilians who were being kept as hostages, ordered the inhabitants to remain in their houses while putting guards at the exits, and, divided into groups, started a systematic massacre in each house–torturing and killing everybody, raping, slaughtering the elderly, stabbing pregnant women, and bayoneting babies in cribs. All inhabitants who were inside the village surrounded by the German armed forces, in total 218 villagers (men, women and children), were murdered, after having been cruelly tortured.

Germany did not pay any compensation for the damage the victims had suffered. Neither Greece nor Germany seemed to be disposed to proceed to negotiations for that purpose (Greece because it could not, Germany because it did not want to). The victims were left abandoned by both countries to their fate.

After having waited in vain for a long time, relatives of the victims started proceedings in 1995 against Germany, bringing claims before Greek Courts.

Leaving aside some particular procedural points, it suffices to say that the Court of First Instance of Livadia rendered a judgment in default (No. 137/1997) against Germany (which didn't appear before the court, although the claim was served on it regularly and lawfully in conformity with the 1965 Hague Service Convention), refusing immunity, and awarding damages to the successors in title of the victims of the massacre, for the moral pain they suffered because of the death of their relatives. Germany brought no appeal against this judgment, but addressed a petition for cassation directly before the Greek Supreme Court (the *Areios Pagos*). The *Areios Pagos* in Plenary (No. 11/2000) dismissed by majority the arguments of Germany (which argued a lack of jurisdiction of the Greek Courts), and confirmed the conclusion of the Court of First Instance.

The claimants tried to enforce the judgment. A judgment against a foreign State, in order to be enforced in Greece, needs permission from the Minister of Justice (Article 923 of the Greek Code of Civil Procedure). The claimants in the *Distomo* case made the relevant application to the Greek Minister of Justice, but received no reply. So the judgment against Germany was not enforced in Greece, as the enforcement proceedings have been stayed by court decisions, because of lack of ministerial permission.

The claimants subsequently brought proceedings against Greece and Germany before the European Court of Human Rights (ECHR), alleging that by refusing to comply with the decision of the Court of First Instance of Livadia (in the case of Germany) and by failing to permit execution of that decision (in the case of Greece), both countries had violated Article 6 § 1 of the Convention for the Protection of Human Rights and Fundamental Freedoms, which provides that "[i]n the determination of his civil rights and obligations [...], everyone is entitled to a fair [...] hearing [...] by an [...] impartial tribunal [...]", and Article 1 of Protocol No. 1, which provides for the peaceful enjoyment of possessions. In its decision of 12 December 2002 in *Kalogeropoulou and others v. Greece and Germany* (Application No. 59021/00), the ECHR [1st Section] declared, by majority concerning Greece, and unanimously concerning Germany, the claimants' application inadmissible, because neither Article 6 of the Convention for the Protection of Human Rights and Fundamental Freedoms nor Article 1 of Protocol No. 1 had been violated. There are serious doubts about the legal and moral correctness of that judgment.

The following text, which is cordially dedicated to the distinguished Secretary General of the Hague Conference on Private International Law, will be necessarily restricted to some aspects only of the reasoning of that decision.

It will not deal with the complaint regarding alleged lack of impartiality on the part of the President of the Greek *Areios Pagos*, or with the complaint regarding Germany (which refers to the question of whether or not the persons concerned were within Germany's jurisdiction according to the meaning of Article 1 of the Convention).

II. THE RIGHT OF ACCESS TO A TRIBUNAL AND ITS LIMITATIONS

A. CRITERIA OF COMPATIBILITY WITH ARTICLE 6 § 1

What infringed Article 6 § 1 of the Convention, according to the applicants, was the refusal of Greece to comply with the judgment of the Court of First Instance of Livadia, approved by *Areios Pagos*, by granting Germany immunity from enforcement of the judgment.

The ECHR stated that this position of the Greek State "amounted to a restriction imposed on the applicants' right of access to a tribunal". But the Court elaborated further that the right of access to the courts is not absolute. It may be subject to limitations.

According to consistent case law of the Court, to be compatible with Article 6 § 1, limitations must satisfy some criteria. The first criterion is a general one, and bears on the extreme limit of any limitation: "it must be satisfied [...] that the limitations applied do not restrict or reduce the access left to the individual in such a way or to such an extent that the very essence of the right is impaired". The second criterion is more specific: the limitation must pursue a legitimate aim. According to the third criterion, there must be "a reasonable relationship of proportionality between the means employed and the aim sought to be achieved".

Nevertheless, one can discern some confusion regarding the above criteria. Could the first criterion be considered as identical to the third one? If this is not the case, and if the first criterion is an additional, autonomous, independent and the most important in relation with the others (and in particular with the third criterion), then the satisfaction of the requirements of a legitimate aim and of proportionality does not necessarily mean that the very essence of the right to access to the courts is not impaired. Consequently the Court should not have restricted itself to tests of legitimate aim and of proportionality, as it actually did, but it should have proceeded further to the determination whether, despite a legitimate aim and proportionality, the very essence of the right of access to the courts was impaired.

It appears that the Court actually ignored or put aside the first criterion, and that it contented itself with the latter two tests. Therefore, it proceeded in the present case to the examination of: (1) whether the restriction "pursued a legitimate aim"; and, (2) whether there is a reasonable relationship of proportionality.

B. THE TWO TESTS APPROACH

1. *Legitimate aim*

The ECHR considered, as it usually does (*e.g.*, *Cudak v. Lithuania* [GC], No. 15869/02 (Judgment of 23 March 2010) (§ 60)), that "the grant of sovereign immunity to a State in civil proceedings pursues the legitimate aim of complying with international law to promote comity and good relations between States [...]".

This may be true, but only from a general and abstract point of view. What is legitimate in general may not be legitimate under specific circumstances. In particular, immunity "[...] has certainly never been intended, by its invocation, to except jurisdiction on, and to cover-up, international crimes, let alone atrocities or grave violations of human rights or of international humanitarian law. It has certainly never been intended to exclude reparations to victims of such atrocities or grave violations".[1] The so-called principle of State immunity (immunity from jurisdiction or from execution), although it appears dubious enough as to whether State immunity constitutes a *principle*, since it is an exception from the fundamental principle of States' jurisdiction, is not absolute. The ECHR itself recognised in *Cudak v. Lithuania* (§ 64), that "the application of absolute State immunity has, for many years, clearly been eroded". The most important (but not unique) restriction of the State immunity privilege regards the *acta jure gestionis*, *i.e.* acts of private law, of a transactional nature, where the foreign State behaves as a fiscus. Another (more recent) restriction regards employment related disputes. Furthermore, there are many, quite clear trends showing that State immunity may not be granted:

(i) When damage is caused in the territory of the forum State (*i.e.* before the courts of which the claim of the injured person is brought), by foreign armed forces being in the territory of that State at the time of the occurrence of the injurious event.

See, *e.g.*, Article 11 of the European Convention on State Immunity done at Basle on 16 May 1972; Article 12 of the then Draft United Nations Convention on the Jurisdictional Immunities of States and Their Property, International Law Commission (1978), which at the time of the *Kalogeropoulou* case was pending before the Legal Committee of the General Assembly and which later became

[1] Judge Cançado Trindade, dissenting (§ 166) in *Jurisdictional Immunities of the State (Germany v. Italy: Greece intervening), I.C.J.* 3 February 2012.

the United Nations Convention on Jurisdictional Immunities of States and Their Property, adopted by the General Assembly on 2 December 2004. Though not yet entered into force, this Convention certainly strengthens the trend towards the creation of a customary international law with relevant content.[2] Further, the domestic law of various Countries, like the U.S.A [*28 U.S.C.* Par. 1605(a)(5), *Foreign Sovereign Immunities Act*], the United Kingdom [*State Immunity Act 1978* (1. 5)] and others, provides that State immunity does not cover proceedings against them for offenses committed on the territory of the forum State. In the same direction is the Resolution of the Institute of International Law on contemporary problems concerning the immunity of States in relation to questions of jurisdiction and enforcement, Article 2 § 2(e) (adopted at its Basle session in 1991), as well as the *Projet de règlement international sur la compétence des tribunaux dans les procès contre les Etats, souverains ou chefs d'Etat étrangers*, Article 4 (adopted by the same Institute at its Hamburg session in 1891).

(ii) Immunity may also not be granted when the State's behaviour infringes rules of international *jus cogens*, such as the rules regarding grave crimes against humanity committed by a State's armed forces, during the occupation of a foreign territory, in that territory. Judges Rozakis and Caflish, joined by Judges Wildhaber, Costa, Cabral Barreto, and Vajić dissenting (§ 3) in *Al-Adsani v. The United Kingdom* [GC], No. 35763/97, ECHR 21 November 2001, correctly supported, that the acceptance of the *jus cogens* nature of the prohibition of torture "entails that a State allegedly violating it cannot invoke hierarchically lower rules (in this case, those on State immunity) to avoid the consequences of the illegality of its actions". To invoke immunity for acts contrary to international *jus cogens* constitutes, further, an abuse of right, which may ground an exemption from immunity.

Various reasons have been advanced in favour of this exemption from State immunity by the Court of First Instance of Livadia (No. 137/1997). *(i)* Acts contrary to international *jus cogens* are invalid and cannot constitute a source of legal rights, like that of immunity (according to the general principle of law, *ex injuria jus non oritur*). *(ii)* The recognition of immunity for acts violating international *jus cogens* is equal to complicity of the domestic Court with an act which is disapproved by the international legal order. *(iii)* Taking into account that the principle of territorial sovereignty is superior in comparison with the "principle" of immunity, a State which offends that superior principle in illicitly occupying a foreign territory, cannot invoke immunity for acts committed during the illicit occupation. *(iv)* Acts of a State contrary to international *jus cogens* do not have the character of sovereign acts. In such cases the defendant State

2 Cf. e.g. Judges Caflish, Cabral Barreto and Vajić dissenting, in *McElhinney v. Ireland* [GC], No. 31253/96, ECHR 21 November 2001.

is considered as not having acted in the frame of its sovereignty. Such acts are sometimes considered as committed not *jure imperii* but simply *jure gestionis*, since they neither were part of the public power of the occupant nor constituted a necessary consequence of the public character of the war occupation.

In my opinion these acts are neither *acta jure imperii* nor *acta jure gestionis*. Judge Cançado Trindade, dissenting in *I.C.J.* 3 February 2012, named them *delicta imperii*. Actually they are acts that are beyond any concept of State sovereignty. Sovereignty does not mean arbitrariness; nor does it mean brutality. Sovereign acts may be contrary to the law; they may even be criminal. They remain nevertheless inside the limits of the behaviour imposed by the participation of a State in the international community. But if these limits are overstepped, if we are beyond any conceivable area of conformity of the obligations of a State emanating from being a member of the international community, then such acts of the State cannot be considered as an exercise of its sovereignty. These thoughts lead to the conclusion that any possibility of immunity should be excluded in such cases.

However, the Court did "not find it established [...] that there is yet acceptance in international law of the proposition that States are not entitled to immunity in respect of civil claims for damages brought against them in another State for crimes against humanity". It referred to its former judgment of 21 November 2001 in *Al-Adsani* (rendered by a majority of nine members against eight), although the facts in that case, as well as in *McElhinney v. Ireland* [GC], no. 31253/96, were far from being comparable with the hideous atrocities perpetrated by the German Armed Forces in *Distomo*,[3] and added that "this is true at least as regards the current rule of public international law, [...] but does not preclude a development in customary international law in the future".

Judge Cançado Trindade, dissenting (§ 297) in *Jurisdictional Immunities of the State (Germany v. Italy: Greece intervening)*, has correctly remarked, that "[i]t is high time to give *jus cogens* the attention it requires and deserves. Its deconstruction, as in the present case, is to the detriment not only of the individual victims of grave violations of human rights and of international humanitarian law, but also of contemporary international law itself".

The above trends (i–ii) have been ignored by the ECHR, which did not proceed, when examining the legitimate aim test, to undertake careful research regarding the existence in international law of such restrictions of State immunity. If such restrictions on State immunity exist, then the refusal to permit enforcement in Greece of the judgments of Greek Courts in this case would not pursue a legitimate aim.

[3] The facts in *Al-Adsani* as well as in *McElhinney* were stated in detail by the Court; on the contrary, the atrocities at Distomo were not even mentioned in *Kalogeropoulou*.

It's worth recalling that the conclusion of the Court in *Kalogeropoulou* was already adopted about one year earlier in *Al-Adsani* (§§ 61–67) (by a vote of 9 to 8), as well as in *Arrest Warrant of 11 April 2000 (Democratic Republic of the Congo* v. *Belgium), Judgment of 14 February 2002, I.C.J. Reports 2002, p. 3 (§ 58)*. It must be noted however, that in *Al-Adsani* as well as in *Congo v. Belgium*, the criminal acts (torture and war crimes respectively) were committed in the defendant State (Kuwait and Congo respectively) and not in the forum State (*i.e.* the United Kingdom or Belgium respectively), a fact that greatly distinguishes those cases from the Greek victims in *Distomo* or elsewhere in Greece.

Regardless, the legitimate aim test is not sufficient. A measure might be grounded on a legal provision; but this very legal provision may not be compatible with the respect owed to human rights. Therefore the proportionality test is necessary as well.

2. *The proportionality test*

In examining whether the refusal of allowing enforcement of the Greek judgments in Greece against Germany's property situated in Greece, the ECHR considered (again in an abstract way, repeating its reasoning in *McElhinney* (§ 37) and in *Al-Adsani* (§ 56)], that "measures taken by a High Contracting Party which reflect generally recognised rules of public international law on State immunity cannot generally be regarded as imposing a disproportionate restriction on the right of access to a court as embodied in Article 6 § 1. Just as the right of access to a court is an inherent part of the fair trial guarantee in that Article, so some restrictions on access must likewise be regarded as inherent, an example being those limitations generally accepted by the community of nations as part of the doctrine of State immunity".[4]

The Court wrongfully confused two different things: the legitimate aim of a measure and its proportionality to the restriction of the right of access to a tribunal. Although a measure is likely to have a legitimate aim, it may however excessively restrict the right to have access to a tribunal or even to frustrate it completely, so that the very essence of Article 6 § 1 be impaired. Actually the Court did not proceed to the proportionality test, as it considered the restriction of the right of access to a court, caused by granting immunity, as an inherent part of the fair trial guarantee of Article 6 § 1. It should however proceed to it, and examine analytically the specific circumstances of the case, as it does in other cases.[5] If the Court had submitted the circumstances of the case to the proportionality

4 This reasoning is used in subsequent cases as well; *e.g. Cudak v. Lithuania* (§ 57).

5 See e.g., *Waite and Kennedy v. Germany* [GC], No. 26083/94, Judgment of 18 February 1999 (§§ 64 ff.); *Cudak v. Lithuania* (§§ 70 ff.).

test, it would have certainly found that it had not been satisfied, all the more as the victims had no alternative means to obtain reparations. Judge Loucaides is right in stating in his dissenting opinions in *Al-Adsani* and in *McElhinney*, that "[a]ny form of blanket immunity, whether based on international law or national law, which is applied by a court in order to block completely the judicial determination of a civil right without balancing the competing interests, namely those connected with the particular immunity and those relating to the nature of the specific claim which is the subject matter of the relevant proceedings, is a disproportionate limitation on Article 6 § 1 of the Convention and for that reason it amounts to a violation of that Article".

The Court concluded that "the Minister of Justice's refusal to give the applicants leave to apply for expropriation of certain German property situated in Greece cannot be regarded as an *unjustified interference* with their right of access to a tribunal, *particularly as it was examined by the domestic courts and confirmed by a judgment of the Greek Court of Cassation*" [emphasis added]. Two remarks must be made on this point.

First remark: The real problem is not whether interference with the right of access to a tribunal is justified or unjustified. The real problem is whether this interference (which might be *justified*, in the sense that it could be provided by a legal provision) has a reasonable relationship of proportionality. And on that very point the Court has not offered any vindication of its conclusion. A crucial question, although it remains sometimes unclear, is, between which matters a relationship of proportionality must exist. One is obviously the means employed and leading to the restriction of the right of access to a tribunal; in our case, the granting of immunity to Germany. The second matter might be the legitimate aim pursued by the concrete measure (by the granting of immunity), which restricts the said fundamental right. Such a position, which seems to be that of the Court in *Kalogeropoulou*, and which has been adopted in *Fayed v. The United Kingdom* (No. 17101/90) (§ 71), where it considered in its judgment of 21 September 1990 that it has to be determined "whether in the circumstances of the particular case there was a reasonable relationship of proportionality between the means employed and the legitimate objectives pursued by the contested limitation", appears quite odd. The aim of the measure is inherent in the measure. We cannot ponder the measure with its aim. We may think at most that we should examine the suitability (or the degree of suitability) of the measure for the realisation of its goal. That goal is securing good relations between States, by granting State immunity (provided that it is legal, which is dubious under the circumstances of the crimes against humanity committed by German armed forces in the occupied Greek territory). However, these very relations between the occupying and the occupied State have to be considered as unsettled, even if not broken off by the unlawful occupation and by the crimes committed,[6] such that refusing immunity would not add anything to the already assumed "bad" relations.

In any case, such an understanding of the proportionality test omits consideration of the main matter. The main matter is the infringement of the fundamental human right of access to a tribunal. This right is limited by the concrete measure. So the real question is whether and to what extent we must tolerate a restriction, in order to satisfy another (hypothetically important) interest. Consequently the proportionality has to be examined between the importance of the aim of the means (granting immunity in order to secure good relations between States) and the extent of the tolerable restriction of the right of access to a tribunal (taking into account the importance of the restricted fundamental human right). The relevant conclusion has to be formed after consideration of the particular circumstances of the case and the relative importance of both aims, *i.e.* the aim of the restricting measure and the aim of the restricted human right. On the last point it must be stressed that the importance or the value of the right of access to a tribunal is far higher than the importance of granting immunity to a State, since the protection of human rights belongs to the international *ius cogens*, while State immunity does not. Regarding the particular circumstances, it should also be taken into account that the specific case had to do on the one hand with securing good relations between an occupying State which perpetrated odious crimes against innocent civilians of the occupied State, and this latter State; and, on the other hand, with denying the essence of the right to access to a court, since any other possibility for the victims to obtain reparation for the losses they suffered was in fact excluded. In *Waite and Kennedy v. Germany* [GC], No. 26083/94 (Judgment of 18 February 1999, § 68) the ECHR considered that for it "a material factor in determining whether granting [...] immunity [...] is permissible under the Convention, is whether the applicants had available to them reasonable alternative means to protect effectively their rights under the Convention". If in *Kalogeropoulou* the Court had taken into account the lack of real (not illusory) and effective (not purely theoretical) alternative means, it should have declared that granting immunity to Germany would impair the essence of the right to a court of the *Distomo* victims, or that it would mean a disproportionate limitation on their access to the Greek courts for the purposes of Article 6 § 1 of the Convention. Unfortunately the ECHR proved itself unable

6 H. Muir Watt, "Les droits fondamentaux devant les juges nationaux à l'épreuve des immunités juridictionnelles – À propos de l'arrêt de la Cour internationale de justice, immunités juridictionnelles de l'État (*Allemagne c/ Italie* [Grèce intervenant]), du 3 février 2012", *Rev. crit. DIP* 2012 552, puts the crucial question: «Quelle est la véritable cause de l'instabilité de l'ordre international : les actions individuelles en réparation ou les crimes qu'elles cherchent à faire sanctionner ?».

to analytically examine and state the circumstances of the case and to analyse correctly the elements between which a relationship of proportionality must exist.

Second remark: What does the last part of the above phrase, when referring to the examination by domestic courts and the confirmation by the *Areios Pagos* of the refusal to permit enforcement in Greece, really mean? Could it really add a ground to the Court's conclusion that there is not an unjustified interference with the right of access to a tribunal? Let us assume that there was such an unjustified interference. Does the fact that Greek courts confirmed the measure justify it? Absolutely not. In confirming (in some way) the ministerial refusal of enforcement, which constitutes an infringement of Article 6 § 1, the Greek Courts (the *Areios Pagos* included) were complicit in this infringement, or they brought it to completion.

III. ARTICLE 1 OF PROTOCOL NO. 1 AND THE PROPORTIONALITY TEST

Regarding the complaints of the applicants under Article 1 of Protocol No. 1 (peaceful enjoyment of possessions) the ECHR examined whether there was a reasonable relationship of proportionality between the means employed and the aim pursued by any measure depriving a person of his possessions. It referred to its conclusion regarding Article 6, and considered further: (i) that "the applicants could not have been unaware of the risk they were taking in bringing enforcement proceedings against the German State without first obtaining the consent of the Minister of Justice"; and (ii) that, having regard to Article 923 Greek Code of Civil Procedure, "their only realistic hope was that Germany would pay the amounts determined by the *Livadia* Court of First Instance of its own accord". The Court added that (iii) "the applicants have not lost the debt owed them by Germany. [...T]hey might be able to enforce it later, at a more appropriate time, or in another country, such as Germany". Regarding this reasoning, three remarks are necessary.

(i) I believe that, contrary to what the Court assumes, the hope that "Germany would pay the amounts determined by the *Livadia* Court of First Instance of its own accord", is not realistic at all. If Germany had the intention of paying compensation to the victims of the massacres perpetrated by its armed forces, it did not need a Court decision to do so. It should have already proceeded to arrangements to fulfil its duties, since otherwise it would risk being considered as approving, tolerating or maintaining without consequences the crimes previously committed by its army. To orally express regret for those crimes (which were, we must not forget, beyond any concept of human behaviour), as Germany did before the International Court of Justice, in *Jurisdictional Immunities of the State*

(*Germany v. Italy: Greece intervening*), does not suffice. Oral repentance not accompanied by acts of repentance is of no value, moral or legal.

(ii) When the Court considered that "by instituting enforcement proceedings, the applicants must have known that, without the prior consent of the Minister of Justice, their application was bound to fail" and that "the situation could not therefore reasonably have founded any legitimate expectation on their part of being able to recover their debt [...]", it appears to think that the protection of the individuals according to Article 1 of the Protocol No. 1 presupposes a reasonable expectation on their part of enforcing the judgment ordering the payment of damages to them. Even if this were true (while it certainly is not, since that additional condition for the applicability of the Protocol does not exist), such a reasonable expectation cannot be excluded by the existence of legal rules in domestic law dissuading the victims from expecting reparation (*e.g.* of Article 923 Greek Code of Civil Procedure), precisely because such rules may *in concreto* be contrary to the Convention. So the reasoning of the Court on this point is completely irrelevant.

(iii) In the Greek government's submissions, it has been pointed out "that the refusal to enforce the judgment was not absolute and that although it could not be enforced in Greece, it could, however, be enforced in Germany". The Court followed in its reasoning a similar way of thinking. Both the Court and Greek government, have been proven wrong. (a) The attempt of the victims to enforce the Greek judgment in Italy failed; (b) their claim for compensation brought before the German Courts has been rejected; and (c) any attempt to enforce the Greek judgment in Germany was fated to fail because of the latter country's immunity.

CONCLUSION

"What a pity!", Judge Ferrari Bravo, dissenting in *Al-Adsani*, exclaimed. We can undoubtedly repeat this in *Kalogeropoulou* as well. The role of Judges is not only to discover an existing rule and to interpret it, but also to contribute to the making of the legal order. Not only to recognize that some trends appear somewhere, but to have the courage, whenever it is needed, to make a step further and to reveal the rule covered by or reflected in the visible trends. The ECHR missed an opportunity to do this. Moreover, instead of showing its capacity to be realistic and to analyse competing interests correctly, it proceeded to a mechanical and deficient argumentation, unconcerned with human suffering and the protection of human dignity. It added, unfortunately, its own contribution to the injustice caused to innocent victims of odious crimes, initially by the German armed forces, and more recently by domestic and international judiciaries.

PRINCIPLE OF CONSENSUS AND EUROPEAN UNION LEGISLATIVE COMPETENCE IN RELATION TO JUDICIAL COOPERATION IN CIVIL MATTERS

Challenges Facing the Hague Conference on Private International Law

Dr. Rolf WAGNER*
Head of Division in the "Private International Law" Division of the Federal Ministry of Justice in Berlin

1. THE LEGISLATIVE COMPETENCE OF THE EUROPEAN UNION IN RELATION TO JUDICIAL COOPERATION IN CIVIL LAW MATTERS

Hardly anyone had seriously expected it to happen, and then suddenly it did, nonetheless. The reference here is to the legislative competence of European legislators covering judicial cooperation in civil matters, established by the Treaty of Amsterdam and in force from 1 May 1999. What a nightmare this must have been for the Secretary General of the Hague Conference on Private International Law, *Dr. Hans van Loon*?

---

* The author would like to thank Mr. Brian Duffett, Barrister, of the Federal Ministry of Justice Translation Service, for his translation of the German original into English. Dr. Hans van Loon's very good command of the German language has enabled the author to refer primarily, in the footnotes, to the literature available in German.

The purpose of the Hague Conference,[1] which still had a very European imprint at that time,[2] consisted, and continues to consist, in compliance with its Statute[3] "[in] work[ing] for the progressive unification of the rules of private international law". All along the term "private international law" has been used in a broad sense in this context and covers not only conflict of laws provisions but also international civil procedure law.

The exact extent and the precise limits of the new competence for the European Community were not even known to Member States' representatives at the time.[4] From the wording of Article 65 ex EC Treaty it was indeed clear that competence for the Community to adopt its own legal instruments (internal competence) would also have a bearing on the conflict of laws rules and on international civil procedure law.[5] What is more, however, in the period that followed, there was a need for substantial input in the effort to identify the impact this new competence was going to have on the conclusion of international agreements with third countries (external competence). This was particularly due to the fact that this external competence was not derived from written law, but primarily from the case law of the ECJ, which first had to be ascertained and examined carefully.[6] But this was not everything, however. In the light of the remaining uncertainties and of the differing opinions regarding the scope of external competence the Opinion[7] of the ECJ had to be sought.[8] Although this Opinion was concerned with the negotiation of the Convention of 30 October 2007 on Jurisdiction and the Enforcement of Judgments in Civil and Commercial Matters (Lugano II Convention),[9] the commissioning of the Opinion was indirectly supposed to bring clarity, too, in respect of the extent of external competence for negotiations in the Hague Conference on Private International Law.

---

1 On the Hague Conference generally see van Loon, Conférence de la Haye de Droit International Privé, *Rép. Internat. Dalloz* 2011, 1.

2 On this see for instance Basedow, "Was wird aus der Haager Konferenz für Internationales Privatrecht", in Rauscher/Mansel (ed.), *Festschrift für Werner Lorenz zum 80. Geburtstag*, 2001, 463 (467).

3 Article 1 of the Statute of the Hague Conference on Private International Law. The Statute can be accessed via the Hague Conference website at www.hcch.net.

4 The same holds true for the special provisions applying to Denmark, the United Kingdom and Ireland, in respect of which there will also be no detailed treatment in the following.

5 Ever since the Treaty of Lisbon competence for judicial cooperation in civil matters emanates from Article 81 of the Treaty on the Functioning of the European Union (TFEU).

6 *EuGHE* 1971, 263 was at the forefront of this discussion.

7 ECJ Opinion 1/03 of 7 February 2006 on the Competence of the Community to Conclude the New Lugano Convention on jurisdiction and the recognition and enforcement of judgments in civil und commercial matters, *EuGHE* 2006, I/1145.

8 Wagner, in Dauses (ed.), *Handbuch des EU-Wirtschaftsrechts (Loseblattsammlung)*, Kapitel Q margin notes 13, 74 and 240.

9 The Convention of 30 October 2007 on jurisdiction and enforcement of judgments in civil and commercial matters (OJ 2009, L 147/5) emerged from the negotiations.

Not only this new competence enjoyed by European legislators, taken in itself, but also the moment of its effective entry was most unfortunate from the Hague Conference aspect because this expansion of competence bounced straight into the ongoing Hague negotiations on the drafting of several Conventions and, particularly amongst the negotiating partners from non-EU Member States, this led to a large measure of uncertainty.[10] In addition to this, overnight the European Community acquired competence in important Hague Conference areas of business – without itself being a Member of the Hague Conference.

2. THE REACTION OF THE HAGUE CONFERENCE

A. GLOBALISATION

Right from the start, the European Commission let there be no doubt that the European Community would be making use of its new competence. For this reason, it became apparent fairly quickly that the Hague Conference would not succeed in convincing the European Community that legal instruments of judicial cooperation ought to be drafted with priority in The Hague and that European legislators should preferably devote their attention to other subjects.

Dr. Hans van Loon very quickly realised that it makes little sense to entrust similar functions to two organisations, each with a similar number of members. Even before any answers had been put forward regarding the exact extent of the competence of the European Community *Dr. Hans van Loon* took off in another direction, deciding to seek new members for his Organisation,[11] in view of the visibly growing number of EC Member States and of the resulting visible dominance within the Hague Conference of EC Member States. The object of this endeavour was to bring about greater detachment from the European Community than formerly the case – i.e. even as regards the outside layer. That his extremely taxing and time-consuming promotion campaign was a success is clear from the fact that, apart from the European Union, since 1 May 1999 the following States have acceded to the Hague Conference:[12]

Albania (4.6.2002), Belarus (12.7.2001), Bosnia and Herzegovina (1.8.2001), Brazil (23.2.2001), Costa Rica (27.1.2011), Ecuador (2.11.2007), Georgia (28.5.2001),

---

10 Primarily from the perspective of the negotiations on a globally oriented jurisdiction, recognition and enforcement instrument, see Wagner, "Das Haager Übereinkommen vom 30.6.2005 über Gerichtsstandsvereinbarungen", *RabelsZ* 73 (2009) 215, 217 et seq.

11 With regard to those reflections of his that go much further, see for instance van Loon, "Unification of private international law in a multi-forum context", in *Denationalisierung des Privatrechts?*, Symposium held on the occasion of the 70th birthday of Karl Kreuzer, 2005, 33.

12 Status as of 1 January 2013.

Iceland (14.11.2003), India (13.3.2008), Jordan (13.6.2001), Lithuania (23.10.2001), Malaysia (2.10.2002), Mauritius (19.1.2011), Montenegro (15.5.2007), New Zealand (5.2.2002), Panama (29.5.2002), Paraguay (28.6.2005), Peru (29.1.2001), Philippines (14.7.2010), Russian Federation (6.12.2001), Serbia (1.6.2001), South Africa (14.2.2002), Sri Lanka (27.9.2001), Ukraine (3.12.2003).

Over this period, EC Member States also had to see how the membership structure of the Hague Conference was "moving further and further away" from the European Community. *Dr. Hans van Loon* cannot be blamed for this, not even when we take his European origins into account. In the final analysis, as the person principally responsible for the Hague Conference, it was his duty to ensure its continued existence. What is more, this expansion ultimately even did justice to the interests of the EC Member States because they also actually cannot have an interest in the European Community and the Hague Conference too closely resembling, and competing with, one another.

B. TRANSITION FROM THE MAJORITY TO THE CONSENSUS PRINCIPLE

Prior to the introduction of European legislator competence in relation to judicial competence in civil matters the EC Member States within the Hague Conference often expressed a diversity of views when conducting Convention negotiations. So – even if only against the backdrop of common allegiance to the *common law* – it was no surprise at all when, for instance, an EC Member State came to express the same view as the United States of America.

The external competence of the European Community in relation to judicial cooperation in civil matters produced the effect that the EC Member States needed to reach a uniform view within the framework of this competence. Not only as regards the quality of law-making itself, but also considering the chances of reaching a consensus, this did not exactly turn out to the advantage of Hague Conference operations because the diversity of ideas amongst EU Member States abruptly went by the board. It was replaced by a uniform view generally requiring a compromise often reached on the basis of the lowest common denominator.

Taking into account the large number of EC Member States, each of which continued to have a vote at the Hague Conference,[13] uniform vote casting by EC

[13] Under Article 3 No. 7 and No. 8 of the new Statute of the Hague Conference, the number of votes of the European Union basically derives, for the purpose of votes regarding matters in respect of which it has an external competence, from the number of Member States who have transferred competence to the European Union. Whenever the European Union exercises its external competence, those EU Member States that have transferred competence to the European Union, will then not exercise their right to vote.

Member States – emanating as it did from the law governing competence – paved the way towards formation of a block; henceforward, this meant it was easy to outvote large non-European States like the U.S. and China – a fact not much appreciated, and not only by the two States just mentioned.

The solution to this problem consisted in the Hague Conference making the transition from the majority principle to the consensus principle, which occurred during the negotiations on the globally oriented jurisdiction, recognition and enforcement instrument.[14] Only after the delay that occurred was this amendment then reproduced in the Hague Conference Statute on 1 January 2007.[15] According to Article 8 para. 2 of the new Statute, the Hague Conference Sessions, Council and Special Commissions are required, to the furthest extent possible, to operate on the basis of consensus.

Through transition to the consensus principle it was also hoped that henceforward a larger number of States than hitherto the case would be in the position to accede to the Hague Conventions, or to ratify them. The consensus principle was intended to avert the situation where outvoted Members of the Hague Conference (perhaps even during a Convention drafting phase) would disengage from the negotiations and (have to) leave ratification out of the calculation from the very outset because of account not being taken of an aspect perceived to be of essential importance perhaps only for those Members themselves.

C. NEW PROFILE FOR THE HAGUE CONFERENCE

With his marketing offensive *Dr. Hans van Loon* gave the Hague Conference on Private International Law a new profile. In the meantime the Hague Conference has turned into a global Organisation. But the growth in its membership has not proved to be a financial boon for the Hague Conference. However, this was not the goal of the expansion policy, nor could it have been so. Also, subsequent to its expansion, the Hague Conference – and this is something the Conference should be consciously aware of from time to time – is still funded in large measure by the 27 Member States of the European Union. After all, these States were responsible for funding nearly half the overall budget for the year 2012/2013.

14 Wagner, *RabelsZ* 73 (2009) 215, 224.

15 Source of the Statute supra in footnote 3.

3. JUXTAPOSITION OF LEGAL INSTRUMENTS FROM THE HAGUE AND FROM BRUSSELS

A. GENERAL MATTERS

Since amendment of the Hague Conference Statute and since the European Community has become a Member of the Hague Conference,[16] the contours of the external competence exercised by European legislators have become somewhat clearer. Since entry into force of the Treaty of Lisbon, the extent of EU external competence no longer derives "only" from ECJ case law but also from Article 216 I and from Article 3 II of the Treaty on the Functioning of the European Union (TFEU) – though in a form still amenable to further improvement.

In the technical legal dimension as well, the coexistence of the two Organisations seems secure. There is even the possibility that the two Organisations will be drafting legal instruments on the same subject and that both instruments will enter into force in parallel. But this only makes sense from the point of view of EU Member States if the Hague Conventions are also ratified by States that are not Members of the European Union.

B. DISTINGUISHING CRITERIA

aa. Jurisdiction

The fact that coexistence is possible with respect to legal instruments concerning procedural law is shown by the Hague Convention on Choice of Court Agreements of 30 June 2005. The innovative rule, in Article 26 VI (a) of that Convention,[17] for distinguishing the jurisdiction regime is conceived in such manner that the Convention's *jurisdiction rules* and those of the Brussels I Regulation[18] each have their own area of application and are able to function alongside each other, without there being any overlapping.

---

[16] On this see the Council Decision of 5 October 2006 on the accession of the Community to the Hague Conference on Private International Law (OJ 2006, L 297/1).

[17] On this and in respect of the statements to follow see Wagner, *RabelsZ* 73 (2009) 100, 137 f.

[18] Regulation (EC) No. 44/2001 of the Council of 22 December 2000 on jurisdiction and the recognition and enforcement of judgments in civil and commercial matters (Brussels I Regulation = EuGVVO; Text: OJ 2001, L 12/1; corrigenda in OJ 2001, L 307/28 and in OJ 2010, L 328/36; new version of the Annexes I–IV in OJ 2012, L 50/3).

bb. *Recognition and enforcement*

In the framework of judicial cooperation in civil matters European legislators have not adopted any provisions on the recognition and enforcement of decisions emanating from third countries.[19] This makes it easier to distinguish the internal EU provisions on recognition and enforcement from those found in the Hague Conventions. That the rules on *recognition and enforcement* of the Hague Convention on Choice of Court Agreements do not apply to the recognition and enforcement of decisions of one EU Member State in another EU Member State, but "only" to the recognition of decisions of EU Member States in non-EU Member States (and vice versa) would seem to be a plain fact (Article 26 VI (b) of the Hague Convention on Choice of Court Agreements). Nevertheless, this also shows that coexistence is possible between the Hague Convention on Choice of Court Agreements and the Brussels I Regulation.

cc. *Conflict of laws*

Important indicators regarding rules on the applicable law emerged from the fact that the EC, after initial uncertainties, gave a broad interpretation of this external competence (see in particular ex Article 61, 65 TEC; now Article 81 TFEU). Also because no clear distinguishing rules have been found, as well as on purely practical grounds, the conflict of laws provisions enjoy validity – having been adopted by European legislators within the framework of judicial cooperation in civil matters – not only in respect of purely internal EU constellations, but also in respect of constellations involving a third country.[20]

So far as the European Union has availed itself of these possibilities, there is no more room at all, in EU Member States, for applying the Hague Conference conflict of laws provisions to one and the same legal field. If within the European Union one still wanted to apply Hague Conference conflict of laws provisions additionally, one would have to restrict the scope of application of the internal EU legal instruments. To this end, there would have to be construction of distinguishing rules that are as straightforward as possible in their application; however, there is no sign of the actual existence of such rules.

Such rules also did not evolve during the drafting of the so-called Rome II Regulation.[21] EU Member States that were Members – at the time this EU

[19] There will be no detailed discussion of the question whether the competence for judicial cooperation in civil matters covers such provisions.

[20] Wagner, "EG-Kompetenz zur Vereinheitlichung des Internationalen Privatrechts in Ehesachen?", *RabelsZ* 68 (2004) 119, 140 ff.

[21] Regulation (EC) No. 864/2007 of the European Parliament and of the Council of 11 July 2007 on the law applicable to non-contractual obligations (OJ 2007, L 199/40).

Regulation was adopted – of the Hague Convention on the Law Applicable to Traffic Accidents and also of the Hague Convention on the Law Applicable to Products Liability were conceded the right to continue applying these Conventions (Article 28 para. 1 Rome II Regulation) in order for such States not to be in breach of their obligations under public international law. Within the EU, this led to a differentiated legal situation: some EU Member States apply the relevant Hague Convention to traffic accidents or, as the case may be, to product liability cases. In these fields, other Member States – for instance Germany – just have to apply the Rome II Regulation.

European legislators' current *modus operandi* in not expecting practitioners in Europe to cope with parallel conflict of laws legal instruments emanating from The Hague on the one hand and from Brussels on the other is not merely occurring at the expense of the Hague Conference, for in areas where there are no internal EU provisions European legislators have already made the decision, on several occasions, to apply the Hague Conference conflict of laws provisions. On the one hand, this is illustrated by the reference, in Article 15 of the Maintenance Regulation,[22] to the rules in the Hague Maintenance Protocol whose application is not confined to internal EU constellations. On the other hand, European legislators have refrained from establishing their own conflict of laws provisions on parental responsibility because, as far this goes, the Convention already in force is the Hague Child Protection Convention of 9 October 1996 (CPC). Insofar as EU Member States are still not members of the latter Convention, they are obliged to ratify it in the interests of the European Union.[23]

As soon as the CPC has entered into force for an EU Member State, the latter is required to apply that Convention's conflict of laws norms not only in its relationships with third countries but also in relation to internal EU constellations.

dd. Cooperation

In relation to cooperation, too, there is room for parallel provisions from Brussels and from The Hague. This is apparent, for example, from the Brussels IIa Regulation[24] and the CPC. However, there are no unequivocal distinguishing rules. From the perspective of EU Member States, the CPC ought to apply in

---

22 Regulation (EC) No. 4/2009 of the Council of 18 December 2008 on jurisdiction, applicable law, recognition and enforcement of decisions and cooperation in matters relating to maintenance obligations (OJ 2009, L 7/1; corrigendum in OJ 2011, L 131/26).

23 On this see the Council Decision of 5 June 2008 (OJ 2008, L 151/36).

24 Regulation (EC) No. 2201/2003 of the Council of 27 November 2003 concerning jurisdiction and the recognition and enforcement of judgments in matrimonial matters and the matters of parental responsibility, repealing Regulation (EC) No. 1347/2000 (Brussels IIa Regulation; OJ 2003, L 338/1; as regards Malta's Treaty with the Holy See: amended in OJ 2004, L 367/1).

cases where the child concerned has his or her habitual residence in a State which, although not a Member State of the Brussels IIa Regulation, is a CPC Member State.[25]

C. PROBLEMS FROM THE PRACTITIONER PERSPECTIVE

Where parallel instruments from Brussels and The Hague have entered into force in the same legal field, this presents a practitioner in the EU Member States with major challenges. This is all the more applicable seeing that competition rules may in fact differ.

Things get really complicated for a practitioner when it comes to a "triad" situation, i.e. when there is yet another legal instrument in addition to the legal instruments from Brussels and The Hague. In the European perspective, this constellation could occur in the event of European legislators drafting a special Convention with the States of the European Free Trade Association, to apply in relationships between EU Member States and EFTA States (and vice versa). The Lugano II Convention[26] is a convention of this kind. This Convention will compete with the Brussels I Regulation and with the Hague Convention on Choice of Court Agreements upon entry into force of the latter. Article 26 of the Convention on Choice of Court Agreements then distinguishes the Brussels I Regulation and the Lugano II Convention from the Hague Convention on Choice of Court Agreements. Article 64 I of the Lugano II Convention governs the relationship between this Convention and the Brussels I Regulation.

The Lugano II Convention, which mirrors the Brussels I Regulation and, from the perspective of EU Member States, would lead to a triad situation in the event of entry into force of the Hague Convention on Choice of Court Agreements, could not stay as just an individual case, for this path is now being considered also for cross-border service, for the taking of evidence, and for generating this kind of third regime in these legal fields too.

[25] Wagner/Janzen, Die Anwendung des Haager Kinderschutzübereinkommens in Deutschland, *FPR* 2011, 110 (111).

[26] Source *supra* in footnote 9. Attention will not be focused here on the Agreement between the European Union and the Kingdom of Denmark on the extension of the Brussels I Regulation to Denmark (OJ 2005, L 299/62), nor will there be treatment of bilateral treaties concerning service and evidence.

4. EFFECTS OF THE INCREASED NUMBER OF MEMBER STATES AND OF THE TRANSITION TO THE CONSENSUS PRINCIPLE

A. SIGNATURE AND RATIFICATION OF NEW CONVENTIONS

What has been the outcome of the increasing number of Hague Conference Member States – and also of the transition made from the majority to the unanimity principle? A reliable answer to this question can probably only be provided in a few years' time. In regard to ratification of the Hague Conventions one has to think in terms of long-term categories. So, in the past, Germany has not been the only State to need a longer build-up before ratifying a Hague Convention. Add to this the fact that a Hague Convention can still turn out successfully in circumstances where it is not signed, or ratified, as soon as it has been adopted but only at a much later stage by a large number of States. Against this backdrop, the statements to come can only give one a view of the momentary situation.

Logically speaking, the question of the cumulative effects produced by both the growth in the number of Hague Conference Members and by the transition from the majority principle to the consensus principle can only be addressed in relation to Conventions that were actually adopted after the transition from the majority to the consensus principle. During this period the Hague Conference adopted five instruments. They all date from the period from 2000 to 2007. How did matters stand by 1 January 2013?[27]

The *Hague Convention on the International Protection of Adults of 13 January 2000*, which was adopted shortly after the transition was made to the consensus principle and, for that reason, still needs to be assigned more to the realm of the majority principle, can point to a growing number of contracting States. However, it is a sobering thought that this Convention, with the exception of Switzerland, has hitherto entered into force in EU Member States only. The States concerned here are the Czech Republic, Estonia, Finland, France, Germany, the United Kingdom of Great Britain and Northern Ireland, whereby the United Kingdom, acting in accordance with Article 55, made a Declaration to the effect that the Convention shall apply to Scotland only.

So far, the *Hague Convention on Choice of Court Agreements of 30 June 2005* has been a success of very modest proportions. To date, it is only the European

[27] The reference date for all statements in the following is therefore always 1 January 2013. Information concerning the signature and ratification status of the individual Conventions is given on the website of the Hague Conference at www.hcch.net.

Union and the United States of America that have actually signed this Convention. Mexico is the only State to have acceded to this Convention. Its entry into force still presupposes one further accession or another ratification (Article 31). This might happen soon. In the United States of America attempts are under way to achieve ratification. For the year 2013, the European Commission has announced a proposal for a mandate to have the European Union accede to this Convention.

The *Hague Convention on the Law Applicable to Certain Rights in Respect of Securities held with an Intermediary of 5 July 2006* has also not been a success so far. Up to now, just Mauritius and Switzerland have ratified it.[28] This Convention can enter into force only when one more State has ratified the Convention (Art. 19). Its failure to date is based on several reasons. One important reason for this is that EU Member States, following long, intensive, internal consultation processes were unable to reconcile themselves with this Convention.

The *Hague Convention on the International Recovery of Child Support and Other Forms of Family Maintenance of 23 November 2007* has been signed by Albania, Bosnia Herzegovina, Burkina Faso,[29] the European Union, Norway, Ukraine and the United States of America. Only Albania, Bosnia Herzegovina and Norway have ratified the Convention to date. Still, the Convention was at least able to enter into force in these three States. The European Union has already decided to accede to the Convention.[30] But before they have deposited their instrument of approval, the EU Member States should still wind up their internal collateral legislative measures in order to enable the Convention to come into operation in these States from the very first day following its entry into force for the European Union.

The *Hague Protocol on the Law Applicable to Maintenance Obligations of 23 November 2007* has also not entered into force yet. It has been signed by the European Union and by Serbia. The European Union has already deposited its instrument of accession. For it to enter into force the Protocol will need just one more ratification (Article 25).

B. WORK IN GENERAL

Hague Conference Member States are becoming more and more accustomed to the European Union entitlement to exercise an external competence in many of the areas with which the Hague Conference itself is concerned. In these negotiations the European Commission carries a substantial responsibility, because in the

28 In addition to this, the Convention has been signed by the United States of America.
29 Burkina Faso is not as yet a Member of the Hague Conference.
30 OJ 2011, L 192/39.

first place it is the European Commission that plays the role of spokesperson for the European Union. EU Member States have, however, stipulated the right to support the European Commission with their own verbal contributions.[31]

In the context of external competence EU Member States at the Hague Conference no longer perform the role they used to play. They need to coordinate their positions on the sidelines and between sessions, which is sometimes extremely difficult within the brief time available. Acting under great pressure to reach agreement, individual Member States are made, even in the context of internal coordination, to accept a compromise, which can then again be amended in the Plenary to their detriment.

By contrast, there has been a noticeable strengthening of the South American Member States. They frequently coordinate their positions in order to give their voice greater weight. Nothing has changed in respect of the particularly strong position enjoyed by the United States of America, Australia, China, Japan, Canada and Russia. This is not supposed to diminish the role of other States that are represented at the Hague Conference, especially as the influence of individual States does not only depend on the country represented but also on the representative concerned.

C. WORK ON INDIVIDUAL PROJECTS

Before drawing brief conclusions, we should take a quick look at the Hague Conference's most important projects.

Those Hague Conference Conventions encompassing only rules governing the applicable law have not had much success to date.[32] The Hague Conference seems to have learned from this. It is currently dealing with provisions on the applicable law for certain international treaties. At least according to the present position, the work being done is not supposed to lead to a Convention but rather to a non-binding legal instrument. From the point of view of the EU Member States this is also to be welcomed for the reason that, in this field, the European Union has at its disposal – in the form of the so-called Rome I Regulation[33] – a soundly functioning legal instrument, which is to be applied independently of where the occurrences that are to be assessed actually took place. So far as EU Member

31 Wagner, "Neues von der Haager Konferenz für Internationales Privatrecht", *IPRax* 2007, 375.

32 E.g. Basedow (footnote 2), 463 (480).

33 Regulation (EC) No. 593/2008 of the European Parliament and the Council of 17 June 2008 on the law applicable to contractual obligations (OJ 2008, L 177/6; corrigendum in OJ 2009, L 309/87).

States want to adhere to the Rome I Regulation, there is no room in their case for a Convention on the law applicable to individual contractual obligations.[34]

The European Union, too, is concerned with the subject of "recognition of foreign protection measures, for instance in connection with domestic violence".[35] The recognition of protection measures from other EU Member States is fully within the focus of these European endeavours. For a start, the Hague Conference would be well-advised carefully to establish whether the subject has a prospect of success.

The consideration being given to determining the status of children (also with regard to surrogacy) could lead to a new Convention. The main difficulty with surrogacy consists in the partially completely antithetical legal solutions pertaining in Hague Conference Member States regarding the actual constellations occurring.[36]

The work of the Hague Conference on a globally conceived recognition and enforcement Convention in civil matters seems promising insofar as, in this Convention, there is no intention – as the name already suggests – of also adopting jurisdiction rules from the very outset. With this narrow approach there is a desire to draw the lessons learned from the fact that previous work on this kind of convention, having also been aimed at the unification of jurisdiction rules, failed primarily for the reason that there were irresolvable differences regarding jurisdiction rules. Here, too, it becomes clear that the growing number of Member States does not necessarily make the European Union politically stronger. A compelling need simultaneously to unify the jurisdiction rules, as was formerly perceived by the EU Member States,[37] is frequently no longer felt to be the case.

But there ought to be an examination as to whether the recognition and enforcement Convention, as yet to be drafted, could still perhaps be enriched with further provisions for instance on international jurisdiction or whether it would seem possible to evolve another, perhaps separate and optional legal instrument on international jurisdiction (under certain circumstances only amongst certain Member States). It remains to be seen whether progress can be made in this respect.

34 As stated above under 3 B) cc), the scope of application of the Rome I Regulation would otherwise have to be curtailed.

35 Proposal for a Regulation of the European Parliament and of the Council on mutual recognition of protection measures in civil matters, Doc. COM(2011) 276 final.

36 For a discussion of these problems see Wagner, "Abstammungsfragen bei Leihmutterschaften in internationalen Sachverhalten – Bemühungen der Haager Konferenz für Internationales Privatrecht", *StAZ* 2012, 294 with further references.

37 Wagner, "Die Bemühungen der Haager Konferenz für Internationales Privatrecht um ein Übereinkommen über die gerichtliche Zuständigkeit und ausländische Entscheidungen in Zivil- und Handelssachen", *IPRax* 2001, 533 (534).

5. CONCLUSIONS

A. STOCKTAKING

(1) The survey has shown that the reception given to the Conventions adopted by the Hague Conference subsequent to transition from the majority to the consensus principle, has been marked for its restraint. At any rate, in the short-term and in relation to the Conventions drafted since the year 2000, the hope that the consensus principle would encourage ratification of Hague Conventions has hardly been fulfilled.[38] The number of six ratifications of the instruments adopted by non-EU Member States in The Hague since 2000 is disappointing.

(2) EU Member States (or the European Union) enjoy inasmuch a somewhat better position than non-EU Member States, although the EU Member States – as far as Hague Conference Members are concerned – find themselves in a minority position. Some EU Member States have ratified the Hague Convention on the International Protection of Adults. What is more, the European Union has acceded to the Hague Protocol on the Law Applicable to Maintenance Obligations and it has decided to accede to the Hague Convention on the International Recovery of Child Support and Other Forms of Family Maintenance. Although the Hague Conference has developed into an Organisation with a global orientation and despite the fact that because of the growing number of its Member States, forming a consensus within the European Union has not become easier in the context of its external competence, the EU Member States (or the European Union) still seem to be the locomotive for the ratification of the Hague Conventions.

(3) The sobering picture in relation to ratification of the new Hague Conventions by non-EU States is certainly a bit distorted. It seems understandable if individual States do not necessarily want to play a pioneering role in relation to ratification of the new Hague Conventions but first want to wait and see whether it will be worthwhile for them to ratify the Convention concerned. Here the reference point is whether the Convention is being ratified by other (large) States. But what cannot be ignored is that, during the period focused on here from 2000 to 2012, many of the more recent Member States of the Hague Conference have started by ratifying particularly successful Hague Conference Conventions, all dating from the period prior to the year 2000. They must, and should, not be blamed for this.

(4) All in all, one can say that there was nevertheless no alternative to the globalisation process initiated by *Dr. Hans van Loon*. With hindsight, too, his

38 The following statements refer to the status pertaining as of 1 January 2013.

approach was absolutely correct and counts amongst his great achievements. The new Member States have to be convinced of the value that lies in ratifying individual Hague Conference Conventions. Here there is a need for considerable patience.

B. FUTURE CHOICE OF SUBJECTS

(1) The increasing number of Members of the Hague Conference makes the selection of new fields of action more difficult. The more global the Hague Conference has become, the greater the likelihood will be of a clash occurring between legal systems that have evolved culturally and traditionally, and the greater the number will be of Member States involved in conceiving new projects. The difficulty in reaching agreement regarding new subjects will be heightened by the consensus principle.

(2) What is surprising is that from amongst the more recent instruments, the Hague Protocol on the Law Applicable to Maintenance Obligations has been relatively successful even though it is the only instrument to have been signed from the period subsequent to 1 May 1999, whereby, at that time, not exactly all Hague Conference Member States had been strongly in favour of drafting this instrument. If the Hague Conference does not want to be forced to a standstill, it must not just stick to drafting such Conventions as have been envisaged – in line with the unanimity principle – by all Member States of the Hague Conference. On the contrary, it must carefully sound out the prospects of success of each individual Convention. Here the Permanent Bureau of the Hague Conference has an important role to play. This does not already suggest that the Hague Conference should keep in step with the desire of individual States for concentration on a new Convention concerning a particular subject. The Members of the Hague Conference should, however, be wise enough not to cut themselves off from a new subject simply for the reason that there are individual States – however important these may be – that are opposed to the project. Greater attention ought to be paid to those States that, in the past, have not only made a contribution to the drafting of instruments but have actually also ratified them.

(3) Where the European Union succeeds – as in the case of the Rome III Regulation[39] in force only for 14 of the EU Member States – in concluding a legal instrument solely within the context of Enhanced Cooperation in relation

[39] Regulation (EU) No. 1259/2010 of the Council of 20 December 2010 implementing enhanced cooperation in the area of the law applicable to divorce and legal separation (OJ 2010, L 343/10).

to certain Member States, because in fact it has not proved possible to achieve consensus with the other EU Member States, a cautious approach will be needed at the Hague Conference as well, for if the EU Member States themselves already cannot agree on uniform provisions, it would seem that such a project would present even fewer prospects of success within the wider framework of the Hague Conference.

C. HAGUE CONFERENCE AND EUROPEAN UNION

(1) Legislative competence on the part of the European Union in relation to judicial cooperation in civil matters certainly does not make the Hague Conference obsolete. The internal European legal instruments have a strong internal market bearing. The global markets and certain family law questions do actually call for Hague Conference regulation. The European Union ought not to regulate legal questions vis-à-vis third countries unilaterally for itself but should rather reach agreement with third countries, and this should not be done directly by way of negotiation with individual third countries but rather at the Hague Conference itself.

(2) The Hague Maintenance Protocol shows that the European Union does not draft its own provisions at all costs and in any event but, to the contrary, is well aware of the quality inherent in Hague Conference operations, a phenomenon to be welcomed as such. Especially in times of limited personnel resources and funding it would seem that intensified and continual contacts of the Hague Conference with the European Commission are most important.

(3) The Hague Maintenance Protocol also shows that with future Hague instruments there will have to be amendment of provisions on entry into force.[40] That the Hague Maintenance Protocol should be able to enter into force after two ratifications is not something to be objected to as a matter of principle, but that the accession of the EU should here count solely as 1 ratification is not a model "with a future", for these provisions have had the consequence that the Maintenance Protocol would have been able to enter into force following ratification by two small non-EU Member States, whereas ratification by the EU, in the exercise of its jurisdiction on this occasion for 25 EU Member States,[41] was not able *per se* to

---

[40] For more detail on this see Mankowski, "Hängepartie dank Kodifikationspolitik – Oder: Die neuen Leitideen des Internationalen Unterhaltsrechts", *FamRZ* 2010, 1487.

[41] On this see Mansel/Thorn/Wagner, "Europäisches Kollisionsrecht 2010: Verstärkte Zusammenarbeit als Motor der Vereinheitlichung? ", *IPRax* 2011, 1 (12).

lead to the Maintenance Protocol's entry into force. If the EU does not avail itself of its own law-making competence, it should be able to allow a Hague Convention to enter into force by means of its own ratification. To say the least, this is also in the interest of the Hague Conference, whose importance is also to be measured in terms of the ratification status achieved by its instruments.

A JAPANESE IMPLEMENTATION BILL FOR THE 1980 CHILD ABDUCTION CONVENTION

Jun YOKOYAMA*
Emeritus Professor, Hitotsubashi University, Tokyo

1. PRELIMINARY REMARKS

On 20 May 2011, the Japanese Cabinet issued the direction that, recognising the need to protect the interests of children who suffered the effects of breakups of international marriages that have been increasing in number in recent years, preparations should be made toward ratifying the Hague Convention of 25 October 1980 on the Civil Aspects of International Child Abduction. In response to it, the Ministry of Justice, in collaboration with the Ministry of Foreign Affairs, prepared a bill designed to implement the 1980 Child Abduction Convention and submitted it to the Diet on 29 May 2012.[1] Unfortunately, the sudden dissolution of the Lower House in December, 2012 left it dead in the water. While I firmly believe that the Convention will turn out to be beneficial to Japanese, it remains to be seen, at this moment, whether the bill will revive in the next session of the Diet.

In this short paper, which is dedicated to Mr van Loon who has served with such devotion the Hague Conference on Private International Law and has contributed much to the development of private international law, I would like to sketch the brief outline of the rules on return proceedings under the bill.[2]

---

* Whereas the author was a member of the Legislative Council for the Ministry of Justice in charge of preparing the bill, the view expressed here is personal.

1 Some of the unofficially translated provisions of the bill are shown at the end of this paper.

2 The bill mainly deals with the roles of Central Authority and the return proceedings. It contains more than 150 articles, most of which are concerned with the return proceedings and reproduce *mutatis mutandis* the provisions of the Act on the Procedures in Family Matters coming into force on 1 January 2013.

2. BACKGROUNDS

In *Giacomo Puccini*'s opera, *Madame Butterfly*, an American naval officer leaves both his Japanese wife and children behind in Japan. It seems that the typical scenario which Japanese people in the 20th century imagined from the expression 'dissolution of international marriage' was not far from that portrayed in the opera. When a mixed marriage breaks down, a father from a western country leaves a Japanese mother and their children behind in Japan. Such association of ideas seems to have lasted long. In the latter half of the 20th-century Japan, where there was domestic labour sufficient for its economic development, witnessed no large-scale immigration. It is true that there were foreigners resident in Japan. However, they were mostly former colonial people from Korea and China and their offspring who seldom crossed the border. It follows that the idea of child abduction from Japan did not come to be seen as a problem that required a legal solution. In other words, the following scenario which the 1980 Child Abduction Convention originally envisaged was seen as foreign to Japan: a non-custodial father of foreign nationality removes the child from its Japanese custodial mother caretaker. Consequently, parental child abduction attracted no attention from politics and media until the mid-2000s, which led to the governmental inertia about ratification of the Convention despite its success-story.

It seems that it was not until 2007 that some western countries, in particular the United States, began to urge Japan to ratify the 1980 Child Abduction Convention. When Japanese politicians and media learnt that Japan was depicted as a paradise for Japanese female abducting caretakers, it seems to have come like a bolt from the blue. It was natural that voices were immediately raised against ratification of the Convention. Particularly, since the United States almost exclusively focused on American left-behind parents, the Convention appeared to have deterrent effect only on abductions to Japan, not on those from Japan. Consequently, the Japanese press could not describe the Convention in words that made it seem as if Japanese had at least nothing to lose in ratifying it. It may be added that many Asian countries such as Mainland China to which children are most likely to be removed are not Contracting States of the Convention.

There were also some doubts about ratification. First, there was concern whether the Convention would prevent Japanese mothers, victims of domestic violence, from fleeing home to Japan with their children or whether such mothers' forum shopping should pay off. Second, some experts on family law doubted that Japanese authorities would be able to implement the Convention properly under the legal machinery available under the current Japanese law. It still remains unsettled, in the court practice relating to purely internal abduction cases, whether enforcement officers should be allowed to take a child physically from an abducting parent. It was argued that one should not expect enforcement officers to do more than they can do in internal situations.

3. CABINET'S DECISION

Despite these objections and doubts, the Japanese Cabinet, as mentioned at the outset, finally decided to make preparations towards ratifying the 1980 Child Abduction Convention.

The decision taken by the Cabinet is welcomed. The number of guest workers has increased in Japan since the 1990s because of the ageing of the population and the consequent labour shortage. In view of this demographic change having revealed itself during the last two decades, it can be expected that abductions from Japan will soon attract attention from media and politicians. Although we have no data proving how many children, to date, have been abducted from Japan, we firmly believe that outgoing abductions already outnumber incoming ones. It seems that the time will soon come when Japan begins to ask some neighbouring countries to join the Convention. Furthermore, whereas it still remains controversial under the current Japanese law whether direct coercive measures can be taken in relation to children, the problem should be legislatively addressed by the Act implementing the Convention.

In addition to its statement, the Cabinet reached a 'common understanding', which was designed to provide the framework for the Ministries of Foreign Affairs and Justice to work within.[3] The second part of the 'common understanding' relates to return proceedings. It reads as follows.

(1) New court proceedings shall be established.
(2) The court may refuse to order the return of the child where:
    a) there is a risk of the child suffering violent acts or other acts physically or psychologically affecting it, done by the applicant in the State of habitual

[3] With regard to the part of the Central Authority (hereafter called the 'JCA'), the following matters were agreed between the Ministers.
(1) The Central Authority of Japan shall be established in the Ministry of Foreign Affairs.
(2) When an application is made for the return of a child, the JCA shall perform the following roles: discovering a child's whereabouts; taking steps necessary to prevent the abuse and other harm to the child; providing advice for the voluntary return of the child or an amicable solution between the parties; and providing information of a general character as to Japanese law including the rules on court proceedings.
(3) For the purpose of performing these roles, the JCA may request relevant authorities to provide information or other assistances if the circumstances so require.
(4) When an application is made for the contact with the child, the JCA shall make necessary arrangements for it.

residence, where the child has suffered such acts done by the applicant there;

b) there is a risk of the respondent suffering such violent or other acts done by the applicant that would result in psychological damage to the child after the respondent returns to the State of habitual residence with the child, where the respondent has suffered such acts done by the applicant within the household in which the child was with them;
c) placement of the child with any person other than the respondent in the State of habitual residence would run counter to the interests of the child in circumstances where the respondent hardly be expected to take care of the child, e.g. because of impossibility for him/her to re-enter that State, fear of arrest or criminal charge, and inability to support him/herself and the child there; or, otherwise,
d) there is a grave risk that his or her return would expose the child to physical or psychological harm or otherwise place the child in an intolerable situation.

It should be noted that the directions shown in above (2) a) and b) reflect concerns as expressed in the Japanese Act on the Prevention, etc. of Child Abuse (Act No. 82 of 2000). It may safely be said that the necessity of explicit provisions which aim to exemplify some critical situations covered by Article 13(b) of the Convention was inspired by Article 5 of the Swiss Federal Act on International Child Abduction and the Hague Conventions on the Protection on Children and Adults.

The directions provided the framework for the Legislative Council for the Ministry of Justice to prepare the bill.

4. RETURN PROCEEDINGS

4.1. PROCEEDINGS

Under the bill, the return proceedings are basically inquisitorial rather than adversarial. It follows that the burden of proof is understood as that of persuasion rather than that of producing evidence, e.g., in the context of Article 13(b) of the Convention.

An application for a return order must be made either to the Tokyo Family Court or to the Osaka Family Court. These courts have the 'Family Divisions' among whose judges experience and expertise are likely to be accumulated. The concentration of jurisdiction on those Family Courts is expected to speed up return proceedings and to lead to a more coherent case law.

An application for a return order must include the identity of the parties and their legal representatives, the effect of application which specifies the child in question and the State to which it shall be returned, and the statement that the application is made pursuant to the proceedings for the return of the child.

If a period of six weeks has elapsed from the date of commencement of the proceedings, the applicant or the JCA may request the court seised with the return application to explain the development of the proceedings.

Once the court is seised with an application for the return of the child, another court before which the proceedings are pending in matters relating to the holder of parental authority or to the custody over a child shall not decide on the merits of the case. The JCA or the former court may give the relevant notice to the court seised with an application relating to the merits of the case.

On the application of one of the parties, the court before which the return proceedings are pending may issue an order prohibiting the other party from taking the child out of Japan where there is a danger of expatriation. The court may order the other party to hand over a passport issued in the child's name to the JCA. Such order ceases to have effect, once the return order becomes binding with final legal force.

4.2. CHILD IN THE PROCEEDINGS

On application or on its own motion, the court may allow the competent child, the subject of the proceedings, to participate in the return proceedings, unless such participation runs counter to the child's interests. The child who participates in the proceedings may, in principle, carry out the same kinds of procedural acts as those of the parties.

4.3. MEDIATION

The court seised with the return application may, on its own motion, initiate family mediation proceedings at every stage of the return proceedings on condition that the parties agree to it. The court which has initiated the family mediation may stay the return proceedings until the end of the mediation proceedings. Under Japanese law, mediation has been defined as the procedure in a family court through which the parties reach an agreement with the assistance and advice of a mediation committee.[4] When the parties reach an agreement as to the return of the child and the agreement is put on record, the mediation is regarded as final and conclusive. The part of the document indicating the agreement as to the return of the child has the same binding force as a court order.

5. RETURN ORDER

Under the bill, the court, in principle, orders a return to the State of a child's habitual residence before the removal or retention. There are, however, exceptions allowing the court not to make such a return order. Apart from the exception set out in Article 20 of the Convention, those exceptions are classified in two groups according to whether concerns about a child's welfare are involved in the course of return and possible litigation on the merits in the State of habitual residence.

The following four situations are ones in which the court has a discretion to order or not to order the return of the child according to the interests of the particular child: (1) where the application is made after the period of one year has elapsed from the date of the wrongful removal or retention and the child is now settled in its new environment; (2) where the applicant was not actually exercising the custody rights at the time of removal or retention unless it is found that the applicant could have been exercising the custody rights in the absence of the removal or retention; (3) where the applicant consented to the removal or retention beforehand or acquiesced in it subsequently; or (4) where the child objects to being returned and has attained an age and degree of maturity at which it is appropriate to take account of its views.

As far as concerns about a child's welfare may be involved in the course of return and possible litigation on the merits in the State of habitual residence, it is regarded as immaterial whether the return order serves a particular child's interests. In identifying the situation which corresponds to that set out in Article 13(b) of the Convention, the court should take into account, particularly, the following three points: (1) whether there is a risk of the child suffering violent acts or other acts physically or psychologically affecting it done by the left-behind parent in the State of its habitual residence; (2) whether there is a risk of the taking parent suffering such violent or other acts done by the left-behind parent that would result in psychological damage to the child after both the taking parent and the child enter the State of habitual residence; and (3) whether there would be circumstances to make it difficult for either the left-behind or taking parent to

[4] For the Japanese mediation in general, see Satotoshi Minamikata, "Resolution of Disputes over Parental Rights and Duties in a Marital Dissolution Case in Japan: A Nonlitigious Approach in Chotei (Family Court Mediation)", 39 *Fam. L.Q.* 489 *et seq.* (2005–2006).

take care of the child in the State of habitual residence. Obviously, the first and second points reflect concerns about the abuse directed towards the child and towards the partner, respectively. The third point stems from the concerns that the child may be placed in foster care in the State of its habitual residence.

6. APPEALS

The return order is subject to only one level of *ordinary* appeal. The appeal is allowed within the period of two weeks after notice of the final order has been given to the person entitled to file an appeal, whereas extraordinary legal challenges whose grounds are limited to points of law are available.

7. ENFORCEMENT OF THE RETURN ORDER

It should be first mentioned that the original copy of the decision ordering the return of the child enables the left-behind parent to request the enforcement without any further proceedings. If an abducting parent refuses to return with a child, the enforcement court may order the abducting parent to pay to a left-behind parent a reasonable amount of money for securing the return of the child where the former fails to perform this obligation. When this indirect coercive measure turns out to be ineffective, in principle, after the period of two weeks has elapsed after the enforcement order became binding, the left behind parent may apply for the 'return order by substitute', which enables a person to perform the return at the expense of the abducting parent. In the application, the left-behind parent may designate himself or herself as a substitute. Once the court appoints the substitute, the return order by substitute continues in force until the child leaves Japan.

In enforcing the return order by substitute, an enforcement officer who finds the child with the abducting parent is, in addition to trying persuasion and with the JCA's assistance, expected to take the steps necessary for the surrender of the child at a place such as the abducting parent's dwelling house: searching for the child there; letting the left-behind parent appointed as a substitute or the abducting parent meet the child; and letting the left-behind parent enter that place. Whereas the enforcement officer who faces resistance is allowed to use force or request police assistance in order to eliminate such resistance, the officer is prohibited from using coercive measures towards the child or towards any other persons when such measures taken against them might have harmful effects on the child.

8. CONCLUDING REMARKS

The Cabinet's directions, which set the framework for the Legislative Council of the Ministry of Justice to work within, are principally concerned with issues concerning the child's welfare, particularly, safety issues surrounding its return. The members of the Cabinet were aware that, without those issues being overcome, the Diet would not approve the ratification of the Convention. Consequently, in making the bill, the Legislative Council acted on the premise that, whereas the State of habitual residence should hold the jurisdictional primacy, there should be exceptions allowing a particular child's interests to be protected until any subsequent litigation on the merits in that State and that those exceptions should be understandable and acceptable for the members of the Diet.

ANNEX: THE BILL FOR IMPLEMENTING THE HAGUE CONVENTION OF 25 OCTOBER 1980 ON THE CIVIL ASPECTS OF INTERNATIONAL CHILD ABDUCTION (abridged translation)

Article 1
For the purpose of implementing the Hague Convention of 25 October 1980 on the Civil Aspects of International Child Abduction which is primarily designed to secure the prompt return of children wrongfully removed to or retained in any State to the State where they were habitually resident, this Bill purports to designate the Central Authority of Japan, to establish its competence and roles, and to establish the procedures necessary to return promptly the children to the States where they were habitually resident, and thereby to serve the interests of children.

Article 3
The Central Authority under Article 6(1) of the Convention shall be the Minister of Foreign Affairs.

...

Article 26
Any person whose rights of custody over a child are violated by removal to or retention in Japan may apply to the Family Court, claiming the return of the child to the State of its habitual residence against the person under whose care and control the child is.

Article 28

1 Notwithstanding the provisions of the preceding Article, the court shall not order the return of the child, when one of the following situations is found to exist. However, situations set out in the subparagraphs from 1 to 3 or subparagraph 5 do not prevent the court from ordering the return of the child, when the return of the child is found to serve the interests of the child under all the circumstances of the case:

(1) the proceedings have been commenced after the period of one year has elapsed from the date of the wrongful removal or retention and the child is now settled in its new environment;

(2) the applicant was not actually exercising the custody rights at the time of removal or retention, unless it is found that the applicant would have been exercising the custody rights in the absence of the removal or retention;

(3) the applicant consented to the removal or retention beforehand or acquiesced in it subsequently;

(4) there is a grave risk that his or her return would expose the child to physical or psychological harm or otherwise place the child in an intolerable situation;

(5) the child objects to being returned and has attained an age and degree of maturity at which it is appropriate to take account of its views; or

(6) The return of the child would not be permitted by the fundamental principles of Japan relating to the protection of human rights and fundamental freedoms.

2 In ascertaining the situation set out in subparagraph 4 of the preceding Article, the court shall take account of all the circumstances, in particular:

(1) whether there is a risk of the child suffering violent acts or other acts physically or psychologically affecting it done by the applicant in the State of its habitual residence;

(2) whether there is a risk of the respondent suffering such violent or other acts done by the applicant that would result in psychological damage to the child after both the respondent and the child enter the State of the habitual residence; or

(3) whether there would be circumstances to make difficult for either the applicant or the respondent to take care of the child in the State of its habitual residence.

3 The sole fact that a decision relating to custody has been given in or is entitled to recognition in Japan shall not be a ground for dismissing the application for the return of the child. However, the court may take account of the reasons for that decision.

...

Article 32

In respect of proceedings relating to the return of the child set out in Article 26, local jurisdiction shall lie with:

(1) the Tokyo Family Court, where the child has its domicile (in the absence of the domicile in Japan, its residence) in a district where the High Court of Tokyo, Nagoya, Sendai or Sapporo has its seat; or

(2) the Osaka Family Court, where the child has its domicile (in the absence of the domicile in Japan, its residence) in a district where the High Court of Osaka, Hiroshima, Fukuoka or Takamatsu has its seat.

...

Article 134

1 The coercive enforcement shall be carried out in accordance with Article 172 (1) of the Civil Execution Act as well as Article 171(1) of the same Act which allows the enforcement court to make a third party perform the return of the child at the expense of the obligor.

2 The coercive enforcement shall be implemented on the basis of an original copy of the decision ordering the return of the child.

Article 135

1 When the child has attained the age of 16 years, the coercive enforcement of the return of the child shall not be implemented in the method set out in Article 171(1) of Civil Execution Act.

2 In the proceedings for the enforcement of the return of the child in the method set out in Article 172(1), the enforcement court shall not order the obligor to pay the amount of money pursuant to the said provision on the ground that he/she does not return the child after the day when it has attained the age of 16 years.

Article 136

The application for the enforcement of the return of the child by substitute may be made after the period of two weeks has elapsed after the decision set out in Article 172(1) off Civil Execution Act became binding with final legal force.

...

Article 137

When the enforcement of the return of the child by substitute is applied for, the applicant shall designate a substitute in charge of returning the child to the State of its habitual residence in lieu of the obligor.

Article 138

When the enforcement court renders the decision set out in Article 134(1), it shall appoint the substitute and the enforcement officer in charge of releasing the child from the obligor's control.

Article 139
The enforcement court shall dismiss the application for enforcement by substitute, when it finds that the appointment of the substitute designated pursuant to Article 137 does not serve the interests of the child.

Article 140
4 The enforcement officer may, if he/she faces resistance when performing his/her duties, use force or request police assistance in order to eliminate such resistance.

Article 141
1 The person appointed as a substitute may make necessary acts, in particular, placing the child under his or her care and control.

Article 142
The Minister of Foreign Affairs may give necessary assistance, in particular, be present at the place of the enforcement.

...

Article 144
The Family Court or the High Court seised with the return application may, on its own motion, initiate the family mediation proceedings at every stage of the return proceedings on condition that the parties agree to it.

Article 145
3 When the parties reach an agreement as to the return of the child and the agreement was put on record, the mediation is regarded as conclusive. The part of the document indicating the agreement as to the return of the child has the same binding force as the court order.

Article 146
The court which has initiated the family mediation proceedings may stay the return proceedings until the end of the former proceedings.

...

Article 151
When the period of six weeks has elapsed from the date of commencement of the proceedings, the applicant or the Minister of Foreign Affairs may request the court seised with the return application to explain the development of the proceedings.

Article 152
The court before which the proceedings are pending in matters relating to the designation or the change of the holder of parental authority or to the custody over a child shall not decide on the merits of the case, after it has received the notice, given by the Minister of Foreign Affairs or by the court before which the proceedings for the return of the child are pending over the same child, to the effect that the child was allegedly wrongfully removed or retained. However, the court may decide on the merits of the case when an application for the return of the child is not lodged within a reasonable time or when the application for the return of the child was finally and conclusively dismissed.

www.ingramcontent.com/pod-product-compliance
Ingram Content Group UK Ltd.
Pitfield, Milton Keynes, MK11 3LW, UK
UKHW051043120926
8556IPUK00031B/870